PHILIP'S

STREET ATLAS

Glasgow

and West Central Scotland

First published in 1995 by

Philip's, a division of
Octopus Publishing Group Ltd
2-4 Heron Quays, London E14 4JP

Second colour edition 2002
Second impression with revisions 2003

ISBN 0-540-08278-3

© Philip's 2003

Ordnance Survey

This product includes mapping data licensed
from Ordnance Survey® with the permission
of the Controller of Her Majesty's Stationery
Office. © Crown copyright 2003. All rights
reserved. Licence number 100011710.

Printed and bound in Spain
by Cayfosa-Quebecor

Contents

Inside front cover: **SPT rail network map**

III **Key to map symbols**

IV **Key to map pages**

VI **Route planning**

VIII **Administrative and Postcode boundaries**

1 **Street maps** at 2½ inches to 1 mile

240 **Street map of Glasgow city centre**
at 5 inches to 1 mile

242 **Index** of towns and villages

243 **Index** of streets, hospitals, industrial estates, railway
stations, schools, shopping centres and universities
and places of interest

Digital Data

The exceptionally high-quality mapping found in this atlas is available as digital data
in TIFF format, which is easily convertible to other bitmapped (raster) image formats.

The index is also available in digital form as a standard database table. It contains all
the details found in the printed index together with the National Grid reference for
the map square in which each entry is named.

For further information and to discuss your requirements, please contact
Philip's on 020 7531 8438 or james.mann@philips-maps.co.uk

Key to map symbols

III

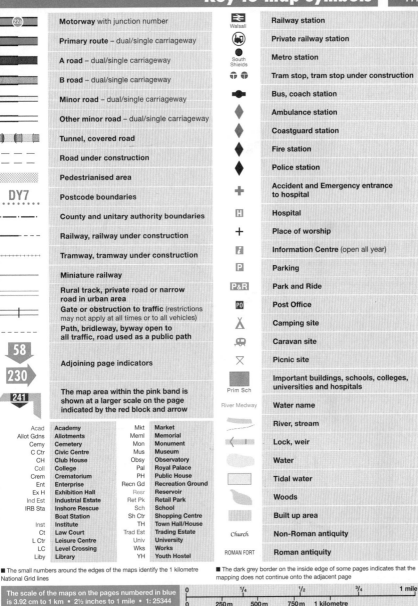

(22a)	**Motorway** with junction number
	Primary route – dual/single carriageway
	A road – dual/single carriageway
	B road – dual/single carriageway
	Minor road – dual/single carriageway
	Other minor road – dual/single carriageway
	Tunnel, covered road
	Road under construction
	Pedestrianised area
DY7	**Postcode boundaries**
	County and unitary authority boundaries
	Railway, railway under construction
	Tramway, tramway under construction
	Miniature railway
	Rural track, private road or narrow road in urban area
	Gate or obstruction to traffic (restrictions may not apply at all times or to all vehicles)
	Path, bridleway, byway open to all traffic, road used as a public path
58 / 230 / 241	**Adjoining page indicators**
	The map area within the pink band is shown at a larger scale on the page indicated by the red block and arrow

Acad	**Academy**	Mkt	**Market**
Allot Gdns	**Allotments**	Meml	**Memorial**
Cemy	**Cemetery**	Mon	**Monument**
C Ctr	**Civic Centre**	Mus	**Museum**
CH	**Club House**	Obsy	**Observatory**
Coll	**College**	Pal	**Royal Palace**
Crem	**Crematorium**	PH	**Public House**
Ent	**Enterprise**	Recn Gd	**Recreation Ground**
Ex H	**Exhibition Hall**	Resr	**Reservoir**
Ind Est	**Industrial Estate**	Ret Pk	**Retail Park**
IRB Sta	**Inshore Rescue Boat Station**	Sch	**School**
		Sh Ctr	**Shopping Centre**
Inst	**Institute**	TH	**Town Hall/House**
Ct	**Law Court**	Trad Est	**Trading Estate**
L Ctr	**Leisure Centre**	Univ	**University**
LC	**Level Crossing**	Wks	**Works**
Liby	**Library**	YH	**Youth Hostel**

Walsall	**Railway station**
	Private railway station
South Shields	**Metro station**
	Tram stop, tram stop under construction
	Bus, coach station
◆	**Ambulance station**
◆	**Coastguard station**
◆	**Fire station**
◆	**Police station**
✚	**Accident and Emergency entrance to hospital**
H	**Hospital**
✛	**Place of worship**
i	**Information Centre** (open all year)
P	**Parking**
P&R	**Park and Ride**
PO	**Post Office**
Ⅹ	**Camping site**
⌒	**Caravan site**
▽	**Picnic site**
Prim Sch	**Important buildings, schools, colleges, universities and hospitals**
River Medway	**Water name**
	River, stream
	Lock, weir
	Water
	Tidal water
	Woods
	Built up area
Church	**Non-Roman antiquity**
ROMAN FORT	**Roman antiquity**

■ The small numbers around the edges of the maps identify the 1 kilometre National Grid lines

■ The dark grey border on the inside edge of some pages indicates that the mapping does not continue onto the adjacent page

The scale of the maps on the pages numbered in blue is 3.92 cm to 1 km • 2½ inches to 1 mile • 1: 25344

0	¼	½	¾	1 mile
0	250 m 500 m	750 m 1 kilometre		

The scale of the maps on pages numbered in red is 7.84 cm to 1 km • 5 inches to 1 mile • 1: 12672

0	220 yards	440 yards	660 yards	½ mile
0	125 m 250 m	375 m ½ kilometre		

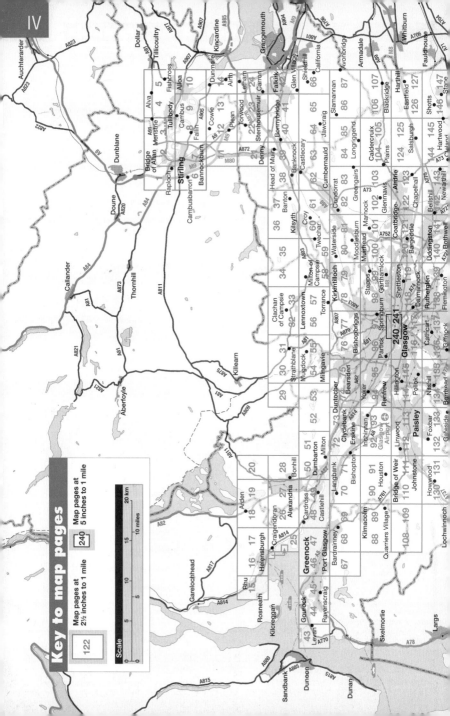

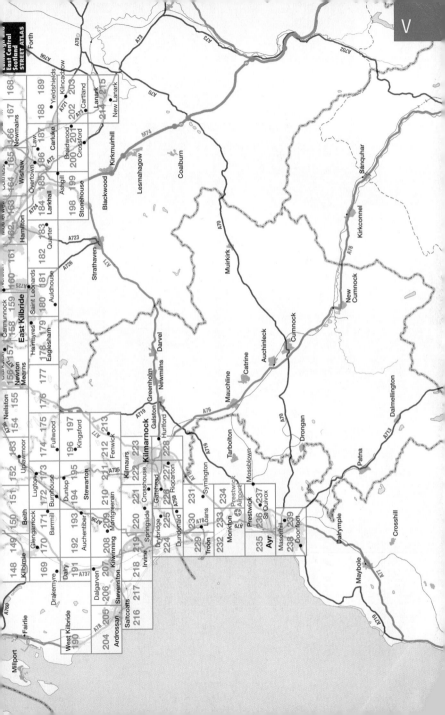

Route planning

Scale

0 1 2 3 4 5 6 7 8km

0 1 2 3 4 5 miles

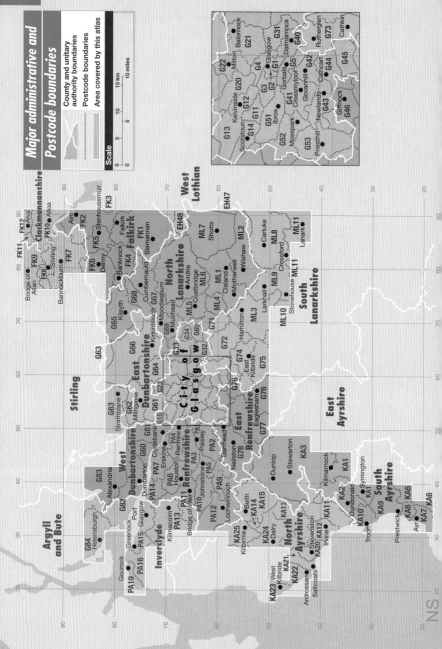

VIII

Major administrative and Postcode boundaries

County and unitary authority boundaries
Postcode boundaries
Area covered by this atlas

Scale
0   5   10   15km
0   5   10 miles

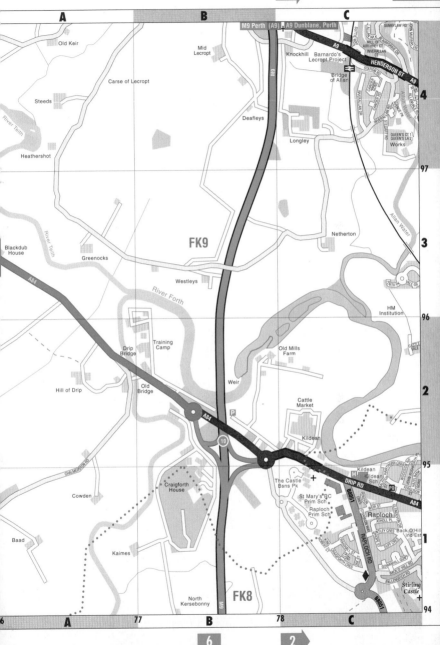

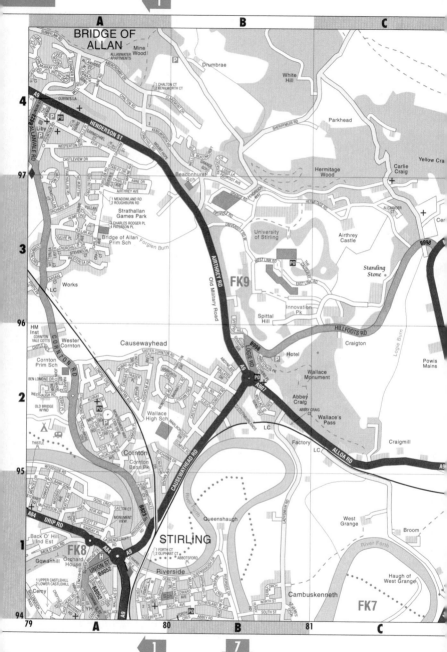

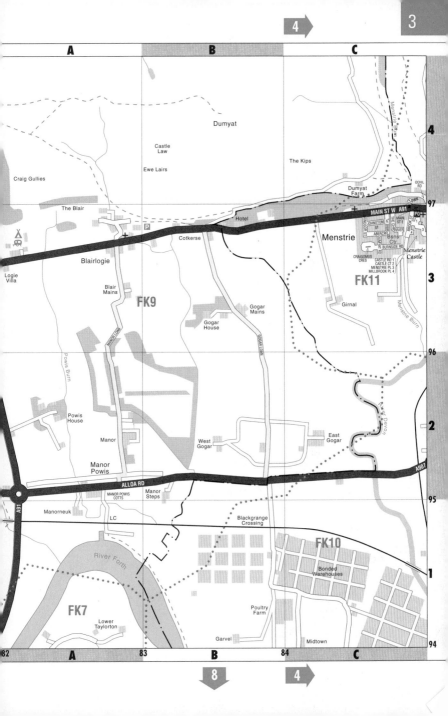

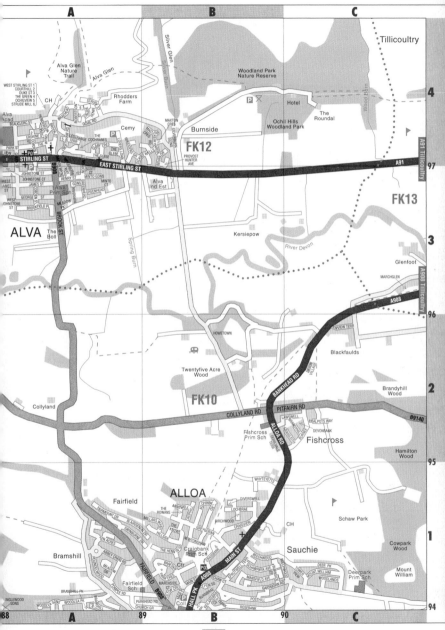

FK9

River Forth

FK8

Falleninch

DUMBARTON RD

B808

King's Knot

King's Park Farm

A811 Alexandria, Loch Lomond

A811

4

Polrogan Bridge

Bankend

White House

South Kersebonny

The Homesteads

THE HOMESTEADS

King's Park

CH

BALMORAL PL

QUEEN'S RD

B8051

93

Hollandbush

Ravloch Burn

ST THOMAS'S WELL

Hayford House

Cemy

ST THOMAS RD

BROOMHILL PL

DOUGLAS TERR

SNOWDON PLACE LA 1
SNOWDON PL 2

PARK PL

Johnny's Bridge

Hillhead

Batterflatts

BATTERFLATTS RD
DALMORGLEN PK

BATTERFLATTS GDNS

Cambusbarron

THOMSON PL

MAIN ST

PO

Liby

Torbrex

SPRINGWOOD

SPRINGWOOD AVE

Johnny's Burn

TOUCH RD

QUARRY RD

GILLINGHAME

OLD DRIVE RD

3

WOODSIDE

UNDERWOOD RD

Polmaise Farm

Abbey Kings Park

FK8

Gartur

Cambusbarron Prim Sch

WALLACE PL

ST NINIANS RD

SYCAMORE

92

Murray's Wood

Gillies Hill

FK7

Polmaise Castle

Bearside

Coxet Hill

CULTENHOVE CRES

TORBREX FARM RD
ST VALERY DR

FK8

2

Touchadam Craig

Fir Park

Haggs Wood

CULTENHOVE PL

Murrayshall Quarry

Castlehill

Murrayshall Farm

GRAYSTALE RD

91

Graystale

1

Sauchie Craig

Moor Burn

Wallstale

Bannock Burn

Chartershall House

Middlethird Wood

Cultenhove

Chartershall Farm

CHARTERSHALL RD

90

76   A   77   B   78   C

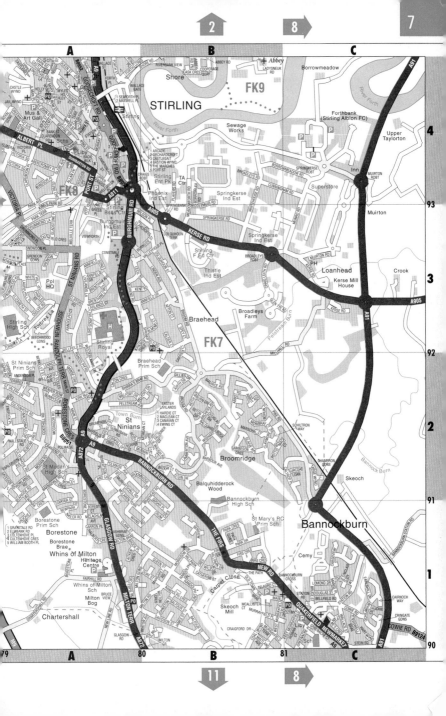

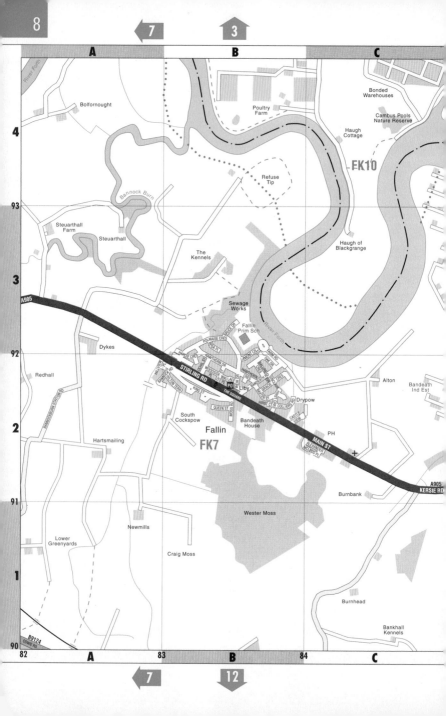

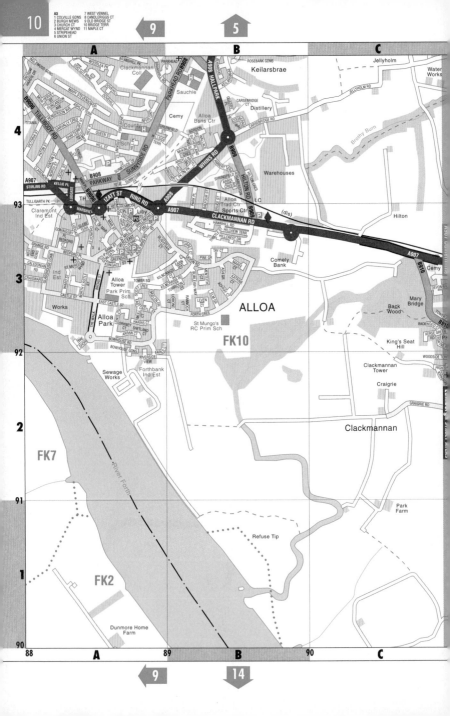

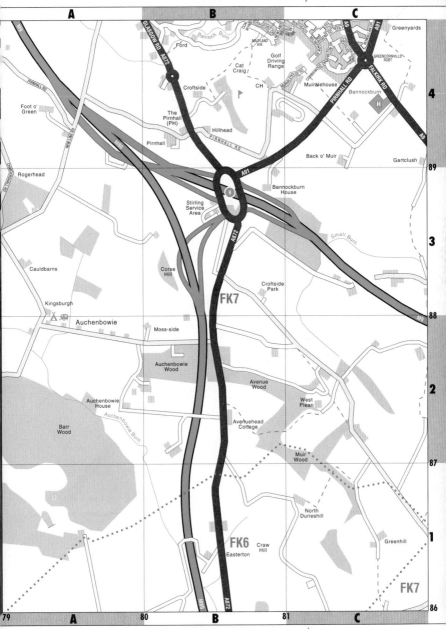

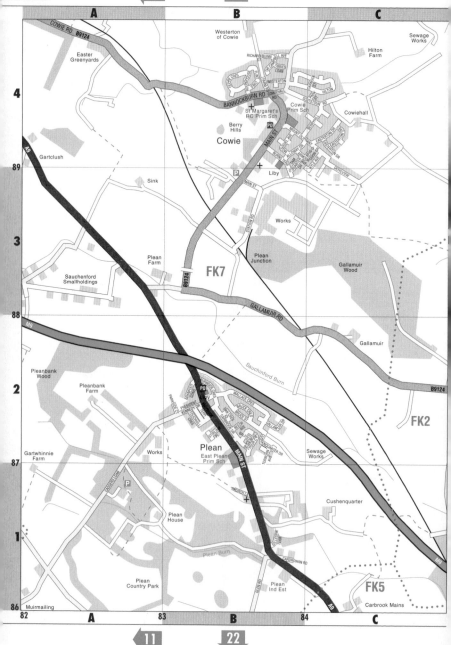

A   B   C

4

89

3

88

2

87

1

86

82   A   83   B   84   C

Cowie
COWIE RD
B9124
Easter Greenyards
Westerton of Cowie
Hilton Farm
Sewage Works
RICHARD D JNN HALL AVE
WESTERTON
BANNOCKBURN RD
St Margaret's RC Prim Sch
Berry Hills
MAIN ST
Cowie Prim Sch
Cowiehall
PO
Liby
Gartclush
A9
Sink
Plean Farm
Plean Junction
STATION RD
Works
B9124
FK7
Gallamuir Wood
Sauchenford Smallholdings
GALLAMUIR RD
Gallamuir
M9
B9124
Sauchinford Burn
Pleanbank Wood
Pleanbank Farm
FK2
PO
Plean
WALLACE CRES
KENNEDY DR
MAIN ST
East Plean Prim Sch
Sewage Works
Gartwhinnie Farm
Works
P
LANGDYKE TERR
Plean House
Cushenquarter
Plean Burn
CARBROWAN RD
A9
FK5
Plean Country Park
GLEN RD
Plean Ind Est
Carbrook Mains
Muirmailing

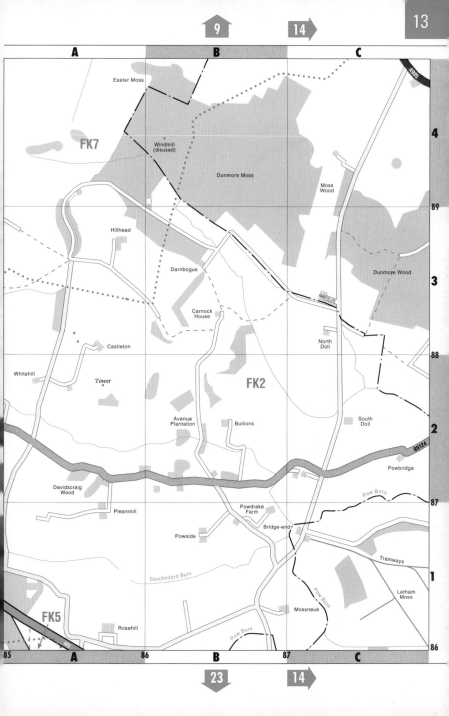

9
14

A B C

Easter Moss

FK7

Windmill
(disused)

Dunmore Moss

Moss
Wood

4

89

Hillhead

Darnbogue

Dunmore Wood

3

Carnock
House

FAIRFIELDS

North
Doll

88

Whitehill

Castleton

Tower

FK2

Avenue
Plantation

Bullions

South
Doll

2

BB124

Powbridge

Davidscraig
Wood

Pow Burn

87

Pleanmill

Powdrake
Farm

Bridge-end

Powside

Sauchinford Burn

Tramways

1

Pow Burn

Letham
Moss

FK5

Mossneuk

Pow Burn

Rosehill

85 86 87 86

A B C

A905

M9

23
14

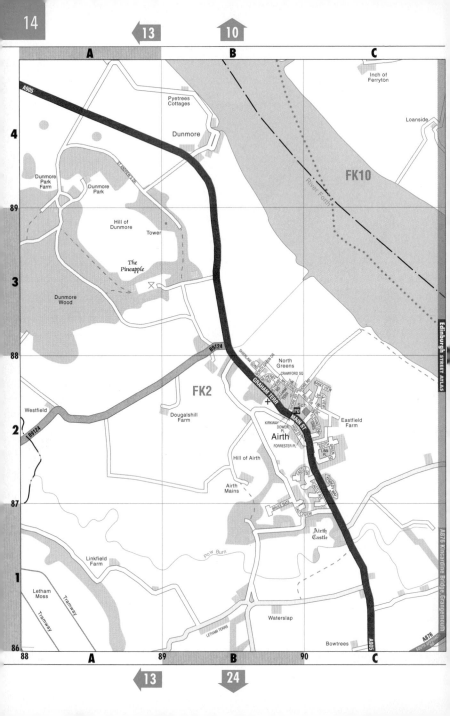

A905

Pyetrees
Cottages

Dunmore

4

Dunmore
Park
Farm

Dunmore
Park

Hill of
Dunmore

Tower

89

The
Pineapple

3

Dunmore
Wood

Inch of
Ferryton

Loanside

FK10

River Forth

B9724

88

North
Greens

GRAHAM TERR

CRAWFORD SQ

BANK'S VIEW

FK2

Dougalshill
Farm

Westfield

B9724

2

KIRKWAY
DOWER
PL

Airth

FORRESTER PL

Eastfield
Farm

MAIN ST

SOUTH
LINN
SQ

GREEN SQ

Hill of Airth

CASTLE RD

Airth
Mains

BRUCE DALE

87

Airth
Castle

POW Burn

Linkfield
Farm

1

Letham
Moss

Tramway

Tramway

Tramway

Waterslap

LETHAM TERRS

Bowtrees

A905

A876

86

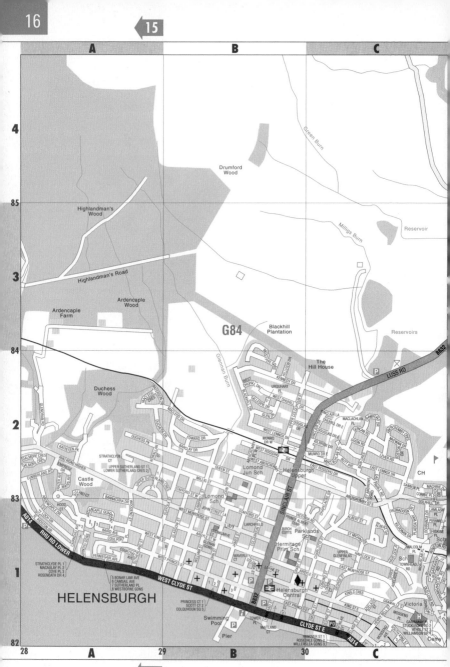

A   B   C

4

85

3

84

2

83

1

82

28   A   29   B   30   C

Green Burn

Drumford
Wood

Highlandman's
Wood

Millig Burn

Reservoir

Highlandman's Road

Ardencaple
Wood

Blackhill
Plantation

G84

Ardencaple
Farm

Reservoirs

Ardencaple
Wood

The
Hill House

LUSS RD

B832

Duchess
Wood

Glennan Burn

WEST DHUIL

Duchess
Wood

STRATHCLYDE
CT

UPPER SUTHERLAND ST 1
LOWER SUTHERLAND CRES 2

Lomond
Jun Sch

Helensburgh
Upper

Castle
Wood

EAST LENNOX DR

CH

Lomond
Sch

Liby

Larchfield

Parklands
Sch

A814

RHU RD LOWER

Hermitage
Prim Sch

UPPER
GLENFINLAS

5 BONAR LAW AVE
6 CAMDAL AVE
7 SUTHERLAND PL
8 WESTBORNE GDNS

Sch
TOWNHEAD
RD

STRATHCLYDE PL 1
MACAULAY PL 2
COVE PL 3
ROSENEATH DR 4

WEST CLYDE ST

Helensburgh
Central

Victoria

HELENSBURGH

KING ST E

KING'S CRES

PRINCESS CT 1
SCOTT CT 2
COLQUHOUN SQ 3

B832

Swimming
Pool

CLYDE ST E

A814

Pier

TOWER
PL

MAITLAND
CT

HANOVER ST 1
ROSEDALE GDNS 2
MILLERSLEA GDNS 3

GARNHAM PL 1
STUCK LOW RD 2
ATHOLE'S 3
WILLIAMSON DR 4

Cemy

G83

Highfields Muir

East
Kilbride

Highfields

Tigh na
Blair

4

Cross
Keys

B831

Inverlauren

Crosskeys
Wood

85

Drumfad

Inverlauren Wood

Callendoun

Fruin Water

Wester
Bannachra

3

Daligan

LUSS RD

G84

84

Bannachra
Woods

Bannachra
Woods

Bannachra
Muir

2

Old Luss Road

83

Garrawy Glen

KENT DR

HORTON PL

PO

1 FROBISHER PL
2 RODNEY PL
3 COCHRANE PL
4 BEATTY PL
5 JERVIS PL

Black
Wood

1

Townhead

G82

Drumfork
Burn

STUCKLECKIE RD

6 WILLIAMSON DR
7 OLD LUSS RD

Quarry
Wood

Northfield
Wood

Colgrain Prim Sch

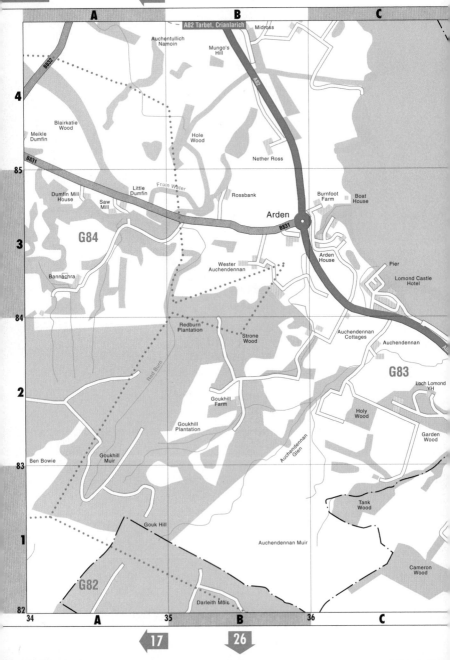

A B C

A82 Tarbet, Crianlarich

Midross

Auchentullich
Namoin

Mungo's
Hill

B82

4

Blairkatie
Wood

Hole
Wood

Meikle
Dumfin

Nether Ross

B831

85

Fruin Water

Dumfin Mill
House

Little
Dumfin

Rossbank

Burnfoot
Farm

Boat
House

Saw
Mill

Arden

B831

G84

3

Arden
House

Pier

Bannachra

Wester
Auchendennan

Lomond Castle
Hotel

84

Redburn
Plantation

Strone
Wood

Auchendennan
Cottages

Auchendennan

Red Burn

G83

2

Goukhill
Farm

Holy
Wood

Loch Lomond
YH

Garden
Wood

Ben Bowie

Goukhill
Muir

Goukhill
Plantation

83

Auchendennan Glen

Tank
Wood

1

Gouk Hill

Auchendennan Muir

Cameron
Wood

G82

82

Darleith Muir

34 A 35 B 36 C

Knockour
Wood

Lorn

4

Knockour
Hill

Boat
Houses

Black
Roundel

85

Boturich
Castle

Meikle
Boturich

3

Whinny Hill

Loch Lomond

84

Ledrishmore
Wood

G83

Burn of Balloch

Over
Balloch

Duck
Bay

Horsehouse
Wood

2

Cameron
Bay

Stable
Wood

Cameron House
(Hotel)

Balloch Castle

83

Cameron House
Farm

Balloch Castle
Country Park

Ledrishbeg

INCHFAD RD

1 McLean Cres
2 Haran Rd
3 Shandon Cres
4 Shandon Brae
5 Dumbain Rd
6 Haldane Terr

CREINCH
DR

HAGGS RD

1

Balloch
Pier

Moss o' Balloch
Plantations

River Leven

PARK AVE

Balloch

Lomond
Shores

Gateway Ctr
(Nat Pk Visitor Ctr)

CASTLE AVE

DRYMEN RD

GALLACHER

BALLOCH RD

82

38
39

A **B** **C**

Tullochan Dam

Tullochan

A811 Stirling

CAMBUSMOON TERR

Burnbrae

Art Gallery

DUNCRYNE

Gartocharn

Tullochan Strip

OLD MILITARY RD   A811

Blairlinnans Strip

West Cambusmoon

Mid Cambusmo

4

Blairennich

85

Blairlinnans

Auchenlinnhe

Water Treatment Plant

Blairlusk

Blackhill Plantation

Ledrishmore Wood

Old Military Road

Little Blairlusk

Dean Plantation

3

Ashfield Farm

Shanacles

G83

Ashfield House

Blairdennan Plantation

84

Ledrishmore

Old Kirk

Blairnyle

Caldarvan Loch

Lochend

AUCHINCARROCH RD

2

Westerton

Ballagan

LOCHEND COTTS

Blairhosh

Blairquhanan

Spittal

83

Nories' Glen

Blairquhom

BLAIRQUHOMRIE COTTS

Blairhosh Strip

Easter Auchincarroch

1

STIRLING RD

A811

1 McKINLAY AVE
2 PETERS AVE
3 BUCHANAN AVE

DUMBAIN RD

DUMBAIN CRES

Dumbain

AUCHINCARROCH RD

Mid Auchencarroch

82

40 **A** **41** **B** **42** **C**

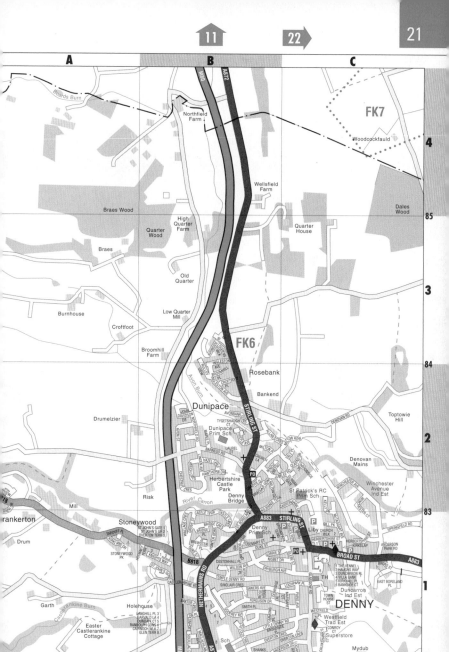

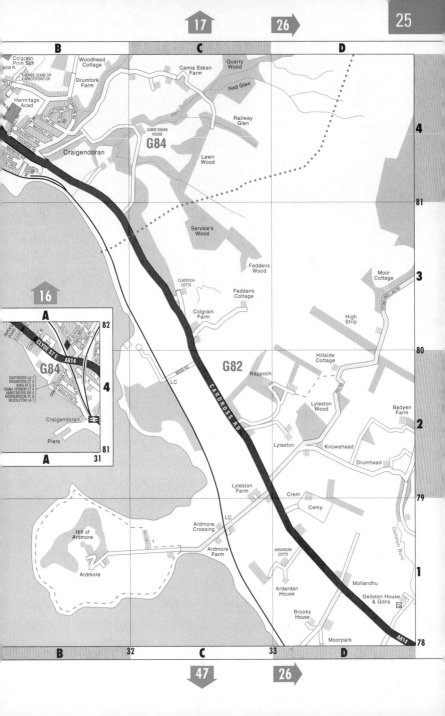

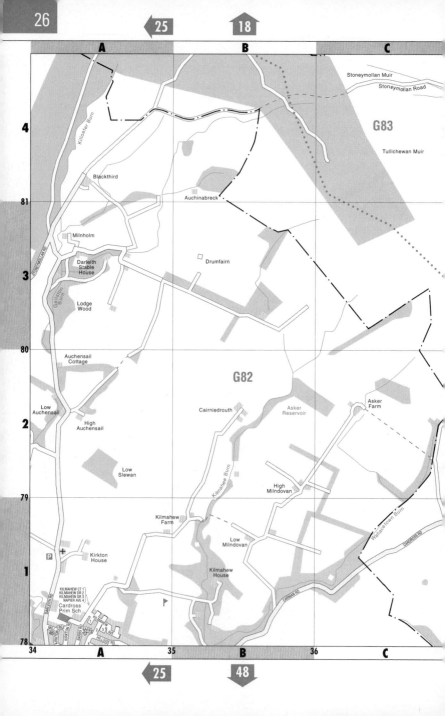

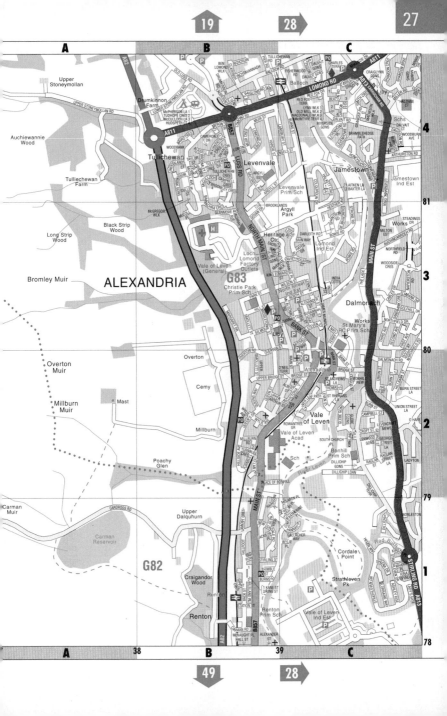

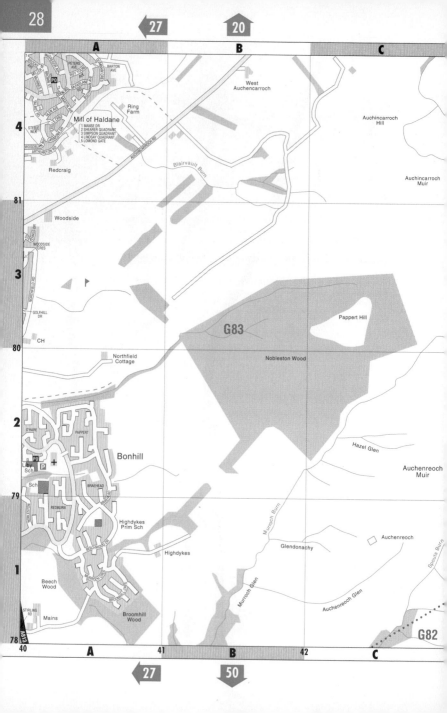

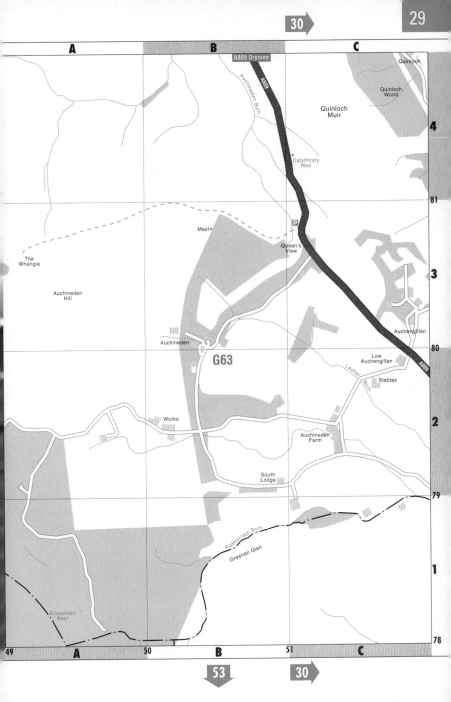

A809 Drymen

A

B

C

Quinloch

Quinloch Wood

Quinloch Muir

4

Auchineden Burn

A809

Catythirsty Well

81

P

Masta

Queen's View

The Whangie

3

Auchineden Hill

Auchengillan

Auchineden

G63

Low Auchengillan

80

A809

Lecher Burn

Stables

Works

2

Auchineden Farm

South Lodge

79

Audmirroch Burn

Greenan Glen

1

Kilmannan Resr

78

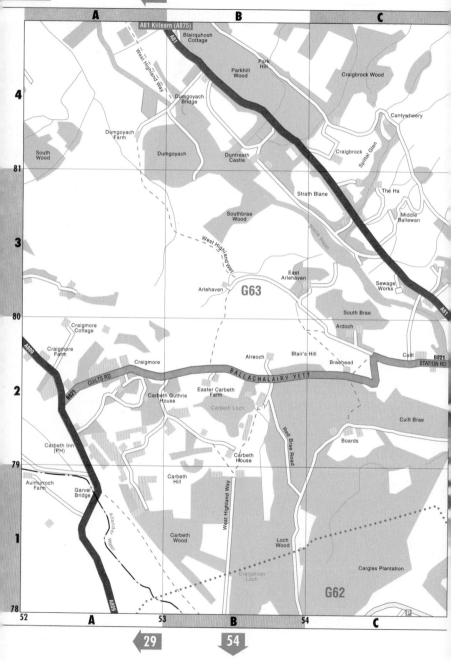

A81 Killearn (A875)
Blairquhosh Cottage
Park Hill
Parkhill Wood
Craigbrock Wood
Cantywheery
Dumgoyach Bridge
West Highland Way
Dumgoyach Farm
Dumgoyach
Duntreath Castle
Craigbrock
Spital Glen
South Wood
Strath Blane
The Ha
Middle Ballewan
Southbrae Wood
West Highland Way
Blane Water
East Arlehaven
Arlehaven
G63
Sewage Works
South Brae
Craigmore Cottage
Ardoch
Craigmore Farm
Cuilt
B821 STATION RD
Craigmore
Alreoch
Blair's Hill
Braehead
CUILTS RD
BALLACHALAIRY YETT
A809
B821
Easter Carbeth Farm
Carbeth Guthrie House
Carbeth Loch
Cuilt Brae
Boards
Carbeth Inn (PH)
Carbeth House
Red Brae Road
Aulmurroch Farm
Garvel Bridge
Carbeth Hill
West Highland Way
Allander Water
Carbeth Wood
Loch Wood
Carglas Plantation
Craigallian Loch
G62
A809
P

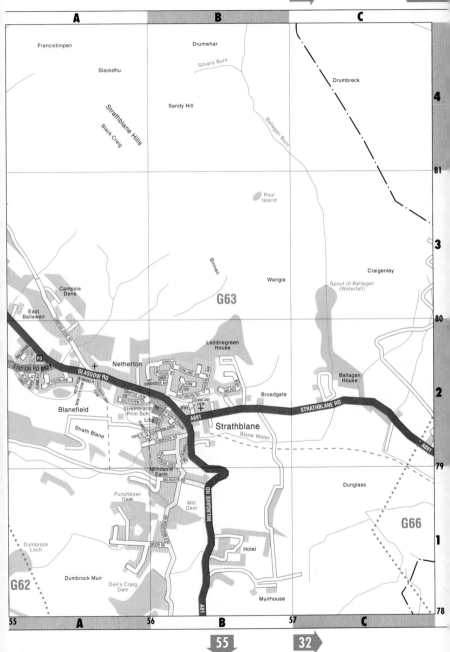

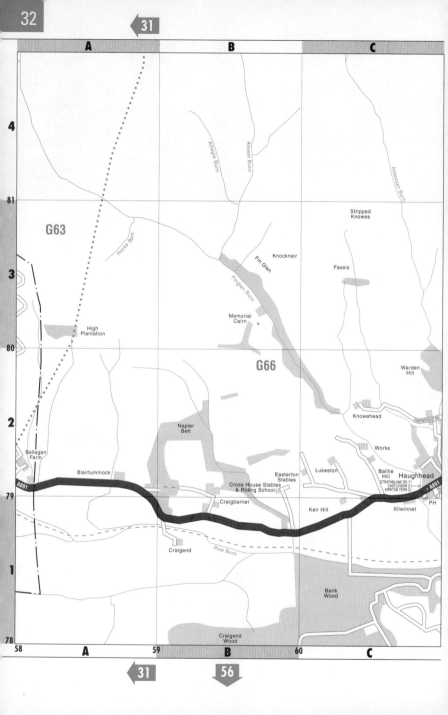

A

B

C

4

81

G63

Altaggle Burn

Almeel Burn

Aldossan Burn

Stripped
Knowes

3

Horse Burn

Finglen Burn

Fin Glen

Knocknair

Fassis

Memorial
Cairn

80

High
Plantation

G66

Warden
Hill

Knowehead

KNOWEHEAD RD

2

Napier
Belt

Works

Ballagan
Farm

Blairtummock

Easterton
Stables

Lukeston

Baillie
Hill

Haughhead

STRATHBLANE RD 1
CASTLEVIEW 2
KIRKTON TERR 3

A891

Cross House Stables
& Riding School

A891

PH

79

Craigbarnet

Keir Hill

Kilwinnet

Craigend

Pow Burn

1

Bank
Wood

Craigend
Wood

78

58

A

59

B

60

C

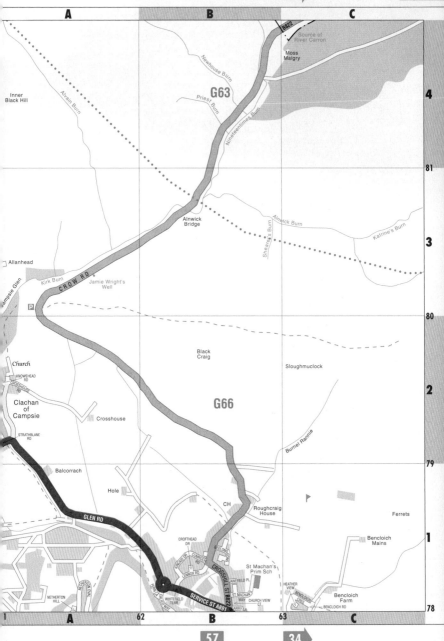

A
B
C

4

81

3

80

2

79

1

78

Source of
River Carron

Moss
Maigry

B822

Newhouse Burn

G63

Priest Burn

Nineteentimes Burn

Inner
Black Hill

Alvain Burn

Alnwick
Bridge

Alnwick Burn

Katrine's Burn

Shearie's Burn

Allanhead

Kirk Burn

C R O W   R D

Jamie Wright's
Well

Campsie Glen

P

Black
Craig

Sloughmuclock

Church

KNOWEHEAD
RD

CROSSBURN
RD

Clachan
of
Campsie

Crosshouse

G66

STRATHBLANE
RD

Burnel Rannie

Balcorrach

Hole

79

GLEN RD

CH

Roughcraig
House

Ferrets

Bencloich
Mains

CROFTHEAD
DR

OSCARD DR

GLENBOIG

STEELE DR

LANEFIELD PL

St Machan's
Prim Sch

HEATHER
VIEW

Bencloich
Farm

LENNOX RD

CROSSHILL ST B821

ST MACHAN'S
WAY

CHURCH VIEW

BENCLOICH
RD

NETHERTON
HILL

NETHERTON DR

LENNOX CASTLE RD

WHITEFIELD
TERR

SERVICE ST A891

QUARRY LA

BENCLOICH RD

A
62
B
63
C

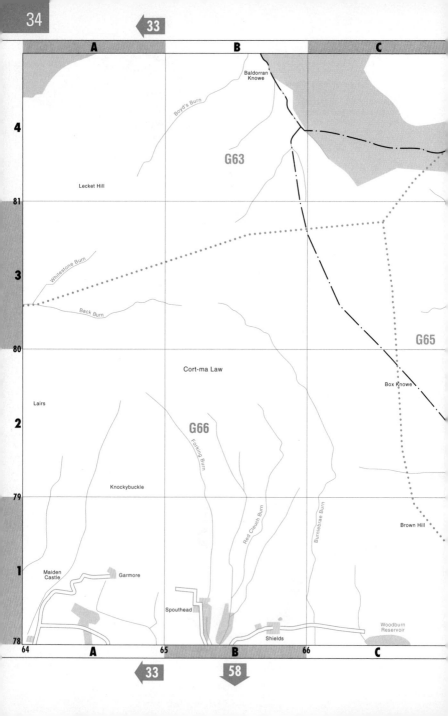

A   B   C

4

G63

Baldorran
Knowe

Boyd's Burn

81

Lecket Hill

3

Whitestone Burn

Back Burn

80

G65

Cort-ma Law

Box Knowe

Lairs

2

G66

Forking Burn

Knockybuckle

79

Red Cleuch Burn

Burniebrae Burn

Brown Hill

1

Maiden
Castle

Garmore

Spouthead

Woodburn
Reservoir

78

Shields

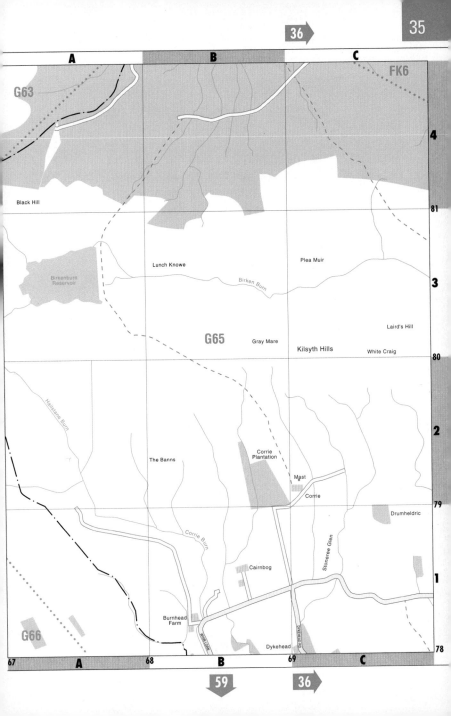

FK6

A   **B**   **C**

Tomtain

Hunt Hill

81

Garrel Hill   Yellow Muir

Green Bank

4

3   Laird's Loup   Little Hill   Money Howes

Black Craig

G65

80

Brockieside

2   Garrel Burn

Bachille Burn

Belt Moss

Baggage Knowe

79   Drumtrocher   Quarries (dis)

Allanfauld

KILSYTH   Highland Park

Five Oaks

Braehead   1 MAIN ST
2 JOHN JARVIS SQ
3 CHARLES ST
4 MAXWELL PL
5 BLENHEIM CT

Colzium House

1   Balcastle Farm   High Balmalloch

Northfield

Dovecotwood

Kilsyth Head

Westfield   Balmalloch   Balmalloch Prim Sch

North Barrwood

STIRLING RD   A803

A803 GLASGOW RD   KINGSTON RD

78

70   71   72

37

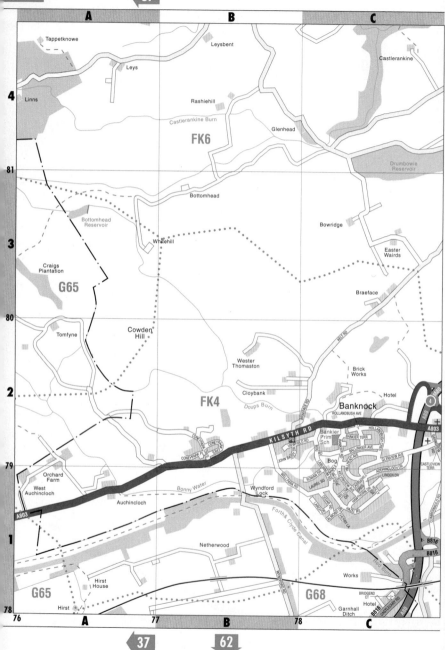

A **B** **C**

Tappetknowe
Leysbent
Castlerankine
Leys
4
Linns
Rashiehill
Castlerankine Burn
Glenhead
FK6
Drumbowie Reservoir
81
Bottomhead
Bowridge
Bottomhead Reservoir
Easter Wairds
3
Whitehill
Craigs Plantation
G65
Braeface
80
Tomfyne
Cowden Hill
Kelty Rd
Wester Thomaston
Brick Works
2
FK4
Cloybank
Hotel
Doups Burn
Banknock
HOLLANDBUSH AVE
A80(M)
KILSYTH RD
Bankier Prim Sch
HOLLANDBUSH DR
A803
Bankier Terr
VIEWFIELD RD
BALVENIE AVE
CONEY PARK PL
CONE Y RD
SCHO RD
John Bassy
Bog
GLENVIEW AVE
79
Orchard Farm
WELL PARK RD
AUCHINLOCH RD
LINDEN DR
CASTLEVIEW TERR
West Auchincloch
LAUREL DR
Bonny Water
Wyndford Lock
Auchincloch
ELM RD
HAZEL RD
Forth & Clyde Canal
CUMBERNAULD RD
1
A803
Netherwood
WYNDFORD RD
B816
B816
Kelty Burn
Works
G68
BRIDGEND CT
Hirst House
G65
Hotel
78
Hirst
Garnhall Ditch
B816
CASTLECARY RD
A80
76 **A** **77** **B** **78** **C**

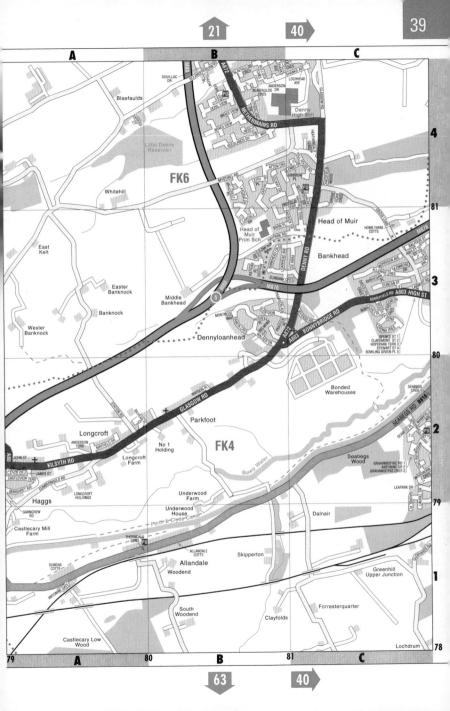

39
22

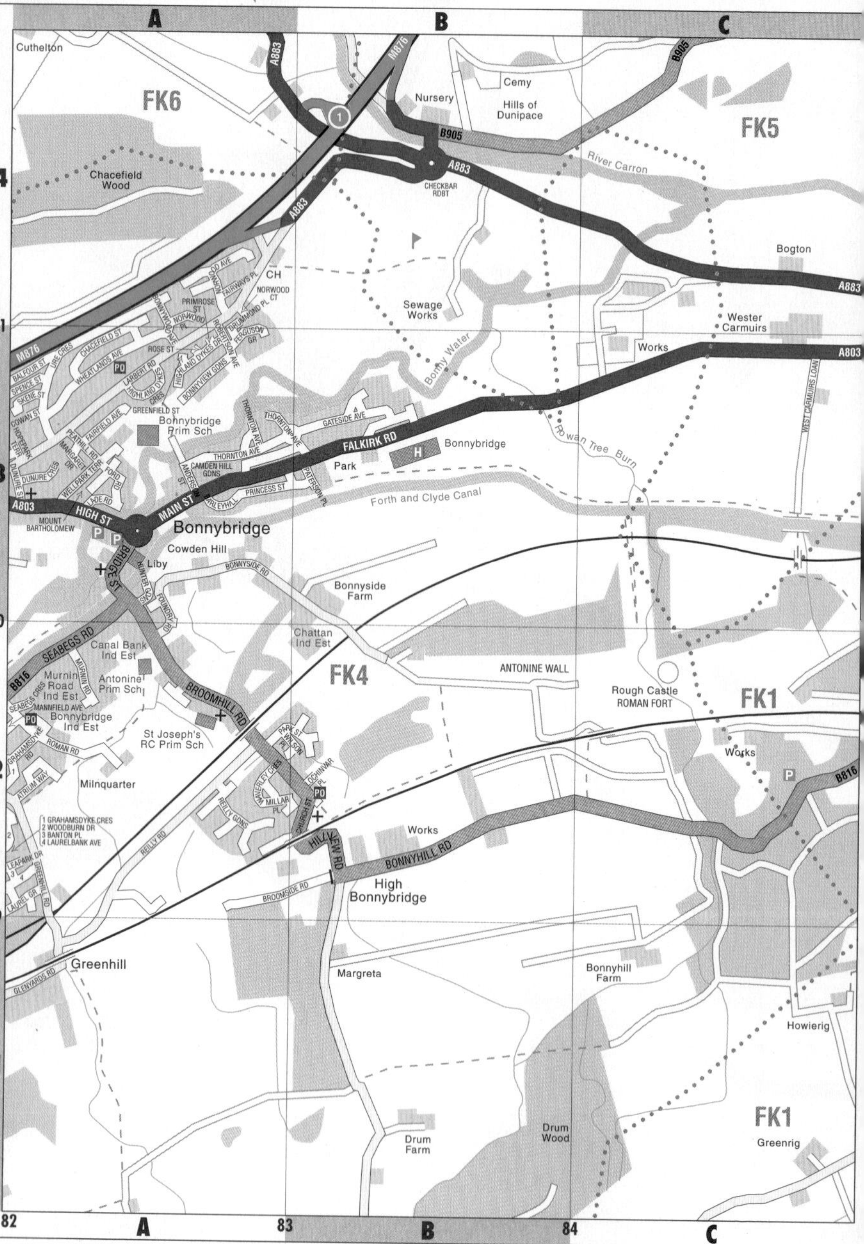

A B C

Cuthelton

FK6

FK5

Cemy
Nursery
Hills of
Dunipace

B905

Chacefield
Wood

4

River Carron

CHECKBAR
RDBT

A883

B905

Bogton

A883

81

CH

Sewage
Works

Bonny Water

Wester
Carmuirs

Works

A803

PRIMROSE
ST
ROSE ST

Greenfield St
Bonnybridge
Prim Sch

GATESIDE AVE

THORNTON AVE

Rowan Tree Burn

3

Camden Hill Sch

FALKIRK RD

Bonnybridge

H

Park

Forth and Clyde Canal

A803

HIGH ST

MAIN ST

Bonnybridge

MOUNT
BARTHOLOMEW

P P
Liby

Cowden Hill

BONNYSIDE RD

Bonnyside
Farm

80

SEABEGS RD

Canal Bank
Ind Est

Chattan
Ind Est

ANTONINE WALL

Rough Castle
ROMAN FORT

FK1

B816

Murnin
Road
Ind Est

Antonine
Prim Sch

BROOMHILL RD

FK4

Works

P

B816

Mannfield
Ave
Bonnybridge
Ind Est

St Joseph's
RC Prim Sch

2

Milnquarter

MILLAR

Works

BONNYHILL RD

1 GRAHAMSDYKE CRES
2 WOODBURN DR
3 BANTON PL
4 LAURELBANK AVE

HILLVIEW RD

High
Bonnybridge

BROOMSIDE RD

79

GLENYARDS RD

Greenhill

Margreta

Bonnyhill
Farm

Howierig

1

Drum
Farm

Drum
Wood

FK1

Greenrig

78

82 A **83** B **84** C

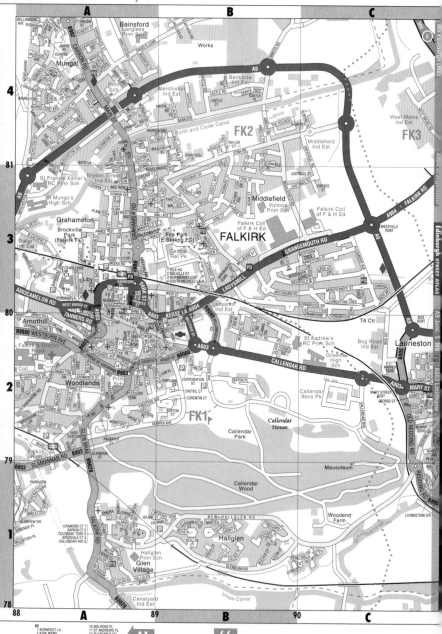

A2
1 BURNFOOT LA
2 KIRK WYND
3 TOLBOOTH ST
4 WOOER ST
5 Callendar Square Sh Ctr
6 ARNOTHILL BANK
7 Howgate Sh Ctr
8 KINGS CT
9 MISSION LA
10 MELROSE PL
11 ST ANDREWS PL
12 PLEASANCE SQ
13 PLEASANCE CT
14 ST MODANS CT
15 COMELY PARK TERR

41   66

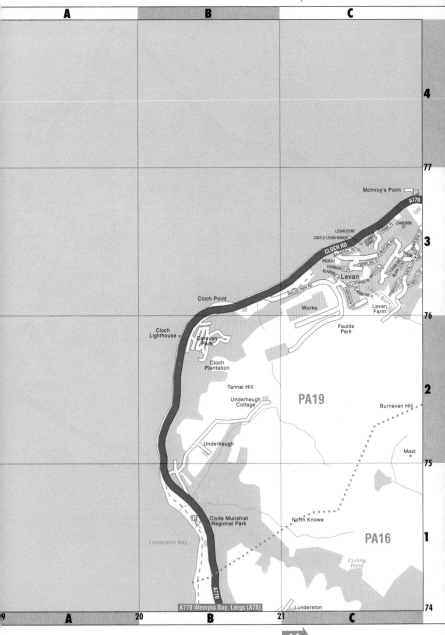

A   B   C

4

77

McInroy's Point   P
A770

LEVAN POINT   CAMERON CT
Castle Levan Manor
CLOCH RD   BALMORAL PL

3

Hotel
EDINBURGH DR
BLAIRMORE
Levan

Cloch Point

FAULDS PARK RD

Works   Levan Farm

Cloch
Lighthouse
Caravan
Park

Faulds
Park

76

Cloch
Plantation

Tannel Hill

Underheugh
Cottage

PA19

Burneven Hill

2

Underheugh

Mast

75

Clyde Muirshiel
Regional Park

North Knowe

PA16

1

Lunderston Bay

Curling
Pond

A770

A770 Wemyss Bay, Largs (A78)

Lunderston

74

9   A   20   B   21   C

A   B   C

Kempock St
PO
Gourock
Liby
1 CASTLE GDNS
2 ADELAIDE ST
3 HOPETON ST

West Bay

ALBERT RD

Tower

Gourock
Bay

SHARP ST 1
MARGARET ST 2
ADAM ST 3
JOHN CAMPBELL ST 4
JOHN CAMPBELL CT 5
RIVERSIDE GDNS 6
CALEDONIA GDNS 7

4

Barr
Hill

Tower
Hill

DRUMSHANTIE
TERR

Pier

A770

ASHTON RD

Ashton

GOUROCK

Gourock
H Sch

CARDWELL RD

MANOR CRES

COVE RD

CALEDONIA CRES

77

CLOCH RD

ASHGROVE AVE 1
ASHTON TERR 2

Victoria Rd

PRESTON PL

Divert

TOWER DR

PO

ARGYLE ST

DEVONPORT RD

COLLINGWOOD
TERR

St Andrews Dr

Cloch Brae

Canal View

Midton

ROSE
CRES

FIR
TERR

ELM TERR

St Ninian's
Prim Sch

GEORGE RD

HILLTOP CRES

GREENPLACE RD

GARVIE AVE

PA19

Moorfoot
Prim Sch

KIRN DR

3

Trumpethill

Mast

Larkfield
Ind Est

Earnhill Rd

Cemy

York Rd

Plymouth Ave

Durham Rd

Bournemouth Rd

Coves
Reservr

1 AVONMOUTH PL
2 LYNMOUTH PL

76

Springfield
Prim Sch

Larkfield

Schs

Inverclyde
Royal

H

14 OBAN TERR
15 MALLAIG TERR
16 PORTREE TERR
17 BROADFORD TERR
18 SUNDERLAND WDK

Coll

Liby

SUFFOLK RD

STAFFORD RD

FANCY FARM PL
GLENIFFER RD

BERWICK RD

2

PA16

Earn Hill

Braeside

Stadium

Branchton

PO

A78

7 KYLEMORE LA
8 BENMORE LA
9 KINLOCH LA
10 MAUCHLINE LA
11 AYR
12 CARRICK LA
13 GLEN ARMOUR LA

MINERVA LA 1
BRAESIDE LA 2
ATHOLE LA 3
JUNO LA 4
JUPITER LA 5
MERCURY LA 6

Banks

Sch

KINTYRE TERR

KYLEMORE LA

INVERKIP RD

Branchton

75

Gallow
Hill

Leitchland
Farm

Flatterton
Farm

Drumillan
Hill

FLATTERTON LA

CRISSWELL CL

Glenburn
Sch

Greenock
High Sch

INVERKIP RD

Spango Burn

A78

1

Flatterton La

Crisswell La

Spango
Valley

Spango

IBM

Howford Glen

Factory

Hole o Spango

Chrisswell

A78

A78 Largs

45

Firth of Clyde

GREENOCK

Swimming Pool & L Complex

1 WILLIAM ST
2 CROSS SHORE ST
3 EAST BREAST
4 BRYMNER ST
5 NEW DOCK LA
6 OPEN SHORE
7 DONALD'S CT

Custom House
Quay Rst
Pk

Superstore

Coll

Custom House
Mus

East India
Harbour

Victoria
Harbour

Garvel
Point

Cathcart
Bldgs

Cathcart
Sq

1 EAST BLACKHALL ST
2 ST ANDREW ST
3 EMPRESS CT
4 EAST STEWART ST

Central

Cartsdyke

Piers

Pier

Great
Harbour

Well Park
Clos

Lynedoch
Ind Est

Cartsdyke

Cartsdyke

Dock

Works

Bridgend

INGLESTON ST

Ladyburn

Stanners

Knowe

Dock

St Lawrence
Prim Sch

Liby

Cappielow
Ind Est
Cappielow Park
(Greenock Morton FC)

Finnieston

Whinhill

Strathclyde
Bsnec Ctr

Grosvenor Rd
Grosvenor La

Bogston

PA15

Castle Rd

St Kenneth
RC Prim Sch

Lady Octavia
Public Park

Gibshill

Sports Ct

Auchmountain
Glen

Strone

King's Glen
Prim Sch

THOMAS MUIR LA
LILYBANK RD
FARQUAR RD
BROADSTONE AVE

Works

Cemy

Knocknairs
Hill

PA1

AUCHMOUNTAIN RD

Craigeneuve Burn

B788

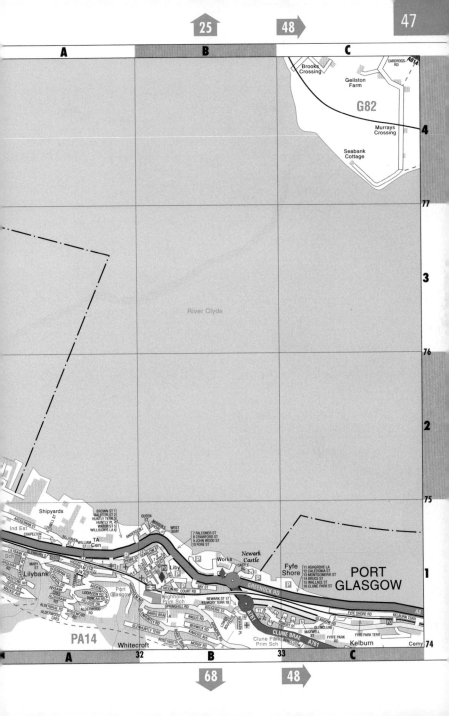

A B C

4

77

3

76

2

75

River Clyde

G82

Brooks Crossing

Geilston Farm

CARDROSS RD

A814

Murrays Crossing

Seabank Cottage

Shipyards

Ind Est

Lilybank

Port Glasgow

PA14

Whitecroft

BROWN ST 1
BALFOUR ST 2
HUNTLY TERR 3
WATER ST 5
WILLISON'S LA 6

QUEEN ST

WEST QUAY

7 FALCONER ST
8 CRAWFORD ST
9 JOHN WOOD ST
10 FORE ST

Works

Newark Castle

Fyfe Shore

11 ASHGROVE LA
12 CALEDONIA ST
13 MONTGOMERIE ST
14 BRUCE ST
15 WALLACE ST
16 CLUNE PARK ST

PORT GLASGOW

GREENOCK RD

Newholm Prim Sch

NEWARK ST 17
KILMORY TERR 18

GLASGOW RD

GLENCLUNE

FYFE SHORE RD

KELBURN TERR

A8

FYFE PARK TERR

Clune Park Prim Sch

Kelburn

Cemy

CLUNE BRAE
A761

A B C

A   B   C

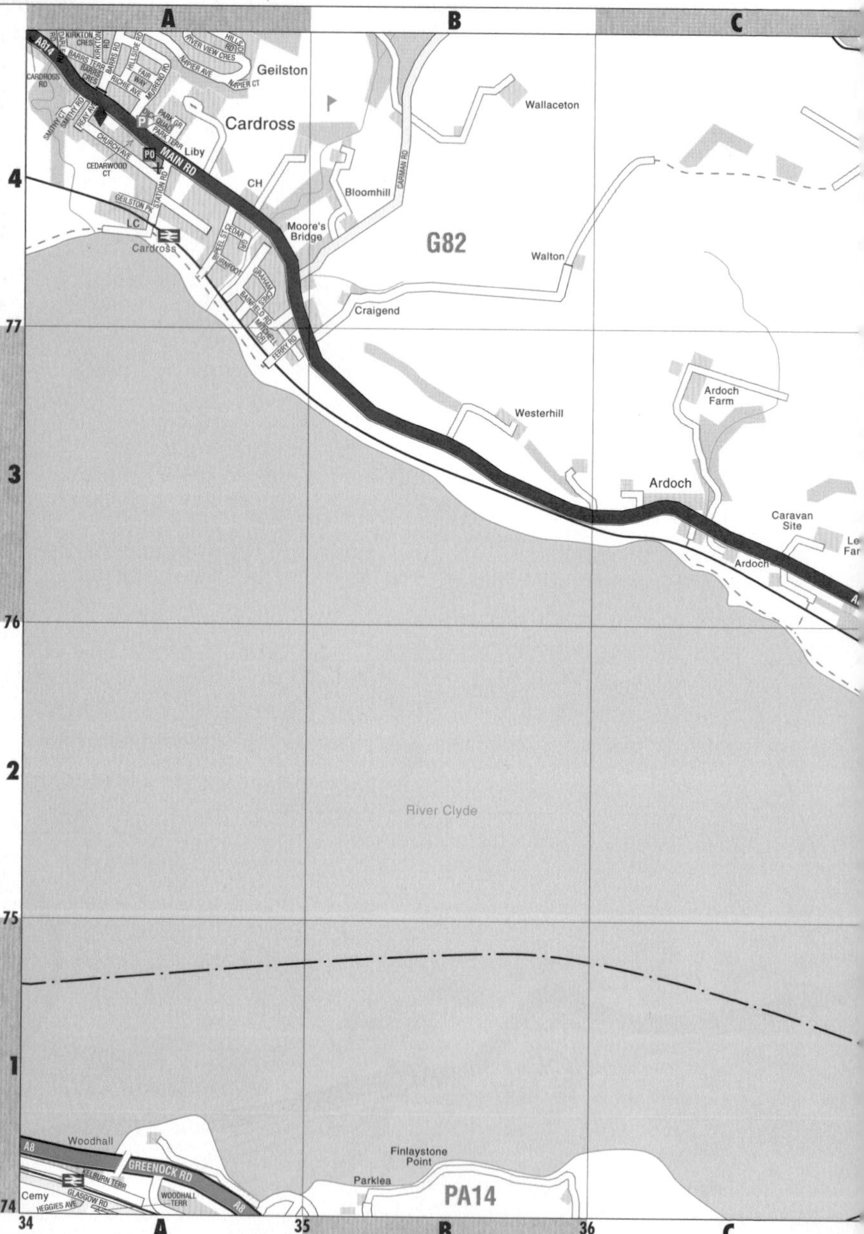

Geilston

Cardross

Wallaceton

P Liby

MAIN RD

PO

CEDARWOOD
CT

CH

Bloomhill

G82

LC

Cardross

Moore's
Bridge

Walton

Craigend

77

Westerhill

Ardoch
Farm

3

Ardoch

Caravan
Site

Le
Far

Ardoch

A

76

2

River Clyde

75

1

Woodhall

A8

GREENOCK RD

Finlaystone
Point

Cemy

GLASGOW RD
A8

WOODHALL
TERR

Parklea

PA14

74

34   A   35   B   36   C

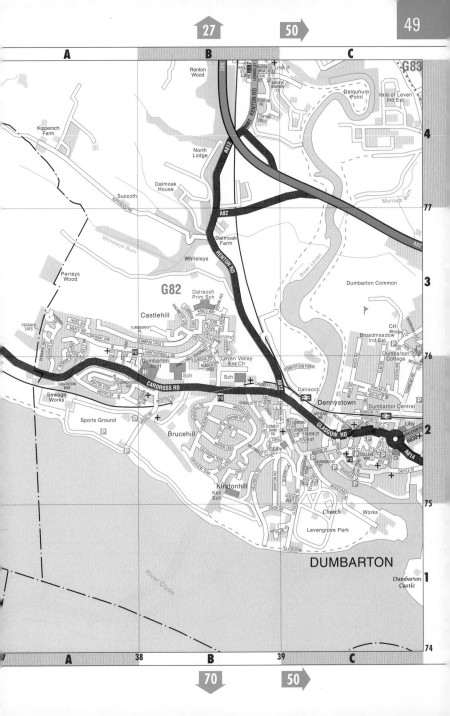

G83

Renton
Wood

Kipperoch
Farm

North
Lodge

Dalmoak
House

Succoth

A82

RENTON RD

B857

A812

A82

Dalquhurn
Point

Vale of Leven
Ind Est

Murroch Burn

4

77

Whiteleys Burn

Dalmoak
Farm

Whiteleys

River Leven

Dumbarton Common

3

Perrays
Wood

G82

Dalreoch
Prim Sch

Castlehill

PERRAYS
CRES

HAZEL AVE
MAPLE AVE
PERRAY AVE

KNOWE RD

TURNBERRY
PL

HAWTHORNHILL RD

CUMBRAE CRES S

KING'S WAY

ROMAN AVE

CUMBRAE CRES

Dumbarton
Joint

CARDROSS RD

Sewage
Works

ASHTON VIEW
WESTCLIFF

CARDROSS RD

WESTFIELD

Sports Ground

Leven Valley
Ent Ctr

Sch

Sch

DALREOCH AVE

Dennystoun Forge

Dalreoch

Dennystown

Dumbarton
Cottage

CH
MEADOW

Broadmeadow
Ind Est

Dumbarton Central

76

Brucehill

Liby

PO

CHARLOTTE ST

COMELY
BANK RD

LOMOND
LEVEN CT

CLYDE ST

ROWIE ST

GLASGOW RD

ARTIZAN
BR

BANKEND
STATION RD

Liby

A814

B830

2

Kirktonhill

Keil
Sch

DIXON AVE

METHLAN RD

CLYDEVIEW

LEVENGROVE CT

Levengrove Park

Church

Works

CASTLE ST

75

River Clyde

DUMBARTON

Dumbarton
Castle

1

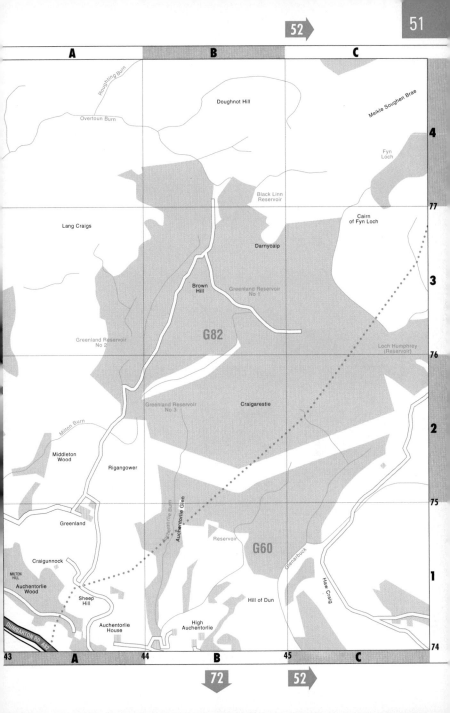

51

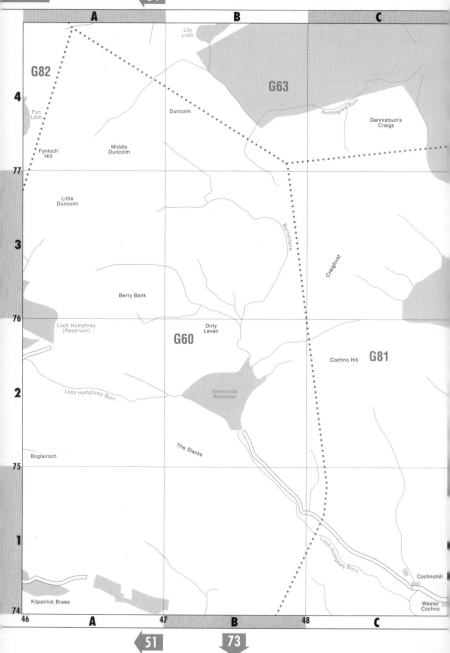

G82

Lily
Loch

G63

4

Fyn
Loch

Duncolm

Auchingree Burn

Dennistoun's
Craigs

Fynloch
Hill

Middle
Duncolm

77

Little
Duncolm

Burnelians

3

Craighirst

Berry Bank

76

Loch Humphrey
(Reservoir)

Dirty
Leven

G60

Cochno Hill

G81

2

Loch Humphrey Burn

Greenside
Reservoir

The Slacks

Boglairoch

75

1

Loch Humphrey Burn

Cochnohill

Kilpatrick Braes

Wester
Cochno

74

51   73

G63

A809

CH

52   A   53   B   54   C

G62

Craigallian Loch

Boat House

Craigallian

Scroggy Hill

Gallow Hill

Craigend Visitor Ctr

Craigend Castle

Moo Hill

Lower Craigallian

Kyber Cottage

Craigallian Bridge

West Highland Way

Mugdock Wood

Mount Zion

Craigton Burn

High Craigton

Shank Burn

Carneddans Wood

Low Craigton

CRAIGTON COTTS

Laighpark

Wks

CH

THE DAM

CARNEDDANS RD

Braval

Field Wood

Craigton Village

Tambowie

Little Balvie

Douglas Acad

CRAIGTON RD

CH

Craigdhu Burn

Balviebank

DOUGLAS AV

Clober Prim Sch

Crossburn

AULDMURROCH DR 1
CRAIGHEAD DR 3

DRUMBROCK RD

DALNAIR

Dumgoyne Sch

Craigdow

CRAIGDHU RD

B8050

8805

Douglas Muir

Mains Plantation

Old Mains Farm

STOCKIEMUIR RD A809

G61

Craighead Knowe

PRESTONFIELD

SOUTH MAINS AVE

BRAEHEAD AVE

B8050

77

3

76

2

75

1

74

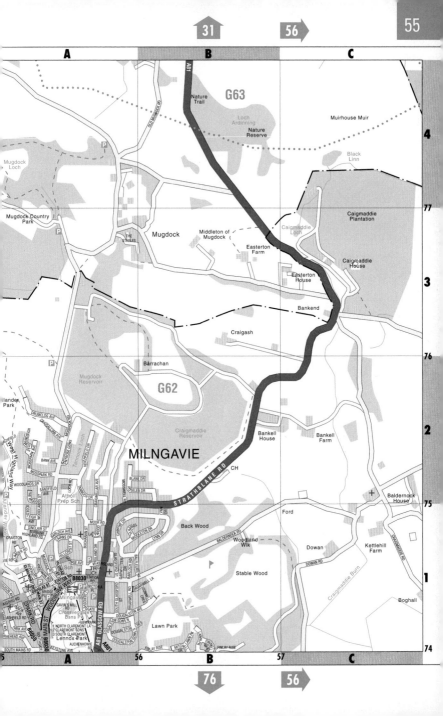

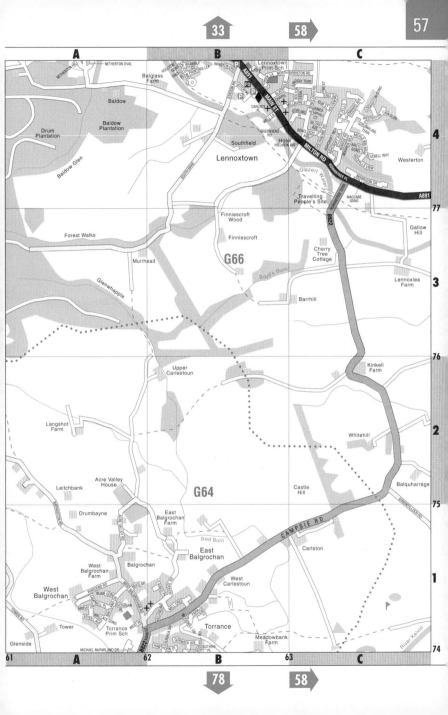

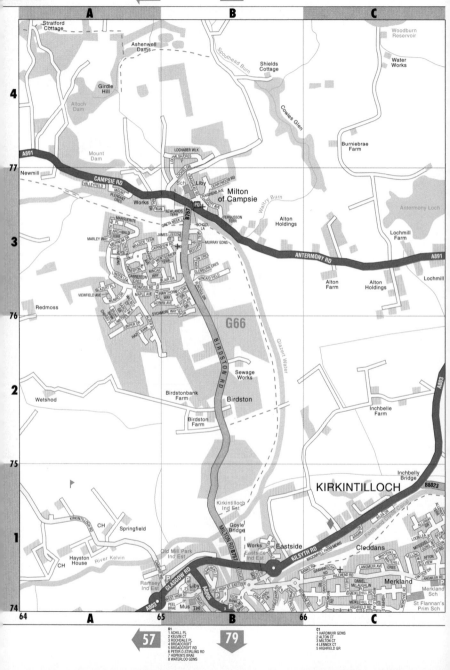

Stratford
Cottage

Woodburn
Reservoir

Ashenwell
Dams

Shields
Cottage

Spouthead Burn

Water
Works

4

Girdle
Hill

Alloch
Dam

Cowies Glen

Burniebrae
Farm

A891

Mount
Dam

LOCHABER WLK
WALSH CRES

77

Newmill

CAMPSIE RD
VALLEYFIELD
PLEASANT
CROFT
MOUNT

LOCHAL DR

Sch Liby
DERRYWOOD RD
CRAIGHEAD AVE
SCOTT AVE
PO

Milton
of Campsie

Walter Burn

Antermony Loch

Works

Alton
Holdings

FERGUSSON
TERR

NEWLANDS
CRES
GRETA MEEK LA

B757

MARGUERITE
ARCHIBALD
TERR

SCHOOL
LA

Lochmill
Farm

MARLEY WAY

JAMES LEESON
LAIRNSVIEW RD

MURRAY GDNS

ANTERMONY RD

A891

Lochmill

3

VIEWFIELD AVE

REDMOSS RD

MONTGOMERIE
TERR
BLAIR DR
GLENBURN CRES
KINCAID FIELD

Alton
Farm

Alton
Holdings

Redmoss

GLAZERT
MUNRO DR
MAPLE AVE
HAWTHORN
BONAN AVE
SYCAMORE WAY

G66

76

HAZEL BANK
JUNIPER DR

Glazert Water

Sewage
Works

BIRDSTON RD

Birdstonbank
Farm

Birdston

2

Wetshod

Inchbelle
Farm

A803

Birdston
Farm

75

Inchbelly
Bridge

KIRKINTILLOCH
B8023

KIRKINTILLOCH IND EST

Kirkintilloch
Ind Est

Goyle
Bridge

KIRKINTILLOCH RD
CH

Springfield

1

CH

Hayston
House

River Kelvin

Old Mill Park
Ind Est

Works
Eastside
Ind Est

Eastside

KILSYTH RD

Cleddans

LANGMUIR AVE

Merkland

Merkland
Sch

Ramsey
Ind Est

GLASGOW RD

Liby
Mus
TH

A803

PEEL
BRAE

B757

St Flannan's
Prim Sch

B1
1 ACHILL PL
2 KELVIN CT
3 ROCHDALE PL
4 BROADCROFT
5 BROADCROFT
6 PETER D.STIRLING RD
7 HOPKIN'S BRAE
8 WATERLOO GDNS

C1
1 HARDMUIR GDNS
2 ALTON CT
3 MILTON CT
4 LENNOX CT
5 HIGHFIELD GR

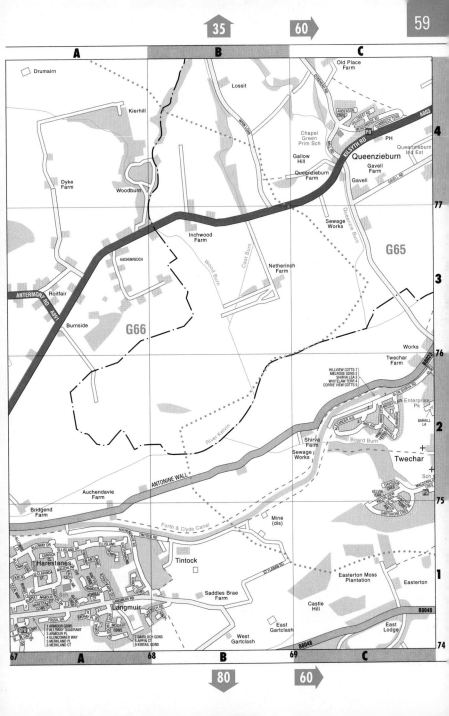

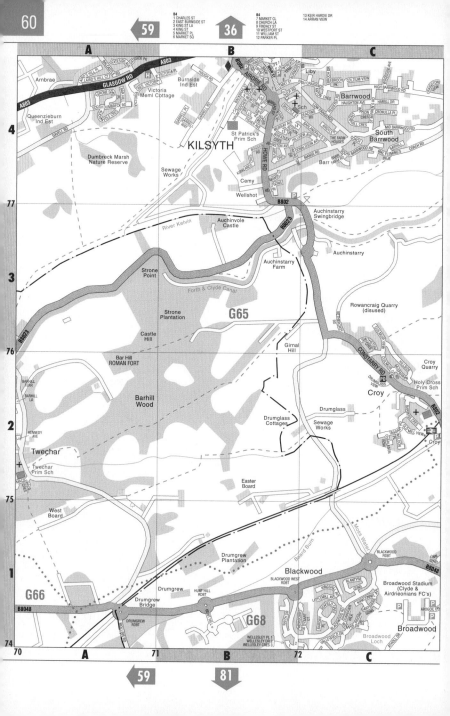

59   36

B4
1 CHARLES ST
2 EAST BURNSIDE ST
3 KING ST LA
4 KING ST
5 MARKET PL
6 MARKET SQ

B4
7 MARKET CL
8 CHURCH LA
9 FINDLAY ST
10 WESTPORT ST
11 WILLIAM ST
12 PARKER PL

13 KEIR HARDIE DR
14 ARRAN VIEW

KILSYTH

Arnbrae

Queenzieburn Ind Est

Dumbreck Marsh Nature Reserve

GLASGOW RD

A803

Burnside Ind Est

Victoria Meml Cottage

St Patrick's Prim Sch

Sewage Works

Cemy

Wellshot

River Kelvin

Auchinvole Castle

Auchinstarry Swingbridge

Auchinstarry Farm

Auchinstarry

Strone Point

Strone Plantation

Forth & Clyde Canal

G65

Castle Hill

Bar Hill ROMAN FORT

Girnal Hill

Rowancraig Quarry (disused)

Barhill Wood

Barhill Farr

Barhill La

Kennedy Ave

Twechar

Twechar Prim Sch

Drumglass Cottages

Drumglass

Sewage Works

Easter Board

Croy Quarry

Holy Cross Prim Sch

Croy

CONSTARRY RD

West Board

Blackwood

Drumgrew Plantation

Board Burn

Moss Water

Blackwood RDBT

Blackwood West RDBT

Broadwood Stadium (Clyde & Airdrieonians FC's)

Broadwood

Broadwood Loch

G66

Drumgrew

Drumgrew Bridge

Drumgrew RDBT

Hunt Hill RDBT

B8048

G68

WELLESLEY PL 1
WELLESLEY DR 2
WELLESLEY CRES 3

B8048

59   81

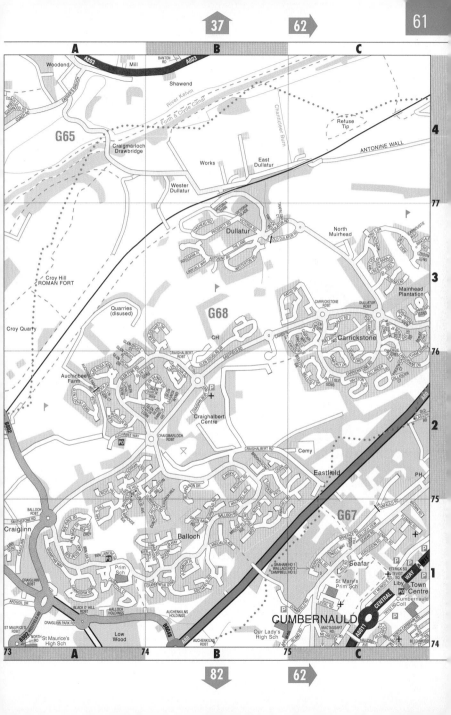

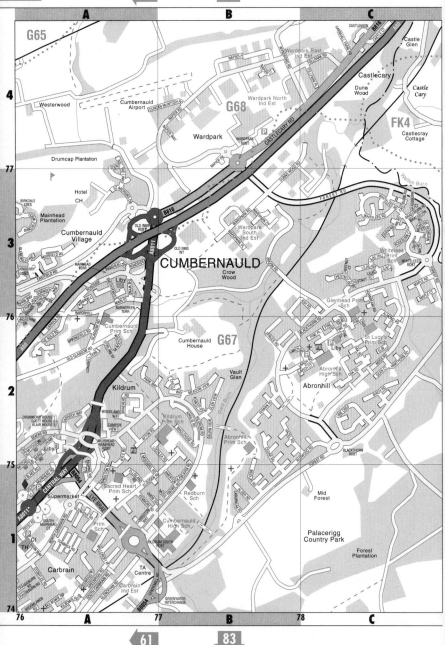

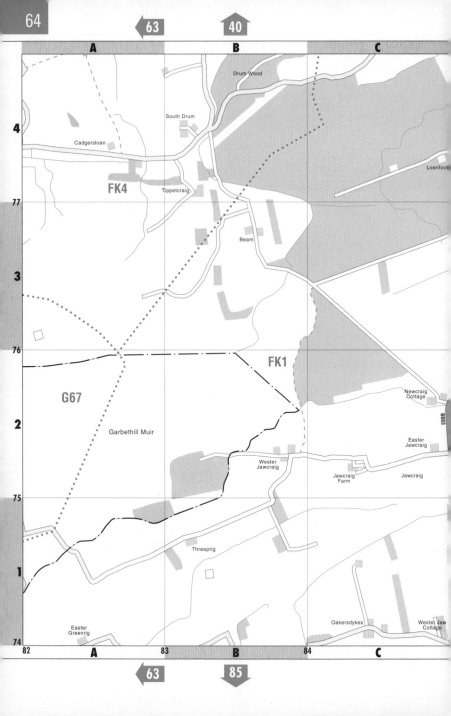

A B C

4

Drum Wood

South Drum

Cadgersloan

FK4

Tippetcraig

Loanfoot

77

Beam

3

76

FK1

G67

Newcraig
Cottage

Garbethill Muir

Easter
Jawcraig

2

B803

Wester
Jawcraig

Jawcraig
Farm

Jawcraig

75

Threaprig

1

Oakersdykes

Wester Jaw
Cottage

Easter
Greenrig

74

82 A 83 B 84 C

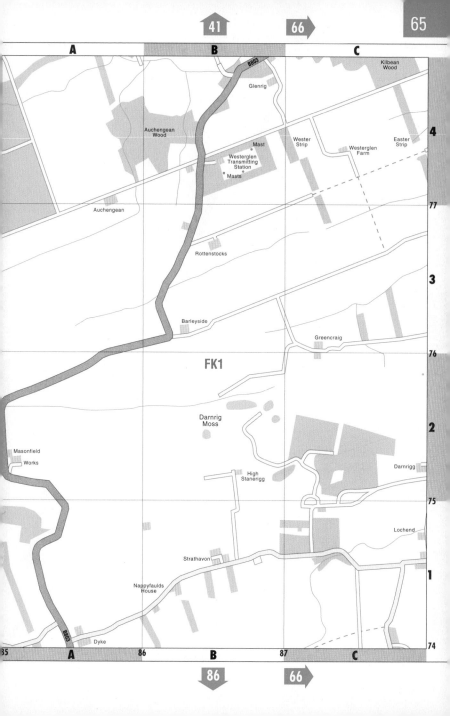

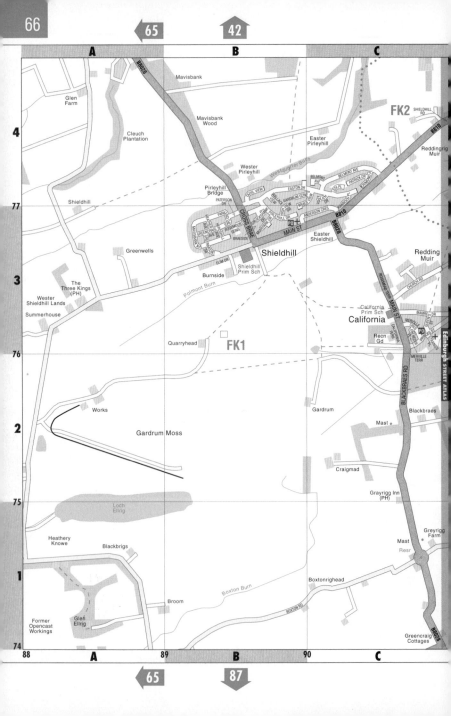

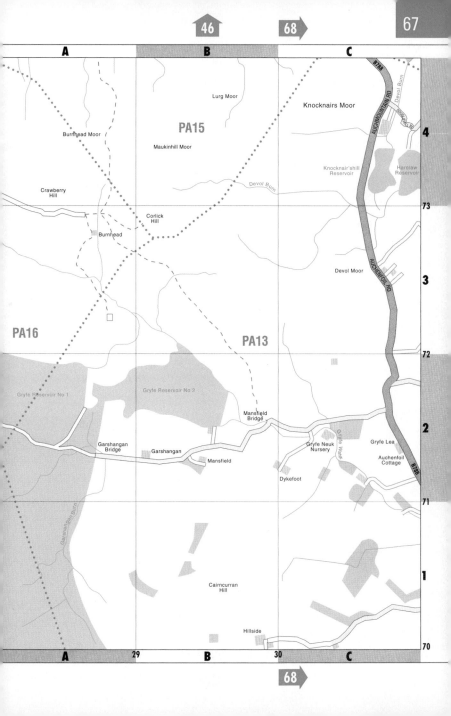

A B C

Lurg Moor

Knocknairs Moor

PA15

Burnhead Moor

Maukinhill Moor

4

Knocknair'shill Reservoir

Harelaw Reservoir

Devol Burn

Crawberry Hill

73

Corlick Hill

Burnhead

Devol Moor

3

PA16

72

PA13

Gryfe Reservoir No 1

Gryfe Reservoir No 2

Mansfield Bridge

2

Garshangan Bridge

Garshangan

Gryfe Neuk Nursery

Gryfe Lea

Mansfield

Auchenfoil Cottage

Dykefoot

71

Cairncurran Hill

1

Hillside

70

A 29 B 30 C

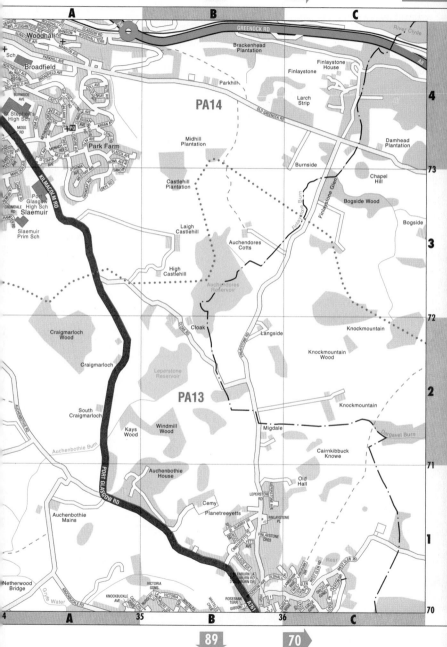

A   B   C

River Clyde

GREENOCK RD

Brackenhead
Plantation

Finlaystone
House

Finlaystone

Woodhall

Broadfield

Parkhill

Larch
Strip

A8

4

PA14

OLD GREENOCK RD

Midhill
Plantation

Damhead
Plantation

St Stephen's
High Sch

MOSS
RD

Park Farm

Burnside

73

Castlehill
Plantation

Chapel
Hill

Port
Glasgow
High Sch

Slaemuir

Bogside Wood

Finlaystone Glen

Finlaystone Burn

Laigh
Castlehill

Bogside

Slaemuir
Prim Sch

Auchendores
Cotts

3

High
Castlehill

Auchendores
Reservoir

Cloak

72

Craigmarloch
Wood

Langside

Knockmountain

KILMACOLM RD

Craigmarloch

Knockmountain
Wood

Leperstone
Reservoir

PA13

Knockmountain

2

South
Craigmarloch

Kays
Wood

Windmill
Wood

Migdale

Gippavel Burn

Auchenbothie Burn

Cairnkibbuck
Knowe

71

PORT GLASGOW RD

Auchenbothie
House

Old
Hall

AUCHENBOTHIE RD

Auchenbothie
Mains

Cemy

Planetreeyetts

Finlaystone
PL

Finlaystone
Cres

Netherwood
Bridge

Gryfe Water

KNOCKBUCKLE RD

VICTORIA
GDNS

KNOCKBUCKLE
AVE

VICTORIA

WHITE LEA
TERR

ROSEBANK
TERR

A761

Res

1

4   A   35   B   36   C   70

70

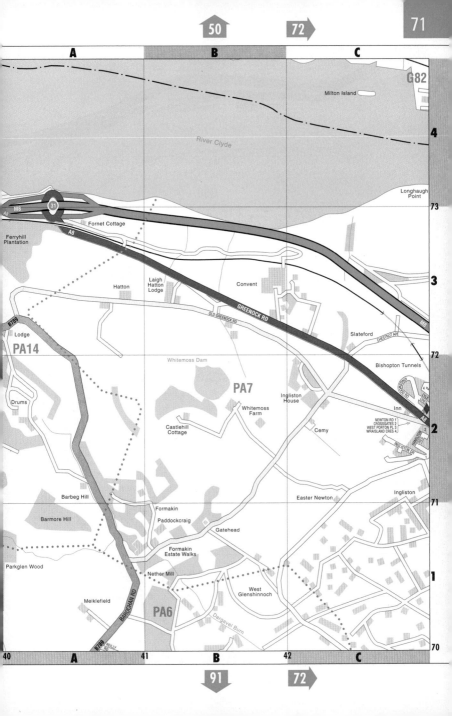

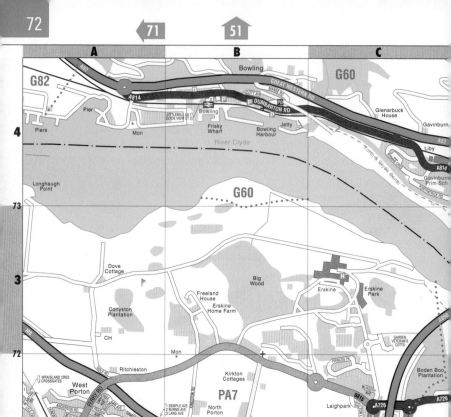

A   B   C

G82

G60

Bowling

GREAT WESTERN RD

Pier

A814

Mon

Littlemill (la 1) Clyde View (2)

Bowling

P P DUMBARTON RD P PO

SCOTT RS MANSE RD

Glenarbuck House

Gavinburn

Piers

Frisky Wharf

Bowling Harbour

Jetty

Liby

A814

Gavinburn Prim Sch

4

River Clyde

A82

Longhaugh Point

G60

73

Dove Cottage

Big Wood

Erskine

Erskine Park

3

Conyston Plantation

Freeland House

Erskine Home Farm

CH

GARDEN VETERAN'S COTTS

M8

Ritchieston

GOLF RD

Mon

Kirkton Cottages

PRINCES PK

Boden Boo Plantation

A726

72

1 WRAISLAND CRES
2 CROSSGATES

West Porton

FERRY RD

PA7

1 SEMPLE AVE
2 BURNS AVE
3 LANG AVE

North Porton

BURGHER AVE

B815

Laighpark

A726

A8

Liby

B815

Golf Inn (PH)

BRIDGEND

ROSSLAND CRES

ANDERSON RD

WALLAC AVE

Bishopton Prim Sch

Kingston

Drumcross

Toll

Bargarran

DARROCH DR

MAXWELL DR

Bargarran Prim Sch

2

Bishopton

Wester Rossland

GREENOCK RD

HAY AVE

OLD GREENOCK RD

M898

St John Bosco Prim Sch

Craigend Hill

PA8

71

Bishopton

Craigton Burn

1 ALMOND PL
2 ROSSLAND PL

Craigton

Linburn

West Craigend

1

Ditch

Gladstone

P PO

Sewage Works

P

Rossland

30

M898

Linburn

Bolerno

Linburn

MILLFIELD

70

43   A   44   B   45   C

A8

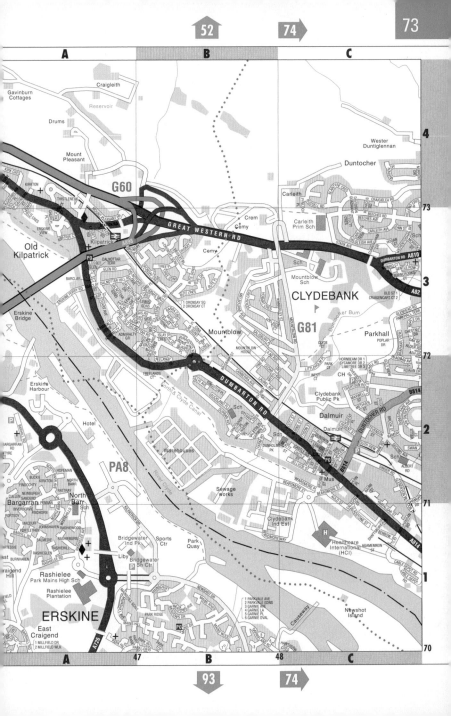

A B C

4

Cochno Filters

Whitehill

Law

Loansdean

Wester Cochno Holdings

Auchnacraig

Duntocher

Southhill

Edinbarnet Prim Sch

Fairley

St Joseph's Prim Sch

73

DUNTOCHER RD

G61

Lawmuir

A810

DUMBARTON RD

Goldenhill Prim Sch

GLASGOW RD

Hardgate CH

Fairday's View

Hutcheson Hill

3

A82

Parkhall

KILBOWIE RD

Cleddans

G81

Garscadden Burn

72

B814

Braidfield

Braidfield

Wr Twr

Lochgoin Prim Sch

DUNTOCHER RD

Liby

Holly St

St Columba's High Sch

Kilmari Prim Sch

Langfaulds Prim Sch

2

Radnor Park

Clydebank High Sch

GREAT WESTERN RD

Kilbowie

Colt

1 Tarbolton Dr
2 Tarbolton Sq
3 Lochlea Ave
4 Duncombe View
5 Garscadden View
6 Gleniffer View
7 Peel View

Laurence PO

Drumry Prim Sch

G15

Liby

71

Dalmuir

DRUMRY RD

B8055

B8055

Singer

St Eunan's Prim Sch

Clydebank Bans Pk

Drumry Cemy

Drumry

Braidfield High Sch

1

CLYDEBANK

A814

DUMBARTON RD

A8014

Clyde Sh Ctr

Works

Forth & Clyde Canal

Greenwood Quadrant

Drumry

70

Works

Liby

Clydebank

Linnvale Prim Sch

Linnvale

Whitecrook Prim Sch

River Clyde

G13

A82

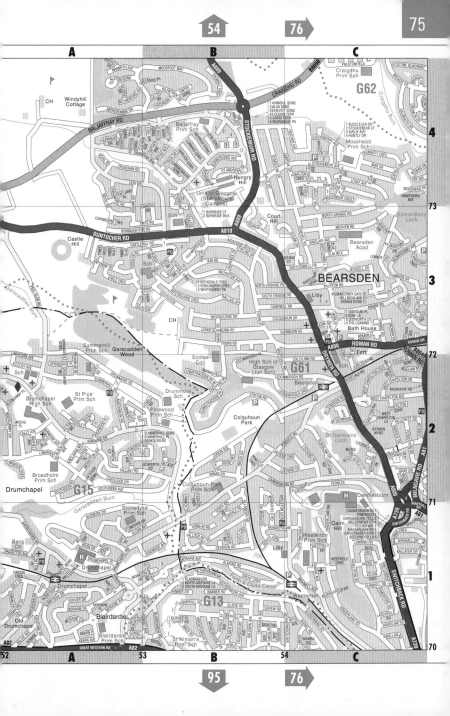

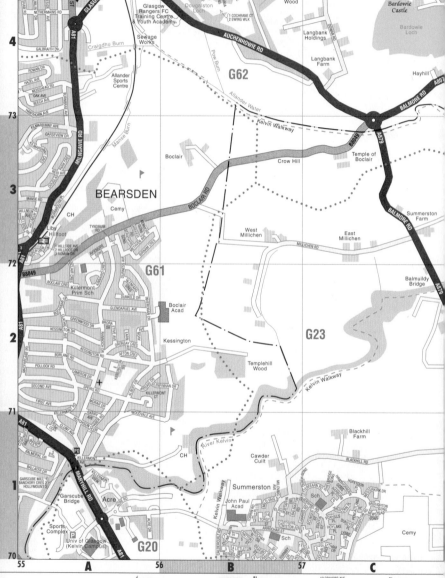

A   B   C

BREADIE DR
KELSTONE QUADRANT
KELSTONE AVE
KEYSTONE AVE

BREADIE DR
NETHERMAINS RD
BRAESIDE AVE
THURLOE AVE
QUEEN
KELSTONE AVE
KEYSTONE AVE

B8030

GLASGOW RD

A81

A807

The Jaw

Bardowie
Mains

Bardowie
Castle

ROWAN DR

HAZEL AVE
MOSSHEAD RD
OAK AVE
BEECH AVE

GALBRAITH DR

Glasgow
Rangers FC
Training Centre
& Youth Academy

Dougalston
Loch

Beech
Wood

Bardowie
Loch

Craigdhu Burn

AUCHENHOWIE RD

Sewage
Works

Langbank
Holdings

Allander
Sports
Centre

G62

Pow Burn

Langbank
Farm

Hayhill

BALMORE RD

A807

73

KILMARDINNY AVE

GARSCUBE RD

Manse Burn

Allander Water

Kelvin Walkway

B8049

A79

Boclair

Crow Hill

Temple of
Boclair

BEARSDEN

CH   Cemy

BOCLAIR RD

Summerston
Farm

BALMORE RD

MANSE RD

3

HILLNEUK

Liby
Hillfoot

TYNDRUM ST

West
Millichen

East
Millichen

1 HILLSIDE AVE
2 HILLFOOT DR
3 ROMAN DR

BELMONT
CLOSE

MILLICHEN RD

Balmuildy
Bridge

72

B8049

A81

BOCLAIR CRES

Killermont
Prim Sch

G61

DUNKELD DR

Boclair
Acad

A79

GLENDARUEL AVE

GREENWOOD DR

BRORA
DR

EARN
GROVE

KESSINGTON DR

KESSINGTON RD

HETON CRES

Kessington

G23

2

BORLAND RD

RANNOCH AVE

BRORA DR

POLLOCK RD

CAMERON DR

SPEIRS RD

GLENFINNAN DR

Templehill
Wood

Kelvin Walkway

SECOND AVE

KILLERMONT

FIRST AVE

MONAR DR

KILLERMONT

GARRY
DR

WOODVALE AVE

71

A81

PO

KILLERMONT

CH

River Kelvin

Blackhill
Farm

BALMORAL DR

KILLERMONT

BLACKHILL RD

Cawder
Cuilt

HOPETOUN

LARKIN DR

GARSCUBE MILL
BANCHORY CRES
HOLLYMOUNT
BALLATER DR

MARYHILL RD

Summerston

Kelvin Walkway

Sch

BREIGHTON DR

1

Garscube
Bridge

Acre

ACRE RD

John Paul
Acad

Sch

FOXHILLS

Cemy

Sports
Complex

P

Univ of Glasgow
(Kelvin Campus)

G20

LITTLETON

A81

ARROCHAR ST

Sch

70

55   A   56   B   57   C

A
B
C

Braeside

CH

Collalis

Works

Balmore

Branziet
Bridge

Whitefauld

Laverockhill

BALMORE RD

A807

Branziet
Farm

Bardowie

Bogside

4

Allander Ave

South
Bardowie

G62

Balmore Haughs

73

Allander Wood

River Kelvin

Cawder House
(CH)

3

Kelvin Walkway

Buchley

G64

BALMULDY RD

72

Easter
Balmuidy

Wilderness
Plantation

Depot

Farm
Bridge

Jellyhill

Mavis Valley Road

Factory

Wester Balmuidy
Farm

G23

2

Marchfield

HILTON TERR

GLENEAGLES
GDNS

HILTON DR

Balmuildy
Prim. Sch

Refuse
Tip

Forth & Clyde Canal

Bishopbriggs

Bishopbriggs Burn

71

LOMOND DR

THE
ROWANS

Works

BALMORE RD

BLACKHILL RD

LOCHFAULD RD

Lochfauld

Turnbull
High Sch

ST ANDREWS
AVE
BISHOP GDNS

CH

CHURCHILL
WAY

DALHOUSIE
GDNS

1

Parkholm
Farm

ST MARYS RD

NOVAR GDNS
BARCHILL DR
POLLOCK
BEAUFORT GDNS

ELDON GDNS

KENMURE AVE

CROSS CT

A879

G22

Kenmure St Mary's
Secure Unit

KENMURE GDNS

HEATHERBRAE
GORSEWOOD

CLOVERGATE

RUSHENTALLOCH RD

A803

Cemy

Possil
Loch

CASTLE BAY
DR

Laigh
Kenmure

70

A
59
B
60
C

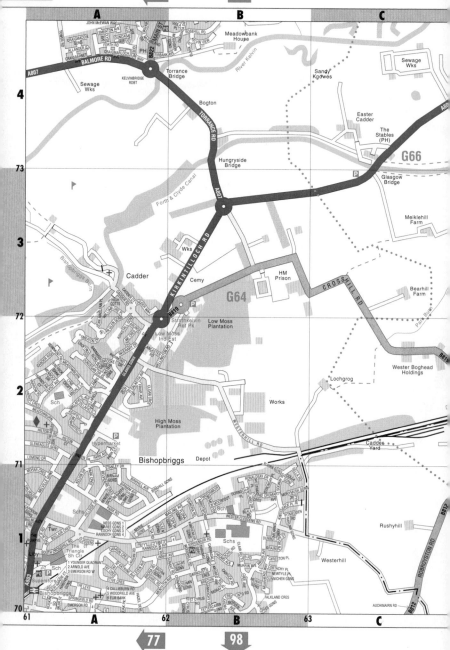

A B C

4

73

3

72

2

71

1

70

Meadowbank House

River Kelvin

John McEwan Way
Smeaton Ave
Forth Rd
Duncanso

Craigmaddie Gdns
Allander Rd
Craigbarnet
Craigmarloch

B822 MAIN ST

Violet Gdns
Rosehill Rd
Pin View
Firbank Ave

PH

Balmore Rd

A807

Kelvinbridge Rdbt

Torrance Bridge

Sewage Wks

Bogton

Sandy Knowes

Sewage Wks

Easter Cadder

The Stables (PH)

A81

G66

Torrance Rd

Hungryside Bridge

Forth & Clyde Canal

A807

Glasgow Bridge

P

Meiklehill Farm

Bishopbriggs Burn

Cadder

Wks

Cemy

Kirkintilloch Rd

G64

HM Prison

Crosshill Rd

Bearhill Farm

Park Burn

B819

Strathkelvin Ret Pk

P

Low Moss Ind Est

Low Moss Plantation

B818

Wester Boghead Holdings

Lochgrog

High Moss Plantation

Sch

Works

Westerhill Rd

Hypermarket

P

Caddes Yard

Bishopbriggs

Depot

Rushyhill

71

Schs

Bishopbriggs

Ness Gdns 1
Maree Gdns 2
Lochy Gdns 3
Rannoch Gdns 4

Wester Cleddens Rd

Westerhill

Twr

Triangle Sh Ctr

Schs

Sch

1 Younger Quadrant
2 Arnold Ave
3 Emerson Rd W

4 Callieburn Rd
5 Woodfield Ave
6 Elm Bank

Robroyston Rd

B812

PO

Superstore

Bishopbriggs

The Leys

Emerson Rd

St Cyrus Rd

Falkland Cres

B812

Auchinairn Rd

A803

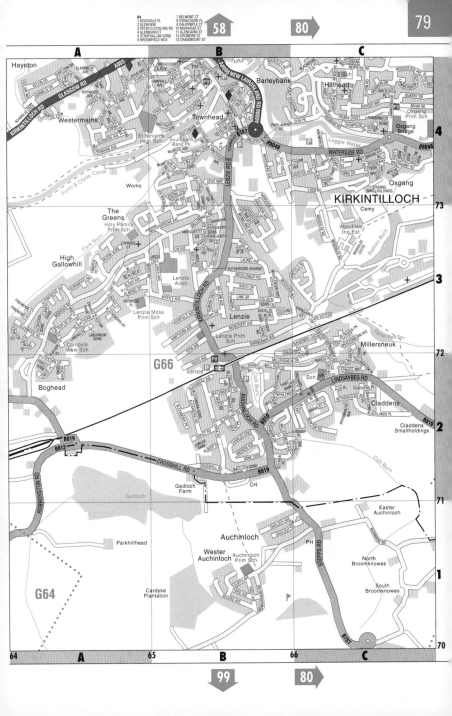

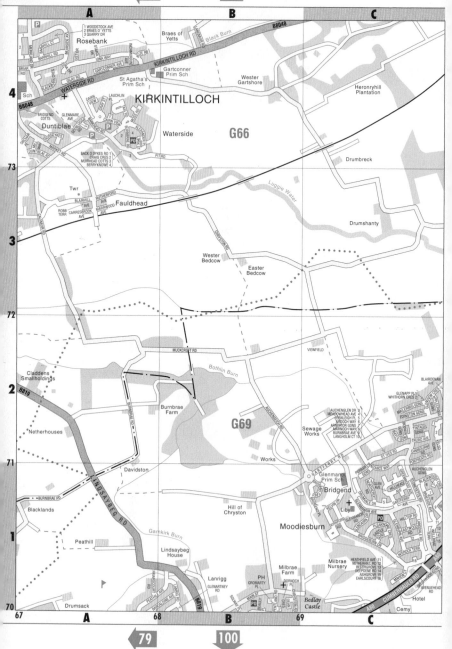

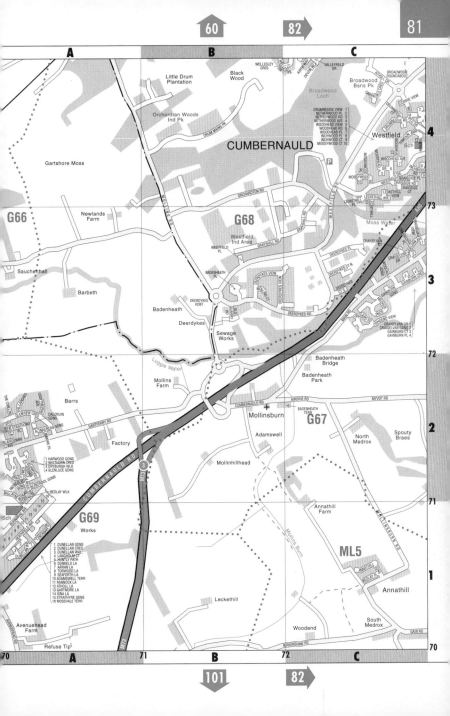

A
B
C

Wellesley Cres
Austin Mace
Doroval Rd

Little Drum Plantation
Black Wood

Valleyfield Dr
Broadwood Roundabout

Broadwood Bsns Pk

Corrie View

Orchardtan Woods Ind Pk

DRUM MAINS PK

Broadwood Loch

DRUMNESSIE VIEW 1
NETHERWOOD PL 2
NETHERWOOD RD 3
NETHERWOOD AVE 4
WOODHEAD VIEW 5
WOODHEAD RD 6
WOODHEAD PL 7
INCHWOOD PL 8
INCHWOOD CT 9
MOSSYWOOD CT 10

CUMBERNAULD

Westfield Sch

Gartshore Moss

ORCHARDTON RD

MOSSYWOOD

WOODHEAD AVE

CRAIGSIDE PL
CRAIGSIDE RD
CRAIGSIDE CT

G66

Newlands Farm

G68

GRAYSHILL RD

LECKETHILL PL
LECKETHILL AVE
LECKETHILL VIEW

Moss Water

73

Sauchenhall

Westfield Ind Area

WESTFIELD PL

GRAYSHILL RD

BADENHEATH PL

DEERDYKES PL

DEERDYKES CT N

CRAIGIEVAR PL

CRAIGIEVAR DR

3

Barbeth

Badenheath

DEERDYKES RDBT

MOLLINS RD
MOLLINS CT

DEERDYKES VIEW

DEERDYKES CT

GAINBURN CRES
GAINBURN GDNS

Deerdykes

DEERDYKES RD

ODSGAND VIEW

CRAIGIEVAR GR 1
CRAIGIEVAR GDNS 2
GAINBURN CT 3
GAINBURN PL 4

Sewage Works

72

Luggie Water

Mollins Farm

Badenheath Bridge

Badenheath Park

THE CHASE

Barrs

DALCRUIN GDNS

GARTFERRY RD

CUMBERNAULD RD

AIRDRIE RD

MYVOT RD

ALTNACREAGH GDNS

BADENHEATH TERR

2

GLENFERN CRES
STRATHORN AVE
SLAUGHENAN AVE

Factory

Mollinsburn

G67

North Medrox

Spouty Braes

1 HARWOOD GDNS
2 WHITDORN WLK
3 DRYBURGH WLK
4 GLENLUCE GDNS

BEDLAY WLK

Adamswell

71

BALLATER...
GLENTUM GDNS

Mollinhillhead

Annathill Farm

WHITELEES RD

Sch

G69

Works

1 DUNELLAN GDNS
2 DUNELLAN CRES
3 DUNELLAN WAY
4 LANGHOLM CT
5 HUNTLY PATH
6 DUNKELD LA
7 ARRAN LA
8 TORWOOD LA
9 SEAFORTH LA
10 ADAMSWELL TERR
11 RANNOCK LA
12 ATHOLL LA
13 GARTMORE LA
14 IONA LA
15 STRATHYRE GDNS
16 MOSSVALE TERR

ML5

Annathill

Leckethill

M73

Avenuehead Farm

Refuse Tip

M73

Woodend

BIRKENSHAW RD

South Medrox

GAIN RD

70

A · B · C

CUMBERNAULD

G68

G67

G66

ML5

ML6

Condorrat

Dalshannan

St Maurices High Sch

Low Wood

St Francis of Assisi Prim Sch

Condorrat Prim Sch

St Helen's Prim Sch

Greenfields High Sch

Greenfaulds

Melrose Prim Sch

Auchenkilns Holdings

North Myvot

Garngibboch House

Wester Blairlinn

Blairlinn Ind Est

Milncroft

North Bellstane Plantation

Madgiscroft Quarry

South Myvot

Craigend Nursery

Wester Myvot

Hallbrae

Loanhead

Summerhill

Summerhill Strips

Shank Bridge

Bellstane

Summerfield

Mossywood

The Grain

Gain Farm

Cleddans

Douglas Glen

Douglas Plantation

South Bellstane Plantation

Luggie Water

Gain Burn

Shank Burn

GLASGOW RD

CONDORRAT RD

CONDORRAT RING RD

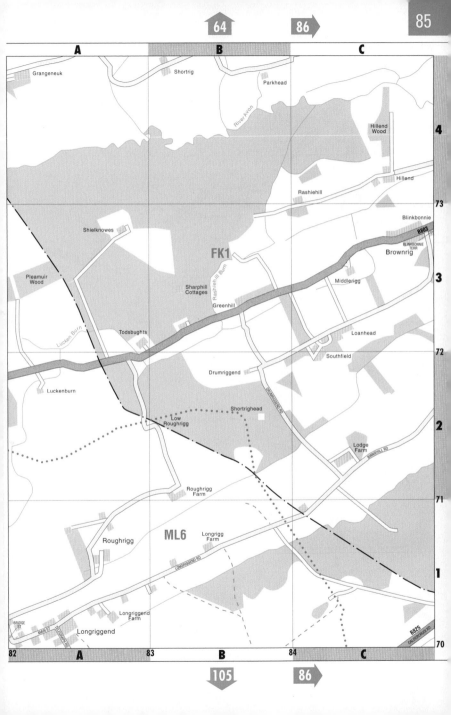

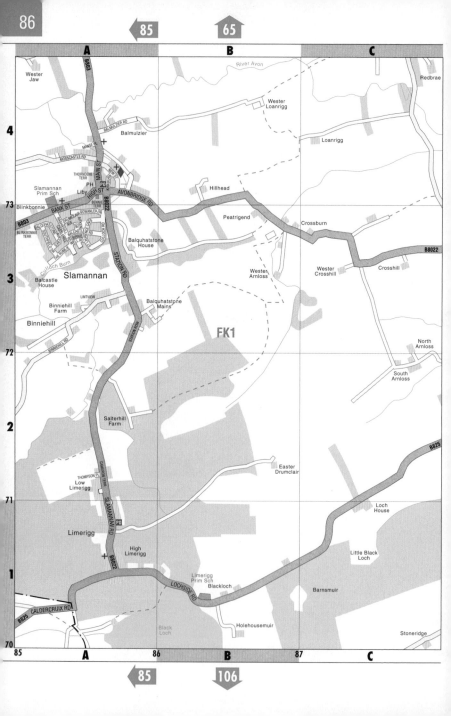

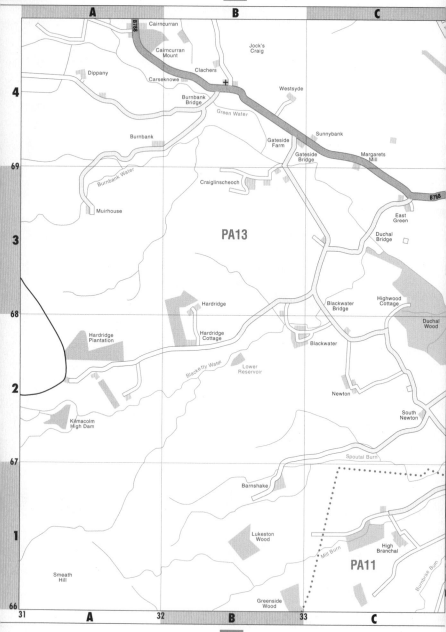

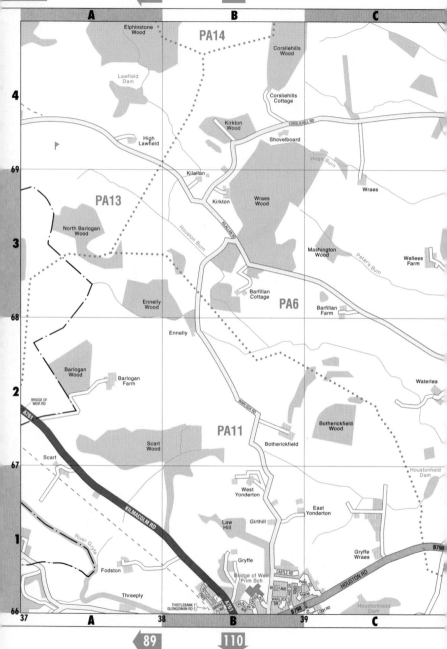

A B C

Elphinstone Wood

PA14

Corsliehills Wood

Lawfield Dam

Corsliehills Cottage

4

Kirkton Wood

CORSLIEHALL RD

Shovelboard

High Lawfield

Hogs Burn

69

Kilallan

Wraes

PA13

Kirkton

Houston Burn

Wraes Wood

North Barlogan Wood

3

Mashington Wood

Peter's Burn

Wellees Farm

Barfillan Cottage

Ennelly Wood

PA6

Barfillan Farm

68

Ennelly

Barlogan Wood

Barlogan Farm

WARLOCK RD

Waterlea

2

BRIDGE OF WEIR RD

A761

Scart Wood

PA11

Botherickfield Wood

Scart

Botherickfield

67

Houstonfield Dam

KILMACOLM RD

West Yonderton

East Yonderton

Law Hill

Girthill

1

River Gryfe

Gryffe Wraes

B790

Gryffe

Fodston

Bridge of Weir Prim Sch

CASTLE RD

BEECH AVE

HOUSTON RD

Threeply

THISTLEBANK 1
GLENGOWAN RD 2

A761

B790

WARLOCK DR

LOCH RD

Houstonhead

66

37 A **38** B **39** C

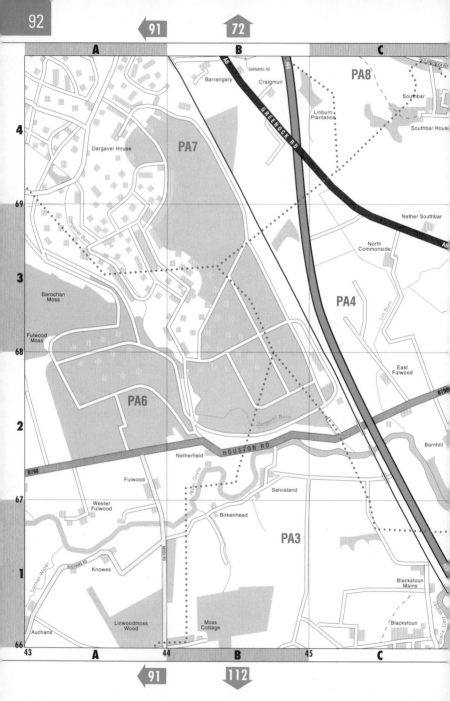

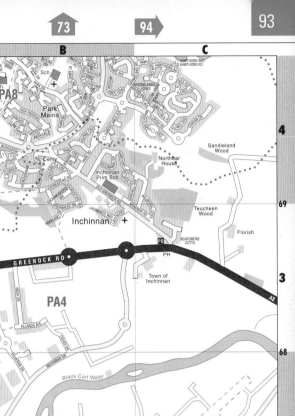

| A | B | C |

4

69

3

68

2

67

1

66

A726

Millfield Wyn 1
Millfield Wlk 2
Millfield Dr 3

PA8

Park Mains

Sch

Park Ridge
Park Gn
Park Gate

Parkway

Cemy

Inchinnan Prim Sch

Northbar House

Sandieland Wood

ERSKINE

Freeland

Inchinnan

Teucheen Wood

Florish

SOUTHBAR RD

Broom Hill

GREENOCK RD

Beardmore Cotts

Town of Inchinnan

PH

PO

A8

A726

New Mains

PA4

Newmains Ave

Allands Ave

Inchinnan Ind Est

Black Cart Water

Works

HOUSTON RD B790

Barnsford Ave

Inchinnan Bsns Pk

Brownsfield

TA Centre

Mast

Camp (dis)

Easter Yonderton

BARNSFORD RD

Barnsford Bridge

Wester Yonderton

Easter Walkinshaw

WALKINSHAW RD

Glasgow Airport

Abbotsinch Rd

White Cart Water

Works

Mill

WRIGHT ST

Blackstone Mains

PA3

A726

West Walkinshaw Farm

CALEDONIA WAY W

St Andrews Cres

BLYTH RD

ST ANDREW'S DR W

CALEDONIA WAY

NEVIS WAY

ARGYLL AVE

ST ANDREW'S DR W

Hotel

Clydesdale Ave 1
Somerled Ave 2

Sewage Wks

i PO

P

P

| 46 | A | 47 | B | 48 | C |

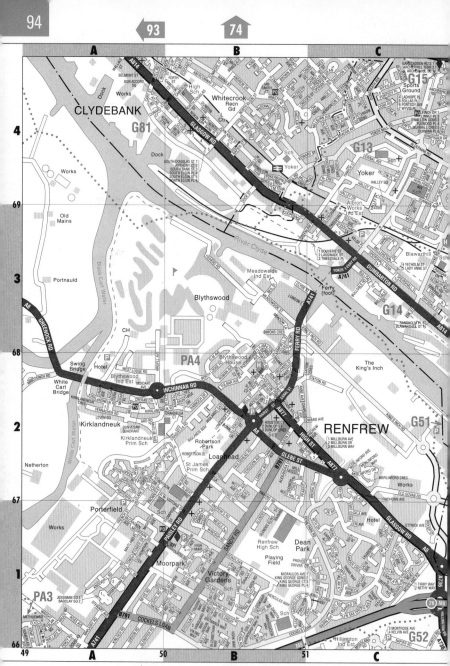

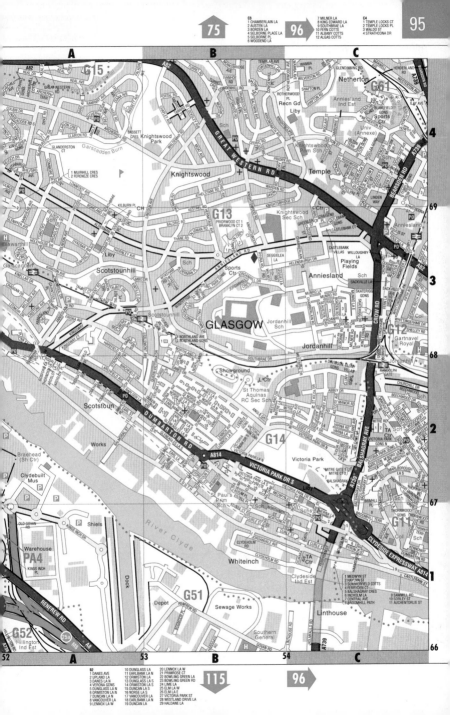

95   76

For full street detail of the highlighted area see page 240

116

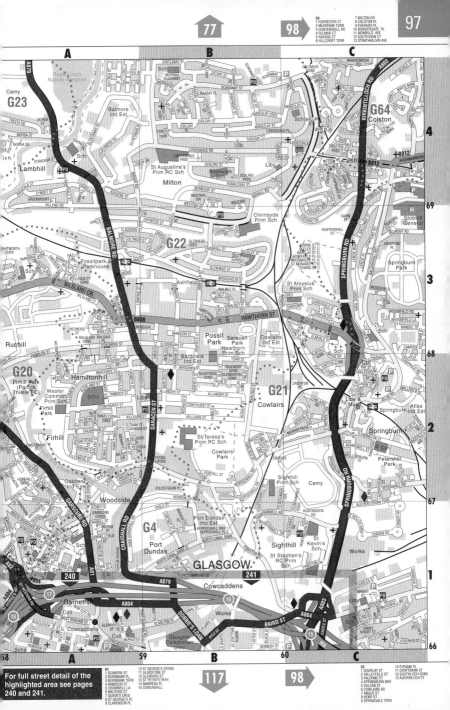

A B C

Drumsack Plantation

Garnkirk Burn

RICHMOND GDNS
BARCALDINE AVE
EVERBEADES

Chryston Bsns Ctr

LINDSAYBEG RD

B819

Chryston
Schs

Chryston
Liby

BOTHLYN RD
MORAY PL
PENTLAND
SOUTH LOAN

Cemy

A80

A752

Bothlin Burn

Holms

4

Glen Cottage

Crow Wood

CH

CUMBERNAULD RD

A752

Hotel

GREENLEA RD
CROW WOOD TERR
POTASELS RD
LILYBANK AVE
MOSS RD
NEUK AVE

CHURCH RD
ELMIRA RD

STATION RD

1 MOORPARK AVE
2 STENHOUSE AVE

Muirhead

St Barbara's Prim Sch

Glaudhall Farm

DRUMROD

69

A80

WOODHEAD TERR
LAUREL RD

DRUMCAVEL RD

Garnkirk Moss

HOLMES PL
BLACKWOOD
SOUTHVIEW PL

Mount Ellen

Lochend House

INCHNOCK AVE

Highpit Plantation

Woodhead Farm

Garnkirk

WOODHEAD

Heathfield Moss

Heathfield Farm

Johnston Loch

LOCHEND RD

B80

3

G33

WHITESIDE
KILPATRICK DR

G69

Lochview Terr

JOHNSTON RD 1
LOCHSIDE 2
WOODNEUK TERR 3
BEARD CRES 4
JARDINE TERR 5
WOODNEUK LA 6

Gartcosh

KIRKHILL RD

MANOR RD

68

Depot

OLD GARTLOCH RD

Prim Sch

M73

B806

A752

2

West Cottages

Mid Cottages

GARTLOCH RD

Gartloch Cottages

Lochview Cottages

Bothlin Burn

COATBRIDGE RD

67

B806

Bishop Loch

Lochwood Cottages

Lochwood Farm

Baillie Moss Wood

1

GLASGOW

Provanhall Prim Sch

St Benedict's Prim RC Sch

Craigend Wood

G34

BALDRAGON RD

Lochwood Plantation

Bishoploch Prim Sch

AUCHINGILL RD
MYROCH
SKELBO
SKELBO PATH

WINLAW

ML5

66

DURRIS
WESTERHOUSE RD

A B C

67 68 69

A · B · C

Refuse Tip

Drumcavel Lodge

BIRKENSHAW RD

Medrox Quarry (disused)

DRUMCAVEL RD

Inchneuk Farm

Shankramuir

Bothlin Burn

Glenboig Farm

4

St Joseph's Sch

1 ASHTON GDNS
2 CROFTFOOT PL

CH

Marnock

69

HILLSIDE COTTS

Glenboig

JOHNSTON RD

Croftfoot

GLENBOIG RD

MAIN ST
PO

Glenboig

Johnston Farm

Recn Gd

2a

G69

PH

3

Garnqueen

Ramoan

COATBRIDGE RD

CARMICHAEL PATH 1
EASDALE PATH 2
BALLATER WAY 3
McGREGOR PATH 4
STRONE PATH 5
CARSAIG LOAN 6
INVERCREE WLK 7
GLENELG PATH 8
EAGLESHAM PATH 9

Garnqueen Farm

1 WOODNEUK RD
2 BEARD CRES

Glenboig Prim Sch

68

ML5

Gartliston Farm

PH

Gartsherrie Holm Farm

COATBRIDGE RD

ML6

2

Refuse Tip

LC

Gartcloss Farm

Heatherbell

Woodend

Gartsherrie Wood

67

Townhead Prim Sch

DUDLEY DR

DOCHART DR

DERWENT DR

WITCHWOOD CT

Woodend Loch

Lochend Cottages

Blacklands

Hollandhurst

P

Drumpellier Country Pk Visitor Centre

TOWNHEAD RD

CRIMAN DR

BELMONT ST

PO

Witch Wood

Freightliner Terminal

CH

Sch

1

Lochend Loch

GARTCOSH RD

A752

LOCHEND RD

Drumpellier Country Park

St Bartholomew's RC Prim Sch

Gartsherrie Ind Est

66

70 · A · 71 · B · 72 · C

A

B

C

G67

Gaindydykehead

East Lodge
Wood

Foot o' Loan
Wood

East
Gartmillan

LC

4

Greenfoot

West
Gartmillan

Shank Burn

Glenmill
Wood

Drumbowie
Farm

Ardaryth

69

ML5

MOLLINSBURN RD

Refuse Tip

Haggmuir
Farm

CONDORRAT RD

Brackenhirst

3

Gas Storage
Depot

PETERSHILL RD

MILLBOYNE RD

Gartverrie Burn

Ryden
Mains

New Monkland

68

Palace

ML6

Cemy

New Monkland
Prim Sch

RAEBOG RD

Rochsoles

2

Gartverrie
Farm

Copse Wood

QUARRYSIDE ST

PH

Braidenhill
Farm

MACARTHUR
AVE

Blackwall
Plantation

Cromlet

COATBRIDGE RD

Dryflat

Glenmavis

67

STRATMUNGO CRES
STAINEYBRAES PL
DYKEHEAD CRES
CRAIGMOCHAN AVE

CH

GLENMAVIS RD

Virtuewell Glen

Golfhill
Prim Sch

ML5

Kippsbyre

BALLOCHNEY LA
LEVEN QUADRANT
LAIDON RD
KATRINE CRES

Burnfoot

1

GARTLISTON RD

Kipps

North Burn

METHVEN
TERR

NORTHBURN RD

WAVERLEY ST

Works

Greenhill
Ind Est

Greenhill

1 CHASSELS ST
2 BRUCE ST
3 GREENSIDE ST
4 BURNBANK ST

LAGGAN
QUADRANT

BALLOCHNEY ST

COMMONHEAD LA

Acad

Sch

COMMONHEAD RD
QUARRY RD

WHINHALL AVE

WILSON
ST

GARTLOSSWOOD RD

Greenhill
Baptist Ctr

CAMERON ST

AFND RD

ARRAN DR

73

A

74

B

75

C

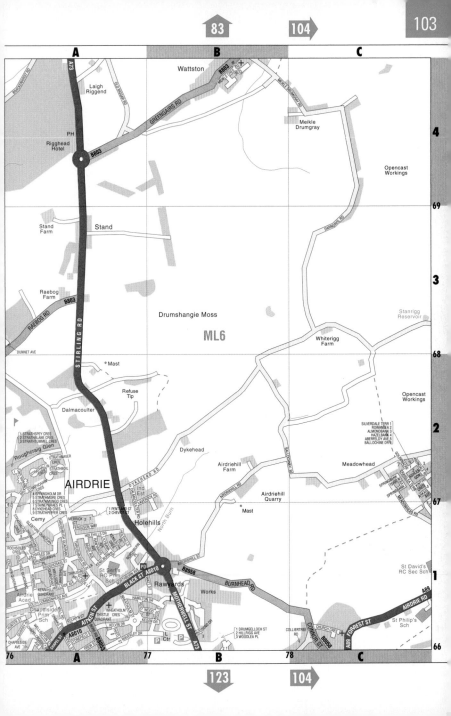

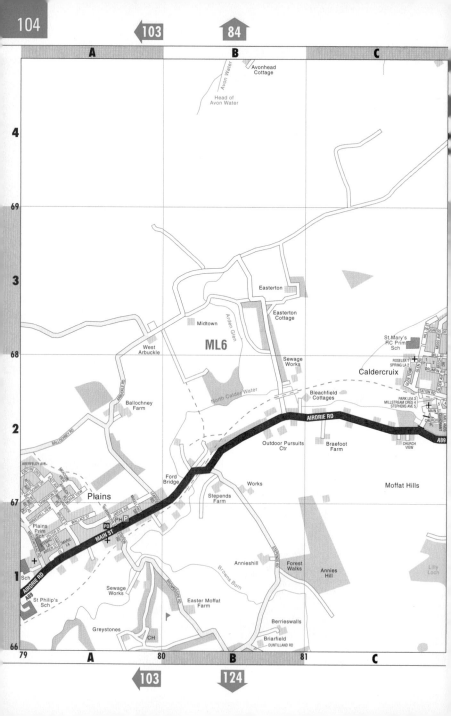

A · B · C

4

69

3

Avonhead
Cottage

Avon Water

Head of
Avon Water

Easterton

Easterton
Cottage

Midtown

ML6

Arden Glen

West
Arbuckle

68

Sewage
Works

St Mary's
RC Prim
Sch

Caldercruix

ROSELEA 1
SPRING LA 2

PROGRESS DR

GLEN TER

DRUMFIN AVE

STATION RD

North Calder Water

Bleachfield
Cottages

PARK LEA 3
MILLSTREAM CRES 4
STEPHENS AVE 5

MAIN ST

LIME AVE

CHURCH
PL

Ballochney
Farm

BALLOCHNEY RD

AIRDRIE RD

A89

2

Outdoor Pursuits
Ctr

Braefoot
Farm

CHURCH
VIEW

Moffat Hills

ABERFELDY AVE.

Plains

Ford
Bridge

Works

67

Plains
Prim
Sch

JARVIE AVE

MEADOWHEAD VIEW

WALLACE ST

MARK LA.

PH P

PO

MAIN ST

Stepends
Farm

REDWOOD RD

BENTS RD.

Sch

AIRDRIE RD

A89

St Philip's
Sch

1

Sewage
Works

Annieshill

Brooms Burn

SPRINGS RD.

Forest
Walks

Annies
Hill

Lilly
Loch

66

Greystones

CH

Easter Moffat
Farm

Berrieswalls

Briarfield

DUNTILLAND RD

79

A

80

B

81

C

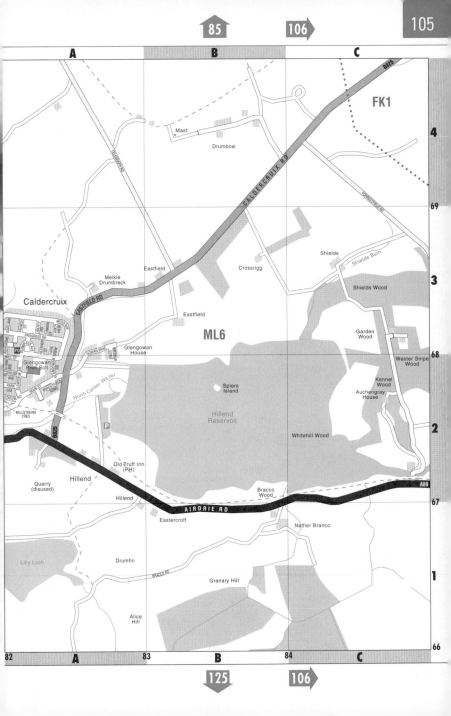

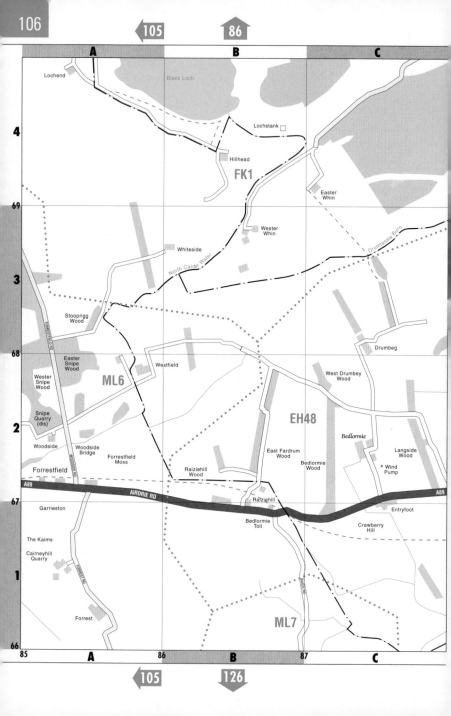

105
86

A　　　　　　B　　　　　　C

Lochend

Black Loch

Lochstank □

4

Hillhead

FK1

Easter Whin

69

Wester Whin

Whiteside

Drumtassie Burn

North Calder Water

3

Stooprigg Wood

Drumbeg

68

Easter Snipe Wood

Westfield

West Drumbey Wood

Wester Snipe Wood

ML6

EH48

Snipe Quarry (dis)

Bedlormie

2

Woodside

Woodside Bridge

Forrestfield Moss

Raiziehill Wood

East Fardrum Wood

Bedlormie Wood

Langside Wood

● Wind Pump

Forrestfield

A89

AIRDRIE RD

Raiziehill

Entryfoot

A89

67

Garrieston

Bedlormie Toll

Crawberry Hill

The Kaims

Cairneyhill Quarry

1

Forrest

ML7

66

85　　　　　A　　　　　86　　　　　B　　　　　87　　　　　C

105
126

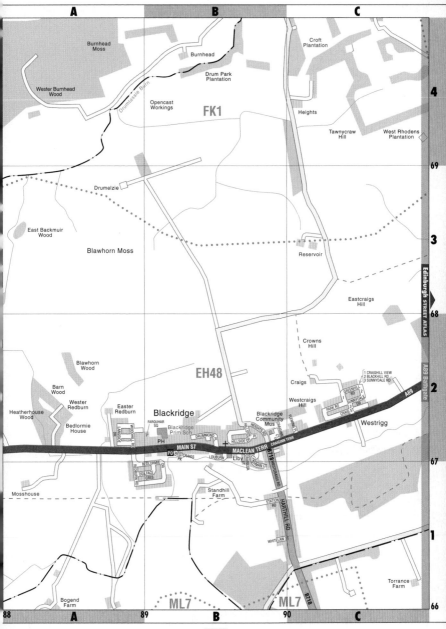

A B C

4

69

3

68

2

67

1

66

Burnhead Moss

Burnhead

Drum Park Plantation

Croft Plantation

Wester Burnhead Wood

Opencast Workings

FK1

Heights

Tawnycraw Hill

West Rhodens Plantation

Drumelzie

East Backmuir Wood

Blawhorn Moss

Reservoir

Eastcraigs Hill

Edinburgh STREET ATLAS

A89 Bathgate

Blawhorn Wood

EH48

Crowns Hill

Barn Wood

Wester Redburn

Easter Redburn

Blackridge

Craigs

Westcraigs Hill

1 CRAIGHILL VIEW
2 BLACKHILL RD
3 SUNNYDALE RD

GREENEND RD
PARK RD
SUNNYDALE DR
CRAIG ST

A89

Heatherhouse Wood

Bedlormie House

Blackridge Prim Sch

FARQUHAR SQ

DRUMMOND

Blackridge Community Mus

HILLSIDE DR

FLEMING ST

CRAIGINN TERR

Westrigg

PH

MAIN ST

MACLEAN TERR

Liby

PO

WESTCRAIGS PK

LOUBURN

B718

BRIGHTSIDE RD

BEDLORMIE DR

OILFACE CRES

REDBURN RD

Mosshouse

Standhill Farm

STATION RD

WHITELAW ST

HARTHILL RD

B718

Bogend Farm

ML7

ML7

Torrance Farm

B718

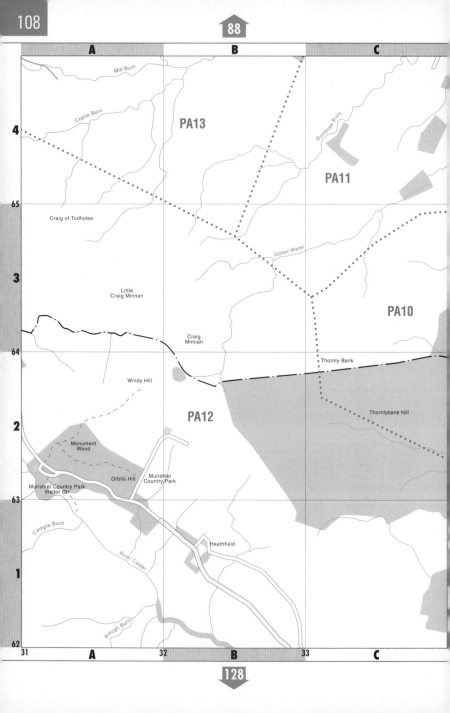

88

A

B

C

Mill Burn

Coplie Burn

PA13

Burnbrae Burn

4

PA11

65

Craig of Todholes

Gotter Water

3

Little
Craig Minnan

PA10

Craig
Minnan

64

Thornly Bank

Windy Hill

Thornlybank Hill

2

PA12

Monument
Wood

Orblis Hill

Muirshiel
Country Park

Muirshiel Country Park
Visitor Ctr

63

Cample Burn

Heathfield

River Calder

1

Rough Burn

62

31

A

32

B

33

C

128

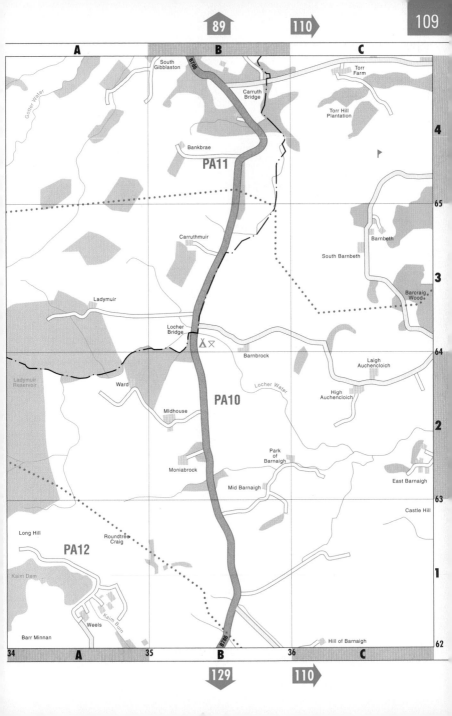

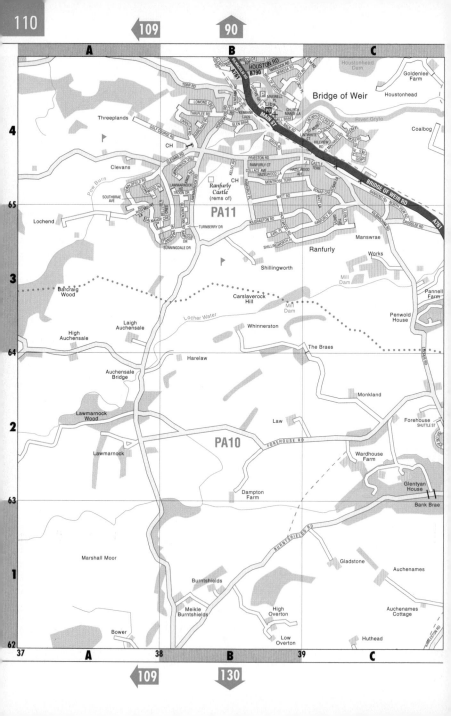

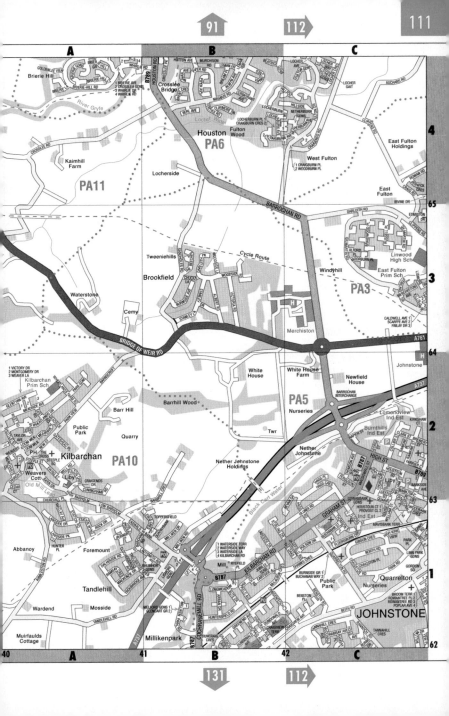

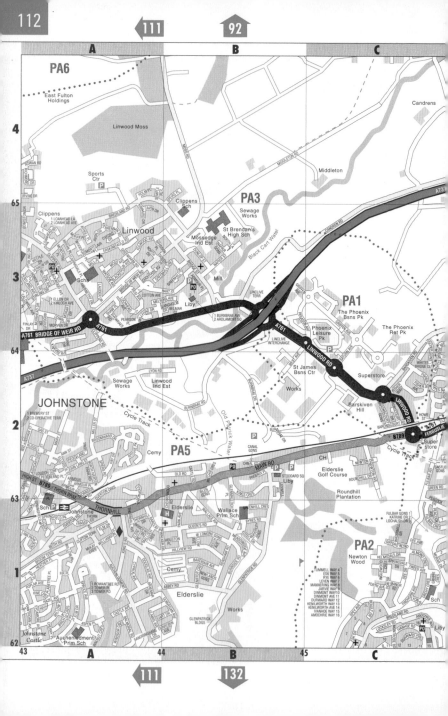

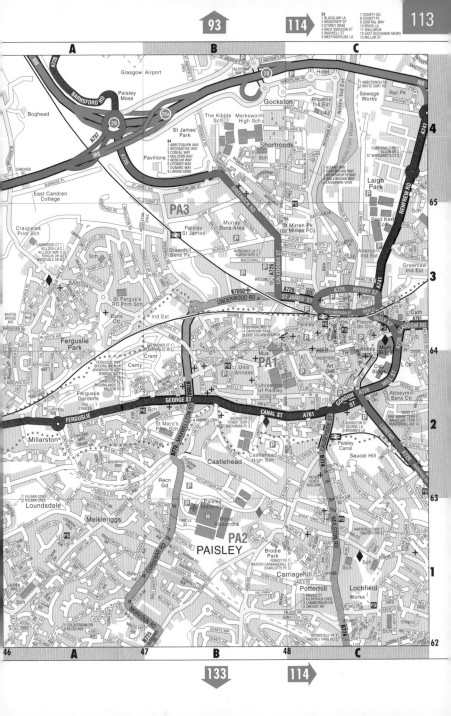

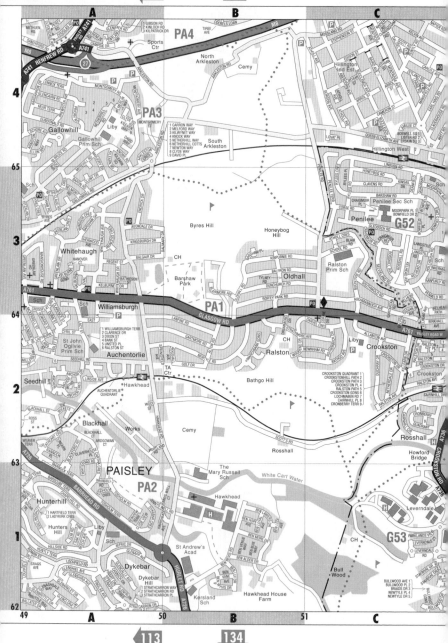

C4
1 LINTHOUSE BLDGS
2 HOLMFAULD RD
3 HOLMFAULDHEAD PL
4 CLACHAN DR
5 CARMOUTH GDNS
6 FAIRFIELD PL

7 FAIRFIELD GDNS
8 ELDERPARK GR
9 CROSSLOAN TERR

A1
1 BULLWOOD DR
2 BULLWOOD CT
3 BALLOCHMYLE DR
4 DEVOL CRES
5 LEITHLAND AVE
6 LEVERNSIDE CRES

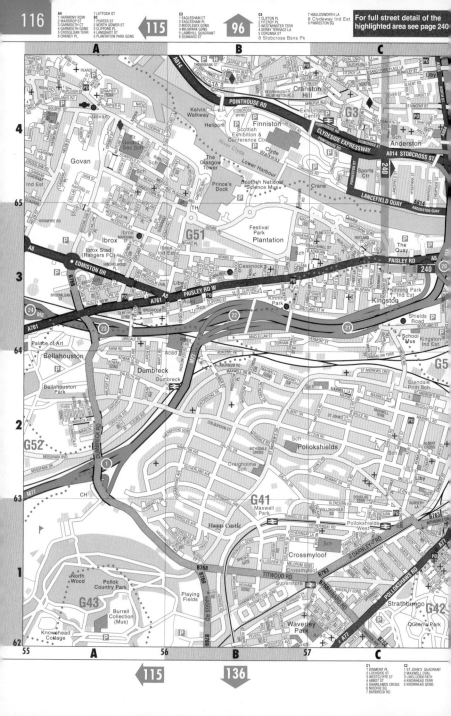

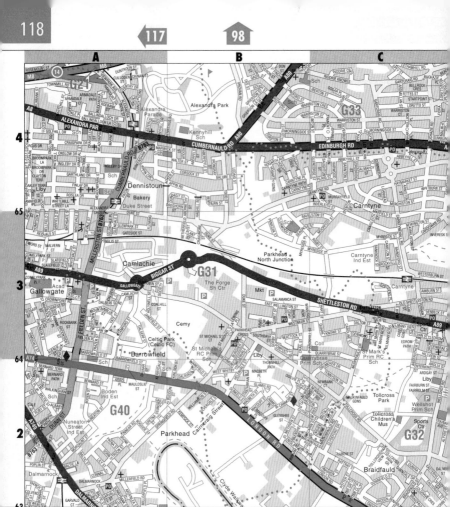

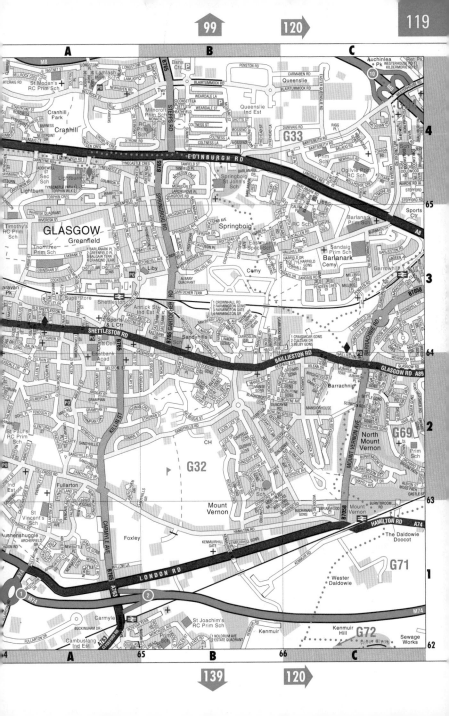

A3
1 SPRINGHILL FARM PL
2 SPRINGHILL FARM WAY
3 SPRINGHILL FARM GR
4 MICKLEHOUSE PL
5 MICKLEHOUSE OVAL
6 MICKLEHOUSE WYND
7 THORNBRIDGE AVE
8 BARONY CT
9 BARONY WYND

10 QUEENSBY AVE
11 BARRACHNIE PL
12 BANNERCROSS GDNS
13 BANNERCROSS AVE
14 THORNBRIDGE GDNS
15 HATHERSAGE GDNS

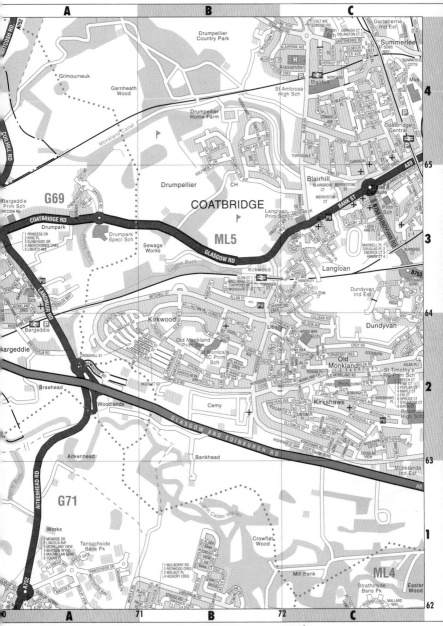

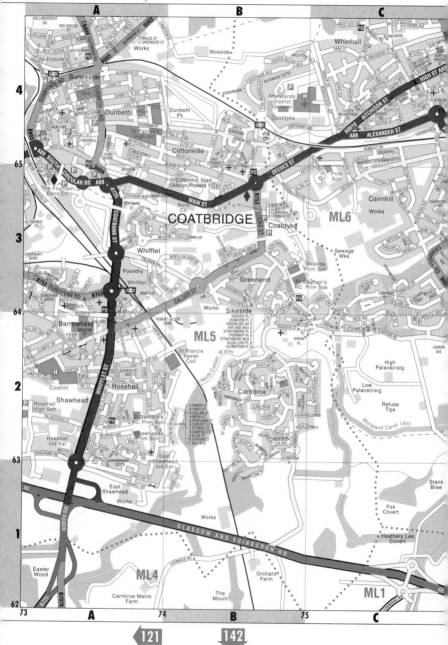

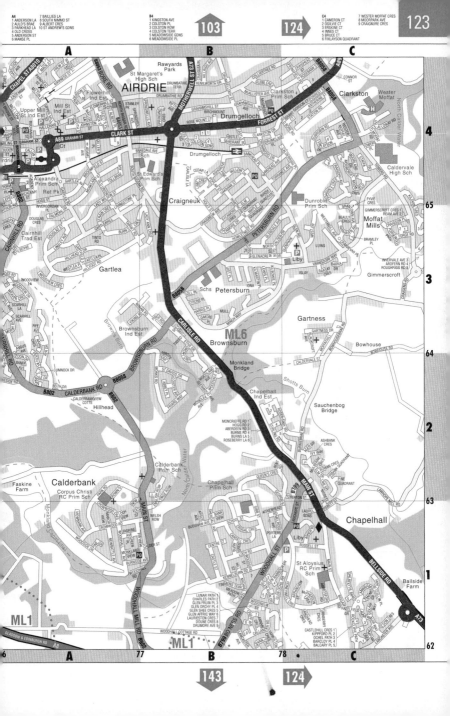

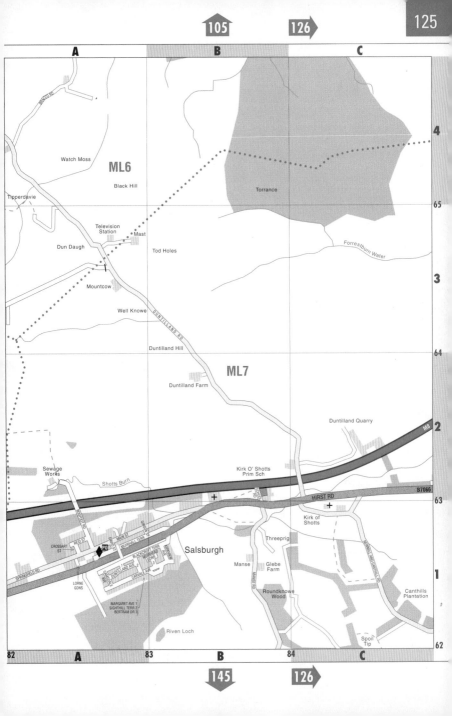

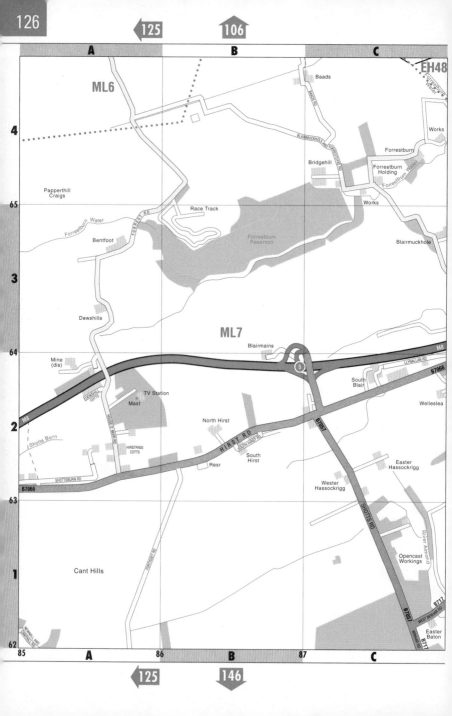

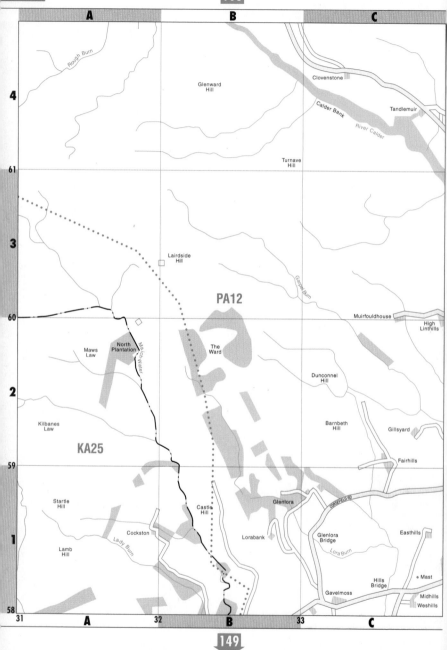

A   **B**   **C**

Rough Burn

Glenward
Hill

Clovenstone

4

Calder Bank

Tandlemuir

River Calder

Turnave
Hill

61

3

Lairdside
Hill

Garpel Burn

PA12

Muirfouldhouse

High
Linthills

60

North
Plantation

Maws
Law

March Water

The
Ward

Dunconnel
Hill

2

Kilbanes
Law

KA25

Barnbeth
Hill

Gillsyard

Fairhills

59

Startle
Hill

Castle
Hill

Glenlora

CORSEFIELD RD

Lamb
Hill

Cockston

Lorabank

Glenlora
Bridge

Easthills

1

Lady Burn

Lora Burn

Hills
Bridge

Mast

Gavelmoss

Midhills

Weshills

58

31   **A**   **32**   **B**   **33**   **C**

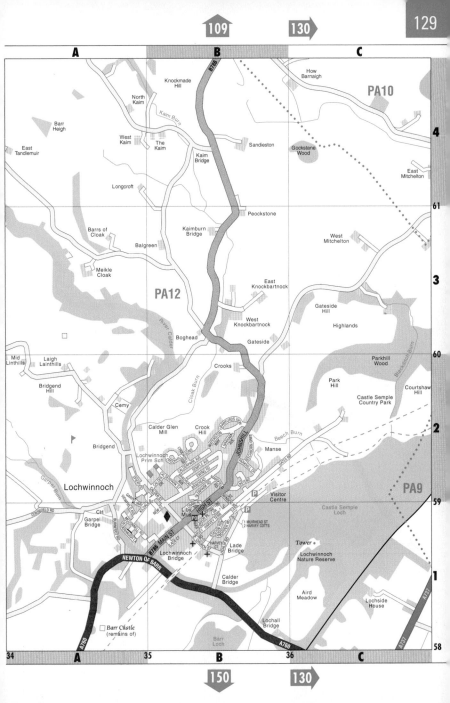

129
110

A **B** **C**

4

Kibbleston

Little Burntshields

Passinglinn

Callochant

Clochodrick

PA10

Corbet Hill

Clochodrick Bridge

Crossflat

St Bride's Burn

Burnfoot

Crossflat Hill

Drygate

ASHGROVE RD

A737

61

Bride's Mill Bridge

Thirdpart Hall

North Gates

Market Hill

St Brydes

Warbowie

Garthland Bridge

Howwood

Markethill Holdings

3

Shields Holdings

Kenmure Hill

Howwood

Howwood

PA12

Temple

MAIN ST

BOWFIELD RD

B776

BETH RD

PO

Sch

East Approach

Black Cart Water

Elliston

BOWFIELD WAY

60

Fancy Bridge

Elliston Bridge

B787

CAPELWOOD AVE

TILLFOUR RD

Low Semple

Castle Semple

East Gavin

B787

Elliston Burn

Castle Semple Loch

PA9

Risk Bridge

North Muirdykes

East Muirdykes

2

Risk Burn

Mid Gavin

Hillcrest

Muirdykes Mount

Gavin Braes

Linnister Burn

South Muirdykes

59

Risk

West Gavin

Hotel

Bowfield Bridge

Burnside

Townhead of Risk

BELLTREES

Bowfield House

APPLETON BRAE

Earlshill

Bowfield

Bowfield Dam

1

Belltrees

Earls Hill

Lorabar

A737

Newtown of Beltrees

PA12

B776

58

Hall

A **B** **C**

37 38 39

129
151

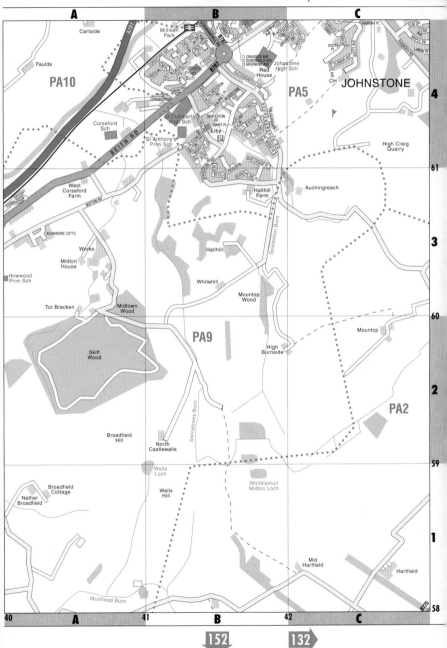

A B C

Cartside

Faulds

PA10

Milliken Park

Fordham Prim Sch

Red House

1 CRAIGSOOD AVE
2 DUNDONALD AVE
3 GREENEND AVE

Johnstone High Sch

CH **JOHNSTONE**

PA5

Corseford Sch

St Cuthbert's High Sch

St Anthony's Prim Sch

Liby

Spateston Rd
Swift Pl
Falcon Rd

BEITH RD

High Craig Quarry

61

West Corseford Farm

Midton Rd

Hallhill Farm

Auchingreach

Spateston Burn

Kilknowe Cotts

Works

Midton House

Howwood Prim Sch

Tor Bracken

Midtown Wood

Hallhill

Whitehill

Mountop Wood

3

60

PA9

Skiff Wood

High Burnside

Mountop

2

PA2

Broadfield Hill

North Castlewalls

Swinefrees Burn

Walls Loch

Whittliemuir Midton Loch

59

Nether Broadfield

Broadfield Cottage

Walls Hill

1

Mid Hartfield

Hartfield

Muirhead Burn

58

40 A 41 B 42 C

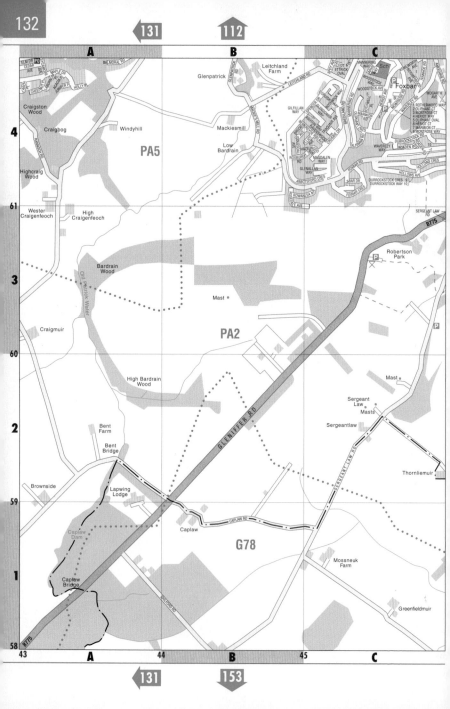

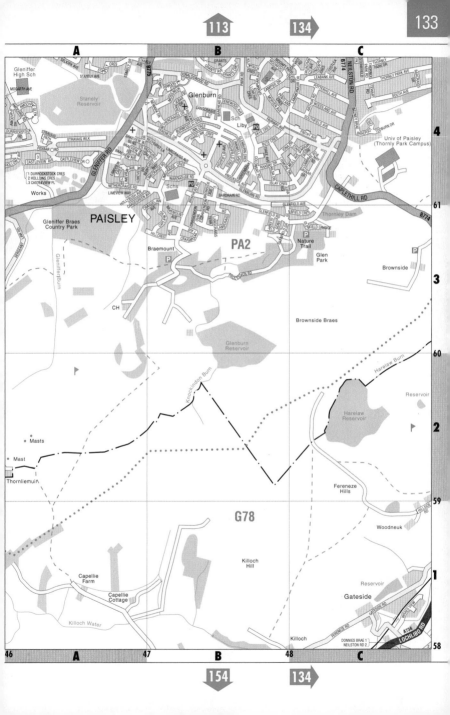

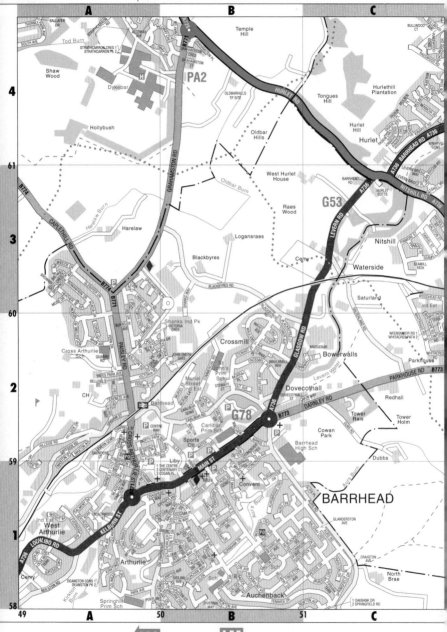

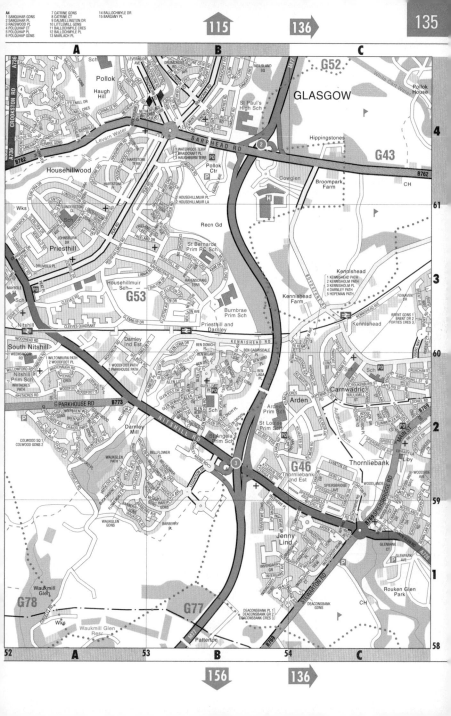

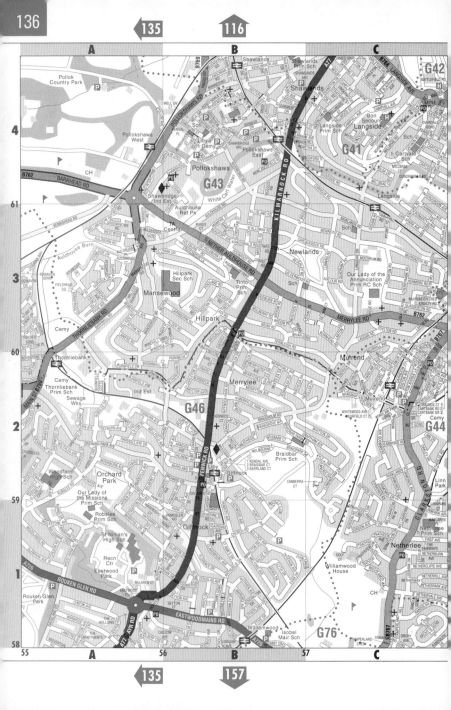

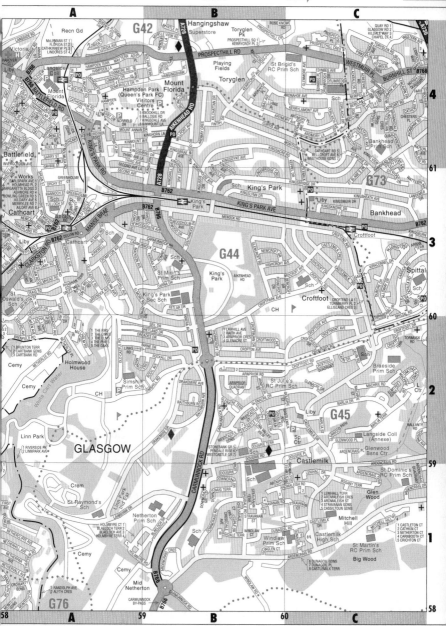

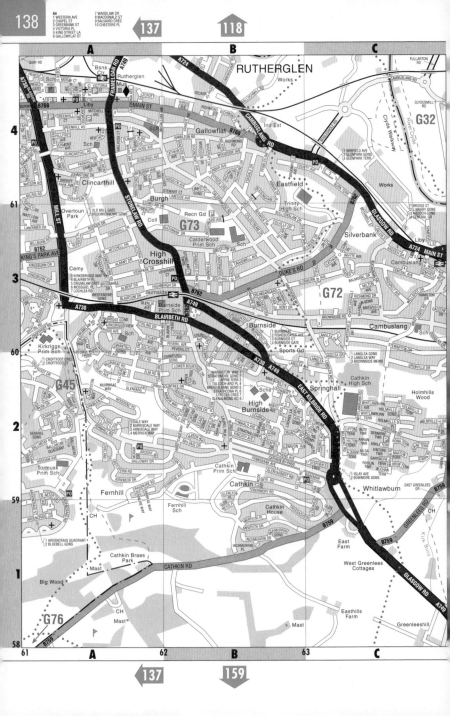

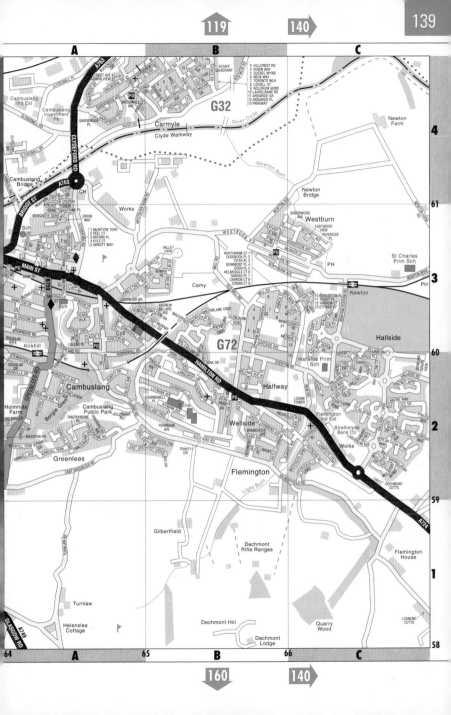

A4
1 YOUNG PL
2 WALKER PATH
3 CHRIGHTON GN
4 MURHEAD GATE
5 PRENTICE LA
6 HADDOW GR

7 CAMPSIE VIEW
8 OCHIL VIEW
9 KILPATRICK WAY
10 RUSSELL GDNS
11 BAILLE WYND

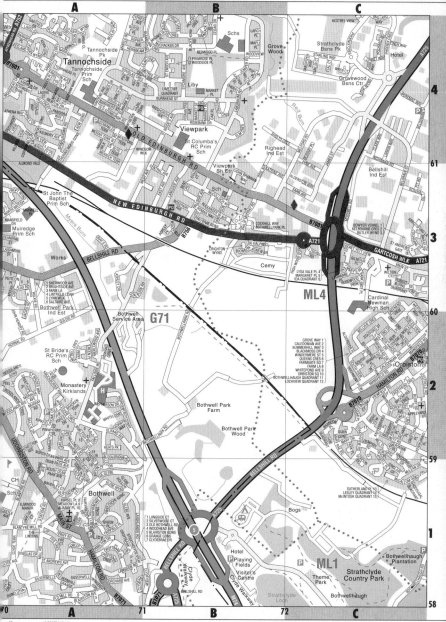

A2
1 KELVIN WAY
2 APPIN WAY
3 MORVEN WAY
4 LIVINGSTON LA
5 BELSTANE PL
6 KATRINE WAY
7 RANNOCH WAY
8 CARRICK WAY
9 TANTALLON RD

10 ROSEBANK LA
11 THORNHILL LA
12 ALDERSIDE PL
13 BARNSWOOD PL
14 MALLARD LA
15 NEWFIELD LA
16 HOZIER PL

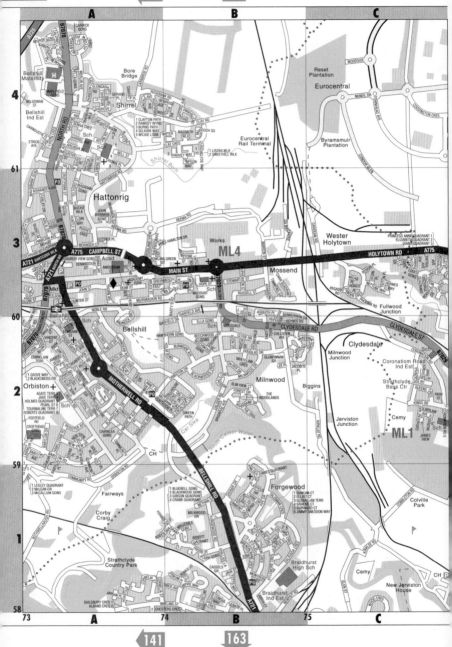

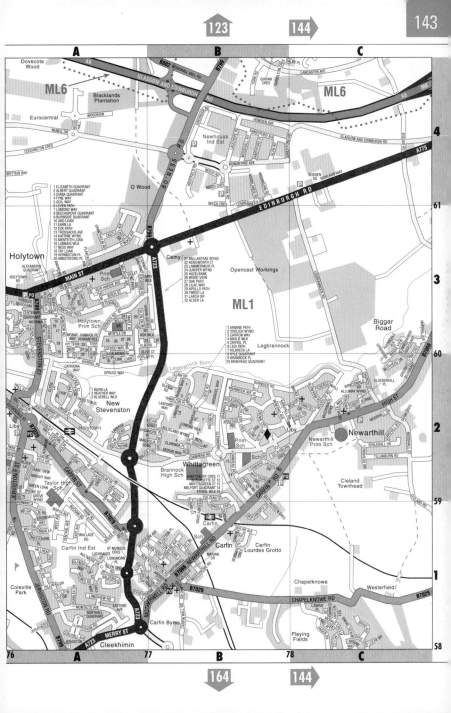

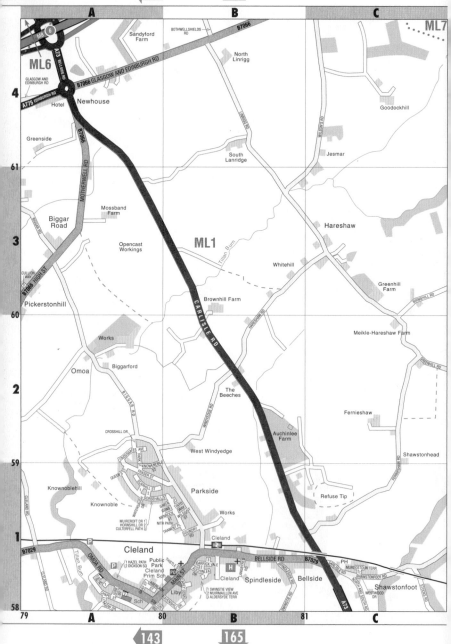

143
124
143
165

ML7

ML6

ML1

A73
BELLSIDE RD
A775 EDINBURGH RD
GLASGOW AND EDINBURGH RD

Sandyford Farm

BOTHWELLSHIELDS RD
B7066

North Linrigg

Newhouse

Hotel

Greenside

GLASGOW AND EDINBURGH RD

B7066 GLASGOW AND EDINBURGH RD

Goodockhill

South Lanridge

Jesmar

MOTHERWELL RD

B7066

Mossband Farm

Biggar Road

Opencast Workings

Tillan Burn

Hareshaw

Whitehill

CULLEN WAY

B7066 HIGH ST

Pickerstonhill

Brownhill Farm

Greenhill Farm

SPINDLEHILL RD

CARLISLE RD

Works

Omoa

Biggarford

Meikle-Hareshaw Farm

GREENHILL RD

BIGGAR RD

WINDYEDGE RD

HARESHAW RD

The Beeches

Fernieshaw

Shawstonhead

CROSSHILL DR

CROSSGATES AVE
KNOWNOBLE ST
QUEEN S
CASSELS ST
SCARFFE ST
FORRESTHALL ST
GREEN CT
JONES
MWCK
DWCK
ST
MWCK
ST
TITTON

West Windyedge

Auchinlee Farm

Refuse Tip

Knownoblehill

Knownoble

MUIRCROFT DR 1
HORNSHILL DR 2
CULTERFELL PATH 3

NITH PATH
TRANENT
ST

Parkside

Works

LOUNCH RD

Cleland

A775 EDINBURGH RD
B7029

CLELAND RD

Tillan Burn

OMOA RD

P

P

Cleland

BELLSIDE RD
B7029

CARLISLE RD

PH

MURDOSTOUN TERR

SHAWSTONFOOT RD

THISTLE ST

1 HAZEL PATH
2 DICKSON SQ

Public Park
Cleland Prim Sch

MAIN ST
PO

CARRICK VALE
CHINLEA

Cleland

Spindleside

Bellside

A73

WESTWOOD DR

Shawstonfoot

LOCKS RD

Sch

Liby

1 SWINSTIE VIEW
2 MUIRMAILLEN AVE
3 ALDERSYDE TERR

79   80   81

58
59
60
61
4
3
2
1

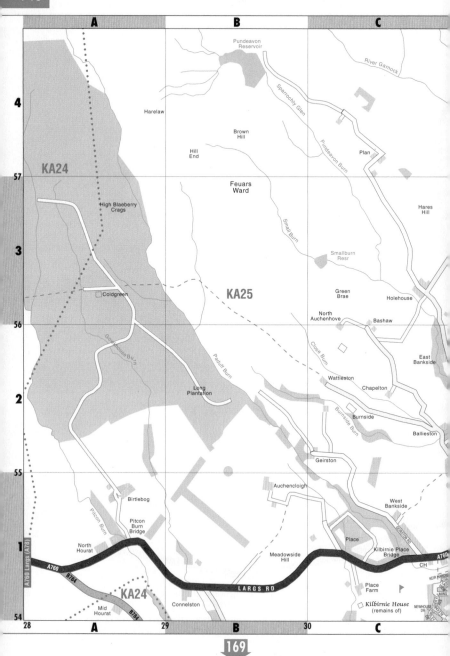

A **B** **C**

KA24

4

Pundeavon
Reservoir

River Garnock

Harelaw

Sparrochy Glen

Brown
Hill

Hill
End

Plan

Pundeavon Burn

57

Feuars
Ward

High Blaeberry
Crags

Hares
Hill

Small Burn

3

Smallburn
Resr

Coldgreen

KA25

Green
Brae

Holehouse

North
Auchenhove

Bashaw

56

Gillhouse Burn

Close Burn

East
Bankside

Paduff Burn

Wattieston

Chapelton

2

Long
Plantation

Burnside Burn

Burnside

Ballieston

Geirston

55

Auchencloigh

West
Bankside

Birtlebog

Pitcon Burn

Pitcon
Burn
Bridge

Place

Kilbirnie Place
Bridge

A760

1

North
Hourat

Meadowside
Hill

LARGS RD

Place
Farm

CH

A760 Largs (A78)

A760

B784

KA24

Connelston

Kilbirnie House
(remains of)

NEWHOUSE
DR

54

Mid
Hourat

B784

28 **A** 29 **B** 30 **C**

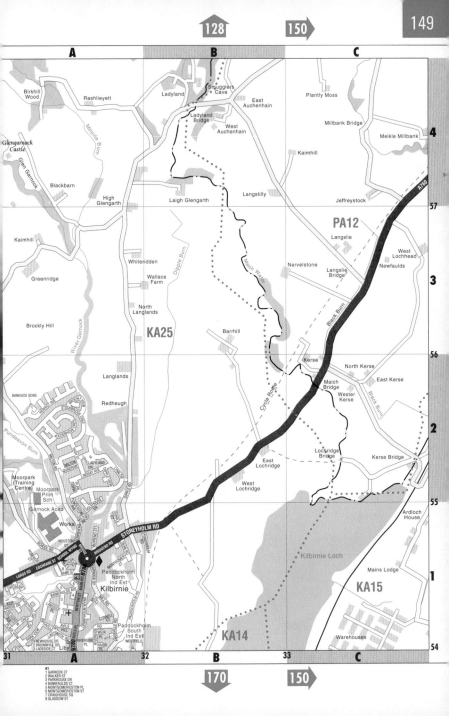

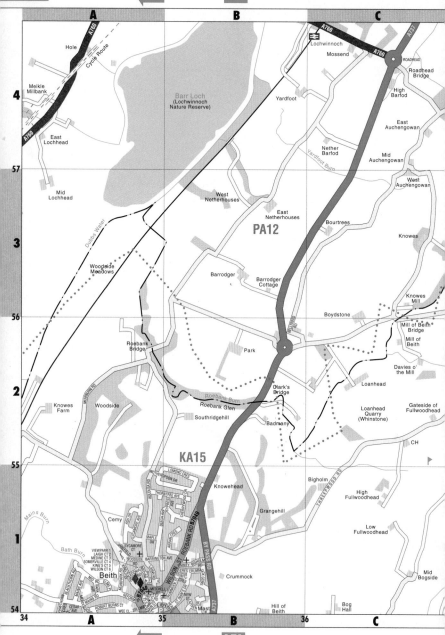

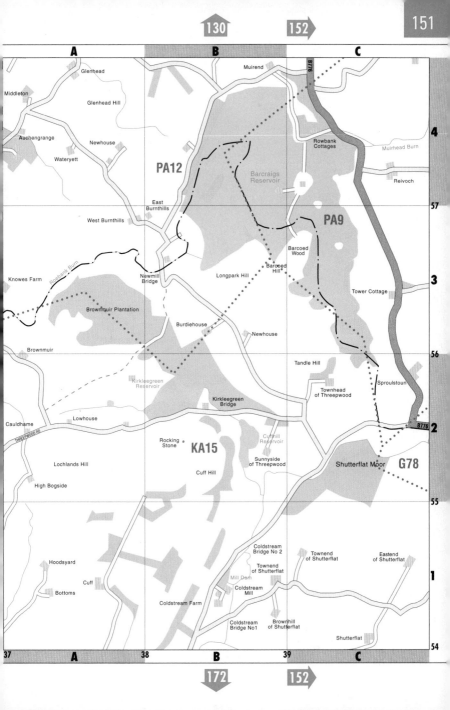

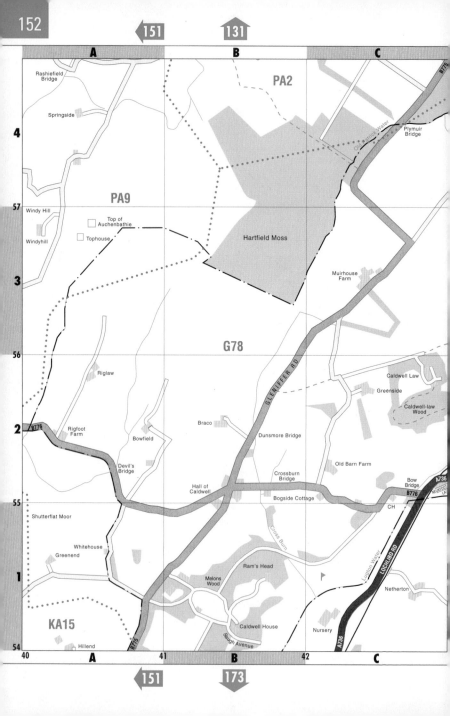

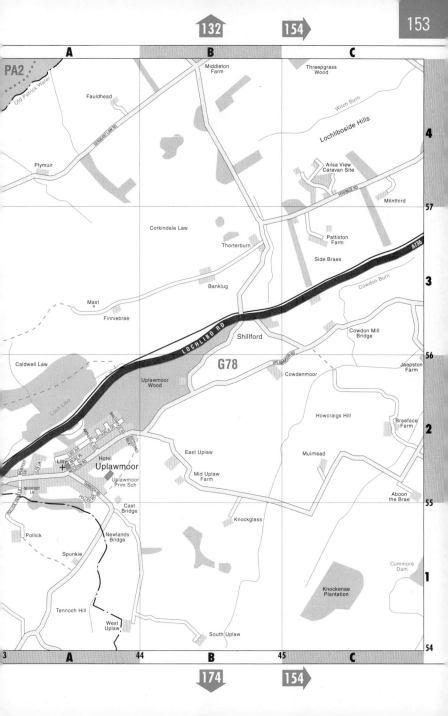

153
133

A **B** **C**

A736

Killoch

Auchentiber

Works

Nether Kirkton

Foreside

FREEZE RD

BARTON BRAE

LOCHLIBO RD

NEILSTON RD

4

Mast

Cowdon Burn

Mill (dis)

St Thomas Sch

GLENFIELD VIEW

MANSE RD

KIRK RD

INGLEBY PL

HATFIELD DR

MOORHILL PK

SPRINGFIELD RD

SYKES TERR

Kirktonfield Bridge

A736

Crofthead Cotts

PO

Liby L Ctr

MADRAS

Neilston Prim Sch

Factory

57

Holehouse

Molendinar Terr

MILLWOOD TERR

Neilston

Neilston

Neilston House

UPLAWMOOR RD

Smiddyhill

Brimstone Bridge

GLEN LUIET RD

GLEN GELL RD

COMMORE PL

GLEN FINLET RD

GLEN MARK

GLEN ESK

Kirkton Bridge

KIRKTON RD

Kirkton Dam

Dyke Greenhill

3

Crumyards

Levern Water

Kilburn

Water Works

P

Loanfoot

Dyke Hill

56

Jaapston Farm

Neilstonside Bridge

Water Works

Craig of Neilston

Muirhead

Neilstonside Hill

Craig of Neilston

Barr Hill

Snypes Dam

2

Neilstonside

Neilston Pad

Snypes

Low Walton

Nort' Walto

Waterside

Craighall Dam

Drumler Craigs

55

Commore

1

Commore Dam

Harelaw

P

West Walton

Straun Hill

High Walton

G77

Commore Bridge

Levern Water

Walton Burn

Walton Glen

54

46 **A** 47 **B** 48 **C**

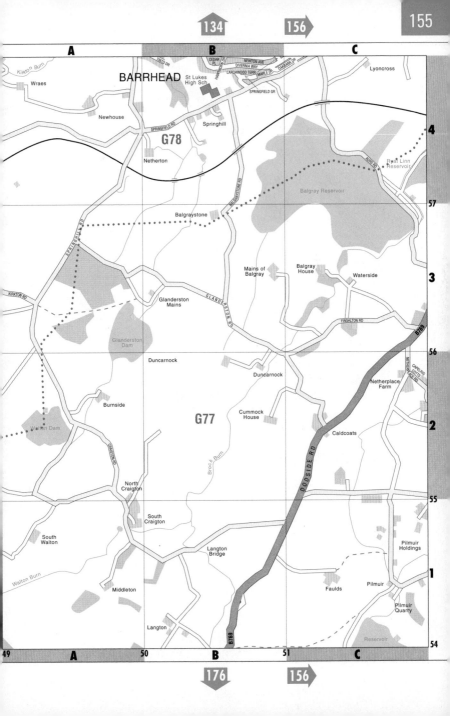

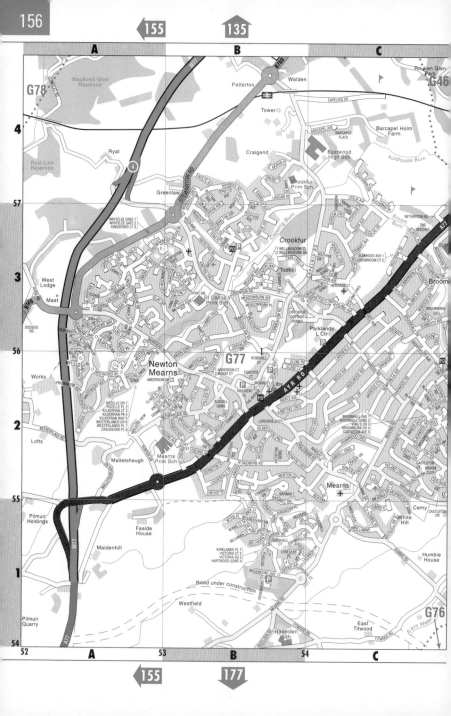

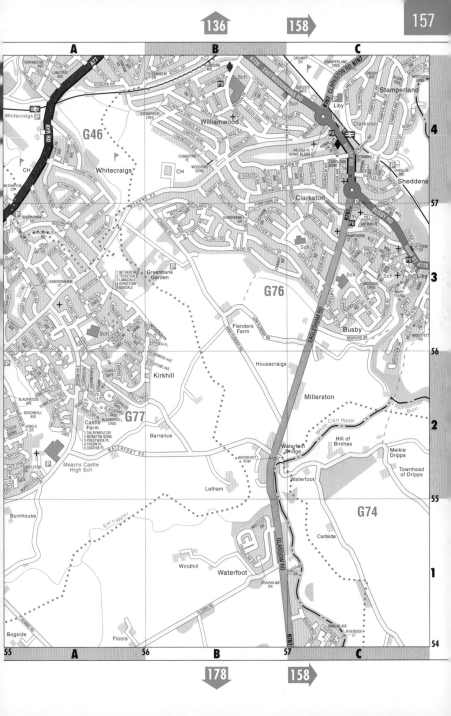

A B C

G45

CARMUNNOCK RD

CATHKIN RD

B759

Netherton
Braes

White Cart Water

Mast

4

Carmunnock

Pedmyre
House

CARMUNNOCK BY-PASS

BUSBY RD

GREENSIDE

WATERSIDE
CT

SYCAMORE WAY

PLEYMYRE LA

Carnbooth
House

Kittoch Water

Carmunnock
Prim Sch

57

Kittoch
Bridge

Picketlaw
Farm

Parklea

WATERSIDE GDNS

Easter
Busby

1 GLENVILLE GATE
2 GLENVILLE TERR
3 PRINTERS LAND

CARMUNNOCK RD

G76

WATERSIDE RD

KITTOCHSIDE RD

B759

3

EAST KILBRIDE RD

Busby

Waterside

Waterbank

Wester
Kittochside

Castle
Hill

Bellcraig
Wood Ct

Kittoch Water

Sewage
Works

WESTERTON
CT

The Peel

The Mus
of Scottish
Country Life

56

Bystone

B766

EAST KILBRIDE RD

Cemy

Philipshill

CASTLEHILL
GN

Castle
Hill

2

Thornmuirhill Burn

Laigh
Braehead

BRAEHEAD RD

Braehead

Thorntonhall

Hotel

Rough
Hill

Thorntonhall

PEEL'S
RD

WELLKNOWE

BISHOPS GATE

WELLKNOWE AVE

THORN AVE

G74

GREENSWAY

A726

GLENEAVON WAY

55

Birkwood

North Hill
of Dripps

South Hill
of Dripps

Ind Est

LINWOOD AVE

Ind Est

Southland

THORNTON RD

Thornton
Farm

Peel
Park

BURLEY

PEEL PARK

HAIRMYRES

B764

1

Road under construction

G75

HAIRMYRES
RDBT

B764

WEST

Little Dripps
Cottage

STRATHPEFFER DR 1
STRATHCONON GDNS 2

Millbrae

REDWOOD AVE
REDWOOD CT

EAGLESHAM RD

B764

H

Hairmyres

54

58 A 59 B 60 C

A B C

G72

G73

G76

4

Muir Farm

South Cathkin Farm

Works

57

Bellcraig

Highflat Farm

CAIRNMUIR RD

NERSTON RD

East Rogerton Lodge Farm

Rogerton

West Rogerton

Kingsgate Ret Pk

MAINS RD

3

Kittochside

Eastend

Dykehead Farm

KITTOCHSIDE RD

CARNBROOE RD

EAST KILBRIDE

Mains Castle

Lee's Burn

High Mains

Law Knowe

Laigh Mains

STEWARTFIELD WAY

56

East Kittochside Farm

MACARTHUR CRES 1
BURNET ROSE CT 2
BURNET ROSE PL 3
MACARTHUR CT 4
WENSLEYDALE 5
WINTERGREEN DR 6
SANDALWOOD CT 8
KILDRUMMY PL 7

James Hamilton Heritage Park

G74

Stewartfield

Nerston

Ind Est

Cemy

B783

2

Ind Est

College Milton

Ind Est

1 GLENSBURN CT
2 GLENBURN WAY

PH

EAST MAINS RD

MARKETHILL RDBT

East Mains

55

Glens Water

HAWBANK RDBT

1 DOONFOOT CT
2 DALMELLINGTON CT

Sch

B783

East Kilbride

B761

Ind Est

THE TENNANT COMPLEX

BROOKLANDS

EAGLESHAM RD

B764

WEST MAINS RD

MAIDPATH EAST 3
MAIDPATH WEST 4

Sch

East Kilbride

1

West Mains

5 ST LAWRENCE PK
6 RAYMOND PL
7 LE FROY GDNS

G75

East Milton Prim Sch

Duncanrig Sec Sch

QUEENSWAY

A726

Dollin Aquacentre

Civic Centre

THE CENTRE RDBT

Rigshead

PRINCES MALL

54

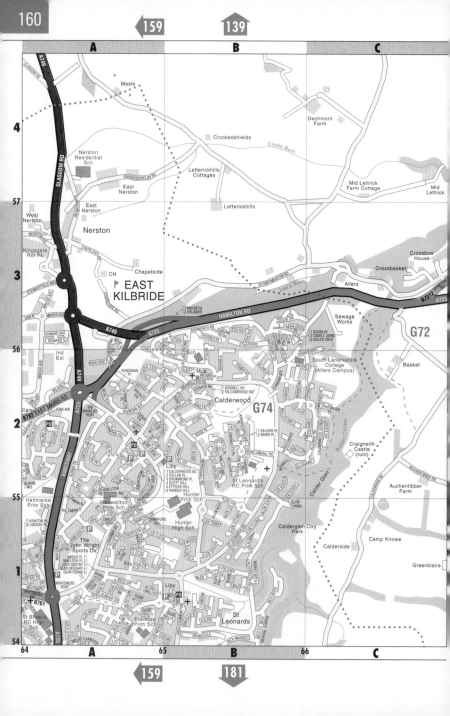

A   B   C

4

GLASGOW RD

Masts

Crookedshields

Cocks Burn

Dechmont
Farm

Nerston
Residential
Sch

CROOKEDSHIELDS RD

East
Nerston

Letterickhills
Cottages

Mid Lettrick
Farm Cottage

Mid
Lettrick

57

West
Nerston

East
Nerston

Letterickhills

NERSTON RD

Kingsgate
Ret Pk

CHAPELSIDE RD

STONEYMEADOW RD

Loo's Burn

Allers

Crossbow
House

STEWARTFIELD WAY

Crossbasket

3

CH

Chapelside

▶ EAST
KILBRIDE

A749

A725

HAMILTON RD

1 MACBETH
2 ORLANDO

PEPLOE DR

FERGUSSON RD

Sewage
Works

1 GOURLAY
2 CADELL GDNS
3 GILLES CRES

B7012 JOHNSTON RD

A725

G72

Basket

56

Ind Est

MAVOR AVE

HOWARD AVE

HOWARD PL

BOSWORTH RD
HORNDEAN

EDGEWARE

STAFFA

KLAN
STRATFORD

KENDGORTH

South Lanarkshire
College
(Allers Campus)

LAW PL

A749

A725

EAST MAINS RD

B783

2

Cem

IONA AVE

THE
WHIRLIES
RDBT

BRAEVIEW PL

RUNCIMAN
PL

BLACKBRAES

MAXWELLTON RD

Sch

MOWBRAY

WINGATE PK

WINGATE

Calderwood

1 BOSWELL PK
2 FALCONBRIDGE RD

G74

CRAIGNEITH

LOCH 2

BALLOCH

Rough Calder

Craigneith
Castle
(ruin)

55

Halfmerke
Prim Sch

GLAMIS
AVE

MAXWELLTON RD

RAEBURN

1 SELKIRK PL
2 NAIRN PL

BRANCUMHALL RD

Auchentibber
Farm

HALFMERK

Maxwellton
Prim Sch

CRAWFORD
HILL

Hunter
Prim Sch

ELLISGARTH

GLEN
TANNER

Calderglen Ctry
Park

Calderside

Camp Knowe

1 KIRKTON PL
2 LINDSAY PL

Liby

1 CALDERWOOD SQ
2 POLLOK PL
3 DRUMMOND PL
4 SCOTT HILL
5 ETTRICK HILL
6 RAMSAY HILL

St Leonard's
RC Prim Sch

Hunter
High Sch

Calder Glen

Greenblairs

1

LINDSAY RD

The
John Wright
Sports Ctr

1 ANGUS PL
2 MALLOCH PL
3 LOCH ASSYNT
4 GLEN DESSARY
5 GLEN FESHIE

GLEN TERRIE

GLEN
FALLOCH

WHITEMOSS

B761

WHITEMOSS
RDBT

Liby

Blacklaw
Prim Sch

GLEN
LYNDON

URQUHART

BENBECULA

St Leonards

St Bride's
RC High
Sch

A725

MOUNT CAMERON

54

64   A   65   B   66   C

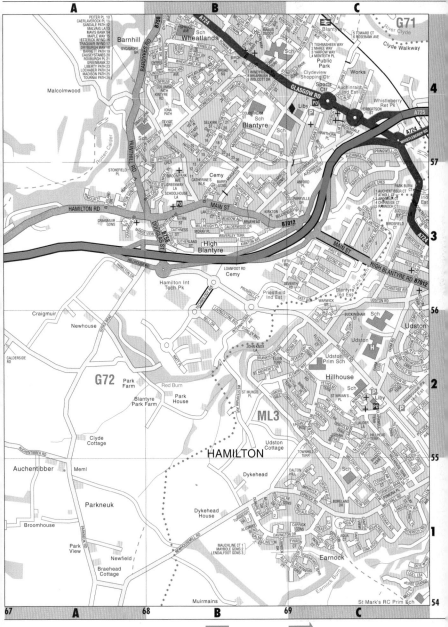

G71
River Clyde
Clyde Walkway

Barnhill
Wheatlands
Malcolmwood
Blantyre
Public Park
Clydeview Shopping Ctr
Sports Ctr
Auchinraith Ind Est
Whistleberry Ret Pk
High Blantyre
Hamilton Int Tech Pk
Craigmuir
Newhouse
Priestfield Ind Est
Blantyre Ind Est
Udston
Udston Prim Sch
Hillhouse
Park Farm
Blantyre Park Farm
Park House
Red Burn
ML3
Clyde Cottage
Auchentibber Rd
Auchentibber
Meml
HAMILTON
Dykehead
Udston Cottage
Parkneuk
Broomhouse
Dykehead House
Park View
Newfield
Braehead Cottage
Muirmains
Earnock
St Mark's RC Prim Sch

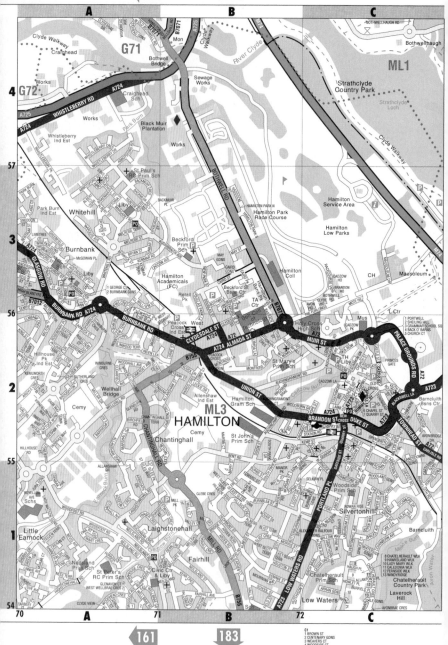

1 BRANDON ARC
2 OAKFIELD DR
3 WATSONVILLE ST
4 WINDMILL CT
5 MACDONALD CT
6 McCLURG CT
7 ELVAN TWR
8 KERR GRIEVE CT
9 CALDER TWR
10 AVON TWR
11 CLYDE TWR
12 ELLIS WAY
13 BLAIR PATH

MOTHERWELL

ML1

Braedale

ML3

ML9

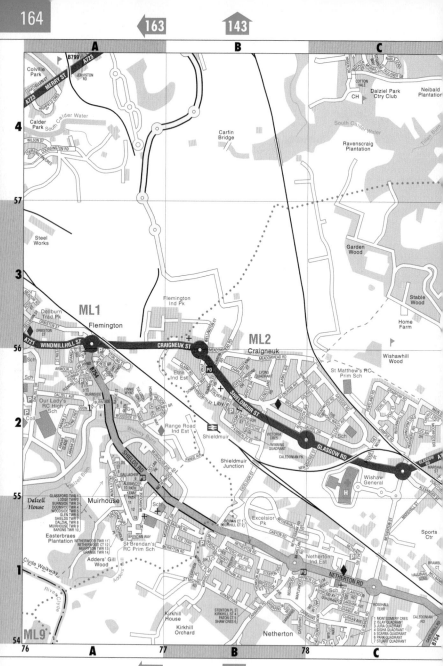

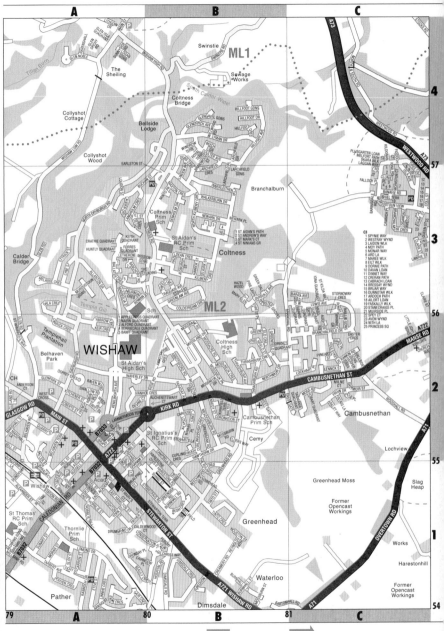

A B C

Swinstie

ML1

Sewage
Works

The
Sheiling

South Calder Water

Coltness
Bridge

Collyshot
Cottage

Bellside
Lodge

Collyshot
Wood

EARLSTON ST

57

HILLFOOT GDNS
HILLFOOT DR
HILLFOOT

GLENGAVEL GDNS
GLENGAVEL AVE
LYMAN DR

4

WESTWOOD RD

A73

PLASGARTEN LOAN
MELFORT PATH
SKARA AVE
LAGGAN AVE

FALLOCH PL

Branchalburn

Calder
Bridge

KEITH
QUADRANT

CRATHIE QUADRANT

FORRES
QUADRANT

HUNTLY QUADRANT

Coltness
Prim
Sch

St Aidan's
RC Prim
Sch

LARCHFIELD
CRES

LARCHFIELD
GDNS

WALKERBURN DR

NEWARK PL

1 ST AIDAN'S PATH
2 ST ANDREW'S WAY
3 ST MARK'S CT
4 ST NINIANS GR

Coltness

3

C3
1 SPYNIE WAY
2 WESTRAY WYND
3 LAIDON WLK
4 MOY PATH
5 MONAR WAY
6 ARD LA
7 MAREE WLK
8 EILT WLK
9 DORNIE PATH
10 DAVAN LOAN
11 DINNET WAY
12 CRERAN PATH
13 CABRACH LOAN
14 BRESSAY WYND
15 BRUAR WAY
16 DUNNOTAR WLK
17 ARDOCH PATH
18 AIORT LOAN
19 FASKALLY WLK
20 STANECRAIGS PL
21 MUIRSIDE PL
22 SPEY CT
23 AVON WYND
24 NITH LA
25 PRINCESS SQ

ML2

HAZEL
WOOD

STORNOWAY
CRES

Temple Gill

Templehall
Plantation

GALA CRES

YARROW
CT

Sch

1 APPLECROSS QUADRANT
2 NAIRN QUADRANT
3 ALFORD QUADRANT
4 BERRIEDALE QUADRANT
5 BANFF QUADRANT

Coltness
High
Sch

56

MANSE RD

A722

WISHAW

St Aidan's
High Sch

Belhaven
Park

CH
ANDERSON
CT

WEST
CROSS

GLASGOW RD

WAVERLEY DR

KIRK RD

CAMBUSNETHAN ST

Cambusnethan

Lochview

2

A71

Camsnethan
Prim Sch

St Ignatius's
RC Prim
Sch

MAIN ST

Liby

A722

Wishaw

Acad

CALEDONIAN RD

St Thomas'
RC Prim
Sch

Thornlie
Prim Sch

Cemy

STEWARTON ST

Greenhead

Greenhead Moss

Former
Opencast
Workings

Slag
Heap

55

OVERTOWN RD

1

Works

Harestonhill

Former
Opencast
Workings

Pather

A721 WISHAW RD

Dimsdale

Waterloo

A71

54

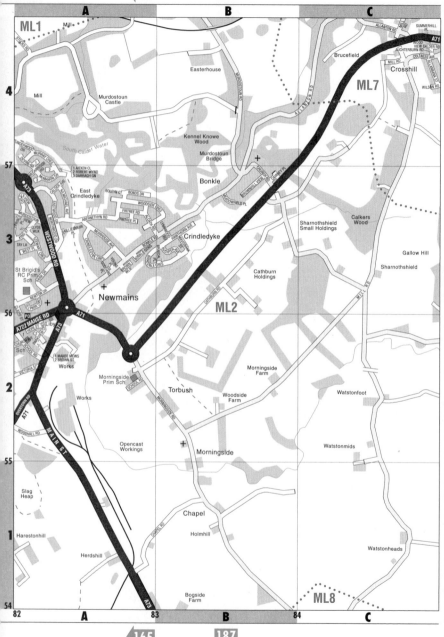

165
145

A   **B**   **C**

ML1

Mill

4

Mill

Murdostoun Castle

Easterhouse

Kennel Knowe Wood

Murdostoun Bridge

ALLANTON RD

SUMMERHILL PL

A71

WOOD VIEW CALDER RD

AUCHTERBURN RD

COLTNESS AVE

Brucefield

MILL RD

Crosshill

WILSON RD

ML7

South Calder Water

57

A73

MURRAY CRES

M MAHON DR

ST MICHAEL DR

1 AITKEN CL
2 ROBERT WYND
3 DARRAGH GDN

East Crindledyke

BOLEYN CT

BONDS DR

WOODSIDE CRES

Bonkle

BROWNLY PL

BROWNFIELD PL

CALDER PK

Calkers Wood

3

WESTWOOD RD

BAILLIE MUIR

MURDOSTOUN AVE

ABERNETHYN RD

FIRTREE RD

FIRTREE PL

WOODSIDE DR

Crindledyke

Sharnothshield Small Holdings

Gallow Hill

Sharnothshield

CLYDE WLK

TAY LA

WEIR LA

St Brigid's RC Prim Sch

Newmains

Cathburn Holdings

CATHBURN RD

ML2

56

A722 MANSE RD

A73

A71

Library

PO

Sch

CHURCH ST

1 MANSE MEWS
2 BROWN ST

Works

Morningside Prim Sch

SCHOOL RD

Torbush

MCKENNAS RD

Woodside Farm

Morningside Farm

Watstonfoot

ML7

2

OVERTOWN RD

A71

MAIN ST

VICTORIA ST

Works

Opencast Workings

Morningside

Watstonmids

WOODHALL RD

55

Slag Heap

Chapel

CHAPEL RD

Holmhill

Watstonheads

1

Harestonhill

Herdshill

A73

Bogside Farm

ML8

54

82   **83**   **84**

A   **B**   **C**

165
187

A B C

KIRK PATH
PO
ALLANTON RD A71
Allanton Prim Sch
Damside (PH)
Allanton
HAWTHORN PL
Coal Burn

Hartfield

ML7

Netherhall

Opencast Workings

4

57

Newark Plantation

3

Upper Daviesdykes

56

Kirkhall

ML2

Lower Daviesdykes

Lodge Hill
Winterhill

Dura

Brow Farm

Mountpleasant

Sunnyside

2

Auchterhead

55

Summerside

Kingshill

Auchter Water

1

ML8

54

85   A   86   B   87   C

167

147

A   B   C

4   Opencast Workings

ML7

Causeyhill

EH47

57

3

Lark Law

56

ML2

2

Cairney   Spoutcross

Addiewell

ML11

Mon

55

Auchterhead Muir

1   Auchterhead

ML8

54

88   A   89   B   90   C

167   189

Edinburgh STREET ATLAS

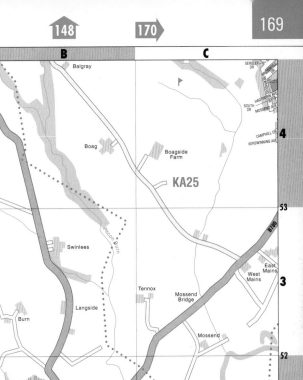

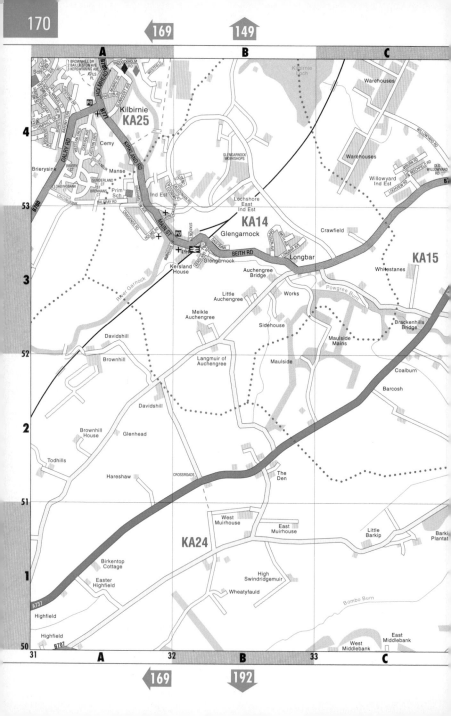

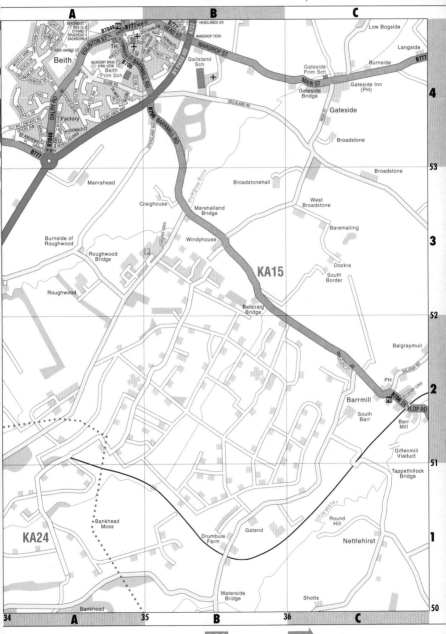

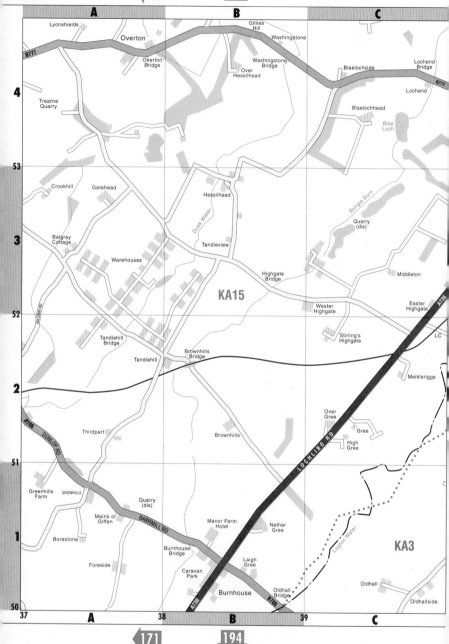

171
151

A
B
C

Lyonshields

Overton

Gillies Hill

Washingstone

B777

Overton Bridge

Over Hessilhead

Washingstone Bridge

Blaelochside

Lochend Bridge

4

Lochend

B777

Trearne Quarry

Blaelochhead

Blae Loch

53

Crookhill

Gatehead

Hessilhead

Bungle Burn

Duck Water

Quarry (dis)

Balgray Cottage

Tandleview

3

Warehouses

Middleton

Highgate Bridge

KA15

Wester Highgate

Easter Highgate

A735

LC

52

BALGRAY RD

Tandlehill Bridge

Stirling's Highgate

Tandlehill

Brownhills Bridge

Meikleriggs

2

B706

DUNLOP RD

Thirdpart

Brownhills

Over Gree

Gree

High Gree

LOCHLIBO RD

51

Greenhills Farm

GREENHILLS

Quarry (dis)

Lugton Water

KA3

Mains of Giffen

BARRMILL RD

Manor Farm Hotel

Nether Gree

1

Borestone

Burnhouse Bridge

Laigh Gree

Oldhall

Foreside

Caravan Park

A736

Burnhouse

Oldhall Bridge

B706

Oldhallside

50

37
A
38
B
39
C

171
194

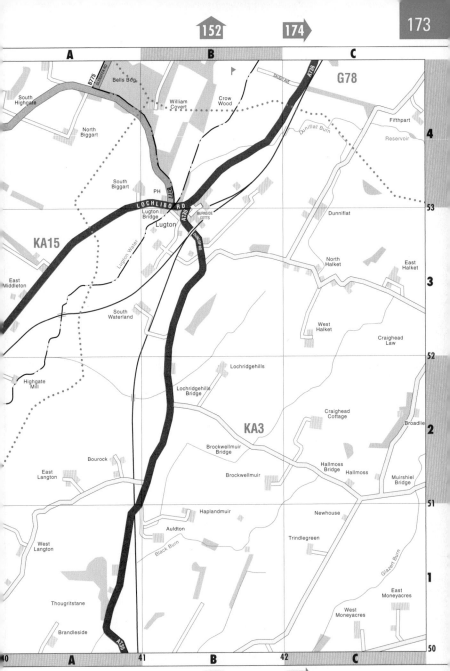

A
B
C

B775 (Stewarton)
Bells Bog
South Highgate
North Biggart
William Covert
Crow Wood
SAUGH AVE
A736
G78
Dunniflat Burn
Fifthpart
Reservoir
4

South Biggart
PH
B775
LOCHLIBO RD
Lugton Bridge
Lugton
A735
BURNSIDE COTTS
Dunniflat
53

KA15
Lugton Water
BURLAND RD
North Halket
East Halket

East Middleton
West Halket
Craighead Law
3

South Waterland
52

Highgate Mill
Lochridgehills
Lochridgehills Bridge
KA3
Craighead Cottage
Broadlie
2

Bourock
Brockwellmuir Bridge
Brockwellmuir
Hallmoss Bridge
Hallmoss
Muirshiel Bridge

East Langton
Haplandmuir
Newhouse
51

West Langton
Auldton
Black Burn
Trindlegreen
Glazert Burn
1

Thougritstane
East Moneyacres
West Moneyacres

Brandleside
A735
50

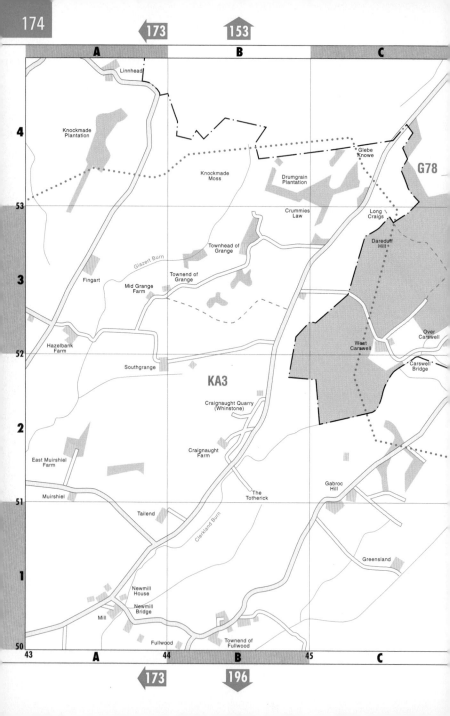

Linnhead

Knockmade
Plantation

4

Knockmade
Moss

Glebe
Knowe

Drumgrain
Plantation

G78

53

Crummies
Law

Long
Craigs

Townhead of
Grange

Dareduff
Hill

Glazert Burn

Townend of
Grange

3

Fingart

Mid Grange
Farm

Over
Carswell

52

Hazelbank
Farm

Southgrange

West
Carswell

Carswell
Bridge

KA3

Craignaught Quarry
(Whinstone)

2

East Muirshiel
Farm

Craignaught
Farm

Gabroc
Hill

51

Muirshiel

The
Totherick

Tailend

Clerkland Burn

Greensland

1

Newmill
House

Newmill
Bridge

Mill

Fullwood

Townend of
Fullwood

50

A **B** **C**

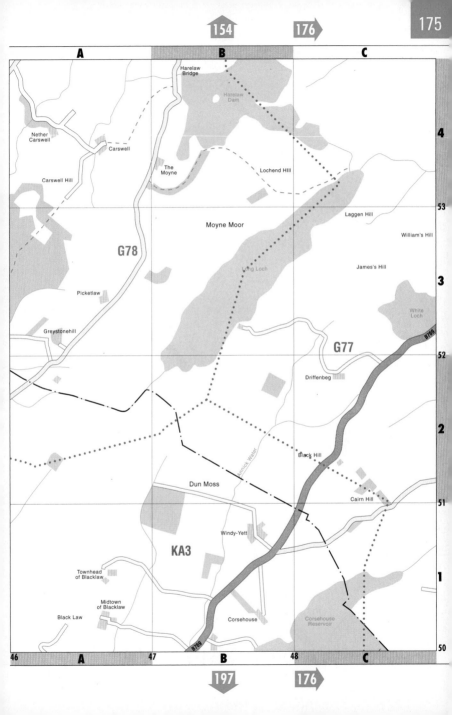

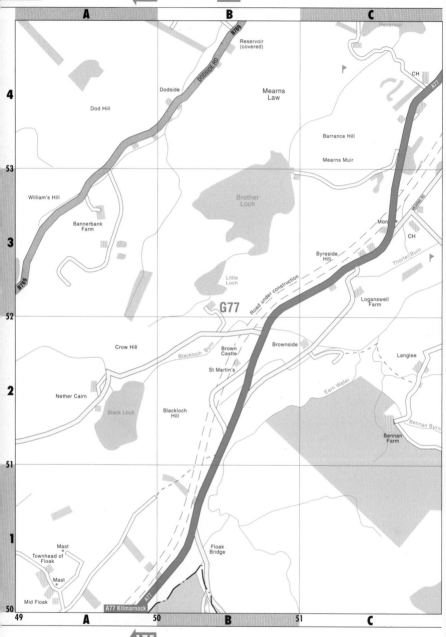

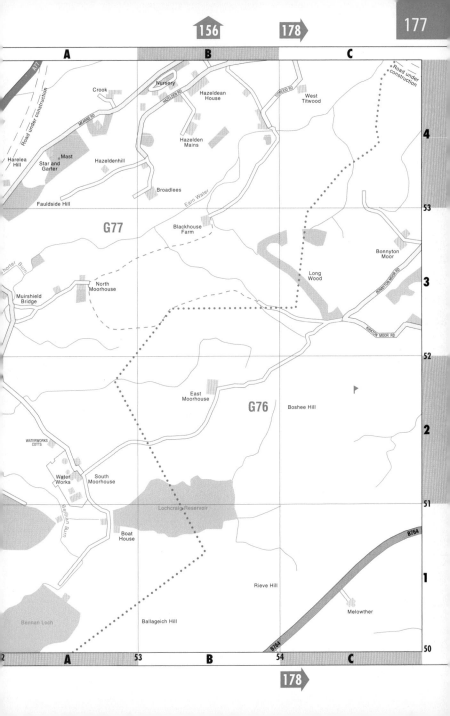

A
B
C

Road under construction

Crook
Nursery
Hazeldean House
West Titwood

Road under construction

MEARNS RD
HAZELDEN RD
TITWOOD RD
BONNYTON MOOR RD

4

Harelea Hill
Star and Garter
Mast
Hazeldenhill
Hazelden Mains

Broadlees
Earn Water

Fauldside Hill

53

G77
Blackhouse Farm

Bonnyton Moor

Whorter Burn

North Moorhouse
Long Wood

3

Muirshield Bridge

KIRKTON MOOR RD

52

East Moorhouse
G76
Boshee Hill

2

WATERWORKS COTTS

Water Works
South Moorhouse

Lochcraig Reservoir

51

Bennan Burn

Boat House

B764

1

Rieve Hill

Melowther

Bennan Loch
Ballageich Hill

B764

50

2
A
53
B
54
C

A B C

Bogside

Brackenrig Burn

B764

Stoneside

4

Bonnyton

G74

WHITE CART WATER

Road under construction

Castlehill
House

FLOORS RD

BONNYTON MOOR RD

KIMBLE RD

Low
Borland

GLASGOW RD

Holehouse

53

Castlehill
Wood

Castlehill

Crosslees

Crosslees
Wood

Borland Burn

Mid
Borland

Cemy

3

High
Borland

Resr

PO

Eaglesham

1 MANSEVIEW TERR
2. BORLAND CRES

CH

Liby

B767

Park Cres

POLNOON
DR

52

G76

KIRKTON MOOR RD

P

GLASGOW RD

Common

B767

CHEAPSIDE ST

EAGLESHAM RD

PH

North
Kirktonmoor

MOOR RD

MONTGOMERY ST

Eaglesham
Prim Sch

2

ALNWICK DR

MONTGOMERY CT 1
KIRKTON CT 2

South
Kirktonmoor

Sewage
Works

Brownmuir
Holding

Picketlaw
Reservoir

Mast

Picketlaw

Low Hill

51

High Dam

High Hill

B764

Woodhouse

1

East
Revoch

Park
Farm

SORN BURN

West
Revoch

50

55 A 56 B 57 C

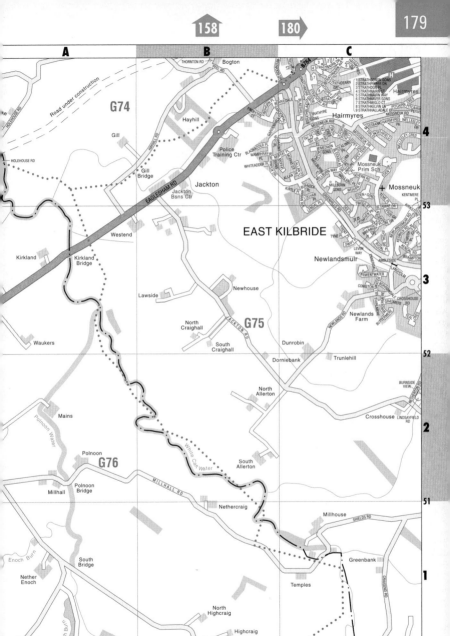

A | B | C

158 | 180

G74

Road under construction

THORNTON RD
Bogton
HOLEHOUSE RD
Gill
Hayhill
Gill Bridge
Police Training Ctr
Jackton
EAGLESHAM RD
Jackton Bsns Ctr
Westend
Kirkland
Kirkland Bridge

EAST KILBRIDE

1 STRATHDON GDNS
2 STRATHPEFFER DR
3 STRATHDOVE
4 STRATHNAIRN CT
5 STRATHNAVER WAY
6 STRATHNAVER GDNS
7 STRATHMIGLO CT
8 STRATHLYON LA
9 STRATHALLADALE RD

Hairmyres
Hairmyres
STRATHYRE
Mossneuk Prim Sch
Mossneuk
KENTMERE PL
MOSSNEUK RD
Newlandsmuir
LEVEN WAY
PINE PL
BRAMPTON
CROSSHOUSE
Crosshouse
LINDSAYFIELD RD
BURNSIDE VIEW

Lawside
Newhouse
North Craighall
JACKTON RD
G75
South Craighall
Dunrobin
Dorniebank
Trunlehill
Waukers
North Allerton
Mains
Polnoon Water
Polnoon
G76
Polnoon Bridge
Millhall
South Allerton
White Cart Water
MILLHALL RD
Nethercraig
Millhouse
SHIELDS RD
Greenbank
CHAPELTON RD
Enoch Burn
South Bridge
Nether Enoch
Temples
Ardoch Burn
Over Enoch
North Highcraig
Highcraig

4 | 53 | 3 | 52 | 2 | 51 | 1 | 50

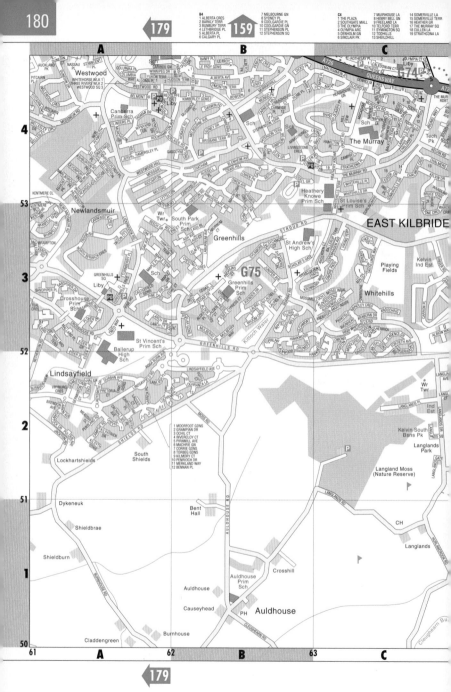

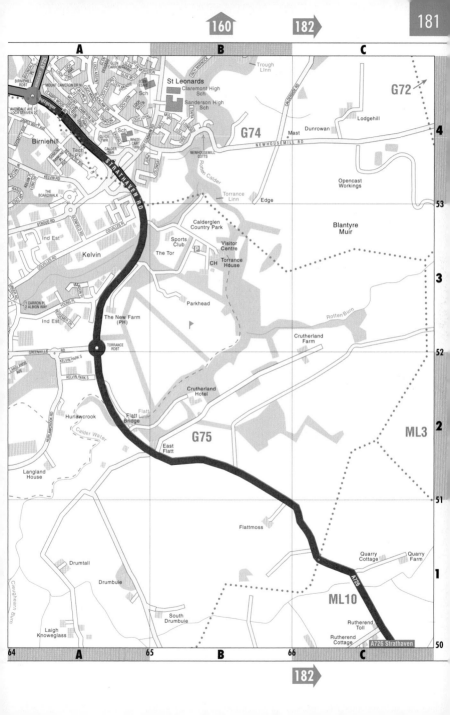

A **B** **C**

Stewartfield

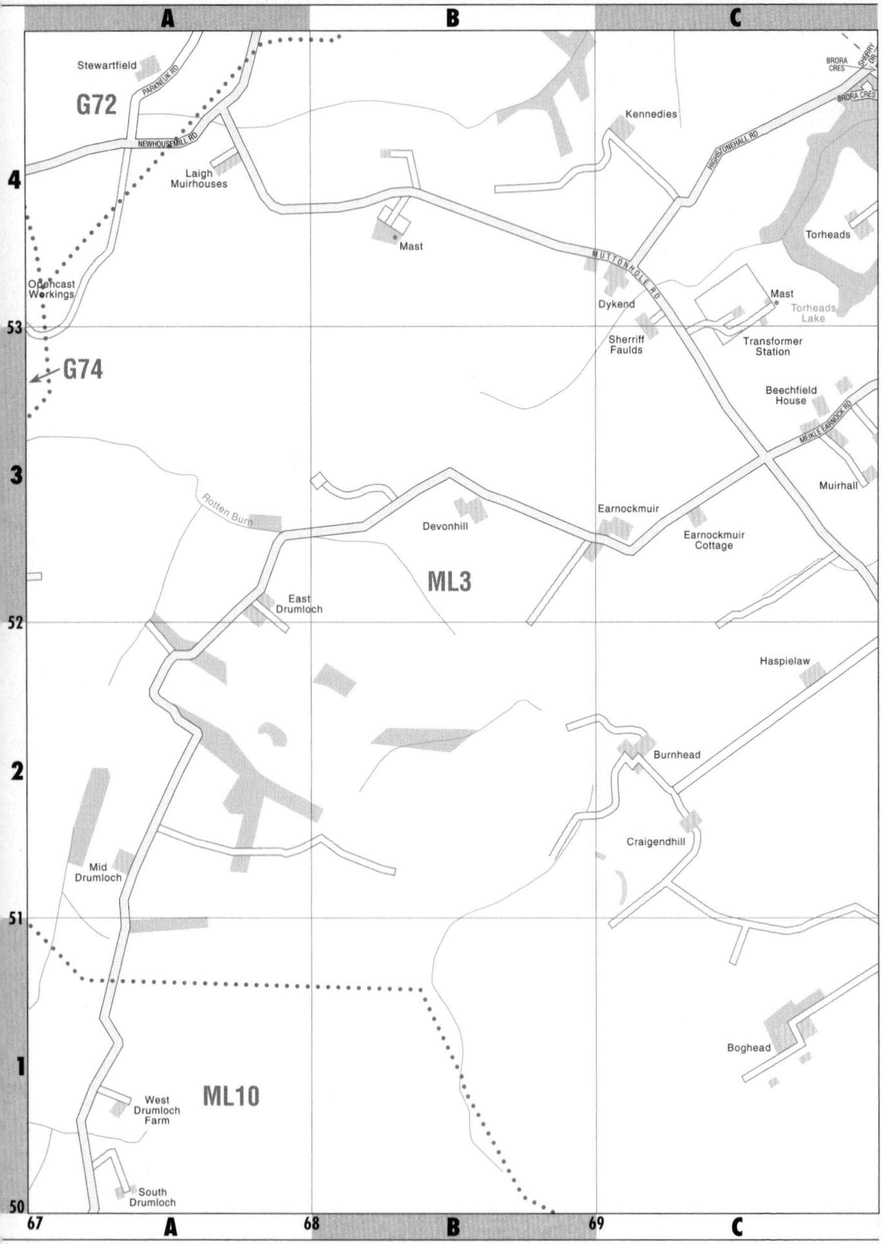

G72

PARKNEUK RD

NEWHOUSE MILL RD

Laigh
Muirhouses

4

Opencast
Workings

Kennedies

HIGH BLANTYRE RD

BRORA
CRES

BRORA CRES

LIBERTY RD

Torheads

Mast

MUTTONHOLE RD

Dykend

Mast
Torheads
Lake

53

G74

Sherriff
Faulds

Transformer
Station

Beechfield
House

MERKLEBANNOCK RD

3

Rotten Burn

Devonhill

Earnockmuir

Earnockmuir
Cottage

Muirhall

ML3

East
Drumloch

52

Haspielaw

2

Burnhead

Craigendhill

Mid
Drumloch

51

1

West
Drumloch
Farm

ML10

Boghead

South
Drumloch

50

67 **A** 68 **B** 69 **C**

A   B   C

Visitor Ctr
Chatelherault
CH
Cadzow Castle

Chatelherault Country Park

ALLANTON TERR

4

High Parks Farm

Merryton

Merryton Farm Cottages

53

LANARK RD

A72

Hamilton High Parks

Belvidere Plantation

Thorney Glen

Avon Braes

High Merryton

3

ML3

Divoty Wood

Beaton's Lodge

ML9

Ramsay's Plantation

Fairholm Bridge

52

Annax Lodge

Avon Water

Merryton Braes

North Quarter

Mid Quarter

2

Fairholm

MOSSBLOWN ST

South Quarter

Raploch

Sunnyside

TRIBBOCH ST
TARBOLTON PATH

MACNEILL ST

51

Knowetop

Little Sunnyside

St Mary's Prim Sch

Knowetop Glen

Darngaber Burn

Thinacre Glen

Millheugh Bridge

Millheugh

Powforth Glen

Powforth Burn

1

Wellbog

Larkhall Acad

Plotcock Glen

Cherry Hill

Wellbog Plantation

Thinacres

Broomelton

BROOMELTON RD

Plotcock Bridge

50

PLOTCOCK RD

73   A   74   B   75   C

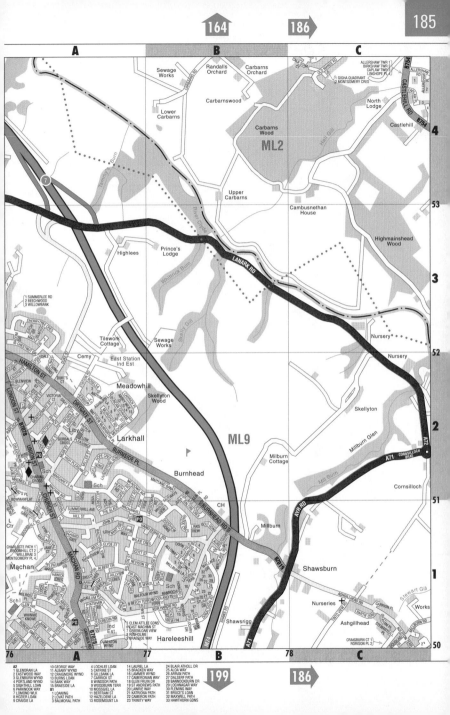

A B C

4

53

3

52

2

51

1

50

Sewage Works
Randalls Orchard
Carbarns Orchard
Carbarnswood
Lower Carbarns
Carbarns Wood

ML2

1 GIGHA QUADRANT
2 MONTGOMERY CRES

ALLERSHAW TWR 1
BIRKSHAW TWR 2
CAPLAW TWD 3
LINGHOPE PL 4

North Lodge

Castlehill

CASTLEHILL RD
B754

Hall Gill

Upper Carbarns

Cambusnethan House

Highmainshead Wood

LANARK RD

Prince's Lodge

Highlees

Five Clyde
Tammy's Burn

1 SUMMERLEE RD
2 BEECHWOOD
3 WILLOWBANK

Whitrick Burn

Tilework Cottage

Cemy

East Station Ind Est

Sewage Works

Skellyton Gill

Nursery

Nursery

Meadowhill

Skellyton Wood

Skellyton

HAMILTON ST

Larkhall

ML9

Millburn Glen

A72

Burnside Pl

Burnhead

Milburn Cottage

Mill Burn

Cornsilloch Brae

A71

CORNSILLOCH BRAE

Cornsilloch

BURNHEAD RD

CH

Millburn

Sch

Shawsburn

AYR RD
B7019

Machan

Charlotte Path 1
Broomhill Ct 2
Wellbrae 3
Montgomery Pl. 4

L Ctr

CHURCH ST
UNION ST

Nurseries

Works

Stewart Gill

Whinnie Knowe

Sch I

Ind Est

5 CLEM ATTLEE GDNS
6 EAST MACHAN ST
7 GREENLOAN VIEW
8 REDHOLME
9 BRAESIDE WAY

Shawsrigg

Hareleeshill

Ashgillhead

CRAIGBURN CT 1
RORISON PL 2

A2
1 GLENORAN LA
2 EASTWOOD WAY
3 GLENBURN WYND
4 PORTLAND WYND
5 SIGHTHILL LOAN
6 PARKNOOK WAY
7 LOMOND WLK
8 HOZIER LOAN
9 CRAIGIE LA

10 GEORGE WAY
11 ALBANY WYND
12 CRAIGMORE WYND
13 BURNS LOAN
14 BANK WAY
15 BRAESIDE LA

B1
1 LOANING
2 LOVAT PATH
3 BALMORAL PATH

4 LOCHLEE LOAN
5 CATRINE ST
6 GILLBANK LA
7 CARRICK ST
8 WINDSOR PATH
9 WOODBURN TERR
10 MOSSGIEL LA
11 BERTRAM ST
12 HAZELDENE LA
13 ROSEMOUNT LA

14 LAUREL LA
15 BRACKEN WAY
16 LAMMER WYND
17 CAMERONIAN WAY
18 GLEN FRUIN DR
19 ST ANDREWS PATH
20 LAWRIE WAY
21 KATRIONA PATH
22 CAMERON PATH
23 TRINITY WAY

24 BLAIR ATHOLL DR
25 ALOA WAY
26 ARRAN PATH
27 DALSERF PATH
28 BANNOCKBURN DR
29 LOCHNAGAR WAY
30 FLEMING WAY
31 BRUCE'S LOAN
32 MAXWELL PATH
33 HAWTHORN GDNS

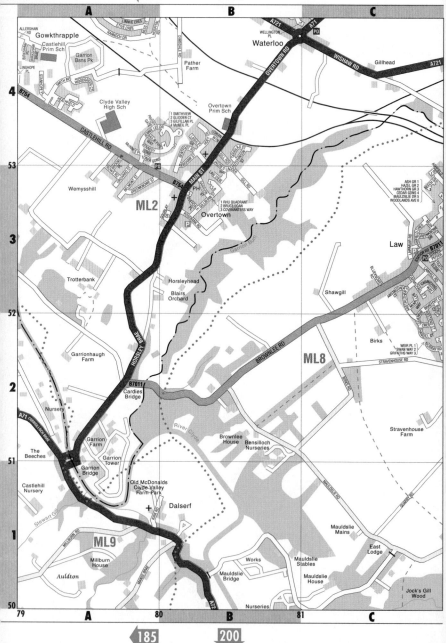

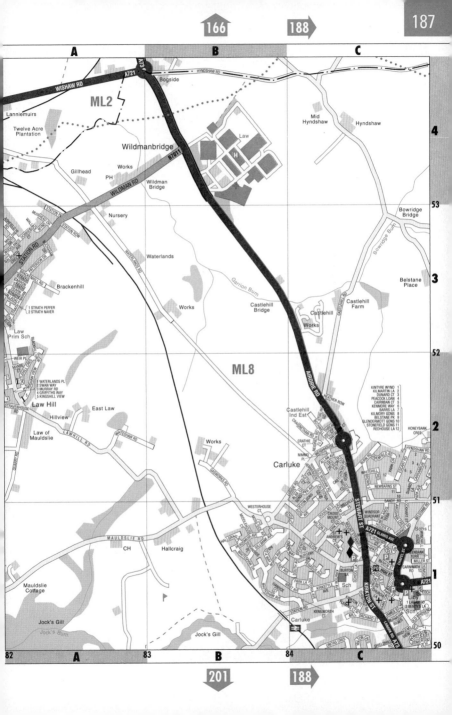

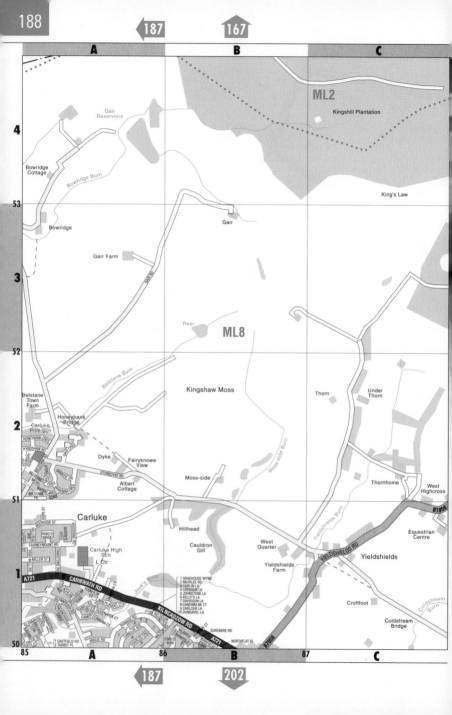

ML2

Kingshill Plantation

Gair Reservoirs

4

Bowridge Cottage

Bowridge Burn

King's Law

53

Bowridge

Gair

Gair Farm

3

Resr

ML8

52

Belstane Burn

Kingshaw Moss

Thorn

Under Thorn

Belstane Town Farm

Honeybank Bridge

Carluke Prim Sch

HONEYBANK CRES

HYNDSHAW RD

2

Dyke

Fairyknowe View

Moss-side Burn

STONEDYKE RD

Albert Cottage

Moss-side

Thornhome

West Highcross

51

Carluke

Hillhead

Cauldron Gill

West Quarter

Yieldshields Burn

YIELDSHIELDS RD

Yieldshields

B7056

Equestrian Centre

Carluke High Sch L Ctr

CAIRNIEMOUNT RD

KING'S CRES

MILLER ST

Yieldshields Farm

1

A721

CARNWATH RD

Jock's Burn

KILNCADZOW RD

1 SRAEHOUSE WYND
2 MUIRLEE RD
3 CARLIN LA
4 CROSSEN LA
5 JOHNSTONE LA
6 KELLY'S LA
7 DAVIDSON LA
8 CANDIMLINE CT
9 CARLOUK LA
10 DUNGAVEL LA

Croftfoot

Coldstream Burn

A721

GOREMIRE RD

NORTHFLAT PL

B7056

Coldstream Bridge

50

1 EASTFIELD RD
2 TARBET PL

ANGUS RD

FOREST BURN

85

86

87

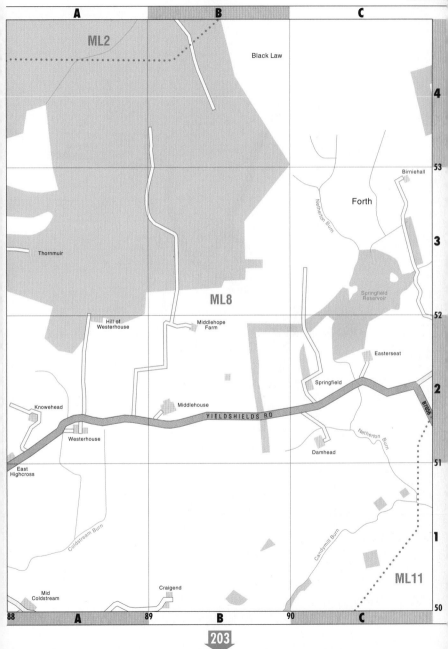

ML2

Black Law

ML8

Thornmuir

Forth

Netherton Burn

Springfield
Reservoir

Hill of
Westerhouse

Middlehope
Farm

Easterseat

Springfield

Knowehead

Middlehouse

YIELDSHIELDS RD

B7056

Westerhouse

Netherton Burn

Damhead

East
Highcross

Coldstream Burn

Candymill Burn

Mid
Coldstream

Craigend

ML11

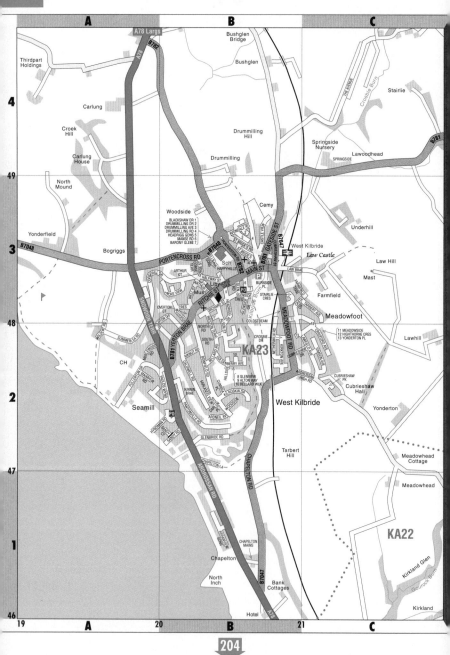

A **B** **C**

A78 Largs

Thirdpart
Holdings

4

Carlung

Croek
Hill

Carlung
House

Yonderfield

North
Mound

49

Bogriggs

Woodside

BLACKSHAW DR 1
DRUMMILLING DR 2
DRUMMILLING AVE 3
DRUMMILLING RD 5
HEADRIGG GDNS 5
MANSE RD 6
BARONY GLEBE 7

3 B7048

PORTENCROSS RD

Bushglen
Bridge

Bushglen

Drummilling
Hill

Drummilling

Cemy

Springside
Nursery

Lawoodhead

SPRINGSIDE

Stairlie

Crosbie Burn

B7047

B781

West Kilbride

Law Castle

Underhill

Law Hill

Mast

Farmfield

Meadowfoot

B7047

Sch

HAPPYHILLS

Museum

ARTHUR
CT

Libwynd

MAIN ST

BURNSIDE

LAW BRAE

11 MEADOWSIDE
12 HIGHTHORNE CRES
13 YONDERTON PL

RITCHIE ST

STAIRLIE
CRES

GLENSIDE
CRES

COLDSTREAM

OVERTON
CT

CROSBIE
DR

Lawhill

48

KA23

CH

North
RD

South
RD

Kinnin
Brae

Seamill

B781 TEROH BRAE

SANDY RD

GLENBRIDE RD

8 GLENVIEW
9 ALTON WAY
10 BELLARD WLK

Cubrieshaw
PK

Cubrieshaw
Hall

West Kilbride

Yonderton

2

ARDNEIL RD

ARROSSAN RD

CHAPELTON RD

Tarbert
Hill

Meadowhead
Cottage

Meadowhead

47

KA22

1

Chapelton
Mains

Chapelton

North
Inch

Bank
Cottages

B7047

Kirkland Glen

Kirkland

Gogarock Burn

46

Hotel

A78

A **B** **C**

19   20   21

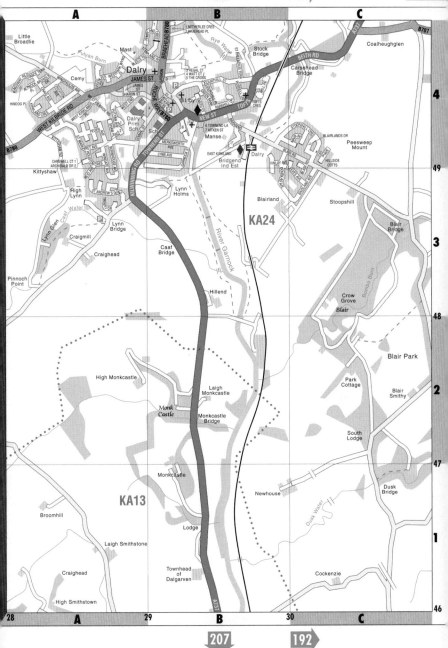

169
192
207
192

Little
Broadlie

Rutyan Burn

Mast

Cemy

Dalry
JAMES ST

1 NETHERLEE CRES
2 BRAEHEAD PL

Rye Water

Stock
Bridge

Coalheughglen

BEITH RD

Carsehead
Bridge

B707

B780

WEST KILBRIDE RD

Dalry
Prim
Sch

Library

1 REGAL CT
4 WATT CT
5 THE CROSS

NEW ST

TOFTS CRES

6 TOWNEND LA
7 AITKEN ST

Manse

EAST KIRKLAND

Dalry

BLAIRLANDS DR

Peesweep
Mount

Bridgend
Ind Est

Kittyshaw

High
Lynn

Hindog Pl

Archibald Dr 2
Carswell Ct 1

49

Merksworth
Ave

Lynn Ave

Lynn
Holms

Blairland

Stoopshill

KA24

Craigmill

Lynn Glen

Caaf Water

Lynn
Bridge

River Garnock

Blair
Bridge

Craighead

Caaf
Bridge

3

Pinnoch
Point

Hillend

Bombo Burn

Crow
Grove
Blair

48

Blair Park

High Monkcastle

Laigh
Monkcastle

Park
Cottage

Blair
Smithy

2

*Monk
Castle*

Monkcastle
Bridge

South
Lodge

Monkcastle

Newhouse

Dusk Water

Dusk
Bridge

47

KA13

Broomhill

Lodge

Laigh Smithstone

1

Craighead

Townhead
of
Dalgarven

Cockenzie

High Smithstown

A7?

46

28   A   29   B   30   C

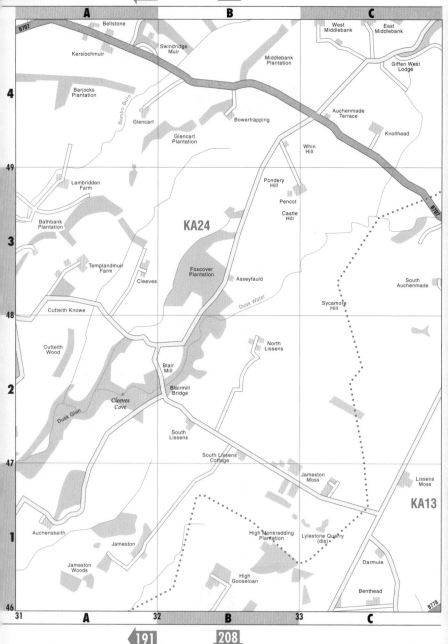

191

170

B707

A

Bellstone

Kerslochmuir

Swindridge Muir

West Middlebank

East Middlebank

C

Giffen West Lodge

Middlebank Plantation

4

Barjocks Plantation

Bombo Burn

Glencart

Bowertrapping

Auchenmade Terrace

Knollhead

Glencart Plantation

Whin Hill

B707

49

Lambridden Farm

Pondery Hill

Pencot

Castle Hill

South Auchenmade

Bathbank Plantation

KA24

3

Templandmuir Farm

Cleeves

Foxcover Plantation

Asseyfauld

Dusk Water

Sycamore Hill

Cutteith Knowe

48

Cutteith Wood

North Lissens

Blair Mill

Blairmill Bridge

2

Cleeves Cove

Dusk Glen

South Lissens

47

South Lissens Cottage

Jameston Moss

Lissens Moss

Auchenskeith

High Monkredding Plantation

Lylestone Quarry (dis)

KA13

1

Jameston

Darmule

Jameston Woods

High Gooseloan

Benthead

B778

46

31

A

32

B

33

C

191

208

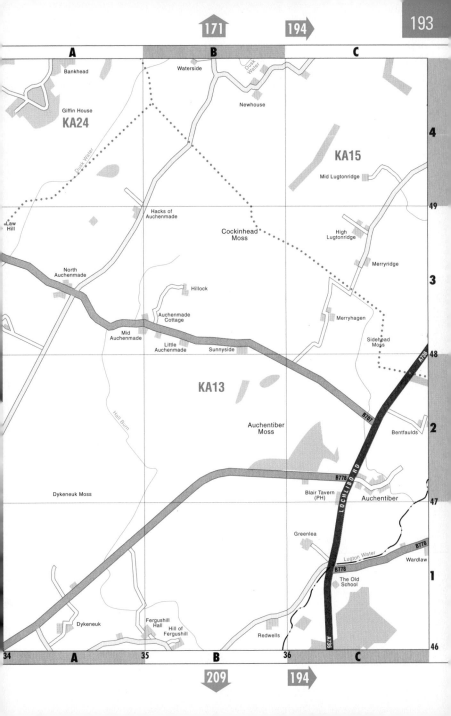

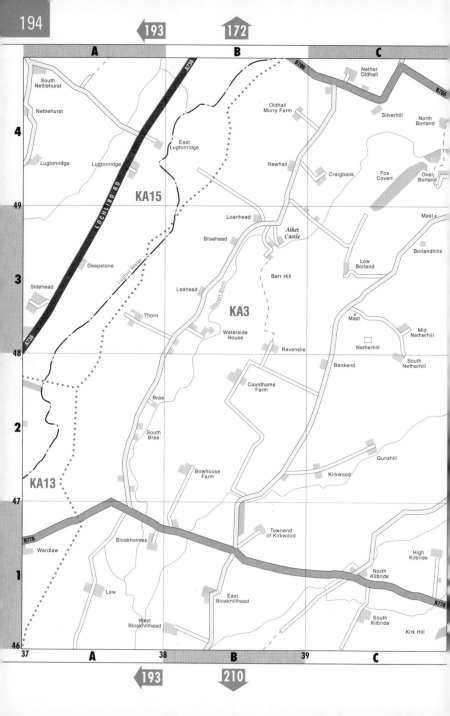

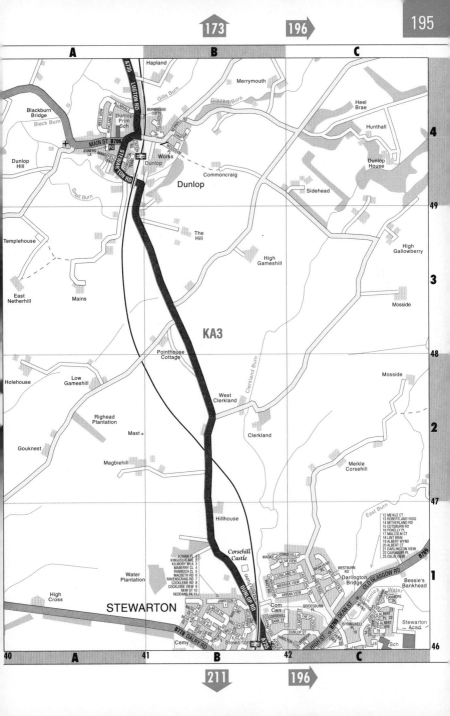

A B C

Titwood

Clerkland Burn

Over
Auchentiber

Over
Auchentiber

Nether
Auchentiber

4

Low
Gallowberry

East Burn

Springbank

West
Whitelee

B7769

49

Auchentiber

Merryhill

Glen Burn

Glenburn
Cottage

Whiteleeburn
Bridge

West Spittal

East
Spittal

3

Upper
Hairshaw

High
Williamshaw

Mid
Hairshaw

Gateside

ANNICK COTTS

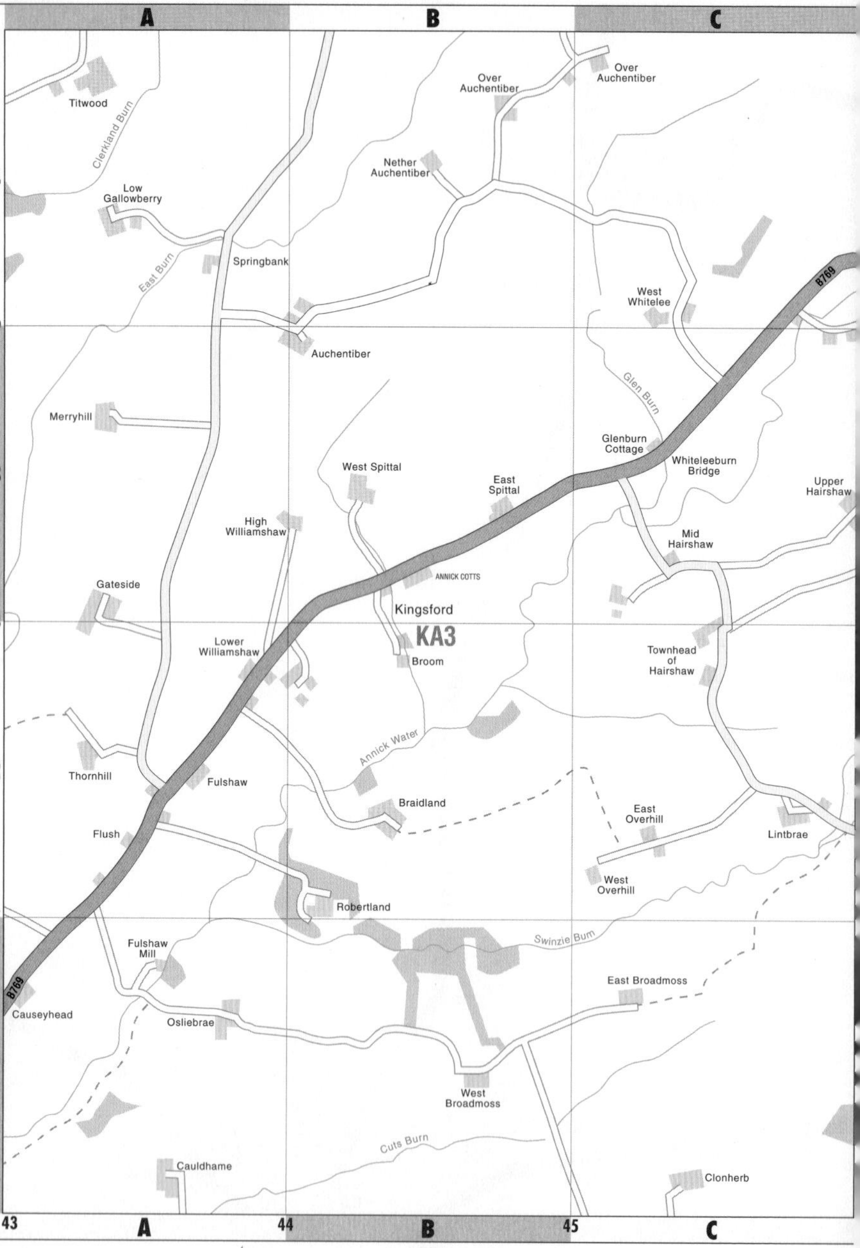

48

Kingsford

KA3

Lower
Williamshaw

Broom

Townhead
of
Hairshaw

Annick Water

2

Thornhill

Fulshaw

Braidland

East
Overhill

Lintbrae

Flush

West
Overhill

Robertland

47

Swinzie Burn

B7769

Fulshaw
Mill

East Broadmoss

Causeyhead

Osliebrae

1

West
Broadmoss

Cauldhame

Cuts Burn

Clonherb

46

43 A 44 B 45 C

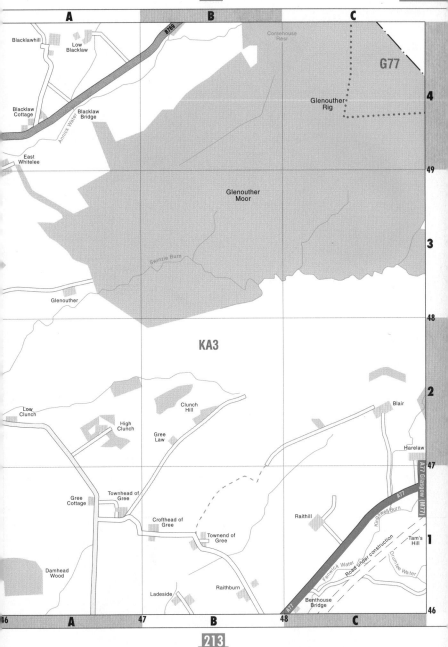

184

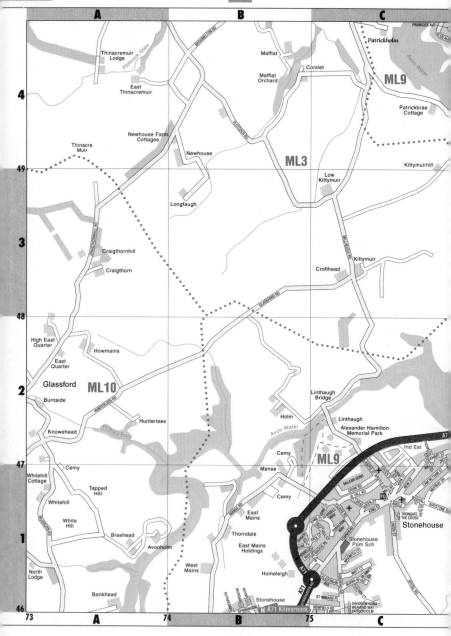

Patrickholm

PRIMROSE AVE.
GLEN AVE.

Avon Water

ML9

Thinacremuir
Lodge

Mafflat

East
Thinacremuir

Corslet

Mafflat
Orchard

Patrickbrae
Cottage

Newhouse Farm
Cottages

Thinacre
Muir

Newhouse

ML3

Kittymuirhill

Low
Kittymuir

Longfaugh

Kittymuirhill

Craigthornhill

Kittymuir

Craigthorn

Crofthead

High East
Quarter

Howmains

East
Quarter

Glassford

ML10

Linthaugh
Bridge

Burnside

Holm

Linthaugh

Hunterlees

Pillar's Burn

Alexander Hamilton
Memorial Park

Avon Water

Knowehead

Ind Est

A7

ML9

Whitehill
Cottage

Cemy

Manse

Whitehill

Tapped
Hill

Cemy

Stonehouse
Prim Sch

Stonehouse

White
Hill

East
Mains

Braehead

Avonholm

Thorndale

North
Lodge

East Mains
Holdings

West
Mains

Homeleigh

Bankhead

Stonehouse

A71 Kilmarnock

NEWFIELD RD

ST NINIANS PL

1 DAVIDSON SONS
2 WEAVERS WAY
3 PATRICKHOLM

199
186

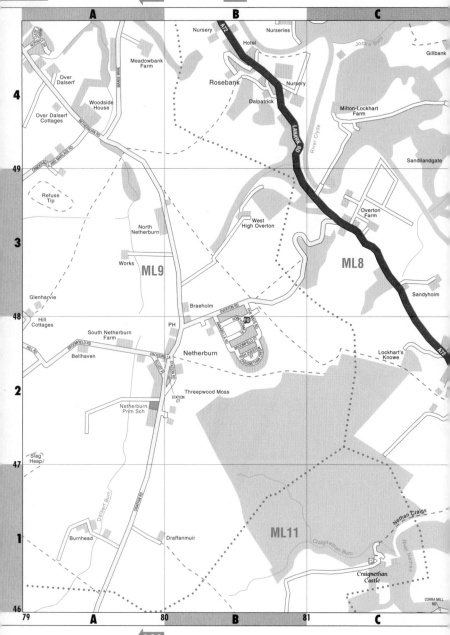

A   B   C

4

Over Dalserf

Over Dalserf
Cottages

Meadowbank
Farm

Woodside
House

Nursery

Nurseries

Gillbank

Jock's Burn

Hotel

Rosebank

Dalpatrick

Nursery

Milton-Lockhart
Farm

River Clyde

LANRK RD

A72

MANSE BRAE

NETHERBURN RD

CANDERMILL AND MARLAGE RD

Sandilandgate

49

Refuse
Tip

North
Netherburn

West
High Overton

Overton
Farm

ML8

3

Works

ML9

Glenharvie

Braeholm

OVERTON RD

Sandyholm

48

Hill
Cottages

HILL RD

BROOMFIELD RD

South Netherburn
Farm

PH

CROSSING LA

STATION RD

ELLIOT RD

HIGH OVERTON

BROOMFIELD

CRAIGNETHAN CT

PO

Lockhart's
Knowe

A72

Bellhaven

Netherburn

2

Netherburn
Prim Sch

STATION
CT

Threepwood Moss

Slag
Heap

47

Dalserf Burn

SHAWTON RD

1

Burnhead

Draffanmuir

ML11

Craignethan Burn

Nethan Craigs

River Nethan

P

Craignethan
Castle

CORRA MILL
RD

46

79   A   80   B   81   C

A B C

Crawforddyke Prim Sch
Caldwell Rd
Roadmeetings
Cemy
NORTHFLAT PL
Northflat Ave
H
A721
Burnhead
YIELDSHIELDS RD
Coldstream Reservoir
West Coldstream
7 CAMERON RD
8 BRAEHEAD LOAN
9 CHARLES CRES
Carluke
KILNCADZOW RD
Burnhead Bridge
FORRESTLEA RD
MAYFIELD GDNS

4

1 SAUCHIESMOOR RD
2 THORNLEA ST
3 BEECHFIELD DR
4 ISLAY GDNS
5 JURA GDNS
6 GIGHA GDNS
Langshaw
Headsmuir
Gowansie
Gateside
A73

BOGHALL RD
A72

49

Fiddler Burn

Nursery
Leemuir

3
PH
B7056
ML8

Lee Meadow

48
Nellfield House
A73

Crossgates
Cartland Muir Plantation

2
Crossgates Plantation
Nursery
Lee Burn
March Bridge
Craigen Hill

47
West Wood
Leewood House
LANARK RD
Mast
MOOR RD

ML11

1
The Lee
New Greentowers Farm
Cartland
Castlehill

46
Auchenglen Burn
Brocklinn Glen
Brocklinn Burn
Brocklinn Bridge
A73
Cartland
CARTLAND RD
GREEN TREES RD
PLATTMOOR RD

85 A 86 B 87 C

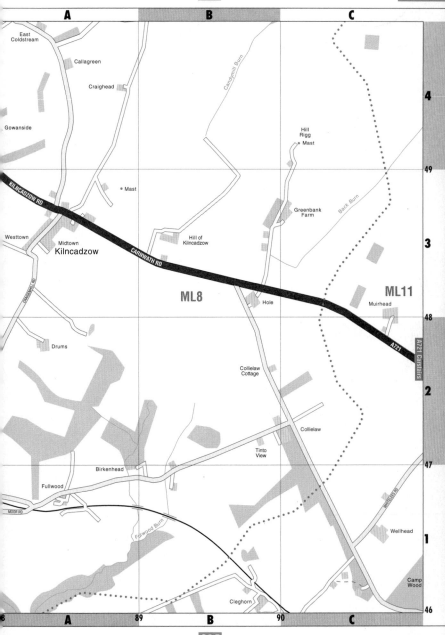

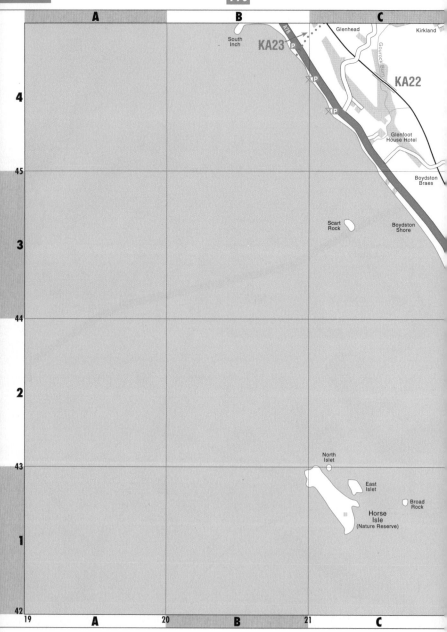

190

| | A | B | C |

South Inch

KA23

KA22

A78

P

P

P

Glenhead

Kirkland

Gourock Burn

Glenfoot House Hotel

Boydston Braes

Scart Rock

Boydston Shore

North Islet

East Islet

Broad Rock

Horse Isle
(Nature Reserve)

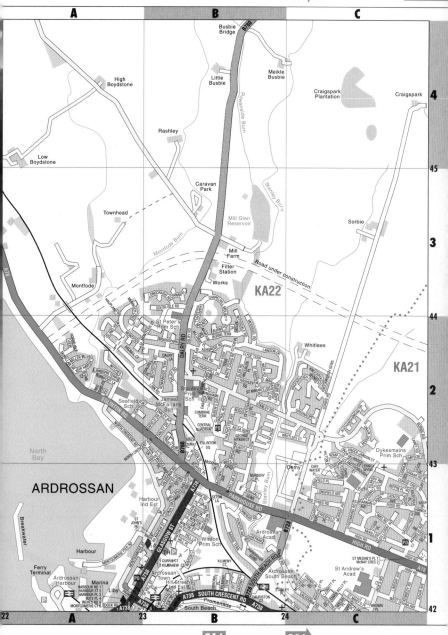

ARDROSSAN

205

KA13

Smithstone
Plantation

KA22

Quarry

Towerlodge

Bankend

Little Laught

Meiklelaught

KA21

Lochwood

West Knockrivoch
Mount

East Knockrivoch
Mount

Knockrivoch

Diddup

Works

Stevenston or
Ashgrove Loch

South Knockrivoch
Mount

The Craigs

Loch Craigs

Glen
Banks

Lochcraigs

Ford

Corsankell

Road under construction

CH

Mast

Sharphill

Glen Burn

Filter
Station

Hillhead

Sharphill
Ind Est

Middlepart

Fellie Hill

STEVENSTON

Greenhead
Holdings

KA20

SALTCOATS

1 ISLAY CRES
2 KEIR HARDIE PL
3 JEAN ARMOUR PL
4 ABBOTSFORD PL
5 TALISMAN WLK
6 MUNRO WLK

MAXWELL PL 1
CLEMENTS PL 2
OAKLAND DR 3
AUCHOHELIE DR 4
ASHGROVE AVE 5
KERELAW AVE 6

LANDSBOROUGH PL

Hawkhill
Ret Pk

Mayfield
Prim Sch

Kerelaw
Sch

Hayocks
Prim Sch

James Reid
Sch

MARY LOVE PL 1
GOLDIE PL 2
CLYDE VIEW AVE 3
CAPONCRAIG AVE 4
GRANGE CT 5
BURNSIDE PL 6
SCHOOLWELL ST 7

Kerelaw
Mains

LOCCARD
RD

St John's
RC Prim Sch

Cemy

1 MORRISON CT
2 ST JAMES' PL
3 ST COLUMBA PL
4 ST JOHN'S PL

Mayfield

Priest
Hill

7 MIDDLEPART CRES
8 DUGUID DR
9 PROSPECTHILL RD
10 McKINNON PL
11 CLARK PL
13 ADAMS AVE
14 LOCHRANZA PL

GLENCAIRN
TERR

HAYOCKS
RDBT

ARDEER
RDBT

Caravan
Park

GLENCAIRN ST

HIGH RD

TOWNHEAD ST

KILWINNING RD

Ardeer Mains

HILLCREST

DUBBS RD

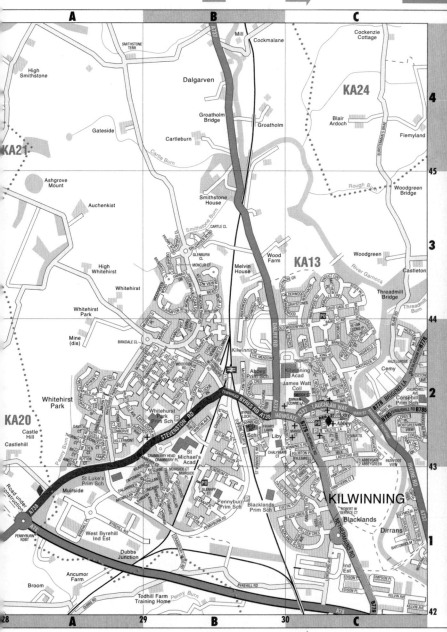

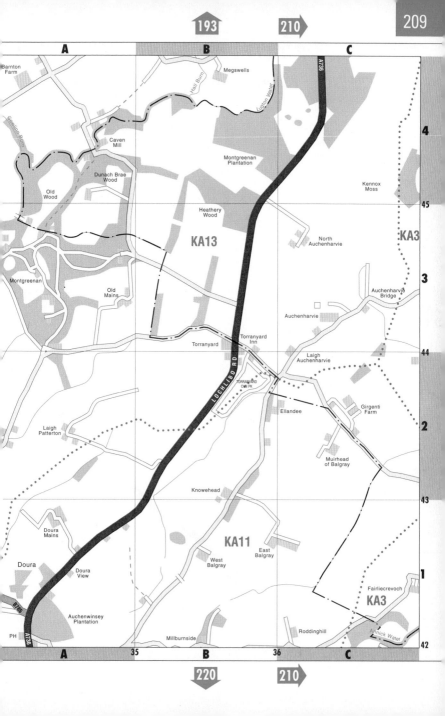

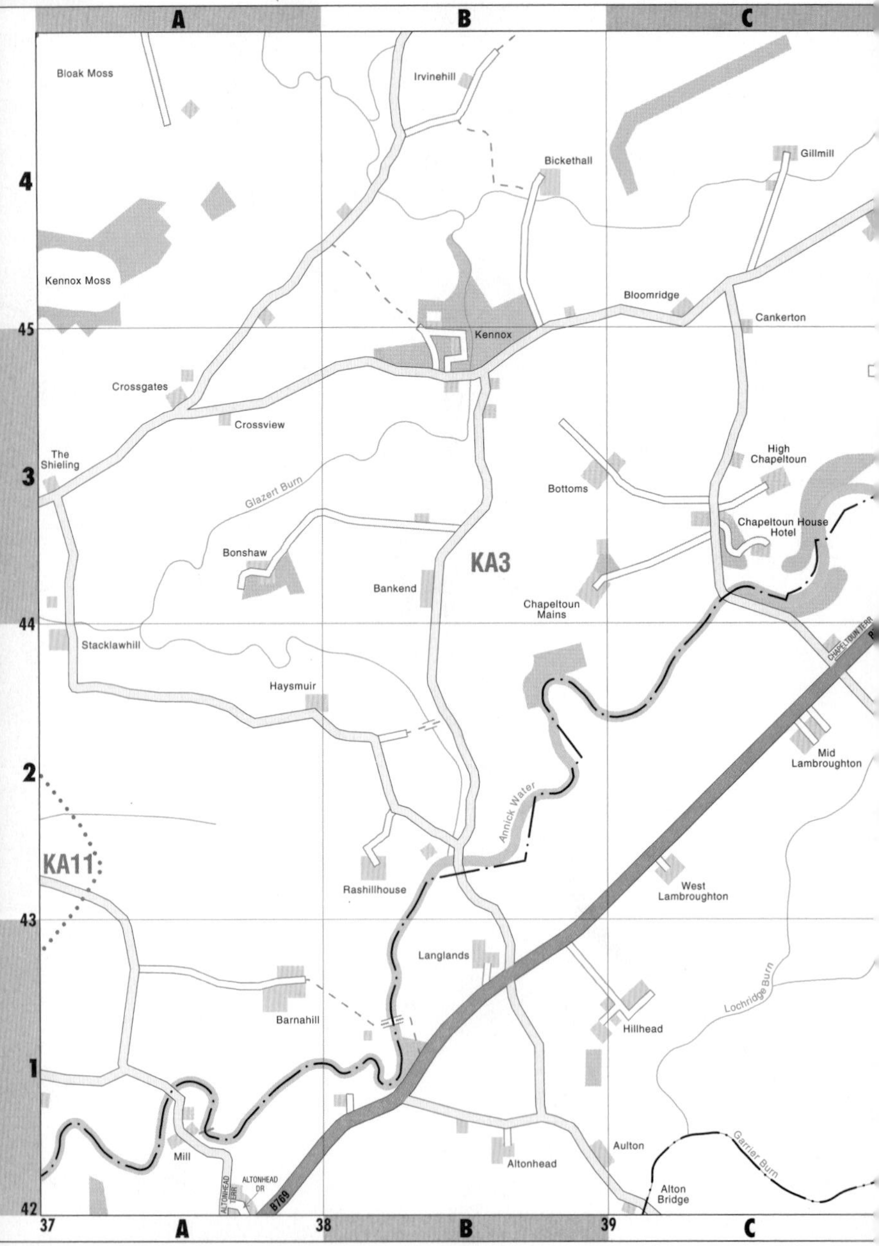

209
194

A
B
C

Bloak Moss

Irvinehill

Bickethall

Gillmill

4

Kennox Moss

Bloomridge

Cankerton

45

Kennox

Crossgates

Crossview

High
Chapeltoun

The
Shieling

Glazert Burn

Bottoms

Chapeltoun House
Hotel

3

Bonshaw

KA3

Bankend

Chapeltoun
Mains

44

Stacklawhill

Haysmuir

Mid
Lambroughton

2

Annick Water

KA11

West
Lambroughton

43

Langlands

Lochridge Burn

Barnahill

Rashillhouse

Hillhead

1

Mill

Aulton

Garrier Burn

ALTONHEAD DR

ALTONHEAD
DRIVE

B769

Altonhead

Alton
Bridge

42

37
A
38
B
39
C

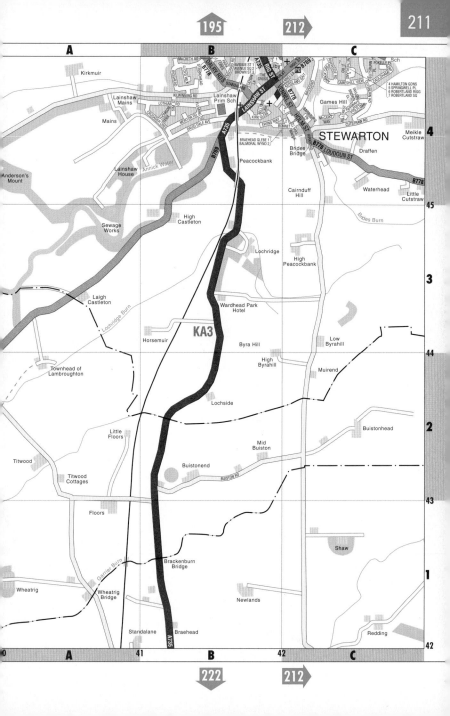

A
B
C

Kirkmuir

MACBETH RD
AVENUE ST 1
AVENUE SQ 2
BROWN ST 3

Lainshaw
Mains

KILWINNING RD

Lainshaw
Prim Sch

THE
CROSS

PO
B769

Lainshaw
House

Mains

LOTHIAN
RD

DAVID DALE AVE

KIRK GLEBE

Games Hill

STEWARTON

Meikle
Cutstraw

Anderson's
Mount

Annick Water

BRAEHEAD GLEBE 1
BALMORAL WYND 2

Peacockbank

Brides
Bridge

LOUDOUN ST

Draffen

4 HAMILTON GDNS
5 SPRINGWELL PL
6 ROBERTLAND RIGG
7 ROBERTLAND SQ

4

Lainshaw
House

Cairnduff
Hill

Waterhead

Little
Cutstraw

45

High
Castleton

Brides Burn

Sewage
Works

Lochridge

High
Peacockbank

Laigh
Castleton

Lochridge Burn

3

Wardhead Park
Hotel

KA3

Horsemuir

Byra Hill

Low
Byrahill

44

Townhead of
Lambroughton

High
Byrahill

Muirend

Little
Floors

Lochside

Mid
Buiston

Buistonhead

2

Titwood

Titwood
Cottages

Buistonend

BUISTON RD

Floors

43

Gartler Burn

Brackenburn
Bridge

Shaw

Wheatrig

Wheatrig
Bridge

Newlands

1

Standalane

Braehead

A735

Redding

42

A
41
B
42
C

211
196

A **B** **C**

Cuts Burn

The Spott

Bogside

West Pokelly

East Pokelly

Darclaboch

Balgray Mill

4

Pokelly Hall

Balgray Mill Burn

B778

Little Cutstraw

45

Burnfoot

Thorn

Burnfoot Resr

Gardrumhill

Blair Hill

Porisken

Over Lochridge

3

Oldhall

Gainford Resr

High Gainford

Gainford Bridge

Glaister

B778

44

High Todhill

Low Gainford

KA3

Shaw Burn

Fenwick Hill

2

Low Todhill

Balgray Mill Burn

Gainhill

Glenleitch

Rowallan Home Farm

43

Little Fenwick

A77

West Tannacrieff

East Tannacrieff

Muirend

B751

1

Rowallan

KILMAURS RD

B7081

Gardrum Mill Burn

Camel Water

Holmepark Plantation

Meikle Mosside

Moss Wood

A77

42

43 **A** **44** **B** **45** **C**

211
223

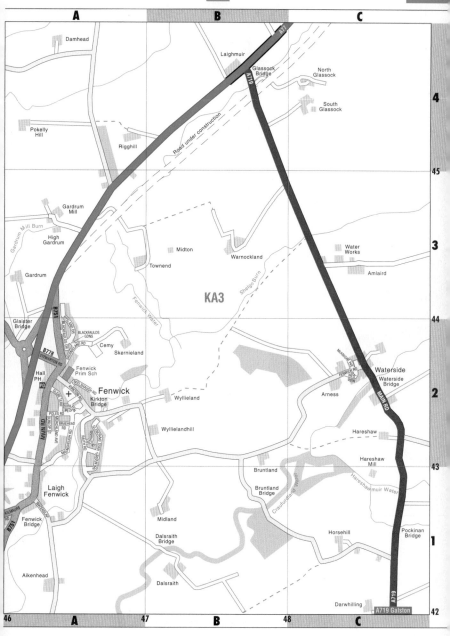

KA3

202

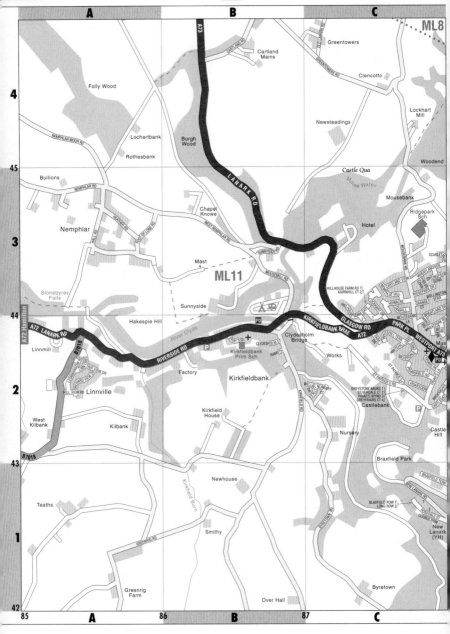

ML8

4

45

3

ML11

44

2

43

1

42

A   85   86   B   87   C

Folly Wood

Greentowers

Cartland Mains

Clencotto

Lockhart Mill

Lochartbank

Burgh Wood

Newsteadings

Woodend

Castle Qua

Mousebank

Ridgepark Sch

Bullions

Nemphlar

Chapel Knowe

Hotel

Stonebyres Falls

Mast

Sunnyside

Hakespie Hill

River Clyde

Kirkfieldbank Brae

Glasgow Rd

Park Pl

Westport A73

Linnmill

Riverside Rd

Clydesholm Bridge

Kirkfieldbank Prim Sch

Works

West Kilbank

Linnville

Factory

Kirkfieldbank

Kilbank

Kirkfield House

Castlebank

Nursery

Castle Hill

Teaths

Newhouse

Braxfield Park

Smithy

Greenrig Farm

Byretown

Over Hall

New Lanark (YH)

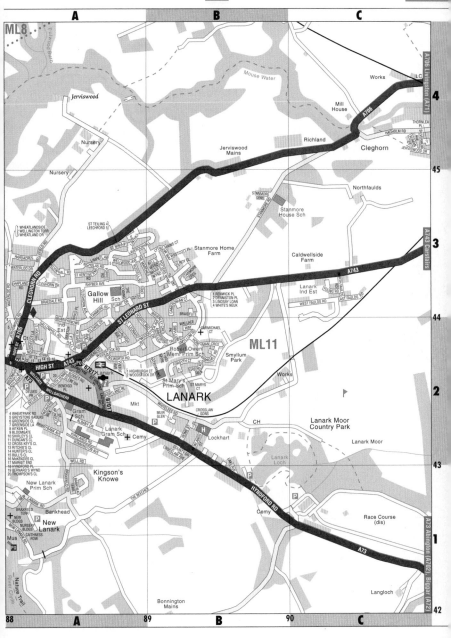

205

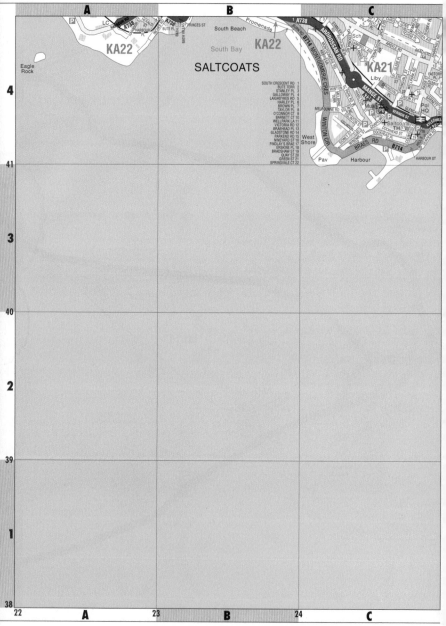

SALTCOATS

KA22

KA22

KA21

Eagle Rock

South Beach

South Bay

Promenade

SOUTH CRESCENT RD 1
BUTE TERR 2
STANLEY PL 3
GALLOWAY PL 4
LAIGHDYKES RD 5
HARLEY PL 6
BROWN PL 7
TAYLOR PL 8
O'CONNOR CT 9
BARNETT CT 10
WELLPARK LA 11
VICTORIA RD 12
BRAEHEAD PL 13
GLADSTONE RD 14
PARKEND RD 15
VINEYARD ST 16
FINDLAY'S BRAE 17
ERSKINE PL 18
BRADSHAW ST 19
QUAY ST 20
GREEN ST 21
SPRINGVALE CT 22

West Shore

Pav

Harbour

STEVENSTON

Auchenharvie
Auchenharvie
Acad

Glencairn
Prim Sch

Ardeer
Park

Park

Harvies
L Ctr

SALTCOATS RD

CANAL ST

Portland Place
Ind Est

Moorpark
Ind Est

Stevenston
Ind Est

KA21

CH

Saltcoats
Campbell

KA20

Caravan
Park

Stevenston

SANDYLANDS PROM

1 THOMAS CAMPBELL ST
2 McISAAC RD
3 PARKEND GDNS
4 CANAL CT
5 PARKEND AVE
6 PARKEND TERR

Ardeer
Prim Sch

CALEDONIAN RD

East
Shore

Beach
Park

Sewage
Works

A B C

DUBBS RD

Ferry Burn

BYREHILL RD A78

A78

Nethermains
Bridge

Garnock Floods
Nature Reserve

KA13

Refuse
Tip

4

B78

41

KA20

GARNOCK RD

River Garnock

WEST RD

POWER PLANT RD

3

NORTH RING RD

CENTRAL AVE

P

P

Works

BURMA RD

MOORPARK RD

SOUTH RING RD

KERELAW RD

Stevenston
Site

40

NEW HILL RD

KA12

CH

Bogside

Crooky's
Point

Bogside
Race Course
(disused)

2

River Irvine

NIBBLE RD

39

Bogside
Flats

1

The Big Idea
(Inventor Ctr)

Irvine
Harbour

River Irvine

HARBOUR ST

Arts
Ctr

P

BEACH DR

Magnum
L Ctr

38

28 A 29 B 30 C

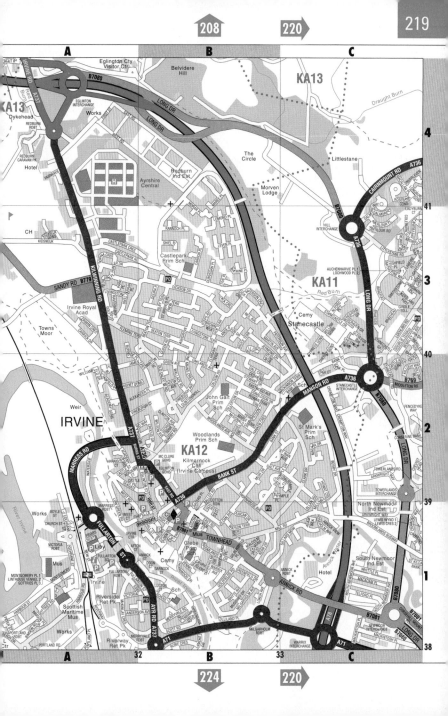

219
209

A   B   C

Draught Burn

A736

Annick Lodge

KA3

4

High Armsheugh

West Wood

Braehead

Sourlie

B7

A736 CAIRNMOUNT RD

SOURLIE RDBT

Lawthorn Plantation

Holehouse

Middleton

41

BRYCE KNOX CT

1 SWINTON PL
2 ORMISTON PL

Overt Farm

Lawthorn Prim Sch

Lawthorn

THE GARDENS

Perceton Mains

Girdle Toll

LAWTHORN RDBT

Perceton House

3

PERCETON RDBT

Perceton

KA2

Cheepy Neuk

1 BONNYTON ROW
2 BONNYTON FOOT
3 SOUTHOOK ROW
4 NEWTONHEAD
5 BUSBIEHEAD
6 OVERTON PL

DARNSHAW

40

MIDDLETON RD

KA11

Warwickdale

B769

LOMOND WAY

Annick Water

IRVINE

Muirhouses

Drummuir

1 SHIELHOPE CT
2 GREENSIDE
3 MID RIG

WHITEWISP CT

2

1 CRAMARJ CT
2 MILLARD CT
3 RODERICK CT
4 CROFTHEAD

WHITEHOPE

Annick Water

Caprington Burn

STATION

Sch

5 NORTH VENNEL
6 CROFTHEAD CT
7 MOORFOOT PL
8 SOUTH VENNEL
9 ELSYTH WLK

CHEVIOT CT

Liby

St John Ogilvie Prim Sch

HEATHERSTANE WLK

39

KILPATRICK CT

HEATHERSTANE BANK

HOPSTOUN BANK

Capringstone

Springside

Springside Prim Sch

FINTRY WLK

Sch

Bourtreehill

GARRIER

COACH BRAE VIEW

MAIN RD

B7U

1

Broomlands Prim Sch

Broomlands

BROOMLANDS BURN

EAST BROOMLANDS

GILPA TERR

HILLSHAW FOOT

CORSEHILL TERR

CORSE AVE

MAIN ST

Mon

Dreghorn Prim Sch

Dreghorn

Greenwood Acad

B7081

Cemy

Liby

TOWNFOOT

B7U

Corsehill

38

CORSEHILL MOUNT

MACROBERT AVE

DUNLOP CRES

B7081

BUTE CT

WOOD GR

34   A   35   B   36   C

219
225

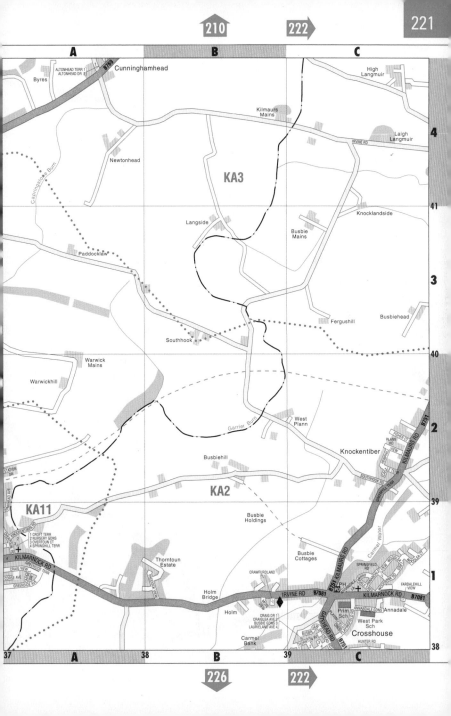

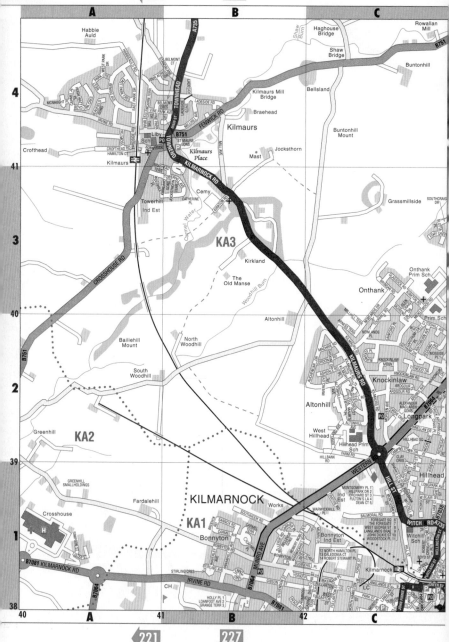

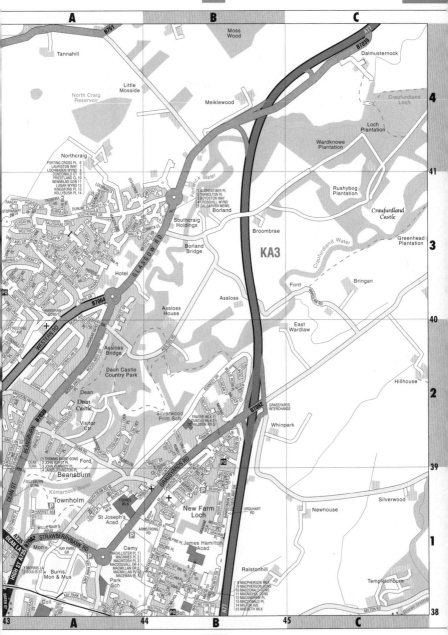

Northcraig
1 PORTING CROSS PL 6
2 LAURISTON WAY 7
3 LOCHMABEN WYND 8
4 DUNDONALD D 9
5 PRIESTLAND CL 10
NEWMILNS GDNS 11
LUGAR WYND 12
KINGSFORD PL 13
HOLLYBUSH PL 14

Borland
1 AUCHENTIBER PL
2 TARBOLTON PL
3 BOYDSTON WAY
4 CROSSHILL WYND
5 DALGARVEN MEWS

KA3

1 THOMAS BAIRD GDNS
2 JOHN SURGT PL
3 JOHN KENNEDY PL
4 JAMES JOHNSTON PL

1 MACALLISTER PL 1
2 MACINNES PL 2
3 MACINTOSH PL 3
4 MACDOUGALL DR 4
5 MACMILLAN DR 5
6 MACMILLAN PV 6
7 MACEWAN PL 7

8 MACPHERSON WLK
9 MACPHERSON GDNS
10 MACDONALD GDNS
11 MACINCHGX GDNS
12 MACANDREW PL
13 MACDONALD D PL
14 MILTON AVE
15 MACBETH WLK

FRASER WLK 1
DUNDAS WLK 2
DONALDSON RD 3

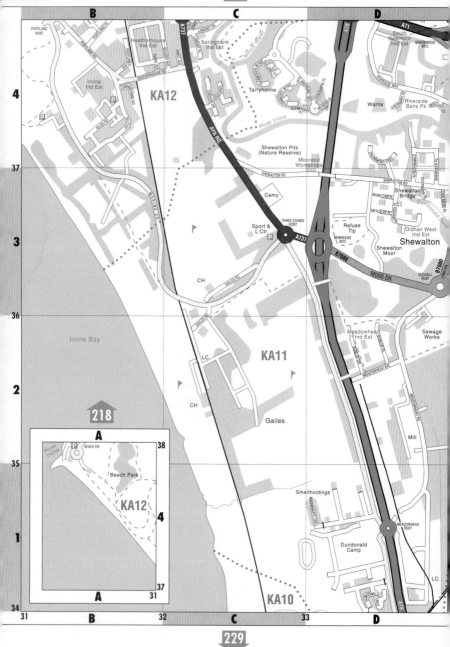

B   C   D

A71

PORTLAND RDBT

PORTLAND RD

Heatherhouse Ind Est

Springbank Ind Est

South Newmoor Ind Est

GREENWOOD INTC

Irvine Ind Est

KA12

Tarryholme

Warrix

Riverside Bsns Pk

River Irvine

Shewalton Pits (Nature Reserve)

Moorend Workshops

SHEWALTON RD

SHEWALTON RD

Shewalton Bridge

Cemy

Dundonald Burn

Three Stanes RDBT

Sport & L Ctr

Refuse Tip

NEWHOUSE INTC

Oldhall West Ind Est

Shewalton

A737

B7080

Shewalton Moor

OLDHALL RDBT

CH

GAILES RD

MOSS DR

B7080

Irvine Bay

GAILES RD

Meadowhead Ind Est

Sewage Works

KA11

LC

CH

Gailes

Mill

218

MEADOWHEAD AVE

A

BEACH DR

38

River Irvine

Beach Park

KA12

4

Smallholdings

MEADOWHEAD RDBT

A

37

31

Dundonald Camp

LC

KA10

31   B   32   C   33   D

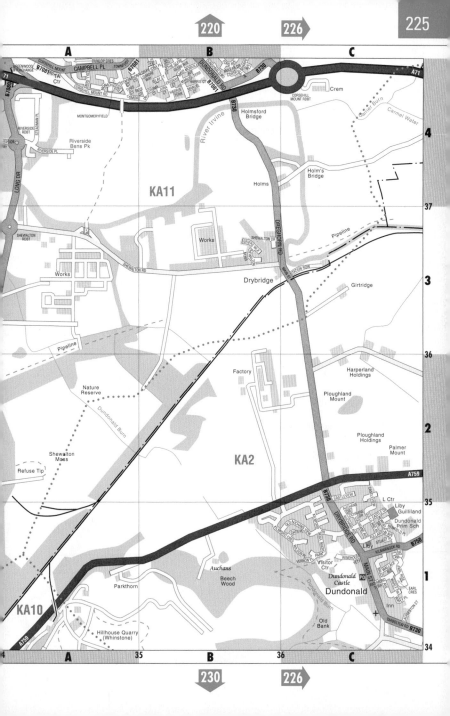

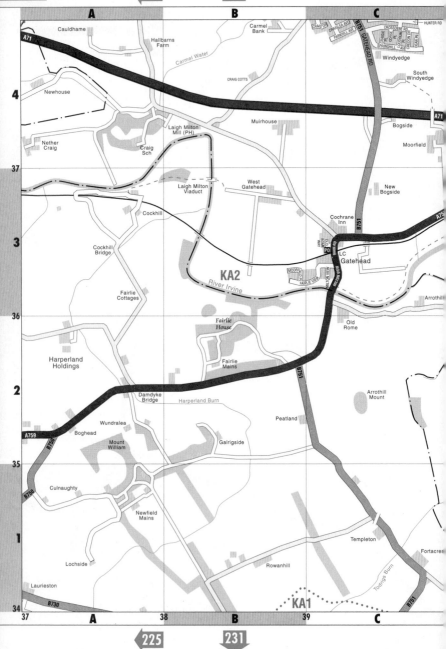

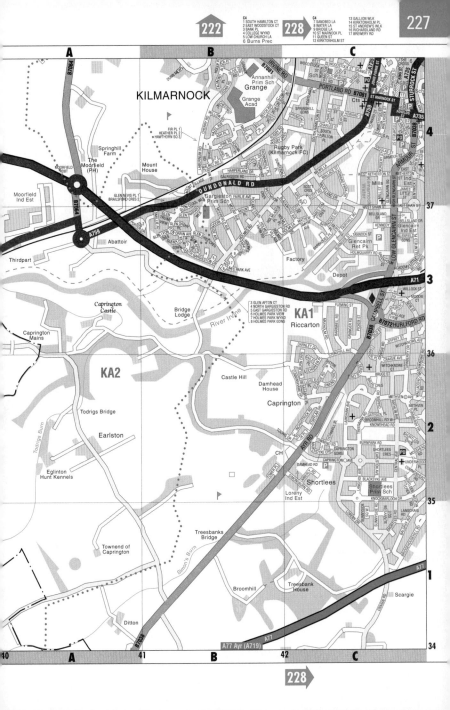

222

228
C4
1 SOUTH HAMILTON CT
2 EAST WOODSTOCK CT
3 BANK PL
4 COLLEGE WYND
5 LOW CHURCH LA
6 Burns Prec

C4
7 SANDBED LA
8 WATER LA
9 BRIDGE LA
10 ST MARNOCK PL
11 QUEEN ST
12 KIRKTONHOLM ST

13 GALLION WLK
14 KIRKTONHOLM PL
15 ST ANDREW'S WLK
16 RICHARDLAND WLK
17 BREWERY RD

227

KILMARNOCK

Grange
Annanhill Prim Sch
Grange Acad

Springhill Farm

The Moorfield (PH)
MOORFIELD RDBT

Moorfield Ind Est

Mount House

FIR PL 1
HEATHER PL 2
HAWTHORN SQ 3

Rugby Park (Kilmarnock FC)

Springhill Gdns

PORTLAND RD B7081

WOODSTOCK ST
STURROCK ST
A735
IRVINE RD
B7081

ST MARNOCK ST
A759
A735
B7038

4

South Hamilton Ct

GLENNEVIS PL 1
BRAILSFORD CRES 2

DUNDONALD RD
Gargieston Fairlie Ave Prim Sch

HARPERLAND RD
GALRIGGSIDE RD

GLEN
ORCHY
VIEW 1
GLEN ORCHY
PL 2 GLEN ROSA
GDNS 3

37

Abattoir

GLEN
AFTON GDNS
ORRIN WLK
GLEN

Thirdpart

A759

GLEN

Factory

WEST SHAW ST

Tannock St

Glencairn Ret Pk

Glencairn Ind Est
GLENFIELD GDNS

HOLMQUARRY RD

Depot

A71

3

Caprington Castle

Bridge Lodge

River Irvine

3 GLEN AFTON CT
4 NORTH GARGIESTON RD
5 EAST GARGIESTON RD
6 HOLMES PARK VIEW
7 HOLMES PARK WYND
8 HOLMES PARK GDNS

WILLOCK ST
MOODIE CT

FLEMING ST

KA1
Riccarton

CAMPBELL ST
B7072 HURLFORD RD

B7038

Caprington Mains

KA2

Castle Hill

Damhead House
Caprington

WITCHKNOWE RD

36

2

Todrigs Bridge

Earlston

Eglinton Hunt Kennels

Todrigs Burn

Simon's Burn

CH

DAMHEAD RD
Shortlees

BURNPARK RD

SHORTLEES CRES
PO

KNOWEHEAD RD

Loreny Ind Est

BLACKSYKE AVE
Shortlees Prim Sch

KNOCKMARLOCH DR

35

Treesbanks Bridge

Townend of Caprington

AYR RD

Broomhill

Treesbank House

A77

A77
Scargie

1

Ditton

B7038

A77 Ayr (A719)

A77

34

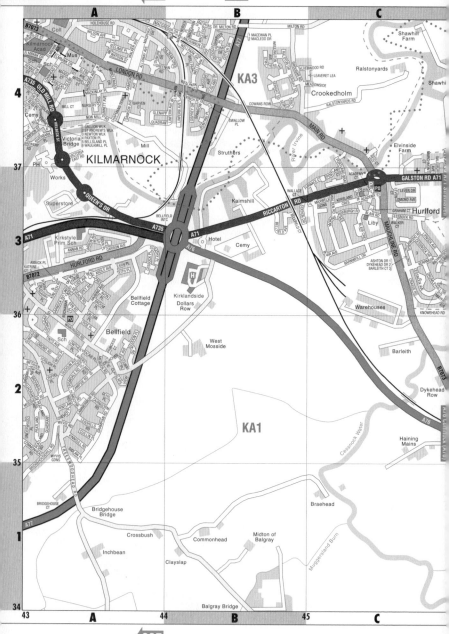

KA3

Crookedholm

KILMARNOCK

Kilmarnock
Acad

Victoria
Bridge

Kaimshill

Struthers

RICCARTON RD

Hurlford

Liby

Galston Rd A71

Bellfield
INTC

Hotel

Cemy

Kirklandside
Dollars
Row

Bellfield
Cottage

Warehouses

Barleith

Bellfield

West
Mosside

KA1

Dykehead
Row

Haining
Mains

Bridgehouse
Bridge

Braehead

Crossbush

Commonhead

Midton of
Balgray

Inchbean

Clayslap

Balgray Bridge

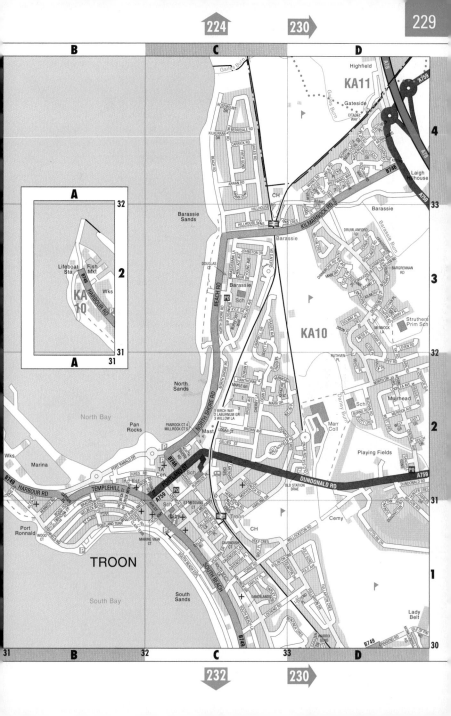

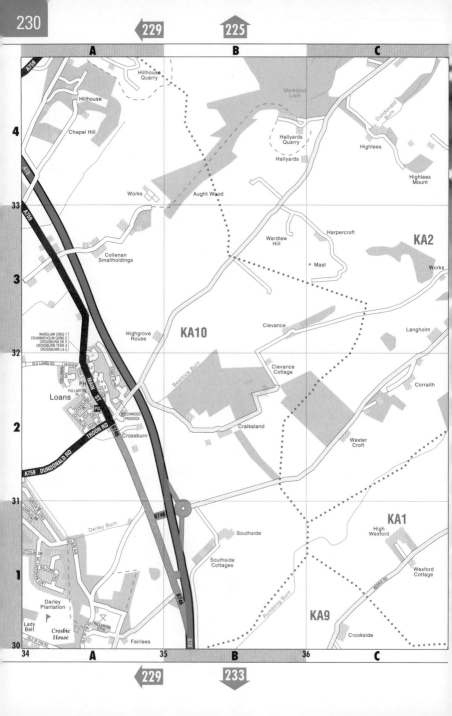

A B C

4

33

3

KA2

32

KA10

2

Loans

31

KA1

KA9

1

30
34 A 35 B 36 C

Hillhouse Quarry

Hillhouse

Chapel Hill

Merkland Loch

Dundonald Burn

Hallyards Quarry

Hallyards

Highlees

Highlees Mount

Works

Aught Wood

Collenan Smallholdings

Wardlaw Hill

Harpercroft

Mast

Works

Highgrove House

Clevance

Langholm

Clevance Cottage

Corraith

WARDLAW CRES 1
CRUMMIEHOLM GDNS 2
CROSSBURN DR 3
CROSSBURN TERR 4
CROSSBURN LA 5

OLD LOANS RD
SEAVIEW
MAIN ST
FULLARTON
PH
PO
TROON RD
B746

Beattock Burn

Craiksland

Wester Croft

Crossburn

BEECHWOOD PADDOCK

A759 DUNDONALD RD

Darley Burn

B746

Southside

High Wexford

Southside Cottages

Wexford Cottage

OTTOLINE DR
MALCOLME
LADY MARGARET DR
WILSON AVE
FULLARTON BLVD

Darley Plantation

Crosbie House

Lady Belt

ISLE OF PIN RD

Fairlees

B746

A71

Rumbling Burn

WEBBOT RD

Crookside

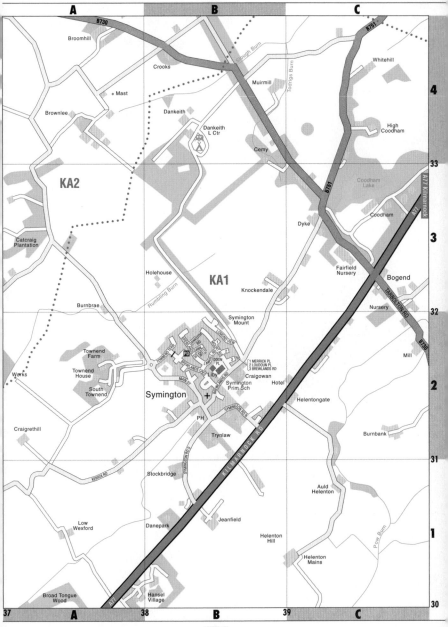

A   B   C

B730

Broomhill

Crooks

Muirmill

Slough Burn

Todrigs Burn

Whitehill

B751

4

Mast

Dankeith

High
Coodham

Brownlee

Dankeith
L Ctr

Cemy

33

KA2

Coodham
Lake

B751

Coodham

3

Catcraig
Plantation

Holehouse

KA1

Dyke

Fairfield
Nursery

Bogend

A77 Kilmarnock

A77

Knockendale

Rumbling Burn

Burnbrae

Symington
Mount

Nursery

TARBOLTON RD

32

B730

Townend
Farm

Townend
House

Works

South
Townend

Symington
Mount

Symington

LONGBIE VIEW

PO

Liby

DOON
PL

Craigowan

Symington
Prim Sch

Hotel

Mill

1 MERRICK PL
2 LOUDOUN PL
3 BREWLANDS RD

Helentongate

2

MAIN ST

TERRACE

BREWLANDS CRES

Craigrethill

PH

Trynlaw

SYMINGTON RD

KILMARNOCK RD

Helentongate

Burnbank

31

KERRIX RD

Stockbridge

SYMINGTON RD S

Auld
Helenton

Low
Wexford

Danepark

Jeanfield

Helenton
Hill

Pow Burn

1

Broad Tongue
Wood

Hansel
Village

A77

Helenton
Mains

30

A   B   C

37   38   39

229

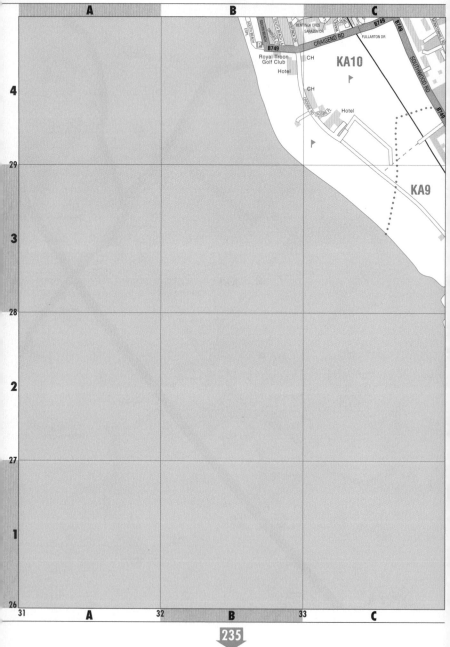

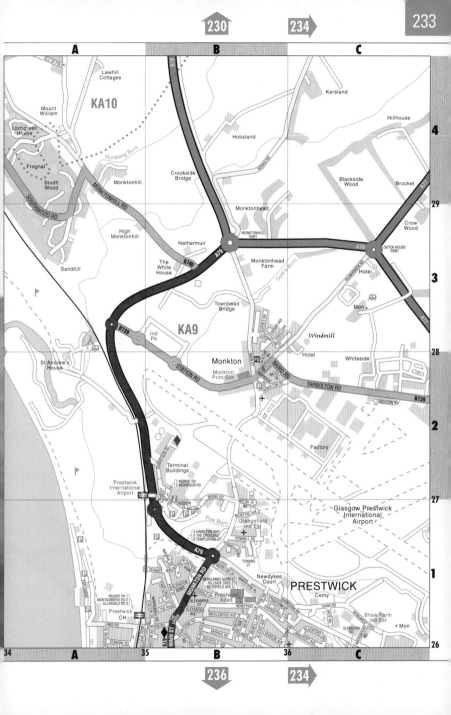

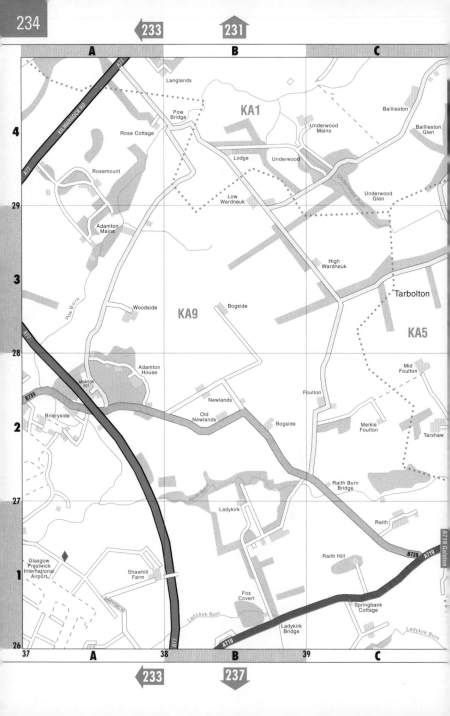

233
231

A   **B**   **C**

A77

KILMARNOCK RD

Langlands

Pow Bridge

KA1

Baillieston

Rose Cottage

Underwood Mains

Baillieston Glen

4

Rosemount

Lodge

Underwood

Low Wardneuk

Underwood Glen

Underwood Burn

29

Adamton Mains

A77

High Wardneuk

3

Pow Burn

Woodside

Bogside

KA9

Tarbolton

KA5

28

Adamton House

Mid Foulton

ADAMTON EST

B739

Foulton

Brieryside

Newlands

Bogside

Meikle Foulton

Tarshaw

2

Old Newlands

Raith Burn

Raith Burn Bridge

27

Ladykirk

Raith

Glasgow Prestwick International Airport

Raith Hill

B739

A719

A719 Galston

Shawhill Farm

1

Fox Covert

Springbank Cottage

Ladykirk Burn

Ladykirk Bridge

Ladykirk Burn

26

37   **A**   **38**   **B**   **39**   **C**

A77

A719

233
237

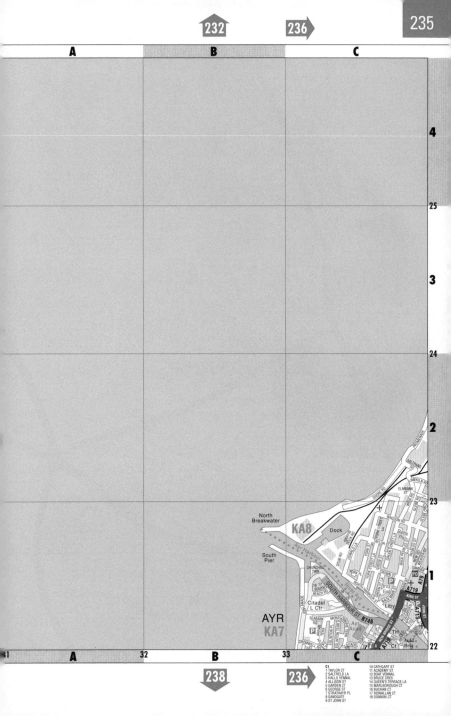

A

B

C

4

25

3

24

2

23

North
Breakwater

KA8

Dock

South
Pier

1

Citadel
L Ctr

AYR
KA7

22

C1
1 TAYLOR CT
2 SALTFIELD LA
3 HALLS VENNAL
4 ALLISON ST
5 GARDEN CT
6 GEORGE ST
7 STRATHAYR PL
8 SANDGATE
9 ST JOHN ST

10 CATHCART ST
11 ACADEMY ST
12 BOAT VENNAL
13 BRUCE CRES
14 QUEEN'S TERRACE LA
15 MARLBOROUGH CT
16 BUCHAN CT
17 ROWALLAN CT
18 DONNINI CT

Glasgow
Prestwick
nt Airport

Shields

Ladykirk Burn

A77

A719

B742

Sandyford
Smithy

Sandyford

KA9

Ladykirk Burn

Clune

Clune Farm
Cottage

Bogend

Raggithill

Mossblown

DRUMLEY
AVE

Mossblown
Farm

25

Factory

Kirklandholm
Farm

B742

RAGGITHILL AVE 1
SANDYFORD RD 2
BARNHEYS DR 3

Barwheys

B743

Highfield

B7035

St Quivox

Brickrow
Holdings

3

24

Hannah
Research Park

B7035

Auchincruive
(West of Scotland
Agricultural Coll)

Oswald's
Temple

Brockle
Wood

White
Gables

KA6

Cutting
Wood

Pheasant
Nook

Mount
Loudoun

Craighall
Wood

2

Oswald's
Bridge

River Ayr

Mount Charles
Wood

Mon

23

Newbarns
Wood

Oaklea

Mount
Scarburgh

River Ayr

1

Laigland

Craighall

Tarholm
Nursery

B744

Mainholm
Holdings

Auchincruive
Holdings

Stanalane

B744

22

Mainholm
Nursery

A   38   B   39   C

AYR

Low Green

Fairfield

Seafield

Longhill
Point

Cunning
Park

Belleisle
Bridge

KA7

Slaphouse

Slaphouse
Bridge

Belleisle

Hotel
CH
Belleisle Park

Rozelle
Park

Rozelle

Burns Cott
(Mus)

Greenan

Doonfoot
Prim Sch

Longhill

Burton
Smithy

High
Greenan

DUNURE RD

Doonfoot

Doonbank
Farm

Mill

Alloway
Prim Sch

Alloway

Liby

Tam O' Shanter
Experience

A719 Turnberry, Girvan (A77)

A719

DOONFOOT RD

RACECOURSE RD

MONUMENT RD

CARRICK RD

ALLOWAY PL

MILLER RD

A70

A719

Wellington
Sch

QUEEN'S TERRACE LA 1
CROMWELL RD 2
AILSA PL 3
BRUCE CRES 4
DOUGLAS LA 5
DOUGLAS ST 6
HOPE ST 7
LORNE ARC 8
BLACKFRIARS WLK 9
KYLE CTR 10
BAINS TERRACE LA 11
ARRAN MALL 12

KILLOCH PL 13
BURNS STATUE SQ 14
SMITH ST 15
PARKHOUSE ST 16

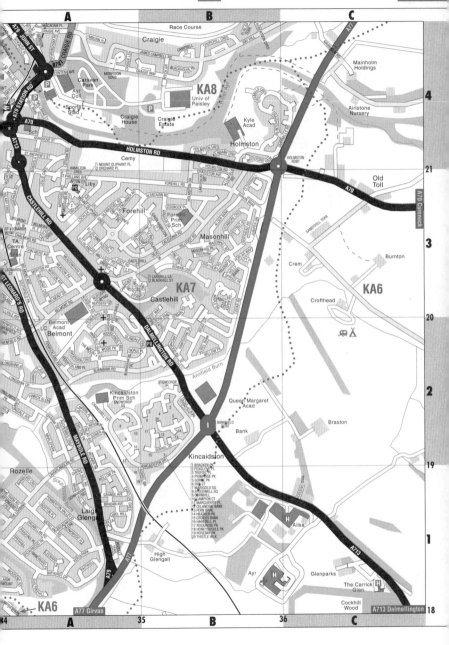

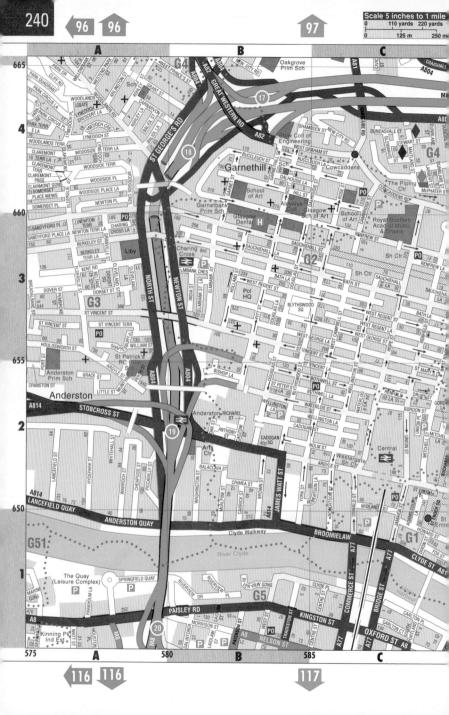

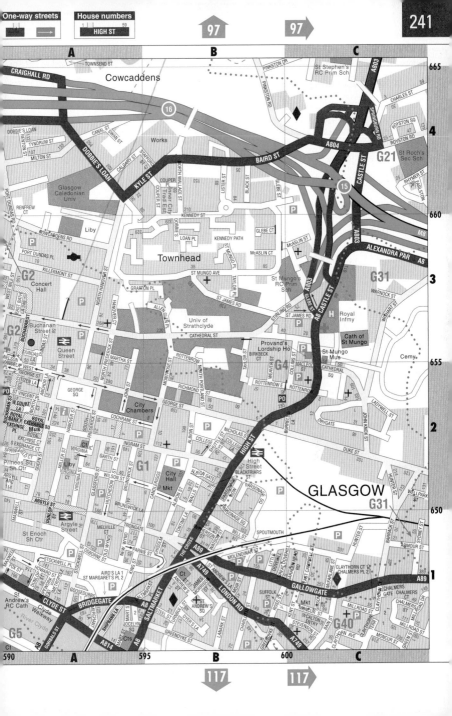

Index

Church Rd **6** Beckenham BR2.........**53** C6

Place name	Location number	Locality, town or village	Postcode district	Page and grid square
May be abbreviated on the map	Present when a number indicates the place's position in a crowded area of mapping	Shown when more than one place has the same name	District for the indexed place	Page number and grid reference for the standard mapping

Public and commercial buildings are highlighted in magenta. Places of interest are highlighted in blue with a star✶

Abbreviations used in the index

Acad	**Academy**	Comm	**Common**	Gd	**Ground**	L	**Leisure**	Prom	**Promenade**
App	**Approach**	Cott	**Cottage**	Gdn	**Garden**	La	**Lane**	Rd	**Road**
Arc	**Arcade**	Cres	**Crescent**	Gn	**Green**	Liby	**Library**	Recn	**Recreation**
Ave	**Avenue**	Cswy	**Causeway**	Gr	**Grove**	Mdw	**Meadow**	Ret	**Retail**
Bglw	**Bungalow**	Ct	**Court**	H	**Hall**	Meml	**Memorial**	Sh	**Shopping**
Bldg	**Building**	Ctr	**Centre**	Ho	**House**	Mkt	**Market**	Sq	**Square**
Bsns, Bus	**Business**	Ctry	**Country**	Hospl	**Hospital**	Mus	**Museum**	St	**Street**
Bvd	**Boulevard**	Cty	**County**	HQ	**Headquarters**	Orch	**Orchard**	Sta	**Station**
Cath	**Cathedral**	Dr	**Drive**	Hts	**Heights**	Pal	**Palace**	Terr	**Terrace**
Cir	**Circus**	Dro	**Drove**	Ind	**Industrial**	Par	**Parade**	TH	**Town Hall**
Cl	**Close**	Ed	**Education**	Inst	**Institute**	Pas	**Passage**	Univ	**University**
Cnr	**Corner**	Emb	**Embankment**	Int	**International**	Pk	**Park**	Wk, Wlk	**Walk**
Coll	**College**	Est	**Estate**	Intc	**Interchange**	Pl	**Place**	Wr	**Water**
Com	**Community**	Ex	**Exhibition**	Junc	**Junction**	Prec	**Precinct**	Yd	**Yard**

Index of localities, towns and villages

Airdrie 123 A4	California 66 C3	Fenwick 213 A2	Lanark 215 B2
Airth 14 B2	Cambus 9 A4	Fishcross 5 C2	Langbank 70 A4
Alexandria 27 A3	Cambusbarron 6 B3	Fluchter 56 A1	Larbert 23 A1
Allandale 39 B1	Cambuslang 139 A2	Forrestfield 106 A2	Larkhall 185 A2
Alloa 10 B3	Cardross 48 A4	Gartcosh 100 C3	Laurieston 42 C2
Alva 5 A3	Carluke 188 A1	Gartocharn 20 C4	Law 186 C3
Annathill 81 C1	Carmunnock 158 C4	Gatehead 226 C3	Lennoxtown 57 B4
Ardrossan 205 A1	Cartland 202 B1	Gateside 171 C4	Letham 24 B4
Ashgill 199 C4	Chapelhall 123 C1	Glasgow 117 B3	Linwood 112 A3
Avonbridge 87 C4	Chryston 100 B4	Glenboig 101 C3	Lochwinnoch 129 A2
Ayr 238 B4	Clachan of Campsie 33 A2	Glengarnock 170 B3	Longcroft 39 A2
Balloch 19 C1	Clackmannan 10 C2	Glenmavis 102 C2	Longriggend 85 A1
Balmore 77 C4	Clarkston 157 C4	Gourock 44 B4	Lugton 173 B3
Banknock 38 C2	Cleghorn 215 C4	Greengairs 83 C1	Luncarty ....
Bannockburn 7 C1	Cleland 144 A1	Greenock 45 B3	Menstrie 3 C3
Banton 37 C2	Clydebank 74 A1	Haggs 39 A2	Millerston 99 A2
Bardowie 77 A4	Coatbridge 122 B3	Hamilton 162 B2	Milngavie 55 B2
Bargeddie 121 A2	Cowie 12 B4	Harthill 127 C3	Milton 50 C1
Barrhead 134 C1	Crookedholm 228 C4	Hartwood 146 A2	Milton of Campsie 58 B3
Barrmill 171 C2	Crossford 201 A1	Helensburgh 16 A1	Monkton 233 B2
Bearsden 75 C3	Crosshouse 221 A2	High Bonnybridge 40 B2	Moodiesburn 80 C1
Beith 150 A1	Croy 21 C1	Houston 91 A1	Mossblown 237 C4
Bellshill 142 A2	Cumbernauld 62 B3	Howwood 130 C3	Motherwell 163 B4
Bishopbriggs 78 A2	Cunninghamhead 221 A4	Hurlford 228 C3	Mugdock 55 B3
Bishopton 72 A2	Dalry 191 A4	Inchinnan 93 B3	Muirhead 100 B4
Blackridge 107 B1	Dalserf 186 B1	Irvine 219 A2	Neilston 154 C3
Blantyre 161 B4	Denny 21 C1	Johnstone 112 A2	Nemphlar 214 A3
Bonhill 28 A2	Drybridge 225 B3	Kilbarchan 111 A2	Netherburn 200 B2
Bonnybridge 40 A3	Dullatur 61 B3	Kilbirnie 149 A1	Newton Mearns 156 A2
Bothwell 141 A1	Dumbarton 49 C1	Kilmacolm 89 B4	Old Kilpatrick 73 A3
Bowling 72 B4	Dundonald 225 C1	Kilmarnock 227 B4	Overtown 186 B3
Braidwood 201 C2	Dunlop 195 B4	Kilmaurs 222 B4	Paisley 113 B1
Bridge of Allan 2 A4	Eaglesham 178 C3	Kilncadzow 203 A3	Perceton 220 B3
Bridge of Weir 110 C4	East Kilbride 180 C3	Kilsyth 60 B1	Plains 104 A2
Brookfield 111 B3	Elderslie 112 B1	Kilwinning 207 C1	Plean 12 B2
Burnhouse 172 B1	Erskine 73 A1	Kirkfieldbank 214 B2	Port Glasgow 47 C1
Calderbank 123 A2	Falkirk 42 B3	Kirkintilloch 79 C1	Prestwick 236 A4
Caldercruix 105 A3	Fallin 8 B2	Knockentiber 221 C2	Quarriers Village 89 C1
			Quarter 183 C2
Queenzieburn 59 C4			
Renfrew 94 C2			
Renton 27 B1			
Rhu 15 B3			
Riggend 83 A1			
Rosneath 15 A2			
Rutherglen 138 B4			
St Quivox 237 A3			
Salsburgh 125 B1			
Saltcoats 216 B4			
Seamill 190 A2			
Shieldhill 66 B3			
Shotts 146 C3			
Skinflats 24 C2			
Slamannan 86 A3			
South Alloa 9 C2			
Springside 220 C1			
Stenhousemuir 23 B2			
Stepps 99 B3			
Stevenston 217 C4			
Stewarton 211 C4			
Stirling 7 B4			
Stonehouse 198 C1			
Strathblane 31 B2			
Symington 231 B2			
Thorntonhall 158 B2			
Throsk 9 A2			
Torrance 57 B1			
Torwood 22 C3			
Troon 229 B1			
Tullibody 4 B2			
Twechar 59 C2			
Uddingston 140 C3			
Uplawmoor 153 A2			
Waterside 213 C2			
West Kilbride 190 B2			
Wishaw 165 A3			

A

Abbey Cl PA1 113 C2
Abbey Craig Ct FK9 2 B2
Abbey Craig Rd FK10 5 A1
Abbey Dr G14 95 C2
Abbey Kings Park Hospl
FK7 6 C3
Abbey Mill FK8 7 B4
Abbey Pl ML6 123 B2
Abbey Prim Sch KA13 207 B2
Abbey Rd Elderslie PA5 112 B1
Stirling FK8 2 B1
Abbey Rd Pl FK8 7 B4
Abbey Wlk ML9 185 A2
Abbeycraig Pk FK9 2 B2
Abbeycraig Rd G34 100 C1
Abbeydale Way G73 138 B2
Abbeygate KA13 207 C2
Abbeygreen KA13 207 C2
Abbeygreen St G34 100 C1
Abbeyhill St G32 118 C4
Abbeylands Rd G81 74 B3
Abbeymill Bsns Ctr PA1 113 C2
Abbot Ct KA9 236 B3
Abbot Rd FK7 7 B2
Abbot St 4 Glasgow G41 116 C1
Greenock PA16 45 B2
Paisley PA3 113 C3
Abbot's Ave KA13 207 C1
Abbot's Pl KA13 207 C2
Abbot's Wlk KA13 207 C2
Abbots Cres KA7 238 A1
Abbots Ct FK2 42 B4
Abbots Moss Dr FK1 41 C1
Abbots Rd FK2 42 B4
Abbots Terr ML6 123 B2
Abbots Way KA7 238 B2
Abbotsburn Way 1 PA3 113 B4
Abbotsford G64 78 B1
Abbotsford Ave
Hamilton ML3 162 A4
Larkhall ML9 185 A1
Rutherglen G73 138 A4
Abbotsford Brae G74 159 C2
Abbotsford Cres
Hamilton ML3 162 A3
Paisley PA2 132 C4
Shotts ML7 146 C3
Wishaw ML2 165 B2
Abbotsford Ct G67 82 C4
Abbotsford Dr
Helensburgh G84 25 A4
Kirkintilloch G66 79 C4
Abbotsford Gdns FK2 24 A1
Abbotsford La ML4 141 C3
Abbotsford Pl
Cumbernauld G67 82 C4
4 Glasgow G5 117 A2
Glasgow, Laurieston G5 117 A3
Motherwell ML1 143 A3
Saltcoats KA21 206 A1
Stirling FK8 2 B1
Abbotsford Rd
Bearsden G61 75 B3
Chapelhall ML6 123 C1
Clydebank G81 74 A1
Cumbernauld G67 82 C4
Hamilton ML3 162 A3
Wishaw ML2 165 B2
Abbotsford St FK2 42 A4
Abbotsford Terr ML11 215 B2
Abbotshall Ave G15 74 C2
Abbotsinch Rd PA3,PA4 93 C1
Abbott Cres G81 94 B4
Aberconway St G81 94 B4
Abercorn Ave G52 114 C4
Abercorn Cres ML3 162 C1
Abercorn Dr ML3 162 C1
Abercorn Ind Est PA3 113 C3
Abercorn Pl G23 76 C1
Abercorn Rd G77 156 B3
Abercorn Sec Sch G4 97 A1
Abercorn St
Clydebank G81 74 C4
Paisley PA3 113 C3
Abercrombie Cres G69 120 C3
Abercrombie Dr G61 75 A4
Abercrombie Pl
Kilsyth G65 36 A1
Menstrie FK11 3 C3
Abercrombie St FK1 41 C3
Abercromby Cres
East Kilbride G74 160 A2
Helensburgh G84 16 C2
Abercromby Dr Ayr KA7 238 B2
Bridge of A FK9 2 A4
Glasgow G40 117 C3
Abercromby Pl
East Kilbride G74 160 A2
Stirling FK8 7 A4
Tullibody FK10 4 A1
Abercromby Pl W G84 16 B2
Abercromby Sq 1 G40 117 C3
Abercromby St 7 G40 117 C3
Abercromby St E G84 16 C1
Aberdalgie Rd G34 120 A4
Aberdeen Rd ML6 123 B2
Aberdour St G31 118 B4
Aberfeldy Ave ML6 103 C2
Aberfeldy St G31 118 B4
Aberfeldy Terr KA11 220 A3
Aberfoyle Rd PA15 46 A1
Aberfoyle St G31 118 B4
Aberlady Rd G51 115 C3
Aberlady St ML1 144 A1
Aberlour Pl KA11 219 C3
Aberlour Rd KA11 219 C3
Abernethy Dr PA3 112 A3
Abernethy Pk G74 159 B1
Abernethy Pl G77 157 A2
Abernethy St G31 118 B4
Abernethyn Rd ML2 166 A3
Aberuthven Dr G32 119 A2
Abiegail Pl G72 140 B1
Aboukir St G51 115 C4
Aboyne Ave FK9 2 B2
Aboyne Dr PA2 113 C1
Aboyne St G51 115 C3
Abronhill High Sch G67 62 C2
Abronhill Prim Sch G67 62 B2
Acacia Dr Barrhead G78 134 A3
Beith KA15 171 A4
Paisley PA2 113 A1
Acacia Pl PA5 132 A4
Acacia Way G72 139 C3
Academy Brae KA15 171 A4
Academy Ct
Coatbridge ML5 122 A4
Hurlford KA1 228 C3
Irvine KA12 219 A2
Academy Gdns KA12 219 A2
Academy Pk Airdrie ML6 123 A4
Glasgow G51 116 B2
Academy Pl
Bannockburn FK7 7 C1
Coatbridge ML5 122 A4
Academy Rd
Glasgow G46 136 B1
Irvine KA12 219 A2
Stirling FK8 7 A4
Academy St Airdrie ML6 123 A4
Alloa FK10 9 C4
11 Ayr KA7 235 C1
Coatbridge ML5 122 A4
Glasgow G32 119 A2
Hurlford KA1 228 C3
Kilmarnock KA1 227 C3
Larkhall ML9 185 A2
Troon KA10 229 C1
Academy Terr ML4 142 A3
Acer Cres PA2 113 A1
Acer Gr ML6 123 C2
Achamore Cres G15 74 C2
Achamore Dr G15 74 C2
Achamore Rd G15 74 C2
Acherhill Gdns G13 95 A4
Achill Pl 1 G66 58 B1
Achnasheen Rd ML6 124 A3
Achray Ave G83 27 B3
Achray Ct FK10 10 B3
Achray Dr Paisley PA2 113 A1
Stirling FK9 2 A2
Achray Pl Coatbridge ML5 101 B1
Milngavie G62 54 B2
Achray Rd G67 82 B3
Acids Rd KA20 218 A3
Acorn Cres FK5 23 B1
Acorn Ct G40 117 C2
Acorn St G40 117 C2
Acre Dr G20 76 A1
Acre Rd G20 76 A1
Acre Valley Rd G64 57 A1
Acredyke Cres G21 98 B4
Acredyke Pl G21 98 B3
Acredyke Rd Glasgow G21 98 B4
Rutherglen G73 137 C4
Acres The ML9 185 A1
Adair Ave KA21 205 C1
Adam Ave ML6 123 A4
Adam Cres FK5 23 C1
Adam St Falkirk FK2 42 B3
Gourock PA19 44 C4
Greenock PA15 46 A2
Adams Ave KA21 205 C1
Adams Ct KA10 229 D3
Adams Gate KA10 229 D3
Adams Loan FK2 24 A1
Adams Pl G65 60 B4
Adams Wlk KA12 219 C1
Adamslie Cres G66 79 A4
Adamslie Dr G66 79 A4
Adamson Pl FK9 2 A2
Adamson St ML4 142 B3
Adamswell St G21 97 C2
Adamswell Terr G69 81 A1
Adamton Est KA9 234 A2
Adamton Road N KA9 236 B4
Adamton Road S KA9 236 B3
Adamton Terr KA9 236 B4
Addie St ML1 163 C4
Addiewell Pl ML5 122 A2
Addiewell St G32 119 A4
Addison Gr G46 135 C2
Addison Pl G46 135 C2
Addison Rd Glasgow G12 96 B2
Glasgow, Thornliebank
G46 135 C2
Adelaide Ct G81 73 B3
Adelaide Rd G75 180 B4
Adelaide St Gourock PA19 44 C4
Helensburgh G84 16 C1
Adele St ML1 163 C2
Adelphi St G5 117 B3
Admiral St G41 116 C3
Admiralty Gdns G60 73 A3
Admiralty Gr G60 73 A3
Admiralty Pl G60 73 A3
Advie Pl G42 137 A4
Affric Ave ML6 104 A2
Affric Dr Falkirk FK2 24 B1
Paisley PA2 114 A1
Affric Loan ML7 146 C3
Afton Ave KA9 236 B3
Afton Cres G61 76 A2
Afton Ct Ayr KA7 239 A3
Irvine KA12 219 A1
Stirling FK7 7 B3
Afton Dr Denny FK6 39 B4
Renfrew PA4 94 C1
Afton Gdns Blantyre G72 161 A3
Coatbridge ML5 122 B3
Troon KA10 229 D2
Afton Pl KA22 205 B2
Afton Rd Cumbernauld G67 62 A2
Stevenston KA20 217 B4
Afton St Glasgow G41 136 C4
Larkhall ML9 185 B1
Afton View G66 58 C1
Agamemnon St G81 73 C1
Agnew Ave ML5 122 B4
Agnew Gr ML4 141 B3
Agnew La G42 117 A1
Aikenhead Ho G44 137 B3
Aikenhead Rd G44 137 B4
Aikman Pl G74 160 A2
Aikman Rd ML1 163 A3
Aiknut Rd KA23 190 B2
Ailean Dr G32 119 C2
Ailean Gdns G32 119 C2
Aileymill Gdns PA16 44 C2
Aillort Pl G74 159 C2
Ailort Ave G44 137 A3
Ailort Loan 18 ML2 165 C3
Ailsa Ave Ashgill ML9 199 C4
Motherwell ML1 163 A4
Ailsa Cres ML1 163 A4
Ailsa Ct Coatbridge ML5 121 C2
Hamilton ML3 161 B1
Ailsa Dr Bothwell G71 141 A2
Clydebank G81 74 B3
Glasgow G42 136 C4
Kirkintilloch G66 58 C1
Paisley PA2 133 B4
Rutherglen G46 157 B4
Rutherglen, Croftfoot G73 137 C3
Stevenston KA20 217 B4
Ailsa Gdns KA22 205 B2
Ailsa Hospl KA6 239 C1
Ailsa Pl Ayr KA7 235 C1
Coatbridge ML5 121 C2
Kilmarnock KA1 223 A3
Ailsa Rd Bishopbriggs G64 78 A1
Coatbridge ML5 121 C2
Gourock PA19 44 B3
Irvine KA12 224 B4
Renfrew PA4 94 B1
Saltcoats KA21 206 A1
Troon KA10 229 B2
Ailsa St KA9 236 A4
Ailsa Twr G72 138 C2
Ailsa View KA3 195 C1
Ailsa View Caravan Site
G78 153 C4
Ainsdale Ct KA13 207 A2
Ainslie Ave G52 115 A4
Ainslie Rd
Cumbernauld G67 62 B2
Glasgow G52 115 A4
Airbles Cres ML1 163 B3
Airbles Dr ML1 163 B3
Airbles Farm Rd ML1 163 B3
Airbles Rd ML1 163 B3
Airbles St ML1 163 C3
Airbles Sta ML1 163 C3
Aird Ave KA1 227 C4
Aird's La G1 241 A1
Airdale Ave G46 136 B1
Airdrie Acad ML6 103 A1
Airdrie Rd
Caldercruix ML6 105 B1
Carluke ML8 187 C2
Cumbernauld G67 82 A3
Cumbernauld, Condorrat
G67 82 A4
Cumbernauld, Mollinsburn
G67 81 C2
Kilsyth G65 60 B4
Plains ML6 103 C1
Airdrie Sta ML6 123 A4
Airdriehill Rd ML6 103 B2
Airdriehill St ML6 103 B1
Airgold Dr G15 74 C2
Airlie Ave G61 75 C4
Airlie Ct KA7 238 C3
Airlie Dr ML4 142 A3
Airlie Gdns G73 138 B2
Airlie La G12 96 A2
Airlie Rd G69 120 A2
Airlie St G12 96 A2
Airlink Ind Est PA3 113 C4
Airlour Rd G43 136 C3
Airth Ct ML1 142 B1
Airth Dr Glasgow G52 115 C2
Stirling FK7 7 B2
Airth La G52 115 C2
Airth Prim Sch FK2 14 C2
Airth Way G68 81 C4
Airthrey Ave
Bridge of A FK9 2 A3
Glasgow G14 95 C2
Airthrey Dr FK5 24 A2
Airthrey La G14 95 C2
Airthrey Rd FK9 2 B3
Airyligg Dr G76 178 C3
Aitchison Ct ML6 122 C4
Aitchison Dr FK5 23 A2
Aitchison St ML6 122 C4
Aitken Cl ML2 166 A4
Aitken Cres FK7 7 A1
Aitken Dr Beith KA15 150 B1
Slamannan FK1 86 A3
Aitken Gdns FK1 41 C3
Aitken La G83 27 C4
Aitken Pl Ardrossan KA22 205 B2
Lanark ML11 215 A2
Aitken Rd Falkirk FK1 41 B3
Hamilton ML3 183 C4
Aitken St Airdrie ML6 103 A1
Dalry KA24 191 B4
Glasgow G31 118 B4
Aitken Terr FK1 41 B3
Aitkenbar Circ G82 50 A3
Aitkenbar Dr G82 50 A3
Aitkenbar Prim Sch G82 50 B3
Aitkenbrae Dr KA9 236 B4
Aitkenhead Ave ML5 121 A2
Aitkenhead Prim Sch
G71 120 C1
Aitkenhead Rd
Chapelhall ML6 123 B1
Uddingston G71 121 A1
Akarit Rd FK5 23 C1
Alasdair Ct G78 134 B1
Alba Gdns ML8 187 C2
Alba Way ML3 183 B3
Albans Cres ML1 163 A4
Albany G74 160 B2
Albany Ave G32 119 B3
Albany Cotts 11 G13 95 C3
Albany Dr Lanark ML11 215 A2
Rutherglen G73 138 A3
Albany Pl G71 141 A1
Albany Quadrant G32 119 B3
Albany Rd ML3 183 B4
Albany St
Coatbridge ML5 121 C4
Glasgow G40 118 A2
Albany Terr G72 138 C2
Albany Way PA3 113 C4
Albany Wynd 11 ML9 185 A2
Albert Ave Glasgow G42 117 A1
Stewarton KA3 195 C1
Albert Cres 9 ML6 123 A4
Albert Cross G41 116 C2
Albert Ct KA3 195 C1
Albert Dr Bearsden G61 76 A2
Glasgow G41 116 B2
Helensburgh G84 16 C1
Larkhall ML9 185 A1
Rutherglen G73 138 A3
Albert Pl Airdrie ML6 123 A4
Stewarton KA3 195 C1
Stirling FK8 7 A4
Albert Prim Sch
Airdrie ML6 123 A4
Glasgow G21 97 C3
Albert Quadrant ML1 143 A3
Albert Rd Brookfield PA5 111 B3
Clydebank G81 74 A2
Falkirk FK1 42 A2
Glasgow G42 117 A1
Gourock PA19 44 B4
Harthill ML7 127 C3
Kirkintilloch G66 79 B2
Renfrew PA4 94 B2
Albert St Alexandria G83 27 C2
Coatbridge ML5 122 A4
Hamilton ML3 162 A3
Helensburgh G84 16 C1
Motherwell ML1 163 C4
Albert Terr Ayr KA8 239 A4
Hamilton ML3 162 A3
Albert Wynd KA3 195 C1
Alberta Ave
Coatbridge ML5 121 C4
East Kilbride G75 180 B4
Alberta Cres 1 G75 180 B4
Alberta Pk G75 180 B4
Alberta Pl 5 G75 180 B4
Albion Ct ML5 122 B3
Albion Gate Glasgow G1 241 B2
Paisley PA3 113 B3
Albion St Coatbridge ML5 122 B3
Glasgow G1 241 B2
Glasgow, North Mount Vernon
G69 119 C2
Motherwell ML1 163 C3
Paisley PA3 113 C3
Albion Way G75 180 C3
Albion Works Ind Est
G13 94 C4
Alcaig Rd G52 115 C1
Alcath Rd ML2 166 A3
Alclutha Ave G82 50 A2
Alder Ave Hamilton ML3 162 C1
Kirkintilloch G66 79 A3
Alder Bank Ayr KA7 239 B3
Uddingston G71 121 B1
Alder Cres G75 180 B3
Alder Ct Barrhead G78 134 B1
East Kilbride G75 180 B3
Alder Gate G72 139 C3
Alder Gn KA11 220 A2
Alder Gr ML5 122 A3
Alder La Motherwell ML1 143 A2
Motherwell ML1 143 B3
Alder Pl East Kilbride G75 180 B3
Glasgow G43 136 B3
Johnstone PA5 112 A1
Kilmarnock KA1 227 B4
Alder Rd Clydebank G81 74 A3
Cumbernauld G67 62 B1
Dumbarton G82 49 C2
Glasgow G43 136 B3
Milton of C G66 58 A2
Alderbank Rd PA14 47 A1
Alderbrae Rd PA14 47 A1
Alderman Pl G13 95 B3
Alderman Rd G13 95 A3
Alderside Gdns G71 140 C4
Alderside Pl 12 G71 141 A2
Alderstocks G75 180 C3
Alderston Ave KA8 236 A2
Alderston Pk KA8 236 A2
Alderston Pl Ayr KA8 236 A2
Bellshill ML4 141 C2
Alderston Way ML4 141 C3
Aldersyde Ave
Troon KA10 229 D2
Wishaw ML2 164 B2
Aldersyde Pl G72 140 B1
Aldersyde Terr ML1 144 B1
Alderwood Cres PA14 47 A1
Alderwood Rd PA14 47 A1
Aldrin Rd G84 25 B4
Alexander Ave
Eaglesham G76 178 C3
Falkirk FK2 42 C3
Stevenston KA20 206 C1
Twechar G65 59 C2
Uddingston G71 141 B3
Alexander Balfour Gdns
ML3 162 B1
Alexander Cres G5 117 B2
Alexander Ct FK9 2 C3
Alexander Dr FK9 2 A4
Alexander Fleming Ave
KA25 148 C1
Alexander Gdns ML3 163 A1
Alexander Gibson Way
ML1 163 B3
Alexander Hospl ML5 121 C4
Alexander Maclaren Gdns
KA3 222 C2
Alexander McLeod Pl FK7 8 C2
Alexander Path ML1 164 A2
Alexander Peden Prim Sch
ML7 127 C3
Alexander Pl Irvine KA12 219 B2
Kirkintilloch G66 80 A4
Rhu G84 15 B3
Alexander Rd ML7 146 B3
Alexander St Airdrie ML6 122 C4
Clydebank G81 74 A1
Coatbridge ML5 122 A4
Dumbarton G82 50 A2
Renton G82 49 B4
Wishaw ML2 165 A1
Alexander Terr G78 154 B3
Alexandra Ave
Kirkintilloch G66 79 B2
Prestwick KA9 233 B1
Stepps G33 99 B3
Alexandra Cross G31 118 A4
Alexandra Ct
Glasgow G31 118 A4
Prestwick KA9 233 B1
Alexandra Dr Alloa FK10 9 C4
Paisley PA2 113 A2
Renfrew PA4 94 B2
Alexandra Gdns G66 79 B2
Alexandra Par G31 118 A4
Alexandra Parade Prim Sch
G31 118 A4
Alexandra Parade Sta
G31 118 A4
Alexandra Park St G31 118 A4
Alexandra Pk G66 79 B2
Alexandra Pl FK8 2 B1
Alexandra Prim Sch
ML6 123 A4
Alexandra Rd G66 79 B2
Alexandra St G66 79 B4
Alexandra Terr Ayr KA8 236 A2
Kilwinning KA13 207 B2
Alexandria Quadrant
ML1 143 A3
Alexandria Sta G83 27 C2
Alford Ave G66 79 A4
Alford Pl Irvine KA11 219 C3
Linwood PA3 111 C3
Alford Quadrant ML2 165 A3
Alford St G21 97 B2
Alfred La 11 G12 96 C2
Algas Cotts 12 G13 95 C3
Algie St G41 136 C4
Algoma Pl G75 180 A4
Alice Ave ML4 142 A2
Alice St PA2 113 C1
Aline Ct G78 134 A2
Alison Lea G74 160 B2
Allan Ave Carluke ML8 187 C2
Renfrew PA4 94 C1
Allan Barr Ct FK1 42 A1
Allan Cres Alexandria G83 27 B2
Denny FK6 21 B2
Dumbarton G82 50 A3
Allan Ct G75 179 C4
Allan Dr G75 179 C4
Allan Glen Gdns G64 78 A2
Allan Pk FK8 7 A4
Allan Pl Ayr KA8 236 B2
Dumbarton G82 50 A2
Glasgow G40 118 A1
Allan Sq KA12 219 C1
Allan St Coatbridge ML5 121 B3
Glasgow G40 118 A1
Motherwell ML1 163 C4
Allan Wlk FK9 1 C4
Allan's Prim Sch FK8 7 A4
Allanbank Rd FK5 23 B1
Allanbank St ML7 166 C4
Allandale Ave ML1 143 C3
Allandale Cotts FK4 39 B1
Allander Ave G62 77 A4

Allander Dr G64 . . . . .78 A4
Allander Gdns G64 . . . . .77 C2
Allander Rd Bearsden G61 .75 B1
Milngavie G62 . . . . .55 A1
Allander St G22 . . . . .97 B2
Allands Ave PA4 . . . . . . .93 B3
Allanfauld Rd
Cumbernauld G67 . . . . . .61 C1
Kilsyth G65 . . . . .36 B1
Allanshaw Gdns ML3 . .162 A2
Allanshaw St ML3 . . . . .162 A1
Allanshaw St ML3 . . . . .162 B2
Allanton Ave PA1 . . . . .114 C2
Allanton Dr G52 . . . . . .115 A3
Allanton Dr ML2 . . . . . .165 A3
Allanton Lea ML3 . . . . .183 B4
Allanton Pl ML3 . . . . . .162 C1
Allanton Prim Sch ML7 .167 A4
Allanton Rd Shotts ML7 .146 B1
Wishaw ML2, ML7 . . . . .166 C4
Allanton Terr ML3 . . . . .184 B4
Allanvale KA3 . . . . .195 A4
Allanvale Rd
Bridge of A FK9 . . . . .1 C4
Prestwick KA9 . . . . .236 A4
Allanwater Apartments
FK9 . . . . .2 A4
Allanwater Gdns FK9 . . . .2 A4
Allanwood Ct FK9 . . . . . . .2 A4
Albany Cres ML1 . . . . . .142 C3
Allen Glen Pl G4 . . . . . .241 B3
Allen Way PA4 . . . . .94 B1
Allendale G74 . . . . .159 B2
Allenfield Rd KA7 . . . . .239 B3
Allenshaw Ind Est ML3 .162 B2
Allerdyce Dr G15 . . . . . .74 C1
Allerdyce Rd G15 . . . . . .74 C1
Allershaw Pl ML2 . . . . .185 C4
Allershaw Rd ML2 . . . . .185 C4
Allershaw Twr ML2 . . . .185 C4
Allerton Gdns G69 . . . .119 C2
Alleysbank Rd G73 . . . .118 A1
Allison Ave PA8 . . . . . . .72 C1
Allison Dr G72 . . . . .139 A4
Allison Pl Gartcosh G69 .100 C2
Glasgow G42 . . . . .117 A1
Newton Mearns G77 . . .156 B2
Allison St Ayr KA8 . . . . .236 A1
Glasgow G42 . . . . .117 A1
Allnach Pl G34 . . . . . . .120 C4
Alloa Acad FK10 . . . . .9 C4
Alloa Rd Falkirk FK2 . . . .24 A2
Fishcross FK10 . . . . .5 B2
Menstrie FK9 . . . . .3 A2
Stenhousemuir FK5 . . . . .23 C2
Alloa Tout Ctr FK10 . . . .10 B4
Alloa Twr* FK10 . . . . . . .10 A3
Alloway KA7 . . . . .238 C1
Alloway Ave
Kilmarnock KA3 . . . . . .228 A4
Paisley PA2 . . . . .134 A4
Alloway Cres
Bonnybridge FK4 . . . . . .39 C2
Paisley PA2 . . . . .134 B4
Rutherglen G73 . . . . . . .137 C3
Alloway Ct G66 . . . . . . .59 A1
Alloway Dr Clydebank G81 .74 B2
Cowie FK7 . . . . .12 B4
Kirkintilloch G66 . . . . . .59 A1
Newton Mearns G77 . . .157 A2
Paisley PA2 . . . . .134 A4
Rutherglen G73 . . . . . . .137 C3
Alloway Gdns
Hamilton ML3 . . . . .161 B1
Kirkintilloch G66 . . . . . .59 A1
Alloway Gr
Kirkintilloch G66 . . . . . .58 C1
Paisley PA2 . . . . .134 B4
Alloway Pk KA7 . . . . . . .238 C4
Alloway Pl
Ardrossan KA22 . . . . . .205 B2
Ayr KA7 . . . . .238 C4
Alloway Place La KA7 . .238 C1
Alloway Prim Sch KA7 . .238 C1
Alloway Quadrant G5 . . .9 A1
Alloway Rd Airdrie ML6 .123 C4
East Kilbride G74 . . . . .160 C2
Glasgow G43 . . . . .136 B3
Alloway St Ayr KA7 . . . .238 C4
Larkhall ML9 . . . . .185 B1
Alloway Terr G66 . . . . . .58 C1
Alloway Wynd
Motherwell ML1 . . . . . .143 C2
Stenhousemuir FK5 . . . . .23 B2
Alma La K7 . . . . .42 A4
Alma St Falkirk FK2 . . . .42 A3
Almada Gr G40 . . . . . . .118 A3
Alma Terr FK2 . . . . .42 A3
Almada La ML3 . . . . . . .162 B3
Almada St ML3 . . . . . . .162 B2
Almond Ave PA4 . . . . . .94 B1
Almond Cres PA2 . . . . .112 C1
Almond Ct Falkirk FK2 . .42 C4
Stirling FK7 . . . . .7 B3
Almond Dr Banknock FK4 .38 C1
Bishopton PA7 . . . . .72 C1
East Kilbride G74 . . . . .160 A1
Kirkintilloch G66 . . . . . .79 B2
Almond Pl
Coatbridge ML5 . . . . . .101 B3
Kilmarnock KA3 . . . . . .227 B4
Motherwell ML1 . . . . . .143 A3
Almond Rd Bearsden G61 .75 B1

Almond Rd continued
Cumbernauld G67 . . . . . .62 C2
Falkirk FK2 . . . . .42 C4
Stepps G33 . . . . .99 B3
Almond St G33 . . . . .98 B1
Almond Terr ML7 . . . . .127 B3
Almond Vale FK1 . . . . .141 A4
Almond Way ML1 . . . . .163 C2
Almondbank ML6 . . . . .103 C2
Almswall Rd KA13 . . . .207 C2
Alness Cres G52 . . . . . .115 C2
Alness St ML3 . . . . .162 B1
Alness Terr ML3 . . . . . .162 B1
Alnwick Dr G76 . . . . . .178 B2
Aloa Way 22 ML9 . . . . .185 B1
Alpha Ctr G81 . . . . .94 B4
Alpine Gr G71 . . . . .140 C4
Alsatian Ave G81 . . . . . .74 B1
Alsh Terr ML3 . . . . .162 A1
Alston Ave ML5 . . . . . .122 A4
Alston Gdns G61 . . . . . .75 A4
Altnacreag Gdns G69 . . .81 A2
Altnock Pl KA24 . . . . . .191 A4
Alton Ct 2 G66 . . . . . . .58 C1
Alton Rd PA1 . . . . .114 B2
Alton St KA23 . . . . .190 B3
Alton Way KA23 . . . . . .190 B2
Altonhead Dr KA3 . . . . .210 A1
Altonhead Terr KA3 . . . .221 A4
Altonhill Ave KA3 . . . . .222 C2
Altry Pl KA7 . . . . .238 A1
Altyre St G32 . . . . .118 C2
Alva Gate G52 . . . . .115 C2
Alva Gdns Bearsden G61 .75 A4
Glasgow G52 . . . . .115 C1
Alva Glen Nature Trail*
FK12 . . . . .5 A4
Alva Ind Est FK12 . . . . . .5 B4
Alva Pl G66 . . . . .79 C2
Alva Prim Sch FK12 . . . . .5 A3
Alwyn Ave PA6 . . . . . . .111 B4
Alwyn Ct G74 . . . . .159 C2
Alwyn Dr G74 . . . . .159 C2
Alyssum Cres ML1 . . . .163 B4
Alyth Cres G76 . . . . . . .158 A4
Alyth Gdns Clarkston G76 .158 A4
Glasgow G52 . . . . .115 C2
Ambassador Way PA4 . .94 B1
Amber Terr ML4 . . . . . .142 A2
Amberside ML5 . . . . . .180 A3
Ambleside Rise ML3 . . .183 B3
Ambrose Ct ML3 . . . . . .162 A1
Amethyst Ave ML4 . . . .142 A2
Amisfield St G20 . . . . . .96 C3
Amlaird Rd KA3 . . . . . .223 A3
Amochrie Dr PA2 . . . . .133 A4
Amochrie Glen PA2 . . . .133 A4
Amochrie Way PA2 . . . .112 C1
Amulree Pl G32 . . . . . .119 A2
Amulree St G32 . . . . . .119 A2
Ancaster Dr G13 . . . . . .95 C3
Ancaster La G13 . . . . . .95 C3
Anchor Ave PA1 . . . . . .114 A2
Anchor Cres PA1 . . . . .114 A1
Anchor Dr PA1 . . . . . . .114 A2
Anchor La G1 . . . . .241 A2
Anchor Wynd PA1 . . . . .114 A1
Ancroft St G20 . . . . .97 A2
Anderson Ct G75 . . . . .180 C3
Anderside G75 . . . . . . .180 C3
Anderson Ave G65 . . . . .36 A1
Anderson Cres Ayr KA7 .239 A4
Prestwick KA9 . . . . .236 C4
Queensheburn G65 . . . . .57 B3
Shieldhill FK1 . . . . .66 C3
Anderson Ct
Bellshill ML4 . . . . .142 A3
Newton Mearns G77 . . .156 B2
Wishaw ML2 . . . . .165 A2
Anderson Dr Denny FK6 .21 C1
Falkirk FK2 . . . . .24 A1
Irvine KA12 . . . . .219 B3
Newton Mearns G77 . . .156 B2
Renfrew PA4 . . . . .94 B2
Saltcoats KA21 . . . . . . .206 A1
Anderson La ML1 . . . . .163 C1
Anderson Park Rd FK6 . .21 C1
Anderson Pl
Kilmarnock KA3 . . . . . .223 B1
Stirling FK7 . . . . .7 A2
Anderson Rd PA7 . . . . . .72 A2
Andrew Ave
Kirkintilloch G66 . . . . . .79 B2
Renfrew PA4 . . . . .94 C2
Andrew Cres FK6 . . . . . .39 B2
Andrew Dr G81 . . . . . . .94 B4
Andrew Hardie Dr FK10 .10 A4
Andrew Pl ML7 . . . . . . .187 C2
Andrew Sillars Ave G72 .139 B3
Andrew St
East Kilbride G74 . . . . .159 C1

Andrew St continued
Paisley PA3 . . . . .113 C3
Anford Pl G72 . . . . .161 C3
Angela Way G71 . . . . . .140 C3
Angle Gate G14 . . . . . . .95 B2
Angle St ML9 . . . . .198 C1
Angus Ave Airdrie ML6 .123 A3
Bishopbriggs G64 . . . . . .78 B1
East Kilbride G74 . . . . .160 A1
Glasgow G52 . . . . .115 B2
Hamilton ML3 . . . . .163 A2
Motherwell ML1 . . . . . .163 B4
Prestwick KA9 . . . . .236 B4
Angus Gdns G71 . . . . . .140 C4
Angus Oval G52 . . . . . .115 A2
Angus Pl
East Kilbride G74 . . . . .160 A1
Glasgow G52 . . . . .115 A2
Angus Rd Carluke ML8 .188 A1
Greenock PA16 . . . . .44 B2
Port Glasgow PA14 . . . . .47 B1
Angus St Alexandria G83 .27 C2
Clydebank G81 . . . . . . .94 C4
Glasgow G21 . . . . .97 C2
Angus Wlk G71 . . . . . . .141 A4
Anish Pl G15 . . . . .74 C2
Ann Ct ML3 . . . . .162 A3
Ann St
Greenock, Central PA15 .45 C2
Hamilton ML3 . . . . .162 A3
Johnstone PA5 . . . . .112 A2
Annan Ave PA3 . . . . . . .114 C2
Annabella Rd ML9 . . . .200 B2
Annan Ave G75 . . . . . . .179 C4
Annan Ct KA1 . . . . .222 C3
Annan Dr Bearsden G61 .75 A4
Glasgow G74 . . . . .159 A4
Annan Glade ML1 . . . . .164 A2
Annan Gr ML1 . . . . . . .164 A2
Annan Pl PA5 . . . . .131 B4
Annan Rd KA1 . . . . . . .228 A3
Annan St Glasgow G42 .137 A4
Paisley PA2 . . . . .112 C1
Rutherglen G73 . . . . . . .138 B4
Annandale Cres KA2 . . .221 C5
Annandale Gdns KA2 . .221 C5
Annandale La KA2 . . . .221 C1
Annandale St G42 . . . . .117 A2
Annandale View KA2 . .221 C5
Annandale Way KA11 . .220 A3
Annanhill Ave KA1 . . . .222 B1
Annanhill Pl KA13 . . . .207 A2
Annanhill Prim Sch KA1 .227 B4
Annathill Gdns ML5 . . . .81 C1
Annbank Pl G31 . . . . . .117 C3
Annbank St Glasgow G31 .117 C3
Larkhall ML9 . . . . .184 C2
Anne Ave PA4 . . . . .94 B2
Anne Cres G66 . . . . . . .79 B2
Anne Dr Bridge of A FK9 . .2 A2
Stenhousemuir FK5 . . . . .23 C2
Annerley Ct ML5 . . . . . .121 C3
Annerley Pl ML5 . . . . . .121 C3
Annes Ct G40 . . . . .117 C2
Annet Rd FK6 . . . . .39 B3
Annette St G42 . . . . . . .117 A2
Annfield Dr FK7 . . . . . . .7 B3
Annfield Gdns
Blantyre G72 . . . . .140 B1
Stirling FK8 . . . . .7 A3
Annfield Glen Rd KA7 . .239 A2
Annfield Gr FK8 . . . . . . .7 A3
Annfield Pl G31 . . . . . . .117 C4
Annfield Rd KA8 . . . . . .236 A4
Annfield Terr KA9 . . . . .236 A4
Annick Cotts KA13 . . . .211 C4
Annick Cres KA3 . . . . . .211 C4
Annick Dr Bearsden G61 .75 B1
Annick St Ind Est G32 . .119 B3
Irvine KA11 . . . . .220 A1
Annick View ML1 . . . . .219 C1
Anniesdale Ave G33 . . . .99 C4
Anniesland Coll (Balshagray
Campus) G11 . . . . .95 C1
Anniesland Cres G14 . . .95 A3
Anniesland Ind Est G13 .95 C3
Anniesland Rd G13 . . . .95 B3
Annieston G65 . . . . .59 C2
Anniversary Ave G75 . .180 B4
Annpit Rd KA8 . . . . . . .236 A2
Annsfield Rd ML3 . . . . .183 B4
Ansdell Ave G72 . . . . . .161 B4
Anson Ave FK1 . . . . .41 C2
Anson St G40 . . . . .117 C2
Anson Way 6 PA4 . . . . .94 B1
Anstruther Ct ML8 . . . .186 C3

Anstruther St
Glasgow G32 . . . . .118 C3
Law ML8 . . . . .186 C3
Antermony Rd G66 . . . .58 C3
Anthony Ct G81 . . . . . . .94 B4
Anthony St G2 . . . . .240 B2
Antigua St FK1 . . . . .46 A2
Antigua Way G75 . . . . .159 A1
Anton Cres G65 . . . . . . .60 C4
Antonine Gate FK4 . . . . .39 A1
Antonine Gdns
Clydebank G81 . . . . .74 A3
Falkirk FK1 . . . . .41 B3
Antonine Gr FK4 . . . . . .39 C2
Antonine Prim Sch FK4 .40 A2
Antonine Rd
Bearsden G61 . . . . .75 A3
Dullatur G68 . . . . .61 B3
Antonine Rd The G15 . . .74 C2
Antonine Wall*
High Bonnybridge FK4 . .40 B2
Kirkintilloch G66 . . . . . .59 A3
Antrim La ML9 . . . . . . .185 A2
Anwoth St G22 . . . . . . .97 C4
Apartments The G46 . . .136 A1
Apollo Path ML1 . . . . . .143 A1
Appian Pl ML1 . . . . . . .142 A1
Appin Cres Glasgow G31 .118 A4
Appin Ct G66 . . . . .79 A3
Appin Rd G31 . . . . .118 B4
Appin Terr Hamilton ML3 .161 C2
Rutherglen G73 . . . . . . .138 A3
Shotts ML7 . . . . .147 A2
Appin Way
2 Bothwell G71 . . . . . .141 A2
Coatbridge ML5 . . . . . .121 C2
Glenmavis ML6 . . . . . .102 C2
Appleby Ct G75 . . . . . .179 C3
Appleby St G22 . . . . . . .97 A2
Applecross Gdns G69 . . .80 C2
Applecross Quadrant
ML2 . . . . .165 A3
Applecross Rd G66 . . . .59 A1
Applecross St G4 . . . . . .97 A2
Appledore Cres G71 . . .141 A2
Appleyard Ct ML4 . . . . .141 C2
Apsley La G11 . . . . .96 A1
Apsley St G11 . . . . .96 A1
Aqua Ave ML3 . . . . . . .161 C1
Aqua Ct ML3 . . . . .161 C1
Aquila Way ML8 . . . . . .187 B1
Araburn Dr G75 . . . . . .180 B4
Aranthrue Cres PA4 . . . .94 B2
Aranthrue Dr PA4 . . . . .94 B2
Aray St G20 . . . . .96 B3
Arbles Road Hospl ML1 .163 C3
Arbroath Ave G52 . . . . .115 A2
Arbroath Cres ML5 . . . .121 A3
Arbroath Gr ML3 . . . . .162 A1
Arbuckle Pl ML6 . . . . . .104 A2
Arbuckle Rd ML6 . . . . .104 A2
Arbuckle St KA1 . . . . . .228 A4
Arbuthnot St FK1 . . . . . .41 C3
Arcade FK8 . . . . .7 A4
Arcadia St Bellshill ML4 .142 A4
Glasgow G40 . . . . .117 C3
Arcan Cres G15 . . . . . . .75 A1
Arch Way G65 . . . . .36 B1
Archerfield Ave G32 . . .119 A1
Archerfield Cres G32 . . .119 A1
Archerfield Gr G32 . . . .119 A1
Archerhill Ave G13 . . . .95 A4
Archerhill Cotts G13 . . .95 A4
Archerhill Cres G13 . . . .95 A4
Archerhill Gdns G13 . . .95 A4
Archerhill Rd G13 . . . . .95 A4
Archerhill Sq G13 . . . . .94 C4
Archerhill Terr G13 . . . .95 A4
Archers Ave FK7 . . . . . . .7 B2
Archibald Craig Pl KA3 .222 C2
Archibald Dr KA24 . . . .191 A4
Archibald Terr G66 . . . .58 A3
Archibald Pl ML4 . . . . .142 B2
Archray Rd G67 . . . . . . .62 B2
Arcon Ave KA6 . . . . . . .237 C3
Ard La G KA2 . . . . .165 C3
Ard Pl PA4 . . . . .94 A1
Ard Rd PA4 . . . . .94 A2
Ard St G32 . . . . .118 C2
Ardardan Cotts G82 . . . .25 C1
Ardargie Dr G32 . . . . . .139 B3
Ardargie Gr G32 . . . . . .139 B4
Ardargie Pl G32 . . . . . .139 B4
Ardayre Rd KA9 . . . . . .236 A4
Ardbeg Ave
Bishopbriggs G64 . . . . . .78 B1
Kilmarnock KA3 . . . . . .222 C2
Rutherglen G73 . . . . . . .138 C2
Ardbeg Ct KA11 . . . . . .219 C3
Ardbeg La G42 . . . . . . .117 A2
Ardbeg St G42 . . . . . . .117 A2
Ardchoille La KA20 . . . .206 C1
Ardchoille La KA20 . . . .206 C1
Ardconnel St G46 . . . . .135 C2
Ardeer La KA20 . . . . . .217 C3
Ardeer Prim Sch KA20 .217 B4
Ardeer Rdbt KA20 . . . .206 C1
Ardeer Terr KA20 . . . . .217 C4
Ardeer Wynd G69 . . . . .80 C1
Arder La KA20 . . . . . . .217 C3
Arden Ave G46 . . . . . . .135 C1
Arden Ct ML3 . . . . .162 B1
Arden Dr G46 . . . . .136 A2
Arden Gr G65 . . . . .36 B2
Arden Hill G84 . . . . .15 B3
Arden Pl G46 . . . . .135 C1

Arden Prim Sch G46 . . .135 B2
Arden Rd Greenock PA15 .46 B1
Hamilton ML3 . . . . .162 B1
Arden St ML6 . . . . .104 A1
Arden Terr ML3 . . . . . . .162 B1
Ardencaple Dr G84 . . . . .16 A1
Ardencaple Quadrant
G84 . . . . .16 A1
Ardenclutha Ave ML3 . .162 A2
Ardenclutha Dr PA14 . . .47 A1
Ardencraig Cres G45 . . .137 B3
Ardencraig Ct G45 . . . .138 A3
Ardencraig Gdns G45 . .137 B3
Ardencraig La G45 . . . .137 B3
Ardencraig Pl G45 . . . .137 C2
Ardencraig Quadrant
G45 . . . . .137 C1
Ardencraig Rd G45 . . . .137 C1
Ardencraig St G45 . . . .138 A1
Ardencraig Terr G45 . . .137 C1
Ardenlea G71 . . . . .140 C4
Ardenlea St G40 . . . . . .118 A2
Ardery St G11 . . . . .96 A1
Ardessie Pl G20 . . . . . . .96 B3
Ardessie St 12 G23 . . . .76 B1
Ardfern Rd ML6 . . . . . .124 A3
Ardfern St G32 . . . . . . .119 A2
Ardfin Ct KA9 . . . . .236 B3
Ardfin Rd KA9 . . . . .236 B3
Ardgare G84 . . . . .15 A4
Ardgay Pl G32 . . . . .119 A2
Ardgay St G32 . . . . . . .119 A2
Ardgay Way G73 . . . . . .138 A2
Ardgour Ct G72 . . . . . .161 C3
Ardgour Dr PA3 . . . . . .113 A3
Ardgour Par ML1 . . . . .143 B1
Ardgour Pl KA3 . . . . . .222 C2
Ardgowan Ave PA2 . . . .113 C2
Ardgowan Ct PA2 . . . . .114 A2
Ardgowan Dr G71 . . . . .140 C4
Ardgowan Pl ML7 . . . . .146 C1
Ardgowan Prim Sch
PA16 . . . . .45 B3
Ardgowan St
Greenock PA16 . . . . .45 B3
Paisley PA2 . . . . .113 C2
Port Glasgow PA14 . . . . .47 A1
Ardgowan Terrace La G3 .96 B1
Ardgryfe Cres PA6 . . . . .91 B1
Ardholm St G32 . . . . . .119 A3
Ardhu Pl G15 . . . . .75 A2
Ardlamont Sq PA3 . . . .112 B3
Ardlaw St G51 . . . . . . .115 C3
Ardle Ave KA1 . . . . . . .228 A3
Ardneil Ave KA23 . . . . .190 B2
Ardneil Ct KA22 . . . . . .205 A2
Ardneil Rd G51 . . . . . . .115 C4
Ardnish St G51 . . . . . . .115 C4
Ardo Gdns G51 . . . . . . .116 A3
Ardoch Cres
Dumbarton G82 . . . . . . .49 B2
Stevenson KA20 . . . . . .217 C3
Ardoch Ct KA20 . . . . . .217 C3
Ardoch Gdns G72 . . . . .138 C3
Ardoch Gr G72 . . . . . . .138 C3
Ardoch Path G67 . . . . .165 C3
Ardoch Rd G61 . . . . . . .75 B2
Ardoch St G22 . . . . . . .97 B2
Ardoch Terr KA20 . . . . .217 C4
Ardoch Way G69 . . . . . .80 C1
Ardochrig G75 . . . . . . .180 C3
Ardressie Pl G20 . . . . . .96 B3
Ardrossan Acad KA22 . .205 B1
Ardrossan Harbour Sta
KA22 . . . . .205 A1
Ardrossan High Rd
KA23 . . . . .190 C2
Ardrossan Rd
Saltcoats KA21 . . . . . . .216 C4
Seamill KA23 . . . . .190 B1
Ardrossan South Beach Sta
KA22 . . . . .205 A1
Ardrossan Town Sta
KA22 . . . . .205 B1
Ardshiel Rd G51 . . . . . .115 C4
Ardsloy La G14 . . . . . . .95 A2
Ardsloy Pl G14 . . . . . . .95 A2
Ardtoe Cres G33 . . . . . .99 C3
Ardtoe Pl G33 . . . . .99 C3
Arduthie Rd G51 . . . . . .115 C4
Ardwreck Pl FK2 . . . . . .24 A2
Ardwell Pl G84 . . . . . . .15 B3
Ardwell Rd G52 . . . . . .115 C2
Argosy Way 8 PA4 . . . . .94 B1
Argus Ave ML6 . . . . . . .123 B1
Argyle Cres Airdrie ML6 .122 C3

Argyle Cres *continued*
Hamilton ML3 161 C2
Argyle Dr ML3 162 A2
Argyle Gdns G66 57 C4
Argyle Pk KA8 236 A1
Argyle Pl Kilsyth G65 60 C4
Saltcoats KA21 216 C4
Argyle Rd Gourock PA19 44 C3
Saltcoats KA21 216 C4
Argyle St Glasgow G2 240 C2
Glasgow, Anderston G3 240 A2
Greenock PA15 45 C3
Paisley PA1 113 B2
Stonehouse ML9 198 C1
Argyle St E G84 16 B1
Argyle St W G84 16 B1
Argyle Street Sta G1 241 A1
Argyll Arc G1 241 A2
Argyll Ave Dumbarton G82 50 B2
Falkirk FK2 42 B3
Renfrew PA3 93 C1
Renfrew, Kirklandneuk PA4 94 A2
Stirling FK8 2 B1
Argyll Ct ML7 127 C3
Argyll Est G83 27 B4
Argyll Gdns ML9 185 A2
Argyll Pl Alloa FK10 10 B4
Bellshill ML4 141 C1
Dumbarton G82 50 B2
East Kilbride G74 160 B2
Argyll Rd Bearsden G61 75 C4
Clydebank G81 74 B1
Rosneath G84 15 A2
Argyll St Alexandria G83 27 B4
Alloa FK10 10 B4
Arisaig Dr Bearsden G61 76 A2
Glasgow G52 115 C2
Arisaig Pl G52 115 C2
Arisdale Cres G77 156 C3
Ark La G31 117 C4
Arkaig Ave ML6 103 C2
Arkaig Pl G77 157 A2
Arkaig St ML2 165 A1
Arkle Terr G72 138 C2
Arkleston Cres PA3 114 A4
Arkleston Prim Sch PA4 94 B1
Arkleston Rd PA3,PA4 114 A4
Arklet Rd G51 115 C4
Arklet Way ML2 165 C2
Arkwright Way KA11 219 C2
Arkwrights Way PA1 113 A2
Arlington St G3 240 A4
Armadale Ct G31 118 A4
Armadale Path G31 118 A4
Armadale Pl
Glasgow G31 118 A4
Greenock PA15 45 C2
Armadale Rd
Lanark ML11 215 B2
Rhu G84 15 C2
Armadale St G31 118 A4
Armine Path ML1 143 B2
Armour Ave Airdrie ML6 122 C4
Cowie FK7 12 B4
Armour Ct Blantyre G72 161 A3
Kirkintilloch G66 59 A1
Armour Dr Ayr KA7 239 B3
Kirkintilloch G66 59 A1
Armour Gdns G66 59 A1
Armour Gr ML1 164 A2
Armour Mews FK5 23 B2
Armour Pl
Ardrossan KA22 205 B2
Johnstone PA5 112 A2
Johnstone, Linwood PA5 112 B3
Kirkintilloch G66 59 A1
Motherwell ML1 143 B2
Stewarton KA3 195 C1
Armour Sq PA5 112 A2
Armour St
Glasgow G4, G31 241 C1
Johnstone PA5 112 A2
Kilmarnock KA1 227 C4
Armstrong Cres G71 141 A4
Armstrong Gr G75 180 B4
Armstrong Rd
Helensburgh G84 25 B4
Kilmarnock KA3 223 B1
Arnbrae Rd G65 36 A1
Arness Terr KA3 222 C2
Arngask Rd G51 115 C4
Arnhall Pl G52 115 C2
Arnhem St G72 139 B3
Arnholm Pl G52 115 C2
Arnisdale Pl G34 120 A4
Arnisdale Rd G34 120 A4
Arnisdale Way G73 138 A2
Arnish PA4 93 B4
Arniston St G32 118 C4
Arniston Way PA3 114 A4
Arnol Pl G33 119 C4
Arnold Ave G64 78 A1
Arnold St G20 97 A3
Arnot St FK1 42 B2
Arnothill FK1 42 A2
Arnothill Bank 6 FK1 42 A2
Arnothill Ct FK1 41 C3
Arnothill Gdns FK1 42 A2
Arnothill La FK1 41 C2
Arnothill Mews FK1 42 A2
Arnott Dr ML5 122 A2
Arnott Quadrant ML1 142 B1
Arnott Way G72 139 A3
Arnprior Cres G44 137 B2
Arnprior Gdns G69 80 C1
Arnprior Pl KA7 238 C1
Arnprior Quadrant G45 137 B2
Arnprior Rd G45 137 B2
Arnprior St G45 137 B2
Arns Gr FK10 9 C4
Arnside Ave G46 136 B2
Arnswell FK10 5 B1
Arnum Gdns ML8 187 C1
Arnum Pl ML8 187 C1
Arnwood Dr G12 96 A3
Aron Terr G72 138 C2
Arondale Rd ML6 103 C2
Aros Dr G52 115 C1
Aros La G52 115 B1
Aros Rd G84 15 B3
Arran G74 160 B1
Arran Ave
Coatbridge ML5 122 B2
Dumbarton G82 49 B3
Kilmarnock KA3 223 A2
Port Glasgow PA14 69 A4
Renfrew PA3 93 C1
Arran Cres KA15 150 B1
Arran Ct Alloa FK10 10 A3
Stevenston KA20 217 B4
Arran Dr Airdrie ML6 102 C1
Cumbernauld G67 82 B4
Glasgow G52 115 C2
Glasgow, Giffnock G46 136 B1
Glenmavis ML6 102 C3
Johnstone PA5 111 B1
Kirkintilloch G66 58 C1
Paisley PA2 133 C4
Arran Gdns Carluke ML8 201 C4
Hamilton ML3 162 C1
Troon KA10 229 C4
Arran La Ardrossan KA22 205 B1
Moodiesburn G69 81 A1
Arran Mall KA7 238 C4
Arran Path 26 ML9 185 B1
Arran Pk KA9 236 A3
Arran Pl Ardrossan KA22 205 B1
Clydebank G81 74 B1
Coatbridge ML6 122 B2
Irvine KA12 219 A3
Linwood PA3 112 A3
Saltcoats KA21 206 A1
Arran Rd Gourock PA19 44 B3
Motherwell ML1 163 B4
Renfrew PA4 94 B1
Troon KA10 229 C4
Arran Terr Ayr KA7 235 C1
Falkirk FK1 41 B2
Rutherglen G73 137 C3
Arran Twr G72 138 C2
Arran View 14 Kilsyth G65 60 B4
Stewarton KA3 195 C1
Arran Way G72 140 C1
Arranview Ct Ayr KA8 236 A2
Irvine KA12 219 A2
Arranview Gdns KA23 190 B1
Arranview St ML6 123 C1
Arrochar Ct G23 96 C4
Arrochar Dr G23 76 B1
Arrochar Path 6 G23 76 B1
Arrochar St G23 76 B1
Arrol Cres FK10 10 B4
Arrol Dr KA7 238 B3
Arrol Pk KA7 238 C3
Arrol Pl G40 118 A2
Arrol St G52 114 C4
Arrothill Dr KA1 227 B4
Arrotshole Ct G74 159 A2
Arrotshole Rd G74 159 A2
Arrowsmith Ave G13 95 B4
Artarman Rd G84 15 C2
Arthur Ave Airdrie ML6 123 A3
Barrhead G78 134 A1
Arthur Ct KA23 190 B3
Arthur Gdns ML6 105 A3
Arthur Pl G76 157 C3
Arthur Rd PA2 133 C4
Arthur St Alexandria G83 27 C2
Ayr KA7 238 C4
Clarkston G76 157 C3
Glasgow G3 96 B1
Greenock PA15 46 A2
Hamilton ML3 162 B3
Paisley PA1 113 B3
Saltcoats KA21 217 A4
Stevenston KA20 217 B4
West Kilbride KA23 190 B3
Arthur's Dr FK5 23 C1
Arthurlie Ave
Barrhead G78 134 B1
Uplawmoor G78 153 A2
Arthurlie Dr
Glasgow G46 136 B1
Newton Mearns G77 156 B2
Uplawmoor G78 153 A2
Arthurlie Gdns G78 134 B1
Arthurlie Pl KA21 216 C4
Arthurlie St
Barrhead G78 134 B1
Glasgow G51 115 C4
Arthurston Rd G83 28 A4
Artizan Br G82 49 C2
Arundel Dr
Bishopbriggs G64 78 A2
Glasgow G42 137 A4
Ascaig Cres G52 115 C1
Ascog Rd G61 75 C1
Ascog St G42 117 A1
Ascot G12 96 A3
Ascot Ave G12 95 C3
Ash Ave G75 180 B3
Ash Ct G75 180 B3
Ash Dr KA15 150 A1
Ash Gr Alloa FK10 10 B3
Bishopbriggs G64 98 A4
Kirkintilloch G66 79 A3
Ash Gr *continued*
Law ML8 186 C3
Stenhousemuir FK5 23 C1
Uddingston G71 141 A4
Ash Pl Banknock FK4 38 C1
East Kilbride G75 180 B3
Johnstone PA5 112 A1
Kilmarnock KA1 227 B4
Ash Rd Clydebank G81 74 A3
Cumbernauld G67 62 C3
Dumbarton G82 49 C2
Glasgow G69 120 A2
Ash Terr FK8 6 C3
Ash Wlk Motherwell ML1 143 A3
Rutherglen G73 138 B2
Ash Wynd G72 139 C3
Ashbank Cres ML6 123 C2
Ashbrae Gdns FK7 7 A1
Ashburn Gate PA19 44 B4
Ashburn Gdns
Gourock PA19 44 B4
Milngavie G62 54 C1
Ashburn Loan ML9 185 A2
Ashburn Rd G62 54 C1
Ashburton La G12 96 A3
Ashburton Pk G75 180 A4
Ashburton Rd G12 96 A3
Ashby Cres G13 75 C1
Ashcraig Sch G33 99 A2
Ashcroft G74 160 B3
Ashcroft Ave G66 57 C4
Ashcroft Dr G44 137 C3
Ashcroft Wlk G66 57 C4
Ashdale Ave KA21 205 C1
Ashdale Dr G52 115 C2
Ashdale Rd KA3 222 C2
Ashdene St G22 97 A4
Asher Rd ML6 123 C1
Ashfield G64 78 A2
Ashfield Cotts G83 20 A2
Ashfield Rd
Clarkston G76 157 C3
Law ML8 187 A3
Milngavie G62 55 A1
Ashfield St G22 97 B2
Ashfield Sta G22 97 B3
Ashgill Pl G22 97 B3
Ashgill Rd G22 97 B4
Ashgillhead Rd ML9 185 C1
Ashgrove Airdrie ML6 123 B4
Caldercruix ML6 105 A3
Coatbridge ML5 122 A2
Hartwood ML7 145 C2
Irvine KA12 219 B3
Moodiesburn G69 80 C1
Ashgrove Ave
Gourock PA19 44 B4
Stevenston KA20 206 C1
Ashgrove La PA14 47 B1
Ashgrove Rd
Ardrossan KA22 205 B2
Bellshill ML4 142 A4
Kilwinning KA13 207 B2
Ashgrove St Ayr KA7 239 A4
Glasgow G73 118 A1
Ashgrove Workshops
KA13 207 B2
Ashiestiel Ct G67 82 C4
Ashiestiel Pl G67 82 C4
Ashiestiel Rd G67 82 C4
Ashkirk Dr Ashgill ML9 199 C4
Glasgow G52 115 C2
Ashland Ave ML3 183 B3
Ashlea Dr G46 136 B2
Ashlea Gdns ML6 103 C2
Ashley Dr G71 141 A3
Ashley La G3 240 A4
Ashley Pk G71 141 B3
Ashley Pl G72 161 B4
Ashley Rise G83 27 C1
Ashley St Bonnybridge FK4 39 C3
Glasgow G3 240 A4
Ashley Terr FK10 10 A4
Ashmore Rd G43 136 C3
Ashton Dr
Helensburgh G84 25 B4
Hurlford KA1 228 C3
Ashton Gdns G69 101 A3
Ashton Gn G74 159 C1
Ashton La N G12 96 B1
Ashton Pl PA19 44 B4
Ashton Rd Glasgow G12 96 B1
Gourock PA19 44 B4
Rutherglen G73 118 A1
Ashton St ML1 142 B1
Ashton Terr PA19 44 B4
Ashton View G82 49 A2
Ashton Way PA2 132 C4
Ashtree Ct G60 73 A3
Ashtree Gr G77 156 B2
Ashtree Rd G43 136 B4
Ashvale Cres G21 97 C2
Ashwood ML2 164 C1
Ashwood Gdns G13 95 C3
Ashworth Terr ML3 162 A2
Aspen Ct KA7 239 B3
Aspen Dr G21 98 A2
Aspen Pl
Cambuslang G72 139 C3
Johnstone PA5 112 A1
Aspen Rd KA7 239 B3
Aspen Way ML3 162 C1
Asquith Pl ML4 142 B3
Assloss Rd KA3 223 B2
Aster Dr G45 138 A2
Aster Gdns Glasgow G53 135 B2
Motherwell ML1 163 C3
Athelstane Dr G67 82 B4
Athelstane Rd G13 95 B4
Athena Way G71 141 A4
Athole Gdns G12 96 B2
Athole La Glasgow G12 96 B2
Gourock PA16 44 B2
Athole St G84 16 C1
Athole Terr PA16 44 B2
Atholl Ave Paisley G52 114 C4
Torrance G64 57 A1
Atholl Cres PA1 114 C3
Atholl Ct G66 59 A1
Atholl Dr Cumbernauld G68 81 C4
Rutherglen G46 157 B4
Atholl Gdns Bearsden G61 75 C4
Bishopbriggs G64 77 C2
Kilwinning KA13 207 C2
Rutherglen G73 138 C2
Atholl La G69 81 A1
Atholl Pl Coatbridge ML5 122 A2
Linwood PA3 112 A3
Stirling FK8 1 C1
Atholl Prep Sch G62 55 A2
Atholl St ML3 162 A3
Atholl Terr G71 120 C1
Atlas Ind Est G21 97 C2
Atlas Pl G21 97 C2
Atlas Rd G21 97 C2
Atlas Sq G21 97 C2
Atlas St G81 94 A4
Atlin Dr ML1 143 A2
Atrium Way FK4 40 A2
Attercliffe Ave ML2 164 B1
Attlee Ave G81 74 C1
Attlee Pl G81 74 C1
Attow Rd G43 136 A3
Auburn Dr G78 134 B1
Auchans Ave KA2 225 C1
Auchans Dr KA2 225 C1
Auchans Pl KA3 213 A2
Auchans Rd PA6 92 A1
Auchanshangan Dr
KA21 205 C2
Auchenback Prim Sch
G78 134 B1
Auchenbeg Cres KA7 239 A2
Auchenbothie Cres G33 98 C3
Auchenbothie Pl G33 98 C3
Auchenbothie Rd PA14 68 C3
Auchencar Dr KA3 222 C2
Auchencrow St G34 120 B4
Auchencruive G62 76 B4
Auchendarroch St PA15 46 B2
Auchendavie Rd G66 59 A1
Auchendoon Cres KA7 238 B2
Auchendores Ave PA14 69 A4
Auchenfoil La PA14 68 B4
Auchenfoil Rd
Port Glasgow PA14 67 C3
Port Glasgow, Devol PA14 68 B4
Auchengate KA10 229 D4
Auchengate Cres KA11 224 D1
Auchengeich Rd G69 80 B2
Auchengilloch G75 180 C3
Auchenglen Dr G69 80 C1
Auchenglen Gdns G69 80 C1
Auchenglen Rd ML8 201 C2
Auchengreoch Ave PA5 131 B4
Auchengreoch Rd PA5 131 B4
Auchenharvie Acad
KA21 217 A4
Auchenharvie Pl
Irvine KA11 219 C3
Stevenston KA20 206 A1
Auchenharvie Rd KA21 217 A4
Auchenhove Cres KA25 149 A2
Auchenhowie Rd G62 76 B4
Auchenkilns Holdings
G68 61 B1
Auchenkilns Rd G67 82 B3
Auchenkilns Rdbt G67 82 B4
Auchenleck La PA14 68 C4
Auchenleck Rd PA14 68 C4
Auchenlodment Prim Sch
PA5 112 A1
Auchenlodment Rd PA5 112 A1
Auchenreoch G66 59 A3
Auchenreoch Ave G82 50 A3
Auchenstewart Ct ML2 165 B2
Auchentibber Rd G72 161 A2
Auchentiber Pl KA3 223 B3
Auchentorlie Quadrant
PA1 114 A2
Auchentorlie St G11 95 C1
Auchentoshan Ave G81 73 C3
Auchentoshan Sch G81 73 C3
Auchentoshan Terr G21 97 C1
Auchentrae Cres KA7 238 B3
Auchentyre Pl FK2 24 B2
Auchinairn Prim Sch
G64 98 A4
Auchinairn Rd G64 98 B4
Auchinbaird FK10 5 B1
Auchinbee Farm Rd G68 61 A2
Auchinbee Way G68 61 A2
Auchincampbell Rd
ML3 162 B2
Auchincarroch Rd
Bonhill G83 28 A4
Gartocharn G83 20 C2
Auchincloch Dr FK4 38 C1
Auchincruive (West of Scotland Agricultural Coll)
KA6 237 B2
Auchincruive Ave KA9 236 B3
Auchineden Ct G61 75 B4
Auchingill Pl G34 100 B1
Auchingill Rd G34 100 B1
Auchingramont Ct ML3 162 B2
Auchingramont Rd ML3 162 B2
Auchingramount Ct
ML3 162 C2
Auchinlea Dr ML1 144 B1
Auchinlea Rd G34 99 C1
Auchinlea Ret Pk G34 99 C1
Auchinleck Ave G33 98 C3
Auchinleck Cres G33 98 C3
Auchinleck Dr G33 98 C3
Auchinleck Gdns G33 98 C3
Auchinleck Rd
Clydebank G81 74 A4
Glasgow G33 98 C4
Auchinleck Terr G81 74 A4
Auchinloch Prim Sch
G66 79 B1
Auchinloch Rd G66 79 B2
Auchinloch St 13 G21 97 C2
Auchinraith Ave ML3 162 B3
Auchinraith Prim Sch
G72 161 B4
Auchinraith Rd G72 161 C3
Auchinraith Terr G72 161 C3
Auchinvole Cres G65 60 A4
Auchmannoch Ave PA1 114 C3
Auchmead Rd PA16 44 C2
Auchmountain Rd
Greenock PA15 46 C1
Greenock, Bridgend PA15 46 B2
Port Glasgow PA15 67 C4
Auchnacraig Rd G81 74 B4
Auchneagh Ave PA16 45 A2
Auchneagh Cres PA16 45 A2
Auchneagh Farm La
PA16 45 A3
Auchneagh Farm Rd
PA16 45 A3
Auchneagh Rd PA16 45 A2
Auchter Ave ML2 166 B3
Auchter Rd ML2 165 C2
Auchterburn Rd ML7 166 C4
Auckland Pk 8 G75 159 A1
Auckland Pl G81 73 B2
Auckland St G22 97 A2
Auld Brig Rd FK10 10 A3
Auld Clay Rd KA21 206 C4
Auld Kirk Mus* G66 58 B1
Auld Kirk Rd G72 139 B2
Auld Nick's View KA7 238 C1
Auld Rd The G67 62 A2
Auld St G81 73 C2
Auld's Brae 2 ML6 123 A4
Auldbar Rd G52 115 C2
Auldbar Terr PA2 114 A1
Auldburn Rd G43 136 A3
Auldearn Rd G21 98 B4
Auldgirth Rd G52 115 C2
Auldhame St ML5 121 C4
Auldhouse Ave G43 136 A3
Auldhouse Ct G43 136 A3
Auldhouse Gdns G43 136 A3
Auldhouse Prim Sch
G75 180 B1
Auldhouse Rd
East Kilbride G75 180 B1
Glasgow G43 136 B3
Auldhouse Ret Pk G43 136 B3
Auldhouse Terr G43 136 B3
Auldlea Rd KA15 150 A1
Auldmurroch Dr G62 54 B1
Auldton Terr ML9 185 C1
Aultbea St G22 97 A4
Aultmore Dr ML1 143 A1
Aultmore Rd G33 119 C4
Aurs Cres G78 134 B1
Aurs Dr G78 134 B1
Aurs Glen G78 134 B1
Aurs Pl G78 134 C1
Aurs Rd G78 134 C1
Aursbridge Cres G78 134 B1
Aursbridge Dr G78 134 B1
Austen La 2 G13 95 C3
Austen Rd G13 95 C3
Austine Dr ML3 183 C4
Aven Dr FK2 42 C2
Avenel Rd G13 75 C1
Avenue End Rd G33 99 A2
Avenue Pk FK9 1 C4
Avenue Sq KA3 211 B4
Avenue St Glasgow G40 118 A3
Rutherglen G73 118 A1
Stewarton KA3 195 B1
Avenue The Bridge of A FK9 2 A4
Falkirk FK2 24 B1
Newton Mearns G77 156 B2
West Kilbride KA23 190 C4
Avenuehead Rd G69 101 A4
Avenuepark St G20 96 C3
Aviemore Gdns G61 76 A3
Aviemore Rd G52 115 C2
Avils Hill KA25 149 A1
Avils Pl KA25 149 A1
Avoch St G34 100 A1
Avon Ave Bearsden G61 76 A2
Carluke ML8 187 C1
Longriggend ML6 84 B2
Avon Ct Falkirk FK1 42 B1
Irvine KA11 220 A2
Avon Dr Bellshill ML4 142 B2
Linwood PA3 112 A3
Avon Ho ML3 162 C3
Avon Pk FK1 87 C3
Avon Pl Coatbridge ML5 101 B1
Kilmarnock KA1 228 A3
Larkhall ML9 199 A4

Avon Rd Bishopbriggs G64 ...**98** A4
Glasgow G46 ....**136** A1
Larkhall ML9 ....**199** A4
Avon St Denny FK6 ......**21** B2
Hamilton ML3 ....**162** C2
Larkhall ML9 ....**184** C2
Motherwell ML1 ......**163** C3
Avon Twr **10** ML1 ......**163** C3
Avon Wynd **22** ML2 ....**165** C3
Avonbank Cres ML3 ....**183** C4
Avonbank Gdns FK6 ....**21** B2
Avonbank
Larkhall ML9 ....**184** C2
Rutherglen G73 ....**137** C4
Avonbrae Cres ML3 ....**183** C4
Avonbridge Dr ML3 ....**162** C2
Avonbridge Prim Sch
FK1 ....**87** C3
Avonbridge Ave G74 ...**159** C1
Avondale Dr PA1 ......**114** A3
Avondale Pl G71 ......**181** A4
Avondale Rd KA23 .....**190** B3
Avondale St G33 ......**99** A1
Avondale G75 ....**180** C3
Avonhead Ave G67 ....**82** B4
Avonhead Gdns G67 ...**82** B4
Avonhead Pl G67 .....**82** B4
Avonhead Rd G67 .....**82** B4
Avonmouth Pl PA19 ...**44** C3
Avonside Dr FK6 ......**21** B3
Avonside Gr ML3 .....**162** C2
Avonspark St G21 ....**98** A2
Aylmer Rd G43 ....**136** C3
Ayr Acad KA7 ....**235** C1
Ayr Coll K48 ....**239** A4
Ayr Coll (Newton Annexe)
K48 ....**236** A1
Ayr Dr ML6 ....**123** A3
Ayr Gram Sch KA7 ....**238** C4
Ayr Hospl KA6 ....**239** B1
Ayr La PA16 ....**44** C2
Ayr Rd Ashgill ML9 ..**185** C1
Irvine KA11,KA12 ....**224** C4
Kilmarnock KA1 .....**227** C2
Newton Mearns G77 ..**156** B2
Prestwick KA9 ....**236** A3
Rutherglen G46 ......**157** A4
Ayr St Glasgow G21 ..**97** C2
Troon KA10 ....**229** C1
Ayr Sta KA7 ....**239** A4
Ayr Terr PA16 ....**44** C2
Ayrshire Central Hospl
KA12 ....**219** A4
Ayton Pk N G74 .....**160** A2
Ayton Pk S G74 .....**160** A2
Aytoun Dr PA8 ......**72** C2
Aytoun Rd G41 ......**116** C2
Azalea Gdns G72 ....**139** C3

B

Baads Rd EH48,ML7 ...**106** B1
Baberton Way KA13 ...**207** A2
Babylon Ave ML4 ....**142** A2
Babylon Dr ML4 .....**142** A2
Babylon Pl ML4 .....**142** A2
Babylon Rd ML4 .....**142** A2
Back Cswy G31 ......**118** B3
Back Hawkhill Ave KA8 .**236** A1
Back Main St KA8 ....**235** C1
Back O Dykes Rd G66 ..**80** A4
Back O Hill FK6 .....**91** A1
Back O' Hill Ind Est FK8 ..**2** A1
Back o' Hill Rd
Fluchter G64 ....**56** C1
Stirling FK8 ....**2** A1
Back O'Barns ML3 ....**162** C2
Back Peebles St KA8 ..**235** C1
Back Rd Alva FK12 ...**4** A2
Bridge of W PA11 ...**110** B4
Back Row ML3 ......**162** C2
Back Sneddon St PA3 ..**113** C3
Back St G82 ....**27** B1
Back Wlk FK8 ....**7** A4
Backbrae St G65 ....**60** B4
Backbrae KA15 ......**171** A4
Backmuir Cres ML3 ..**162** A3
Backmuir Pl ML3 ....**162** A3
Backmuir Rd Glasgow G15 **75** A2
Hamilton ML3 ....**162** A3
Backwood Ct FK10 ...**10** C3
Badenheath Pl G68 ..**81** B3
Badenheath Terr G67 ..**81** C2
Badenoch Rd G66 ....**59** B1
Bagnell St G21 .....**97** C3
Bahamas Way **5** G75 **159** A1
Baidland Ave KA24 ..**191** C3
Bailie Dr G61 ......**75** B4
Bailie Fyfe Way ML2 ..**186** A4
Bailiehill Pl KA11 ...**222** B1
Bailie Wynd **10** G71 ..**141** A4
Bailie Dr Bothwell G71 ..**141** A2
East Kilbride G74 ...**160** B2
Baillie Gdns ML2 ....**165** C2
Baillie Waugh Rd FK7 ..**7** B2
Baillies La **7** ML6 ..**123** A4
Bailliesmuir Pl ML2 ..**166** A3
Baillieston Ave KA25 ..**170** A4
Baillieston Rd
Glasgow G32 ....**119** C2
Glasgow, Broomhouse
G71 ....**120** A3

Baillieston Sta G69 ...**120** A2
Bain Cres G84 ....**16** C2
Bain St G40 ....**241** C1
Bain Way G83 ....**27** C3
Bainfield Rd G82 ....**48** A4
Baingle Brae FK10 ...**4** A2
Baingle Cres FK10 ...**4** A2
Bainsford Prim Sch FK2 ..**42** A4
Bainsford St G32 ....**118** C3
Baird Ave Airdrie ML6 ..**103** A1
Helensburgh G84 ....**16** A1
Kilwinning KA13 ....**207** C2
Larkhall ML9 ....**199** B4
Paisley G52 ....**114** C4
Baird Brae G4 ......**97** A2
Baird Cres Alexandria G83 ..**27** B4
Cumbernauld G67 ..**82** A4
Baird Ct G81 ....**74** A1
Baird Dr Bearsden G61 ..**75** B3
Erskine PA8 ....**72** C2
Baird Hill G75 .....**180** C4
Baird Meml Prim Sch
G67 ....**82** B4
Baird St G5 ....**117** B2
Baird St G5 ....**117** B2
Bairds Dr Bearsden G61 **76** A1
Inchinnan PA4 ....**93** B4
Paisley PA3 ....**114** A1
Stirling FK9 ....**2** B2
Ballater Dr G5 .....**117** B2
Ballater St G5 .....**117** B2
Ballayne Dr G69 ....**81** A2
Ballengeich Pass FK8 ..**2** A1
Ballengeich Rd FK8 ..**1** C1
Ballentrae Wynd ML1 ..**143** A3
Ballerup High Sch G75 ..**180** A2
Ballerup Terr G75 ...**180** C3
Ballewan Cres G63 ..**31** A2
Ballindalloch Dr G31 ..**118** A4
Ballindalloch La G31 ..**118** A4
Ballinkier Ave G65 ..**58** C2
Balloch Castle* G83 ..**19** B1
Balloch Castle Ctry Pk*
G83 ....**19** B1
Balloch Gdns G52 ...**115** C2
Balloch Holdings G68 ..**61** A1
Balloch Rd Airdrie ML6 ..**124** A3
Balloch G68 ....**27** B4
Cumbernauld G68 ...**61** B1
Greenock PA15 ......**46** A1
Shotts ML7 ....**146** C3
Balloch St G68 .....**61** A1
Balloch Sta G83 ....**27** C4
Balloch View G67 ...**61** C1
Ballochmill Rd G73 ..**138** B4
Ballochmyle G74 ....**160** B2
Ballochmyle Cres **11**
G53 ....**135** A4
Ballochmyle Dr **14** G53 **135** A4
Ballochmyle Gdns G53 **135** A4
Ballochmyle Pl **12** G53 **135** A4
Ballochney La ML6 ..**102** C1
Ballochney St ML6 ..**103** C2
Ballochnie Dr ML6 ..**104** A2
Ballochney Rd PA19 ..**43** C3
Ballogie Rd G44 ....**137** A4
Ballot Rd KA12 .....**219** B2
Balmalloch Prim Sch
G65 ....**59** B1
Balmalloch Rd G65 ..**36** B1
Balmartin Rd G23 ...**76** B1
Balmedie PA8 ......**73** A1
Balmeg Ave G46 ....**157** B4
Balmerino Pl G64 ...**98** B4
Balminnoch Pk KA7 ..**238** B1
Balmoral Ave ML6 ..**102** C3
Balmoral Cres
Coatbridge ML5 ....**121** B2
Inchinnan PA4 ......**93** C3
Balmoral Dr Bearsden G61 ..**76** A1
Bishopton PA7 ......**72** B1
Cambuslang G72 ...**138** C3
Falkirk FK1 ....**41** C2
Glasgow G32 ....**139** A4
Balmoral Gdns
Blantyre G72 ....**140** B1
Uddingston G71 ....**120** C1
Balmoral Path **8** ML9 ..**185** B1
Balmoral Pl
East Kilbride G74 ...**159** B1
Gourock PA19 ......**44** C3
Stenhousemuir FK5 ..**23** C2
Stirling FK8 ....**7** A4
Balmoral Rd
Elderslie PA5 ....**112** A1
Kilmarnock KA3 ....**222** C1
Balmoral St Falkirk FK1 ..**41** C2
Glasgow G14 ......**95** A2
Balmoral Wynd KA3 ..**211** C4
Balmore Dr ML3 ....**183** A4
Balmore Ind Est G22 ..**97** A2
Balmore Pl G22 ....**97** A3
Balmore Rd Glasgow G22 **97** A3
Greenock PA15 .....**46** B1
Bardowie G62,G64 ..**77** B4
Balmore Sq G22 ....**97** A3
Balmuildy Prim Sch G64 **77** C2
Balmuildy Rd G64 ...**77** B3
Balmulzier Rd FK1 ..**86** A4
Balornock Prim Sch G21 **98** A2
Balornock Rd G21 ...**98** A3
Balquhidder Cres FK1 ..**86** A3
Balquhidderock FK7 ..**7** B2
Balrossie Dr PA13 ..**89** A4
Balruddery Pl G64 ..**98** B4
Balshagray Ave G11,G14 ..**95** C1
Balshagray Dr G11 ..**95** C1
Balshagray La G11 ..**95** C2
Balshagray Pl G11 ..**95** C2
Baltersan Gdns ML3 ..**183** C2
Baltic Ct G40 ......**118** A2
Baltic La G40 .....**118** A2
Baltic Pl G40 .....**117** C2
Baltic St G40 .....**118** A2
Balure Cres FK7 ...**8** B2
Balure St G33 .....**118** B4
Balvaird Cres **8** G73 **138** A4
Balvaird Dr G73 ...**138** A4
Balvenie Dr ML1 ...**143** A1
Balvenie St ML5 ...**122** A2
Balveny St G33 ....**99** B1
Balvicar Dr G42 ...**116** C1
Balvicar St G42 ...**116** C1
Balvie Ave Glasgow G15 ..**75** A1
Glasgow, Giffnock G46 ..**136** B1
Balvie Cres G62 ...**54** C1
Balvie Rd G62 ....**54** C1
Banavie Rd Glasgow G11 **96** A2
Wishaw ML2 ....**165** A3
Banchory Ave
Glasgow G43 ......**136** A3
Glennavis ML6 .....**102** C3
Inchinnan PA4 .....**93** B4
Banchory Cres G61 ..**76** A1
Banchory Pl FK10 ..**4** B2
Banchory Rd FK10 ..**4** B2
Banchory Rd ML1 ..**165** A3
Bandeath Ind Est
Fallin FK7 ....**8** C2
Throsk FK7 ....**9** A3
Bandeath Rd FK7 ..**9** A3
Baneberry Path G74 ..**159** B2
Banff Ave ML6 ....**123** A2
Banff Pl East Kilbride G75 **180** B4
Greenock PA16 .....**44** B3
Banff Quadrant ML2 ..**165** A3
Banff Rd PA16 ....**44** B3
Banff St G33 ......**99** A1
Bangorshill St G46 ..**135** C2
Bank Ave G62 .....**55** A2
Bank Ct KA12 .....**219** C2
Bank Pk G75 .....**180** B4
Bank Rd Glasgow G32 ..**139** A4
Alexandria G83 ....**27** C4
Alloa FK10 ....**10** A3
Barrhead G78 .....**134** B1
Cambuslang G72 ..**139** A3
Coatbridge ML5 ...**121** C3
Falkirk FK1 ....**42** A3
Glasgow G12 ....**96** C1
Greenock PA15 ....**45** C2
Irvine KA12 ......**219** B2
Kilbirnie KA25 ....**149** A1
Neilston G78 .....**154** B4
Paisley PA1 ....**113** C3
Prestwick KA9 ....**236** A4
Slamannan FK1 ...**86** A3
Stirling FK8 ......**7** A4
Troon KA10 ....**229** B1
Bank View ML6 ...**123** B1
Bank Way **14** ML6 ..**123** A4
Bankbrae Ave G53 ..**135** A3
Bankend PA1 KA13 ..**223** A3
Bankend Rd
Bridge of W PA11 ..**110** C4
Dumbarton G82 ...**49** A4
Bankes Ave KA1 ....**227** A3
Bankfaulds Ave KA15 ..**149** A1
Bankfaulds Ct **4** KA25 **149** A1
Bankfield Dr ML3 ..**183** B4
Bankfield RdM KA7 ..**239** B2
Bankfoot Dr G52 ...**115** A3
Bankfoot Pl G77 ...**156** C2
Bankfoot Rd
Glasgow G52 .....**115** A2
Paisley PA3 ......**113** A3
Bankglen Rd G15 ...**75** A2
Bankhall St G42 ...**117** A1
Bankhead Ave
Airdrie ML6 ......**123** A4
Barrhead G78 .....**134** A1
Coatbridge ML5 ..**121** B2
Glasgow G13 .....**95** A3
Springwside KA11 ..**221** A3
Bankhead Cres FK4 ..**39** B3
Bankhead Dr Ayr G73 ..**137** C4
Coatbridge ML5 ..**121** B2
Stewarton KA3 ....**195** C1
Bankhead Prim Sch
Glasgow G13 ......**95** A3
Glasgow, Bankhead G73 ..**137** C4
Bankhead Rd
Carmunnock G76 ..**158** A4
Fishcross FK10 ....**5** B2
Kilwinning KA13 ..**207** C2
Kirkintilloch G66 ..**80** A4
Rutherglen G73 ...**137** C4
Bankhead Terr ML11 ..**215** A1
Bankholm Pl G76 ..**157** C3
Bankier Prim Sch FK4 ..**38** C2
Bankier Rd FK4 ...**38** C2
Bankier Terr FK4 ..**38** C2
Banknock St G32 ..**118** C3
Banks Rd G66 ....**58** B1
Banks View FK2 ...**14** C2
Bankside Ave PA5 ..**112** A1
Bankside Rd ML6 ..**126** C1
Bankside Gdns KA25 **149** A2
Bankside Ind Est FK2 ..**42** A4
Banktop PA5 .....**111** C2
Bankview Cres G66 ..**79** A4
Bankview Dr G66 ...**79** A4
Bannachra Cres G83 ..**27** B3
Bannachra Dr G84 ...**16** A1
Bannatyne Ave G31 ..**118** A4
Bannatyne St ML11 ..**215** A2
Banner Dr G13 ....**75** B1
Banner Rd G13 ....**75** B1
Bannercross Ave **13**
G69 ....**120** A3
Bannercross Dr G69 ..**120** A3
Bannercross Gdns **12**
G69 ....**120** A3
Bannerman Dr
Bellshill ML4 .....**142** B3
Kilmarnock KA3 ..**223** B1
Bannerman High Sch
G69 ....**120** A2
Bannerman Pl G81 ..**74** A1
Bannock Gdns KA13 ..**208** A2
Bannoch Pl KA13 ..**208** A2
Bannoch Rd KA13 ..**208** A2
Bannock Rd FK7 ...**8** B2
Bannockburn Cross FK7 ..**7** C1
Bannockburn Heritage Ctr*
FK7 ....**7** A1
Bannockburn High Sch
FK7 ....**7** B1
Bannockburn Hospl FK7 **11** C4
Bannockburn Pl
Kilmarnock KA3 ...**223** A2
Motherwell ML1 ...**143** A1
Bannockburn Prim Sch
FK7 ....**7** C1
Bannockburn Rd
Cowie FK7 ....**12** B4
Stirling FK7 ....**7** B2
Bannockburn St PA16 ..**45** B2
Bannockburn Station Rd
FK7 ....**8** A2
Bantaskin St G20 ..**96** B4
Bantaskine Dr FK1 ..**41** C2
Bantaskine Gdns FK1 ..**41** C2
Bantaskine Rd FK1 ..**41** C2
Bantaskine St FK1 ..**41** C1
Banton Pl
Bonnybridge FK4 ..**40** A2
Glasgow G33 .....**120** A4
Banton Prim Sch G65 ..**37** C2
Banton Rd G65 ...**37** B1
Banyan Cres G71 ..**121** B1
Bar Hill Pl G65 ...**60** A4
Bar Hill Roman Fort*
G65 ....**60** A2
Barassie Cres G68 ..**61** C3
Barassie Ct G72 ...**140** C1
Barassie Dr PA11 ..**110** B3
Barassie Pl KA1 ...**227** C2
Barassie Prim Sch
KA10 ....**229** C3
Barassie St KA10 ..**229** C2
Barassie Sta KA10 ..**229** C3
Barassiebank La KA10 ..**229** C3
Barassiebank La KA10 ..**229** C3
Barbadoes Pl KA1 ..**227** C3
Barbadoes Rd KA1 ..**227** C3
Barbados Gn **5** G75 ..**159** A1
Barbae Pl G71 .....**141** C2
Barbana Rd G74 ...**158** C2
Barbegs Cres G65 ..**60** C2
Barberry Ave G53 ..**135** A1
Barberry Dr KA15 ..**171** A4
Barberry Gdns G53 ..**135** A1
Barberry Pl G53 ...**135** B1
Barbeth Gdns G67 ..**82** B3
Barbeth Pl
Cumbernauld G67 ..**82** A3
Irvine KA11 ......**220** A3
Barbeth Rd G67 ...**82** A3
Barbeth Way G67 ..**82** A3
Barbour Ave FK7 ..**7** B2
Barbour's Pk KA3 ..**211** C4
Barbreck Rd **7** G42 ..**116** C1
Barcaldine Ave G69 ..**80** A1
Barcapel Ave G77 ..**156** C4
Barcarp_ Flats G77 ..**156** C4
Barclaven Rd PA13 ..**89** C4
Barclay Ave PA5 ..**112** A1
Barclay Ct G60 ...**73** A3
Barclay Dr
Helensburgh G84 ..**16** B2
Kilmarnock KA3 ..**223** B1
Barclay Pl KA3 ...**195** B1
Barclay Rd ML1 ...**163** A3
Barclay Sq PA4 ...**94** A1
Barclay St Glasgow G21 ..**97** C3
Old Kilpatrick G60 ..**73** A3
Barclay Way PA12 ..**129** C3
Barcloy Pl ML6 ....**123** C1
Barcraigs Dr PA2 ..**133** C4
Bard Ave G13 .....**95** A4
Bardowie Ind Est G22 ..**97** B2
Bardrain Ave PA5 ..**112** B1
Bardrain Rd PA2 ..**133** B4
Bardrainney Ave PA14 ..**68** C4
Bardrill Dr G64 ...**77** C1
Bardykes Rd G72 ..**161** A4
Barefield St ML9 ..**185** A3
Barfillan Dr G52 ..**115** C3
Barfillan Rd G53 ..**115** A1
Bargany Ct G53 ...**115** A1
Bargany Pl G53 ...**115** A1
Bargany Rd G53 ...**115** A1
Bargaran Rd G53 ..**115** A4
Bargarran Prim Sch PA8 ..**72** C1
Bargarran Rd PA8 ..**72** C2

Bargarron Dr PA3 114 A4
Barge Ct G84 15 B3
Bargeddie Prim Sch G69 121 A3
Bargeddie St G33 98 B1
Bargeddie Sta G69 121 A2
Bargeny KA13 207 A1
Bargrennan Rd KA10 229 D3
Barhill La G65 59 C2
Barhill Rd PA8 73 A1
Barhill Terr G65 60 A2
Barholm Sq G33 99 B1
Barke Rd G67 62 A2
Barkin Ct FK1 42 A1
Barkly Terr 2 G75 180 B4
Barlae Ave G76 178 C4
Barlanark Ave G32 119 B3
Barlanark Cres G33 119 B4
Barlanark Dr G33 119 B4
Barlanark Pl
Glasgow G33 119 C4
Glasgow, Greenfield G32 119 A3
Barlanark Prim Sch G33 119 C3
Barlanark Rd G33 119 C4
Barlandfauld St G65 60 C4
Barleith Ct KA1 228 C3
Barleyhill FK4 40 A3
Barlia Dr G45 137 C2
Barlia St G45 137 C2
Barlia Terr G45 137 C2
Barloan Cres G82 50 A3
Barloan Pl G82 50 A3
Barloch Ave G62 55 A1
Barloch Rd G62 55 A1
Barloch St G22 97 B2
Barlogan Ave G52 115 C3
Barlogan Quadrant G52 115 C3
Barmore Ave ML8 202 A4
Barmouth Ave PA19 44 C3
Barmulloch Prim Sch G21 98 B2
Barmulloch Rd G21 98 A2
Barn Gn PA10 111 A2
Barn Rd FK8 7 A4
Barnard Gdns G64 78 A2
Barnardo's Lecropt Project FK9 1 C4
Barnbeth Rd G53 115 A1
Barncluith Bsns Ctr ML3 162 C2
Barncluith Rd ML3 162 C1
Barnego Rd FK6 21 B2
Barnes Rd G20 97 A3
Barnes St G78 134 A1
Barness Pl G33 119 A4
Barnett Cres KA21 216 C4
Barnett Ct KA21 216 C4
Barnett Path G72 161 B4
Barnflat St G73 118 A1
Barnford Cres KA7 239 A1
Barnhill Ct G77 156 B2
Barnhill Dr Hamilton ML3 161 B1
Newton Mearns G77 156 B2
Tullibody FK10 4 B1
Barnhill Rd G82 50 B2
Barnhill St PA15 46 B2
Barnhill Sta G21 98 A2
Barnkirk Ave G15 75 A2
Barns Cres KA7 238 C4
Barns Pk KA7 238 C4
Barns St Ayr KA7 238 C4
Clydebank G81 94 B4
Barns Street La KA7 238 C4
Barns Terr KA7 238 C4
Barns Terrace La KA7 238 C4
Barnscroft PA10 111 A2
Barnsdale Rd FK7 7 A2
Barnsford Ave PA4 93 A2
Barnsford Rd PA3,PA4 93 A2
Barnswood Pl 13 G71 141 A2
Barnton La FK1 42 A2
Barnton St Glasgow G32 118 C4
Stirling FK8 7 A4
Barnweil Rd
Kilmarnock KA1 227 C3
Prestwick KA9 236 B3
Barnweill Dr KA1 228 C3
Barnwell Rd FK9 2 B2
Barnwell Terr G51 115 C4
Barochan Cres PA3 113 A2
Barochan Pl G53 115 A2
Barochan Rd
Bellshill ML4 142 B3
Bishopton PA6 71 A1
Glasgow G53 115 A2
Houston PA6 91 A3
Barochan Way PA3 113 A2
Baron Ct ML3 163 A1
Baron Path G69 120 C3
Baron Rd PA3 114 A3
Baron St PA4 94 B1
Baron's Haugh Nature Reserve* ML1 163 C1
Baronald Dr G12 96 A3
Baronald Gate G12 96 A3
Baronald St G73 118 A1
Barone Dr G76 157 B4
Baronhall Dr G72 161 B4
Baronhill G67 62 A3
Barons Gate G71 140 C2
Barons Rd ML1 164 B1
Barons Twr ML1 164 A2
Baronscourt Dr PA1 112 C2
Baronscourt Gdns PA1 112 C2
Baronscourt Rd PA1 112 C2
Barony Ct
Ardrossan KA22 205 B1
Barony Ct *continued*
8 Glasgow G69 120 A3
Irvine KA11 219 C3
Barony Dr G69 120 A3
Barony Gdns G69 120 A3
Barony Glebe KA23 190 B3
Barony Pl G68 60 C1
Barony Rd KA9 236 B3
Barony Terr KA25 170 A4
Barony Wynd 9 G69 120 A3
Barr Ave G78 154 C4
Barr Cres G81 74 A3
Barr Farm Rd G65 60 C4
Barr Gr G71 141 A4
Barr Pl
Newton Mearns G77 156 B3
Paisley PA1 113 B2
Barr St Ardrossan KA22 205 B1
Glasgow G20 97 A2
Motherwell ML1 163 C4
Barr Terr G74 159 C1
Barr's Brae
Kilmacolm PA13 69 B1
Port Glasgow PA14 68 B4
Barra Ave
Coatbridge ML5 121 C2
Renfrew PA4 94 B1
Wishaw ML2 165 C3
Barra Cres Irvine KA11 220 B1
Old Kilpatrick G60 73 B3
Barra Dr ML6 123 C3
Barra Gdns G60 73 B3
Barra La KA11 220 B1
Barra Pl Coatbridge ML5 121 C2
Irvine KA11 220 B1
Stenhousemuir FK5 24 A2
Stevenston KA20 206 C1
Barra Rd G60 73 B3
Barra St G20 96 B4
Barra Wynd KA11 220 B1
Barrachnie Ave G69 120 A3
Barrachnie Cres G69 119 C3
Barrachnie Ct G69 119 C3
Barrachnie Dr G69 120 A3
Barrachnie Gr G69 120 A3
Barrachnie Pl 11 G69 120 A3
Barrachnie Rd G69 119 C3
Barrack St Glasgow G4 241 C1
Hamilton ML3 162 B2
Barraston Rd G64 57 A1
Barrbridge Rd G69 121 A2
Barrcraig Rd PA11 110 B4
Barrhead High Sch G78 134 B2
Barrhead Rd
Glasgow G53 135 B4
Newton Mearns G77 156 A3
Paisley PA2 114 A1
Barrhead Sta G78 134 A2
Barrhill Cres PA10 111 B2
Barrhill Ct G66 80 A4
Barrhill Rd Erskine PA8 93 A4
Gourock PA19 44 B4
Kirkintilloch G66 80 A4
Barrie Quadrant G81 74 A2
Barrie Rd
East Kilbride G74 160 B3
Glasgow G52 115 A4
Stenhousemuir FK5 23 C2
Barrie St ML1 163 C3
Barrie Terr KA22 205 B1
Barriedale Ave ML3 162 A2
Barrington Ave KA15 150 A1
Barrington Dr G4 96 C1
Barrisdale Rd
Glasgow G20 96 B4
Wishaw ML2 165 C3
Barrisdale Way G73 138 A2
Barrland Ct G46 136 B2
Barrland Dr G46 136 B2
Barrland St G41 117 A2
Barrmill Rd Beith KA15 171 B4
Burnhouse KA15 172 A1
Glasgow G43 136 A3
Barrochan Intc PA5 111 C2
Barrochan Rd PA3,PA5, PA6 111 C3
Barrowfield Prim Sch G40 118 A3
Barrowfield St
Coatbridge ML5 121 C2
Glasgow G40 118 A3
Barrpath G65 60 C4
Barrs Brae La PA14 47 B1
Barrs Cres G82 48 A4
Barrs Ct G82 26 A1
Barrs La ML8 187 C2
Barrs Terr G82 48 A4
Barrwood Pl G71 141 A4
Barrwood St G33 98 C1
Barry Gdns G72 161 B3
Barsail Prim Sch PA8 93 B4
Barscube Ave PA14 68 C4
Barscube Terr PA2 114 A1
Barshaw Dr PA1 114 A3
Barshaw Pl PA1 114 B3
Barshaw Rd G52 114 C3
Barskiven Rd PA1,PA3 112 C2
Barterholm Rd PA2 113 C1
Bartholomew St G40 118 A2
Bartie Gdns ML9 185 C1
Bartiebeith Rd G33 119 C4
Bartlands Pl G76 178 C2
Barton Ave G83 28 A4
Bartonhall Rd ML2 165 B1
Bartonholm Terr KA13 207 C1
Barty's Rd ML4 142 B3
Barwheys Dr KA6 237 C3
Barwood Hill G82 50 A3
Bassett Ave G13 95 A4
Bassett Cres G13 95 A4
Bastion Wynd FK8 7 A4
Bath La G2 240 B3
Bath Pl KA7 238 C4
Bath Sq KA22 216 B4
Bath St Glasgow G2 240 C3
Gourock PA19 44 C4
Kilmarnock KA3 222 C1
Bath Villas KA22 216 B4
Bathgate St G31 118 A3
Bathgo Ave PA1 114 C2
Bathurst Dr KA7 239 A1
Bathville Rd KA25 149 A1
Baton Rd ML7 146 B3
Batson St G42 117 A1
Batterflats Gdns FK7 6 C3
Batterflats Ho FK7 6 C3
Battery Park Ave PA16 45 A4
Battery Park Dr PA16 45 A4
Battismains ML11 215 B2
Battle Pl G42 136 C4
Battlefield Ave G42 137 A4
Battlefield Gdns G42 137 A4
Battlefield Prim Sch G42 136 C4
Battlefield Rd G42 137 A4
Bavelaw St G33 99 B1
Bawhirley Rd PA15 46 B2
Baxter Cres FK6 21 B1
Baxter La Alexandria G83 27 C4
Lanark ML11 215 A2
Baxter St Fallin FK7 8 B2
Greenock PA15 46 B2
Baxter's Wynd FK1 42 A2
Bay St PA14 47 B1
Bay View Rd PA19 44 C4
Bay Willow Ct G72 139 C2
Bayfield Ave G15 75 A2
Bayfield Terr G15 75 A2
Bayne St FK8 2 A1
Beach Dr KA12 218 C1
Beach Pk* KA12 224 A4
Beach Rd KA10 229 C3
Beacon Pl G33 118 C4
Beaconcroft FK9 2 B4
Beaconhurst Sch FK9 2 B3
Beaconsfield Rd G12 96 A3
Beagle Cres KA7 238 B2
Bean Row FK1 42 A2
Beansburn KA3 223 A2
Beanshields Rd ML8 201 C2
Beard Cres G69 100 C3
Beardmore Cotts PA4 93 C3
Beardmore Pl G81 73 C2
Beardmore St G81 73 C2
Beardmore Way G81 73 B1
Bearford Dr G52 115 A3
Bearhope St PA15 45 C3
Bearsden Acad G61 75 C3
Bearsden Bath Ho* G61 75 C3
Bearsden Prim Sch G61 75 C2
Bearsden Rd G13 95 C4
Bearsden St G61 75 C2
Bearside Rd FK7 7 A2
Beaton Ave FK7 7 B1
Beaton Rd Balloch G83 27 C4
Glasgow G41 116 C1
Beaton St ML9 184 C3
Beaton Terr KA12 219 B3
Beatrice Dr ML1 142 C3
Beatrice Gdns PA6 111 B4
Beatson Wynd G71 121 A1
Beattock St G31 118 B3
Beattock Wynd ML3 162 A2
Beatty Ave FK8 2 A1
Beatty Pl G84 17 A1
Beatty St G81 73 C2
Beauclerc St FK12 5 A4
Beaufield Gdns KA3 222 A4
Beaufort Ave G43 136 B3
Beaufort Dr Falkirk FK2 24 A2
Kirkintilloch G66 79 A4
Beaufort Gdns G64 77 C1
Beauly Cres Airdrie ML6 123 C3
Kilmacolm PA13 89 B4
Kilmarnock KA1 228 A3
Newton Mearns G77 157 A2
Wishaw ML2 165 A1
Beauly Ct FK1 42 B1
Beauly Dr PA2 112 C1
Beauly Pl Chryston G69 80 B1
Coatbridge ML5 122 A2
East Kilbride G74 159 B1
14 Glasgow G20 96 B3
Motherwell ML1 143 A3
Beauly Rd G69 120 A2
Beaumont Dr FK2 24 A1
Beaumont Gate 17 G12 96 B2
Beckfield Cres G33 98 B4
Beckfield Dr G33 98 B4
Beckfield Gate G33 98 B4
Beckfield Gr G33 98 B4
Beckfield Wlk G33 98 B4
Beckford La ML3 162 B3
Beckford Prim Sch ML3 162 B3
Beckford St ML3 162 B3
Beckford St Bsns Ctr ML3 162 B3
Beda Pl FK7 8 B3
Bedale Rd G69 119 C2
Bedcow View G66 79 C4
Bedford Ave G81 74 B1
Bedford Ct FK10 10 A3
Bedford La 6 G5 117 A3
Bedford Pl FK10 10 A3
Bedford St Glasgow G5 117 A3
Greenock PA16 45 B4
Bedlay Ct G69 81 A2
Bedlay Pl ML5 81 C1
Bedlay View G71 141 A4
Bedlay Wlk G69 81 A2
Bedlormie Dr EH48 107 B1
Beech Ave Bearsden G61 76 A4
Beith KA15 150 A1
Bridge of W PA11 90 B1
Elderslie PA5 112 B1
Glasgow G69 120 A3
Glasgow, Dumbreck G41 116 A2
Irvine KA12 219 B1
Kilmarnock KA1 227 B4
Larkhall ML9 185 B1
Motherwell ML1 143 A2
Newton Mearns G77 156 C2
Paisley PA2 114 A1
Plean FK7 12 B2
Quarter ML3 183 C2
Rutherglen, Cambuslang G72 138 C3
Rutherglen, High Burnside G73 138 B2
Beech Cres
Cambuslang G72 139 C2
Denny FK6 21 B2
Larbert FK5 41 B4
Motherwell ML1 143 B4
Newton Mearns G77 156 C2
Beech Ct ML5 121 C2
Beech Dr
Caldercruix ML6 104 C2
Clydebank G81 74 A3
Beech Gdns G69 120 A3
Beech Gr Ayr KA8 239 B4
East Kilbride G75 180 A3
Gartcosh G69 101 A3
Law ML8 186 C3
Rhu G84 15 B3
Wishaw ML2 165 B4
Beech La FK9 2 A2
Beech Pl Bishopbriggs G64 98 A4
Blantyre G72 161 C4
Gourock PA19 44 B3
Beech Rd
Bishopbriggs G64 98 A4
Johnstone PA5 111 B1
Kirkintilloch G66 79 B3
Motherwell ML1 143 B4
Beech Terr ML9 185 A1
Beechbank Ave ML6 102 C1
Beechburn Cres PA12 129 B2
Beeches Ave G81 73 C3
Beeches Rd G81 73 C3
Beeches Terr G81 74 A3
Beeches The
Brookfield PA5 111 B3
Houston PA6 91 B1
Lanark ML11 215 A1
Newton Mearns G77 156 C3
Beechfield Dr ML8 202 A4
Beechfield Rd KA15 170 C4
Beechgrove G69 80 C1
Beechgrove Ave G71 141 B4
Beechgrove Pl G84 25 B4
Beechgrove Quadrant ML1 143 A3
Beechgrove St G40 118 A1
Beechlands Ave G44 136 C1
Beechlands Dr G76 157 B3
Beechmount Ct ML7 147 A1
Beechmount Rd G66 79 B2
Beechtree Terr G66 58 B3
Beechwood Alloa FK10 5 B1
Kilwinning KA13 207 B3
Larkhall ML9 185 A3
Wishaw ML2 164 B1
Beechwood Ave
Clarkston G76 157 B3
Hamilton ML3 183 A4
Langbank PA14 70 B4
Rutherglen G73 138 B3
Beechwood Cres ML2 165 B1
Beechwood Ct
Bearsden G61 75 C2
Cumbernauld G67 61 C1
Cumbernauld G67 82 C4
Beechwood Dr
Bonhill G83 28 A1
Coatbridge ML5 122 B3
Glasgow G11 95 C2
Renfrew PA4 94 B1
Beechwood Gdns
Bellshill ML4 142 B2
Moodiesburn G69 80 C1
Stirling FK8 7 A3
Beechwood Gr G78 134 B1
Beechwood La G61 75 C2
Beechwood Paddock KA10 230 A2
Beechwood Pl
Bellshill ML4 142 B2
Glasgow G11 95 C2
Beechwood Rd G67 82 C4
Beechworth Dr ML1 143 B1
Beecroft Pl G72 140 C1
Begg Ave FK1 41 C2
Beggs Terr KA22 205 B2
Beil Dr G13 94 C4
Beith Dr ML6 123 A2
Beith Prim Sch KA15 171 A4
Beith Rd Dalry KA24 191 C4
Glengarnock KA14 170 B3
Greenock PA16 45 C1
Johnstone PA5 111 C1
Beith St G11 96 A1
Belford Ct G77 156 B1
Belford Gr G77 156 B1
Belgowan St ML4 141 C4
Belgrave La G12 96 C2
Belgrave St ML4 141 C3
Belhaven Ct G77 156 B1
Belhaven Pk G69 100 B4
Belhaven Pl G77 156 B1
Belhaven Rd
Hamilton ML3 161 C2
Wishaw ML2 165 A2
Belhaven St PA14 47 A1
Belhaven Terr
40 Glasgow G12 96 B2
Wishaw ML2 165 A2
Belhaven Terr W 36 G12 96 B2
Belhaven Terrace La 39 G12 96 B2
Belhaven Terrace West La 37 G12 96 B2
Bell Coll of Technology ML3 162 B2
Bell Cres KA12 219 B3
Bell Dr ML3 161 B2
Bell Gn E G75 180 C4
Bell Gn W G75 180 C4
Bell St Airdrie ML6 122 C4
Bellshill ML4 142 A4
Clydebank G81 94 B4
Glasgow G1 241 B1
Greenock PA15 46 C1
Renfrew PA4 94 B2
Wishaw ML2 165 A2
Bell Trees Rd PA9 130 B1
Bell View Ct PA4 94 B2
Bell's Wynd Falkirk FK1 42 A2
Lanark ML11 215 B3
Bellahouston Acad G41 116 B3
Bellahouston Acad Annexe G51 116 B3
Bellahouston Dr G52 115 C2
Bellahouston Prim Sch G51 116 B3
Bellairs Pl G72 140 B1
Bellard Rd KA23 190 B2
Bellard Wlk KA23 190 B2
Bellas Pl ML6 104 A1
Bellcraig Ct G76 158 A3
Belleaire Dr PA16 45 B4
Bellefield Rd ML11 215 A3
Belleisle Ave G71 140 C4
Belleisle Cl KA13 207 B2
Belleisle Cres PA11 110 B3
Belleisle Dr G68 61 C2
Belleisle Gdns G68 61 C2
Belleisle Gr G68 61 C2
Belleisle Pk* KA7 238 C2
Belleisle Pl Gourock PA19 44 A3
Kilmarnock KA1 227 C2
Belleisle St G42 117 A1
Bellesleyhill Ave KA8 236 A2
Bellesleyhill Rd KA8 236 A2
Bellevale Quadrant KA7 238 C3
Bellevue Ave G66 79 A4
Bellevue Cres Ayr KA7 238 C4
Prestwick KA9 236 B4
Bellevue Gdns KA1 222 B1
Bellevue La KA7 238 C4
Bellevue Rd Alloa FK10 9 C3
Ayr KA7 238 C4
Kilmarnock KA1 222 B1
Kirkintilloch G66 79 A4
Prestwick KA9 236 B4
Bellevue St Ayr KA7 238 C4
Falkirk FK1 42 B2
Bellfield Ave KA1 228 B3
Bellfield Cres G78 134 A2
Bellfield Ct
Barrhead G78 134 A2
Hurlford KA1 228 B3
Bellfield Dr ML2 165 B1
Bellfield Intc KA1 228 B3
Bellfield La KA9 236 A4
Bellfield Prim Sch KA1 228 A2
Bellfield Rd
Bannockburn FK7 7 C1
Kirkintilloch G66 79 A4
Stirling FK8 7 A3
Bellfield St G31 118 A3
Bellflower Ave G53 135 B2
Bellflower Ct G74 159 B2
Bellflower Gdns G53 135 B2
Bellflower Gr G74 159 B2
Bellflower Pl G53 135 B2
Bellgrove St G31 117 C3
Bellgrove Sta G31 117 C3
Bellisle Terr ML3 183 A4
Bellrock Ave KA9 236 A3
Bellrock Cres G33 119 A4
Bellrock Ct G33 119 A4
Bellrock Path G33 119 A4
Bellrock Rd KA8 236 A2
Bellrock St G33 119 A4
Bellscroft Ave G73 137 C4
Bellsdyke Hospl FK5 23 B3
Bellsdyke Rd Airdrie ML6 123 A3
Falkirk FK2 24 B3
Stenhousemuir FK5 23 B2
Bellsdyke Rdbt FK5 23 A2
Bellsfield Dr G72 161 C3
Bellshaugh Gdns G12 96 B3
Bellshaugh La G12 96 B3
Bellshaugh Pl 2 G12 96 B3
Bellshaugh Rd G12 96 B2
Bellshill Acad ML4 142 A3
Bellshill Ind Est ML4 141 C3

Bellshill Maternity Hospl
ML4 ....142 A4
Bellshill Rd
Bellshill G71,ML4 ....141 B1
Bothwell G71 ....141 A1
Motherwell ML1,ML4 ....142 B1
Bellshill Sta ML4 ....142 A3
Bellside Rd
Chapelhall ML6 ....123 C1
Cleland ML1 ....144 A4
Morningside ML1 ....144 A4
Bellsland Dr KA1 ......227 C3
Bellsland Gr KA1 ......227 C3
Bellsland Pl KA1 ......228 A4
Bellsmeadow Rd FK1 ..42 B2
Bellsmyre Ave G82 ....50 A3
Belltree Ave KA3 ......211 B4
Belltrees Cres PA3 ....13 A2
Belltrees Rd PA12 ....150 B2
Bellvale Ave KA7 ......239 A3
Bellvue Cres ML4 ......141 C2
Bellvue Way ML5 ......122 B2
Bellwood St G41 ......136 C4
Bellziehill Rd ML4 ....141 C3
Belman's Cl KA15 ......150 A1
Belmont Ave G42 ......137 A3
Belmont Acad KA7 ....239 A3
Belmont Ave Ayr KA7 ..239 A3
Bonnybridge FK4 ....39 B3
Shieldhill FK1 ....66 C4
Uddingston G71 ....140 C4
Belmont Cres Ayr KA7 .239 A3
Glasgow G12 ....96 C2
Kilmaurs KA3 ....222 A4
Belmont Ct Kilmaurs KA3 .222 B4
7 Kirkintilloch G66 ....79 B4
Belmont Dr Ayr KA7 ....239 A3
Barrhead G78 ....134 B1
East Kilbride G75 ....180 A4
Glasgow G46 ....136 A2
Rutherglen G73 ....138 A4
Shotts ML7 ....147 A1
Belmont House Sch
G77 ....157 A3
Belmont La G12 ....96 C2
Belmont Pl E KA7 ......239 A3
Belmont Pl W KA7 ....239 A3
Belmont Rd Ayr KA7 ...239 A3
Cambuslang G72 ....138 C2
Glasgow G21 ....97 C3
Kilmacolm PA13 ....89 B4
Paisley PA3 ....114 A3
Belmont St Clydebank G81 .74 A1
Coatbridge ML5 ....101 B1
Falkirk FK1 ....42 B2
Glasgow G12,G20 ....96 C2
Kilsyth G65 ....36 B1
Wishaw ML2 ....186 A3
Belses Dr G52 ....115 B3
Belses Gdns G52 ......115 B3
Belstane Mews ML8 ...188 A2
Belstane Pk ML8 ......187 C2
Belstane Pl 8 G71 ....141 C2
Belstane Rd Carluke ML8 .188 A2
Cumbernauld G67 ....82 C3
Belsyde Ave G15 ......75 A1
Beltane St Glasgow G3 .240 A3
Wishaw ML2 ....165 A1
Beltrees Ave G53 ......115 A1
Beltrees Cres G53 ....115 A1
Beltrees Rd G53 ......115 A1
Belvidere Cres
Bellshill ML4 ....142 A2
Bishopbriggs G64 ....78 A1
Belvidere Prim Sch
ML4 ....142 A2
Belvidere Rd ML4 ......142 A2
Belvidere Terr KA8 ....236 A1
Belville Ave PA15 ......46 B2
Belville Dr PA15 ....46 A2
Belville St PA15 ....46 A2
Belvoir Pl G72 ....161 B4
Bemersyde G64 ....78 B1
Bemersyde Ave G43 ..136 A3
Bemersyde Pl ML9 ....185 A1
Bemersyde Rd PA2 ....132 C4
Ben Aigan Pl G53 ......135 B2
Ben Alder Dr PA2 ......114 B1
Ben Bouie Dr G84 ......16 C5
Ben Buie Way PA2 ....114 B1
Ben Donich Pl G53 ....135 B2
Ben Edra Pl G53 ....135 B2
Ben Garrisdale Pl G53 .135 B2
Ben Glas Pl G53 ....135 B2
Ben Hope Ave PA2 ....114 B1
Ben Laga Pl G53 ....135 B2
Ben Lawers Dr
Cumbernauld G68 ....61 A1
Paisley PA2 ....114 B1
Ben Ledi Ave PA2 ......114 B1
Ben Ledi Cres G68 ....61 A1
Ben Lomond Dr FK9 ...2 A2
Ben Lomond Wlk G83 .27 B4
Ben Loyal Ave PA2 ....114 B1
Ben Lui Dr PA2 ....114 B1
Ben Lui Pl
Cumbernauld G68 ....61 A1
Glasgow G53 ....135 B2
Ben Macdui Gdns G53 .135 B2
Ben More Dr
Cumbernauld G68 ....61 A1
Paisley PA2 ....114 B1
Ben Nevis Rd PA2 ......114 B1
Ben Nevis Way G68 ...61 A1
Ben Oss Pl G53 ....135 B2

Ben Uird Pl G53 ....135 B2
Ben Vane Ave PA2 ....114 B1
Ben Venue Rd G68 ....61 A1
Ben Venue Way PA2 ..114 B1
Ben Vorlich Dr G53 ....135 B2
Ben Vorlich Pl G53 ....135 B2
Ben Wyvis Dr PA2 ....114 B1
Benalder St G11 ....96 B1
Benarty Gdns G64 ....78 A1
Benbain Pl KA11 ......220 A3
Benbecula G74 ....160 B1
Benbecula Rd KA3 ....223 A3
Benbow Rd G81 ....73 C1
Bencleuch Pl FK1 ......220 A2
Bencloich Ave G66 ....57 C4
Bencloich Cres G66 ...33 C1
Bencloich Rd G66 ......57 C4
Benclutha PA14 ....47 C1
Bencroft Dr G44 ......137 C2
Bendigo Pl ML11 ......215 A2
Benford Ave ML1 ......143 B2
Benford Knowe ML1 ..143 C2
Bengairn St G31 ......118 B4
Bengal Pl G43 ....136 B4
Bengal St G43 ....136 B4
Benhar Pl G33 ....118 C4
Benhar Prim Sch ML7 .127 B3
Benhar Rd Harthill ML7 .126 C1
Shotts ML7 ....147 A3
Benholm St G32 ......118 C2
Benmore KA9 ....236 B3
Benmore La PA16 ......44 C2
Benmore Twr G22 ....138 C2
Bennan Ho KA9 ....236 A3
Bennan Pl G75 ....180 B2
Bennan Sq G42 ....117 B1
Bennie Terr FK1 ....86 A4
Bennoch Pl KA9 ....236 B3
Benny Lynch Ct G5 ...117 B3
Benrig Ave KA3 ....220 A4
Bensley Ave KA11 ....219 C3
Bensley Rise KA11 ....219 C3
Benson St ML5 ....122 A2
Benston Pl PA5 ....111 C1
Benston Rd PA5 ....111 C1
Bent Cres G71 ....141 B3
Bent Rd Chapelhall ML6 .123 B2
Hamilton ML3 ....162 B2
Bentfield Ave KA7 ....238 C3
Bentfield Dr KA9 ......236 A3
Bentfoot Rd ML2 ......186 B4
Benthall St G5 ....117 B2
Bentheads FK7 ....11 C4
Bentinck Cres KA10 ...229 D1
Bentinck Dr KA10 ....229 C1
Bentinck St Glasgow G3 .95 C1
Greenock PA16 ....45 A4
Kilmarnock KA1 ....227 C4
Bents Rd G69 ....120 A3
Benty's La ML8 ....201 C4
Benvie Gdns G64 ......78 A1
Benview FK7 ....7 B1
Benview Ave PA14 ....68 C4
Benview Rd
Clarkston G76 ....157 C4
Glasgow PA14 ....68 C4
Benview St G20 ....96 C2
Benview Terr
Fishcross FK10 ....5 C2
Paisley PA2 ....114 A1
Benvue Rd G66 ....57 C4
Berchem Pl KA21 ....216 C4
Bereland Ave KA9 ....236 B4
Berelands Cres G73 ...137 C4
Berelands Gdns KA9 ..233 B1
Berelands Pl G73 ......137 C4
Berelands Rd KA9 ....233 B1
Berenice Pl G82 ....50 B1
Beresford Ave G14 ...95 C2
Beresford Ct KA7 ......238 C4
Beresford Dr KA11 ....219 C3
Beresford La KA7 ......238 C4
Beresford Terr KA7 ...238 C4
Berkeley St Glasgow G3 .240 A3
Stirling FK7 ....7 A2
Berkeley Terrace La G3 .240 A3
Berkley Dr G72 ....140 B1
Berl Ave PA6 ....111 B4
Bernadette Cres ML1 .143 B1
Bernadette St ML1 ....143 B1
Bernard Path G40 ....118 A2
Bernard St G40 ....118 A2
Bernard Terr G40 ......118 A2
Bernard's Wynd ML11 .215 A2
Berneray St G22 ......97 B4
Berridale Ave G44 ....137 A3
Berridale Rd KA10 ....229 C4
Berriedale G75 ....179 C4
Berriedale Ave G69 ...120 A2
Berriedale Quadrant
ML2 ....165 A3
Berry Dr KA12 ....219 C2
Berryburn Rd G21 ....98 B2
Berryhill Ave KA11 ...220 A3
Berryhill Dr G46 ......136 A1
Berryhill Pl ML7 ....147 A1
Berryhill Prim Sch ML2 .164 C2
Berryhill Rd
Cumbernauld G67 ....67 A1
Glasgow G46 ....136 A1
Berryknowe G66 ......80 A4
Berryknowe Ave G69 .100 B4
Berryknowes Ave G52 .115 B3
Berryknowes La G52 ..115 B3
Berryknowes Rd G52 ..115 B3
Berryyards Rd PA15 ..45 C2
Bertram Dr ML7 ....125 B1

Bertram Pl ML7 ....146 B3
Bertram St Glasgow G41 .116 C1
Hamilton ML3 ....162 A3
Harthill ML7 ....127 B3
1 Larkhall ML9 ....185 B1
Shotts ML7 ....146 C3
Bervie St G51 ....116 A3
Berwick Cres
Airdrie ML6 ....122 C3
Linwood PA3 ....111 C4
Berwick Dr Glasgow G52 .115 A2
Rutherglen G73 ....138 B3
Berwick Pl
Coatbridge ML5 ....122 A2
East Kilbride G74 ....160 B2
Greenock PA16 ....44 B2
Berwick Rd
Coatbridge ML5 ....122 A2
Port Glasgow PA14 ......47 B1
Berwick St
Coatbridge ML5 ....122 A2
Hamilton ML3 ....162 A3
Bessemer Dr G75 ....181 A3
Beta Ctr G81 ....94 B4
Bethal La G75 ....180 A2
Betula Dr G81 ....74 A3
Bevan Dr FK12 ....5 B4
Bevan Gdns KA13 ....207 C2
Bevan Gr PA5 ....111 C1
Beveridge Terr ML4 ..142 B2
Beverley Rd G43 ......136 B3
Bevin Ave G81 ....74 B1
Bideford Cres G32 ....119 B2
Bield The ML2 ....165 B1
Big Idea (Inventor Ctr) The*
KA12 ....6 A2
Big Land 2 G74 ....159 C1
Biggar Rd
Chapelhall ML6 ....123 C1
Chapelhall, Biggar Road
ML6 ....143 C4
Biggar St G31 ....118 A3
Biggart Hospl KA9 ...236 B4
Bigholm Pl KA15 ......150 B1
Bigholm Rd KA15 ....150 B1
Bigton St G33 ....99 A1
Bilby Terr KA12 ....219 B3
Billings Rd ML1 ....163 A3
Bilsland Ct G20 ....97 A3
Bilsland Dr G20 ....97 A3
Bilsland Pl G82 ....27 B1
Bimson Pl KA12 ......219 A1
Binend Rd G53 ....135 B4
Binnie La PA19 ....4 C1
Binnie Pl Glasgow G40 .117 C3
Skinflats FK2 ....24 C1
Binniehill Rd
Cumbernauld G68 ....61 B1
Slamannan FK1 ....85 C2
Binns Rd G33 ....99 B1
Birch Ave Clarkston G76 .157 C3
Stirling FK8 ....6 C3
Birch Brae ML3 ....162 C1
Birch Cotts G84 ......16 B1
Birch Cres Clarkston G76 .157 C3
Johnstone PA5 ....111 B1
Birch Ct ML5 ....121 C2
Birch Dr Cambuslang G72 .139 B3
Kirkintilloch G66 ....79 B3
Birch Dr Larkhall ML9 ...185 A3
Uddingston G71 ....141 B4
Birch Knowe G64 ......98 A4
Birch Pl Blantyre G72 ..161 B4
Cambuslang G72 ....139 C2
Kilmarnock KA1 ....227 B4
Birch Quadrant ML6 ..122 B3
Birchfield G72 ....161 C3
Birchfield Dr G14 ......95 A2
Birchfield St ML1 ......161 C3
Birdston Rd Glasgow G21 .98 B3
Milton of Campsie G66 .58 B2
Birgidale Pl G45 ......137 B1
Birgidale Rd G45 ......137 B1
Birkbeck Ct G4 ....240 A4
Birkdale G74 ....159 B2
Birkdale Cl KA13 ......207 B2
Birkdale Cres G69 ....120 C1
Birkdale Wood G68 ...62 A3
Birken Rd G66 ....80 A3
Birkenburn Rd G67 ...62 C3
Birkenshaw Rd G69,ML5 .81 C1
Birkenshaw St G31 ...118 A4

Birkenshaw Way PA3 ..113 C4
Birkfield Loan ML8 ....188 B1
Birkfield Pl ML8 ....188 B1
Birkhall Ave
Glasgow G52 ....115 A2
Inchinnan PA4 ....93 B4
Birkhall Dr G61 ....75 C1
Birkhall Ave G64 ......78 A1
Birkhill Gdns G64 ....78 A1
Birkhill Rd
Crossford ML8,ML11 ...201 B1
Hamilton ML3 ....183 B4
Stirling FK7 ....6 C3
Birkmyre Ave PA14 ...47 A2
Birkmyre Rd G51 ......115 C3
Birks Cl ML6 ....186 C3
Birks Hill KA11 ....220 A2
Birks Rd Larkhall ML9 .199 A4
Birkshaw Brae ML2 ..186 A4
Birkshaw Pl ML2 ......186 A4
Birkshaw Twr ML2 ...185 C4
Birkwood Pl G77 ......156 B1
Birkwood St G40 ......118 A1
Birmingham Rd PA4 ..94 A1
Birnam Ave G64 ......78 A1
Birnam Cres G61 ......76 A3
Birnam Ct FK2 ....24 B1
Birnam Gdns G64 ....78 A1
Birnam Rd Hamilton ML3 .161 C2
Newton Mearns G77 ....157 A2
Birnam Rd G31 ....118 B2
Birnie Ct G21 ....98 B2
Birnie Rd G21 ....98 B2
Birnie Well Rd FK1 ....84 B4
Birniehill Rd ML1,ML7 .145 A3
Birniehill Rdbt G74 ...181 A4
Birnock Ave PA4 ......94 C1
Birny Hill Ct G81 ......74 A4
Birrell Rd G62 ....54 B3
Birrens Rd ML1 ....163 B4
Birsay Rd G22 ....97 B4
Bishop Gdns
Bishopbriggs G64 ....77 C1
Hamilton ML3 ....183 C4
Bishop La G2 ....240 B2
Bishopbriggs High Sch
G64 ....78 A1
Bishopbriggs Ind Est
G21 ....98 A4
Bishopbriggs Sta G64 .78 A1
Bishopdale G74 ......159 B2
Bishoploch Prim Sch
G34 ....100 B1
Bishopmill Pl G21 ....98 B2
Bishopmill Rd G21 ....98 B2
Bishops Gate G74 ....158 B2
Bishops Pk G74 ......158 A2
Bishopsgate Dr G21 ..97 C4
Bishopsgate Gdns G21 .97 C4
Bishopsgate Pl 10 G21 .97 C4
Bishopsgate Rd G21 ..97 C4
Bishopton Rd PA7 ....72 A2
Bishopton Sta PA7 ...72 A1
Bissett Cres G81 ......73 C3
Black O' Hill Rdbt G68 .61 A4
Black St Airdrie ML6 ..100 A1
Glasgow G4 ....241 B4
Blackadder Pl G75 ....179 B4
Blackbog Rd ML6 ......82 C1
Blackbraes Rd
California FK1 ....66 C2
East Kilbride G74 ....160 A2
Blackburn Cres
Kirkintilloch G66 ....80 A4
Blackburn Dr KA7 ....238 C3
Blackburn Pl KA7 ....238 C3
Blackburn Rd KA7 ....238 C3
Blackburn Sq G78 ...134 A2
Blackbyres Ct G78 ...134 B2
Blackbyres Rd G78 ...134 B3
Blackcraig Ave G15 ..75 A2
Blackcroft Ave ML6 ..123 C3
Blackcroft Gdns G32 .119 B2
Blackcroft Rd G32 ....119 B2
Blackdyke Rd G66 ....79 C4
Blackfarm Rd G77 ....156 C2
Blackfaulds Dr KA3 ...213 A2
Blackfaulds Gdns KA3 .213 A2
Blackfaulds Rd G73 ..137 B4
Blackfaulds St G73 ...137 B4
Blackford Rd PA2 ....114 A2
Blackfriars Ct KA7 ....238 C4
Blackfriars Prim Sch
G15 ....75 A1
Blackfriars St G1 ......241 B2
Blackfriars Wlk KA7 ..238 C4
Blackhall La PA1 ......114 A2
Blackhall St Paisley PA1 .114 A2
Shotts ML7 ....147 A1
Blackhill Pl G33 ....98 B1
Blackhill Rd
Blackridge EH48 ....107 C2
Blackhill St KA7 ......239 A3
Blackhill View ML8 ...187 A2
Blackhouse Ave G77 .156 C2
Blackhouse Gdns G77 .156 C2
Blackhouse Rd KA8 ..239 B4

Blackhouse Rd G77 ...156 C2
Blacklands Ave KA13 .207 C3
Blacklands Cres KA13 .207 C1
Blacklands Pl G66 ....79 C2
Blacklands Prim Sch
KA13 ....207 B1
Blacklands Rd G74 ...159 B1
Blacklaw Dr KA3 ......223 A4
Blacklaw La 1 PA3 ...113 C3
Blacklaw Prim Sch G74 .160 A1
Blackmill Cres FK2 ...24 A2
Blackmoor Pl ML1 ....143 A2
Blackmuir Ave ML4 ..142 A2
Blackmuir Pl FK10 ....4 B2
Blackness St ML5 ....122 A2
Blackridge Com Mus*
EH48 ....107 B2
Blackridge Prim Sch
EH48 ....107 B2
Blackshaw Dr KA23 ..190 B3
Blackstone Ave G53 ..115 B4
Blackstone Cres G53 ..115 B3
Blackstone Rd PA3 ...113 A4
Blackstoun Ave PA3 ..113 A3
Blackstoun Oval PA3 .113 A3
Blackstoun Rd PA3 ...113 A3
Blacksyke Ave KA1 ..227 C2
Blackthorn Ave
Beith KA15 ....150 A1
Kirkintilloch G66 ....79 A3
Blackthorn Gr G66 ....79 A3
Blackthorn Rd
Cumbernauld G67 ....62 C2
Uddingston G71 ....141 B4
Blackthorn Rdbt G67 ..62 C2
Blackthorn St G22 ....97 C3
Blacktongue Farm Rd
ML6 ....83 C1
Blackwood G75 ....180 B3
Blackwood Ave
Kilmarnock KA1 ....227 C3
Linwood PA3 ....112 A3
Newton Mearns G77 ...156 C2
Blackwood Gdns ML1 .142 B3
Blackwood Rd
Cumbernauld G68 ....60 C1
Milngavie G62 ....54 C2
Blackwood Rdbt G68 ..60 C1
Blackwood St
Barrhead G78 ....134 A1
Glasgow G13 ....95 C4
Blackwood Terr PA5 ..131 B4
Blackwood West Rdbt
G68 ....60 B1
Blackwoods Cres
Bellshill ML4 ....142 B2
Moodiesburn G69 ....80 C1
Bladda La PA1 ....113 C2
Blades Ct G69 ....101 B3
Bladnoch Dr G15 ......75 B1
Blaefaulds Cres FK6 ..39 B4
Blaeloch Ave G45 ....137 B1
Blaeloch Dr G45 ......137 B1
Blaeloch Terr G45 ....137 B1
Blair Atholl Dr 2 ML9 .185 B1
Blair Ave KA11 ....228 C3
Blair Cres Glasgow G69 .120 A2
Hurlford KA1 ....228 C3
Blair Dr G66 ....58 B3
Blair Gdns Gourock PA19 .43 C3
Newton Mearns G77 ....156 A4
Torrance G64 ....57 A1
Blair Ho G67 ....62 A2
Blair Linn View G67 ..63 A3
Blair Path 8 ML1 ......163 C3
Blair Rd Coatbridge ML5 .122 A2
Crossford ML8 ....201 A1
Dalry KA24 ....191 C4
Hurlford KA1 ....228 C3
Kilwinning KA13 ....207 C3
Paisley PA1 ....114 C2
Blair St Glasgow G32 ..118 C3
Kilmarnock KA3 ....222 C1
Blair Terr FK5 ....24 A2
Blairatholl Wynd KA13 .207 B3
Blairatholl Ave G11 ..96 A2
Blairatholl Cres G77 ..157 A2
Blairatholl Gdns G77 ..157 A2
Blairatholl Gdns 11 G11 .96 A2
Blairbeth Dr G44 ......137 A4
Blairbeth Pl ML9 ......43 C3
Blairbeth Rd G73 ......138 A3
Blairbeth Terr G73 ...138 B3
Blairbuie Dr G20 ......96 B3
Blairdardie Rd
G15 ....75 A1
Blairdenan Ave G69 ..81 A2
Blairdenon Cres FK1 ..41 C2
Blairdenon Dr Alloa FK10 .5 A1
Cumbernauld G68 ....61 A2
Blairdenon Way KA11 .220 A1
Blairgowrie Rd G52 ..115 B2
Blairgrove Ct ML5 ....121 C3
Blairhall Ave G66 ......80 A3
Blairhill Ave ML5 ......80 A3
Blairhill Pl ML5 ....121 C4
Blairhill St ML5 ....121 C4
Blairholm Dr ML4 ....142 B2
Blairlands Dr KA24 ...191 C4
Blairlinn Ind Est G67 .82 C3

Blairlinn G67 ....82 C3
Blairlogie St G33 ......99 A1
Blairmore Ave PA1 ...114 B3
Blairmore Cres PA15 ...46 B1
Blairmore Pl PA19 .....43 C3
Blairmore Rd PA15 .....46 B1
Blairmuckhole & Forrestdyke
  Rd ML7 ....126 C2
Blairpark Ave G71 ....141 A1
Blairston Ave G71 ....141 A1
Blairston Gdns G71 ...141 A1
Blairtum Dr G73 ......138 A3
Blairtummock Prim Sch
  G34 ....120 A4
Blairtummock Rd
  Glasgow G33 ......119 B4
  Glasgow, Queenslie G33 ..119 C4
Blake Rd G67 ....62 A1
Blakely Rd KA21 ......217 A4
Blane Ave G63 ....31 A2
Blane Cres G63 ....31 A2
Blane Dr G62 ....31 A2
Blane Pl G63 ....31 A2
Blane St ML5 ....122 A4
Blanefield Ave KA9 ...236 A3
Blanefield Gdns G13 ...95 A3
Blaneview G69 ....99 B2
Blantyre Cres G81 .....73 C4
Blantyre Dr PA11 ......73 A2
Blantyre Dr PA7 ....72 A2
Blantyre Farm Rd G71,
  G72 ....140 B3
Blantyre Gdns G68 ....60 C1
Blantyre High Sch G72 161 B4
Blantyre Ferme Rd G72 161 C3
Blantyre Mill Rd G71 ..141 A1
Blantyre Rd G71 .....141 A1
Blantyre St G3 ....96 B1
Blantyre Sta G72 ....161 C4
Blaven Ct G69 ......120 B2
Blaven Head KA11 ....220 A2
Blawarthill Hospl G14 ..95 A3
Blawarthill St G14 .....94 C3
Blaxfield Row ML11 ...214 C1
Bleachfield Falkirk FK2 ..42 A3
  Milngavie G62 ....55 A2
Bleeze Rd KA24 ......191 A4

Blenheim Ave
  East Kilbride G75 ...180 B4
  Stepps G33 ....99 C3
Blenheim Ct
  Carluke ML8 ....188 A1
  Kilsyth G65 ....36 B1
  Stepps G33 ....99 B3
Blenheim Pl FK5 ....23 B3
Blindwells FK12 ....4 C3
Blinkbonnie Terr FK1 ...86 A3
Blinkbonny Rd FK1 ....141 A2
Blinny Ct ML7 ....147 A2
Blochairn Rd G21 ......98 A1
Block 13 G61 ....75 C2
Bloomgate ML11 .....215 A2
Bluebell Gdns
  Glasgow G45 ....138 C3
  Motherwell ML1 .....142 B1
Bluebell Way
  Airdrie ML6 ....102 C1
  Carluke ML8 ....201 C4
  Lennoxtown G66 .....57 C4
Bluebell Wlk ML1 ....143 A2
Blueknowes Rd ML8 ..186 C3
Bluevale St G31 ......118 A3
Blyth Rd G33 ....119 C3
Blythe Pl G33 ....119 B3
Blythswood Ave PA4 ..94 B2
Blythswood Dr PA3 ...113 C3
Blythswood Ho Hospl
  PA4 ....94 B2
Blythswood Ind Est PA4 94 A2
Blythswood Rd PA4 ....94 B2
Blythswood Sq G2 ...240 B3
Blythswood St G2 ....240 B3
Bo'ness Rd
  Chapelhall ML6 .....123 B1
  Motherwell ML1 .....143 B4
Boardwalk The G75 ...181 A4
Boat Vennel KA7 .....235 C1
Bobbin Wynd FK7 ......6 B3
Bobbins Gate PA1 ....113 A2
Boclair Acad G61 ......76 B2
Boclair Ave G61 ....75 C2
Boclair Cres
  Bearsden G61 ....76 A2
  Bishopbriggs G64 .....78 A1
Boclair Rd
  Bearsden G23,G61 ....76 B3
  Bishopbriggs G64 .....78 A3
Boclair St G13 ....95 C4
Bodden Sq ML1 ......143 C4
Boden Ind Est G40 ...118 A2
Boden Quadrant ML1 .142 B1
Boden St G40 ....118 A2
Bodesbeck Ct KA11 ..220 A2
Bodmin Gdns G69 .....80 C2
Bog Rd Banknock FK4 ..38 C2
  Laurieston PA3 ....42 C2
Bog Rbt FK2 ....42 C2
Bog Road Ind Est FK2 ..42 C2
Bogany Terr G45 .....137 C1
Bogbain Rd G34 .....120 A4
Bogend Rd
  Bannockburn FK7 .....11 C4
  Larbert FK2 ....23 A4
  Torwood FK5 ....22 C4
Bogfoot Rd ML7 ......125 A1
Boggknowe G71 ....140 B4
Boghall Rd Carluke ML8 .202 A4

Boghall Rd continued
  Glasgow G69 ......120 A2
  Stonehouse ML9 .....198 C1
Boghall St Glasgow G33 ..99 A1
Boghead KA15 ....171 A4
Boghead Rd 50 A2
Boghead Rd
  Dumbarton G82 ......50 A2
  Glasgow G21 ....98 A2
  Kirkintilloch G66 .....79 A3
Bogie St PA15 ....46 A2
Bogle St PA15 ....46 A2
Boglemart St KA20 ..217 B4
Bogleshole Rd G72 ..138 C4
Boglestone Ave PA14 ..68 C4
Boglestone Prim Sch
  PA14 ....68 C4
Bogmoor Pl G51 ......95 B1
Bogmoor Rd G51 .....114 A2
Bogside Rd Ashgill ML9 199 C4
  Kilsyth G65 ....60 A2
  Millerston G33 ....99 A3
  Port Glasgow PA14 ...68 C4
Bogside St G40 ......118 A2
Bogston La PA15 ......46 C1
Bogstonhill Rd PA6 ...91 B1
Bogton Ave G44 .....136 C2
Bogton Avenue La G44 136 C2
Bohun Ct FK7 ....7 B2
Boleyn Ct ML2 ....166 A3
Boleyn Rd G41 ....116 C1
Bolingbroke G74 .....160 A3
Bolivar Terr G42 .....137 B3
Bolton Dr G42 ....137 A4
Bolton Terr G66 ....57 C4
Boman Rd ML2 ....195 B1
Bon Accord Cres ML7 .146 C3
Bon Accord Rd G76 ..157 C3
Bon Accord Sq G81 ...94 A4
Bon Secours Hospl G41 116 C4
Bonar Cres PA11 .....110 C4
Bonar La PA11 ....110 C4
Bonar Law Ave G84 ..16 C1
Bonawe St G20 ....96 C2
Bond St FK10 ....4 A1
Bonds Rd ML2 ....166 A3
Boness St G40 ....118 A2
Bonhill Prim Sch G83 ..27 C2
Bonhill Rd G82 ....50 A2
Bonhill St G22 ....97 A2
Bonkle Gdns ML2 ....166 A3
Bonkle Rd ML2 ....166 A3
Bonnar St G40 ....118 A2
Bonnaughton Rd G61 ..75 A3
Bonnet Ct KA3 ....211 C4
Bonnet Rd ML11 .....215 A3
Bonnington View G83 ....27 C2
Bonnington Ave ML11 215 A2
Bonnybridge Hospl FK4 40 B3
Bonnybridge Ind Est FK4 40 A2
Bonnybridge Prim Sch
  FK4 ....40 A3
Bonnybridge Rd FK4 ..39 C3
Bonnyfield Rd FK4 ....39 C3
Bonnyhill Rd Falkirk FK1 41 A2
  High Bonnybridge FK4 40 B2
Bonnyholm Prim Sch
  G53 ....115 A2
Bonnyrigg Dr G43 ...136 A3
Bonnyside Rd FK4 .....40 A3
Bonnyton Dr G76 ....178 B3
Bonnyton Foot KA11 .220 A3
Bonnyton Ind Est KA1 220 A3
Bonnyton Moor Rd G76 178 A4
Bonnyton Pl Irvine KA11 220 A3
  Kilmarnock KA1 .....222 B1
Bonnyton Rd KA11 ...220 A3
Bonnyvale Pl FK4 .....40 A3
Bonnywood Gdns FK4 ..40 A3
Bontine Ave G82 ......49 B2
Bonyton Ave G13 .....94 C3
Boon Dr G15 ....75 A1
Booth Pl FK1 ....42 A2
Boquhanran Pl G81 ...74 A2
Boquhanran Rd G81 ..74 A2
Borden La G13 ....95 C3
Borden Rd G13 ....95 C3
Border Ave KA21 ....216 C4
Border Pl KA21 ......216 C4
Border St PA15 ....46 B2
Border Way G66 ....79 C4
Bore Rd ML1 ....123 A4
Boreland Dr Glasgow G13 95 A3
  Hamilton ML3 ....161 C1
Boreland Ave KA25 ..170 A4
Borestone Cres FK7 ....7 A2
Borestone Ct FK7 ......7 A1
Borestone Pl FK7 ......7 A1
Borgie Cres G72 .....139 A3
Borgie Cres G76 .....178 D3
Borland Dr ML9 ......199 A4
Borland Rd G61 ....76 A2
Borron St G4 ....97 A3
Borrowdale G75 .....179 C3
Borrowlea Rd FK7 .....7 C4
Borrowmeadow Rd FK7 ..7 C4
Borthwick Dr G75 ...179 B4
Borthwick St G33 .....99 A1
Bosfield Cnr G74 ....159 C2
Bosfield Pl G74 ......159 C2

Bosfield Rd G74 .....159 C2
Boston Dr G84 ....16 C2
Boswell Ct G42 .....136 C4
Boswell Dr G72 .....161 B4
Boswell Pk Ayr KA7 ..238 C4
  East Kilbride G74 ...160 B2
Boswell Sq G52 .....114 C4
Bosworth Rd G74 ...160 B3
Botanic Cres G20 .....96 B2
Botanic Crescent La G20 96 B2
Bothkennar Prim Sch
  FK2 ....24 C2
Bothkennar Rd FK2 ...24 C2
Bothlin Dr G33 ....99 B3
Bothlyn Ave G66 ......79 C4
Bothlyn Cres G69 ....100 C4
Bothlyn Rd G69 ....80 A1
Bothwell Castle * G72 140 B2
Bothwell Ho ML3 ....162 C3
Bothwell La Glasgow G2 240 C2
  Glasgow, Kelvingrove
  G12 ....96 B1
Bothwell Park Ind Est
  G71 ....141 A2
Bothwell Pl
  Coatbridge ML5 .....121 C4
  Paisley PA2 ....132 C4
Bothwell Prim Sch G71 141 A1
Bothwell Rd
  Bothwell G71 ....140 C2
  Carluke ML8 ....187 C2
  Hamilton ML3 ....162 B3
Bothwell St
  Cambuslang G72 ....138 C3
  Glasgow G2 ....240 C2
  Hamilton ML3 ....162 B3
Bothwellhaugh Quadrant
  ML4 ....141 C2
Bothwellhaugh Rd ML4 141 C3
Bothwellpark Pl ML4 ..141 B3
Bothwellpark Rd G71 .141 B2
Bothwellpark Sch G71 141 B3
Bothwellshields Rd
  ML1 ....124 B1
Bothwick Way PA2 ...133 C4
Botterill Dr G31 ......119 C1
Boundary Rd KA8 ....236 B2
Bourhill Ct ML2 ......164 B1
Bourne Cres PA4 ......93 B4
Bourne St ML3 ....162 C3
Bournemouth Rd PA19 44 C3
Bourock Sq G78 .....134 C1
Bourtree Pk KA7 ....239 A4
Bourtree Rd ML3 ....161 C1
Bouverie St Glasgow G14 94 C3
  Port Glasgow PA14 ...47 B1
  Rutherglen G73 .....137 C4
Bow Rd PA16 ....45 B2
Bowden Dr G52 .....115 A3
Bowden Pk G75 .....180 B4
Bower St G22 ....96 C2
Bowerwalls St G78 ..134 C2
Bowes Cres G69 .....119 C2
Bowes Rigg KA3 .....195 C1
Bowfield Cres G52 ..114 C3
Bowfield Dr G52 ....114 C3
Bowfield Pl G52 .....114 C3
Bowhill Rd
  Howwood PA9 .....130 C3
  West Kilbride KA23 ..190 B2
Bowhill Way KA9 ....236 A2
Bowhouse Gdns FK10 ..10 A3
Bowhouse Head KA11 .220 A3
Bowhouse Rd
  Airdrie ML6 ....123 C3
  Alloa FK10 ....10 A3
Bowhouse Rise KA11 .220 A3
Bowhousebog or Liquo
Bowhousebrae Rd ML6 123 C3
Bowie Rd G83 ....27 C3
Bowhousemuir Prim Sch
  ML4 ....146 A1
Bowling Green La G21 ..98 A1
Bowling Green Pl
  G14 ....95 B2
Bowling Green Pl FK4 ..39 C3
Bowling Green Rd
  Chryston G69 ....100 A4
  Glasgow G44 ....137 A3
  Glasgow, Barrachnie G32 119 B2
  Glasgow, Whiteinch G14 95 B2
  Kilmaurs KA3 ....127 A3
Bowling Green St ML4 142 A3
Bowling Green View
Bowling Green Prim Sch
  ML1 ....146 C4
Bowling Sta KA7 ....238 C3
Bowman Rd KA7 ....238 C3
Bowmanflat ML9 ....185 A2
Bowmont Gdns G G12 ..96 B2
Bowmont Hill G64 ....78 A2
Bowmont Pl
  Cambuslang G72 ....139 B3
  East Kilbride G75 ...179 B4
Bowmont Terr G12 ...96 B2
Bowmore Ct G12 .....220 A3
Bowmore Gdns
  Rutherglen G73 .....138 C2
  Uddingston G71 ....140 C4
Bowmore Rd G52 ....115 A4
Bowmore Wlk ML7 ...147 A2
Bowyer Vennel ML4 .141 C3
Boxton Rd FK1 ....166 B3
Boyd Ct ML1 ....143 A4
Boyd Dr ML1 ....163 A4

Boyd Orr Cres KA3 ..222 A4
Boyd Orr Rd KA21 ...206 A1
Boyd St Falkirk FK2 ...42 A3
  Glasgow G42 ....117 B1
  Kilmarnock KA3 ....223 A1
  Prestwick KA9 .....236 B4
Boydston Ct KA22 ...205 B2
Boydston Rd ML3 ....223 B3
Boydstone Pl G46 ...136 A3
Boydstone Rd G43 ..135 C3
Boyle St Clydebank G81 94 B4
Boylestone Rd G78 ..134 A2
Boyndie St G34 ......120 A4
Brabloch Cres PA3 ..113 C3
Bracadale Dr G69 ...120 B2
Bracadale Gdns G69 120 B2
Bracadale Gr G69 ...120 B2
Bracadale Rd G69 ...120 B2
Bracco Rd ML1 ......105 B1
Brachelston St PA16 ..45 B2
Bracken Pk KA7 .....239 B2
Bracken Rd PA14 ....169 A4
Bracken St Glasgow G22 97 A3
  Motherwell ML1 ....143 A2
Bracken Terr G71 ...141 A2
Bracken Way ML9 ...185 B1
Brackenbrae Ave G64 77 C1
Brackenbrae Rd G64 .77 C1
Brackendene PA6 .....91 B1
Brackenhill Ave KA3 .222 A3
Brackenhill Dr ML3 ..183 B4
Brackenhill Rd ML8 ..187 A3
Brackenhirst St G82 .50 B3
Brackenknowe Rd ML6 .83 B2
Brackenrig Cres G76 157 C1
Brackenrig Rd G46 ..135 B2
Brackla Ave G81 ......94 C4
Bradan Ave Ayr KA7 .239 A1
  Clydebank G13,G81 ..94 C4
Bradan Ct KA10 .....229 B1
Bradan Cres KA9 ....228 C1
Bradbury Glebe KA12 219 B1
Bradbury St FK2 .....24 A1
Bradda Ave G73 ......138 B2
Bradfield Ave G12 ....96 B3
Bradshaw Cres ML3 .161 C2
Bradshaw St KA21 ..216 C4
Brady Cres G69 ......81 A2
Brae The Bannockburn FK7 ..7 B1
  Cambusbarron FK7 ....6 A3
Braeadae Ave
  Milngavie G62 ....76 A4
  Moodiesburn G69 ....80 C1
  Rutherglen G73 .....138 B4
Braeside Cres
  Barrhead G78 ......134 C1
  Glasgow G69 ....120 C2
Braeside Dr
  Barrhead G78 ......134 C1
  Dumbarton G82 ......50 A3
Braeside Gdns ML3 ..183 C4
Braeside La G Gourock PA16 .44 B2
Braeside Pl G72 .....139 A2
Braeside Prim Sch G45 137 C2
Braeside Rd Ayr KA8 .236 B1
  Greenock PA16 ......45 B3
  Motherwell ML1 ....143 B2
Braeside St Glasgow G20 .96 C2
  Kilmarnock KA3 ....228 A4
Braeside Way ML9 ..185 A1
Braeview Lauriestion FK2 .42 C2
  Stenhousemuir FK5 ..23 B1
Braeview Ave PA2 ...133 A4
Braeview Dr PA2 ....133 A4
Braeview Pl G74 ....160 A2
Braeview Rd PA2 ...133 A4
Braid Ave ML1 ....143 C1
Braid Ct KA13 ....207 A4
Braid Sq G4 ....97 A1
Braid St G4 ....97 A1
Braid's Rd PA2 ......113 C1
Braidbar Ct G46 .....136 B2
Braidbar Farm Rd G46 136 B2
Braidbar Prim Sch G46 136 B2
Braidcraft Pl G53 ...135 B4
Braidcraft Rd G53 ...115 B1
Braidcraft Terr G53 ..115 C1
Braidfauld Gdns G32 118 C2
Braidfauld Pl G32 ...118 C1
Braidfauld St G32 ...118 C2
Braidfield Gr G81 .....74 A3
Braidfield High Sch G81 .74 A3
Braidfield Rd G81 .....74 A3
Braidfute ML11 .....215 B3
Braidholm Cres G46 .136 B2
Braidholm Rd G46 ...136 B2
Braidhurst High Sch
  ML1 ....142 B1
Braidhurst St ML1 ...163 C4
Braidley Cres G75 ..180 C3
Braids Cait H2 ....113 B1
Braids Dr PA2 ....113 C1
Braids Gait PA2 .....113 C1
Braids Rd PA2 ....113 C1
Braidwood Pl PA3 ..111 C3
Braidwood Prim Sch
  ML8 ....201 C2
Braidwood Rd
  Kilwinning KA13 ....207 C2
  Law ML8 ....201 B2
Braidwood St ML2 ..165 B4
Bramble Ct G66 ......57 B4
Bramblehedge Path G83 17 C2
Brambling Ct ML2 ...165 A1
Bramley Pl Airdrie ML6 123 C3
  Kirkintilloch G66 .....79 C2
Bramah Ave G75 ....180 B4
Brampton G75 ......179 C3
Branchal Rd ML2 ....165 B2
Branchalfield Dr ML2 165 C2
Branchalmuir Cres ML2 165 C3
Branchline Ind Est
  KA10 ....229 B2
Branchock Ave G72 .139 B2
Branchton Rd PA16 ...44 C2

Branchton Sta PA16 44 C2
Brancumhall Rd G74 160 B2
Brand Pl G51 116 B3
Brand St G51 116 B3
Brandon Arc 1 ML1 163 C3
Brandon Ct ML3 162 B2
Brandon Dr G61 75 C4
Brandon Gdns
 Cambuslang G72 138 C3
 Prestwick KA9 236 A4
Brandon Ho ML3 162 C3
Brandon Par E ML1 163 C4
Brandon Par S ML1 163 C3
Brandon Pl ML4 141 C2
Brandon St Glasgow G31 117 C3
 Hamilton ML3 162 C2
 Motherwell ML1 163 C3
Brandon Way ML5 121 B2
Brandyhill FK10 5 C2
Brankholm Brae ML3 161 B2
Branklyn Cres G13 95 B3
Branklyn Ct G13 95 B3
Brannock Ave ML1 143 B2
Brannock High Sch ML1 143 B2
Brannock Pl ML1 143 B2
Brannock Rd ML1 143 B2
Branshill Pk FK10 10 A4
Branshill Rd FK10 10 A4
Brassey St G20 96 C3
Braxfield Rd ML11 215 A1
Braxfield Terr ML11 214 C1
Breadalbane Cres ML1 142 B1
Breadalbane Gdns G73 138 B2
Breadalbane St G3 240 A3
Breadie Dr G62 75 C4
Bream Pl PA6 111 B4
Breamish Pl G75 179 C3
Brechin Rd G64 78 B1
Brechin St G3 116 C4
Breck Ave PA2 132 B4
Brediland Prim Sch PA2 113 A1
Brediland Rd
 Linwood PA3 112 A3
 Paisley PA2 112 C1
Bredin Way ML1 163 A4
Bredisholm Cres G71 121 B1
Bredisholm Dr G69 120 B2
Bredisholm Rd
 Bargeddie G69 121 A2
 Coatbridge G69 120 C2
 Glasgow G69 120 B2
Bredisholm Terr G69 120 B2
Brendan Way ML1 164 A1
Brendon Ave G75 180 A2
Brenfield Ave G44 136 C2
Brenfield Dr G44 136 C2
Brenfield Rd G44 137 A2
Brent Ave G46 135 C3
Brent Cres PA6 111 B4
Brent Ct G74 159 C2
Brent Dr G46 135 C3
Brent Gdns G46 135 C3
Brent Rd
 East Kilbride G74 159 C2
 Glasgow G46 135 C3
Brent Way G46 135 C3
Brentham Ave FK8 7 A3
Brentham Cres FK8 7 A3
Brentwood Ave G53 135 A2
Brentwood Dr G53 135 A2
Brentwood Sq G53 135 A2
Brereton St G42 117 B1
Breslin Terr ML7 127 B3
Bressay G74 159 C2
Bressay Pl KA3 223 A3
Bressay Rd G33 119 C3
Bressay Wynd 14 ML2 165 C3
Breton Ct FK1 42 B2
Breval Cres G81 74 A4
Breval Ct G69 120 B2
Brewery Rd 17 KA1 227 C4
Brewery St PA5 111 C2
Brewlands Cres KA1 231 B2
Brewlands Dr KA1 231 B2
Brewlands Rd KA1 231 B2
Brewster Ave PA3 114 A4
Brewster Pl Denny FK6 21 B1
 Irvine KA11 224 D3
Briar Bank G66 58 A3
Briar Dr G81 74 A2
Briar Gdns G43 136 B3
Briar Gr Ayr KA7 239 B2
 Glasgow G43 136 B3
Briar Neuk G64 98 A4
Briar Pl PA19 44 B3
Briar Rd Glasgow G43 136 B3
 Kirkintilloch G66 79 C4
Briarbush Way G72 161 B4
Briarcroft Dr G33 98 B4
Briarcroft Pl G33 98 C3
Briarcroft Rd G33 98 C3
Briarhill Ct KA9 236 B4
Briarhill Rd KA9 236 B4
Briarhill St KA9 236 B4
Briarlea Dr G46 136 B2
Briars Rd FK10 4 C1
Briarwell La G62 55 A1
Briarwell Rd G62 55 A1
Briarwood Ct G32 119 C1
Briarwood Rd ML2 164 C2
Brick La 10 PA3 113 C3
Bridesburn Pl KA3 195 C1
Bridge Cres FK6 21 B1
Bridge End ML7 146 B3
Bridge La
 9 Kilmarnock KA1 227 C4
 Paisley PA2 113 A2
Bridge of Allan Prim Sch FK9 2 A3
Bridge of Allan Sta FK9 1 C4
Bridge of Weir Prim Sch PA11 90 B1
Bridge of Weir Rd
 Bridge of W PA11 110 C4
 Brookfield PA3,PA5,PA11 111 B3
 Houston PA6 91 A1
 Kilmacolm PA13 89 C3
 Linwood PA3 112 A3
Bridge Pl Denny FK6 21 B1
 Milngavie G62 55 A1
 Shotts ML7 147 A2
Bridge Rd PA14 68 C4
Bridge St Alexandria G83 27 C2
 Bonnybridge FK4 40 A3
 Cambuslang G72 139 A3
 Clydebank G81 73 C2
 Dumbarton G82 49 C2
 Glasgow G5 240 C1
 Hamilton ML3 162 B1
 Kilbirnie KA25 149 A1
 Linwood PA3 112 B3
 Longriggend ML6 84 C1
 Paisley PA1 113 C2
 Prestwick KA9 236 A4
 Wishaw ML2 164 C2
Bridge Street Underground Sta G5 117 A3
Bridge Terr 10 FK10 10 A3
Bridgebar St G78 134 C2
Bridgeburn Dr G69 80 C1
Bridgeford Ave ML4 142 B4
Bridgegait G62 76 B4
Bridgegate Glasgow G1 241 A1
 Irvine KA12 219 B1
Bridgehaugh Rd FK9 2 A1
Bridgehouse Ct KA1 228 A1
Bridgehousehill Rd KA1 227 C1
Bridgend Bishopton PA7 72 A2
 Dalry KA24 191 B4
 Kilwinning KA13 207 C2
 Stewarton KA3 211 C4
Bridgend Ave PA14 68 C4
Bridgend Cotts G66 80 A4
Bridgend Cres G69 80 C1
Bridgend Ct G68 38 C1
Bridgend Ind Est KA24 191 B4
Bridgend La KA13 207 C2
Bridgend Pl G69 80 C1
Bridgend Rd
 Greenock PA15 46 B1
 Kilbirnie KA25 149 A1
Bridgend View ML8 187 C1
Bridgend Wlk G78 153 A2
Bridgepark KA22 205 B1
Bridgeton Bsns Ctr 6 G40 117 C3
Bridgeton Sta G40 117 C2
Bridgewater Ind Pk PA8 73 B1
Bridgewater Sh Ctr PA8 73 B1
Bridgeway Ct G66 79 C4
Bridgeway Pl G66 79 C4
Bridgeway Rd G66 79 C4
Bridgeway Terr G66 79 C4
Bridie Terr G74 160 B2
Brierie Ave PA6 91 A1
Brierie Gdns PA6 111 A4
Brierie La PA6 111 A4
Brierie-Hill Ct PA6 111 A4
Brierie-Hill Gr PA6 111 A4
Brierie-Hill Rd PA6 111 A4
Briery Ct KA25 170 A4
Brierybank Ave ML11 215 A2
Brig O'Lea Terr G78 154 B3
Brig-O-Doon Gr FK7 12 C4
Brigbrae Ave ML4 142 B2
Brigham Pl G23 96 C4
Bright St G21 97 C1
Brighton Pl G51 116 A3
Brighton St G51 116 A3
Brightside Ave
 Port Glasgow PA14 69 A4
 Uddingston G71 140 C3
Brigside Gdns ML3 163 A1
Bringan Rd KA3 222 C3
Brisbane Ct G46 136 B2
Brisbane Rd PA7 72 A2
Brisbane St Clydebank G81 73 B2
 Glasgow G42 137 A4
 Greenock PA16 45 B3
Brisbane Terr G75 180 B4
Britannia Pl KA8 236 A1
Britannia Way PA4 94 B1
Briton St G51 116 A4
Broad Sq G72 161 B4
Broad St Alloa FK10 10 A3
 Denny FK6 21 C1
 Glasgow G40 118 A3
 Stirling FK8 7 A4
Broad Way The ML2 164 C2
Broadcroft
 Kirkintilloch G66 79 B4
 4 Kirkintilloch, Eastside G66 58 B1
Broadcroft Rd 5 G66 58 B1
Broadfield Ave PA14 69 A4
Broadford St G4 97 B1
Broadford Terr PA16 44 C2
Broadholm Prim Sch G15 75 A2
Broadholm St G22 97 B3
Broadleys Ave G64 77 C1
Broadleys Rd FK7 7 B4
Broadleys Rdbt FK7 7 B3
Broadlie Ct G78 154 B4
Broadlie Dr Dalry KA24 191 A4
 Glasgow G13 95 A3
Broadlie Rd G78 154 B4
Broadloan PA4 94 B1
Broadmeadow Ind Est G82 49 C3
Broadmoss Ave G77 157 B2
Broadside Pl FK6 21 B1
Broadstone Ave PA14 47 A1
Broadway KA22 205 B2
Broadwood Bsns Pk G68 81 C4
Broadwood Dr G44 137 A3
Broadwood Pk KA7 239 A1
Broadwood Rdbt G68 81 C4
Broadwood Stad (Clyde & Airdrieonians FC's) G68 60 C1
Brock Oval G53 135 B3
Brock Pl Glasgow G53 135 B4
 Stirling FK7 7 A1
Brock Rd G53 135 B3
Brock Terr G53 135 B3
Brockburn Cres G53 135 A4
Brockburn Rd G53 135 B4
Brockburn Terr G53 135 B4
Brocklinn Pk G75 179 C4
Brockly View KA25 149 A2
Brockville Pk (Falkirk FC) FK1,FK2 42 A3
Brockville St G32 118 C3
Brodick Ave
 Kilwinning KA13 207 B2
 Motherwell ML1 163 A4
Brodick Cl KA13 207 B2
Brodick Dr
 East Kilbride G74 159 B2
 Gourock PA19 43 C3
 Helensburgh G84 16 C2
Brodick Pl Falkirk FK1 41 B2
 Newton Mearns G77 156 A2
Brodick Rd KA1 222 B1
Brodick St G21 98 A1
Brodie Ave KA10 229 C2
Brodie Park Ave PA2 113 C1
Brodie Park Cres PA2 113 B1
Brodie Park Gdns PA2 113 C1
Brodie Pl
 East Kilbride G74 159 B2
 Kilmarnock KA3 223 B1
 Stonehouse ML9 198 C1
Brodie Rd G21 98 B4
Brodie St FK2 42 A4
Brogan Cres ML1 163 A4
Broich The FK12 4 C4
Bron Way G67 62 A1
Bronte Pl FK5 24 A2
Brook St Alva FK10,FK12 5 A3
 Clydebank G81 73 C2
 Glasgow G40 117 C3
 Menstrie FK11 3 C3
Brookbank Terr ML8 188 A1
Brooke Ave G83 28 A4
Brookfield Ave G33 98 B4
Brookfield Cnr G33 98 B4
Brookfield Dr G33 98 B4
Brookfield Gate G33 98 B4
Brookfield Gdns G33 98 B4
Brookfield Pl Alva FK12 5 A3
 Glasgow G33 98 C4
Brookfield Rd PA14 68 C4
Brooklands
 Alexandria G83 27 B3
 East Kilbride G74 159 A1
Brooklands Ave G71 140 C4
Brooklea Dr G46 136 B3
Brooklime Dr G74 159 B2
Brooklime Gdns G74 159 B2
Brooklyn Pl ML2 186 A4
Brookside St G40 118 A3
Broom Ave PA8 93 A4
Broom Cliff G77 156 C2
Broom Cres
 Barrhead G78 134 A3
 East Kilbride G75 180 B3
Broom Ct FK7 7 B2
Broom Dr Clydebank G81 74 A2
 Larkhall ML9 185 A3
Broom Gdns G66 79 A3
Broom Path G69 119 C2
Broom Pk E FK11 4 A3
Broom Pk W FK11 4 A3
Broom Pl
 Bridge of W PA11 110 C4
 Coatbridge ML5 121 C2
 Glasgow G43 136 B3
 Kilmarnock KA1 228 A3
 Motherwell ML1 143 B2
Broom Rd
 Cumbernauld G67 62 B3
 Glasgow G43 136 B3
 Newton Mearns G77 157 A3
 Rosneath G84 15 A2
 Stirling FK7 7 B2
Broom Rd E G77 157 A2
Broom Terr PA5 112 A1
Broom Wynd ML7 146 C3
Broomage Ave FK5 23 A2
Broomage Cres FK5 23 A2
Broomage Dr FK5 23 A2
Broomage Pk FK5 23 B1
Broomberry Dr PA19 44 C4
Broomburn Dr G77 157 A2
Broomcroft Rd G77 157 A3
Broomdyke Way 2 PA3 113 B4
Broomelton Rd ML3,ML9 184 B1
Broomfauld Gdns G82 50 A2
Broomfield PA6 91 B1
Broomfield Ave
 Cambuslang G72 138 B4
 Newton Mearns G77 156 C2
Broomfield Ct G21 98 B2
Broomfield Gdn KA7 238 C3
Broomfield Gdns G84 15 B4
Broomfield La G21 97 C3
Broomfield Pl G21 97 C3
Broomfield Rd Ayr KA7 238 C3
 Glasgow G21 98 A2
 Netherburn ML9 199 C2
 Netherburn, Strutherhill ML9 199 A4
 Rutherglen G46 157 A3
Broomfield St
 Airdrie ML6 123 A4
 Kilwinning KA13 207 C2
 Netherburn ML9 200 B2
Broomfield Terr G71 120 C1
Broomfield Wlk 6 G66 79 B4
Broomgate ML11 215 A2
Broomhill Ave
 Glasgow G32 139 A4
 Glasgow, Whiteinch G11 95 C1
 Larbert FK5 23 A1
 Newton Mearns G77 156 C2
Broomhill Cres
 Bellshill ML4 141 C2
 Bonhill G83 28 A1
 Erskine PA8 93 A4
Broomhill Ct
 Kilwinning KA13 207 B3
 Larkhall ML9 185 A1
Broomhill Dr
 Dumbarton G82 50 A3
 Glasgow G11 95 C2
 Rutherglen G73 138 A3
Broomhill Farm Mews G66 58 C1
Broomhill Gate ML9 185 A1
Broomhill Gdns
 Glasgow G11 95 C2
 Newton Mearns G77 156 C2
Broomhill La G11 95 C1
Broomhill Path G11 95 C1
Broomhill Pl Denny FK6 21 B2
 Glasgow G11 95 C1
 Stirling FK7 6 C3
Broomhill Prim Sch G11 95 C2
Broomhill Prim Sch Annexe G11 95 C2
Broomhill Quadrant KA1 228 A2
Broomhill Rd
 Bonnybridge FK4 40 A2
 Larkhall ML9 185 A1
Broomhill Rd E KA1 228 A2
Broomhill Rd W KA1 227 C2
Broomhill St
 Greenock PA15 45 C2
 Harthill ML7 127 B3
Broomhill Terr G11 95 C1
Broomhill View ML9 184 C1
Broomhill Way PA15 45 C2
Broomieknowe FK10 4 B2
Broomieknowe Dr G73 138 A3
Broomieknowe Rd G73 138 A3
Broomielaw G1, G2 240 C1
Broomknoll St ML6 123 A4
Broomknowe G68 61 B2
Broomknowe Rd PA13 89 B4
Broomknowe Terr PA13 89 B4
Broomknowes Ave G66 79 C2
Broomknowes Prim Sch G21 98 A2
Broomknowes Rd G21 98 A2
Broomland Ct PA1 113 B2
Broomlands Ave PA8 93 C4
Broomlands Busway KA11 220 A1
Broomlands Cres PA8 93 C4
Broomlands Ct KA11 220 A1
Broomlands Dr KA12 219 B1
Broomlands Gdns PA8 93 B4
Broomlands La PA1 113 A2
Broomlands Pl KA12 219 B1
Broomlands Prim Sch KA11 220 A1
Broomlands Rd
 Cumbernauld G67 83 A4
 Irvine KA11 220 A1
Broomlands St PA1 113 B2
Broomlands Way PA8 93 C4
Broomlea Cres PA4 93 B4
Broomlea Sch G11 95 C1
Broomlee Rd G67 82 C3
Broomley Cres G83 27 B4
Broomley Dr G46 136 B1
Broomley La G46 136 B1
Broomloan Ct G51 116 A3
Broomloan Pl G51 116 A3
Broomloan Rd G51 116 A3
Broompark Ave
 Blantyre G72 161 B3
 Prestwick KA9 236 B4
Broompark Cir 8 G31 117 C4
Broompark Cres
 Airdrie ML6 103 A2
 Prestwick KA9 236 B4
Broompark Dr
 Glasgow G31 117 C4
 Inchinnan PA4 93 B4
 Newton Mearns G77 157 A3
Broompark Gdns FK6 21 C1
Broompark La 7 G31 117 C4
Broompark Rd
 Blantyre G72 161 B4
Broompark Rd *continued*
 Wishaw ML2 164 B2
Broompark St 6 G31 117 C4
Broomridge Rd FK7 7 A2
Broomside Cres ML1 163 C2
Broomside Pl FK5 23 B1
Broomside Rd FK4 40 A2
Broomside St ML1 163 C2
Broomstone Ave G77 156 C2
Broomton Rd G21 98 B4
Broomvale Dr G77 156 C3
Broomward Dr PA5 112 A2
Brora Cres ML3 182 C4
Brora Dr Bearsden G61 76 A2
 Glasgow G46 136 B1
 Renfrew PA4 94 C2
Brora Gdns G64 78 A1
Brora Rd G64 78 A1
Brora St G33 98 B1
Brosdale Ct FK1 42 A1
Brougham St PA16 45 C4
Broughton G75 180 C3
Broughton Dr G23 96 C4
Broughton Gdns G23 76 C1
Broughton Gn KA11 220 A3
Broughton Pl
 Coatbridge ML5 122 A2
 Hamilton ML3 162 A2
Broughton Rd G23 76 C1
Broun Dr KA7 238 C1
Brouster Gate 16 G74 159 C1
Brouster Hill G74 159 C1
Brouster Pl G74 159 C1
Brown Ave Alloa FK10 4 C1
 Clydebank G81 94 C4
 Dumbarton G82 50 B2
 Stirling FK9 2 A1
 Troon KA10 229 C2
Brown Pl
 Cambuslang G72 139 A3
 Saltcoats KA21 205 C1
Brown Rd G67 61 C1
Brown St Balloch G83 28 A4
 Carluke ML8 187 C2
 Coatbridge ML5 122 A3
 Falkirk FK1 41 B3
 Glasgow G2 240 B2
 Greenock PA15 46 B2
 1 Hamilton ML3 162 C1
 Larkhall ML9 185 A2
 Motherwell ML1 163 C4
 Paisley PA1 113 B3
 Port Glasgow PA14 47 A1
 Renfrew PA4 94 A2
 Shotts ML7 147 A2
 Stewarton KA3 211 B4
 Wishaw ML2 166 A2
Brown Wlk Irvine KA12 219 B3
 Wishaw ML2 166 A3
Brown's La PA1 113 C2
Browncarrick Dr KA7 238 A1
Brownhill Dr KA25 169 C4
Brownhill Rd G43 136 A2
Brownhill View ML2 166 B3
Brownieside Pl ML6 104 A2
Brownieside Rd ML6 104 B1
Brownlee Rd ML8 186 B2
Brownlie St G42 137 A4
Brownmuir Ave G76 178 C2
Brownsburn Ind Est ML6 123 A3
Brownsburn Rd ML6 123 B3
Brownsdale Rd G73 137 C4
Brownsfield Cres PA4 93 A3
Brownsfield Rd PA4 93 A3
Brownshill Ave ML5 121 C2
Brownside Ave
 Barrhead G78 134 A3
 Cambuslang G72 138 C3
Brownside Cres G78 134 A3
Brownside Dr
 Barrhead G78 134 A3
 Glasgow G13 94 C3
Brownside Gr G78 134 A3
Brownside Mews G72 138 C3
Brownside Rd G72 138 C3
Brownsland Ct G69 100 C3
Browside Ave PA2 133 B4
Bruar Way 15 ML2 165 C3
Bruart Ave FK5 23 C2
Bruce Ave
 Dundonald KA2 225 C1
 Johnstone PA5 131 C4
 Motherwell ML1 163 B4
 Paisley PA3 114 A4
 Prestwick KA9 236 A3
Bruce Cres 13 Ayr KA7 235 C1
 Falkirk FK2 24 A2
 Kilmarnock KA1 227 C2
 Plean FK7 12 B2
Bruce Ct 5 ML6 123 C4
Bruce Dr Fallin FK7 8 B3
 Stenhousemuir FK5 23 C2
Bruce Gate FK2 14 B1
Bruce La KA9 236 A3
Bruce Loan ML2 186 B3
Bruce Pl G75 180 C4
Bruce Rd Bishopton PA7 72 A2
 Glasgow G41 116 C2
 Motherwell ML1 143 A1
 Paisley PA3 114 A4
 Renfrew PA4 94 A1
Bruce St Alloa FK10 10 B4
 Bannockburn FK7 7 C1
 Bellshill ML4 142 A3
 Clydebank G81 74 A1
 Coatbridge ML5 122 A4
 Dumbarton G82 50 A1

Bruce St continued
Falkirk FK2 .....42 B3
Greenock PA15 .....45 C3
Kilmarnock KA1 .....227 C2
Plains ML6 .....104 A1
Plean FK7 .....12 B2
Port Glasgow PA14 .....47 B1
Stirling FK8 .....2 A1
Bruce Terr Blantyre G72 .....140 C1
Cambuslnorton FK7 .....6 A3
East Kilbride G75 .....180 C4
Irvine KA12 .....219 B3
Bruce View FK7 .....7 A1
Bruce's Loan 51 ML9 .....185 B1
Brucefield Pl G34 .....120 B4
Brucehill Rd G82 .....49 B2
Brunel Way G75 .....180 C4
Brunstane Rd G34 .....100 A1
Brunswick La G1 .....241 A2
Brunswick St G1 .....241 A2
Brunton St G44 .....137 A3
Brunton Terr G44 .....137 A2
Bruntsfield Ave
Glasgow G53 .....135 A2
Kilwinning KA13 .....207 A2
Bruntsfield Gdns G53 .....135 A2
Bryan St ML3 .....162 A3
Bryce Ave FK2 .....24 A1
Bryce Gdns ML9 .....185 A2
Bryce Knox Ct KA11 .....220 A3
Bryce Pl G75 .....180 B3
Brydson Pl PA3 .....112 A3
Brymner St PA15 .....46 A3
Bryon Ct G71 .....141 A1
Bryony The FK10 .....4 A1
Bryson Ct ML3 .....183 B4
Bryson St Clydebank G81 .....74 C4
Falkirk FK2 .....42 A3
Bryson Street Ind Est
FK2 .....42 A2
Buccleuch Ave
Clarkston G76 .....157 B4
Paisley PA2 .....114 C4
Buccleuch Dr G61 .....75 C4
Buccleuch La G3 .....240 B4
Buccleuch St PA15 .....45 C3
Buchan Ct 16 KA7 .....235 C1
Buchan Gn G74 .....160 A2
Buchan Rd
Motherwell ML1 .....143 A1
Troon KA10 .....229 D2
Buchan St Hamilton ML3 .....143 A1
Wishaw ML2 .....165 A3
Buchan Terr G72 .....138 C2
Buchanan Ave
Balloch G83 .....28 A4
Bishopton PA7 .....72 A2
Buchanan Bsns Pk G33 .....99 C3
Buchanan Cres
Bishopbriggs G64 .....98 B4
Hamilton ML3 .....162 A1
Buchanan Ct Falkirk FK2 .....42 A4
Stepps G33 .....99 C3
Buchanan Dr
Bearsden G61 .....76 A2
Bishopbriggs G64 .....98 B4
Carluke ML8 .....202 B4
Kirkintilloch G66 .....79 B2
Law ML8 .....187 A3
Newton Mearns G77 .....156 C4
Rutherglen, Burgh G73 .....138 B3
Rutherglen G73 .....138 B3
Stirling FK9 .....2 A2
Buchanan Gdns G32 .....119 C1
Buchanan Gr G69 .....120 A3
Buchanan Pl
Kilmarnock KA1 .....228 A3
Torrance G64 .....57 A1
Buchanan Rd G84 .....17 A1
Buchanan St Airdrie ML6 .....123 A4
Coatbridge ML5 .....121 C3
Dumbarton G82 .....50 A1
Glasgow G1 .....240 C2
Glasgow, Baillieston G69 .....120 A2
Greenock PA16 .....45 A2
Johnstone PA5 .....111 C1
Milngavie G62 .....55 A1
**Buchanan Street
Underground Sta** G1 .....241 C2
Buchanan Way PA15 .....111 C1
Buchandyke Rd G74 .....160 A2
Buchlyvie Gdns G64 .....97 C4
Buchlyvie Rd PA1 .....114 C3
Buchlyvie St G34 .....120 A4
Buckie PA8 .....73 A2
Buckie Wlk ML4 .....142 A4
Buckingham Ct ML3 .....161 C2
Buckingham Dr
Glasgow G32 .....139 A4
Rutherglen G73 .....138 B4
Buckingham St G12 .....96 B2
Buckingham Terr G12 .....96 B2
Bucklaw Gdns G52 .....115 B2
Bucklaw Pl G52 .....115 B2
Bucklaw Terr G52 .....115 B2
Bucksburn Rd G21 .....98 B2
Buckthorne Pl G53 .....135 A2
Buddon St G40 .....118 B2
Budhill Ave G32 .....119 A3
Budshaw Ave ML6 .....123 B1
Buiston Rd KA3 .....211 B2
Bull Rd G76 .....157 C3
Bull's Cl ML11 .....215 A2
Bulldale Ct G14 .....94 C3
Bulldale Rd G14 .....94 C3
Bulldale St G14 .....94 C3

Buller Cres G72 .....140 B2
Bullionslaw Dr G73 .....138 B3
Bulloch Ave G46 .....136 B3
Bulloch Cres FK6 .....21 B1
Bullwood Ave G53 .....134 C4
Bullwood Ct 2 G53 .....115 A1
Bullwood Dr G53 .....114 C1
Bullwood Gdns G53 .....114 C1
Bullwood Pl G53 .....114 C1
Bunbury Terr 3 G75 .....180 B4
Bunessan St G52 .....115 C3
Bungalows The FK5 .....23 A1
Bunhouse Rd G3 .....96 B1
Buntine Cres FK7 .....7 A2
Bunting Pl KA1 .....228 B4
Burbank G62 .....55 A1
Burbank Terr PA14 .....68 B4
Burder Pk G42 .....24 A1
Burgh Hall La G11 .....96 A1
Burgh Hall St G11 .....96 A1
Burgh La 4 G12 .....96 B2
Burgh Mews 2 FK10 .....10 A3
Burgh Prim Sch G73 .....138 A4
Burgh Rd KA9 .....236 A4
Burgh Wlk PA19 .....44 C4
Burghead Dr G51 .....115 C4
Burghead Pl G51 .....115 C4
Burgher St G31 .....118 B3
Burghmuir Ind Est FK8 .....7 A3
Burghmuir Rd FK7 .....7 A3
Burleigh Rd G71 .....141 A2
Burleigh St
Coatbridge ML5 .....122 A4
Glasgow G51 .....116 A4
Burleigh Way FK10 .....10 B3
Burley Pl G75 .....158 C1
Burlington Ave G12 .....96 A3
Burma Rd KA20 .....218 A3
Burmola St G22 .....97 A2
Burn Cres Chapelhall ML6 .....123 B1
Motherwell ML1 .....143 A2
Burn Dr FK7 .....7 B2
Burn La ML1 .....143 A2
Burn Rd Carluke ML8 .....187 C2
Saltcoats KA21 .....205 C2
Burn St G83 .....27 C2
Burn Street La G83 .....27 C2
Burn Terr G72 .....138 C4
Burn View 62 B2
Burn's Cres ML6 .....123 A3
Burn's Pl KA21 .....206 C1
Burn's Wicket KA7 .....238 C1
Burnacre Gdns G71 .....140 C4
Burnawn Gdns G33 .....98 B4
Burnawn Gr G33 .....98 B4
Burnawn Pl G33 .....98 B4
Burnbank Braes ML8 .....187 C1
Burnbank Ctr ML3 .....162 A3
Burnbank Dr G78 .....134 B1
Burnbank Gdns
Hamilton ML3 .....162 A3
Glasgow G20 .....96 C1
Burnbank La G20 .....96 C1
Burnbank Pl KA7 .....239 A2
Stewarton KA3 .....195 C1
Burnbank Quadrant
ML6 .....122 C4
Burnbank Rd Ayr KA2 .....239 A2
Falkirk FK2 .....42 A4
Hamilton ML3 .....162 A3
Burnbank St Airdrie ML6 .....122 C4
Coatbridge ML5 .....122 A4
Stevenston KA20 .....217 B4
Burnbank Terr
 Kilsyth G65 .....36 B1
Burnblea Gdns ML3 .....162 C1
Burnblea St ML3 .....162 B1
Burnbrae Alloa FK10 .....10 B4
Clydebank G81 .....74 A3
Twechar G65 .....59 C2
Burnbrae Ave
Bearsden G61 .....76 A4
Linwood PA3 .....112 B3
Moodiesburn G69 .....81 A1
Burnbrae Dr
Eldersley PA1,PA3,PA5 .....112 B2
Perceton KA11 .....220 B3
Rutherglen G73 .....138 B3
Burnbrae Pl G74 .....159 B1
Burnbrae Prim Sch G53 .....135 B3
Burnbrae Rd
Blantyre G72 .....161 B4
Chryston G69,G66 .....80 A2
Eldersley PA3 .....112 A3
Falkirk FK1 .....42 A3
Harthill ML7 .....127 C3
Kirkintilloch, Auchinloch
G66 .....79 C1
Shotts ML7 .....146 C2
Burnbrae St
Clydebank G81 .....74 B4
Glasgow G21 .....98 A2
Larkhall ML9 .....185 A2
Burnbridge Wynd KA3 .....195 C1
Burnbrae Wynd 2 G72 .....139 A2
Burncrooks Ave
Bearsden G61 .....75 B4
East Kilbride G74 .....159 C1
Burndale La PA13 .....89 B4
Burndyke Ct G51 .....116 B4
Burndyke Sq G51 .....116 B4
Burnee FK10 .....5 C2

Burness Ave KA7 .....238 C1
Burnet Rose Ct G74 .....159 B2
Burnet Rose Gdns G74 .....159 B2
Burnet Rose Pl G74 .....159 B2
Burnett Rd G33 .....119 C4
Burnett Terr KA8 .....236 A1
Burnfield Ave G46 .....136 A2
Burnfield Cotts G46 .....136 A2
Burnfield Gdns G46 .....136 B2
Burnfield Pl FK2 .....42 B4
Burnfield Rd G43 .....136 A2
Burnfoot G82 .....48 A4
Burnfoot Cres
Paisley PA2 .....133 B4
Rutherglen G73 .....138 B3
Burnfoot Dr G52 .....115 A3
Burnfoot La
Ardrossan KA22 .....205 A2
 Falkirk FK1 .....42 A4
Burnfoot Rd Airdrie ML6 .....122 C4
Lochwinnoch PA12 .....129 A1
Burnfoot Way KA10 .....229 C3
Burngreen G65 .....60 B4
Burngreen Terr G67 .....62 A4
Burnhall Pl ML2 .....165 B1
Burnhall Rd ML2 .....165 B1
Burnhall St ML2 .....165 B1
Burnham Rd G14 .....95 A2
Burnhaven PA8 .....73 A1
Burnhead La Falkirk FK1 .....42 B2
Port Glasgow PA14 .....68 B4
Burnhead Prim Sch
G71 .....141 B4
Burnhead Rd
Airdrie ML6 .....103 B1
Cumbernauld G68 .....61 B1
Glasgow G43 .....136 C3
Larkhall ML9 .....185 B1
Port Glasgow PA14 .....68 B4
Stenhousemuir FK5 .....23 B2
Burnhead St
Greenock PA15 .....46 A1
Uddingston G71 .....141 B4
Burnhill Quadrant G73 .....137 C4
Burnhill St G73 .....137 C4
Burnhouse Ave
Cumbernauld G68 .....61 A1
Dally KA24 .....191 A4
Burnhouse Brae G77 .....157 A2
Burnhouse Cotts KA3 .....195 A4
Burnhouse Rd
East Kilbride G75 .....180 A1
Hamilton ML3 .....162 A1
Burnhouse St G20 .....96 B3
Burniebrae Rd ML6 .....123 C2
Burnlea Cres PA6 .....91 A2
Burnlip Rd KA20 .....206 C2
Burnlip Pl G64 .....102 A2
Burns Ave Bishopton PA7 .....72 A2
Kilmarnock KA3 .....223 A2
Saltcoats KA21 .....205 C2
Stenhousemuir FK5 .....23 B2
Burns Cres Harthill ML7 .....127 C3
Irvine KA11 .....220 A3
Laurieston PA2 .....42 C2
Burns Ct G66 .....59 A1
Burns Dr Johnstone PA5 .....131 C4
Burns Gdns G72 .....140 B1
Burns Gr G46 .....136 A1
Burns La ML6 .....123 B2
Burns Loan 13 ML9 .....185 A2
Burns Park ML4 .....142 A4
Burns Pk G74 .....160 A2
Burns Pl Kilwinning KA13 .....207 A2
Shotts ML7 .....146 A3
Burns Prec 6 KA1 .....227 C4
Burns Rd Chapelhall ML6 .....123 B2
Cumbernauld G67 .....62 A1
Greenock PA16 .....45 A1
Troon KA10 .....229 D2
Burns Sq Ardrossan KA22 .....205 B2
Greenock PA16 .....44 B2
Burns St Alexandria G83 .....27 C4
Hamilton ML3 .....162 B2
Burns Statue Sq KA7 .....238 C4
Burns Terr
Ardrossan KA22 .....205 B2
Cowie FK7 .....12 C4
Burns Way ML1 .....143 B2
Burns Wynd ML1 .....198 C1
Burnside
Barrhead G78 .....134 A4
Bellshill ML4 .....141 B3
Brookfield PA5 .....111 B3
Calderbank ML6 .....123 A1
Kirkintilloch G66 .....79 A4
Port Glasgow PA14 .....68 B4
Burnside Cotts KA3 .....173 B3

Burnside Cres
Balloch G83 .....27 C4
Clydebank G81 .....74 A4
Hamilton G72 .....161 C3
Plean FK7 .....12 B2
Shotts ML7 .....146 B3
Burnside Ct Bearsden G61 .....75 B3
Coatbridge ML5 .....121 C3
Hamilton ML3 .....164 A2
Rutherglen G73 .....138 B3
Burnside Gate G73 .....138 B3
Burnside Gdns
Clarkston G76 .....157 B4
Johnstone PA10 .....111 A1
Prestwick KA9 .....233 B1
Burnside Gr PA5 .....111 C1
Burnside Ind Est G65 .....60 B4
Burnside La ML3 .....162 C1
Burnside Pl
Dumbarton G82 .....50 A1
Falkirk FK2 .....24 A2
Irvine KA12 .....219 A2
Larkhall ML9 .....185 A2
Paisley PA3 .....113 A4
Stevenston KA20 .....206 C1
Troon KA10 .....229 C2
West Kilbride KA23 .....190 B3
Burnside Prim Sch G73 .....138 A3
Burnside Quadrant ML1 .....143 A3
Burnside Rd
Elderslie PA5 .....112 B1
Glenmavis ML6 .....102 B1
Gourock PA19 .....44 C3
Menstrie PA10 .....3 C3
Monkton KA9 .....233 B2
Newton Mearns ML1 .....143 B2
Rutherglen G46 .....157 A3
Rutherglen, High Burnside
G73 .....138 B2
Burnside St Alloa FK10 .....5 B3
Dumbarton G82 .....50 A1
Glengarnock KA14 .....170 A3
Kilmarnock KA1 .....227 C3
Motherwell ML1 .....164 A2
Stirling FK7 .....7 B3
Burnside Sta G73 .....138 B3
Burnside Terr FK1 .....41 C3
Burnside Twr ML3 .....164 A2
Burnside View
Coatbridge ML5 .....121 C3
East Kilbride G75 .....180 A2
Burnthills ind Est PA10 .....110 B1
Burntbroom Dr G69 .....119 C2
Burntbroom Gdns G69 .....119 C2
Burntbroom St G33 .....119 B4
Burntbroom St G33 .....119 C2
Burnthills Ind Est PA10 .....110 B1
Burntshields Rd PA10 .....110 B1
Burnwood Dr ML6 .....124 A3
Burra Dr KA3 .....223 A3
Burra Gdns G64 .....78 B1
Burrell Collection (Mus)*
G43 .....116 A1
Burrell's La G4 .....241 C2
Burrelton Rd G43 .....136 C3
Bursnten's Brae
East Kilbride G74 18
Glasgow G20 .....96 B3
Burton La G42 .....117 A2
Busbie Gdns KA2 .....221 C1
Busbie Rd KA2 .....221 C1
Busbiehead ML11 .....220 A3
Busbiehill Pl KA3 .....222 B1
Busby Pl KA13 .....207 C2
Busby Rd Bellshill ML4 .....141 C1
Carmunnock G76 .....158 B4
Clarkston G76 .....157 C3
Glasgow G76 .....158 B4
Bush Cres ML2 .....165 B1
Bush Rd G64 .....99 A3
Bushelhead Rd ML8 .....201 C3
Bushes Ave PA2 .....113 B1
Bushes Prim Sch PA2 .....113 A1
Bushyhill St G72 .....139 A3
Bute G74 .....160 B1
Bute Cres Bearsden G61 .....75 C2
Old Kilpatrick G60 .....73 B3
Paisley PA2 .....113 B2
Bute Ct KA3 .....223 A3
Bute Dr Johnstone PA5 .....111 B1
Old Kilpatrick G60 .....73 B3
Bute Gdns Glasgow G44 .....136 C2
Glasgow, Kelvingrove G12 .....96 B1
Old Kilpatrick G60 .....73 B3
Bute La G12 .....96 B1
Bute Pl Ardrossan KA22 .....205 B1
Old Kilpatrick G60 .....73 B3
Bute Rd Kirkintilloch G66 .....80 A4
Old Kilpatrick G66 .....73 B3
Paisley PA2 .....113 A4
Bute Terr Rutherglen G73 .....138 A3
Uddingston G71 .....141 A4
Bute Twr G72 .....138 C2
Butler Wynd ML4 .....141 C3
Butt Ave G84 .....16 C2
Butterbiggins Rd G42 .....117 A2

Butterburnpark St ML3 .....162 B1
Butterfield Pl 13 G41 .....117 A2
Buttermere G75 .....179 C3
By Pass Rd KA15 .....150 B1
By-Pass Rd FK4 .....39 C3
Byars Rd G66 .....79 A4
Byrebush Rd G53 .....115 B1
Byrehill Ave KA13 .....207 A1
Byrehill Rd KA13 .....207 B1
Byrehill Rd Irvine KA13 .....218 C4
Kilwinning KA13,KA20 .....207 B1
Byres Ave PA3 .....114 A3
Byres Cres PA3 .....114 A3
Byres Loch KA13 .....207 B2
Byres Rd Eldersile PA5 .....112 B1
Glasgow G11, G12 .....96 B1
Kilwinning KA13 .....207 B2
Motherwell ML1 .....143 C2
Byresknowe La ML1 .....143 A1
Byrestone Ave G77 .....157 B2
Byretown Rd ML11 .....214 C1
Byron Rd ML7 .....146 A3
Byron St Clydebank G81 .....74 A2
Glasgow G11 .....95 C1
Byshot St G22 .....97 B2

C

Cable Depot Rd G81 .....73 C1
Cables Dr G83 .....27 C3
Cabrach Loan 18 ML2 .....165 C3
Cadder Ct G64 .....78 A3
Cadder Pl G20 .....96 C4
Cadder Rd
Bishopbriggs G64 .....78 A3
Glasgow G20 .....96 C4
Cadder Way G64 .....78 A3
Caddel Pl KA1 .....228 B3
Caddellhill St PA16 .....45 B3
Cadell Dr FK2 .....24 A3
Cadell Gdns G74 .....160 B3
Cadger's Sheuch G65 .....61 A4
Cadgers Loan FK7 .....12 A1
Cadoc St G72 .....139 A3
Cadogan Sq G2 .....240 B2
Cadogan St G2 .....240 B2
Cadzow Ave
Hamilton ML3 .....162 B3
Rutherglen G46 .....157 A4
Cadzow Cres ML5 .....121 C2
Cadzow Dr Bellshill ML4 .....142 B2
Cambuslang G72 .....139 A3
Cadzow Gn G74 .....159 B1
Cadzow Gn G74 .....159 B1
Cadzow Ho ML3 .....162 C3
Cadzow Ind Est ML3 .....183 B4
Cadzow La ML3 .....162 C2
Cadzow Pk ML3 .....162 C2
Cadzow Rd ML3 .....183 C2
Cadzow Rd Glasgow G42 .....240 B2
Hamilton ML3 .....162 C2
Larkhall ML9 .....185 A2
Motherwell ML1 .....163 B3
Caerlaverock Ave KA9 .....236 B4
Caerlaverock Pl G72 .....139 A2
Caerlaverock Rd KA9 .....236 B4
Caff Water Pl KA1 .....205 C1
Caird Ave KA16 .....45 B4
Caird Dr G11 .....96 A1
Caird Gdns ML3 .....162 B3
Caird Pk ML3 .....162 B3
Caird St ML3 .....162 B3
Caird Terr G61 .....75 B4
Cairn Ave PA4 .....94 C1
Cairn Ct G74 .....195 B1
Cairn Ct G74 .....238 B1
Cairn Dr PA3 .....112 A3
Cairn Pl G74 .....159 C2
Cairn St G21 .....97 C3
Cairn View Airdrie ML6 .....122 C2
Kirkintilloch G66 .....80 A4
Cairnban St ML6 .....123 A4
Cairnban St G51 .....115 B3
Cairnbrook Ind Est G34 .....120 B4
Cairnbrook Rd G34 .....120 B4
Cairncurran PA15 .....45 C2
Cairndhu Ave G84 .....16 A1
Cairndhu Gdns G84 .....16 A1
Cairndow Ave G44 .....136 C2
Cairndow Avenue La
G44 .....136 C2
Cairndow Pl G44 .....136 C2
Cairndow Pl ML3 .....162 B1
Cairney Pl KA3 .....195 C1
Cairney Pl KA3 .....195 C1
Cairneymount Rd ML8 .....188 A2
Cairnfore Ave KA10 .....229 D3
Cairngorm Cres
Barrhead G78 .....134 A1
Bearsden G61 .....75 A4
Paisley PA2 .....133 C4
Wishaw ML2 .....164 C2
Cairngorm Ct KA11 .....220 A3
Cairngorm Gdns G68 .....61 A1
Cairngorm Pl ML2 .....180 A2
Cairngorm Rd
Glasgow G43 .....136 B3
Kilmarnock KA1 .....228 A2
Cairnhill Ave ML6 .....123 A3
Cairnhill Cir G52 .....114 C2
Cairnhill Cres ML5 .....122 B2
Cairnhill Ct ML8 .....188 A1
Cairnhill Dr G52 .....114 C2

Cairnhill Pl G52 . . . . .114 C2
Cairnhill Rd Airdrie ML6 . .123 A3
  Bearsden G61 . . . . .75 C1
Cairnhill Trad Est ML6 . .123 A3
Cairnlea Ave ML6 . . . . . .122 C3
Cairnlea Dr G51 . . . . . . .116 A3
Cairnlea Gdns ML4 . . . .142 A2
Cairnlea Rd G62 . . . . .54 C1
Cairnmount Rd G74 . . .159 B3
Cairnoch Hill G68 . . . . . .61 B1
Cairnoch Way FK7 . . . . . . .7 C1
Cairnoch Wlk FK6 . . . . . .21 B1
Cairnryan G74 . . . . .159 B2
Cairns Ave G72 . . . . .139 A3
Cairns Dr G62 . . . . .55 A1
Cairns Prim Sch The
  G72 . . . . .139 B2
Cairns Rd Bishopton PA7 . .72 A2
  Cambuslang G72 . . . . .139 A2
Cairns St ML1 . . . . .163 C3
Cairns Terr KA1 . . . . .222 C1
Cairnview Rd G66 . . . . . .58 B3
Cairnwood Dr ML6 . . . . .122 C3
Cairnsgarroch Way
  KA11 . . . . .220 A1
Cairnsmore Dr Air KA7 . .238 B1
  Bearsden G61 . . . . .75 C1
Cairnsmore Rd G15 . . . .74 C1
Cairnsmore Way KA11 . .220 A1
Cairnswell Pl G72 . . . . . .139 B2
Cairntoul Ct G68 . . . . . . .61 A1
Cairntoul Dr G14 . . . . . . .95 A3
Cairntoul Pl G14 . . . . . . .95 A3
Cairnview Rd G66 . . . . . .58 B3
Cairnwood Dr ML6 . . . .122 C3
Caithness Rd
  East Kilbride G74 . . . . .160 B2
  Greenock PA16 . . . . . . .44 A2
Caithness Row ML11 . .215 A1
Caithness St
  Blantyre G72 . . . . .161 B3
  Glasgow G20 . . . . .96 C2
Cala Sona Ct ML2 . . . . . .165 C4
Calcots Path G34 . . . . . .100 B1
Calcots Pl G34 . . . . .100 B1
Caldarvan St G22 . . . . . .97 A2
Caldeen Rd ML5 . . . . .122 A3
Calder Ave Barrhead G78 . .134 B1
  Caldercruix ML6 . . . . . . .104 C2
  Coatbridge ML5 . . . . . . .122 A2
  Troon KA10 . . . . .229 D3
  Wishaw ML2 . . . . .166 A3
Calder Ct Coatbridge ML5 . .122 A2
  Stirling FK7 . . . . .7 B3
Calder Dr Bellshill ML4 . .142 B2
  Cambuslang G72 . . . . . .139 A2
  Lochwinnoch PA12 . . . .129 B2
  Shotts ML7 . . . . .147 A2
Calder Gate G64 . . . . . . .77 C2
Calder Pl Falkirk FK1 . .42 B1
  Glasgow G69 . . . . .101 A2
  Kilmarnock KA1 . . . . . . .228 A3
Calder Prim Sch ML1 . .163 C4
Calder Rd Bellshill ML4 . .142 B3
  Paisley PA3 . . . . .113 A3
  Shotts ML7 . . . . .146 A4
  Uddingston G72 . . . . . . .140 B3
Calder St Blantyre G72 . .161 B4
  Calderbank ML6 . . . . . . .123 B1
  Coatbridge ML5 . . . . . . .122 B3
  Glasgow G42 . . . . .117 A1
  Lochwinnoch PA12 . . . .129 B2
Calder Twr
  East Kilbride G74 . . . . .181 A4
  9 Motherwell ML1 . . .163 C3
Calder View ML3 . . . . . .183 A4
Calderbank Prim Sch
  ML6 . . . . .123 A2
Calderbank Rd ML6 . . . .123 A2
Calderbank Terr ML1 . .163 C3
Calderbank View G69 . .120 B2
Calderbankview Cotts
  ML6 . . . . .123 A2
Calderbraes Ave G71 . .140 C4
Caldercruix Rd FK1,ML6 . .105 B4
Caldercuilt Prim Sch
  G23 . . . . .76 C1
Caldercuilt Rd G20,G23 . .96 B4
Calderglen Ave G72 . . .140 B2
Calderglen Ctry Pk*
  G75 . . . . .181 B3
Calderglen Ctry Pk Visitor
  Ctr* G75 . . . . .181 B3
Calderglen Rd G74 . . . .160 B1
Caldergrove ML1 . . . . . .163 C4
Calderhaugh La PA12 . .129 A1
Calderhead High Sch
  ML7 . . . . .147 A3
Calderhead Rd ML7 . . . .146 B4
Calderpark Ave
  Glasgow G71 . . . . .120 A1
  Lochwinnoch PA12 . . . .129 C1
Calderpark Cres G71 . .120 A1
Calderpark St PA12 . . . .129 B2
Caldergrigg Pl ML6 . . . .123 C4
Calderside Gr G74 . . . . .160 C2
Calderside Rd G72,G74 . .160 C2
Caldervale High Sch
  ML6 . . . . .123 C4
Caldervale St ML6 . . . . .123 C2
Calderview ML6 . . . . . . .163 C4
Calderview Ave ML5 . . .122 C2
Calderwood KA13 . . . . .207 C3
Calderwood Ave G69 . .120 A2

Calderwood Ct ML2 . . . .165 A1
Calderwood Dr
  Blantyre G72 . . . . .161 B3
  Glasgow G69 . . . . .120 A2
Calderwood Gdns
  East Kilbride G74 . . . . .160 C2
  Glasgow G69 . . . . .120 A2
Calderwood Jewish Prim Day
  Sch G43 . . . . .136 A3
Calderwood Prim Sch
  G73 . . . . .138 B3
Calderwood Rd
  East Kilbride G74 . . . . .160 A1
  Glasgow G43 . . . . .136 B3
  Rutherglen G73 . . . . . . .138 A4
Calderwood Sq G74 . . .160 A2
Caldon Rd KA12 . . . . .219 B2
Caldwell Ave
  Glasgow G13 . . . . .95 A3
  Linwood PA3 . . . . .112 A3
Caldwell Gr ML4 . . . . . . .142 A4
Caldwell Pl G84 . . . . .15 C3
Caldwell Quadrant ML1 . .163 B3
Caldwell Rd Carluke ML8 . .202 A4
  West Kilbride KA23 . . .190 B2
Caledon La G72 . . . . .96 B1
Caledon St G22 . . . . .96 B2
Caledonia Ave
  Glasgow G5 . . . . .117 B2
  Rutherglen G73 . . . . . . .138 A4
Caledonia Cres
  Ardrossan KA22 . . . . . .205 B1
  Gourock PA19 . . . . .45 A4
Caledonia Ct
  Kilmarnock KA1 . . . . . .222 C1
  Paisley PA3 . . . . .113 B3
Caledonia Dr
  Glasgow G69 . . . . .120 A2
  Motherwell ML1 . . . . . . .143 C2
Caledonia Gdns
  Carluke ML8 . . . . .187 C2
  Gourock PA19 . . . . .44 C4
Caledonia Prim Sch
  KA21 . . . . .216 C4
Caledonia Rd
  Ardrossan KA22 . . . . . .205 B1
  Ayr KA7 . . . . .239 B3
  Beith KA15 . . . . .150 A1
  Glasgow G69 . . . . .120 A2
  Glasgow, Gorbals G5 . .117 B2
  Saltcoats KA21 . . . . . . .216 C4
  Shotts ML7 . . . . .146 C3
Caledonia St
  Clydebank G81 . . . . .73 C2
  Glasgow G5 . . . . .117 B2
  Paisley PA3 . . . . .113 B3
  Port Glasgow PA14 . . . .47 B1
  Rutherglen G73 . . . . . . .138 A4
Caledonia Terr ML2 . . . .49 B2
Caledonia Way E PA3 . .93 C1
Caledonia Way E PA3 . .93 B1
Caledonia Wlk ML3 . . . .162 C1
Caledonian Ave
  Bellshill ML4 . . . . .141 C2
  Stonehouse ML9 . . . . . .198 C1
Caledonian Cres **6** G12 . .96 C1
Caledonian Ct
  East Kilbride G74 . . . . .180 C4
  Falkirk FK2 . . . . .42 B4
Caledonian Pk ML1 . . .164 B2
Caledonian Pl KA14 . .170 B4
Caledonian Prim Sch
  G69 . . . . .120 A2
Caledonian Rd Alloa FK10 . .9 C3
  Glengarnock KA14 . . . .170 B4
  Larkhall ML9 . . . . .185 A2
  Stevenston KA20 . . . . .217 C4
  Wishaw ML2 . . . . .165 A1
Caley Brae G71 . . . . .140 C3
Caley Ct KA20 . . . . .217 B4
Caifhill Rd G53 . . . . . . .115 A1
Calfmuir Rd G66 . . . . . .80 A3
Calgary PA5 . . . . .180 B4
Calgary Pl **6** G75 . . . . .180 B4
Calgary St G4 . . . . .241 A4
Calico Way G66 . . . . . . .33 B1
California Prim Sch FK1 . .66 C3
California Terr FK1 . . . . .66 C3
Callaghan Wynd G72 . .140 B1
Callander Ct G68 . . . . . .61 C2
Callander Dr FK5 . . . . . .41 B4
Callander Rd
  Chapelhall ML6 . . . . . . .123 B1
  Cumbernauld G68 . . . .61 C2
Callander St G20 . . . . . .97 A2
Callendar Ave FK1 . . . .42 A1
Callendar Bsns Pk FK1 . .42 C2
Callendar Bvd FK1 . . . .42 C2
Callendar Ho* FK1 . . . .42 B2
Callendar Rd FK1,FK2 . .42 B2
Callendar Riggs FK1 . .42 B2
Callendar Square Sh Ctr
  FK1 . . . . .42 A2
Callender Rd KA8 . . . . .236 B3
Callieburn Ct G64 . . . . .98 A4
Callieburn Rd G64 . . . .98 A4
Callon St ML6 . . . . .123 A4
Cally Ave G15 . . . . .75 A2
Calside PA2 . . . . .113 C2
Calside Ave PA2 . . . . . .113 B2
Calton Cres FK7 . . . . . .7 A2
Calton Entry G40 . . . .241 C1
Caltrop Pl FK7 . . . . .7 C2
Calvay Cres G33 . . . . . .119 B4
Calvay Pl G33 . . . . .119 C4
Calvay Rd G33 . . . . .119 C4
Calvinston Rd KA9 . . . .236 B3

Cam'nethan St ML9 . . . .198 C1
Cambourne Rd G69 . . .80 C2
Cambridge Ave
  Clydebank G81 . . . . .74 A2
  Gourock PA19 . . . . .45 A4
Cambridge Rd
  Greenock PA16 . . . . . . .44 B2
  Renfrew PA4 . . . . .94 B3
Cambridge St G22 . . . .240 C3
Camburn St G32 . . . . . .118 C3
Cambus Pl G33 . . . . .99 B1
Cambus Pools Nature
  Reserve* FK10 . . . . . . .8 C4
Cambusbarron Prim Sch
  FK7 . . . . .7 B4
Cambusdoon Dr KA7 . .238 C1
Cambusdoon Pl KA13 . .207 B2
Cambuskenneth Rd KA20 . .206 C2
Cambuskenneth Abbey*
  FK9 . . . . .7 B4
Cambuskenneth Gdns
  G32 . . . . .119 B3
Cambuskenneth Pl G33 . .99 B1
Cambuslang Coll Allers
  Annexe G74 . . . . .160 B2
Cambuslang Coll Annexe
  G74 . . . . .159 C1
Cambuslang Ind Est
  G32 . . . . .119 A4
Cambuslang Investment Pk
  G32 . . . . .139 A4
Cambuslang Rd
  Cambuslang G72 . . . . .138 C4
  Rutherglen G72,G73 . .138 C3
  Cambuslang Sta G72 . .138 C3
Cambuslea Rd KA8 . . .236 A3
Cambusmoon Terr G83 . .20 C4
Cambusnethan Prim Sch
  ML2 . . . . .165 B2
Cambusnethan St ML2 . .165 B2
Camden Hill Gdns FK4 . .40 A3
Camden Terr G5 . . . . . . .117 B2
Camelia Dr ML2 . . . . . . .164 C1
Camelon Cres G72 . . . .161 B4
Camelon Ed Ctr FK1 . .41 C3
Camelon Rd FK1 . . . . . .41 B3
Camelon St G32 . . . . . .118 C3
Camelon Sta FK1 . . . . .41 B3
Cameron Ave Port PA7 . .72 A2
Cameron Cres
  Carmunnock G76 . . . . .158 C4
  Hamilton ML3 . . . . .162 B2
Cameron Ct
  Clydebank G81 . . . . .94 B4
  Gourock PA19 . . . . .43 C3
  Rutherglen G73 . . . . . . .138 A4
Cameron Dr
  Alexandria G83 . . . . . . .27 B4
  Bearsden G61 . . . . .76 A2
  Kilmarnock KA3 . . . . . . .223 B1
  Newton Mearns G77 . .156 C4
Cameron Path **22** ML9 . .185 B1
Cameron Pl FK2 . . . . . .24 A1
Cameron Rd
  Carluke ML8 . . . . .202 A4
  Greenock ML5 . . . . .83 B1
Cameron Sq G81 . . . . . .74 B3
Cameron St
  Clydebank G81 . . . . .94 B4
  Coatbridge ML5 . . . . . . .122 A4
  Motherwell ML1 . . . . . . .163 B3
  Paisley G52 . . . . .114 C4
Cameron Terr FK1 . . . . .86 A2
Cameron Way G72 . . . .161 B4
Canal Bank Ind Est FK4 . .40 A2
Canal Cres KA20 . . . . .217 B4
Canal Ct KA21 . . . . .217 A4
Canal Gdns PA5 . . . . . .112 B2
Canal La G66 . . . . .58 B1
Canal Pl KA21 . . . . .217 A4
Canal Rd PA5 . . . . .112 A1
Canal St Eldersie PA5 . .112 B2
  Falkirk FK2 . . . . .42 A4
  Falkirk, Camelon FK1 . .41 B3
  Glasgow G4 . . . . .241 A4
  Johnstone PA5 . . . . . . .112 A2
  Kirkintilloch G66 . . . . .58 B1
  Paisley PA1 . . . . .113 B2
  Renfrew PA4 . . . . .94 B2
  Saltcoats KA21 . . . . . . .217 A4
Canavan Ct FK7 . . . . . .7 B2
Canberra Ave G81 . . . .73 B2
Canberra Ct G46 . . . . .136 C2
Canberra Dr G75 . . . . .180 B4
Canberra Prim Sch G75 . .180 A4
Cander Ave ML9 . . . . . .199 A2
Cander Rigg G64 . . . . .78 A4
Canderside St ML9 . . .199 A2
Canderside Toll ML9 . .199 A3
Candimilne Ct ML8 . . .188 A1
Candleriggs Alloa FK10 . .10 A3
  Glasgow G1 . . . . .241 B2
Candleriggs Ct **6** G71 . .241 B2
Candren Rd Linwood PA3 . .112 C3
  Paisley PA3 . . . . .113 A2
Candren Way PA3 . . . . .113 A2
Caneluk Ave ML8 . . . . .188 A1
Cangillan Ct KA9 . . . . .236 B3
Canmore Cres PA16 . .45 A2
Canmore Pl Glasgow G31 . .118 B2

Canmore Pl continued
  Stewarton KA3 . . . . .195 C1
Canmore St G31 . . . . . .118 B2
Cannerton Cres G66 . .58 A3
Cannerton Pk G66 . . . .58 A3
Cannich Dr PA2 . . . . . . .114 A1
Cannich Pl ML2 . . . . . . .165 C3
Canniesburn Hospl G61 . .75 C2
Canniesburn Rd G61 . .75 B2
Canniesburn Sq G61 . .75 C2
Canniesburn Toll G61 . .75 C2
Cannons Way FK2 . . . .24 A1
Canon Ct ML1 . . . . .143 B1
Canonbie Ave G74 . . . .159 C2
Canonbie St G34 . . . . .100 B1
Canongate G74 . . . . . . .160 B2
Canterbury G75 . . . . . .180 B4
Canthill Gdns ML7 . . . .146 A2
Cantieslaw Dr G74 . . . .160 A2
Canting Way G51 . . . . .116 B4
Canyon Rd ML2 . . . . . . .164 B1
Capel Ave G77 . . . . .156 C3
Capel Gr G74 . . . . .160 A2
Capel Pl KA11 . . . . .220 A1
Capelrig Cotts G77 . . .155 C2
Capelrig Dr
  East Kilbride G74 . . . . .160 A2
  Newton Mearns G77 . .156 C4
Capelrig La G77 . . . . . .156 B3
Capelrig Rd G77 . . . . . .156 B3
Capelrig St G46 . . . . . .135 C2
Caplaw Pl ML2 . . . . .185 C4
Caplaw Rd
  Johnstone G78 . . . . . . .132 B1
  Paisley PA2 . . . . .133 B3
Caplaw Twr ML2 . . . . .185 C4
Caplethill Rd
  Barrhead G78 . . . . .134 A3
  Paisley PA2 . . . . .133 C4
Cappuccino Ave KA20 . .206 B1
Capper View KA9 . . . .233 B1
Cappielow Ind Est PA15 . .46 B2
Cappielow Pk (Greenock
  Morton FC) PA15 . . . .46 B2
Caprington Foot
  KA11 . . . . .220 A3
Caprington Ave KA1 . .227 C2
Caprington Gdns KA1 . .227 C2
Caprington St G33 . . .99 A1
Captain St PA15 . . . . . .45 C2
Cara Dr G51 . . . . .115 C4
Caravelle Way **17** PA4 . .94 B1
Carbarns ML4 . . . . .164 C1
Carbarns E ML2 . . . . . .164 B1
Carbarns Rd ML2 . . . .164 B1
Carbarns W ML2 . . . . .164 B1
Carberry Rd G41 . . . . .116 B1
Carbeth Rd G62 . . . . . .54 C1
Carbeth St G22 . . . . . .97 A2
Carbisdale St G22 . . .97 C3
Carbost St G23 . . . . . .76 B1
Carbrain Ind Est G67 . .62 A1
Carbrain Prim Sch G67 . .62 A1
Carbrook Dr FK7 . . . . .12 B2
Carbrook St Glasgow G21 . .98 A1
  Paisley PA1 . . . . .113 B2
Carbrook Terr FK5 . . .23 B2
Carcluie Cres KA7 . . .239 A1
Cardarrach St G21 . . .98 A2
Cardean Rd ML4 . . . . . .142 C3
Cardell Ave PA2 . . . . .113 A2
Cardell Cres ML6 . . . .123 B1
Cardell Dr PA2 . . . . . . .113 A2
Cardell Rd PA2 . . . . . . .113 A2
Cardinal Newman High Sch
  ML4 . . . . .141 C3
Cardon Pl KA11 . . . . . . .220 A1
Cardonald Coll G52 . .115 B2
Cardonald Dr G52 . . .115 A2
Cardonald Gdns G52 . .115 A2
Cardonald Place Rd
  G52 . . . . .115 A2
Cardonald Prim Sch
  G52 . . . . .115 B3
Cardonald Sta G52 . .115 B3
Cardow Cres KA11 . . .220 A3
Cardowan Dr
  Cumbernauld G68 . . . .60 C1
  Stepps G33 . . . . .99 C3
Cardowan Rd
  Glasgow G32 . . . . .119 A4
  Stepps G33 . . . . .99 C3
Cardrona St G33 . . . . .99 A2
Cardross Ave PA15 . . .46 B1
Cardross Cres PA15 . .46 B1
Cardross Ct G31 . . . . .117 C4
Cardross Pl FK15 . . . .46 B1
Cardross Prim Sch G82 . .26 B1
Cardross Rd
  Alexandria G82 . . . . . . .26 C1
  Dumbarton G82 . . . . . . .49 A2
  Helensburgh G82 . . . . .25 C2
  Renton G82 . . . . .27 A1
Cardross St G31 . . . . .117 C4
Cardross Sta G82 . . . .48 A4
Cardrowan Rd FK7 . . .12 B1
Cardwell Rd PA19 . . . .44 C4
Cardwell St G5 . . . . . . .117 A2
Cardyke St G21 . . . . . .98 A2
Carelcoch Rd PA14 . .68 C4
Carerron G72 . . . . .161 B4
Carey Gdns ML1 . . . . .144 B1
Carey Rd KA21 . . . . . . .205 C2
Carfin Dr ML8 . . . . .201 B1
Carfin Ind Est ML1 . .143 A1

Carfin Lourdes Grotto*
ML1 ....143 B1
Carfin Mill Rd ML1 ......143 B1
Carfin Rd
Motherwell ML1 ....143 B2
Wishaw ML2 ....164 B2
Carfin St Coatbridge ML5 .122 A2
Glasgow G42 ....117 A1
Motherwell ML1 ....143 A2
Carfin Sta ML1 ....143 B1
Carfrae St G3 ....116 B4
Cargil Ave PA13 ....89 B4
Cargill Dr KA9 ....236 B3
Cargill Sq G64 ....98 B4
Carham Cres G52 ....115 B3
Carham Dr G52 ....115 B3
Caribou Gn G75 ....180 A4
Carillon Rd G51 ....116 B3
Carisbrooke Cres G64 .....78 A2
Carlaverock Rd G43 ......136 C3
Carleith Ave G81 ....73 C3
Carleith Prim Sch G81 ...73 C3
Carleith Quadrant G51 ..73 B4
Carleith Terr G81 ....73 C3
Carleston St G21 ....97 C2
Carleton Ct G46 ....136 B2
Carleton Dr G46 ....136 B2
Carleton Gate G46 ....136 B2
Carleton Gdns KA9 ......236 B4
Carlibar Ave G13 ....94 C4
Carlibar Dr G78 ....134 B2
Carlibar Gdns G78 ....134 B2
Carlibar Prim Sch G78 ..134 B2
Carlibar Rd G78 ....134 B2
Carlie Ave PA9 ....2 A3
Carlile Pl PA3 ....113 C3
Carlin La ML6 ....188 A1
Carlin's Pl G66 ....57 B4
Carlisle La ML6 ....123 B4
Carlisle Rd Airdrie ML6 .123 B3
Cleland ML1 ....144 B3
Hamilton ML3 ....163 A2
Larkhall ML3,ML9 ....184 C4
Stonehouse ML9 ....199 B2
Carlisle St G21, G22 ....97 B2
Carlouk La ML8 ....188 A1
Carlowrie Ave G72 ....140 B1
Carlton Ct Glasgow G5 ...240 C1
[6] Hamilton ML3 ....162 C1
Carlton Pl G5 ....240 C1
Carluke High Sch ML8 ...188 A1
Carluke Prim Sch ML8 ...188 A2
Carluke Sta ML8 ....187 C1
Carlung Pl KA23 ....190 B2
Carlyle Ave G52 ....114 C4
Carlyle Dr G74 ....160 A1
Carlyle Terr
East Kilbride G74 ....160 A1
Rutherglen G73 ....118 A1
Carnaben Rd G33 ....119 C4
Carman Rd Cardross G82 ..48 B4
Renton G82 ....26 C2
Carman View G82 ....50 A3
Carmel Ave KA1 ....222 B1
Carmel Dr KA11 ....221 A1
Carmel Pl
Kilmarnock KA1 ....222 B1
Kilmaurs KA3 ....222 A4
Carmel Terr KA1 ....222 B2
Carment Dr Glasgow G41 .136 B4
Stevenston KA20 ....217 C4
Carmichael Ct
Bridge of A FK9 ....2 A4
Lanark ML11 ....215 C4
Carmichael Path ML5 ....101 B3
Carmichael Pl G42 ....136 C4
Carmichael St
Glasgow G51 ....116 B3
Greenock PA16 ....45 B3
Law ML8 ....186 C3
Carmichael Way ML8 ....186 C3
Carmona Dr G83 ....28 A4
Carmuirs Ave FK1 ....41 B3
Carmuirs Dr FK1 ....41 B3
Carmuirs Prim Sch FK1 ..41 B3
Carmuirs St FK1 ....41 B3
Carmunnock By-Pass
G76 ....158 B4
Carmunnock La G44 ....137 B3
Carmunnock Prim Sch
G76 ....158 A3
Carmunnock Rd
Clarkston G76 ....158 A3
Glasgow G44 ....137 B4
Carmyle Ave G32 ....139 A4
Carmyle Gdns ML5 ....121 C2
Carmyle Pl KA20 ....217 B4
Carmyle Prim Sch G32 ..119 B1
Carmyle Sta G32 ....119 A1
Carna Dr G44 ....137 B3
Carnarvon St G3 ....240 A4
Carnaughton Pl FK12 .....4 C3
Carnbooth Ct G45 ....137 C1
Carnbroe Prim Sch ML5 .122 B2
Carnbroe Rd ML5 ....122 B2
Carneddans Rd G62 ....54 B2
Carnegie Dr FK1 ....41 B3
Carnegie Hill G75 ....180 B4
Carnegie Rd G52 ....115 A3
Carnell Cres KA9 ....236 B4
Carnell Terr KA9 ....236 B4
Carnock St [9] G63 ....76 B1
Carnock Cres G78 ....134 A1
Carnock Gdns G62 ....54 C1
Carnock Rd G53 ....135 B4
Carnock St Cowie FK7 .....7 C4
Greenock PA15 ....46 A2

Carnoustie Ave PA19 ......44 A3
Carnoustie Cres
Bishopbriggs G64 ....78 B1
East Kilbride G75 ....180 A3
Carnoustie Ct
Bothwell G72 ....140 C1
Kilwinning KA13 ....207 A2
Carnoustie Pl
Bellshill ML4 ....142 A4
Glasgow G5 ....116 C3
Irvine KA11 ....224 D4
Carnoustie St G5 ....116 C3
Carnoustie Way G68 ......61 C3
Carntyne Ind Est G32 ...118 C3
Carntyne Path G32 ....118 B4
Carntyne Pl G32 ....118 B4
Carntyne Prim Sch G33 .118 B4
Carntyne Sta G32 ....118 C3
Carntynehall Rd G32 ....118 C3
Carnwadric Prim Sch
G46 ....135 C2
Carnwadric Rd G46 ......135 C2
Carnwath Ave G43 ....136 C3
Carnwath Rd
Carluke ML8 ....188 A1
Kilncadzow ML8 ....203 B3
Caroline Cres FK12 ....4 C3
Caroline St G31 ....118 C3
Carolside Ave G76 ....157 C4
Carolside Dr G15 ....75 A2
Carolside Gdns G76 ......157 C4
Carolside Prim Sch
G76 ....157 C3
Carousel Cres PA2 ....165 B2
Carpenters Wynd FK10 ...9 C3
Carr Quadrant ML4 ....142 B3
Carradale Ave PA1 ....114 C2
Carradale Cres G68 ....81 C4
Carradale Dr KA7 ....236 B3
Carradale Gdns
Bishopbriggs G64 ....78 B1
Carluke ML8 ....202 A4
Carradale Ct FK10 ....108 B4
Carradale St ML5 ....121 C4
Carranbuie Rd ML6 ....187 C2
Carrbridge Dr [9] G20 ...96 B3
Carresbrook Ave G66 .....98 A3
Carriagehill Ave PA2 .....113 C1
Carriagehill Dr PA2 ......113 C1
Carrick Ave Ayr KA7 ......238 C3
Saltcoats KA21 ....206 A2
Carrick Cres
Glasgow G46 ....136 A2
Wishaw ML2 ....165 A2
Carrick Ct Kirkintilloch G66 ..59 A1
Stirling FK7 ....7 B3
Carrick Dr
Coatbridge ML5 ....121 B4
Irvine KA12 ....219 A3
Rutherglen G73 ....138 A4
Carrick Gdns Ayr KA7 ..238 C3
Bellshill ML4 ....142 A4
Coatbridge ML5 ....121 B4
Blantyre G72 ....140 B3
Carluke ML8 ....202 A4
Hamilton ML3 ....161 C1
Carrick Glen Hospl The
KA6 ....239 C1
Carrick Gr G32 ....119 C2
Carrick La PA16 ....44 C2
Carrick Pk KA7 ....238 C3
Carrick Pl
Ardrossan KA22 ....205 B2
Bellshill ML4 ....142 A4
Coatbridge ML5 ....121 B4
Falkirk FK2 ....24 A2
Falkirk, Tamfourhill FK1 ...41 A2
Glenboig ML5 ....101 C3
Larkhall ML9 ....185 A2
Prestwick KA9 ....236 A3
Carrick Rd Ayr KA7 ....238 C3
Bishopbriggs G64 ....78 B1
Bishopton PA7 ....72 A1
Cumbernauld G67 ....62 A2
East Kilbride G74 ....159 C2
Rutherglen G73 ....138 B4
Troon KA10 ....229 C4
Carrick Road La KA7 ......238 C4
Carrick St KA7 ....238 C4
[7] Larkhall ML9 ....185 B1
Carrick Terr
Dumbarton G82 ....49 A2
Greenock PA16 ....44 C2
Carrick Vale ML5 ....101 C3
Carrick Way ML4 [1] 141 A2
Carrickarden Rd G61 ......61 C2
Carrickstone Rd G68 ......61 C4
Carrickstone Rdbt G68 ..61 C4
Carrickstone View G68 ..61 C3
Carrington St G4 ....96 C1
Carroch Rd G83 ....27 C4
Carrochan Cres G83 ....27 C4
Carrochan Rd G83 ....27 C4
Carroglen Gdns G32 .....119 B3
Carroglen Gr G32 ....119 B3
Carroll Cres ML1 ....143 B1
Carron Cres Bearsden G61 .75 B2
Bishopbriggs G64 ....78 A1
Glasgow G22 ....78 A2
Carron Ct
Cambuslang G72 ....139 B3
Hamilton ML3 ....162 A1
Carron Dr PA7 ....72 B1
Carron Pl Coatbridge ML5 .101 B1

Carron Pl continued
East Kilbride G75 ....180 C3
Glasgow G22 ....97 C3
Irvine KA12 ....219 B3
Stirling FK7 ....7 A1
Carron Prim Sch FK2 ......24 A1
Carron Rd FK2 ....42 A4
Carron St Glasgow G22 ...97 C3
Wishaw ML2 ....165 A1
Carron Way
Motherwell ML1 ....143 B2
Paisley PA3 ....114 A4
Carronbank Ave FK2 ....24 A1
Carronbank Cres FK6 .....21 C2
Carronbank Ct FK2 ....24 A1
Carronflats Rd FK2 ....24 A2
Carrongrange Ave FK5 ..23 C1
Carrongrange Gdns FK5 .23 C1
Carrongrange Gr FK5 .....23 C1
Carrongrange Prim Sch
FK5 ....23 C1
Carrongrange Rd FK5 .....23 C1
Carrongrove Ave FK2 ....24 A1
Carrongrove Bsns Pk
FK2 ....24 A1
Carrongrove Rd FK2 ......24 A1
Carronhall Ave FK2 ....24 A2
Carronlea Dr FK2 ....24 A1
Carronshore Prim Sch
FK2 ....24 B2
Carronshore Rd FK2 ....24 A1
Carronside Pl FK6 ....21 C2
Carronside St ML5 ....121 C4
Carronvale Ave FK5 ....23 B1
Carronvale Rd FK5 ....23 B1
Carronview FK5 ....23 B1
Carrour Gdns G64 ....77 C1
Carruth Rd PA11 ....110 B4
Carruth St PA11 ....110 B4
Carsaig Ct FK9 ....2 A3
Carsaig Dr G52 ....115 C3
Carsaig Loan ML5 ....101 B3
Carscallan Rd ML3 ....183 C3
Carse Terr FK10 ....9 A2
Carse View FK2 ....14 C2
Carsebridge Ct FK10 ....10 B2
Carsebridge Rd FK10 ......10 B4
Caresgreen Ave PA2 ......133 A4
Carseloch Rd KA7 ....238 C2
Carsemeadow PA11 ....89 C1
Carsewood Ave PA9 ....130 C3
Carson Dr KA12 ....224 C4
Carson Rd G83 ....27 C4
Carstairs St G40 ....141 B1
Carswell Ct KA24 ....191 A4
Carswell Gdns G41 ....116 C1
Carswell Rd G77 ....156 A3
Cart La PA3 ....113 A3
Cart St G81 ....94 A4
Cartbank Gdns G44 ....137 A2
Cartbank Gr G44 ....136 C2
Cartbank Rd G44 ....136 C2
Cartcraigs Rd G43 ....136 A3
Carters Pl KA12 ....219 B1
Cartha Cres PA2 ....114 A2
Cartha St G41 ....136 C4
Cartland Ave ML8 ....201 C4
Cartland Rd ML11 ....214 B4
Cartland View ML11 ......214 C3
Cartle Cl KA13 ....207 B3
Cartsbridge Rd G76 ......157 C3
Cartsburn St PA15 ....46 A2
Cartsdyke Ave G76 ....46 B2
Cartsdyke Sta PA15 ....46 B2
Cartside Ave
Inchinnan PA4 ....93 A2
Johnstone PA5 ....111 B1
Cartside Dr G76 ....158 A3
Cartside Pl G76 ....157 C3
Cartside Quadrant G42 .137 A4
Cartside Rd G76 ....157 C3
Cartside St G42 ....137 A4
Cartvale La PA3 ....113 C3
Cartvale Rd G42 ....137 A4
Cartvale Sch G42 ....136 C4
Cartview Ct G76 ....157 C3
Carvale Ave ML7 ....147 C1
Carwinshoch View KA7 ..238 B3
Carwood St PA15 ....46 B2
Cask Cres FK6 ....7 B4
Caskie Dr G72 ....140 C1
Cassels Gr ML1 ....143 B2
Cassels St Carluke ML8 ..187 C1
Motherwell ML1 ....163 C4
Cassillis St KA7 ....239 A2
Cassillon Gdns G45 ....137 B1
Cassley Ave PA4 ....94 C1
Castburn Rd G67 ....62 C3
Castings Ave FK2 ....42 A3
Castings Ct Falkirk FK2 ...42 A4
Falkirk, Middlefield FK2 ..42 C3
Castings Dr FK2 ....42 A3
Castings Rd FK2 ....42 A3
Castle Ave Airth FK2 ....14 C3
Bailloch G83 ....19 C4
Bothwell G71 ....140 C2
Elderslie PA5 ....112 A1
Falkirk FK2 ....16 A1
Helensburgh G84 ....16 C1
Motherwell ML1 ....164 B1
Stevenston KA20 ....206 C1
Castle Bsns Pk The PA1 ..1 C1
Castle Chimmins Ave
G72 ....139 B2
Castle Chimmins Rd
G72 ....139 B2

Castle Cres Bishopton PA7 .72 A1
Denny FK6 ....21 B1
Falkirk FK2 ....42 B4
Torwood FK5 ....22 C4
Castle Ct Cumbernauld G68 .62 C4
Falkirk FK2 ....42 B4
Kirkintilloch G66 ....79 B4
Menstrie FK11 ....3 C3
Stirling FK8 ....7 A4
Castle Dr Airth FK2 ....14 C2
Dundonald KA2 ....225 C1
Falkirk FK2 ....42 B4
Kilbirnie KA25 ....149 A1
Kilmarnock KA3 ....223 A2
Motherwell ML1 ....143 A3
Stenhousemuir FK5 ....23 C1
West Kilbride KA23 ....190 B3
Castle Farm Cl KA3 ....195 B1
Castle Gait PA1 ....113 C2
Castle Gate
Newton Mearns G77 ......157 A2
Uddingston G71 ....140 C3
Castle Gdns Chryston G69 .80 C1
Gourock PA19 ....44 C4
Paisley PA2 ....113 A2
Kilsyth G65 ....36 B1
Castle Gr Kilbirnie KA25 .149 A1
Kilsyth G65 ....36 B1
Castle Levan Manor
PA19 ....43 C3
Castle Mains Rd G62 .....54 B3
Castle Pl Falkirk FK2 ....42 B4
Irvine KA12 ....219 A2
Castle Quadrant ML1 .....143 B1
Castle Rd Airdrie ML6 ....123 B4
Ardrossan KA22 ....205 B2
Bridge of W PA11 ....90 B1
Dumbarton G82 ....50 A1
Elderslie PA5 ....112 B2
Falkirk FK2 ....42 B4
Greenock PA15 ....46 B1
Menstrie FK11 ....3 C3
Newton Mearns G77 ......156 B2
Newton Mearns G77 ......156 C2
Stirling FK9 ....2 A2
Castle Semple Ctry Pk*
PA12 ....129 C2
Castle Semple Loch Visitor
Ctr* PA12 ....129 B2
Castle Sq Ayr KA7 ....238 A2
Clydebank G81 ....73 C2
Castle St Alloa FK10 ......10 A3
Chapelhall ML6 ....123 B1
Clydebank G81 ....73 C2
Dumbarton G82 ....49 C2
Glasgow G4 ....241 C3
Glasgow, Baillieston G69 .120 A2
Glasgow, Kelvinhaugh G11 ..96 B1
Hamilton ML3 ....162 C2
Irvine KA12 ....219 A2
Paisley PA1 ....113 B2
Rutherglen G73 ....138 A4
Castle Terr
Bridge of W PA11 ....110 C4
Denny FK6 ....21 B1
Knockentiber KA2 ....221 C2
Castle Vale FK9 ....2 A3
Castle View Airth FK2 .....14 B1
Ayr KA7 ....238 A2
West Kilbride KA23 ....190 B3
Wishaw ML2 ....166 A3
Castle Way
Coatbridge G69 ....120 C3
Cumbernauld G67 ....62 B4
Castle Wynd
Bothwell G71 ....141 A1
Quarter ML3 ....183 C2
Stirling FK8 ....7 A4
Castlebank Cres G13 ......95 C3
Castlebank Ct G13 ....95 C3
Castlebank Gdns G13 .....96 A1
Castlebank Villas G13 ....95 C3
Castlebay Dr G22 ....77 B1
Castlebay Pl G22 ....77 B1
Castlebay St G22 ....77 B1
Castlebrae G82 ....49 B3
Castlebrae Gdns G44 ....137 A3
Castlecary Rd G68 ....62 B4
Castlecroft Gdns G71 ....140 C3
Castlefern Rd G73 ....138 A2
Castlefield Ct G33 ....99 A2
Castlefield Gdns G75 ....180 A3
Castlefield Prim Sch
G75 ....180 A3
Castlegait FK8 ....7 A4
Castleglen Rd G74 ....159 A2
Castlegreen Cres G82 .....49 B3
Castlegreen Gdns G82 ...50 A1
Castlegreen La G82 ....50 A1
Castlegreen St G82 ....50 A1
Castlehead High Sch
PA1 ....113 B2
Castlehill Ave
Port Glasgow PA14 ....69 B4
Slamannan FK1 ....86 A3
Castlehill Cres Ayr KA7 ..239 B3
Banknock FK4 ....38 C1
Chapelhall ML6 ....123 C1
Hamilton ML3 ....162 A4
Hamilton, Allanton ML3 ..163 B1
Kilmacolm PA13 ....89 A4
Law ML8 ....187 A2
Renfrew PA4 ....94 B2

Castlehill Ct KA7 ....239 A3
Castlehill Dr G77 ....156 C2
Castlehill Gdns ML3 ......162 C1
Castlehill Gn G81 ....73 B3
Castlehill Ind Est ML8 ...187 C2
Castlehill Rd
Bearsden G61 ....75 B3
Wishaw ML2 ....186 A4
Castlehill Quadrant G82 .49 B3
Castlehill Rd Ayr KA7 .....239 A3
Bearsden G61 ....75 B3
Carluke ML8 ....187 C3
Dumbarton G82 ....49 B3
Kilmacolm PA13 ....89 B4
Overtown ML2 ....185 C4
Stewarton KA3 ....195 C1
Castlehill View G65 ....36 B1
Castleknowe Gdns ML8 .187 C2
Castlelaurie St FK2 ....42 A4
Castlelaw Gdns G32 ....119 A3
Castlelaw St G32 ....119 A3
Castlemilk Ave G44 ....137 B2
Castlemilk Arc G45 ....137 B2
Castlemilk Cres G44 .....137 C2
Castlemilk Dr G45 ....137 C2
Castlemilk High Sch
G45 ....137 C1
Castlemilk Rd G44 ....137 C1
Castlemilk Terr G45 ......137 C1
Castlemount Ave G77 ....137 C2
Castlepark Cres KA12 ...219 A3
Castlepark Prim Sch
KA12 ....219 A3
Castlepark Rd KA12 ......219 A3
Castlerankine Rd FK6 .....21 B1
Castleton Ave
Bishopbriggs G64 ....97 C4
Newton Mearns G77 ......156 C2
Castleton Cres G77 ....156 C2
Castleton Ct
Glasgow G45 ....137 C1
Newton Mearns G77 ......156 C2
Castleton Dr G77 ....156 C2
Castleton Prim Sch G45 .137 C2
Castleview
Clachan of C G66 ....32 C2
Cumbernauld G68 ....62 C4
Dundonald KA2 ....225 C2
Castleview PA2 ....133 A4
Castleview Dr
Bridge of A FK9 ....2 A4
Paisley PA2 ....133 A4
Castleview Terr FK4 ....39 A2
Catacol Ave KA21 ....205 C2
Cath of St Mungo* G4 ..241 C3
Cathay St G22 ....97 B4
Cathburn Rd ML2 ....166 B3
Cathcart Cres PA2 ....114 A2
Cathcart Pl G73 ....137 C4
Cathcart Rd
Glasgow G42 ....117 A1
Rutherglen G73 ....138 A3
Cathcart Sq PA15 ....45 C3
Cathcart St [10] Ayr KA7 .235 C1
Greenock PA15 ....46 A3
Cathcart Sta G44 ....137 A2
Cathedral Rd Prim Sch
ML1 ....163 C4
Cathedral Sq G4 ....241 C2
Cathedral St G1, G4 ......241 B3
Catherine Pl KA3 ....222 B3
Catherine St
Bannockburn FK7 ....7 B1
Kirkintilloch G66 ....79 B4
Motherwell ML1 ....163 C2
Catherine's Wlk G72 .....141 C2
Cathkin Ave
Rutherglen G72 ....138 C3
Rutherglen, Gallowflat
G73 ....138 B4
Cathkin By-Pass G73 ....138 B2
Cathkin Cres G68 ....61 C2
Cathkin Ct G45 ....137 C1
Cathkin Dr G76 ....157 B4
Cathkin Gdns G71 ....121 A1
Cathkin Pl
Cambuslang G72 ....138 C3
Kilwinning KA13 ....207 A2
Cathkin Prim Sch G73 ..138 B1
Cathkin Rd Glasgow G42 .136 C4
Rutherglen G73 ....138 B1
Uddingston G71 ....121 A1
Cathkin View G32 ....139 A4
Cathkinview Pl G42 ....137 A4
Cathkinview Rd G42 ......137 A4
Catrine G74 ....160 B2
Catrine Ave G81 ....74 B2
Catrine Ct G53 ....135 A4
Catrine Cres ML1 ....163 A3
Catrine Gdns G53 ....135 A4
Catrine Pl G53 ....135 A4
Catrine St [9] G53 ....135 A4
Catrine St G53 ....185 B1
Catriona Pl G82 ....50 A2
Catter Gdns G62 ....54 C2
Cauldhame Cres FK7 ....6 B3
Cauldhame Rigg KA3 ....211 C4
Cauldstream Pl G62 ....54 C1
Causeway The PA9 ....2 B3
Causeway St G82 ....119 B4
Causewayside Cres G32 .119 A3
Causewayside St G32 ....119 A3
Causeyfoot Dr KA25 ......149 A1

Causeyside St PA1 . . . . .113 C2
Causeystanes G72 . . . . .161 B4
Cavendish Ct
  5 Glasgow G5 . . . . .117 A2
Troon KA10 . . . . .229 C1
Cavendish Dr G77 . . . . .156 C3
Cavendish La KA10 . . . . .229 C1
Cavendish Pl
  Glasgow G5 . . . . .117 A2
  Troon KA10 . . . . .229 C1
Cavendish St G5 . . . . .117 A2
Cavin Dr G45 . . . . .137 C2
Cavin Rd G45 . . . . .137 C2
Cawder Ct G68 . . . . .61 B3
Cawder Gdns FK9 . . . . .1 C4
Cawder Pl G68 . . . . .61 C3
Cawder Rd Bridge of A FK9 . . . .1 C4
  Cumbernauld G68 . . . . .61 C3
Cawder View G68 . . . . .61 C3
Cawder Way G68 . . . . .61 C3
Cawdor Cres
  Bishopton PA7 . . . . .72 A1
  Greenock PA16 . . . . .45 A4
Cawdor Pl PA16 . . . . .45 A2
Cawdor Way G74 . . . . .159 B2
Cayton Gdns G69 . . . . .119 C2
Cecil St Clarkston G76 . . . . . . .157 C4
  Coatbridge ML5 . . . . .122 A3
  Glasgow G12 . . . . .96 B2
  Stirling FK7 . . . . .7 A3
Cedar Ave Beith KA15 . . . . .171 A4
  Clydebank G81 . . . . .73 B2
  Johnstone PA5 . . . . .132 A4
  Stirling FK8 . . . . .6 C3
  Uddingston G71 . . . . .141 A4
Cedar Cres Greenock PA15 . .46 C1
  Hamilton ML3 . . . . .162 C1
Cedar Ct
  Cambuslang G72 . . . . .139 C2
  East Kilbride G75 . . . . .180 B3
  Glasgow G20 . . . . .97 A1
  Kilbarchan PA10 . . . . .111 A2
Cedar Dr
  East Kilbride G75 . . . . .180 B3
  Kirkintilloch G66 . . . . .79 B3
  Milton of C G66 . . . . .58 B3
Cedar Gdns Law ML8 . . . . .186 C3
  Motherwell ML1 . . . . .143 B2
  Rutherglen G73 . . . . .138 B2
Cedar Gr Cardross G82 . . . . . . .48 A4
  Stenhousemuir FK5 . . . . .23 B1
Cedar La Airdrie ML6 . . . . .123 B4
  Motherwell ML1 . . . . .143 B2
Cedar Pl Barrhead G78 . . . . . . .155 B4
  Blantyre G72 . . . . .140 B1
  East Kilbride G75 . . . . .180 B3
  Gourock PA19 . . . . .44 B3
Cedar Rd Ayr KA7 . . . . .239 B3
  Banknock FK4 . . . . .38 C1
  Bishopbriggs G64 . . . . .98 A4
  Cumbernauld G67 . . . . .62 B2
  Irvine KA12 . . . . .219 B2
  Kilmarnock KA1 . . . . .227 B4
Cedar St G20 . . . . .97 A1
Cedar View G84 . . . . .16 C3
Cedar Wlk G64 . . . . .98 A4
Cedar Wynd ML7 . . . . .147 A2
Cedars The FK10 . . . . .4 A1
Cedarwood Ave G77 . . . . .156 C3
Cedarwood Ct G82 . . . . .48 A4
Cedarwood Rd G77 . . . . .156 C2
Cedric Pl G13 . . . . .95 B4
Cedric Rd G13 . . . . .95 B4
Celandine Bank KA7 . . . . .239 B2
Celtic Pk (Celtic FC)
  G40 . . . . .118 A3
Celtic St G20 . . . . .96 B4
Cemetery Rd
  Blantyre G72 . . . . .161 B3
  Glasgow G52 . . . . .115 C2
  Shotts ML7 . . . . .147 A2
Centenary Ave ML6 . . . . .122 B4
Centenary Ct
  Barrhead G78 . . . . .134 A1
  Clydebank G81 . . . . .74 A1
Centenary Gdns
  Coatbridge ML5 . . . . .122 A3
  2 Hamilton ML3 . . . . .162 C1
Centenary Pl KA27 . . . . .205 D2
Centenary Quadrant
  ML1 . . . . .143 A3
Centenary Rd KA11 . . . . .224 C4
Central Ave
  Ardrossan KA22 . . . . .205 B2
  Cambuslang G72 . . . . .138 C3
  Clydebank G81 . . . . .74 A1
  Glasgow G11 . . . . .95 C1
  Glasgow, North Mount Vernon
    G32 .119 C2
  Hamilton ML3 . . . . .161 C3
  Kilbirnie KA25 . . . . .170 A4
  Kilmarnock KA1 . . . . .227 C2
  Motherwell ML1 . . . . .143 A1
  Motherwell, Holytown
    ML1 .143 C4
  Stevenston KA20 . . . . .218 A3
  Troon KA10 . . . . .229 D2
  Uddingston G71 . . . . .141 B3
Central Terr FK5 . . . . .23 A2
Central Cres ML9 . . . . .199 C4
Central Dr FK5 . . . . .23 C2
Central Gr
  Cambuslang G72 . . . . .138 C3
  Glasgow G32 . . . . .119 B2

Central Park Ave FK5 . . . . .23 A2
Central Park Bsns Pk
  FK5 . . . . .23 A2
Central Path G32 . . . . .119 C2
Central Quadrant KA22 . . . . .205 B2
Central Rd PA1 . . . . .113 C3
Central Ret Pk FK1 . . . . .42 B3
Central Sta Glasgow G2 . . . . . .240 C2
  Hamilton ML3 . . . . .162 C2
Central Way
  Cumbernauld G67 . . . . .61 C1
  9 Paisley PA1 . . . . .113 C3
Centre Rdbt The G74 . . . . .159 C1
Centre St Chapelhall ML6 . . . .123 B1
  Glasgow G5 . . . . .117 A2
  Glenboig ML5 . . . . .101 B3
Centre The ML4 . . . . .134 A1
Centre Way G78 . . . . .134 A2
Centrum (Sports Arena)
  KA9 . . . . .236 A3
Centurion Way FK2 . . . . .41 B3
Century Ct KA11 . . . . .224 D4
Ceres Gdns G64 . . . . .78 B1
Cessnock Ave KA1 . . . . .228 C3
Cessnock Dr KA1 . . . . .228 C3
Cessnock Pl Ayr KA7 . . . . .239 B3
  Cambuslang G72 . . . . .139 B3
Cessnock Rd
  Hurlford KA1 . . . . .228 C3
  Millerston G33 . . . . .99 A2
  Troon KA10 . . . . .229 C2
Cessnock St G51 . . . . .116 B3
Cessnock Underground Sta
  G51 . . . . .116 B3
Cessnock Pl FK44 . . . . .40 A3
Chacefield St PK44 . . . . .40 A3
Chacefield Wood FK6 . . . . .39 C4
Chalmers Ave KA7 . . . . .239 A3
Chalmers Cres G75 . . . . .180 C4
Chalmers Ct
  Glasgow G40 . . . . .241 C1
  Uddingston G71 . . . . .140 C3
Chalmers Dr G75 . . . . .180 C4
Chalmers Gate G40 . . . . .241 C1
Chalmers Pl
  Glasgow G40 . . . . .241 C1
  Irvine KA11 . . . . .224 D3
Chalmers Rd KA7 . . . . .239 A3
Chalmers St
  Clydebank G40 . . . . .241 C1
  Gourock PA19 . . . . .44 C4
Chalmerston Rd FK9 . . . . .1 A2
Chalton Ct FK9 . . . . .2 A4
Chalton Rd FK9 . . . . .2 A4
Chalybeate Ct KA13 . . . . .207 B2
Chamberlain La 11 G12 . . . . . . .95 C3
Chamberlain Rd G13 . . . . .95 C3
Chambers Dr FK2 . . . . .24 A1
Chamfron Gdns FK7 . . . . .7 C2
Chancellor St G11 . . . . .96 A1
Chantinghall Rd ML3 . . . . .162 A2
Chantinghall Terr ML3 . . . . . . .162 A2
Chapel Cres FK2 . . . . .24 A2
Chapel Ct G73 . . . . .137 C4
Chapel Dr FK5 . . . . .23 C2
Chapel Green Prim Sch
  G65 . . . . .59 C4
Chapel La Falkirk FK1 . . . . .42 A3
  Irvine KA12 . . . . .219 B1
Chapel Pl G78 . . . . .134 A1
Chapel Rd Clydebank G81 . . . . .74 A3
  Houston PA6 . . . . .91 A2
  Wishaw ML2 . . . . .165 A3
Chapel St Airdrie ML6 . . . . .123 A4
  Carluke ML8 . . . . .187 C1
  Carluke ML8 . . . . .144 A1
  Glasgow G20 . . . . .96 C3
  Gourock PA19 . . . . .44 C4
  Lennoxtown G66 . . . . .57 B4
  Rutherglen G73 . . . . .137 C4
  Hamilton ML3 . . . . .162 C2
Chapel Street Ind Est
  G20 . . . . .96 C3
Chapelacre Gr G84 . . . . .16 C1
Chapelcross Ave ML6 . . . . .103 A1
Chapelgill Pl KA11 . . . . .220 A2
Chapelhall Ind Est ML6 . . . . . .123 A2
Chapelhall Prim Sch
  ML6 . . . . .123 B1
Chapelhill Mount KA27 . . . . . .205 D3
Chapelhill Rd PA2 . . . . .114 A1
Chapelknowe Rd ML1 . . . . .143 C1
Chapelpark Rd KA7 . . . . .238 C1
Chapelside Ave ML6 . . . . .123 A4
Chapelside Prim Sch
  ML6 . . . . .123 A4
Chapelside Rd G74 . . . . .160 A3
Chapelton Ave
  Bearsden G61 . . . . .75 C2
  Dumbarton G82 . . . . .50 A3
Chapelton Gdns
  Bearsden G61 . . . . .75 C2
  Dumbarton G82 . . . . .50 A3
Chapelton La KA23 . . . . .190 B2
Chapelton Mains KA23 . . . . . .190 B1
Chapelton Rd
  Cumbernauld G67 . . . . .82 B3
  West Kilbride KA23 . . . . .190 B1
Chapelton St
  Glasgow G22 . . . . .97 A3
  Port Glasgow PA14 . . . . .47 A1
Chapelton Terr KA1 . . . . .210 C2
Chapelwell St KA21 . . . . .216 C4
Chapland Rd ML11 . . . . .215 A3
Chaplet Ave G13 . . . . .95 B4
Chapman Ave ML5 . . . . .101 B3
Chapman St 4 G42 . . . . .117 A1

Chapmans Terr KA1 . . . . .228 A4
Chappell St G78 . . . . .134 A2
Charing Cross ML9 . . . . .185 A2
Charing Cross La G3 . . . . .240 A3
Charing Cross Sta G2 . . . . .240 B3
Charles Ave Bridge of A FK9 . . .2 A3
  Monkton KA9 . . . . .233 B3
  Renfrew PA4 . . . . .94 B2
Charles Cres
  Carluke ML8 . . . . .188 A1
  Kirkintilloch G66 . . . . .79 B2
Charles Dr Larbert FK5 . . . . .41 A4
  Troon KA10 . . . . .229 D1
Charles Path ML6 . . . . .123 B1
Charles Pl Greenock PA15 . . . . .45 C3
  Kilmarnock KA1 . . . . .227 C4
Charles Quadrant ML1 . . . . . .143 A3
Charles Rodger Pl FK9 . . . . .2 A3
Charles St Alloa FK10 . . . . .9 C4
  Glasgow G21 . . . . .97 C1
  Kilmarnock KA1 . . . . .227 C4
  Kilsyth G65 . . . . .36 B1
  Shotts ML7 . . . . .147 A2
  Stirling FK8 . . . . .7 A3
Charles Terr G83 . . . . .27 C4
Charleson Row G65 . . . . .60 C2
Charlotte Ave G64 . . . . .78 A4
Charlotte Hill Ct PA15 . . . . .46 C4
Charlotte Path ML9 . . . . .185 A1
Charlotte Pl PA2 . . . . .113 C1
Charlotte St Ayr KA7 . . . . .238 C4
  Dumbarton G82 . . . . .49 B2
  Glasgow G1 . . . . .241 B1
  Helensburgh G84 . . . . .16 C1
  Shotts ML7 . . . . .147 A2
  Stirling FK8 . . . . .7 A3
Charlotte Street La KA7 .238 C4
Charnwood Ave PA5 . . . . .131 B4
Charrier The FK11 . . . . .3 A2
Charter St FK7 . . . . .7 C2
Chartershall Rd
  Bannockburn FK7 . . . . .7 A1
  Bannockburn FK7 . . . . .11 A3
Chartwell Rd PA7 . . . . .72 A2
Chassels St ML5 . . . . .101 C4
Chateau Gr ML3 . . . . .163 A1
Chatelherault Ave G72 . . . . . . .138 B3
Chatelherault Country Pk*
  ML3 . . . . .184 A4
Chatelherault Country Pk
  Visitor Ctr* ML3 . . . . .184 A4
Chatelherault Cres ML3 . . . . .162 C1
Chatelherault Prim Sch
  ML3 . . . . .162 C1
Chatelherault Wlk ML3 . . . . . .162 C1
  Chatham G75 . . . . .180 B4
Chatton Ave FK9 . . . . .2 A2
Chatton Ind Est FK4 . . . . .40 B2
Chatton St G23 . . . . .76 B1
Chatton Wlk ML5 . . . . .122 B2
Cheapside St
  Eaglesham G76 . . . . .178 C3
  Glasgow G3 . . . . .240 A2
Checkbar Rdbt FK5 . . . . .40 B4
Chelmsford Dr G12 . . . . .96 A3
Cherry Bank G66 . . . . .79 A2
Cherry Cres G81 . . . . .74 A2
Cherry Gdns KA11 . . . . .219 C3
Cherry Gr G69 . . . . .121 A3
Cherry Hill Rd KA7 . . . . .239 A1
Cherry La Banknock FK4 . . . . . .38 C1
  Cumbernauld G67 . . . . .229 C2
Cherry Pl
  Bishopbriggs G64 . . . . .98 A4
  Johnstone PA5 . . . . .112 A1
  Milton of C G66 . . . . .58 A2
  Uddingston G71 . . . . .141 B4
Cherry Rd KA1 . . . . .227 B4
Cherry Wlk ML1 . . . . .163 C2
Cherrybank Rd G43 . . . . .136 C3
Cherrybank Wlk ML6 . . . . .122 B4
Cherryhill View ML4 . . . . .184 C2
Cherryridge Dr G69 . . . . .121 A3
Cherrytree Cres ML9 . . . . .185 A3
Cherrytree Dr G72 . . . . .139 C2
Cherrywood Dr KA15 . . . . .150 B1
Cherrywood Rd PA5 . . . . .112 B1
Chester Rd PA16 . . . . .44 C2
Chester St G32 . . . . .119 A3
Chesterfield Ave G12 . . . . .96 A3
Chesters Cres ML1 . . . . .164 B3
Chesters Pl 10 G73 . . . . .138 A4
Chesters Rd G61 . . . . .75 B2
Chestnut Ave Beith KA15 . . . . .171 A4
  Bishopton PA7 . . . . .71 C3
  Cumbernauld G67 . . . . .62 B3
Chestnut Cres Denny PA16 . . . .21 B2
  East Kilbride G75 . . . . .180 B4
  Hamilton ML3 . . . . .162 C1
  Uddingston G71 . . . . .141 B4
Chestnut Ct
  Cumbernauld G67 . . . . .62 C3
  Milton of C G66 . . . . .58 B3
Chestnut Dr
  Clydebank G81 . . . . .74 A3
  Kirkintilloch G66 . . . . .79 A3
Chestnut Gdns KA11 . . . . .219 C3
Chestnut Gr
  Blantyre G72 . . . . .161 B4
  Carluke ML8 . . . . .187 C1
  Glenboig ML5 . . . . .101 B3
  Hamilton ML3 . . . . .162 C1
  Larkhall ML9 . . . . .185 A3
  Motherwell ML1 . . . . .163 B2
  Stenhousemuir FK5 . . . . .23 C2
Chestnut La G62 . . . . .54 C1
Chestnut Pl
  Cumbernauld G67 . . . . .62 C3

Chestnut Pl continued
  Johnstone PA5 . . . . .132 A4
  Kilmarnock KA1 . . . . .227 B4
Chestnut Rd KA7 . . . . .239 B3
Chestnut St G22 . . . . .97 B3
Chestnut Way
  Cambuslang G72 . . . . .139 C2
  Hamilton ML3 . . . . .183 C2
Cheviot Ave G78 . . . . .134 A1
Cheviot Cres
  East Kilbride G75 . . . . .180 A2
  Wishaw ML2 . . . . .164 C2
Cheviot Ct Airdrie ML6 . . . . . . .103 A1
  Coatbridge ML5 . . . . .122 B2
  Irvine KA11 . . . . .220 A2
Cheviot Dr G77 . . . . .156 B2
Cheviot Gdns G66 . . . . .75 B4
Cheviot Head KA11 . . . . .219 C2
Cheviot Rd Glasgow G43 . . . . .136 B3
  Hamilton ML3 . . . . .162 C1
  Larkhall ML9 . . . . .185 B1
  Paisley PA2 . . . . .113 C1
Cheviot St G72 . . . . .161 B4
Cheviot Way KA11 . . . . .220 A2
Chillin Pl ML9 . . . . .185 B1
Chiremorie Cres G53 . . . . .115 A1
Chirmorie Pl G53 . . . . .115 A1
Chirnside Ct G72 . . . . .161 A4
Chirnside Pl G52 . . . . .115 A3
Chirnside Rd G52 . . . . .115 A3
Chirnsyde Prim Sch G22 . . . . .97 B3
Chisholm Ave
  Bishopton PA7 . . . . .72 B2
  Stirling FK9 . . . . .2 A2
Chisholm Dr G77 . . . . .156 C3
Chisholm Pl ML1 . . . . .164 A1
Chisholm St G1 . . . . .241 B1
Chisolm St G1 . . . . .241 A2
Chrighton Gn 3 G71 . . . . .141 A4
Chriss Ave ML3 . . . . .183 A1
Christ the King Prim Sch
  ML1 . . . . .143 A3
Christchurch Pl G75 . . . . .180 A4
Christian St G43 . . . . .136 B3
Christie Gdns KA21 . . . . .216 C4
Christie La PA3 . . . . .113 C3
Christie Park Prim Sch
  G83 . . . . .27 B3
Christie Pl G72 . . . . .139 A3
Christie St Bellshill ML4 . . . . . .142 B3
  Paisley PA1 . . . . .113 C3
Christie Terr FK5 . . . . .23 C2
Christopher St G21 . . . . .98 A1
Chromars Pl PA15 . . . . .45 C2
Chryston Gdns G69 . . . . .100 B4
Chryston High Sch G69 . . . . .100 A4
Chryston Prim Sch G69 . . . . .100 B4
Chryston Rd
  Chryston G69 . . . . .100 A4
  Kirkintilloch G69,G66 . . . . .80 B3
Chuckie La ML1 . . . . .142 A3
Church Ave Cardross G82 . . . . .48 A4
  Rutherglen G73 . . . . .138 B3
  Stepps G33 . . . . .99 B3
Church Cres Airdrie ML6 . . . . .103 C1
  Hamilton ML3 . . . . .183 B3
Church Ct 3 Alloa FK10 . . . . . .10 A3
  Ayr KA8 . . . . .236 A1
  Dumbarton G82 . . . . .49 C2
Church Dr G66 . . . . .79 B3
Church Gr FK10 . . . . .5 B1
Church Hill PA1 . . . . .113 C3
Church La Carluke MLB 187 C1
  Coatbridge ML5 . . . . .122 A4
  Denny FK6 . . . . .21 B2
  Kilmarnock KA3 . . . . .227 C3
  8 Kilsyth G65 . . . . .60 B4
  Plean FK7 . . . . .12 B1
Church Manse La PA11 . . . . . .110 B4
Church Pl
  Ardrossan KA22 . . . . .205 B1
  Caldercruix ML6 . . . . .104 C2
  Falkirk FK2 . . . . .42 A3
  Old Kilpatrick G60 . . . . .73 A3
  Rhu G84 . . . . .15 C2
Church Rd
  Bridge of W PA11 . . . . .110 C4
  California FK1 . . . . .66 C3
  Clarkston G76 . . . . .157 C3
  Glasgow G46 . . . . .136 B1
  Muirhead G69 . . . . .100 B4
  Quarriers Village PA11 . . . . . . .89 C1
  Rhu G84 . . . . .15 C2
  Wishaw ML2 . . . . .166 C2
Church St Alexandria G83 . . . . .27 C2
  Alloa FK10 . . . . .10 A3
  Blantyre G72 . . . . .161 C4
  Clydebank G81 . . . . .74 A2
  Coatbridge ML5 . . . . .122 A4
  Dumbarton G82 . . . . .49 C2
  Falkirk FK1 . . . . .42 A2
  Glasgow G11 . . . . .96 B1
  Glasgow, Muirhead G69 . . . . . .44 C4
  Gourock PA19 . . . . .44 C4
  Harthill ML7 . . . . .127 C3
  High Bonnybridge FK4 . . . . . . .40 B2
  Irvine KA12 . . . . .219 B1
  Johnstone PA5 . . . . .111 C2
  Kilmarnock KA3 . . . . .222 C1
  Kilmarnock KA3 . . . . .227 C3
  Kilsyth G65 . . . . .60 B4
  Kilwinning KA13 . . . . .207 C2
  Larkhall ML9 . . . . .185 A1
  Lochwinnoch PA12 . . . . .129 B1

Church St continued
  Motherwell ML1 . . . . .143 C2
  Port Glasgow PA14 . . . . .47 B1
  Stenhousemuir FK5 . . . . .23 C2
  Stonehouse ML9 . . . . .229 C1
  Troon KA10 . . . . .229 C1
  Uddingston G71 . . . . .140 C3
Church View
  Caldercruix ML6 . . . . .104 C2
  Cambuslang G72 . . . . .139 A4
  Coatbridge ML5 . . . . .122 A4
Church View Ct G66 . . . . .33 B1
Church View Gdns ML4 . . . . . .142 A3
Church Wlk FK5 . . . . .21 C1
Churchill Ave
  East Kilbride G74 . . . . .159 C1
  Johnstone PA5 . . . . .131 B4
  Kilwinning KA13 . . . . .208 A2
Churchill Cres Ayr KA8 . . . . . . .239 B4
  Bothwell G71 . . . . .141 A2
Churchill Dr
  Ardrossan KA22 . . . . .205 B2
  Bishopton PA7 . . . . .72 A2
  Bridge of A FK9 . . . . .2 A3
Churchill Pl Falkirk FK2 . . . . . . .42 B4
  Kilbarchan PA10 . . . . .111 A2
Churchill Rd PA13 . . . . .89 B4
Churchill Sq G84 . . . . .17 A1
Churchill St G10 . . . . .96 C1
Churchill Twr KA7 . . . . .235 C1
Churchill Way G64 . . . . .77 C1
Churchyard Ct ML7 . . . . .146 C2
Circus Dr G31 . . . . .117 C4
Circus Pl G31 . . . . .117 C4
Circus Place La G31 . . . . .117 C4
Citadel L Ctr KA7 . . . . .235 C1
Citadel Pl KA10 . . . . .229 D4
Citadel Way KA10 . . . . .229 D4
Citizen La G1 . . . . .241 A2
Citrus Cres G71 . . . . .141 B4
Cityford Cres G73 . . . . .137 C4
Cityford Dr G73 . . . . .137 C3
Civic St G4 . . . . .97 A1
Civic Way G66 . . . . .79 B4
Clachan Dr 5 G51 . . . . .115 C4
Clachan Rd G84 . . . . .15 A2
Clachan The ML2 . . . . .165 A2
Clackmannan Coll of F Ed
  FK10 . . . . .10 A4
Clackmannan Rd FK10 . . . . .10 B3
Clackmannan Twr*
  FK10 . . . . .10 C2
Claddens Pl G66 . . . . .79 C2
Claddens Quadrant G22 . . . . . .97 C3
Claddens St G22 . . . . .97 A3
Claddoch Cotts G82 . . . . .25 C2
Cladence Gr G75 . . . . .180 C3
Clair Rd G64 . . . . .78 B1
Claire St ML2 . . . . .166 A3
Clairinsh G83 . . . . .27 B4
Clairinsh Gdns 1 PA4 . . . . .94 B1
Clairmont Gdns G3 . . . . .240 A4
Clamp Rd ML2 . . . . .164 B2
Clamps Gr G74 . . . . .181 A4
Clamps Terr G74 . . . . .181 A4
Clamps Wood G74 . . . . .181 A4
Clanranald Pl FK1 . . . . .41 C1
Clanrye Dr ML5 . . . . .122 A2
Clapperhow Rd ML1 . . . . .143 A1
Clare St G21 . . . . .98 A1
Claremont FK10 . . . . .9 C4
Claremont Ave G66 . . . . .79 A4
Claremont Cres KA13 . . . . .207 B2
Claremont Dr
  Bridge of A FK9 . . . . .2 B4
  Milngavie G62 . . . . .55 A1
Claremont Gdns G62 . . . . .55 A1
Claremont High Sch
  G74 . . . . .181 B4
Claremont Ind Est FK10 . . . . . .10 A3
Claremont Pass G3 . . . . .240 A4
Claremont Pl G3 . . . . .240 A4
Claremont Prim Sch FK10 . . . . .9 C4
Claremont St
  Bonnybridge FK4 . . . . .39 C3
  Glasgow G3 . . . . .116 C4
Claremont Terr G3 . . . . .240 A4
Claremont Terrace La
  G3 . . . . .240 A4
Claremount Ave G46 . . . . .136 B1
Clarence Dr Glasgow G11 . . . . . .96 A2
  Paisley PA1 . . . . .114 A2
Clarence Gdns G11 . . . . .96 A2
Clarence La G12 . . . . .96 A2
Clarence St Clydebank G81 . . . .74 B2
  Greenock PA15 . . . . .45 C3
  Paisley PA1 . . . . .114 A3
Clarendon La 9 Glasgow G20 . .97 A1
Clarendon Pl
  9 Glasgow G20 . . . . .97 A1
  Stepps G33 . . . . .99 B3
  Stirling FK8 . . . . .7 A3
Clarendon St G20 . . . . .97 A1
Clarinda Ave FK1 . . . . .41 A3
Clarinda Ct G66 . . . . .59 A1
Clarinda Pl
  Motherwell ML1 . . . . .143 B2
  Stenhousemuir FK5 . . . . .23 B2
Clarion Cres G13 . . . . .95 A4
Clarion Rd G13 . . . . .95 A4
Clark Cres KA20 . . . . .217 B4
Clark Dr KA12 . . . . .219 C2
Clark Pl
  Newton Mearns G77 . . . . .156 A2
  Saltcoats KA21 . . . . .206 A1
  Torrance G64 . . . . .78 B4

Clark St Airdrie ML6 .....123 A4
Bannockburn FK7 ....7 A1
Clydebank G81 ....73 C2
Johnstone PA5 ....111 C2
Kilmarnock KA1 ....227 C4
Paisley PA3 ....113 B3
Renfrew PA4 ....94 A2
Wishaw ML2 ....165 C3
Clark Way ML4 ....141 C4
Clarke Ave KA7 ....238 C3
Clarkin Ave G75 ....180 A2
Clarkston Ave G44 ....136 C2
Clarkston Dr ML6 ....123 B4
Clarkston Prim Sch
ML6 ....123 B4
Clarkston Rd G44 ....136 C2
Clarkston Sta G76 ....157 C4
Clarkwell Rd ML3 ....145 B1
Clarkwell Terr ML3 ......161 C2
Clathic Ave G61 ....76 A2
Claud Rd PA3 ....114 A3
Claude Ave G72 ....139 C2
Claude St ML9 ....185 A4
Clavens Rd G52 ....114 C3
Claverhouse Pl PA2 ......114 C4
Claverhouse Rd G52 ......114 C4
Clavering St E PA1 ......113 B3
Clavering St W PA1 ......113 B2
Clay Cres Bellshill ML4 .142 B4
Kilmarnock KA3 ....222 C1
Clay Ct ML1 ....163 C2
Clay Rd ML4 ....142 B4
Claycrofts Pl FK7 ....7 A3
Claymore Dr
Houston PA6 ....111 B4
Stirling FK7 ....7 A3
Claypotts Pl G33 ....99 A1
Claypotts Rd G33 ....99 A1
Clayslaps Rd G3 ....96 A1
Clayslaps View KA1 ......228 A2
Claythorn Ave G40 ....241 C1
Claythorn Cir 9 G40 .....117 C3
Claythorn Ct G40 ....241 C1
Claythorn Pk G40 ....117 C3
Claythorn St G40 ....241 C1
Claythorn Terr G40 ......241 C1
Clayton Ave KA12 ....219 B2
Clayton Path ML4 ....142 A4
Clayton Terr 3 G31 .....117 C4
Clearfield Ave ML3 ......162 A2
Cleaves The FK11 ....4 A1
Cleddans Cres G81 ....74 B3
Cleddans Rd
Clydebank G81 ....74 B3
Kirkintilloch G66 ......58 C1
Cleddans View
Clydebank G81 ....74 B3
Glenmavis ML6 ....102 C2
Cleddens Ct G64 ....78 A1
Cleeves Ave KA24 ....191 C3
Cleeves Quadrant G53 ...135 A3
Cleeves Rd G53 ....135 A3
Cleghorn Ave ML11 ......215 A3
Cleghorn Dr ML1 ....143 A2
Cleghorn Rd ML11 ....215 A3
Cleghorn St G22 ....97 A2
Cleish Ave G61 ....75 B4
Cleland Hospl ML1 ....144 B1
Cleland La G5 ....117 B3
Cleland Pl G74 ....160 A2
Cleland Prim Sch ML1 ....144 A1
Motherwell ML1 ....143 B1
Wishaw ML2 ....165 C3
Clelland Ave G64 ....98 A4
Clem Attlee Gdns ML9 ...185 A1
Clements Pl KA20 ....206 C1
Clerkland Rd KA3 ....195 B1
Clerwood St G32 ....118 B3
Cleuch Ave FK10 ....4 A1
Cleuch Dr FK12 ....4 C4
Cleuch Gdns G76 ....157 B4
Cleuch Rd G52 ....114 B3
Cleughearn Rd G75 ......180 B1
Clevans Rd PA11 ....110 B4
Cleveden Cres G12 ......96 A3
Cleveden Crescent La
G12 ....96 A3
Cleveden Dr Glasgow G12 .96 B2
Rutherglen G73 ....138 B3
Cleveden Drive La G12 ...96 B2
Cleveden Gdns G12 ......96 A3
Cleveden Pl G12 ....96 A3
Cleveden Rd G12 ....96 A3
Cleveden Sec Sch G12 ...96 B3
Cleveland La G3 ....240 A3
Cleveland St G3 ....240 A3
Cliff Rd G3 ....240 A4
Clifford Gdns G51 ......116 A3
Clifford La G51 ....116 B3
Clifford Pl 3 G51 ......116 B3
Clifford Rd PA8 ....7 A3
Clifford St G51 ....116 B3
Clifton Pl Coatbridge ML5 .122 B3
1 Glasgow G3 ....116 C4
Clifton Rd G46 ....136 A2
Clifton St G3 ....96 C1
Clifton Terr
Cambuslang G72 ....138 C2
Johnstone PA5 ....112 A1
Cliftonhill Stad (Albion
Rovers FC) ML5 ....122 B3
Cliftonville Ct ML5 ....122 B3
Climie Pl KA3 ....228 A4

Clincart Rd G42 ....137 A4
Clincarthill Rd G73 ....138 A4
Clippens Rd PA3 ....112 A3
Clippens Sch PA3 ....112 A3
Clive St ML7 ....146 C3
Cloak Rd PA13 ....69 B2
Cloan Ave G15 ....75 A4
Cloan Cres G64 ....78 A2
Clober Farm La G62 .....54 C2
Clober Prim Sch G62 ....54 C1
Clober Rd G62 ....55 A1
Cloberfield G62 ....54 C2
Cloberfield Gdns G62 ...54 C2
Cloberhill Rd G13 ......75 B1
Cloch Brae PA19 ....44 A3
Cloch Pl PA19 ....43 C3
Cloch St G33 ....119 A4
Clochbar Ave G62 ......54 C2
Clochbar Gdns G62 .....54 C1
Clochoderick Ave PA10 ..111 A1
Clochranhill Rd KA7 ....238 C1
Clockerhill Pl ML1 .....143 C2
Cloister Ave ML6 ....123 B2
Clonbeith St G33 ......99 C1
Cloncaird KA13 ....207 B1
Closeburn St G22 ......97 B3
Cloth St G78 ....134 B1
Clouden Rd G67 ....62 A1
Cloudhowe Terr G72 ....140 B1
Clouston Ct 8 G20 .....96 C2
Clouston La G20 ....96 C2
Clouston St G20 ....96 C2
Clova Pl G71 ....140 C3
Clova St G46 ....135 C2
Clove Mill Wynd ML9 ...184 C1
Clover Leaf Path G83 ...27 C2
Cloverbank St G21 .....98 A4
Clovergate G64 ....77 C1
Cloverhill Pl G69 ......100 B4
Cloverhill Terr G74 ....159 C1
Cloverhill View G74 ....159 B1
Cloves The FK11 ....4 A3
Cluanie Ave ML7 ....146 C3
Cluanie Dr ML7 ....47 C3
Clune Brae PA14 ....47 C1
Clune Dr KA9 ....236 B4
Clune Park Prim Sch
PA14 ....47 C1
Clune Park St PA14 ....47 C1
Clunie Pl Coatbridge ML5 .122 A2
Wishaw ML2 ....165 C3
Cluny Ave Bearsden G61 .76 A1
Cluny Dr Bearsden G61 ..76 A1
Newton Mearns G77 .....156 A3
Paisley PA3 ....114 A3
Stenhousemuir FK5 ......23 C2
Cluny Gdns Glasgow G14 ..95 C2
Glasgow, Baillieston G69 .120 A2
Cluny Villas G14 ......95 C2
Clutha Pl G75 ....180 A4
Clutha St G51 ....116 B3
Clyde Ave Barrhead G78 .134 B1
Bothwell G72 ....141 A3
Torrance G64 ....78 A4
Clyde Ct Carluke ML8 ...187 C1
Clydebank G81 ....74 A2
Coatbridge ML5 ....122 B3
Dumbarton G82 ....49 C2
Clyde Dr Bellshill ML4 .142 B2
Shotts ML7 ....146 C3
Clyde Ho ML3 ....162 C3
Clyde La ML1 ....143 A2
Clyde Muirshiel Regional
Pk* PA13 ....70 C2
Clyde Pl Ardrossan KA22 .205 B2
Cambuslang G72 ....139 B2
Glasgow G5 ....240 C1
Johnstone PA5 ....131 B4
Kilmarnock KA1 ....228 A3
Motherwell ML1 ....143 A2
Troon KA10 ....229 D3
Clyde Rd Gourock PA19 ..44 C3
Paisley PA3 ....114 A4
Clyde Shopping Ctr G81 .74 A1
Clyde St Carluke ML8 ...187 C1
Coatbridge ML5 ....122 B4
Falkirk FK1 ....41 C3
Glasgow PA1 ....241 A1
Renfrew PA4 ....94 B3
Clyde Terr
Ardrossan KA22 ....205 B2
Bothwell ML1 ....141 A1
Motherwell ML1 ....164 B1
Clyde Twr
East Kilbride G74 .....181 A4
1 Motherwell ML1 .....163 C3
Clyde Valley Ave ML1 ...163 C2
Clyde Valley Ctry Est*
ML2 ....186 A4
Clyde View Ashgill ML9 .200 A4
Hamilton ML3 ....162 A1
Paisley PA2 ....114 B2
Clyde View Ave KA20 ...206 B1
Clyde View Ct G60 .....72 B4
Clyde Wlk G4 ....166 A3
Clyde Wynd PA15 ....45 B2
Clydebank Bsns Pk G81 ..74 A2
Clydebank Coll G81 ....74 A1

Clydebank High Sch G81 .74 A2
Clydebank East G81 ....73 B1
Clydebank Mus G81 .....73 C2
Clydebank Sta G81 .....74 A1
Clydebrae Dr G71 ......162 A4
Clydebrae St G51 ......116 A4
Clydebuilt Mus* G51 ...95 A2
Clydeford Dr
Glasgow G32 ....118 C2
Uddingston G71 ....140 C4
Clydeford Rd G32, G72 ..139 A4
Clydeholm Rd G14 ......95 B1
Clydeholm Terr G81 ....94 B4
Clydemuir Prim Sch G81 .73 B2
Clydeneuk Dr G71 ......140 B4
Clydesdale Ave
Hamilton ML3 ....183 B3
Paisley PA3,PA4 ....94 A4
Wishaw ML2 ....164 B1
Clydesdale Pl ML3 .....183 B3
Clydesdale Rd ML4 .....142 B2
Clydesdale St
Hamilton ML3 ....162 B2
Larkhall ML9 ....185 A2
Motherwell ML1,ML4 ....142 B1
Clydesholm Ct ML11 ....214 B2
Clydeshore Rd G82 .....49 C1
Clydeside Expressway
G3 ....116 C4
Clydeside Ind Est G14 ..95 C1
Clydeside Rd G73 ......117 C1
Clydesmill Dr G32 .....139 A4
Clydesmill Gr G32 .....139 A4
Clydesmill Pl G32 .....139 A4
Clydesmill Rd G32 .....139 A4
Clydevale G71 ....141 A1
Clydeview Bothwell G71 .141 B3
Dumbarton G82 ....49 C1
Clydeview Sch
Greenock PA15 ....46 A1
Port Glasgow PA14 .....68 C4
Clydeview Shopping Ctr
G72 ....161 C4
Clydeview Terr G32 ....139 A4
Clydeway Ind Est 8 G3 ..116 C4
Clynder Rd PA15 ....46 B1
Clynder St G51 ....116 A3
Clyth Dr G46 ....136 B1
Co-operative Terr PA5 ..112 A2
Coach Brae View ML1 ...220 C1
Coach Cl G65 ....60 C4
Coach Rd G65 ....60 C4
Coal Wynd FK7 ....7 B1
Coalburn Rd G71 ....141 A3
Coalhall Ave ML1 ......143 A1
Coalhill Rd KA22 ......205 A2
Coalhill St G31 ....118 A3
Coalpots Way FK10 .....5 C2
Coatbank St ML5 ....122 A3
Coatbank Way ML5 .....122 A3
Coatbridge Central Sta
ML5 ....121 C4
Coatbridge Coll ML5 ...122 A4
Coatbridge High Sch
ML5 ....122 A4
Coatbridge Rd
Coatbridge G69 ....120 C3
Glasgow G69 ....120 C3
Glenboig G69 ....101 A2
Glenboig, Garnqueen ML5 .101 C3
Glenmavis ML6 ....102 B4
Coatdyke Sta ML5 .....122 B4
Coathill Hospl ML5 ....122 A3
Coathill St ML5 ....122 A3
Coats Cres G69 ....120 A3
Coats Dr PA2 ....113 A2
Coats Pl ML6 ....225 C1
Coats St ML5 ....122 A3
Coatshill Ave G72 .....140 B1
Cobbett Rd ML1 ....163 A2
Cobblebrae Cres FK2 ...24 A1
Cobblerigg Way G71 ....140 C3
Cobblerush Pl ML4 .....142 C2
Coburg St 8 G5 ....117 A3
Cochno Rd G81 ....74 A4
Cochno St G81 ....94 B4
Cochran St G1 ....113 C2
Cochrane Ave
Dundonald KA2 ....225 C1
Falkirk FK2 ....42 A2
Cochrane Castle Prim Sch
PA5 ....131 B4
Cochrane Cres FK12 ....4 C4
Cochrane Ct G62 ....76 A4
Cochrane Sq PA3 ......225 C1
Cochrane Pl
Helensburgh G84 ....16 B1
Prestwick KA9 ....236 A4
Cochrane Sq PA3 ......112 A3
Cochrane St
Barrhead G78 ....134 A1
Bellshill ML4 ....141 C3
Falkirk FK1 ....42 A2
Glasgow G1 ....241 A2
Irvine KA12 ....219 A1
Kilbirnie KA25 ....149 A1

Cochranemill Rd PA5 ...111 B1
Cochranes The FK12 ....5 A4
Cochrie PI FK10 ....4 B1
Cockaine View G63 .....31 B2
Cockburn Pl
Coatbridge ML5 ....121 C2
Irvine KA11 ....224 D3
Cockburn St FK1 ......42 A2
Cockels Loan PA4 ......94 A1
Cockenzie St G32 .....119 A3
Cockhill Way ML4 ......141 B3
Cocklebie Rd KA3 .....195 B1
Cocklebie View KA3 ...195 B1
Cockmuir St G21 ......98 A2
Cockrane Castle Prim Sch
PA5 ....111 B1
Coddington Cres ML1 ..142 C4
Cogan Pl G78 ....134 A1
Cogan Rd G43 ....136 B3
Cogan St Barrhead G78 .134 A1
Glasgow G43 ....136 B4
Coila Ave KA9 ....236 B3
Coire Loan ML7 ....147 A2
Colbert St G40 ....117 C2
Colbreggan Ct G81 ....74 B3
Colbreggan Gdns G81 ..74 B3
Colchester Dr G12 ....96 A3
Coldgreen Ave KA25 ...149 A1
Coldingham Ave G14 ...94 C3
Coldstream KA23 ......190 B3
Coldstream Cres ML2 ..165 B3
Coldstream Dr
Paisley PA2 ....113 A1
Rutherglen G73 ....138 B3
Coldstream Pl G21 ....96 C2
Coldstream Rd G81 ....74 A1
Coldstream St G72 ....161 A4
Colebrooke Pl G12 ....96 C2
Colebrooke St
Cambuslang G72 ....139 A3
12 Glasgow G12 ......96 C2
Colebrooke Terr G12 ..96 C2
Coleburn Ct KA11 .....219 C3
Coleridge G75 ....180 A4
Coleridge Ave G71 ....141 A2
Colfin St G34 ....100 B1
Colgrain Prim Sch G84 .25 B4
Colgrave Cres G32 ....118 C2
Colinbar Ave G78 .....133 C2
Colinslee Cres PA2 ...113 C1
Colinslee Dr PA2 .....113 C1
Colinslie Rd G53 .....135 B4
Colinton Pl G32 ......119 A4
Colintraive Ave G33 ..98 C2
Colintraive Cres G33 ..98 C2
Coll G21 ....181 B4
Coll Ave
Port Glasgow PA14 ....69 A4
Renfrew PA4 ....94 B1
Coll Dr ML5 ....121 B2
Coll Gdns KA11 ....225 A4
Coll Lea ML3 ....161 C1
Coll of Nautical Studies
G51 ....116 A4
Coll Pl Airdrie ML6 ...123 B3
Glasgow G21 ....98 A1
Coll St Glasgow G21 ...98 A1
Wishaw ML2 ....165 C3
Colla Gdns G64 ......78 A2
Collace Ave PA11 .....110 B4
College Cres FK2 .....42 B4
College Gate G61 .....75 B3
College La G1 ....241 B2
College La PA10 ......229 D4
College St Dumbarton G82 .49 C2
Glasgow G1 ....241 B2
College Way 4 KA1 ....227 C4
Colleran Ave KA10 ....141 C4
Collessie Dr G33 .....99 B1
Collier St PA5 ....111 C2
Colliers Rd FK7 ......7 B2
Colliertree Rd ML6 ...123 B4
Collina St G20 ....96 B3
Collingwood Ct KA11 ..43 C3
Collingwood Pl G84 ...17 A1
Collingwood Terr PA19 .44 C3
Collins Dr KA10 ......230 A2
Collins St G4 ....241 C2
Collins St Clydebank G81 .74 B3
Glasgow G4 ....241 C2
Collylinn Rd G61 .....75 B2
Colmonell Ave G13 ....94 C4
Colonay Ave
Port Glasgow PA14 ....69 A4
Renfrew PA4 ....94 B1
Colonsay Cres ML5 ...121 B2
Colonsay Ho KA9 .....236 A4
Colonsay Pl KA3 .....223 A3
Colonsay Rd
Glasgow G52 ....115 C3
Paisley PA2 ....133 B4
Colonsay Terr ML1 ....42 C4
Colquhoun Ave G52 ...115 A4
Colquhoun Ct G41 ....116 C2
Colquhoun Dr
Alexandria G83 ....27 C4
Bearsden G61 ....75 B3
Colquhoun Park Prim Sch
G61 ....75 C3
Colquhoun Pk G52 ....115 A4
Colquhoun Rd
Kilmarnock KA3 ....223 B1
Milton G82 ....50 C1

Colquhoun Sq G84 .....16 B1
Colquhoun St
Dumbarton G82 ....50 A2
Helensburgh G84 ......16 B1
Stirling FK7 ....7 B3
Colquhoun Terr FK7 ...7 B3
Colsnaur FK11 ....4 A3
Colson Pl ML4 ....142 B2
Colston Ave G64 .....97 C4
Colston Dr G64 ......97 C4
Colston Gdns
Airdrie ML6 ....123 B4
Bishopbriggs G64 ....97 C4
Colston Pl
3 Airdrie ML6 ....123 B4
8 Bishopbriggs G64 ..97 C4
Colston Rd Airdrie ML6 .123 B4
Bishopbriggs G64 ....97 C4
Colston Row 3 ML6 ...123 B4
Colston Terr 4 ML6 ..123 B4
Colt Ave ML5 ....101 C1
Colt Pl ML5 ....122 A4
Colt Terr ML5 ....122 A4
Coltmuir Cres G64 ...97 C4
Coltmuir Dr G64 .....97 C4
Coltmuir Gdns G64 ...97 C4
Coltmuir St G22 .....97 A3
Coltness Ave ML7 ....166 C4
Coltness Dr ML4 .....142 A2
Coltness High Sch ML2 .165 B2
Coltness La G33 .....119 B4
Coltness Prim Sch ML2 .165 B3
Coltness Rd ML2 .....165 B3
Coltness St G33 .....119 B4
Coltpark La G64 .....97 C4
Coltsfoot Dr G53 ....135 A2
Coltswood Ct ML5 ....122 A4
Coltswood Rd ML5 ...122 A4
Columba Ave G84 .....142 B1
Columba High Sch ML5 .122 A2
Columba Path G81 ....161 B4
Columba St Glasgow G51 .116 A4
Greenock PA16 ....45 B2
Helensburgh G84 ....16 B1
Columbia Pl G75 .....180 A4
Columbia Way G75 ...180 A4
Columbine Way ML8 ...201 C4
Colvend La G40 ......117 C2
Colvend St G40 ......117 C2
Colville Ct ML1 ......143 B1
Colville Dr G73 ......138 B3
Colville Gdns 1 FK10 .10 A3
Colvilles Pl G75 .....181 A3
Colvilles Rd G75 ....181 A3
Colwood Ave G53 ....135 A2
Colwood Gdns G53 ...135 A2
Colwood Path G53 ...135 A2
Colwood Sq G53 .....135 A2
Colwyn Ct ML6 ....103 A1
Colzium Ho* G65 .....36 C1
Colzium View G65 ....60 C4
Combe Quadrant ML4 ..141 C2
Comedie Rd G33 .....99 C2
Comely Bank ML3 ....161 B1
Comely Park Prim Sch
FK1 ....42 A2
Comely Park Terr 15 FK1 .42 A2
Comelybank La G82 ...49 B2
Comelybank Rd G82 ..49 B2
Comelypark Pl G31 ..118 A3
Comelypark St G31 ..118 A3
Commerce St G5 .....240 C1
Commercial Ct G5 ...117 B3
Commercial Rd
Barrhead G78 ....134 B2
Glasgow G5 ....117 B3
Common Gn ML3 .....162 C2
Commonhead & St Colettes
Schs G34 ....120 B4
Commonhead Ave ML6 .102 C1
Commonhead La ML6 ..102 C1
Commonhead St ML6 ..102 C1
Commonhead Rd
Glasgow G69 ....120 C4
Kilmarnock KA1 ......199 C1
Commore Ave G78 ...134 B1
Commore Dr G13 .....95 A4
Commore Pl G78 .....154 B3
Community Ave ML4 ..142 A1
Community Pl ML4 ...142 A1
Community Rd ML4 ...142 A1
Comrie Cres ML3 ....161 B1
Comrie Rd G33 ......99 B3
Comrie St G32 ......119 A2
Cona St G46 ....135 C2
Conan Ct G72 ....139 B3
Condor Glen ML1 ....143 A2
Condorrat Intc G67 ..82 B4
Condorrat Prim Sch G67 .82 A4
Condorrat Rd ML6 ...102 B3
Condorrat Ring Rd G67 .82 B4
Coney Pk FK7 ....6 C3
Coneyhill Rd FK9 ....2 A4
Coneypark Cres FK4 .38 B2
Coneypark Pl FK4 ...38 B2
Congress Rd G3 ....116 B4
Congress Way G3 ...116 B4
Conifer Pl G66 ......79 A3
Coningsby Pl FK10 ..10 A3
Conisborough Cl G34 .100 A1
Conisborough Path G34 .99 C1

Conisborough Rd G34 . . .100 A1
Coniston G75 . . . . .179 C3
Coniston Cres ML3 . . . . . .183 B3
Coniston Dr ML4 . . . . .142 A2
Conistone Cres G69 . . . . .119 C2
Connal St G40 . . . . .118 A2
Connell Cres G62 . . . . .55 B1
Connell Ct KA25 . . . . .149 A1
Conner Ave FK2 . . . . .42 A4
Connor St G32 . . . . .118 C4
Connor Rd G78 . . . . .134 A2
Connor St ML6 . . . . .103 C1
Conon Ave G61 . . . . .75 B2
Conroy Cr FK6 . . . . .21 C1
Conservation Pl ML2 . . . . .165 B1
Constable La G33 . . . . . . .119 B4
Consett St G33 . . . . .119 B4
Constable Rd FK7 . . . . .7 A3
Constantine Way ML1 . . . .142 B1
Constarry Rd G65 . . . . .60 C2
Consul Way ML1 . . . . .142 B1
Container Way PA15 . . . . . .45 C3
Content Ave KA8 . . . . . . .239 A4
Content St KA8 . . . . .236 A1
Contin Pl G20 . . . . .96 B3
Convair Way PA4 . . . . .94 B1
Conval Way 3 PA3 . . . . . .113 B4
Conway St FK1 . . . . .41 C2
Coo La G76 . . . . .178 C3
Coodham Pl KA13 . . . . . . .207 B2
Cook Rd G83 . . . . .28 A4
Cook St G5 . . . . .117 A3
Coolgardie In 10 G75 . . . .180 B4
Coolgardie Pl 9 G75 . . . . .180 B4
Cooper Ave ML8 . . . . .187 C2
Cooper's Well St G11 . . . . . .96 B1
Cooperage Ct G14 . . . . . . .94 B3
Cooperage La FK1,FK2 . . . .42 A3
Cooperage Pl G3 . . . . .116 B4
Cooperage Way FK8 . . . . . . .7 B4
Cooperage Way FK10 . . . . .10 B4
Coopers Cres KA1 . . . . . . .195 C1
Copeland Prim Sch
  G51 . . . . .116 A4
Copenhagen Ave G75 . . . .180 C3
Copland Pl Alva FK12 . . . . . .4 C4
  Glasgow G51 . . . . .116 A3
Copland Quadrant G51 . . .116 A3
Copland Rd G51 . . . . .116 A3
Coplaw St G42 . . . . .117 A2
Copperfield La G71 . . . . . .141 A4
Coralmount Gdns G66 . . . . .79 C4
Coranbae Pl KA7 . . . . . . .238 A1
Corbett Ct G32 . . . . .118 C2
Corbett St G32 . . . . .119 A2
Corbie Pl G62 . . . . .54 B1
Corbiewood Dr FK7 . . . . . .11 C4
Corbiston Way G67 . . . . . .62 A1
Cordale Ave G82 . . . . .27 C1
Cordiner La G44 . . . . .137 A3
Cordiner St G44 . . . . .137 A4
Cordon Rd KA3 . . . . .222 C2
Corentin Ct FK1 . . . . .42 B2
Corkerhill Gdns G52 . . . . .115 C2
Corkerhill Pl G52 . . . . .115 C1
Corkerhill Rd G52 . . . . . . .115 C2
Corkerhill Sta G52 . . . . . .115 B1
Corlaich Ave G42 . . . . . . .137 C4
Corlaich Dr G42 . . . . .137 C4
Corlic St PA15 . . . . .46 A1
Corlic Way PA13 . . . . .89 B4
Cormack Ave G64 . . . . .57 B1
Cormorant Ave PA6 . . . . . .111 B4
Corn Exchange Rd FK8 . . . . .7 A4
Corn St G4 . . . . .97 A1
Cornaig Rd G53 . . . . .135 A4
Cornalee Gdns G53 . . . . . .135 A4
Cornalee Pl G53 . . . . .135 A4
Cornalee Rd G53 . . . . .135 A4
Cornelia St ML1 . . . . .142 A1
Cornelian Terr ML4 . . . . . .142 A2
Cornhaddock St PA15 . . . . .45 C2
Cornhill KA7 . . . . .239 A2
Cornhill Cres FK7 . . . . .7 A2
Cornhill Dr ML5 . . . . .121 C4
Cornhill St G21 . . . . .98 A3
Cornish Ct ML5 . . . . .121 C4
Cornmill Ct G81 . . . . .74 A3
Cornock Cres G81 . . . . . . .74 A2
Cornock St G81 . . . . .74 A2
Cornsilloch Brae ML9 . . . .186 A2
Cornton Bsns Pk FK9 . . . . . .2 A2
Cornton Cres FK9 . . . . .2 A3
Cornton Prim Sch FK9 . . . . .2 A2
Cornton Rd FK9 . . . . .2 A2
Cornton Vale Cotts FK9 . . . .2 A2
Cornwall Dr G72 . . . . .138 B3
Cornwall St 1 G74 . . . . . .159 C1
Cornwall St
  East Kilbride G74 . . . . . .159 C1
  Glasgow G41 . . . . .116 B3
Cornwall St S G41 . . . . . . .116 B3
Cornwall Way G74 . . . . . . .159 C1
Corona Cres FK4 . . . . .39 C3
Coronation Ave ML9 . . . . .199 A4
Coronation Cres ML9 . . . . .199 A4
Coronation Pl
  Gartcosh G69 . . . . .100 C4
  Larkhall ML9 . . . . .199 A4
  Skinflats FK2 . . . . .24 C2
Coronation Rd ML1,ML4 . .142 C2
Coronation Rd E ML1 . . . .142 C2
Coronation Road Ind Est
  ML1 . . . . .142 C2

Coronation St
  Monkton KA9 . . . . .233 B3
  Wishaw ML2 . . . . .165 B2
Coronation Way G61 . . . . . .76 A1
Corpach Pl G34 . . . . .100 B1
Corporation St FK1 . . . . . . .42 B2
Corpus Christi RC Prim Sch
  Airdrie ML6 . . . . .123 A2
  Glasgow G13 . . . . .95 B3
Corra Linn ML3 . . . . .162 A2
Corran Ave G77 . . . . .156 B3
Corran St G33 . . . . .118 C4
Correen Gdns G61 . . . . . . .75 A4
Corrie Ave FK5 . . . . .23 C2
Corrie Brae G65 . . . . .36 B1
Corrie Cres
  Kilmarnock KA3 . . . . . . .222 C2
  Saltcoats KA21 . . . . .205 C1
Corrie Dr
  Motherwell ML1 . . . . . . .163 A4
  Paisley PA1 . . . . .114 C2
Corrie Gdns G75 . . . . .180 A2
Corrie Gr G68 . . . . .61 C4
Corrie Pl Falkirk FK1 . . . . . .41 B2
  Helensburgh G84 . . . . . . .16 C2
  Kirkintilloch G66 . . . . . . .79 C2
  Troon KA10 . . . . .229 D4
Corrie Rd G65 . . . . .36 B1
Corrie View G68 . . . . .61 C4
Corrie View Cotts G65 . . . .59 C2
Corrie Way ML3 . . . . .183 A1
Corrour Rd Glasgow G43 . .136 C4
  Newton Mearns G77 . . . .156 B3
Corruna St ML8 . . . . .188 A1
Corsankell Wynd KA21 . . .205 C2
Corse Ave KA11 . . . . .221 A1
Corse Dr G78 . . . . .134 A2
Corse Pl KA2 . . . . .224 B2
Corse Rd G52 . . . . .114 C3
Corse St KA23 . . . . .190 B3
Corse Terr KA23 . . . . .190 B3
Corsebar Ave PA2 . . . . . . .113 B1
Corsebar Cres PA2 . . . . . .113 B1
Corsebar Dr PA2 . . . . .113 B1
Corsebar La PA2 . . . . .113 A1
Corsebar Rd PA2 . . . . .113 A1
Corsebar Way PA2 . . . . . . .113 B2
Corsefield Rd PA12 . . . . . .128 C1
Corseford Ave PA5 . . . . . .131 B4
Corseford Sch PA10 . . . . .131 A4
Corsehill KA13 . . . . .208 A2
Corsehill Dr KA23 . . . . . . .190 A3
Corsehill Mount Rd
  KA11 . . . . .225 A1
Corsehill Pl Ayr KA7 . . . . .238 C3
  Irvine KA11 . . . . .225 B4
Corsehill Rd Ayr KA7 . . . . .238 C3
  Stewarton KA3 . . . . .195 C1
Corsehill Prim Sch
  KA13 . . . . .207 C2
Corsehill Rd KA7 . . . . .238 C3
Corsehill St G34 . . . . .120 B4
Corsehillbank St KA3 . . . .195 B1
Corselet Rd G53 . . . . .135 A2
Corserine Bank KA11 . . . .219 C2
Corserine Rd KA7 . . . . . . .238 A1
Corsewall Ave G32 . . . . . .119 C2
Corsewall St ML5 . . . . .121 C4
Corsford Dr G53 . . . . .135 B3
Corsliehill Rd PA6 . . . . .90 B4
Corsock Ave ML3 . . . . .161 C1
Corsock St G31 . . . . .118 B4
Corston St G33 . . . . .118 B4
Cortachy Ave FK2 . . . . .24 A2
Cortachy Pl G64 . . . . .78 B1
Coruisk Dr G76 . . . . .157 B4
Coruisk Way PA2 . . . . .132 C4
Corunna St 5 G3 . . . . . . .116 C4
Cosy Neuk ML9 . . . . .185 B1
Cottage Cres FK1 . . . . .41 C3
Cottar St G20 . . . . .96 C4
Cotter Dr KA3 . . . . .228 B4
Cotton Ave PA3 . . . . .112 A3
Cotton Row KA12 . . . . . . .219 B1
Cotton St Glasgow G40 . . .118 A1
  Paisley PA1 . . . . .113 C2
Cotton Street Ent Pk
  G40 . . . . .118 A1
Cotton Vale ML1 . . . . .143 C1
Coulport Pl G84 . . . . .16 A1
Coulter Ave
  Coatbridge ML5 . . . . . . .121 C4
  Wishaw ML2 . . . . .165 B4
Coulthard Dr KA9 . . . . . . .236 B3
Countess St KA1 . . . . .216 C4
County Ave G72 . . . . .138 C4
County Dr ML11 . . . . .215 B2
County Hospl FK10 . . . . . . .10 A4
County Pl 11 PA1 . . . . . . .113 C3
County Sq 4 PA1 . . . . . . .113 C3
Couper Dr G21 . . . . .241 B4
Couper St G21 . . . . .241 B4
Coursington Cres ML1 . . . .164 A4
Coursington Gdns ML1 . . .163 C4
Coursington Pl ML1 . . . . . .163 C4
Coursington Rd ML1 . . . . .164 A4
Court Hill G84 . . . . .15 A2
Court Rd PA14 . . . . .47 B1
Courthill Alva FK12 . . . . .5 A4
  Bearsden G61 . . . . .75 B3
Courthill Ave G44 . . . . . . .137 A3

Courthill Cres G65 . . . . . . .60 C4
Courthill Pl KA24 . . . . . . .191 B4
Courthill St KA24 . . . . . . .191 B4
Courtrai Ave G84 . . . . .16 A1
Coustonholm Rd G43 . . . .136 B4
Couther Quadrant ML6 . . .103 A1
Covanburn Ave ML3 . . . . .162 C1
Cove Cres ML7 . . . . .146 C3
Cove Pl G84 . . . . .16 A1
Cove Rd PA19 . . . . .44 C4
Coveland Dr G73 . . . . .138 A2
Covenant Cres ML9 . . . . . .185 A1
Covenant Pl ML2 . . . . .164 B1
Covenanter Rd ML7 . . . . . .127 B2
Covenanters Way ML2 . . . .186 B3
Coventry Dr G31 . . . . .118 A4
Cow Wynd FK1 . . . . .42 A2
Cowal Cres Gourock PA19 . .44 A3
  Kirkintilloch G66 . . . . .59 A1
Cowal Dr PA3 . . . . .112 A3
Cowal Gdns FK7 . . . . .7 C2
Cowal Pl G20 . . . . .96 B4
Cowal St G20 . . . . .96 B4
Cowal View Ayr KA8 . . . . .236 B2
Cowan La G12 . . . . .96 C1
Cowan Rd G68 . . . . .61 B1
Cowan St Bonnybridge FK4 . .40 A3
  Glasgow G12 . . . . .96 C1
Cowan Wilson Ave G72 . . .161 B4
Cowan Wynd
  Uddingston G71 . . . . . . .141 A4
  Wishaw ML2 . . . . .186 A4
Cowans Row KA3 . . . . .7 A4
Cowans Row KA3 . . . . . . .228 B4
Cowcaddens Rd G3 . . . . . . .97 A1
Cowcaddens Underground
  Sta G4 . . . . .240 C4
Cowden Dr G64 . . . . .78 A2
Cowden St G51 . . . . .115 B4
Cowdenhill Cir G13 . . . . . . .95 B4
Cowdenhill Pl G13 . . . . . . .95 B4
Cowdenhill Rd G13 . . . . . . .95 B4
Cowdray Cres PA4 . . . . .94 B2
Cowgate G66 . . . . .79 B4
Cowglen Hospl G53 . . . . . .135 B4
Cowglen Rd G53 . . . . .135 B4
Cowie Prim Sch FK7 . . . . . .12 B4
Cowie Rd Bannockburn FK7 . .7 C1
  Cowie FK7 . . . . .12 A4
Cowiehall Rd FK7 . . . . .12 A4
Cowlairs Ind Est G22 . . . . .97 B3
Cowlairs Rd 6 G21 . . . . . . .97 C2
Coxton Pl G33 . . . . .99 B1
Coyle Pk KA10 . . . . .229 D3
Coylebank KA7 . . . . .236 B3
Coylton Ave G76 . . . . .157 C2
Coylton Rd G43 . . . . .136 C3
Crabb Quadrant ML1 . . . . .142 B1
Cragdale G74 . . . . .159 B2
Craggan Dr G14 . . . . .95 A3
Craigannon Pl FK10 . . . . . . .4 A1
Crags Ave PA2 . . . . .113 C1
Crags Cres PA2 . . . . .113 C1
Crags Rd PA2 . . . . .113 C1
Cragwell Pk G76 . . . . .158 C4
Craig Ave Alexandria G83 . .27 B4
  Dalry KA24 . . . . .191 A4
Craig Cres
  Kirkintilloch G66 . . . . .80 A4
  Stirling FK9 . . . . .2 B2
Craig Dr KA2 . . . . .226 C4
Craig Gdns G77 . . . . .156 B3
Craig Hill G75 . . . . .180 B4
Craig Leith Rd FK7 . . . . .7 B3
Craig Pl G77 . . . . .156 A3
Craig Rd Glasgow G44 . . . .137 A3
  Linwood PA3 . . . . .111 C4
  Neilston G78 . . . . .154 B3
  Troon KA10 . . . . .229 B2
Craig St Airdrie ML6 . . . . .122 C4
  Blackridge EH48 . . . . . . .107 C2
  Blantyre G72 . . . . .161 C4
  Coatbridge ML5 . . . . . . .121 B1
Craig Valley KA11 . . . . . . .221 A1
Craigallian Ave
  Cambuslang G72 . . . . . . .139 B2
  Milngavie G62 . . . . .55 A3
Craigard Pl G73 . . . . .138 B2
Craigash Quadrant G62 . . .54 C2
Craigash Rd G62 . . . . .54 C2
Craigbank FK10 . . . . .5 B1
Craigbank Dr G76 . . . . . . .178 C3
Craigbank Dr G53 . . . . . . .135 A3
Craigbank Prim Sch
  Alloa FK10 . . . . .5 B1
  Larkhall ML9 . . . . .199 A4
Craigbank Rd ML9 . . . . . . .199 A4
Craigbank St ML9 . . . . . . .199 A4
Craigbanzo St G81 . . . . . . .74 B4
Craigbarnet Ave G64 . . . . . .77 C3
Craigbarnet Cres G33 . . . . .99 A2
Craigbarnet Rd G62 . . . . . .54 C1
Craigbet Ave PA11 . . . . .89 C1
Craigbet Cres PA11 . . . . . . .89 C1
Craigbet Pl PA11 . . . . .89 C1
Craigbo Ave 10 G23 . . . . . .76 B1
Craigbo Ct G23 . . . . .76 B1
Craigbo Dr 9 G23 . . . . .76 B1
Craigbo Pl G23 . . . . .96 B4
Craigbo Rd G23 . . . . .76 B1

Craigbo St G23 . . . . .76 B1
Craigbog Ave PA5 . . . . . . .131 B4
Craigburn Ave PA6 . . . . . .111 B4
Craigburn Cres PA6 . . . . . .111 B4
Craigburn Ct Ashgill ML9 .185 C1
  Falkirk FK1 . . . . .41 C1
Craigburn Pl PA6 . . . . .111 C4
Craigburn St ML3 . . . . .183 B4
Craigdene Dr KA20 . . . . . .206 C3
Craigdhu Ave
  Airdrie ML6 . . . . .123 C4
  Milngavie G62 . . . . .54 C1
Craigdhu Prim Sch G62 . . .75 C4
Craigdhu Rd
  Bearsden G61 . . . . .75 C4
  Milngavie G62 . . . . .54 C1
Craigdonald Pl PA5 . . . . . .111 C2
Craigellan Rd G43 . . . . . . .136 B3
Craigelvan Ct G67 . . . . .81 C3
Craigelvan Dr G67 . . . . . . .81 C3
Craigelvan Gdns G67 . . . . .81 C3
Craigelvan Gr G67 . . . . . . .81 C3
Craigelvan Pl G67 . . . . . . .81 C3
Craigelvan View G67 . . . . .81 C3
Craigenbay Cres G66 . . . . .79 C3
Craigenbay Rd G66 . . . . . . .79 C3
Craigenbay St G21 . . . . . . .98 A2
Craigencart Ct G81 . . . . . . .73 C3
Craigend Ave FK1 . . . . . . .104 B2
Craigend Dr ML5 . . . . .121 B2
Craigend Dr W G62 . . . . . .54 C1
Craigend Pl G13 . . . . .95 C3
Craigend Rd
  Cumbernauld G67 . . . . . . .81 C1
  East Kilbride G75 . . . . . .179 C1
  Stirling FK7 . . . . .7 A2
  Troon KA10 . . . . .232 C4
Craigend St G13 . . . . .95 C3
Craigend View G67 . . . . . . .81 C1
Craigend Visitor Ctr*
  G62 . . . . .55 A4
Craigendmuir Rd G33 . . . . .99 C2
Craigendmuir St G33 . . . . .98 B1
Craigendon Oval PA2 . . . . .133 B3
Craigendon Rd PA2 . . . . . .133 B3
Craigendoran Ave G84 . . . .25 A4
Craigendoran Sta G84 . . . . .25 A4
Craigends Ave PA11 . . . . . .89 C2
Craigends Dr PA10 . . . . . . .111 A2
Craigends Pl PA11 . . . . .89 C2
Craigends Rd
  Glengarnock KA14 . . . . .170 A3
  Houston PA6 . . . . .111 C4
Craigenfeoch Ave PA5 . . . .111 B1
Craigenhill Rd ML8 . . . . . .203 A3
Craigenlay Ave G63 . . . . . .31 B2
Craigens Ave PA2 . . . . .113 A1
Craigens Rd ML1,ML6 . . . .124 B2
Craigfaulds Ave PA2 . . . . .113 A1
Craigfell Ct ML3 . . . . .161 C1
Craigfern Dr G63 . . . . .31 B2
Craigfin Ct KA9 . . . . .236 B3
Craigflower Gdns G53 . . . .135 A2
Craigflower Gdns G53 . . . .135 A2
Craigflower Rd G53 . . . . . .135 A2
Craigford Dr FK7 . . . . .7 B1
Craigforth Cres FK8 . . . . .1 C1
Craighalbert Rd G68 . . . . . .61 B2
Craighalbert Rdbt G68 . . . .61 B2
Craighalbert Way G68 . . . .61 B2
Craighall Pl KA7 . . . . .239 A1
Craighall Quadrant G78 . . .154 B3
Craighall Rd G4 . . . . .97 A1
Craighall St FK8 . . . . .1 C1
Craighaw St G81 . . . . .74 B4
Craighead Ave
  Glasgow G33 . . . . .98 B2
  Milton of C G66 . . . . .58 B3
Craighead Dr G62 . . . . .54 B1
Craighead Prim Sch G66 . .58 B3
Craighead Rd
  Bishopton PA7 . . . . .72 A1
  Milton of C G66 . . . . .58 B3
Craighead Sch ML3 . . . . . .162 A4
Craighead Way G78 . . . . . .134 A1
Craighill Dr G76 . . . . .157 B3
Craighill Gr G76 . . . . .157 B3
Craighirst Dr G81 . . . . .73 C4
Craighirst Rd G62 . . . . .54 B1
Craighlaw Ave G76 . . . . . .157 B1
Craighlaw Dr G76 . . . . . . .157 B1
Craigholm Pl PA6 . . . . .91 B1
Craigholme Sch G41 . . . . .116 B2
Craighorn Dr FK1 . . . . .41 C1
Craighorn Rd FK12 . . . . .4 C3
Craighouse Sq 7 KA25 . . .149 A1
Craighouse St G33 . . . . . . .99 A1
Craighton Gdns G66 . . . . . .58 C4
Craighurst Rd G62 . . . . .54 B1
Craighview KA7 . . . . .239 A1
Craighwell Rd KA7 . . . . . . .236 A3
Craigie Ave Ayr KA8 . . . . .239 A4
  Kilmarnock KA1 . . . . . . .227 C2
Craigie Ct FK5 . . . . .23 C2
Craigie Dr G77 . . . . .156 B2
Craigie La 8 ML9 . . . . . . .185 C2
Craigie Lea KA8 . . . . .239 A4
Craigie Pl
  Crosshouse KA2 . . . . . . .226 C4
  Kilmarnock KA1 . . . . . . .227 C2
Craigie Rd Ayr KA8 . . . . . .236 A1
  Hurlford KA1 . . . . .228 C4
  Kilmarnock KA1 . . . . . . .227 C1
  Kilmarnock, Riccarton KA1 .227 C1
Craigie St Glasgow G42 . . .117 A2
  Prestwick KA9 . . . . .236 A4

Craigie Way KA8 . . . . .239 B4
Craigieburn Gdns G20 . . . .75 C3
Craigieburn Rd G67 . . . . . .61 C1
Craigiehall Ave PA8 . . . . . .93 A4
Craigiehall Cres PA8 . . . . . .93 A4
Craigiehall Pl G51 . . . . . . .116 C3
Craigiehall St G51 . . . . . . .116 C3
Craigiehall Way PA8 . . . . . .93 A4
Craigieknowes St PA15 . . . .46 B2
Craigielea Cres G62 . . . . . .54 C1
Craigielea Ct PA4 . . . . .94 B2
Craigielea Dr PA3 . . . . .113 B3
Craigielea Pk PA4 . . . . .94 B2
Craigielea Prim Sch
  PA3 . . . . .113 A3
Craigielea Rd
  Clydebank G81 . . . . .73 C4
  Renfrew PA4 . . . . .94 B2
Craigielea St G31 . . . . . . .118 A4
Craigielinn Ave PA2 . . . . . .133 B4
Craigievar Ave FK2 . . . . . . .24 A2
Craigievar Pl
  Airdrie ML6 . . . . .123 C3
  Newton Mearns G77 . . . .156 A3
Craigievar St G33 . . . . .99 C1
Craiginn Ct EH48 . . . . .107 B2
Craiginn Terr EH48 . . . . . .107 B2
Craiglea Ave PA14 . . . . . . .47 A1
Craiglea Ct KA1 . . . . .226 C4
Craiglea Cres KA1 . . . . . . .148 A1
Craiglea Pl ML6 . . . . .123 B4
Craiglea Terr ML6 . . . . . . .103 C2
Craiglee G75 . . . . .180 C3
Craigleith FK10 . . . . .5 C2
Craigleith Ave FK1 . . . . . . .41 C1
Craigleith St G32 . . . . .118 C3
Craiglinn G68 . . . . .61 A1
Craiglinn Park Rd G68 . . . .61 A1
Craiglockhart St G33 . . . . . .99 B1
Craiglockhart St G33 . . . . . .99 B1
Craiglomond Gdns G83 . . . .27 B4
Craiglynn Gdns G83 . . . . . .27 C4
Craigmaddie Gdns G64 . . . .78 A4
Craigmaddie Rd G64 . . . . . .56 A1
Craigmaddie Terrace La 7
  G4 . . . . .76 C1
Craigmark Pl KA11 . . . . . .219 C3
Craigmarloch Ave G64 . . . .78 A4
Craigmarloch Rdbt G68 . . .61 B2
Craigmarloch View G61 . . .31 A2
Craigmillar Ave G62 . . . . . .55 A2
Craigmillar Pl FK5 . . . . . . .23 C2
Craigmillar Rd G42 . . . . . .137 A4
Craigmochan Ave ML6 . . . .102 C1
Craigmont Dr G20 . . . . .96 C3
Craigmont St G20 . . . . .96 C3
Craigmore Pl ML5 . . . . . . .121 C2
Craigmore Rd G61 . . . . . . .75 A4
Craigmore St G31 . . . . . . .118 B4
Craigmore Wynd 12
  ML9 . . . . .185 A2
Craigmount Ave PA2 . . . . .133 B3
Craigmuir Cres G52 . . . . . .114 C3
Craigmuir Gdns G72 . . . . .161 A3
Craigmuir Pl G52 . . . . .114 C3
Craigmuir Rd
  Blantyre G72 . . . . .161 A3
  Glasgow G52 . . . . .114 C3
Craigmuschat Rd PA19 . . . .44 C4
Craigneil St G33 . . . . .99 C1
Craigneith Ct G74 . . . . . . .160 C2
Craignethan Castle*
  ML9 . . . . .200 C3
Craignethan Rd ML9 . . . . .200 B2
Craignethan Rd
  Carluke ML8 . . . . .187 C2
  Rutherglen G46 . . . . .157 A4
Craigneuk Ave ML6 . . . . . .123 C3
Craigneuk St ML1,ML2 . . .164 B3
Craigneure Cres 9 G64 . .123 C4
Craigneure Rd G73 . . . . . .138 A2
Craigniven Cres FK1 . . . . . .3 C3
Craigpark G31 . . . . .118 A4
Craigpark Ave KA9 . . . . . .236 A3
Craigpark Dr G31 . . . . . . .118 A4
Craigpark Sch KA7 . . . . . .239 A3
Craigpark St G81 . . . . .74 B4
Craigpark Way G71 . . . . . .141 A4
Craigpark Terr FK1 . . . . . . .10 C2
Craigs Ave G81 . . . . .74 B3
Craigs Pl KA21 . . . . .217 A4
Craigs Rd FK7 . . . . .7 B4
Craigsbank KA10 . . . . .229 D3
Craigsheen Ave G76 . . . . .158 B4
Craigside Pl KA7 . . . . .238 B2
Craigside Ct G68 . . . . .81 C4
Craigside Rd G68 . . . . .81 C4
Craigskeen PA9 KA9 . . . . .236 B3
Craigson Pl ML6 . . . . .123 C3
Craigspark KA21 . . . . .205 C2
Craigstewart Cres KA7 . . .238 B1
Craigston Pl PA5 . . . . .111 C1
Craigston Rd KA1 . . . . .217 A4
Craigthornhill Rd ML3,
  ML10 . . . . .198 A3
Craigton Ave
  Barrhead G78 . . . . .134 C1
  Milngavie G62 . . . . .54 C1
Craigton Cotts G62 . . . . . . .54 C1
Craigton Cres Alva FK12 . . . .4 C2
  Newton Mearns G77 . . . .156 A3

Craigton Dr
Barrhead G78 134 C1
Glasgow G51 115 C3
Newton Mearns G77 156 B3
Craigton Gdns G62 54 C1
Craigton Ind Est G52 115 C3
Craigton Pl Blantyre G72 140 B1
Glasgow G51 115 C3
Craigton Prim Sch G52 115 C3
Craigton Rd
Glasgow G51 115 C4
Kilbirnie KA25 170 A4
Milngavie G62 54 C2
Neilston G77 155 A2
Craigton St G81 74 B4
Craigvale Cres ML6 123 C4
Craigvicar Gdns G32 119 B2
Craigview FK10 5 B1
Craigview Ave PA5 111 C1
Craigview Rd ML1 163 C4
Craigview Terr PA5 111 B1
Craigward FK10 10 A3
Craigweil Pl KA7 238 C4
Craigweil Rd KA7 238 C4
Craigwell Ave G73 138 B3
Craiksland Pl KA10 230 A2
Crail St G31 118 B3
Cramalt Ct KA11 220 A2
Crammond Ave ML5 121 B2
Cramond Ave PA4 94 C1
Cramond Ct FK1 42 A1
Cramond Pl KA11 219 C1
Cramond St G5 117 C1
Cramond Terr G32 119 A3
Cramond Way KA11 219 C1
Cranberry Moss Rd
Kilwinning KA13 207 B2
Kilwinning KA13,KA20 207 B1
Cranberry Rd KA13 207 A1
Cranborne Rd G12 96 A3
Cranbrooke Dr G20 96 B4
Crandleyhill Rd KA9 236 A3
Cranesbill Ct KA7 239 A2
Crannog Ct G82 50 C1
Crannog Rd G82 50 C1
Crannog Way KA13 207 B2
Cranston St G3 240 A2
Cranworth La G12 96 B2
Cranworth St G12 96 B2
Crarae Ave G61 75 C1
Crathes Ave FK5 24 A2
Crathes Ct G44 136 C2
Crathie Ct ML8 187 C2
Crathie Dr
Ardrossan KA22 205 B1
Denny FK6 21 B2
Glasgow G11 96 A1
Glenmavis ML6 102 C2
Crathie Pl G77 157 A2
Crathie Quadrant ML2 165 A3
Crathie Rd KA3 222 C1
Crauford Ave KA23 190 C2
Craufurd Cres KA15 171 C2
Craufurdland Rd KA3 223 A3
Craven Gr KA11 219 C3
Craw Pl PA12 129 B1
Craw Rd PA2 113 B2
Crawberry Rd PA15 46 A1
Crawford Ave
Kirkintilloch G66 79 C2
Prestwick KA9 236 B3
Crawford Cres
Blantyre G72 140 B1
Uddingston G71 140 C4
Crawford Dr
East Kilbride G74 160 A1
Glasgow G15 75 A1
Helensburgh G84 16 C2
Crawford Hill G74 160 A1
Crawford Rd Houston PA6 91 B1
Milngavie G62 54 C2
Crawford Sq FK2 14 B2
Crawford St Glasgow G11 96 A1
Hamilton ML3 162 A3
Motherwell ML1 163 B3
Port Glasgow PA14 47 B1
Crawforddyke Prim Sch
ML8 202 A4
Crawfurd Ave G73 138 A3
Crawfurd Dr PA3 113 A3
Crawfurd Gdns G73 138 B2
Crawfurd Rd G73 138 A2
Crawfurd St PA15 45 C3
Crawfurdland Pl KA2 221 B1
Crawfurds View PA12 129 B2
Crawhin Gdns PA15 45 B2
Crawriggs Ave G66 79 B3
Creamery Rd ML2 165 B1
Crebar Dr G78 134 B1
Crebar St G46 135 C2
Credon Dr Airdrie ML6 123 A2
Crosshouse KA2 226 C4
Credon Gdns G73 138 B2
Cree Ave G64 78 B1
Cree Gdns G32 118 C3
Cree Pl G75 159 A1
Creebank Pl KA10 229 D3
Creelshaugh Rd KA3 213 A2
Creighton Gr G74 159 C1
Creigton Ct KA3 223 A3
Creinch Dr G83 19 C1
Creran Ct Hamilton ML3 162 A1
Prestwick KA9 236 B3
Creran Dr Denny FK6 39 B3
Renfrew PA4 94 A2
Creran Path 12 ML2 165 C3
Crescent Rd G13 95 A3
Crescent St PA15 46 A2
Crescent The
Clarkston G76 158 A3
Clydebank G81 73 C2
Longriggend ML6 84 B1
Prestwick KA9 233 B1
Stewarton KA3 195 C1
Cressdale Ave G45 137 B1
Cressdale Ct G45 137 B1
Cressdale Dr G45 137 B1
Cresswell Gr G77 156 B2
Cresswell La G12 96 B2
Cresswell Pl G77 156 C1
Cresswell St 5 G12 96 B2
Cressy St G51 115 C4
Crest Ave G13 95 A4
Crestlea Ave PA2 133 C4
Creteil Ct FK1 42 B2
Creveul Ct G83 27 C3
Crichton Ave KA24 191 A4
Crichton Ct G45 137 C1
Crichton Pl G21 97 C2
Crichton St
Coatbridge ML5 122 A4
Glasgow G21 97 C2
Cricketfield La PA6 91 A2
Crieff Ave ML6 123 B1
Criffel Pl Kilmarnock KA1 228 A2
Motherwell ML1 143 B2
Criffell Gdns G32 119 B2
Criffell Rd G32 119 B2
Crighton Wynd ML4 141 B3
Crimea St G2 240 B2
Crimond Pl Kilsyth G65 36 A1
Shieldhill FK1 66 C4
Crinan Cres ML5 101 B1
Crinan Gdns G64 78 B1
Crinan Pl
Ardrossan KA22 205 B3
Bellshill ML4 142 A2
Coatbridge ML5 101 B1
Crinan Rd G64 78 B1
Crinan St G31 118 A4
Crindledyke Cres ML2 166 A3
Cringate Gdns FK7 7 C1
Cripps Ave G81 74 B1
Crisswell Cl PA16 44 B1
Crisswell Cres PA16 44 B1
Crocus Bank KA7 239 B2
Crocus Gr KA12 219 B2
Croe Pl KA1 228 A2
Croft ML9 184 C1
Croft Pl ML9 184 C2
Croft Rd Balmore G64 77 C4
Cambuslang G72 139 A3
East Kilbride G75 180 C4
Larkhall ML9 184 C2
Croft St Alexandria G83 27 C2
Kilmarnock KA1 222 C1
Croft Terr KA11 220 C1
Croft Way PA4 94 C1
Croft Wynd G71 141 A3
Croft's Rd FK10 4 A2
Croftbank Ave G71 141 A1
Croftbank Cres
Bothwell G71 141 A1
Uddingston G71 140 C3
Croftbank Gate G71 141 A1
Croftbank St 11 G21 97 C2
Croftburn Dr G44 137 B2
Croftcot Ave ML4 141 C2
Croftcroighn Rd G33 99 A1
Croftcroighn Sch G33 99 C1
Croftend Ave G44 137 C3
Croftend La G44 137 C3
Croftfoot Cres G45 138 A2
Croftfoot Dr G45 137 C2
Croftfoot Pl Denny FK6 21 B2
Gartcosh G69 101 A3
Croftfoot Quadrant G45 137 C2
Croftfoot Rd G44 137 C2
Croftfoot Sch G44 137 C3
Croftfoot St G45 138 A2
Croftfoot Sta G44 137 C3
Croftfoot Terr G45 137 C2
Crofthead KA11 220 A2
Crofthead Ave KA3 223 A3
Crofthead Cotts G78 154 B4
Crofthead Cres ML4 141 C2
Crofthead Ct Irvine KA11 220 A2
Stirling FK8 2 A1
Crofthead Dr G66 33 B1
Crofthead Pl
Bellshill ML4 141 C2
Newton Mearns G77 156 C2
Crofthead Rd Ayr KA7 239 B3
Kilmaurs KA3 222 A4
Prestwick KA9 233 B1
Stirling FK8 2 A1
Crofthead St G71 140 C3
Crofthill Ave G71 140 C3
Crofthill Ct ML9 198 C1
Crofthill Rd G44 137 C3
Crofthouse Dr G44 137 C2
Croftmont Ave G44 137 C2
Croftmoraig Ave G69 81 A2
Crofton Ave G44 137 B2
Croftpark Ave G44 137 B3
Croftpark Cres G72 161 C3
Croftpark Rd G81 74 A4
Croftpark St ML4 142 A3
Croftshaw Rd FK12 5 A4
Croftside Ave G44 137 C2
Croftspar Ave G32 119 B3
Croftspar Ct G32 119 B3
Croftspar Dr G32 119 B3
Croftspar Gate G32 119 B3
Croftspar Gr G32 119 B3
Croftspar Pl G32 119 B3
Croftwood G64 78 A2
Croftwood Ave G44 137 B2
Croftwood Rd ML3 162 B1
Crogal Cres ML6 123 B1
Cromalt Ave G75 180 A2
Cromalt Cres G61 75 B4
Cromarty Ave
Bishopbriggs G64 78 B1
Glasgow G43 136 C3
Cromarty Cres G61 75 C4
Cromarty Gdns G76 137 A1
Cromarty Pl Chryston G69 80 B1
East Kilbride G74 160 B2
Cromarty Rd ML6 122 C3
Crombie Gdns G69 120 A2
Cromdale Rd
Kilmarnock KA1 228 A2
Port Glasgow PA14 69 A3
Cromdale St G51 115 C4
Cromdale Way ML1 143 A1
Cromer Way 6 PA3 113 B4
Crompton Ave G44 137 A3
Crompton Way KA12 219 C2
Cromptons Gr PA1 113 A2
Cromwell Dr FK1 42 B2
Cromwell La 5 G20 97 A1
Cromwell Rd Ayr KA7 235 C1
Falkirk FK1 42 B2
Cromwell Rd W FK1 42 B2
Cromwell St G20 97 A1
Crona Dr ML3 161 C2
Cronberry Quadrant
G52 114 C2
Cronberry Terr G52 114 C2
Cronin Pl ML4 142 A4
Cronulla Pl G65 60 C4
Crookedshields Rd G72,
G74 160 A4
Crookfur Cottage Homes
G77 156 B3
Crookfur Prim Sch G77 156 B4
Crookfur Rd G77 156 B3
Crookhill Dr PA12 129 B2
Crookhill Gdns PA12 129 B2
Crookston Ave G52 115 A2
Crookston Castle* G53 115 A1
Crookston Ct G52 115 A2
Crookston Dr PA1,G52 114 C2
Crookston Gdns G52 114 C2
Crookston Gr G52 115 A2
Crookston Path G52 114 C2
Crookston Pl G52 114 C2
Crookston Quadrant
G52 115 A2
Crookston Rd G53 135 A4
Crookston Sta G52 114 C2
Crookston Terr G52 115 A2
Crookstonhill Path G52 114 C2
Crophill FK10 5 B1
Crosbie Ct KA10 232 B4
Crosbie Dr Paisley PA2 132 C4
West Kilbride KA23 190 B2
Crosbie La G20 96 B4
Crosbie Pl KA10 232 C4
Crosbie Rd KA10 232 C4
Crosbie St G20 96 B4
Crosbie Terr KA9 236 B4
Crosbie Wood PA2 113 A1
Crosbies Ct FK8 7 A4
Cross KA15 171 A4
Cross Arthurlie Sch
G78 134 A2
Cross Arthurlie St G78 134 A2
Cross Brae FK1 66 B3
Cross Ct G64 77 C1
Cross Gates ML4 142 A2
Cross House Stables & Riding
Sch* G66 32 B2
Cross Key's Cl ML11 215 A2
Cross Rd PA2 113 A1
Cross Shore St PA15 46 A3
Cross St Falkirk FK2 24 A1
Glasgow G32 119 B1
Cross Stone Pl ML1 163 C3
Cross The Dalry KA24 191 B4
Glasgow G1 241 B1
Kilmarnock KA1 227 C4
Prestwick KA9 233 B1
Stewarton KA3 211 B4
Stonehouse ML9 198 C1
Cross Wynd 1 G74 159 C1
Crossart St ML7 125 A1
Crossbank Ave G42 117 C1
Crossbank Dr G42 117 B1
Crossbank Rd G42 117 B1
Crossbank Terr G42 117 B1
Crossburn KA7 238 A1
Crossburn Ave G62 54 C1
Crossburn Dr KA10 230 A2
Crossburn La KA10 230 A2
Crossburn Terr KA10 230 A2
Crossclyde View ML8 201 B1
Crossdene Rd KA2 226 C4
Crossdykes G66 80 A4
Crossen La ML8 188 A1
Crossflat Cres PA1 114 A3
Crossford Dr 8 G23 76 C1
Crossford Hawk Ctr*
ML8 201 A1
Crossgate G66 58 B1
Crossgates PA7 72 A2
Crossgates Ave ML1 144 A2
Crossgates St ML9 184 C2
Crosshill Ave
Glasgow G42 117 A1
Kirkintilloch G66 79 B3
Crosshill Dr Cleland ML1 144 A2
Rutherglen G73 138 A3
Crosshill Pl PA14 68 C4
Crosshill Rd
Bishopbriggs G64,G66 78 C3
Kirkintilloch G66 79 B2
Port Glasgow PA14 68 C3
Port Glasgow, Boglestone
PA14 68 C4
Crosshill St Airdrie ML6 122 C4
Coatbridge ML5 121 A2
Lennoxtown G66 33 B1
Motherwell ML1 163 C3
Crosshill Sta G42 117 A1
Crosshill Wynd KA3 223 B3
Crosshouse Hospl KA2 222 A1
Crosshouse Prim Sch
Crosshouse KA2 221 C1
East Kilbride G75 180 A3
Crosshouse Rd
Clachan of C G66 33 A2
East Kilbride G75 180 A3
Kilmaurs KA3 222 A3
Crossing La ML9 200 A2
Crosslaw Ave ML11 215 B2
Crosslaw Gdns ML11 215 B2
Crosslea Gdns PA6 91 A1
Crosslee Cres PA6 91 B1
Crosslee Pk PA6 111 B4
Crosslee Rd PA11 111 A4
Crosslee St G52 115 B3
Crosslees Dr G46 135 C2
Crosslees Pk G46 135 C2
Crosslees Rd G46 135 C1
Crosslet Ave G82 50 B2
Crosslet Ct G82 50 A2
Crosslet Pl G82 50 A2
Crosslet Rd G82 50 A2
Crossloan Rd G51 115 C4
Crossloan Terr 5 G51 116 A4
Crossmill Ave G78 134 B2
Crossmount Ct ML8 187 C1
Crossmyloof Gdns G41 116 B1
Crossmyloof Sta G41 116 C1
Crosspoint Dr 7 G23 76 C1
Crossroads KA24 170 B2
Crosstobs Rd G53 115 A1
Crossveggate Bsns Pk
G62 55 A1
Crossview Ave G69 120 B3
Crossview Pl G69 120 B3
Crossways PA6 91 B1
Crosveggate G62 55 A1
Crovie Rd G53 135 A4
Crow Ave ML1 143 A3
Crow Rd Glasgow G11 96 A1
Lennoxtown G66 33 A3
Stonehouse ML9 198 C1
Crow Wood Rd G69 100 A4
Crow Wood Terr G69 100 A4
Crowflat View G71 121 B1
Crowflats Rd G71 140 C3
Crowhall Dr G33 119 C3
Crowhill Cres ML6 102 C1
Crowhill Rd G64 97 C4
Crowhill St G22 97 B3
Crowlin Cres G33 119 A4
Crown Ave G81 74 A2
Crown Cir 19 G12 96 B2
Crown Gdns Alloa FK10 9 C4
Glasgow G12 96 B2
Crown Rd N G12 96 B2
Crown Rd S G12 96 B2
Crown St Ayr KA8 235 C1
Calderbank ML6 123 A2
Coatbridge ML5 122 B4
Glasgow G69 119 C2
Glasgow, Gorbals G1,G5 117 B3
Greenock PA15 45 C3
Crown Terr G12 96 B2
Crownest Loan FK5 23 C1
Crownhall Pl G32 119 B3
Crownhall Rd G32 119 B3
Crownpoint Rd G40 117 C3
Crowwood Cres ML6 123 A1
Crowwood Dr ML6 123 B4
Crowwood Rd ML6 123 A1
Croy G74 159 B2
Croy Ave G77 157 A3
Croy Hill Roman Fort*
G68 61 A3
Croy Pl G21 98 B3
Croy Rd Coatbridge ML5 121 C2
Glasgow G21 98 B3
Croy Sta G68 60 C2
Cruachan Ave
Paisley PA2 133 C4
Renfrew PA4 94 B1
Stirling FK9 2 A2
Cruachan Ct FK1 42 B1
Cruachan Dr
Barrhead G78 134 B1
Newton Mearns G77 156 C2
Cruachan Pl KA1 228 A2
Cruachan Rd
Bearsden G61 75 A4
Rutherglen G73 138 B2
Cruachan St G46 135 C2
Cruachan Way G78 134 B1
Cruckburn Wynd FK7 6 C2
Cruden St G51 115 C3
Cruickshank Dr FK1 66 B3
Cruikshank's Ct FK6 21 C1
Crum Ave G46 136 A2
Crum Cres FK7 7 B1
Crummieholm Gdns
KA10 230 A2
Crummock Gdns KA15 150 B1
Crummock St KA15 150 B1
Crusader Ave G13 75 B1
Crusader Cres KA3 211 B4
Cubie St G40 117 C3
Cubrieshaw Dr KA23 190 B2
Cubrieshaw Pk KA23 190 C2
Cubrieshaw St KA23 190 B3
Cuckoo Way ML1 143 A3
Cuff Cres KA15 171 A4
Cuilhill Rd G69 121 A4
Cuillin Ct FK1 42 B1
Cuillin Pl Chapelhall ML6 123 C1
Irvine KA11 220 A2
Kilmarnock KA1 228 A2
Cuillin Way G78 134 B1
Cuillins Ave PA14 68 C3
Cuillins The
Moodiesburn G69 81 A2
Uddingston G71 120 C1
Cuilmuir Terr G65 60 C2
Cuilmuir View G65 60 C3
Cuilt Pl G63 31 A2
Cuilts Rd G63 30 A2
Culbin Dr G13 95 A4
Cullen PA8 73 A2
Cullen La 18 G75 180 C4
Cullen Pl G71 141 A4
Cullen Rd
East Kilbride G75 180 B4
Motherwell ML1 163 B3
Cullen St Alexandria G83 27 B4
Glasgow G32 119 A2
Cullin Gdns G22 97 B2
Cullins Rd G73 138 B2
Cullion Way ML1 144 A3
Culloch Rd Bearsden G61 75 B4
Slamannan FK1 86 A3
Cullochrig Rd G67 82 C1
Culloden Ave ML4 142 B2
Culloden Pl KA3 223 A2
Culloden St G31 118 A4
Culmore Pl FK1 42 C1
Culrain Gdns G32 119 A3
Culrain St G32 119 A2
Culross Hill G74 159 B1
Culross Pl
Coatbridge ML5 121 C4
East Kilbride G74 159 B1
Culross St G32 119 B2
Culross Way G69 81 A2
Cult Rd G66 79 C2
Cultenhove Cres FK7 7 A2
Cultenhove Pl FK7 7 A2
Cultenhove Rd FK7 7 A2
Culterfell Path ML1 144 B1
Cults St G51 115 C3
Culvain Ave G61 75 A4
Culvain Pl FK1 42 B1
Culzean ML6 102 C3
Culzean Ave
Coatbridge ML5 121 C2
Prestwick KA9 236 B4
Culzean Cres
Glasgow G69 120 A2
Kilmarnock KA3 228 B4
Newton Mearns G77 157 A2
Culzean Ct ML5 121 C3
Culzean Dr
East Kilbride G74 159 B2
Glasgow G32 119 B2
Gourock PA19 43 C3
Motherwell ML1 143 B2
Culzean Pl
East Kilbride G74 159 B2
Kilwinning KA13 207 B1
Stenhousemuir FK5 23 C2
Culzean Rd KA7 238 B2
Cumberland Arc 9 G5 117 B2
Cumberland Ave G84 16 A2
Cumberland Pl
Coatbridge ML5 121 B2
13 Glasgow G5 117 B2
Cumberland Rd
Greenock PA16 44 C2
Rhu G84 15 B3
Cumberland St
Glasgow G5 117 B2
Glasgow, Laurieston G5 117 A3
Cumberland Terr G84 15 B3
Cumberland Wlk PA16 44 C2
Cumbernauld Airport
G68 62 A4
Cumbernauld Coll G67 61 C1
Cumbernauld High Sch
G67 62 B1
Cumbernauld Prim Sch
G67 62 A2
Cumbernauld Rd
Chryston G69 100 B4
Cumbernauld G67 81 B2
Glasgow G31,G33 118 B4
Haggs FK4 39 A2
Moodiesburn G68,G69 81 A2
Stepps G33 99 B3
Cumbernauld Sta G67 83 A4
Cumbrae G74 160 B1
Cumbrae Ave PA14 69 A4
Cumbrae Cres ML5 122 C3
Cumbrae Cres N G82 49 B3
Cumbrae Cres S G82 49 B3
Cumbrae Ct
Clydebank G81 74 A1
Irvine KA11 225 B4
Cumbrae Dr Falkirk FK1 41 B2
Kilmarnock KA3 223 A3
Motherwell ML1 163 B4
Cumbrae Ho KA9 236 A3

Cumbrae Pl
Coatbridge ML5 .122 C2
Gourock PA19 .44 B3
West Kilbride KA23 .190 B2
Cumbrae Rd Paisley PA2 .133 C4
Renfrew PA4 .94 B1
Saltcoats KA21 .205 C1
Cumbrae St G33 .119 A4
Cumlodden Dr G20 .96 B4
Cumming Ave ML8 .202 B4
Cumming Dr G42 .137 A4
Cumnock Dr Airdrie ML6 .123 A2
Barrhead G78 .134 B1
Hamilton ML3 .161 B1
Cumnock Rd G33 .98 C3
Cumroch Rd G66 .33 B1
Cunard Ct G81 .94 A4
Cunard St G81 .94 A4
Cuninghame Dr KA20 .206 A1
Cuninghame Rd
Ardrossan KA22 .205 B2
Kilbarchan PA10 .111 A2
Saltcoats KA21 .217 A4
Cunning Park Dr KA7 .238 B2
Cunningair Dr ML1 .163 C2
Cunningham Cres KA7 .239 B3
Cunningham Dr
Clydebank G81 .73 C3
Glasgow G46 .136 C2
Harthill ML7 .127 B3
Cunningham Gdns
Falkirk FK2 .42 C3
Houston PA6 .91 B1
Cunningham Pl KA7 .239 B3
Cunningham Rd
Paisley G52 .114 C4
Stenhousemuir FK5 .24 A2
Stirling FK7 .7 B4
Cunningham St ML1 .163 B3
Cunningham Watt Rd
KA3 .195 B1
Cunninghame Dr KA1 .227 C2
Cunninghame Rd
East Kilbride G74 .159 C1
Irvine KA12 .224 B4
Prestwick KA9 .236 B4
Rutherglen G73 .138 B4
Cupar Dr PA16 .44 C2
Cuparhead Ave ML5 .121 C2
Cuppleton Brae PA9 .130 A1
Curfew Rd G13 .75 B1
Curle St G14 .95 B1
Curlew Cres PA16 .45 A2
Curlew La PA16 .45 A2
Curlew Pl PA5 .131 B4
Curling Cres G44 .137 B4
Curlinghaugh Cres ML2 .165 B2
Curlingmire G75 .180 C4
Curran Ave ML2 .164 C1
Currie Ct KA22 .205 B1
Currie St G20 .96 C3
Currieside Ave ML7 .146 C2
Currieside Pl ML7 .146 B2
Curtecan Pl KA7 .238 C3
Curtis Ave G44 .137 B4
Curzon St G20 .96 C3
Cushenquarter Dr FK7 .12 B2
Custom House Mus*
PA15 .46 A3
Custom House Quay Ret Pk
PA15 .46 A3
Customhouse Pl PA15 .46 A3
Custonhall Pl FK6 .21 B1
Cut The G71 .140 C3
Cuthbert Pl KA3 .223 A1
Cuthbert St G71 .141 A4
Cuthbertson Prim Sch
G42 .117 A2
Cuthbertson St G42 .117 A1
Cuthelton Dr G31 .118 C2
Cuthelton St G31 .118 B2
Cuthelton Terr G31 .118 B2
Cutsburn Pl KA3 .211 C4
Cutsburn Rd KA3 .211 C4
Cutstraw Rd KA3 .211 C4
Cutty Sark Pl G82 .50 B1
Cuttyfield Pl FK2 .24 B2
Cypress Ave Beith KA15 .150 B1
Blantyre G72 .140 B1
Uddingston G71 .141 A4
Cypress Cres G75 .180 B3
Cypress Ct
East Kilbride G75 .180 B3
Hamilton ML3 .162 C1
Kirkintilloch G66 .79 A3
Cypress Gdns KA11 .219 C3
Cypress Pl G75 .180 B3
Cypress St G22 .97 B3
Cypress Way G72 .139 C2
Cyprus Ave PA5 .112 A1
Cyril St PA1 .114 A2

D

Daer Ave PA4 .94 C1
Daer Way ML3 .162 A2
Daer Wlk ML9 .199 A4
Daffodil Way ML1 .163 C4
Dairsie Ct G44 .136 C2
Dairsie Gdns G64 .98 B4
Dairsie House Sch G43 .136 C3
Dairsie St G44 .136 C2
Daisy Cotts KA8 .236 A2
Daisy St G42 .117 A1
Daisybank KA14 .170 B3
Dakala Ct ML2 .165 A1
Dakota Way PA4 .94 B1
Dalbeattie Braes ML6 .123 C1
Dalbeth Pl G32 .118 C1
Dalbeth Rd G32 .118 C1
Dalblair Rd KA7 .238 C4
Dalcharn Pl G34 .120 A4
Dalcross St G11 .96 B1
Dalcruin Gdns G69 .81 A2
Dalderse Ave FK2 .42 A3
Daldowie Ave G32 .119 B2
Daldowie Doocot The*
G69 .119 C1
Daldowie Rd G71 .120 A1
Daldowie St ML5 .121 C2
Dale Ave G75 .180 B3
Dale Cres KA12 .219 B2
Dale Ct ML2 .164 B1
Dale Dr ML1 .143 A2
Dale Path G40 .117 C2
Dale St G40 .118 A2
Dale Way G73 .138 A2
Daleview Ave G12 .96 A3
Daleview Dr G76 .157 B3
Daleview Gr G76 .157 B3
Dalfoil Ct PA1 .114 C2
Dalgain Ct KA11 .220 A3
Dalgarroch Ave G81 .94 C4
Dalgarven Mews KA3 .223 B3
Dalgarven Mill* KA13 .207 B4
Dalgarven Wynd KA13 .207 B3
Dalgleish Ave G81 .73 C3
Dalgleish Ct FK8 .7 A4
Dalgraig Cres G72 .140 B1
Dalhousie Gdns G64 .78 A1
Dalhousie La G3 .240 B4
Dalhousie Rd PA10 .111 A1
Dalhousie St G3 .240 C4
Dalilea Dr G34 .100 B1
Dalilea Pl G34 .100 B1
Dalintober St G5 .240 B1
Daljarrock Ave KA13 .207 A1
Dalkeith Ave
Bishopbriggs G64 .78 A2
Glasgow G41 .116 A2
Dalkeith Rd G64 .78 A2
Dallas Ct KA10 .229 C1
Dallas La KA10 .229 C1
Dallas Pl KA10 .229 C1
Dallas Rd KA10 .229 C1
Dalmacoulter Rd ML6 .103 A2
Dalmahoy Cres PA11 .110 B3
Dalmahoy St G32 .118 C4
Dalmahoy Way KA13 .207 A2
Dalmailing Ave KA11 .220 A1
Dalmally St Glasgow G20 .96 C2
Greenock PA15 .46 C1
Dalmarnock Ct G40 .118 A2
Dalmarnock Prim Sch
G40 .118 A2
Dalmarnock Rd G40 .118 A2
Dalmarnock Road Trad Est
G73 .118 A1
Dalmarnock Sta G40 .118 A2
Dalmary Dr PA1 .114 A3
Dalmellington Ct
East Kilbride G74 .159 B1
Hamilton ML3 .161 B1
Dalmellington Dr
East Kilbride G74 .159 B1
9 Glasgow G53 .135 A4
Dalmellington Rd
Ayr KA7 .239 B2
Glasgow G53 .115 A1
Dalmeny Ave G46 .136 B2
Dalmeny Dr G78 .134 A1
Dalmeny Rd ML3 .162 B1
Dalmeny St G5 .117 C1
Dalmilling Cres KA8 .236 B1
Dalmilling Dr KA8 .236 C1
Dalmilling Rd KA8 .236 C1
Dalmoak Rd PA15 .46 B1
Dalmonach Rd G83 .27 C2
Dalmore Cres G84 .16 A2
Dalmore Dr Airdrie ML6 .123 A3
Alva FK12 .4 C3
Dalmore Pl KA11 .219 C3
Dalmore Way KA11 .219 C3
Dalmorglen Pk FK7 .6 C3
Dalmuir Sta G81 .73 C2
Dalnair Pl G62 .54 B1
Dalnair St G3 .96 B1
Dalness St G32 .119 A2
Dalnottar Ave G60 .73 A3
Dalnottar Dr G60 .73 A3
Dalnottar Gdns G60 .73 A3
Dalnottar Hill Rd G60 .73 A3
Dalnottar Terr G60 .73 A3
Dalreoch Ave G69 .120 B3
Dalreoch Ct G82 .49 B2
Dalreoch Path G69 .120 B3
Dalreoch Prim Sch G82 .49 B3
Dalreoch Sta G82 .49 C2
Dalriada Cres ML1 .142 B1
Dalriada Dr G64 .78 B4
Dalriada Rd PA16 .44 B2
Dalriada St G40 .118 B2
Dalry Gdns ML3 .161 B1
Dalry La KA22 .205 B2
Dalry Pl ML6 .143 C4
Dalry Prim Sch KA24 .191 A4
Dalry Rd Ardrossan KA22 .205 B2
Beith KA15 .171 A4
Kilbirnie KA25 .170 A4
Kilwinning KA13 .207 B2
Saltcoats KA21 .206 A1
Stewarton KA3 .195 B1
Dalry Rd *continued*
Uddingston G71 .141 A4
Dalry St G32 .119 A2
Dalry Sta KA24 .191 B4
Dalrymple Ct
Irvine KA12 .219 C2
2 Kirkintilloch G66 .79 B4
Dalrymple Dr
Coatbridge ML5 .121 C2
East Kilbride G74 .159 C1
Newton Mearns G77 .157 A2
Dalrymple Pl KA12 .219 B2
Dalrymple St PA15 .46 A3
Dalserf Cres G46 .136 A1
Dalserf Ct G31 .118 A3
Dalserf Gdns G31 .118 A3
Dalserf Path 27 ML9 .185 B1
Dalserf Prim Sch ML9 .199 C4
Dalserf St G31 .118 A3
Dalsetter Ave G15 .75 A1
Dalsetter Pl G15 .75 A1
Dalshannon Pl G67 .82 A4
Dalshannon Rd G67 .82 A4
Dalshannon View G67 .82 A4
Dalshannon Way G67 .82 A4
Dalsholm Ave G20 .96 A4
Dalsholm Ind Est G20 .96 A4
Dalskeith Ave PA3 .113 A3
Dalskeith Cres PA3 .113 A3
Dalskeith Rd PA3 .113 A3
Dalswinton St G34 .120 B4
Dalton Ave G81 .74 C1
Dalton Hill ML3 .161 C1
Dalton St G31 .118 C3
Dalvait Ct G83 .27 C4
Dalvait Gdns G83 .27 C4
Dalvait Rd G83 .27 C4
Dalveen Ct G78 .134 B1
Dalveen Dr G71 .140 C4
Dalveen Quadrant ML5 .122 B3
Dalveen St G32 .118 C3
Dalveen Way G73 .138 B2
Dalwhinnie Ave G72 .140 B1
Dalwhinnie Ct KA11 .219 C3
Dalwood Rd KA9 .236 A4
Daly Gdns G72 .140 C1
Dalzell Ave ML1 .164 A2
Dalzell Dr ML1 .164 A2
Dalzell Pk* ML1 .163 C2
Dalzial Twr ML1 .164 A2
Dalziel Ct ML3 .162 A2
Dalziel Dr G41 .116 B2
Dalziel High Sch ML1 .163 B3
Dalziel Rd G52 .114 C4
Dalziel St Hamilton ML3 .162 A3
Motherwell ML1 .163 C4
Damhead Rd KA1 .227 C2
Dampark KA3 .195 B4
Damshot Cres G53 .115 B1
Damshot Rd G53 .135 B4
Damside KA8 .235 C1
Danby Rd G69 .119 C2
Danes Ave 1 G14 .95 B2
Danes Cres G14 .95 A3
Danes Dr G14 .95 B2
Danes La N 3 G14 .95 B2
Danes La S G14 .95 B2
Daniel McLaughlin Pl
G66 .58 C1
Dankeith Dr KA1 .231 B2
Dankeith Rd KA1 .231 B2
Darg Rd KA20 .217 B4
Dargarvel Ave G41 .116 A2
Dargavel Ave PA7 .72 A2
Dargavel Rd PA7,PA8 .72 B1
Dark Brig Rd ML8 .201 A1
Darkwood Cres PA3 .113 A3
Darkwood Ct PA3 .113 A3
Darkwood Dr PA3 .113 A3
Darleith Rd
Alexandria G83 .27 C3
Cardross G82 .26 A1
Darleith St G32 .118 C3
Darley Cres KA10 .229 C1
Darley Pl Hamilton ML3 .183 A4
Troon KA10 .229 C1
Darley Rd G68 .61 C3
Darlington View KA3 .195 C1
Darluith Pk PA5 .111 B3
Darluith Rd PA3 .111 C3
Darmeid Pl ML7 .167 A4
Darmule Dr KA13 .207 B3
Darnaway Ave G33 .99 B1
Darnaway Dr G33 .99 B1
Darnaway St G33 .99 B1
Darndaff Rd PA15 .46 A1
Darngaber Gdns ML3 .183 C2
Darngaber Rd ML3 .183 C2
Darngavil Rd ML6 .103 C3
Darnick St G21 .98 A1
Darnley Cres G64 .77 C2
Darnley Dr KA1 .227 C3
Darnley Gdns G41 .116 C1
Darnley Ind Est G53 .135 A3
Darnley Mains Rd G53 .135 B2
Darnley Path G46 .135 C3
Darnley Pl G41 .116 C1
Darnley Prim Sch No 1
G53 .135 B2
Darnley Rd
Barrhead G78 .134 C2
Glasgow G41 .116 C1
Darnley St Glasgow G41 .116 C2
Stirling FK8 .7 A4
Darnshaw Cl KA11 .220 B3
Darrach Dr FK6 .21 A1
Darragh Gn ML2 .166 A3
Darroch Ave PA19 .44 C4
Darroch Dr Erskine PA8 .72 C2
Gourock PA19 .44 C4
Darroch Way G67 .62 A2
Dartford St G22 .97 A2
Dartmouth Ave PA19 .44 C3
Darvel Ave KA3 .223 A3
Darvel Cres PA1 .114 C2
Darvel Dr G77 .157 A3
Darvel St G53 .134 C3
Darwin Pl G81 .73 B2
Darwin Rd G75 .180 B4
Dava St G51 .116 A4
Davaar G74 .160 B1
Davaar Dr
Coatbridge ML5 .121 B4
Kilmarnock KA3 .223 A3
Motherwell ML1 .142 B1
Paisley PA2 .133 C4
Davaar Pl Falkirk FK1 .41 B2
Newton Mearns G77 .156 B3
Davaar Rd Greenock PA16 .44 B2
Renfrew PA4 .94 B1
Saltcoats KA21 .205 C1
Davaar St G40 .118 A2
Davan Loan 10 ML2 .165 C3
Dave Barrie Ave ML9 .184 C3
Daventry Dr G12 .96 A3
Davey St PA16 .45 B3
David Dale Ave KA3 .211 B4
David Gage St KA13 .207 C3
David Livingstone Ctr*
G72 .140 C1
David Livingstone Meml Prim
Sch G72 .140 B1
David Orr St KA1 .222 C1
David Pl Glasgow G69 .119 C2
Paisley PA3 .114 A4
David St Coatbridge ML5 .122 B4
Glasgow G40 .118 A3
Salsburgh ML7 .125 A1
David Way PA3 .114 A4
David's Cres KA13 .207 B1
David's Loan FK2 .24 B1
Davidson Ave KA14 .170 B3
Davidson Cres G65 .59 C2
Davidson Dr PA19 .44 C4
Davidson Gdns G14 .95 C2
Davidson La ML8 .188 A1
Davidson Pl Ayr KA8 .236 A1
Glasgow G32 .119 B3
Davidson Quadrant G81 .73 C4
Davidson Rd G83 .27 C4
Davidson St Airdrie ML6 .122 C4
Bannockburn FK7 .7 B1
Clydebank G81 .94 C4
Coatbridge ML5 .122 A2
Glasgow G40 .118 A2
Davidston Pl G66 .79 C2
Davie's Acre G74 .158 C2
Davieland Rd G46 .136 A1
Davies Dr G83 .27 C3
Davies Quadrant ML1 .142 B1
Davies Row FK6 .21 C1
Davington Dr ML3 .161 B1
Daviot St G51 .115 B3
Dawsholm Rd G20 .96 A4
Dawson Ave Alloa FK10 .9 C4
East Kilbride G75 .159 A1
Dawson Pl G4 .97 A2
Dawson Rd G4 .97 A2
Dawson St FK2 .42 A4
De Morville Pl KA15 .171 A4
De Walden Terr KA3 .223 A1
Deacons Rd G65 .60 C4
Deaconsbank Ave G46 .135 C1
Deaconsbank Cres G46 .135 B1
Deaconsbank Gdns G46 .135 C1
Deaconsbank Gr G46 .135 B1
Deaconsbank Pl G46 .135 B1
Dealston Rd G78 .134 A2
Dean Castle* KA3 .223 B2
Dean Castle Ctry Pk*
KA3 .223 A2
Dean Cres Chryston G69 .80 B1
Hamilton ML3 .162 B1
Stirling FK8 .2 B1
Dean Ct KA3 .222 C1
Dean La KA3 .223 A1
Dean Park Ave G71 .141 A1
Dean Park Dr G72 .139 B2
Dean Park Rd PA4 .94 C1
Dean Pl KA2 .226 C4
Dean Rd Kilbirnie KA25 .149 A1
Kilmarnock KA3 .223 A2
Dean St Bellshill ML4 .142 A3
Clydebank G81 .74 B1
Kilmarnock KA3 .223 A1
Stewarton KA3 .195 C1
Dean Terr KA3 .223 A2
Dean View KA3 .223 B2
Deanbank Sch ML5 .101 B1
Deanbrae St G71 .140 C3
Deanfield Quadrant
G52 .114 C3
Deanhill La KA3 .223 A2
Deans Ave G72 .139 B2
Deanside Rd G52 .115 A4
Deanston Ave G78 .134 A1
Deanston Dr G41 .136 C4
Deanston Gdns G78 .134 A1
Deanston Gr ML5 .121 C2
Deanston Pk G78 .134 A1
Deanstone Pl ML5 .122 B2
Deanstone Wlk ML5 .122 B1
Deanwood Ave G44 .136 C2
Deanwood Rd G44 .136 C2
Deas Rd ML7 .146 B3
Dechmont G75 .180 B3
Dechmont Ave
Cambuslang G72 .139 B2
Motherwell ML1 .163 B4
Dechmont Cotts G72 .139 C2
Dechmont Gdns G72 .140 B1
Dechmont Pl G72 .139 B2
Dechmont Rd G71 .120 C1
Dechmont St
Glasgow G31 .118 B2
Hamilton ML3 .162 B1
Dechmont View
Bellshill ML4 .141 C2
Uddingston G71 .141 A4
Dee Ave Kilmarnock KA1 .228 A2
Paisley PA2 .112 C1
Renfrew PA4 .94 C2
Dee Dr PA2 .112 C1
Dee Path Larkhall ML9 .199 A4
Motherwell ML1 .143 A3
Dee Pl East Kilbride G75 .179 C3
Johnstone PA5 .131 B4
Dee St Coatbridge ML5 .101 B1
Glasgow G33 .118 B4
Greenock PA16 .45 A3
Shotts ML7 .146 B3
Dee Terr ML3 .183 A4
Deedes St ML6 .122 B3
Deep Dale G74 .159 B2
Deepdene Rd
Bearsden G61 .75 B1
Chryston G69 .80 C1
Deer Park Ave KA20 .217 C4
Deer Park Ct ML3 .183 B4
Deer Park Pl ML3 .183 C4
Deer Path ML7 .127 C3
Deer Pk FK10 .5 C1
Deerdykes Ct N G68 .81 C3
Deerdykes Ct S G68 .81 C3
Deerdykes Pl G68 .81 C3
Deerdykes Rd G68,G69 .81 C3
Deerdykes Rdbt G68 .81 B3
Deerdykes View G68 .81 B3
Deerpark Prim Sch FK10 .5 C1
Deeside Dr ML8 .188 A2
Deeside Pl ML5 .122 B2
Delfie Dr PA16 .45 A2
Delhi Ave G81 .73 B2
Dell The Bellshill ML4 .142 B2
Newton Mearns G77 .157 A3
Dellburn St ML1 .164 A3
Dellburn Trad Pk ML1 .164 A3
Dellingburn St PA15 .46 A2
Delny Pl G33 .119 C4
Delph Rd FK10 .4 B1
Delphwood Cres FK10 .4 B1
Delves Pk ML11 .215 A2
Delves Rd ML11 .215 A2
Delvin Rd G44 .137 A3
Dempsey Rd ML4 .141 C2
Dempster St PA15 .45 C2
Den La ML7 .146 B3
Denbak Ave ML3 .162 A1
Denbeck St G32 .118 C3
Denbrae St G32 .118 C3
Denewood Ave PA2 .133 B4
Denham St G22 .97 A2
Denholm Cres G75 .180 C4
Denholm Dr
Glasgow G46 .136 B1
Wishaw ML2 .165 B3
Denholm Gdns
Greenock PA16 .45 B3
Quarter ML3 .183 C2
Denholm Gn 5 G75 .180 C4
Denholm St PA16 .45 B3
Denholm Terr
Greenock PA16 .45 B3
Hamilton ML3 .161 C2
Denholm Way KA15 .171 A4
Denmark St G22 .97 B2
Denmilne Gdns G34 .120 B4
Denmilne Path G34 .120 B4
Denmilne Rd G34 .120 B4
Denmilne St G34 .120 B4
Denniston Pl ML11 .215 B3
Dennistoun Cres G84 .25 B4
Dennistoun Rd PA14 .70 B4
Dennistoun St ML4 .142 A3
Denny High Sch FK6 .39 C4
Denny Prim Sch FK6 .21 B1
Denny Rd Denny FK4,FK6 .39 C3
Larbert FK5 .23 A1
Denny Tank Mus* G82 .50 A2
Dennyholm Wynd KA25 .149 A1
Dennystoun Forge G82 .49 C2
Denovan Rd FK6 .21 C2
Dentdale G74 .159 B2
Deramore Ave G46 .157 A4
Derby St G3 .116 C4
Derby Terrace La 4 G3 .116 C4
Deroran Pl FK8 .6 C3
Derrywood Rd G66 .58 B3
Dervaig Gdns ML6 .84 B2
Derwent Ave FK1 .41 C2
Derwent Dr ML5 .101 B1
Derwent St G22 .97 A2
Derwentwater G75 .179 C3
Despard Ave G32 .119 C2
Despard Gdns G32 .119 C2
Deveron Ave G46 .136 B1
Deveron Cres ML3 .161 C2
Deveron Rd Bearsden G61 .75 B1
East Kilbride G74 .160 A1
Kilmarnock KA1 .228 A3
Motherwell ML1 .143 A3
Troon KA10 .229 D3
Deveron St
Coatbridge ML5 .101 B1

Deveron St continued
Glasgow G33 ....98 B1
Devilla Ct KA9 ....236 B3
Devine Ct ML2 ....165 A2
Devine Gr ML2 ....166 A4
Devlin Gr G72 ....161 C4
Devol Ave PA14 ....47 A1
Devol Cres G53 ....135 A4
Devol Rd PA14 ....68 B3
Devon Ct FK10 ....4 A1
Devon Dr Bishopton PA7 ....72 B2
  Tullibody FK10 ....4 C2
Devon Gdns
  Bishopbriggs G64 ....77 C2
  Carluke ML8 ....187 C1
Devon Pl Cambus FK10 ....4 A1
  Glasgow G41 ....117 A2
Devon Rd Alloa FK10 ....10 B3
  Greenock PA16 ....44 B2
Devon St G5 ....117 A2
Devon Village FK10 ....5 C2
Devon Way ML1 ....163 A3
Devonbank FK10 ....5 C4
Devondale Ave G72 ....140 B1
Devonhill Ave ML3 ....183 B4
Devonport Pk G75 ....180 A4
Devonshire Gardens La [2]
  G12 ....96 A2
Devonshire Gdns La [3] G12 ....96 A2
Devonshire Terr G12 ....96 A2
Devonshire Terrace La
  G12 ....96 A2
Devonview Pl ML6 ....122 C3
Devonview St ML6 ....122 C3
Devonway FK10 ....10 C3
Dewar Cl G71 ....121 A1
Dewar Wlk ML8 ....201 A1
Dewshill Cotts ML7 ....126 A2
Dhuhill Dr E G84 ....16 C2
Diamond St ML4 ....142 A2
Diana Ave G13 ....95 A3
Diana Quadrant ML1 ....143 A3
Diana Vernon Ct G84 ....25 A4
Dick Cres KA12 ....219 B3
Dick Ct ML9 ....198 C1
Dick Inst Mus* KA1 ....222 C1
Dick Quad G82 ....48 A4
Dick Rd KA1 ....228 A4
Dick St G20 ....96 C2
Dick Terr KA12 ....219 B3
Dickburn Cres FK4 ....39 C3
Dickens Ave G81 ....74 A2
Dickens Gr ML1 ....143 B1
Dickies Wells FK12 ....5 A4
Dicks Pk G75 ....180 B4
Dickson Dr G13 ....219 B3
Dickson Sq ML1 ....144 A1
Dickson St ML9 ....185 B1
Diddup Dr KA20 ....206 A1
Differ Ave G65 ....59 C1
Dillichip Cl G83 ....27 C1
Dillichip Gdns G83 ....27 C2
Dillichip Loan G83 ....27 C2
Dillichip Terr G83 ....27 C2
Dilwara Ave G14 ....95 C1
Dimity St M5 ....111 C2
Dimsdale Cres ML2 ....165 B1
Dimsdale Rd ML2 ....165 B1
Dinard Dr G44 ....137 A4
Dinart St G33 ....98 B1
Dinduff St G34 ....100 B1
Dingwall Dr PA16 ....44 C2
Dinmont Ave PA2 ....112 C1
Dinmont Cres ML1 ....162 C1
Dinmont Pl G41 ....116 C1
Dinmont Rd G41 ....116 B1
Dinmont Way PA2 ....112 B1
Dinmurchie Rd KA10 ....229 D3
Dinnet Way [1] ML2 ....165 C3
Dinwiddie St G21 ....98 B1
Dinyra Pl ML6 ....101 B3
Dipple Ct G15 ....79 A1
Dipple Pl G15 ....79 A1
Dipple View KA25 ....149 A2
Dirleton Dr Glasgow G41 ....136 C4
  Paisley PA2 ....113 A1
Dirleton Gate G61 ....75 B1
Dirleton Gdns FK10 ....9 C3
Dirleton Lane G41 ....136 C4
Dirleton Pl G41 ....136 C4
Dirrans Terr KA13 ....207 C1
Ditton Rd KA1 ....227 C2
Divernia Way G78 ....155 B4
Diverswell FK10 ....6 B3
Divert Rd PA19 ....44 B3
Divert Wlk PA19 ....44 B3
Dixon Ave Dumbarton G82 ....49 C2
  Glasgow G42 ....117 A1
Dixon Dr G82 ....49 B1
Dixon Pl G74 ....159 A2
Dixon Rd Glasgow G42 ....117 B1
  Helensburgh G84 ....16 C2
Dixon St Coatbridge ML5 ....122 A4
  Glasgow G1 ....240 C1
  Hamilton ML3 ....162 B2
  Paisley PA1 ....113 C2
Dixons Blazes Ind Est
  G42,G5 ....117 B2
Dobbie Ave FK5 ....23 B1
Dobbie's Loan G4 ....241 A4
Dobbie's Loan Pl G4 ....241 B3
Dobbies Ct ML8 ....187 A3
Dochart Ave PA4 ....94 B2
Dochart Dr ML5 ....101 B1
Dochart Pl FK1 ....42 B1

Dochart St G33 ....98 C1
Dock Breast PA15 ....46 A3
Dock Rd KA22 ....205 A1
Dock St Clydebank G81 ....94 B4
  Falkirk FK2 ....24 B1
Dockhead Pl KA21 ....216 C4
Dockhead St KA21 ....216 C4
Dodhill Pl G13 ....95 A3
Dodside Gdns G32 ....119 B2
Dodside Pl G32 ....119 B2
Dodside Rd G77 ....155 C2
Dodside St G32 ....119 B2
Dolan St G69 ....120 A3
Dollan Aquacentre G74 ....159 C1
Dollar Ave FK2 ....42 A4
Dollar Gdns FK2 ....42 A4
Dollar Pk FK2 ....42 A4
Dollar Terr G20 ....96 B4
Dolphin Rd G41 ....116 B1
Dominica Gn [4] G75 ....159 A1
Don Ave PA4 ....94 C1
Don Ct ML3 ....183 A4
Don Dr PA2 ....112 C1
Don Path ML9 ....199 A4
Don Pl PA5 ....131 B4
Don St Glasgow G33 ....98 B1
Donald Cres KA10 ....229 C2
Donald Terr ML3 ....162 B1
Donald Way G71 ....141 A4
Donald's Ct PA15 ....46 A3
Donaldfield Rd PA11 ....110 A4
Donaldson Ave Alloa FK10 ....4 C1
  Kilsyth G65 ....60 C4
  Saltcoats KA21 ....216 C4
  Stevenston KA20 ....206 C1
Donaldson Cres G66 ....79 B1
Donaldson Dr
  Irvine KA12 ....219 B2
  Kilmarnock KA3 ....223 B2
  Renfrew PA4 ....94 B2
Donaldson Gn G71 ....141 A4
Donaldson Pl
  Cambusbarron FK7 ....6 B3
  [8] Kirkintilloch G66 ....79 B3
Donaldson Rd
  Kilmarnock KA3 ....223 B2
  Larkhall ML9 ....185 B1
Donaldson St
  Hamilton ML3 ....162 A3
  Kirkintilloch G66 ....79 B4
Donaldswood Pk PA2 ....133 B4
Donaldswood Rd PA2 ....133 B4
Doncaster St G20 ....97 A2
Dongola Rd KA7 ....239 A4
Donnelly Way ML2 ....164 B2
Donnies Brae G78 ....154 C4
Donnini Ct [18] KA7 ....235 C1
Doo'cot Brae FK10 ....110 A4
Doon Ave KA9 ....236 A3
Doon Cres G61 ....75 B2
Doon Ct KA12 ....219 B1
Doon Dr PA2 ....112 C1
Doon Pl Kilmarnock KA1 ....228 A2
  Kirkintilloch G66 ....79 B1
  Saltcoats KA21 ....206 A2
  Symington KA1 ....231 B2
  Troon KA10 ....229 D3
Doon Rd G66 ....59 A1
Doon Side G67 ....74 B2
Doon St Clydebank G81 ....74 B2
  Motherwell ML1 ....185 B1
Doon Way G66 ....59 A1
Doonfoot Ct G74 ....159 B1
Doonfoot Gdns G74 ....159 B1
Doonfoot Rd Ayr KA7 ....238 C2
  Glasgow G43 ....136 B3
Doonholm Pl KA7 ....238 C1
Doonholm Rd KA7 ....238 C1
Doonside Twr ML1 ....164 A2
Doonview Gdns KA7 ....238 B3
Doonview Wynd KA7 ....238 B3
Dora St G21 ....117 C2
Dorain Rd ML1 ....142 C1
Dorchester Ave [2] G12 ....96 A3
Dorchester Ct G12 ....96 A3
Dorchester Pl G12 ....96 A3
Dorian Dr G76 ....157 B4
Dorlin Rd G33 ....99 C3
Dormanside Ct G53 ....115 A2
Dormanside Gate G53 ....115 A2
Dormanside Pl G53 ....115 A2
Dormanside Rd G53 ....115 A2
Dornal Ave G13 ....94 C4
Dornal Dr KA10 ....229 D3
Dornford Ave G32 ....119 B1
Dornford Rd G32 ....119 B1
Dornie Ct KA3 ....195 B1
Dornie Path [8] ML2 ....165 C3
Dornie Wynd ML7 ....147 A2
Dornoch Ave G46 ....136 A1
Dornoch Ct Bellshill ML4 ....142 A3
Dornoch Pl Bearsden G61 ....75 B3
  [17] Kirkintilloch G66 ....79 B3
Dornoch Rd ML1 ....162 C1
Dornoch Way
  Airdrie ML6 ....122 C3
  Cumbernauld G68 ....62 A3

Dorrator Ct FK1 ....41 C3
Dorrator Rd FK1 ....41 C2
Dorset Rd PA16 ....44 C2
Dorset Sq G3 ....240 A3
Dorset St G3 ....240 A3
Dosk Ave G13 ....94 C4
Dosk Pl G13 ....94 C4
Double Edges Rd G78 ....154 B3
Double Row ML11 ....214 C1
Dougalston Ave G62 ....55 A1
Dougalston Cres G62 ....55 A1
Dougalston Gdns N G62 ....55 A1
Dougalston Gdns S G62 ....55 A1
Dougalston Rd G23 ....76 C1
Douglas Acad G62 ....54 B2
Douglas Ave Dalry KA24 ....191 B3
  Elderslie PA5 ....112 A1
  Glasgow G46 ....136 A2
  Glasgow, Carmyle G32 ....119 A1
  Kirkintilloch G66 ....79 B3
  Langbank PA14 ....70 B2
  Prestwick KA9 ....236 A3
  Rutherglen G73 ....138 B3
Douglas Cres
  Airdrie ML6 ....123 A3
  Bishopton PA8 ....72 C2
  Hamilton ML3 ....183 B3
  Uddingston G71 ....141 A4
Douglas Ct
  [1] Kirkintilloch G66 ....79 B3
Douglas Dr Ashgill ML9 ....199 C4
  [2] Bearsden G61 ....75 C2
  Glasgow G69 ....136 B3
  Glasgow G71 ....140 C4
  Glasgow G72 ....138 C2
  Newton Mearns G77 ....156 C3
  Stirling FK7 ....7 B2
Douglas Dr E G84 ....16 C2
Douglas Drive La G84 ....137 B2
Douglas Gate G72 ....138 B4
Douglas Muir Dr G62 ....54 B2
Douglas Muir Gdns G62 ....54 B2
Douglas Muir Pl G62 ....54 B2
Douglas Muir Rd
  Clydebank G81 ....74 B4
  Milngavie G62 ....54 B2
Douglas Park Cres G61 ....76 A3
Douglas Park La ML3 ....162 B2
Douglas Pl [5] Bearsden G61 ....75 C3
  Coatbridge ML5 ....121 C3
  Hamilton ML3 ....183 B3
  Kirkintilloch G66 ....79 B3
  Stenhousemuir FK5 ....23 C2
Douglas Rd
  Dumbarton G82 ....50 A2
  Renfrew PA4 ....114 A4
Douglas St Airdrie ML6 ....123 A4
  Ayr KA7 ....238 C4
  Bannockburn FK7 ....7 C1
  Blantyre G72 ....161 B3
  Carluke ML8 ....187 C1
  Glasgow G2 ....240 B3
  Hamilton ML3 ....162 B2
  Kilmarnock KA1 ....227 C4
  Larkhall ML9 ....185 A2
  Milngavie G62 ....55 A1
  Paisley PA1 ....113 B3
  Stirling FK8 ....2 A1
  Wishaw ML2 ....186 B4
Douglas Terr
  Glasgow G41 ....116 C2
  Stirling FK7 ....6 C3
Douglasdale G74 ....159 B1
Douglaston Woodland Wlk*
  G62 ....55 B1
Dougliehill Pl PA14 ....68 A4
Dougliehill Rd PA14 ....68 A4
Dougliehill Terr PA14 ....68 B4
Dougray Pl G78 ....134 B1
Dougrie Dr G45 ....137 B2
Dougrie Gdns G45 ....137 B1
Dougrie Pl G45 ....137 C2
Dougrie Rd G45 ....137 B2
Dougrie St G45 ....137 C2
Dougrie Terr G45 ....137 B2
Doune Cres
  Bishopbriggs G64 ....78 A2
  Chryston G69 ....100 C4
  Newton Mearns G77 ....156 C3
  Stenhousemuir FK5 ....23 C3
Doune Gardens La G20 ....96 C2
Doune Gdns G20 ....96 C2
Doune Gr G75 ....180 A2
Doune Park Way ML5 ....121 C2
Doune Quadrant [10] G20 ....96 C2
Doune Terr 101 B1
Doura Dr KA11 ....219 C3
Doura Pl KA12 ....219 B3
Dove Pl G75 ....179 C3
Dove St G53 ....135 A3
Dove Wynd ML4 ....141 C4
Dovecot G43 ....136 B4
Dovecot La
  Kilwinning KA13 ....207 C2

Dovecot continued
  Lanark ML11 ....215 A2
Dovecot Pl PA10 ....4 A2
Dovecot Rd FK10 ....4 A2
Dovecote View G78 ....79 C4
Dovecothall St G78 ....134 B2
Dovecotwood G65 ....36 B1
Dovehill KA10 ....10 A4
Dovehill FK10 ....10 A4
Dovenholm G82 ....50 A3
Dovenholm Ave G82 ....50 A3
Dover St Coatbridge ML5 ....101 B1
  Glasgow G3 ....240 A3
Dowan Pl FK7 ....6 C2
Dowan Rd G62 ....55 C1
Dowanfield Rd G67 ....61 C1
Dowanhill Prim Sch G11 ....96 B1
Dowanhill St G11 ....96 B1
Dowanside La [7] G12 ....96 B2
Dowanside Rd G12 ....96 B2
Dower Pl FK2 ....14 C2
Downcraig Dr G45 ....137 B3
Downcraig Gr G45 ....137 B3
Downcraig Rd G45 ....137 B3
Downcraig Terr G45 ....137 B3
Downfield Dr ML3 ....183 A4
Downfield Gdns G72 ....140 C1
Downfield St G32 ....118 C2
Downhill St G12 ....96 B2
Downie St ML3 ....162 B1
Downiebrae Rd G73 ....118 A4
Downs Cres FK10 ....9 C3
Downs St G21 ....97 C3
Dowrie Cres G53 ....115 A2
Dr Campbell Ave FK7 ....12 B4
Draffan Rd ML9 ....200 A1
Draffen St ML1 ....163 C4
Draffen St ML1 ....163 C4
Drake St G40 ....117 C3
Drakemire Ave G45 ....137 B2
Drakemire Dr G45 ....137 B2
Dreghorn Prim Sch KA11 ....220 B1
Dreghorn Rd KA11 ....225 B3
Dreling St G31 ....118 B4
Dresling Rd ML1 ....45 C2
Drimnin Rd G33 ....99 C3
Drip Rd FK8,FK9 ....1 C1
Drive David Gray G66 ....59 A1
Drive Rd G51 ....115 C4
Drochil St G34 ....100 A1
Dromore St [12] G66 ....79 B4
Drossie Rd FK1 ....42 A2
Drove Hill G68 ....61 A2
Drove Rd G78 ....153 A2
Drove Loan FK4,FK6 ....39 C3
Drove Loan Cres FK6 ....39 C4
Druid Dr KA13 ....207 C2
Drum Mains Pk G68 ....81 B4
Drumadoon Dr G84 ....16 C1
Drumbathie Rd ML6 ....123 B4
Drumbathie Terr ML6 ....123 B4
Drumbeg Dr G53 ....135 A3
Drumbeg Pl G53 ....135 A3
Drumbeg Terr G62 ....54 B1
Drumbottie Rd G21 ....98 A3
Drumbreck Pl G66 ....79 C2
Drumbrock Rd G62 ....54 B1
Drumby Cres G76 ....157 B4
Drumby Dr G76 ....157 B4
Drumcarn Dr G62 ....54 C1
Drumcavel Rd G69 ....100 C4
Drumchapel Gdns G15 ....75 A1
Drumchapel High Sch
  G15 ....75 A2
Drumchapel Hospl G15 ....75 A1
Drumchapel Rd G15 ....75 A1
Drumchapel Sh Ctr G15 ....75 A1
Drumchapel Sta G15 ....75 A1
Drumclair Ave FK1 ....86 A3
Drumclair Pl ML6 ....123 B4
Drumclog Ave G62 ....55 A2
Drumclog Gdns G33 ....98 C3
Drumcross Pl G53 ....115 B1
Drumcross Rd
  Bowling G60 ....72 C4
  Glasgow G53 ....115 B1
Drumduff G75 ....180 B3
Drumellan Rd KA7 ....239 A1
Drumelzier Ct KA11 ....220 A2
Drumfin Ave ML6 ....104 C2
Drumfork Ct G84 ....25 C4
Drumfork Rd G84 ....25 C4
Drumfrochar Pl PA15 ....45 C2
Drumfrochar Rd PA15 ....45 B2
Drumgarve Ct G84 ....16 B1
Drumgelloch St ML6 ....123 B4
Drumgelloch Sta ML6 ....123 B4
Drumglass View G65 ....60 C2
Drumgray Gdns ML6 ....83 B1
Drumgray La ML6 ....83 B1
Drumgrew Rdbt G68 ....81 C2
Drumhead Pl G32 ....118 C1
Drumhead Rd G32 ....118 C1
Drumhill KA3 ....59 A1
Drumilaw Cres G73 ....138 A3
Drumilaw Way G73 ....138 A3
Drumilaw Hill G44 ....51 A1
Drumlaken Ave [1] G23 ....76 B1
Drumlaken Ct [1] G23 ....76 B1
Drumlaken Path [7] G23 ....76 B1
Drumlaken Pl [5] G23 ....76 B1
Drumlaken St G23 ....76 B1
Drumlanford Rd KA10 ....229 D3

Drumlanrig Pl
  Glasgow G34 ....100 B1
  Stenhousemuir FK5 ....23 C2
Drumlanrig Quadrant
  G34 ....100 B4
Drumley Ave KA6 ....237 C3
Drumleyhill Dr KA1 ....228 C3
Drumlin Dr G62 ....76 A4
Drumloch Gdns G75 ....180 C3
Drumlochy Rd G33 ....99 A1
Drummilling Ave KA23 ....190 B3
Drummilling Dr KA23 ....190 B3
Drummilling Rd KA23 ....190 B3
Drummond Ave G73 ....137 C4
Drummond Cres
  Ayr KA8 ....236 C3
  Irvine KA11 ....224 D4
Drummond Dr
  Paisley PA1 ....114 B2
  Wishaw ML2 ....165 A1
Drummond Hill G74 ....160 A2
Drummond Ho G67 ....62 A2
Drummond La FK8 ....7 A3
Drummond Pl
  Blackridge EH48 ....107 B2
  Bonnybridge FK4 ....40 A4
  East Kilbride G74 ....160 A2
  Falkirk FK1 ....41 C1
  Kilmarnock KA3 ....223 B1
  Stirling FK8 ....7 A3
Drummond Place La [1] FK7 ....7 A3
Drummond Way G77 ....156 A3
Drummore Rd G15 ....75 B2
Drummore Sch G15 ....75 B2
Drummuir Foot KA11 ....220 A3
Drumness Ct G68 ....81 C4
Drumnessie Rd G68 ....81 C4
Drumnessie View G68 ....81 C4
Drumore Ave ML6 ....123 B1
Drumover Dr G31 ....118 C2
Drumoyne Ave G51 ....115 C3
Drumoyne Cir G51 ....115 C3
Drumoyne Dr G51 ....115 C4
Drumoyne Pl G51 ....115 C3
Drumoyne Prim Sch
  G51 ....115 C3
Drumoyne Quadrant
  G51 ....115 C3
Drumoyne Rd G51 ....115 C3
Drumoyne Sq G51 ....115 C4
Drumpark St
  Coatbridge ML5 ....121 B2
  [3] Glasgow G46 ....135 C2
  Stirling FK7 ....7 A2
Drumpellier Ave
  Coatbridge ML5 ....121 B3
  Cumbernauld G67 ....82 B4
  Glasgow G69 ....120 A2
Drumpellier Country Pk*
  ML5 ....101 C1
Drumpellier Country Pk
  Visitor Ctr* ML5 ....101 A1
Drumpellier Cres ML5 ....121 B3
Drumpellier Ct G67 ....82 B4
Drumpellier Gdns G67 ....82 B4
Drumpellier Pl
  Cumbernauld G67 ....82 B4
  Glasgow G69 ....120 A2
Drumpellier Rd G69 ....120 A2
Drumreoch Dr G42 ....137 C4
Drumreoch Pl G42 ....137 C4
Drumriggend Rd FK1 ....85 B2
Drumry Rd G15 ....74 B2
Drumry Rd E G15 ....74 B2
Drumry Sta G81 ....74 B3
Drums Ave PA3 ....113 B3
Drums Cres PA3 ....113 B3
Drums Rd G53 ....115 A3
Drumsack Ave G69 ....100 B3
Drumsargard Rd G73 ....138 B3
Drumshangie Pl ML6 ....103 A1
Drumshangie St ML6 ....103 A1
Drumshantie Rd PA19 ....44 C3
Drumshantie Terr PA19 ....44 C4
Drumshaw Dr G32 ....139 B4
Drumslea PA16 ....45 B4
Drumtrocher St G65 ....60 B4
Drury La G69 ....24 C2
Drury St G2 ....240 C2
Dryad St G46 ....135 C3
Drybridge Rd KA2 ....225 C1
Dryburgh Ave Denny FK6 ....21 C1
  Rutherglen G73 ....138 A4
Dryburgh Gdns G20 ....96 C2
Dryburgh Hill G74 ....159 B1
Dryburgh La G74 ....159 B1
Dryburgh Pl
  Coatbridge ML5 ....121 C4
  Kirkintilloch G66 ....79 C4
Dryburgh Rd
  Bearsden G61 ....75 B3
  Wishaw ML2 ....165 C2
Dryburgh St ML3 ....162 A3
Dryburgh Way G72 ....161 B4

Dryburgh Wlk G69 .....81 A2
Dryburn Ave G52 .....115 A3
Dryden St ML3 .....162 A3
Drygait PA9 .....131 A3
Drygate G4 .....241 C2
Drygate St ML9 .....185 A2
Drygrange Rd G33 .....99 B1
Drymen Pl G66 .....79 B2
Drymen Rd Balloch G83 .....19 C1
  Bearsden G61 .....75 C2
Drymen St G52 .....115 C3
Drymen Wynd G61 .....75 C2
Drynoch Pl G22 .....97 A4
Drysdale St Alloa FK10 .....10 A3
  Glasgow G14 .....94 C3
Duart Ave KA9 .....236 B4
Duart Cres KA9 .....236 B4
Duart Dr
  East Kilbride G74 .....159 B2
  Elderslie PA5 .....112 B1
  Newton Mearns G77 .....157 A3
Duart St G20 .....96 B4
Dubbs Rd
  Kilwinning KA13 .....207 A1
  Port Glasgow PA14 .....68 C4
  Stevenston KA20 .....206 C1
Dubs Rd G78 .....134 C2
Dubton St G34 .....100 A1
Duchal Rd ML3 .....89 B4
Duchal St PA14 .....68 B4
Duchall Pl G14 .....95 A2
Duchess Ct ML3 .....163 A1
Duchess Dr G84 .....16 A2
Duchess Rd G73 .....138 B4
Duchess Pk G84 .....16 A2
Duchess Rd G73 .....118 B1
Duchray Dr PA1 .....114 C2
Duchray La G33 .....98 B1
Duchray St G33 .....98 B1
Ducraig St G32 .....119 A3
Duddingston Ave KA13 .....207 A2
Dudhope St G33 .....99 B1
Dudley Dr
  Coatbridge ML5 .....101 B1
  Glasgow G12 .....96 A2
Dudley La G12 .....96 A2
Duff Cres KA8 .....1 C1
Duff Pl Kilmarnock KA3 .....223 B2
  Saltcoats KA21 .....206 A1
Duff St PA15 .....46 A3
Duffus Pl G32 .....139 B4
Duffus St G34 .....100 A1
Duffus Terr G32 .....139 B4
Duguid Dr KA21 .....206 A1
Duich Gdns G23 .....76 C1
Duisdale Rd G32 .....139 B4
Duke St Alva FK12 .....5 A4
  Bannockburn FK7 .....7 C1
  Denny FK6 .....21 B1
  Glasgow G31 .....118 A3
  Hamilton ML3 .....162 C2
  Larkhall ML9 .....185 A2
  Motherwell ML1 .....163 C4
  Paisley PA2 .....113 C1
  Wishaw ML2 .....165 C3
Duke Street Sta G31 .....118 A4
Duke Terr KA8 .....236 A4
Duke's Ct ML9 .....185 A2
Duke's Rd G72,G73 .....138 B3
Dukes Gate G71 .....140 C2
Dukes Pl ML3 .....183 B3
Dukes Rd Coatbridge G69 .....120 C3
  Troon KA10 .....229 B2
Dulatur Rd G68 .....61 B3
Dullatur Rdbt G68 .....61 C3
Dulnain St G72 .....139 C3
Dulsie Rd G21 .....98 B3
Dumbain Cres G83 .....28 A4
Dumbain Rd G83 .....28 A4
Dumbarton Acad G82 .....50 A2
Dumbarton Castle* G82 .....49 B2
Dumbarton Central Sta
  G82 .....49 C2
Dumbarton Cottage Hospl
  G82 .....49 C1
Dumbarton Joint Hospl
  G82 .....49 B2
Dumbarton Rd
  Bowling G60 .....72 B4
  Cambusbarron FK8 .....6 C4
  Clydebank G60,G81 .....73 B2
  Glasgow G14 .....94 C3
  Glasgow, Partick G11 .....96 A1
  Milton G82 .....50 C1
  Stirling FK8 .....7 A4
Dumbreck Ave G41 .....116 A2
Dumbreck Ct G41 .....116 A2
Dumbreck Marsh Nature
  Reserve* G65 .....60 A4
Dumbreck Pl G41 .....116 A2
Dumbreck Rd G41 .....116 A2
Dumbreck Sq G41 .....116 A2
Dumbreck Sta G41 .....116 B2
Dumbreck Terr G65 .....59 C4
Dumbrock Cres G63 .....31 B2
Dumbrock Dr G63 .....31 B2
Dumbrock Rd G63 .....31 B2
Dumbuck Cres G82 .....50 B1
Dumbuck Gdns G82 .....50 A1
Dumbuck Rd G82 .....50 A2
Dumbuie Ave G82 .....50 A2
Dumfries Cres ML6 .....122 C3
Dumfriespark KA6 .....239 A1
Dumgoyne Ave G62 .....54 C1

Dumgoyne Dr G61 .....75 B4
Dumgoyne Gdns G62 .....54 C1
Dumgoyne Pl G76 .....157 B4
Dumgoyne Rd KA1 .....228 A2
Dumyat Ave FK10 .....4 A1
Dumyat Dr FK1 .....41 C2
Dumyat Rd Alva FK12 .....4 C3
  Menstrie FK11 .....3 B2
  Stirling FK9 .....2 C2
Dumyat Rise FK5 .....23 B3
Dumyat St FK10 .....4 C1
Dun Cann PA4 .....93 B4
Dun Pk G66 .....79 C4
Dunagoil Gdns G45 .....137 C1
Dunagoil Pl G45 .....137 C1
Dunagoil Rd G45 .....137 C1
Dunagoil St G45 .....137 C1
Dunalastair Dr G33 .....99 A3
Dunalistair Dr G33 .....99 A3
Dunan Pl G33 .....119 C4
Dunard Ct ML8 .....187 C2
Dunard Prim Sch G20 .....96 C2
Dunard Rd G73 .....138 A4
Dunard St G20 .....96 C2
Dunard Way 7 PA3 .....113 B4
Dunaskin St G11 .....96 B1
Dunavon Pl ML5 .....122 B2
Dunbar Ave
  Coatbridge ML5 .....121 B2
  Johnstone PA5 .....131 C4
  Rutherglen G73 .....138 B4
Dunbar Cres ML5 .....23 C2
Dunbar Dr
  Kilmarnock KA3 .....223 B1
  Motherwell ML1 .....164 A2
Dunbar Gate FK6 .....21 C2
Dunbar Hill G74 .....159 B1
Dunbar La ML1 .....143 A1
Dunbar Pl G74 .....159 B1
Dunbar Rd PA2 .....113 A1
Dunbar St ML3 .....162 A3
Dunbeith Ave G74 .....156 C3
Dunbeith Pl 8 G20 .....96 B3
Dunbeth Ave G81 .....74 A4
Dunbeth Ct ML5 .....122 A4
Dunbeth Rd ML5 .....122 A4
Dunblane Dr G74 .....159 C1
Dunblane Pl
  Coatbridge ML5 .....121 C2
  East Kilbride G74 .....159 C1
Dunblane St G4 .....240 C4
Dunbrach Rd G68 .....61 B1
Dunbreck Ave ML6 .....103 A3
Dunbritton Rd G82 .....50 B2
Duncairn Ave PA4 .....93 A3
Duncan Ave Falkirk FK2 .....24 A2
  Glasgow G14 .....95 B2
Duncan Ct
  Kilmarnock KA3 .....223 B2
  Motherwell ML1 .....142 B1
Duncan Dr KA12 .....219 B1
Duncan Graham St ML9 .....185 A2
Duncan La G G14 .....95 B2
Duncan La N 9 G14 .....95 B2
Duncan La S G14 .....95 B2
Duncan McIntosh Rd
  G68 .....62 B4
Duncan Rd
  Helensburgh G84 .....16 C2
  Port Glasgow PA14 .....47 A1
Duncan St
  Bonnybridge FK4 .....39 C3
  Clydebank G81 .....74 A2
  Greenock PA15 .....45 C3
Duncan's Cl ML11 .....215 A2
Duncanrig Sec Sch G75 .....159 B1
Duncansby Rd G33 .....119 B3
Duncanson Ave FK10 .....10 A4
Duncarnock Ave G78 .....154 C4
Duncarnock Cres G78 .....154 C4
Duncarron Ind Est FK6 .....21 C1
Duncarron Pl FK6 .....21 C1
Dunchattan Ave KA10 .....229 D1
Dunchattan Pl G31 .....117 C4
Dunchattan St G31 .....117 C4
Dunchattan Way KA10 .....229 D1
Dunchurch Rd PA1 .....114 B3
Dunclutha Dr G71 .....141 A1
Dunclutha St G40 .....118 A1
Duncolm Pl G62 .....54 B1
Duncombe Ave G81 .....74 A4
Duncombe View G81 .....74 B2
Duncraig Cres PA5 .....131 B4
Duncrub Dr G64 .....77 C1
Duncruin St G20 .....96 B4
Duncruin Terr G20 .....96 B4
Duncryne Ave G32 .....119 C2
Duncryne Gdns G32 .....119 C2
Duncryne Pl G64 .....97 C4
Duncryne Rd
  Alexandria G83 .....27 C3
  Gartocharn G83 .....20 C4
  Glasgow G32 .....119 B2
Dundaff Ct FK6 .....21 B1
Dundaff Hill G68 .....61 B1
Dundarroch St FK5 .....23 A1
Dundas Ave G64 .....78 A4
Dundas Cotts FK4 .....39 A1
Dundas Ct G34 .....160 C1
Dundas La G31 .....241 A3
Dundas Pl G34 .....159 C1
Dundas Rd G34 .....2 A2
Dundas Wlk KA3 .....223 B2
Dundashill G4 .....240 C4
Dundasvale Ct G4 .....240 C4
Dundee Dr FK2 .....42 A4

Dundee Dr G52 .....115 A2
Dundee Path G52 .....115 B2
Dundee Pl FK2 .....42 A4
Dundonald Ave PA5 .....111 B1
Dundonald Castle*
  KA2 .....225 C1
Dundonald Cres
  Newton Mearns G77 .....157 A2
  Troon KA11 .....224 D1
Dundonald Ct KA3 .....223 A3
Dundonald Dr ML3 .....183 B4
Dundonald Pl
  Kilmarnock KA1 .....227 B4
  Neilston G78 .....154 B4
Dundonald Prim Sch
  KA2 .....225 C1
Dundonald Rd
  Glasgow G12 .....96 B2
  Irvine KA11 .....220 B1
  Kilmarnock KA1,KA2 .....227 B4
  Paisley PA3 .....114 A4
  Troon KA10 .....229 D2
Dundonald St G72 .....119 C4
Dundrennan Rd G42 .....136 C4
Dundyvan Gate ML5 .....122 A3
Dundyvan Ind Est ML5 .....121 C3
Dundyvan La ML2 .....165 A1
Dundyvan Rd ML5 .....121 C3
Dundyvan St ML2 .....165 A1
Dundyvan Way ML5 .....121 C3
Dunean St G4 .....96 C1
Dunearn Pl PA2 .....114 A2
Duneaton Wynd ML9 .....185 A1
Dunedin Ct G75 .....180 A4
Dunedin Dr G75 .....180 A4
Dunedin Rd ML9 .....185 A1
Dunedin Terr G81 .....94 B4
Dunellan Ave G69 .....81 A1
Dunellan Cres G69 .....81 A1
Dunellan Dr G81 .....74 A4
Dunellan Gdns G69 .....81 A1
Dunellan Rd G62 .....54 B1
Dunellan St G52 .....115 C3
Dunellan Way G69 .....81 A1
Dungavel Gdns ML3 .....183 C4
Dungavel La ML8 .....188 A1
Dungavel Rd KA1 .....228 A2
Dungeonhill Rd G34 .....120 B4
Dunglass Ave
  East Kilbride G74 .....159 C2
  Glasgow G14 .....95 B2
Dunglass La G G14 .....95 B2
Dunglass La N 8 G14 .....95 B2
Dunglass La S G14 .....95 B2
Dunglass Pl Milngavie G62 .....54 C2
  Newton Mearns G77 .....156 A3
Dunglass Rd PA7 .....72 B1
Dunglass Sq G74 .....159 C2
Dunglass View G63 .....31 B2
Dungoil Ave G68 .....61 A2
Dungoil Rd G66 .....79 C2
Dungourney Dr PA16 .....45 B4
Dungoyne St G20 .....96 B4
Dunholme Pk G81 .....73 B2
Dunipace Prim Sch FK6 .....21 B2
Dunira St G32 .....118 C2
Dunivaig Rd G33 .....119 C4
Dunkeld Ave G33 .....138 A4
Dunkeld Dr G61 .....76 A2
Dunkeld Gdns G64 .....78 A1
Dunkeld La G69 .....81 A1
Dunkeld Pl
  Coatbridge ML5 .....121 C2
  Falkirk FK2 .....24 B1
  Hamilton ML3 .....161 C2
  Newton Mearns G77 .....157 A2
Dunkeld St G31 .....118 B2
Dunkenny Rd G15 .....74 C2
Dunkenny Sq G15 .....74 C2
Dunkirk St ML6 .....105 A3
Dunlin East Kilbride G74 .....159 C1
  Glasgow G12 .....96 A3
Dunlin Cres PA6 .....91 B1
Dunlop Cres Ayr KA8 .....236 C1
  Bothwell G71 .....141 A1
  Irvine KA11 .....220 A1
  Renfrew PA4 .....94 B2
Dunlop Dr ML1 .....183 C4
Dunlop Pl KA1 .....224 D2
Dunlop Pl G71 .....121 A1
Dunlop Halt ML1 .....195 A4
Dunlop Prim Sch KA3 .....195 A4
Dunlop Rd Barrmill KA15 .....172 A2
  Lugton KA3 .....173 B3
  Stewarton KA3 .....195 B1
Dunlop St
  Cambuslang G72 .....139 C3
  Fenwick KA3 .....213 A2
  Glasgow G1 .....241 A1
  Greenock PA16 .....45 B4
  Kilmarnock KA1 .....222 C1
  Linwood PA3 .....112 A3
  Renfrew PA4 .....94 B3
  Stewarton KA3 .....195 C1
Dunlop Terr KA8 .....236 B1
Dunmar Cres PA5 .....111 C1
Dunmar Dr FK10 .....4 C1
Dunmore Dr G62 .....76 B4
Dunmore St G81 .....94 B4
Dunn Mews KA1 .....227 B4
Dunn St Clydebank G81 .....73 C3
  Clydebank, Dalmuir G81 .....73 C2
  Glasgow G40 .....118 A2
  Greenock PA15 .....45 C2

Dunn St continued
  Paisley PA1 .....114 A2
Dunn Terr ML7 .....127 C3
Dunnachie Dr ML5 .....121 A2
Dunnet Ave ML6 .....102 C3
Dunnet Dr PA6 .....91 A1
Dunnett Ave KA11 .....228 A4
Dunnichen Gdns G64 .....78 B1
Dunnikier Wlk G68 .....60 C1
Dunning Pl FK2 .....24 B3
Dunnottar Wlk 10 ML2 .....165 C3
Dunnottar Cres G74 .....159 B2
Dunnottar Dr FK5 .....23 C2
Dunnottar St
  Bishopbriggs G64 .....78 B1
  Glasgow G33 .....99 A1
Dunns Wood Rd G67 .....62 B3
Dunollie Gdns KA3 .....223 A3
Dunolly Dr G77 .....156 C3
Dunolly St G21 .....98 A1
Dunoon Ave KA3 .....222 C2
Dunottar Ave ML5 .....122 A1
Dunottar St G33 .....99 A1
Dunphail Dr G34 .....100 B1
Dunphail Rd G34 .....120 B4
Dunragit St G31 .....118 B4
Dunrobin Ave
  Elderslie PA5 .....112 B1
  Stenhousemuir FK5 .....23 C3
Dunrobin Cres G74 .....159 B2
Dunrobin Ct
  Clydebank G81 .....74 A1
  East Kilbride G74 .....159 B2
Dunrobin Dr
  East Kilbride G74 .....159 B2
  Gourock PA19 .....43 C3
Dunrobin Pl ML5 .....121 C4
Dunrobin Prim Sch
  ML6 .....123 C4
Dunrobin Rd ML6 .....123 C4
Dunrobin St G31 .....118 A3
Dunrod Hill G74 .....159 C2
Dunrod St G32 .....119 A2
Duns Cres ML2 .....165 B4
Duns Path ML5 .....122 B2
Dunscore Brae ML3 .....161 C1
Dunside Dr G53 .....135 A3
Dunsiston Rd ML6 .....123 C4
Dunskaith Pl G34 .....120 B4
Dunskaith St G34 .....120 B4
Dunskey Rd KA3 .....223 A3
Dunsmore Rd PA7 .....72 A2
Dunsmuir St G51 .....116 A4
Dunster Gdns G64 .....78 B2
Dunster Rd FK2 .....2 B2
Dunswin Ave G81 .....73 C2
Dunsyre Pl G23 .....76 C1
Dunsyre St G33 .....118 C4
Duntarvie Ave G34 .....120 B4
Duntarvie Cl G34 .....120 B4
Duntarvie Cres G34 .....120 B4
Duntarvie Dr G34 .....120 B4
Duntarvie Gdns G34 .....120 B4
Duntarvie Pl G34 .....120 B4
Duntarvie Rd G34 .....120 B4
Dunterlie Ave G13 .....95 A3
Dunterlie Ct G78 .....134 B2
Dunthblae Rd G66 .....60 A4
Duntiglennan Rd G81 .....74 A3
Duntilland Ave ML7 .....125 A1
Duntilland Rd
  Airdrie ML6 .....124 C4
  Salsburgh ML6,ML7 .....125 B3
Duntocher Rd
  Bearsden G61 .....75 A3
  Clydebank G81 .....74 A2
  Clydebank, Radnor Pk G81 .....74 A2
Duntonknoll KA12 .....219 B2
Duntreath Gdns G15 .....74 C1
Duntreath Gr G15 .....74 C1
Duntreath Terr G65 .....60 B4
Duntroon Pl ML4 .....142 C4
Duntroon St G31 .....118 A4
Dunure Cres PA4 .....40 A3
Dunure Dr Hamilton ML3 .....161 B1
  Kilmarnock KA3 .....228 A4
  Newton Mearns G77 .....157 A2
Dunure Pl
  Coatbridge ML5 .....121 C2
  Kilmarnock KA3 .....223 A3
  Newton Mearns G77 .....157 A2
Dunure Rd KA7 .....238 B1
Dunure St
  Bonnybridge FK4 .....40 A3
  Coatbridge ML5 .....121 C2
  Glasgow G20 .....96 B4
Dunvegan Ave
  Coatbridge ML5 .....101 B1
  Elderslie PA5 .....112 B1
  Gourock PA19 .....43 C3
  Stenhousemuir FK5 .....23 C2
Dunvegan Ct FK10 .....10 A3
Dunvegan Dr
  Bishopbriggs G64 .....78 A2
  Falkirk FK2 .....24 B1
  Newton Mearns G77 .....157 A3
  Stirling FK9 .....2 A3
Dunvegan Pl
  Bonnybridge FK4 .....39 C3
  East Kilbride G74 .....159 B2
  Irvine KA12 .....219 B3
  Uddingston G71 .....140 B4

Dunvegan Quadrant PA4 .....94 A2
Dunwan Ave G13 .....94 C4
Dunwan Pl G13 .....94 C4
Dura Rd ML2,ML7 .....167 B3
Durban Ave Clydebank G81 .....73 B2
  East Kilbride G75 .....180 A2
Durham Rd PA16 .....44 C3
Durham St G41 .....116 B3
Durisdeer Dr ML3 .....161 C1
Durness Ave G61 .....76 A2
Duror St G32 .....119 A3
Durris Gdns G32 .....119 B2
Durrockstock Cres PA2 .....132 C4
Durrockstock Rd PA2 .....132 C4
Durrockstock Way PA2 .....132 C4
Durward G74 .....160 C2
Durward Ave G41 .....116 B1
Durward Cres PA2 .....112 C1
Durward Ct Glasgow G41 .....116 B1
  Motherwell ML1 .....142 B1
Durward Way PA2 .....112 C1
Dutch House Rdbt KA9 .....233 C3
Duthie Rd PA19 .....45 A4
Duthil St G51 .....115 B3
Dyce Ave ML6 .....122 C2
Dyce La G11 .....96 A1
Dyer's La G1 .....241 B1
Dyers' Wynd PA1 .....113 C3
Dyfrig St Blantyre G72 .....161 B4
  Shotts ML7 .....146 C3
Dyke Rd G13 .....95 A4
Dyke St Coatbridge ML5 .....121 A2
  Glasgow G69 .....120 B3
Dykebar Ave G13 .....95 A3
Dykebar Cres PA2 .....114 A1
Dykebar Hospl PA2 .....134 A4
Dykehead Cres ML6 .....102 C1
Dykehead La G33 .....119 C4
Dykehead La G33 .....119 B4
Dykehead Prim Sch
  ML7 .....146 C3
Dykehead Rd
  Airdrie ML6 .....103 A2
  Bargeddie G69 .....121 A3
  Dullatur G68 .....61 B3
  Queenzieburn G65 .....59 C4
Dykehead Sq ML3 .....161 C2
Dykehead St G33 .....119 B4
Dykehead Way PA2 .....132 C4
Dykemuir Pl G21 .....98 A2
Dykemuir Quadrant G21 .....98 A2
Dykemuir St G21 .....98 A2
Dykeneuk Rd PA14 .....68 B4
Dykes Pl KA21 .....205 C1
Dykes Rd KA21 .....205 C1
Dykesfield Pl KA21 .....205 C1
Dykesmains Prim Sch
  KA21 .....205 C1
Dykesmains Rd KA21 .....205 C1
Dysart Ct G68 .....60 C1
Dysart Way ML6 .....124 A3

E

Eagle Cres G61 .....75 A3
Eagle St G4 .....97 B1
Eaglesham Ct 1 ML5 .....101 B1
Eaglesham Path ML5 .....101 B3
Eaglesham Pl 2 G51 .....116 B3
Eaglesham Prim Sch
  G76 .....178 C2
Eaglesham Rd
  Clarkston G76 .....157 C3
  East Kilbride GL75,GL76 .....179 B4
  Newton Mearns G77 .....156 B2
Earl Ave ML6 .....102 C3
Earl Cres KA2 .....225 C1
Earl Haig Rd G52 .....114 C4
Earl La G14 .....95 B2
Earl Of Mar Ct FK10 .....10 A3
Earl Pl Bridge of W PA11 .....110 B3
  Glasgow G14 .....95 B2
Earl Rise KA2 .....225 C1
Earl St G14 .....95 A2
Earl View ML1 .....143 A2
Earl's Gate G71 .....140 C2
Earl's Hill G68 .....61 A2
Earlbank Ave G14 .....95 B2
Earlbank La N
  1 Glasgow G14 .....95 B2
  10 Glasgow G14 .....95 B2
Earlbank La S G14 .....95 B2
Earls Ct FK10 .....10 A3
Earls Way KA7 .....238 B1
Earlsburn Rd G66 .....79 C2
Earlsburn Rd G66 .....79 C2
Earlscourt G69 .....80 C1
Earlsgate PA6 .....91 A1
Earlshill Dr
  Bannockburn FK7 .....7 C1
  Howwood PA9 .....130 C3
Earlspark Ave G43 .....136 C3
Earlston Ave Glasgow G21 .....97 C1
  Kilmarnock KA1 .....227 C2
Earlston Cres ML5 .....122 B2
Earlston Pl G21 .....241 C4
Earlston St ML2 .....165 B3
Earlybraes Dr G33 .....119 C3
Earlybraes Gdns G33 .....119 B3
Earn Ave Bearsden G61 .....76 A2
  Bellshill ML4 .....141 C3
  Renfrew PA4 .....94 C1
Earn Cres ML2 .....165 A1
Earn Gdns ML9 .....199 A4
Earn La ML1 .....143 A3
Earn Pl Denny FK6 .....39 B3

Earn Pl *continued*
Kilmarnock KA1 228 A3
Earn Rd
Newton Mearns G77 156 B4
Troon KA10 229 D2
Earn St G33 98 C1
Earn Terr ML7 146 C3
Earncraig Gn KA11 220 A2
Earnhill La PA16 44 B3
Earnhill Pl PA16 44 B3
Earnhill Rd PA16 44 B3
Earnock Ave ML1 163 B3
Earnock High Sch ML3 162 A1
Earnock Rd ML3 161 C1
Earnock St Glasgow G33 98 B2
Hamilton ML3 162 A2
Earnside St G32 119 A3
Easdale G74 181 A4
Easdale Dr G32 119 A2
Easdale Path
Coatbridge ML5 122 B2
Glenboig ML5 101 B3
Easdale Pl G77 156 A3
Easdale Rise ML3 161 C2
East Academy St ML2 165 A1
East Ave Carluke ML8 187 B1
Hamilton G72 161 C3
Motherwell ML1 143 A1
Plains ML6 104 A2
Renfrew PA4 94 B2
Uddingston G71 141 B3
East Barmoss Ave PA14 68 C4
East Barns St G81 94 B4
East Bath La G2 241 A3
East Blackhall St PA15 46 A2
East Boreland Pl FK6 21 C1
East Bowhouse Head KA11 220 A3
East Bowhouse Way KA11 220 A3
East Breast PA15 46 A3
East Bridge St FK1 42 B2
East Broomlands KA11 220 A1
East Buchanan Mews 12 PA1 113 C3
East Buchanan St PA1 113 C3
East Burnside St 2 G65 60 B4
East Campbell St G1 241 C1
East Castle St FK10 10 A3
East Crawford St PA15 46 B2
East Dean St ML4 142 A3
East Dr FK5 23 B1
East Faulds Rd ML11 215 C3
East Fulton Prim Sch PA3 111 C3
East Gargieston Ave KA1 227 B3
East Gate Glenboig ML5 101 B4
Wishaw ML2 165 B2
East George St ML5 122 A4
East Glebe Terr ML3 162 B1
East Gr KA10 229 D2
East Greenlees Ave G72 139 B2
East Greenlees Cres G72 139 B2
East Greenlees Dr G72 139 B2
East Greenlees Gr G72 138 C2
East Greenlees Rd G72 139 A2
East Hallhill Rd G33 120 B3
East Hamilton St
Greenock PA15 46 B2
Wishaw ML2 165 A1
East High St Airdrie ML6 123 A4
Kirkintilloch G66 58 B1
East India Breast PA15 46 A3
East Kilbride Rd
Rutherglen G73 138 C2
Thorntonhall G74,G76 158 B2
East Kilbride Sta G74 159 C1
East Kirkland KA24 191 B4
East La PA1 114 A2
East Lennox Dr G84 16 C2
East Link Rd FK9 2 B3
East Machan St ML9 185 A1
East Main St ML7 127 C3
East Mains FK11 4 A3
East Mains Rd G74 159 C2
East Milton Gr G75 159 A1
East Milton Prim Sch G75 159 B1
East Montrose St G84 16 A1
East Murrayfield FK7 7 C1
East Netherton St KA1 227 C4
East Park Cres KA3 222 A4
East Park Dr KA3 222 A4
East Park Rd KA8 236 A2
East Plean Prim Sch FK7 12 B2
East Princes St G84 16 B1
East Rd Irvine KA12 219 A4
Irvine KA12 219 B2
Kilbarchan PA10 111 A2
Motherwell ML1 143 A2
Port Glasgow PA14 68 C4
Prestwick KA9 236 B3
East Rossdhu Dr G84 16 C2
East Scott Terr ML3 162 B1
East Shaw St
Greenock PA15 45 C3
Kilmarnock KA1 227 C3
East Shawhead Ind Est ML5 122 A2
East Springfield Terr G64 98 A4
East St PA14,PA15 46 C1
East Station Ind Est ML9 185 A2
East Stewart Gdns ML5 122 B4
East Stewart Pl ML5 122 B4
East Stewart St
Coatbridge ML5 122 B3
Greenock PA15 46 A2
East Stirling St FK12,FK13 5 A4
East Thomson St G81 74 A2
East Thornlie St ML2 165 A1
East Vennel FK10 10 A3
East Wellbrae Cres ML3 162 A1
East Wellington St G31 118 B3
East William St PA15 46 B2
East Woodside Ave PA14 69 A4
East Woodstock Ct 2 KA1 227 C4
Eastbank Acad G32 119 A2
Eastbank Dr G32 119 B3
Eastbank Pl G32 119 B3
Eastbank Prim Sch G32 119 B3
Eastbank Rise G32 119 B3
Eastburn Cres G21 98 A3
Eastburn Dr FK1 42 B2
Eastburn Pl G21 98 A3
Eastburn Rd G21 98 A3
Eastcote Ave G14 95 C2
Eastcroft G73 138 A4
Eastcroft St FK5 23 A1
Eastcroft Terr G21 98 A2
Eastend PA12 129 B2
Eastend Ave ML1 143 A1
Easter Carmuirs Prim Sch FK1 41 A3
Easter Cornton Rd FK9 2 A2
Easter Craigs G31 118 A4
Easter Cres ML2 165 C2
Easter Garngaber Rd G66 79 C3
Easter Livilands FK7 7 B2
Easter Mews G71 140 C3
Easter Queenslie Rd G33 119 C4
Easter Rd Clarkston G76 158 A3
Shotts ML7 146 B3
Easter Wood Cres G71 121 B1
Eastergreens Ave G66 79 B4
Easterhill Pl G32 118 C2
Easterhill Rd G84 16 C2
Easterhill St G32 119 A1
Easterhouse Pl G34 120 B4
Easterhouse Quadrant G34 120 B4
Easterhouse Rd G34 120 B4
Easterhouse Sta G69 120 B3
Eastermains G66 59 A1
Eastern Cres KA25 170 A4
Easterton Ave G76 158 A3
Easterton Cres FK7 12 C4
Easterton Dr FK7 12 C4
Easterton Gr FK7 12 C4
Easterton Stables* G66 32 B2
Eastfield Ave G72 138 C3
Eastfield Cres G82 50 A1
Eastfield Pl G82 50 A1
Eastfield Prim Sch G68 61 A1
Eastfield Rd
Caldercruix ML6 105 A3
Carluke ML8 202 A4
Cumbernauld G68 61 B2
Glasgow G21 97 C2
Eastfield Terr ML4 142 B2
Eastgate G69 101 A3
Easthall Prim Sch G34 119 C4
Eastlea Pl ML6 123 A3
Eastmuir Specl Sch G33 119 B3
Eastmuir St Glasgow G32 119 A3
Wishaw ML2 165 C2
Easton Ct FK8 2 A1
Easton Dr FK1 66 B4
Easton Pl ML5 122 A3
Eastside G66 58 B1
Eastside Ind Est G66 58 B1
Eastvale Pl G3 116 B4
Eastwood Ave
Glasgow G41 136 B4
Glasgow, Giffnock G46 136 B1
Irvine KA12 219 B2
Eastwood Cres G46 135 C2
Eastwood Dr ML2 166 A3
Eastwood High Sch G77 156 C4
Eastwood La G84 25 A4
Eastwood Rd G69 80 C1
Eastwood Toll G46 136 A1
Eastwood View G72 139 C3
Eastwood Way 2 ML9 185 A2
Eastwoodmains Rd
Clarkston G76 157 B4
Glasgow G46 136 B1
Easwald Bank PA10 111 B1
Ebenezer Pl FK1 66 C3
Ebroch Dr G65 60 C4
Ebroch Pk G65 60 C4
Eccles Ct FK7 7 A2
Eccles St G22 97 C3
Eck Path ML1 143 A3
Eckford St G32 119 A2
Eday Cres KA3 222 C3
Eday St G22 97 B3
Edderton Pl G34 120 A4
Edderton Way G34 120 A4
Eddington Dr G77 156 B2
Eddleston Pl G72 139 C3
Eddlewood Ct G33 120 A4
Eddlewood Path G33 119 C4
Eddlewood Pl G33 119 C4
Eddlewood Rd G33 119 C4
Eden Ct KA13 207 A2
Eden Dr G75 179 C3
Eden Gdns G75 179 C4
Eden Gr G75 179 C4
Eden La G33 98 B1
Eden Pk G72 140 C1
Eden Pl Cambuslang G72 139 B3
Kilmarnock KA1 228 A3
Renfrew PA4 94 C1
Eden Rd FK10 9 C4
Eden St G33 98 B1
Edenhall Ct G77 156 B1
Edenhall Gr G77 156 B1
Edenhall Rd KA8 236 A2
Edenkill Pl G63 31 B2
Edenside G68 62 A4
Edenwood St G31 118 C3
Edgam Dr G52 115 B3
Edgefauld Ave G21 97 C2
Edgefauld Dr G21 97 C2
Edgefauld Pl G21 97 C3
Edgefauld Rd G21 98 A2
Edgehill La G11 96 A2
Edgehill Rd Bearsden G61 75 C3
Glasgow G11 96 A2
Edgemont Pk ML3 183 B4
Edgemont St G41 136 C4
Edinbarnet Prim Sch G81 74 B4
Edinbeg Ave G42 137 C4
Edinbeg Pl G42 137 C4
Edinburgh Dr PA19 43 C3
Edinburgh Rd
Glasgow G33 119 B4
Harthill ML7 127 B3
Motherwell ML1 143 B4
Edington Gdns G69 80 C2
Edington St G4 97 A1
Edison Pl KA13 207 C1
Edison St G52 114 C4
Edmiston Ave KA9 236 A4
Edmiston Dr
Glasgow G51 116 A3
Linwood PA3 112 A3
Edmonstone Dr G65 60 B4
Edmonton Terr G75 180 B4
Edmund Kean G74 160 B3
Edrom Ct G32 118 C3
Edrom Path G32 118 C3
Edrom St G32 118 C3
Edward Ave Renfrew PA4 94 C2
Stenhousemuir FK5 23 C2
Stirling FK8 2 B1
Edward Dr G84 16 B2
Edward Pl FK2 24 C2
Edward Rd FK8 2 A1
Edward St Clydebank G81 94 B4
Coatbridge G69 120 C3
Hamilton ML3 162 B1
Kilsyth G65 36 B1
Motherwell ML1 163 C2
Edwin St G51 116 B3
Edzell Ct G14 95 B1
Edzell Dr Elderslie PA5 112 B1
Newton Mearns G77 156 C2
Edzell Gdns
Bishopbriggs G64 98 B4
Wishaw ML2 165 A1
Edzell Pl G14 95 B2
Edzell Row KA13 207 A2
Edzell St Coatbridge ML5 121 B2
Glasgow G14 95 B1
Egidia Ave G46 136 B1
Egilsay Cres G22 97 B4
Egilsay Pl G22 97 B4
Egilsay St G22 97 B4
Egilsay Terr G22 97 B4
Eglington Cty Visitor Ctr* KA12 219 A4
Eglinton Cres KA10 229 C1
Eglinton Ct Glasgow G5 117 A3
Saltcoats KA21 216 C4
Eglinton Ctry Pk KA13 208 A1
Eglinton Dr
Eaglesham G76 178 C2
Glasgow G46 136 B1
Troon KA10 229 D1
Eglinton Gdns KA12 219 B2
Eglinton Intc KA12 219 A4
Eglinton Pl Ayr KA7 235 C1
Kilwinning KA13 207 C2
Saltcoats KA21 216 C4
Eglinton Rd KA22 205 A2
Eglinton Sq KA22 205 B2
Eglinton St Beith KA15 171 A4
Coatbridge ML5 122 A4
Glasgow G5 117 A2
Irvine KA12 219 B2
Saltcoats KA21 216 C4
Eglinton Terr KA7 235 C1
Eglinton Wlk G76 178 C2
Egmont Pk G75 180 A4
Eider G12 96 A4
Eider Ave G75 180 A3
Eider Gr G75 180 A3
Eider Pl G75 180 A2
Eighth St G71 120 C1
Eildon Cres ML6 123 C1
Eildon Dr G78 134 B1
Eildon Rd G66 79 C4
Eileen Gdns G64 78 A1
Eilt Wlk 8 ML2 165 C3
Elba Ct KA8 236 A1
Elba Gdns KA8 236 A1
Elba St KA8 236 A1
Elcho St G40 117 C3
Elder Ave KA15 171 A4
Elder Cres G72 139 C2
Elder Gr G71 141 A4
Elder Grove Ave G51 115 B4
Elder Grove Ct G51 115 B4
Elder Grove Pl G51 115 B4
Elder Park Prim Sch G51 115 C4
Elder St G51 115 C4
Elderbank G61 75 C2
Elderpark Gdns G51 115 C4
Elderpark Gr 8 G51 115 C4
Elderpark St G51 115 C4
Elders Way ML2 165 B2
Elderslea Rd ML8 202 A4
Elderslie Cres KA1 227 C2
Elderslie Hospl PA5 112 B1
Elderslie St G3 240 A3
Eldin Pl Bridge of W PA11 110 C3
Elderslie PA5 112 A1
Eldon Ct G11 96 A1
Eldon Gdns G64 77 C1
Eldon Pl PA16 45 B4
Eldon St Glasgow G3 96 C1
Greenock PA16 45 B4
Elgin Ave
East Kilbride G74 159 C2
Stewarton KA3 195 B1
Elgin Dr FK7 7 B2
Elgin Gdns G76 157 C4
Elgin Pl Airdrie ML6 122 C3
Coatbridge ML5 122 A2
East Kilbride G74 159 C2
Falkirk FK1 42 B2
Kilsyth G65 36 B1
Elgin Rd G61 75 C4
Elgin Terr ML3 161 C2
Elgin Way ML4 142 A3
Elibank St G33 99 A1
Elie St G11 96 B1
Elim Dr FK1 66 B3
Eliot Cres ML3 162 B1
Eliot Terr ML3 162 B1
Elison Ct ML1 164 A2
Elive Ct ML5 122 A2
Elizabeth Ave
Milton of C G66 58 A3
Stenhousemuir FK5 23 B1
Elizabeth Cres Falkirk FK1 41 A3
Glasgow G46 136 A2
Elizabeth Quadrant ML1 142 C3
Elizabeth St
Glasgow G51 116 B3
Stirling FK8 7 A3
Elizabeth Wynd ML3 183 B4
Elizabethan Way PA4 94 B1
Ella Gdns ML4 142 B2
Ellangowan Rd
Glasgow G41 136 B4
Milngavie G62 55 A1
Ellergreen Rd G61 75 C2
Ellerslie St PA5 112 A2
Ellesmere St G22 97 A2
Elliot Ave Glasgow G46 136 B2
Paisley PA2 132 C4
Elliot Cres G74 160 A1
Elliot Dr G46 136 B2
Elliot Pl Glasgow G3 116 C4
Netherburn ML9 200 A2
Elliot St G3 116 C4
Elliot Terr FK2 42 A4
Ellis St Coatbridge ML5 122 A3
Kilmarnock KA1 227 C4
Ellis Way 12 ML1 163 C3
Ellisland
East Kilbride G74 160 C2
Kirkintilloch G66 59 A1
Ellisland Ave G81 74 B2
Ellisland Cres G73 137 C3
Ellisland Dr Blantyre G72 161 A3
Kilmarnock KA3 228 B4
Kirkintilloch G66 59 A1
Ellisland Pl Ayr KA7 239 A3
Saltcoats KA21 206 A2
Ellisland Rd
Clarkston G76 157 C3
Cumbernauld G67 62 A1
Glasgow G43 136 B3
Ellisland Sq KA7 239 A3
Ellisland Wynd ML1 143 B2
Ellismuir Farm Rd G69 120 B2
Ellismuir Pl G69 120 B2
Ellismuir Rd G69 120 B2
Ellismuir St ML5 121 C2
Ellismuir Way G71 121 A1
Elliston Ave G53 135 B3
Elliston Cres G53 135 B3
Elliston Dr G53 135 B3
Elliston Pl PA9 130 C3
Elliston Rd PA9 130 C3
Ellon Dr PA3 112 A3
Ellon Gr PA3 113 C4
Ellon Way PA3 114 A4
Ellrig G75 180 B3
Elm Ave Kirkintilloch G66 79 B3
Renfrew PA4 94 B2
Elm Bank
Bishopbriggs G64 78 A1
Kirkintilloch G66 58 B1
Elm Cres G71 141 B4
Elm Ct ML3 183 C2
Elm Dr Cambuslang G72 139 B3
Chapelhall ML6 123 C2
Cumbernauld G67 62 C2
Johnstone PA5 112 A1
Elm Gdns Bearsden G61 75 C3
Troon KA10 230 A1
Elm Gr Alloa FK10 10 B3
Langbank PA14 70 B4
Stenhousemuir FK5 23 B1
Elm La E 26 G14 95 B2
Elm La W 25 G14 95 B2
Elm Pk KA22 205 B2
Elm Pl G75 180 B3
Elm Quadrant ML6 123 B4
Elm Rd Bridge of W PA11 110 C4
Clydebank G81 74 A3
Dumbarton G82 49 C2
Motherwell ML1 143 A1
Motherwell ML1 143 A3
Paisley PA2 114 A1
Rutherglen G73 138 A2
Elm St Blantyre G72 161 C4
Clarkston G76 157 C3
Coatbridge ML5 122 B3
Glasgow G14 95 B2
Lennoxtown G66 57 C4
Motherwell ML1 163 B4
Stirling FK8 1 C1
Elm Terr PA19 44 C3
Elm View Ct ML4 142 B2
Elm Way G72 139 C2
Elm Wlk G61 75 C3
Elmbank FK11 4 A3
Elmbank Ave
Kilmarnock KA1 228 A4
Uddingston G71 141 A4
Elmbank Cres
Bonnybridge FK4 39 B3
Glasgow G2 240 B3
Hamilton ML3 162 A2
Elmbank Dr
Alexandria G83 27 C3
Kilmarnock KA1 228 A4
Larkhall ML9 185 B1
Elmbank Rd
Langbank PA14 70 B4
Stirling FK7 7 A2
Elmbank St Ayr KA8 236 A2
Bellshill ML4 142 A2
Carluke ML8 202 A4
Glasgow G2 240 B3
Elmbank Street La G2 240 B3
Elmbank Terr KA12 219 B2
Elmfoot St G5 117 B1
Elmhurst ML1 163 B2
Elmira Rd G69 100 B4
Elmore Ave G44 137 A3
Elms Pl Beith KA15 150 A1
Stevenston KA20 206 C1
Elms The G44 137 A2
Elmslie Ct G69 120 B2
Elmtree Gdns G45 137 C2
Elmvale Prim Sch G22 97 C3
Elmvale Row G21 97 C3
Elmvale St G21 97 C3
Elmway ML9 185 A3
Elmwood ML2 164 C1
Elmwood Ave
Glasgow G11 95 C2
Newton Mearns G77 156 C3
Elmwood Ct G71 141 A1
Elmwood Gdns G66 79 A3
Elmwood La G14 95 C2
Elmwood Manor G71 141 A1
Elmwood Rd ML7 147 A1
Elphin St G23 76 B1
Elphinstone Cres
Airth FK2 14 C2
East Kilbride G75 180 C3
Elphinstone Ct PA13 89 B4
Elphinstone Mews PA13 89 B4
Elphinstone Pl G51 116 B4
Elphinstone Rd G46 157 A4
Elrig Rd G44 137 A3
Elsinore Path G75 180 C3
Elspeth Gdns G64 78 B1
Elswick Dr ML6 105 A2
Eltham St G22 97 A2
Elvan Pl G75 179 C4
Elvan St Glasgow G32 118 C3
Motherwell ML1 163 B3
Elvan Twr 7 ML1 163 C3
Elvis St KA9 233 B1
Embo Dr G13 95 A3
Emerald Terr ML4 142 A2
Emerson Rd G64 78 A1
Emerson Rd W G64 78 A1
Emerson St G20 97 A3
Emily Dr ML1 163 C2
Emma Jay Rd ML4 142 A3
Empire Way ML1 142 B1
Empress Ct PA15 46 A2
Empress Dr G84 16 A2
Empress Rd G84 15 B3
Endfield Ave G12 96 A3
Endrick Bank G64 78 A2
Endrick Ct ML5 121 C3
Endrick Dr Balloch G83 19 C1
Bearsden G61 75 C2
Denny FK6 39 C3
Paisley PA1 114 A3
Endrick Gdns G62 54 C1
Endrick Pl FK7 7 A2
Endrick Rd PA15 46 A1
Endrick St G21 97 B2
Endrick Way G83 27 C3
Engelen Dr FK10 10 A3
Engels St G83 27 C4
Englewood Ave KA8 236 A3
English Row ML6 123 B2
English St ML2 164 B2
Ennerdale G75 179 C3
Ennisfree Rd G72 161 B4
Ensay St G22 97 B4
Enterkin St G32 118 C2
Enterkine KA13 207 A1

Enterprise Pk G65 ....59 C2
Eribol Wlk ML1 ....143 B2
Eriboll Pl G22 ....97 A4
Eriboll St G22 ....97 A4
Ericht Pl ML7 ....146 C3
Ericht Rd G43 ....136 B3
Eriska Ave G14 ....95 A3
Eriskay Ave
Hamilton ML3 ....161 C1
Newton Mearns G77 ....156 A3
Port Glasgow PA14 ....69 A4
Eriskay Cres G77 ....156 A3
Eriskay Ct Falkirk FK1 ....42 B1
Irvine KA11 ....225 B4
Eriskay Dr G60 ....73 B3
Eriskay Pl
Kilmarnock KA3 ....223 A3
Old Kilpatrick G60 ....73 B3
Ermelo Gdns G75 ....180 A2
Erradale St G22 ....97 A4
Errogie St G34 ....120 A4
Erskin View G60 ....73 A3
Erskine Ave G41 ....116 A2
Erskine Cres ML6 ....122 C3
Erskine Ct 3 ML6 ....123 C4
Erskine Ferry Rd G60 ....73 A3
Erskine Hospl PA7 ....72 C3
Erskine Pl
Clackmannan FK10 ....10 C3
Kilmarnock KA3 ....223 B1
Saltcoats KA21 ....216 C4
Erskine Rd G46 ....157 A3
Erskine Sq G52 ....114 C4
Erskine St Alloa FK10 ....10 A4
Alva FK12 ....5 A4
Erskine Way ML7 ....146 C2
Erskinefauld Rd PA3 ....112 A3
Ervie St G34 ....120 B4
Escart Rd ML8 ....187 C2
Esdaile Ct ML1 ....143 A2
Esk Ave PA4 ....94 C1
Esk Dale G74 ....159 B2
Esk Dr PA2 ....112 C1
Esk Rd Kilmarnock KA1 ....228 A2
Troon KA10 ....229 D3
Esk St G14 ....94 C3
Esk Way PA2 ....112 C1
Eskbank St G32 ....119 A3
Eskdale G77 ....157 A3
Eskdale Dr G73 ....138 B4
Eskdale Rd G61 ....75 B1
Eskdale St G42 ....117 A1
Esmond St G3 ....96 B1
Espedair St PA2 ....113 C2
Espieside Cres ML5 ....121 B4
Esplanade Ayr KA7 ....238 C4
Greenock PA16 ....45 B4
Prestwick KA9 ....233 A1
Essenside Ave G15 ....75 B1
Essex Dr G14 ....95 C2
Essex La G14 ....95 C2
Essex Rd PA16 ....44 C2
Esslemont Ave G14 ....95 B2
Esson Pl KA3 ....223 A2
Estate Ave FK1 ....42 B2
Estate Quadrant G32 ....139 B4
Estate Rd G32 ....119 B1
Etive Ave Bearsden G61 ....76 A2
Hamilton ML3 ....162 A1
Etive Cres
Bishopbriggs G64 ....78 A1
Cumbernauld G67 ....82 A3
Etive Ct Clydebank G81 ....74 B3
Cumbernauld G67 ....82 A3
Etive Dr Airdrie ML6 ....123 B3
Bishopton PA7 ....72 B1
Cumbernauld G67 ....82 A3
Glasgow G46 ....136 B1
Etive Pl Cumbernauld G67 ....82 B3
Irvine KA12 ....219 B3
Stirling FK9 ....2 A2
Etive St Glasgow G32 ....119 A3
Wishaw ML2 ....165 A1
Etive Way ML7 ....147 A2
Etna Ct FK2 ....42 B4
Etna Ind Est ML2 ....164 B2
Etna Rd FK2 ....42 B4
Etna St ML2 ....164 B2
Eton La 3 G12 ....96 C1
Etrick Ave ML4 ....142 A4
Etterick Wynd G72 ....161 B4
Ettrick Ave PA4 ....94 C1
Ettrick Cres
Kilmarnock KA3 ....222 C2
Rutherglen G73 ....138 B4
Ettrick Ct
Cambuslang G72 ....139 C2
Coatbridge ML5 ....122 B2
Falkirk FK1 ....42 B1
Ettrick Dr Bearsden G61 ....75 B4
Bishopton PA7 ....72 B1
Ettrick Hill G74 ....160 A2
Ettrick Oval PA2 ....132 C4
Ettrick Pl Ayr KA8 ....236 A2
Glasgow G43 ....136 B4
Ettrick Sq G67 ....61 C1
Ettrick St ML2 ....165 A3
Ettrick Terr PA5 ....131 B4
Euchan Pl KA10 ....229 D3
Eurocentral Rail Terminal
ML1 ....142 B4
Evan Cres G46 ....136 B1
Evan Dr G46 ....136 B1
Evans St FK5 ....23 B2
Evanton Dr G46 ....135 C2
Evanton Pl G46 ....135 C2
Evelyn Terr KA13 ....207 C1
Everard Ct G21 ....97 C4
Everard Dr G21 ....97 C3
Everard Pl 9 G21 ....97 C4
Everard Quadrant G21 ....97 C3
Everglades The G69 ....100 A4
Eversley St G32 ....119 A2
Everton Rd G53 ....115 B1
Ewart Cres ML3 ....162 A1
Ewart Terr ML3 ....162 A1
Ewenfield Ave KA7 ....239 A2
Ewenfield Gdns KA7 ....239 A2
Ewenfield Pk KA7 ....238 C2
Ewenfield Rd KA7 ....239 A2
Ewing Ave FK2 ....42 A4
Ewing Ct Hamilton ML3 ....183 B4
Stirling FK7 ....7 B2
Ewing Dr FK2 ....42 A4
Ewing Pl Falkirk FK2 ....42 A4
Glasgow G31 ....118 B3
Ewing Rd PA12 ....129 B2
Ewing St Kilbarchan PA10 ....111 A2
Rutherglen G73 ....138 A4
Ewing Way KA3 ....211 B4
Ewing Wlk G62 ....55 B1
Excelsior Pk ML2 ....164 B1
Excelsior St ML2 ....164 B2
Exchange Pl G1 ....241 A2
Exeter Dr G11 ....96 A1
Exeter La G11 ....96 A1
Exeter St ML5 ....122 A3
Exhibition Centre Sta
G3 ....116 C4
Exmouth Pl PA19 ....44 C3
Eynort St G22 ....97 A4
Eyrepoint Ct G33 ....119 A4

F

Factory Pl KA21 ....216 C4
Factory Rd ML1 ....163 C3
Fagan Ct G72 ....140 C1
Faifley Rd G81 ....74 B4
Failford Pl KA3 ....223 A2
Fair Isle Pl KA3 ....223 A3
Fair Oaks G76 ....158 C4
Fair View Dr ML11 ....214 A2
Fair Way G82 ....48 A4
Fairbairn Cres G46 ....136 A1
Fairbairn Path G40 ....118 A2
Fairburn St G32 ....118 C2
Fairfax Ave G44 ....137 B3
Fairfield FK10 ....5 B1
Fairfield Ave FK4 ....40 A3
Fairfield Ct G76 ....157 C3
Fairfield Dr
Clarkston G76 ....157 C3
Renfrew PA4 ....94 B1
Fairfield Gdns 7 G51 ....115 C4
Fairfield Pk KA7 ....238 C4
Fairfield Pl Bothwell G71 ....141 A1
East Kilbride G74 ....159 B1
Falkirk FK2 ....42 B3
6 Glasgow G51 ....115 C4
Hamilton ML3 ....162 C1
Fairfield Rd KA7 ....238 C4
Fairfield Sch FK10 ....5 A1
Fairfield St G51 ....115 C4
Fairfields FK2 ....13 C3
Fairford Dr G67 ....82 B4
Fairgreen Pl FK7 ....11 C4
Fairhaven KA10 ....229 D4
Fairhaven Ave ML6 ....123 C3
Fairhaven Rd G23 ....96 C4
Fairhaven Sq KA13 ....207 A2
Fairhill Ave Glasgow G53 ....135 B4
Hamilton ML3 ....162 B1
Fairhill Cres ML3 ....162 B1
Fairhill Pl ML3 ....183 B4
Fairhill Rd FK7 ....7 A1
Fairholm Ave ML3 ....163 B1
Fairholm St
Glasgow G32 ....118 C2
Larkhall ML9 ....184 C2
Fairley St G51 ....116 A3
Fairlie G74 ....159 B2
Fairlie Ave KA1 ....227 B4
Fairlie Dr Falkirk FK1 ....41 B3
Irvine KA11 ....220 A3
Fairlie Gdns FK1 ....41 B3
Fairlie Park Dr G11 ....96 A1
Fairlie St FK1 ....41 B3
Fairlie View KA2 ....226 C3
Fairmount Dr FK10 ....5 A1
Fairrie St PA15 ....46 B2
Fairview Ct G62 ....55 A1
Fairway G61 ....75 B3
Fairway Ave PA2 ....133 B4
Fairways Irvine KA12 ....219 A4
Larkhall ML9 ....185 B2
Stewarton KA3 ....211 C4
Fairways Pl FK4 ....40 A4
Fairways The
Glasgow G44 ....136 C1
Johnstone PA5 ....131 B4
Fairways View G81 ....74 B3
Fairweather Pl G77 ....156 B2
Fairyburn Rd FK10 ....9 C4
Fairyhill Pl KA1 ....227 C3
Fairyhill Rd KA1 ....227 C3
Fairyknowe Ct G71 ....141 A1
Fairyknowe Gdns G71 ....141 A1
Faith Ave PA11 ....89 C1
Falcon Cres
Greenock PA16 ....45 A3
Paisley PA3 ....113 A3
Falcon Dr FK5 ....23 A2
Falcon La PA16 ....45 A3
Falcon Rd PA5 ....131 B4
Falcon Terr G20 ....96 B4
Falcon Terrace La G20 ....96 B4
Falconbridge Rd G74 ....160 B2
Falconer Ct FK7 ....7 B2
Falconer St PA14 ....47 B1
Falconer Terr ML3 ....162 B1
Falfield St 6 G5 ....117 A2
Falkirk & District Royal Infmy
FK1 ....42 A2
Falkirk Coll of F & H Ed
Flexible Learning Ctr
FK2 ....42 C3
Falkirk High Sch FK1 ....41 C2
Falkirk High Sta FK1 ....42 A2
Falkirk Rd
Bannockburn FK7 ....11 C4
Bonnybridge FK4 ....40 B3
Falkirk FK1,FK3 ....42 C3
Falkirk, Glen Village FK1 ....42 A1
Larbert FK5 ....41 B4
Falkirk Wheel* FK1 ....41 A3
Falkland Ave G77 ....157 A3
Falkland Cres G64 ....98 B4
Falkland Dr G74 ....159 B1
Falkland La G12 ....96 A2
Falkland Park Rd KA8 ....236 A2
Falkland Pk G74 ....159 B1
Falkland Pl Ayr KA8 ....236 A2
Coatbridge ML5 ....122 A2
East Kilbride G74 ....159 B1
Stenhousemuir FK5 ....23 C2
Falkland Rd KA8 ....236 A2
Falkland St G12 ....96 A2
Fallin Prim Sch FK7 ....8 B3
Falloch Pl ML2 ....165 B3
Falloch Rd Bearsden G61 ....75 B1
Glasgow G42 ....137 A4
Milngavie G62 ....54 C2
Fallside Ave G71 ....141 B3
Fallside Rd G71 ....141 A2
Falmouth Dr PA19 ....44 C3
Falside Ave PA2 ....113 C1
Falside Rd Glasgow G32 ....119 A1
Paisley PA2 ....113 C1
Falstaff G74 ....160 B3
Fancy Farm Pl PA16 ....44 C2
Fancy Farm Rd PA16 ....45 A2
Fara St G23 ....96 C4
Faraday Ave ML2 ....165 B2
Faransay Pl KA3 ....223 A3
Fardalehill View KA2 ....221 C1
Farden Pl KA9 ....236 B3
Farie St G73 ....138 A4
Farlands View KA23 ....190 B2
Farm Cres ML1 ....143 C2
Farm Ct G71 ....141 A2
Farm Houses The G65 ....60 C4
Farm La ML4 ....141 C2
Farm Pk G66 ....79 B2
Farm Rd Blantyre G72 ....140 B1
Clydebank G81 ....73 B2
Clydebank, Duntocher G81 ....74 A4
Cowie FK7 ....12 B4
Fallin FK7 ....8 B3
Glasgow G41 ....116 A3
Hamilton ML3 ....161 C2
Kilmarnock KA3 ....222 C2
Port Glasgow PA14 ....68 C4
Prestwick KA9 ....233 B1
Farm St Falkirk FK2 ....24 A1
Motherwell ML1 ....163 B4
Farm Terr ML3 ....161 C2
Farme Castle Ct G73 ....118 B1
Farme Castle Est G73 ....118 B1
Farme Cross G73 ....118 A1
Farmeloan Rd G73 ....138 A4
Farmfield Terr KA23 ....190 B3
Farmgate Sq ML4 ....141 C2
Farmington Ave G32 ....119 B3
Farmington Gate G32 ....119 B2
Farmington Gdns G32 ....119 B3
Farmington Gr G32 ....119 B3
Farndale G74 ....159 B2
Farne Dr G44 ....137 B2
Farnell St G4 ....97 A1
Farquhar Rd PA14 ....47 A1
Farquhar Sq EH48 ....107 B2
Farquharson Way FK1 ....41 C1
Farrell Pl KA8 ....236 A1
Farrier Ct PA5 ....111 C2
Faskally Ave G64 ....77 C2
Faskally Wlk 10 ML2 ....165 C3
Faskin Cres G53 ....134 C4
Faskin Pl G53 ....134 C4
Faskin Rd G53 ....134 C4
Faskine Ave Airdrie ML6 ....122 C3
Calderbank ML6 ....123 A1
Faskine Cres ML6 ....122 C3
Fasque Pl G15 ....74 C2
Fastnet St G33 ....119 A4
Fauldhouse St G5 ....117 B2
Faulds G69 ....120 B3
Faulds Gdns G69 ....120 B3
Faulds Park Rd PA19 ....43 C3
Faulds St ML5 ....121 C2
Faulds Wynd KA23 ....190 B2
Fauldshead Rd PA4 ....94 B2
Fauldspark Cres G69 ....120 B3
Fauldswood Cres PA2 ....113 A1
Fauldswood Dr PA2 ....113 A1
Faulkner Gr ML1 ....164 C4
Fearnach Pl G20 ....96 A4
Fearnan Pl PA16 ....45 A2
Fearnmore Rd G20 ....96 B4
Fearnoch KA9 ....236 B3
Fellhill St KA7 ....239 A3
Fells The G66 ....57 C4
Fellsview Ave G66 ....58 C1
Felton Pl G13 ....94 C4
Fencedyke Prim Sch
KA11 ....220 A2
Fencedyke Way KA11 ....220 A2
Fendoch St G32 ....119 A2
Fenella St G32 ....119 A3
Fennsbank Ave G73 ....138 B2
Fenton St FK10 ....10 A4
Fenwick Cl KA3 ....223 B3
Fenwick Dr
Barrhead G78 ....134 B1
Hamilton ML3 ....183 C4
Fenwick Pl G46 ....136 A1
Fenwick Prim Sch KA3 ....213 A2
Fenwick Rd Glasgow G46 ....136 B2
Kilmaurs KA3 ....222 B4
Waterside KA3 ....213 C2
Fenwickland Ave KA7 ....239 A2
Fenwickland Pl KA7 ....239 A2
Ferclay St G81 ....74 B4
Fereneze Ave
Barrhead G78 ....134 A2
Clarkston G76 ....157 B4
Renfrew PA4 ....114 A4
Fereneze Cres
Glasgow G13 ....95 A4
Hamilton ML3 ....161 C2
Fereneze Dr PA2 ....133 B4
Fereneze Rd G78 ....154 B4
Fergus Ave PA3 ....113 A3
Fergus Ct G20 ....96 C2
Fergus Dr Glasgow G20 ....96 C2
Greenock PA16 ....45 A2
Paisley PA3 ....113 A3
Fergus Gdns ML3 ....162 C1
Fergus La G20 ....96 C2
Fergus Pl PA16 ....45 A2
Fergus Rd PA16 ....45 A2
Fergushill Rd KA13 ....208 A2
Ferguslie PA1 ....113 A2
Ferguslie Park Ave PA3 ....113 A3
Ferguslie Park Cres
PA3 ....113 A2
Ferguslie Prim Sch PA3 ....113 A3
Ferguslie Wlk PA1 ....113 A2
Ferguson Ave
Milngavie G62 ....55 A1
Prestwick KA9 ....236 B4
Renfrew PA4 ....94 B2
Ferguson Dr Denny FK6 ....21 B1
Falkirk FK2 ....24 A3
Motherwell ML1 ....163 C2
Ferguson Gr FK4 ....40 A3
Ferguson St Ayr KA8 ....236 B2
Johnstone PA5 ....111 C2
Renfrew PA4 ....94 B2
Stirling FK8 ....1 C1
Ferguson Way ML6 ....103 A1
Fergusson Pl G74 ....160 B3
Fergusson Rd G67 ....61 C1
Fergusson Terr G66 ....58 B3
Ferguston Rd G61 ....75 C2
Fern Ave Bishopbriggs G64 ....98 A4
Erskine PA8 ....93 A4
Kirkintilloch G66 ....79 B3
Fern Brae KA7 ....239 B2
Fern Cotts 10 G13 ....95 C3
Fern Dr G78 ....134 A2
Fern Gr G69 ....101 A3
Fern La Glasgow G13 ....95 C3
Lennoxtown G66 ....33 B1
Fern Lea Gr FK2 ....24 B2
Fern Pl KA1 ....227 B4
Fern St ML1 ....164 A2
Fernan St G32 ....118 C3
Fernbank KA9 ....236 A3
Fernbank Ave G72 ....139 B2
Fernbank Ct KA9 ....236 A3
Fernbank St G21 ....97 C3
Fernbrae Ave G73 ....138 B2
Fernbrae Way G73 ....138 A2
Ferncroft Dr G44 ....137 B3
Ferndale ML9 ....185 A1
Ferndale Ct G23 ....96 B4
Ferndale Dr G23 ....96 B4
Ferndale Gdns G23 ....96 B4
Ferndale Pl G23 ....96 B4
Ferness Oval G21 ....98 B4
Ferness Pl G21 ....98 B4
Ferness Rd G21 ....98 B3
Ferngrove Ave G12 ....96 A3
Fernhill Grange G71 ....141 A1
Fernhill Rd G73 ....138 A2
Fernhill Sch G73 ....138 B2
Fernie Gdns G20 ....96 C4
Ferniegair Ave G84 ....16 A1
Fernieshaw Rd ML1 ....144 C1
Fernlea G61 ....75 C2
Fernleigh Pl G69 ....80 C1
Fernleigh Rd G43 ....136 B3
Fernside Wlk ML3 ....162 C1
Fernslea Ave G72 ....161 B4
Ferry Ct FK9 ....2 A2
Ferry Loan G83 ....27 C3
Ferry Orch FK9 ....2 B1
Ferry Rd Bishopton PA7 ....72 A2
Bothwell G71 ....141 A1
Cardross G82 ....48 A3
Glasgow G3 ....96 A1
Renfrew PA4 ....94 B3
Rosneath G84 ....15 A2
South Alloa FK7 ....9 C2
Stirling FK9 ....2 B1
Uddingston G71 ....140 C3
Ferryden Ct G14 ....95 C1
Ferryden St G14 ....95 C1
Fersit Ct G43 ....136 B3
Fersit St G43 ....136 B3
Fetlar Dr Glasgow G44 ....137 B3
Kilmarnock KA3 ....223 A3
Fetlar Rd PA11 ....110 B4
Fettercairn Ave G15 ....74 C2
Fettercairn Gdns G64 ....78 B1
Fettes St G33 ....118 C4
Fiddison Pl KA9 ....236 C3
Fiddoch Ct ML2 ....165 C4
Fidra St G33 ....118 C4
Field Gr G76 ....157 C3
Field Rd Clarkston G76 ....157 C3
Clydebank G81 ....74 B4
Larkhall ML9 ....185 A1
Field St ML3 ....162 B1
Fielden Pl G40 ....118 A3
Fielden St G40 ....118 A3
Fieldhead Dr G43 ....136 A3
Fieldhead Sq G43 ....136 A3
Fieldings The KA3 ....195 B4
Fields La PA6 ....91 A2
Fife Ave Airdrie ML6 ....123 A3
Glasgow G52 ....115 A2
Fife Cres G71 ....141 A1
Fife Ct G71 ....141 A1
Fife Dr Greenock PA16 ....44 B3
Motherwell ML1 ....142 B1
Fife Rd PA16 ....44 B3
Fife Way G64 ....98 B4
Fifth Ave Airdrie ML6 ....123 B4
Glasgow G12 ....95 C3
Millerston G33 ....99 A3
Renfrew PA4 ....94 B1
Fifth Rd G72 ....161 C3
Fifty Pitches Pl G51 ....115 B4
Fifty Pitches Rd G51,
G52 ....115 A4
Finart Dr PA2 ....114 A1
Finaven Gdns G61 ....75 A4
Finbraken Dr PA19 ....43 C3
Finch Dr G13 ....95 A4
Finch Pl Johnstone PA5 ....131 B4
Kilmarnock KA1 ....228 B4
Finch Rd PA16 ....45 A3
Finch Way ML4 ....141 C4
Findhorn PA8 ....73 A1
Findhorn Ave
Paisley PA2 ....112 C1
Renfrew PA4 ....94 C2
Findhorn Ct G75 ....179 B4
Findhorn Pl
East Kilbride G75 ....179 B4
Falkirk FK1 ....42 B1
Troon KA10 ....229 D3
Findhorn Rd KA9 ....233 C2
Findhorn St G33 ....118 B4
Findlay Ct ML1 ....163 B4
Findlay St 9 Kilsyth G65 ....60 B4
Motherwell ML1 ....163 C3
Findlay's Brae KA21 ....216 C4
Findochty PA8 ....73 A2
Findochty St G33 ....99 C1
Fingal La G20 ....96 B4
Fingal St G20 ....96 B4
Fingalton Rd G77 ....155 C3
Fingask St G32 ....119 B2
Finglas Ave PA2 ....114 A1
Finglen Gdns G62 ....54 C1
Finglen Pl G53 ....135 A3
Fingleton Ave G78 ....134 B1
Finhaven St G32 ....118 C2
Finistere Ave FK1 ....42 A2
Finlarig Ct FK5 ....23 C2
Finlarig St G34 ....120 B4
Finlas Ave KA7 ....239 A2
Finlas St G22 ....97 B2
Finlay Ave KA24 ....191 B4
Finlay Dr Glasgow G31 ....118 A4
Linwood PA3 ....111 C3
Finlay Rise G62 ....76 B4
Finlayson Dr Airdrie ML6 ....123 C4
Kilmarnock KA3 ....223 B2
Finlayson Quadrant 6
ML6 ....123 C4
Finlaystone* PA14 ....69 C4
Finlaystone Cres PA13 ....69 B1
Finlaystone Rd
Kilmacolm PA13 ....69 B2
Port Glasgow PA14 ....69 A4
Finlaystone St ML5 ....121 C4
Finnart Cres PA19 ....44 B3
Finnart Rd PA16 ....45 B3
Finnart Sq G40 ....117 C2
Finnart St Glasgow G40 ....117 C2
Greenock PA16 ....45 B3
Finneston La PA15 ....46 A2
Finneston St PA15 ....46 A2
Finneston Way PA15 ....46 A2
Finnick Glen KA7 ....239 A2
Finnie Terr Gourock PA19 ....44 B3
Springside KA11 ....220 C1
Finnie Wynd ML1 ....164 A2
Finnieston Sq 9 G3 ....116 C4
Finnieston St G3 ....116 C4
Finsbay St G51 ....115 C3
Fintaig La ML2 ....165 C2
Fintrie Terr ML3 ....161 C2
Fintry Ave PA2 ....133 C4
Fintry Cres Barrhead G78 ....134 B1
Bishopbriggs G64 ....78 B1
Fintry Ct ML5 ....122 B2
Fintry Dr G44 ....137 B4
Fintry Gdns G61 ....75 B4
Fintry Pl
East Kilbride G75 ....180 A2
Irvine KA11 ....220 A1

Fin – Gal 263

Fintry Rd PA15 46 A1
Fintry Terr KA11 220 A2
Fintry Wlk KA11 220 A1
Fir Bank KA7 239 B3
Fir Bank Ave ML9 185 A1
Fir Ct Cambuslang G72 139 C2
Coatbridge ML5 121 C2
Fir Dr G75 180 A3
Fir Gr Motherwell ML1 143 A1
Uddingston G71 141 B4
Fir La FK5 23 B1
Fir Park St ML1 163 C2
Fir Pk (Motherwell FC) ML1 163 C2
Fir Pl Cambuslang G72 139 B3
Cleland ML1 144 A1
Glasgow G69 120 A2
Johnstone PA5 112 A1
Kilmarnock KA1 227 B4
Fir St PA15 46 C1
Fir Terr PA19 44 B3
Fir View ML6 123 A1
Firbank Ave G64 78 A4
Firbank Quadrant ML6 123 C2
Firbank Terr G78 134 C1
Firdon Cres G15 75 A1
Firhill Ave ML6 122 C3
Firhill Dr KA9 233 B3
Firhill Pk (Partick Thistle FC) G20 97 A2
Firhill Rd G20 97 A2
Firhill St G20 97 A2
Firlee G75 179 C4
Firpark Rd G64 98 A4
Firpark Sch ML1 163 C2
Firpark St G31 117 C4
Firpark Terr
Cambusbarron FK7 6 B3
Glasgow G31 117 C4
Firs Cres FK7 7 B1
Firs Entry FK7 7 B1
Firs Pk (East Stirlingshire FC) FK2 42 B3
Firs Rd FK10 4 B1
Firs St FK2 42 B3
Firs The Bannockburn FK7 7 B1
Glasgow G44 137 A2
First Ave Alexandria G83 27 C3
Bearsden G61 76 A2
Dumbarton G82 50 B1
Glasgow G44 136 C1
Irvine KA12 224 C4
Kirkintilloch G66 79 B1
Millerston G33 99 A2
Renfrew PA4 94 B1
Stevenston KA20 217 C4
Uddingston G71 140 C4
First Gdns G41 116 A2
First Rd G72 161 C3
First St Irvine KA12 219 A4
Uddingston G71 140 C4
First Terr G81 74 A2
Firth Cres PA19 44 B3
Firth Gdns KA10 229 C4
Firth Rd KA10 229 C4
Firth View Terr KA22 205 B2
Firthview Terr G82 49 B2
Firtree Pl ML2 166 A3
Firtree Rd ML2 166 A3
Firwood Cts G77 156 C2
Firwood Dr G44 137 B3
Firwood Rd G77 156 C2
Fischer Gdns PA1 112 C3
Fishcross Prim Sch FK10 5 B2
Fisher Ave Kilsyth G65 60 B4
Paisley PA1 112 C2
Fisher Cres G81 74 A3
Fisher Ct Glasgow G31 117 C4
Knockentiber KA2 221 C2
Fisher Dr PA1 112 C2
Fisher Pl G84 17 A1
Fisher St ML9 185 A1
Fisher Way PA1 112 C2
Fishers Rd PA4 94 B3
Fisherwood Rd G83 27 C4
Fishescoates Ave G73 138 B3
Fishescoates Gdns G73 138 B3
Fitzalan Dr PA3 114 A3
Fitzalan Rd PA4 94 A1
Fitzroy La G3 116 C4
Fitzroy Pl 2 G3 116 C4
Five Roads KA13 208 A2
Five Ways Rd ML9 200 B2
Flakefield G74 159 A1
Flanders St G81 74 B4
Flanigan Gr ML4 142 A3
Flatterton La PA16 44 B1
Flatterton Rd PA16 44 B1
Flax Mill Rd ML7 127 C3
Flax Rd G71 141 A3
Flaxfield Gr ML1 142 B1
Flaxmill Ave ML2 164 B2
Fleck Ave KA21 206 A1
Fleet Ave PA4 94 C1
Fleet St G32 119 A2
Fleming Ave
Chryston G69 100 B4
Clydebank G81 94 B4
Fleming Cres KA21 206 A2
Fleming Ct Carluke ML8 187 C1
Clydebank G81 74 A1
Hamilton ML3 161 C2
Motherwell ML1 164 A2
Fleming Dr
Stenhousemuir FK5 24 A2
Stewarton KA3 211 B4
Fleming Gdns FK1 41 C3
Fleming Pl
Blackridge EH48 107 C2
East Kilbride G75 180 C4
Fleming Rd Bellshill ML4 142 A4
Bishopton PA7 72 A2
Cumbernauld G67 61 C1
Houston PA6 91 A1
Fleming St Glasgow G31 118 A3
Kilmarnock KA1 227 C3
Paisley PA3 113 C4
Fleming Terr KA12 219 A3
Fleming Way
Hamilton ML3 161 C2
30 Larkhall ML9 185 B1
Flemington Ind Est G72 139 C2
Flemington Ind Pk ML1 164 B3
Flemington St G21 97 C2
Flenders Ave G76 157 B3
Flenders Rd G76 157 B3
Fletcher Ave PA19 44 C4
Fleurs Ave G41 116 A2
Fleurs Rd G41 116 A2
Flinders Pl G75 180 A4
Flint Cres FK7 12 B4
Flint Mill La PA15 46 A1
Flloyd St ML5 121 C4
Floors Rd G76 157 B1
Floors St PA5 111 C1
Floors Street Ind Est PA5 111 C1
Floorsburn Cres PA5 111 C1
Flora Gdns G64 78 B1
Florence Dr
Glasgow G46 136 B1
Kilmacolm PA13 89 A4
Florence Gdns G73 138 B2
Florence St Glasgow G5 117 B3
Greenock PA16 45 A2
Florida Ave G42 137 A4
Florida Cres G42 137 A4
Florida Dr G42 137 A4
Florida Gdns G69 120 A3
Florida Sq G42 137 A4
Florida St G42 137 A4
Florish Rd PA8 93 C4
Flotta Pl KA3 222 C3
Flowerdale Pl G53 135 A2
Flowerhill Ind Est ML6 123 A4
Flowerhill St ML6 123 A4
Flures Ave PA8 93 C4
Flures Cres PA8 93 C4
Flures Dr PA8 93 C4
Flures Pl PA8 93 C4
Fochabers Dr G52 115 B3
Fogo Pl G20 96 B3
Foinaven Dr G46 136 A3
Foinaven Gdns G46 136 A3
Foinaven Way G46 136 A3
Foinavon Rd ML3 183 C2
Foot Of Lone Rd ML11 214 A3
Footfield Rd ML4 141 C2
Forbes Cres FK5 23 B1
Forbes Ct FK2 42 C3
Forbes Dr Ayr KA8 236 B2
3 Glasgow G40 117 C3
Motherwell ML1 142 B1
Forbes Pl
Kilmarnock KA3 223 A1
Paisley PA1 113 C2
Forbes Rd FK1 42 B2
Forbes St Alloa FK10 9 C3
Glasgow G40 117 C3
Forbes Wlk KA3 223 A1
Ford Ave KA11 225 B4
Ford Rd Bonnybridge FK4 40 A3
Glasgow G12 96 B2
Newton Mearns G77 156 B2
Fordbank Prim Sch PA5 131 B4
Forde Cres KA20 206 C1
Fordneuk St G40 118 A3
Fordoun St G34 120 B4
Fordyce Ct G77 156 B2
Fordyce Gdns FK1 41 C2
Fordyce St G11 96 B1
Fore Row ML3 162 C2
Fore St Glasgow G14 95 B2
Port Glasgow PA14 47 B1
Forebraes FK10 10 A4
Foregate Sq KA1 222 C1
Foregate The KA1 222 C1
Forehill Prim Sch KA7 239 B3
Forehill Rd KA7 239 B3
Forehouse Rd PA10 110 B2
Foremount Terrace La 18 G12 96 B2
Forest Ave ML3 183 B3
Forest Dr Bellshill ML4 142 B2
Bothwell G71 141 A2
Forest Gdns G66 79 A2
Forest Gr KA3 223 A3
Forest Kirk ML8 202 A4
Forest La ML3 183 B3
Forest Pk ML2 165 B3
Forest Pl Crossford ML8 201 A1
Kirkintilloch G66 79 A2
Paisley PA2 113 C1
Forest Rd
Cumbernauld G67 62 C3
Larkhall ML9 185 A2
Forest View G67 62 B2
Forest Walks* G66 57 A3
Forest Way KA7 239 B3
Forester Gr FK10 4 C1
Forestfield Gdns ML6 105 A2
Foresthall Cres G21 98 A2
Foresthall Dr G21 98 A2
Forfar Ave G52 115 A2
Forfar Cres G64 98 B4
Forfar Rd PA16 44 C2
Forgan Gdns G64 98 B4
Forge Dr ML5 121 C4
Forge Pl G21 98 A1
Forge Rd Airdrie ML6 123 C3
Ayr KA8 236 A2
Forge Row ML6 123 B2
Forge Sh Ctr The G31 118 B3
Forge St Glasgow G21 98 A1
Kilmarnock KA1 222 C1
Forge Vennal KA13 207 B2
Forgewood Path ML6 123 C3
Forgewood Rd ML1 142 B1
Forglen Cres FK9 2 A3
Forglen Rd FK9 2 A3
Forglen St G34 100 A1
Formakin Estate Walks* PA7 71 B1
Formby Dr G23 76 B1
Forres Ave G46 136 B2
Forres Cres ML4 142 A3
Forres Gate G46 136 B1
Forres Quadrant ML2 165 A3
Forres St Blantyre G72 161 B3
1 Glasgow G23 76 C1
Forrest Dr G61 75 A4
Forrest Gate
Hamilton ML3 162 A1
Uddingston G71 121 A1
Forrest Pl ML7 127 C3
Forrest Rd
Forrestfield ML6 106 A1
Lanark ML11 215 A3
Salsburgh ML7 126 A3
Stirling FK8 2 A1
Forrest St Airdrie ML6 123 B4
Blantyre G72 161 C4
Glasgow G40 118 A3
Shotts ML7 146 C3
Forrester Ct 1 G64 97 C4
Forrester Pl FK2 14 B2
Forrestfield Cres G77 156 C3
Forrestfield Gdns G77 156 C3
Forrestfield Rd ML6 106 A3
Forrestfield St G21 98 A1
Forrestlea Rd ML8 202 A4
Forsa Ct G75 180 B2
Forsyth Ct ML11 215 B2
Forsyth Gr PA16 45 B3
Forsyth St Airdrie ML6 123 A4
Greenock PA16 45 B3
Fort Matilda Pl PA16 45 A4
Fort Matilda Sta PA16 45 A4
Fort Matilda Terr PA16 45 A4
Fort St Ayr KA7 235 C1
Motherwell ML1 163 B4
Fortacre Pl KA11 220 A3
Forteviot Ave G69 120 B3
Forteviot Pl G69 120 B3
Forth Ave Larbert FK5 23 A2
Paisley PA2 112 C1
Forth Cres Alloa FK10 10 B3
East Kilbride G75 179 C4
Stirling FK8 7 A4
Forth Ct East Kilbride G75 179 C4
Stirling FK8 2 A1
Forth Gr G75 179 C4
Forth Pk FK9 2 A3
Forth Pl Johnstone PA5 131 B4
Kilmarnock KA1 228 A3
Larkhall ML9 199 A4
Stirling FK8 7 A4
Forth Rd Bearsden G61 75 B1
Torrance G64 78 A4
Forth St Cambus FK10 9 A4
Clydebank G81 94 B4
Fallin FK7 8 B2
Glasgow G41 116 C2
Greenock PA16 45 A3
Stirling FK8 2 A1
Forth Terr ML3 183 A4
Forth Valley Coll of Nursing & Midwifery FK1 42 A2
Forth View FK8 2 A1
Forthbank (Stirling Albion FC) FK7 7 C4
Forthbank Ind Est FK10 10 A2
Forthvale FK11 4 A3
Forthvale Ct FK9 2 A1
Forthview FK7 7 C1
Forthview Ct FK1 41 C1
Forties Cres G46 136 A3
Forties Gdns G46 136 A3
Forties Rd PA6 111 B4
Forties Way G46 136 A3
Fortieth Ave G75 180 C3
Fortingale Ave G12 96 B3
Fortingale Pl G12 96 B3
Fortingall Rd G72 161 C3
Fortissat Ave ML7 146 B3
Fortisset Rd ML7 126 A1
Fortrose St G11 96 A1
Fortuna Ct FK1 42 B2
Forum Pl ML1 142 B1
Forum Sh Ctr The PA15 45 C3
Fossil Gr G66 59 A1
Foswell Dr G15 74 C3
Foswell Pl G15 74 C3
Fotheringay La G41 116 B1
Fotheringay Rd G41 116 C1
Fothringham Rd KA8 239 A4
Foulburn Rd ML7,ML2, ML1 145 B1
Foulis La G13 95 C3
Foulis St G13 95 C3
Foulsykes Rd ML2 165 C2
Foundry La G78 134 B1
Foundry Loan FK5 23 A1
Foundry Rd
Bonnybridge FK4 40 A3
Cleland ML1 144 B1
Shotts ML7 146 C2
Foundry St FK2 42 A4
Foundry Wynd KA13 207 B2
Fountain Ave PA4 93 A2
Fountain Bsns Ctr The ML5 122 A3
Fountain Cres PA4 93 B3
Fountain Dr PA4 93 B2
Fountain Rd FK9 2 A4
Fountainwell Ave G21 97 B2
Fountainwell Dr G21 97 B1
Fountainwell Pl G21 97 B2
Fountainwell Rd G21 97 B1
Fountainwell Sq G21 97 C1
Fountainwell Terr G21 97 C1
Four Acres Dr KA3 222 A4
Four Windings PA6 91 A1
Fourth Ave
Dumbarton G82 50 B1
Kirkintilloch G66 79 B1
Millerston G33 99 A3
Renfrew PA4 94 B1
Fourth Gdns G41 116 A2
Fourth St G71 120 C1
Fowlds St KA1 227 C4
Fowlis Dr G77 156 B3
Fox Gr ML1 163 A4
Fox St Glasgow G1 240 C1
Greenock PA16 45 B4
Foxbar Cres PA2 132 C4
Foxbar Dr Glasgow G13 95 A3
Paisley PA2 132 C4
Foxbar Rd PA2 132 C4
Foxes Gr G66 79 C3
Foxglove Pl Ayr KA7 239 B2
Glasgow G53 135 A2
Foxhills Pl G23 76 C1
Foxley St G32 119 B1
Foyers Terr G21 98 A2
Franchi Dr FK5 23 C3
Francis St 7 G5 117 A2
Frankfield Rd G33 99 C3
Frankfield St G33 98 C1
Frankfort St G41 116 C1
Franklin Pl G75 159 A1
Franklin Rd KA21 205 C1
Franklin St G40 117 C2
Fraser Ave Bishopton PA7 72 A2
Dumbarton G82 50 B2
Johnstone PA5 112 A1
Newton Mearns G77 156 C3
Rutherglen G73 138 B4
Troon KA10 229 C3
Fraser Cres ML3 162 A1
Fraser Gdns G66 79 A4
Fraser Pl FK9 2 A2
Fraser St
Cambuslang G72 138 C3
Cleland ML1 144 A1
Fraser Wlk KA3 223 B2
Frazer Ave G84 16 A2
Frazer St G40 118 A3
Frederick St ML5 121 C4
Freeland Cres G53 135 A3
Freeland Ct G53 135 B3
Freeland Dr
Bridge of W PA11 90 B1
Glasgow G53 135 A3
Inchinnan PA4 93 B3
Freeland La 9 G75 180 C4
Freeland Pl G66 79 B4
Freeland Rd PA8 93 A4
Freelands Cres G60 73 B3
Freelands Ct G81 73 B2
Freelands Rd G60 73 B2
Freesia Ct ML1 163 C3
French St Clydebank G81 73 C2
Glasgow G40 117 C2
Renfrew PA4 94 A1
Wishaw ML2 165 A2
Freuchie St G34 120 A4
Frew Terr KA12 219 B3
Friar Ave G64 78 A2
Friar's La ML11 214 C2
Friar's Wynd ML11 214 C2
Friars Croft Irvine KA12 219 A1
Kirkintilloch G66 79 C4
Friars Lawn KA13 207 B2
Friars Pk ML11 214 C2
Friars Pl G13 95 B4
Friars St FK8 7 A4
Friars Way ML6 123 B2
Friarscourt Ave G13 95 B4
Friarscourt Rd G69 80 A1
Friarsdene ML11 214 C2
Friarsfield Rd ML11 214 C2
Friarton Rd G43 136 C3
Friendship Gdns FK2 24 B2
Friendship Way PA4 94 B1
Frobisher Ave FK1 41 C2
Frobisher Pl G84 17 A1
Frood St ML1 142 B1
Fruin Ave G77 156 C3
Fruin Dr ML2 165 C2
Fruin Rd G15 74 C1
Fruin Rise ML3 161 C1
Fruin St G22 97 B2
Fudstone Dr KA25 170 A4
Fulbar Ave PA4 94 B2
Fulbar Cres PA2 112 C1
Fulbar Ct PA4 94 B2
Fulbar Gdns PA2 112 C1
Fulbar La PA4 94 B2
Fulbar Rd Glasgow G51 115 B4
Paisley PA2 112 C2
Fulbar St PA4 94 B2
Fullarton Ave
Dundonald KA2 225 C1
Glasgow G32 119 A1
Fullarton Cres KA10 229 D1
Fullarton Ct KA1 222 C1
Fullarton Dr
Glasgow G32 119 A1
Troon KA10 229 D1
Fullarton La G32 119 A1
Fullarton Pl
Coatbridge ML5 121 C2
Stevenston KA20 217 B4
Troon KA10 230 A2
Fullarton Rd
Cumbernauld G68 61 C3
Glasgow G32 119 A1
Prestwick KA9 236 B3
Fullarton Rdbt KA12 219 A1
Fullarton Sq KA12 219 A1
Fullarton St Ayr KA7 238 C4
Coatbridge ML5 121 C2
Irvine KA12 219 A1
Kilmarnock KA1 222 C1
Fullers Gate G81 74 B4
Fullerton Ctyd KA10 230 A1
Fullerton Dr KA23 190 A2
Fullerton La PA15 46 C2
Fullerton Sq KA22 205 B1
Fullerton St PA3 113 B4
Fullerton Terr PA3 113 C4
Fulmar Ct 4 G64 97 C4
Fulmar Pk G74 159 B2
Fulmar Pl PA5 131 B3
Fulshaw Cres KA8 236 C1
Fulshaw Ct KA9 236 B3
Fulshaw Pl KA8 236 C2
Fulton Cres PA10 111 A2
Fulton Dr PA6 111 C4
Fulton Gdns PA6 111 C4
Fulton Rd G62 55 A1
Fulton St G13 95 C4
Fulton's La KA3 222 C1
Fulwood Ave Glasgow G13 94 C4
Linwood PA3 112 A3
Fulwood Pk Ind Est ML3 162 A2
Fulwood Pl G13 94 C4
Furlongs The ML3 162 C3
Furnace Ct KA1 228 C3
Furnace Rd ML3 183 C2
Fyfe Park Terr PA14 47 C1
Fyfe Shore Rd PA14 47 C1
Fyffe Park Rd PA14 47 C1
Fyne Ave ML4 141 C3
Fyne Cres ML9 184 C3
Fyne Ct ML3 162 A1
Fyne La ML7 146 C3
Fyne Way ML1 143 A3
Fyneart St ML2 165 C2
Fynloch Pl G81 73 C4
Fyvie Ave G43 136 A3
Fyvie Cres ML6 123 C3

G

Gaberston Ave FK10 10 B4
Gabriel St PA15 46 A1
Gadburn Sch G21 98 B3
Gadie Ave PA4 94 C1
Gadie St G33 118 B4
Gadloch Ave G66 79 B1
Gadloch Gdns G66 79 B2
Gadloch St G22 97 B3
Gadloch View G66 79 B1
Gadsburn Ct G21 98 B3
Gadshill St G21 97 C1
Gael St PA16 45 B2
Gagarin Terr KA13 207 C1
Gailes Pk G72 140 C1
Gailes Pl KA1 227 C2
Gailes Rd
Cumbernauld G68 61 C3
Irvine KA11 224 C3
Troon KA10 229 C4
Gailes St G40 118 A2
Gain & Shankburn Rd G67 82 B1
Gain Rd G67, ML5 82 A1
Gainburn Cres G67 81 C3
Gainburn Ct G67 81 C3
Gainburn Gdns G67 81 C3
Gainburn Pl G67 81 C3
Gainburn View G67 82 A3
Gainford Pl KA3 222 C2
Gainside Rd ML5 101 B3
Gair Cres Carluke ML8 188 A2
Wishaw ML2 165 A1
Gair Rd ML8 188 A3
Gair Wynd ML7 147 A2
Gairbraid Ave G20 96 B3
Gairbraid Ct G20 96 B3
Gairbraid Pl G20 96 B3
Gairbraid Terr G69 121 A3
Gairdoch Dr FK2 24 B2
Gairdoch St FK2 42 A4
Gairloch Gdns G66 59 A1
Gaitskell Ave G83 27 B4
Gala Ave PA4 94 C1
Gala Cres ML2 165 A3
Gala St G33 98 C1
Galbraith Cres ML8 187 A3
Galbraith Dr
Glasgow G51 115 C4

Galbraith Dr *continued*
Milngavie G62 .75 C4
Galdenoch St G33 .99 A1
Gallacher Ave PA2 .113 A1
Gallacher Cres G83 .19 C1
Gallacher Ct
Motherwell ML1 .164 A2
Paisley PA1 .113 B3
Gallacher Way G82 .27 B1
Gallahill Ave PA14 .69 A4
Gallamuir Dr FK7 .12 B2
Gallamuir Rd FK7 .12 B3
Gallan Ave 3 G23 .76 C1
Gallion Wlk 13 KA1 .227 C4
Galloway Ave Ayr KA8 .236 B1
Hamilton ML3 .183 B4
Galloway Ct
Falkirk FK1,FK2 .42 A3
Irvine KA11 .220 A3
Galloway Dr G73 .138 A2
Galloway Pl KA21 .216 C4
Galloway Rd Airdrie ML6 .122 C2
East Kilbride G74 .160 B2
Galloway St Falkirk FK1 .42 A3
Glasgow G21 .97 C3
Gallowflat St 6 G73 .138 A4
Gallowgate G1,G4,G40 .117 C3
Gallowhill ML9 .185 A1
Gallowhill Ave G66 .79 B3
Gallowhill Gr G66 .79 B4
Gallowhill Prim Sch
PA3 .114 A4
Gallowhill Rd
Carmunnock G76 .158 C4
Kirkintilloch G66 .79 B3
Lanark ML11 .215 A2
Paisley PA3 .114 A3
Galrigside Rd KA1 .227 B4
Galston Ave G77 .157 A3
Galston Ct ML3 .183 C4
Galston Pl KA3 .223 A3
Galston Rd KA1 .228 C3
Galston St G53 .134 C3
Galt Ave KA12 .219 B2
Galt Pl G75 .180 B4
Galt St PA15 .46 B2
Gambeson Cres FK7 .7 B2
Gameshill View KA3 .211 C4
Gamrie Dr G53 .135 A4
Gamrie Gdns G53 .135 A4
Gamrie Rd G53 .135 A4
Gannochy Dr G64 .78 B1
Gantock Cres G33 .119 A4
Ganton Ct KA13 .207 A2
Garden Ct 5 KA8 .235 C1
Garden Pl KA10 .229 B2
Garden Square La KA13 .207 C2
Garden Square Wlk
ML6 .122 B4
Garden St Ayr KA8 .235 C1
Falkirk FK1 .42 B3
Kilmarnock KA3 .222 C1
Garden Terr FK1 .42 B3
Garden Veteran's Cotts
PA8 .72 C3
Gardenhall G75 .179 C4
Gardenhall Ct G75 .179 C4
Gardens The KA11 .220 B3
Gardenside ML4 .142 A2
Gardenside Ave
Glasgow G32 .139 A4
Uddingston G71 .140 C3
Gardenside Cres G32 .139 A4
Gardenside Pl G32 .139 A4
Gardenside Rd ML3 .162 B1
Gardenside St G71 .140 C3
Gardiner St KA9 .236 B4
Gardner Gr G71 .141 A4
Gardner St G11 .96 A1
Gardrum Gdns FK1 .66 B4
Gardrum Pl KA3 .222 C2
Gardyne St G34 .100 A1
Gare Rd G84 .15 A2
Garelet Pl KA11 .220 A1
Gareloch Ave PA2 .113 A1
Gareloch Cl PA15 .46 A1
Gareloch Cres ML6 .102 C1
Gareloch La PA14 .68 B4
Gareloch Rd
Greenock PA15 .46 A2
Port Glasgow PA14 .68 C4
Rhu G84 .15 C2
Garfield Ave ML4 .142 B3
Garfield Dr ML4 .142 B2
Garfield Pl G33 .99 C3
Garfield St G31 .118 A3
Garforth Rd G69 .119 C2
Gargieston Prim Sch
KA2 .227 B3
Gargrave Ave G69 .119 C2
Garion Dr G13 .95 A3
Garlieston Rd G33 .119 C3
Garmouth Ct 3 G51 .116 A4
Garmouth Gdns 4 G51 .116 A4
Garmouth St G51 .115 C4
Garnet St G3 .240 B4
Garnetbank Prim Sch
G3 .240 B4
Garnethill Convent Sec RC Sch G3 .240 B4
Garnethill St G3 .240 B4
Garngaber Ave G66 .79 B3
Garngaber Ct G66 .79 C3
Garngrew Rd FK4 .38 C2
Garnhall Ditch* G68 .38 C1
Garnhall Farm Rd G68 .62 C4
Garnie Ave PA8 .93 B4
Garnie La PA8 .93 B4
Garnie Oval PA8 .73 B1
Garnie Pl PA8 .73 B1
Garnieland Rd PA8 .73 B1
Garnkirk La G33 .99 C3
Garnock Acad KA25 .149 A1
Garnock Ct Irvine KA12 .219 B1
1 Kilbirnie KA25 .149 A1
Garnock Pk G74 .160 A1
Garnock Rd
Kilmarnock KA1 .228 A3
Stevenston KA20 .217 B4
Stevenston, Stevenston Site
KA20 .218 B3
Garnock St Dalry KA24 .191 B4
Glasgow G21 .97 C1
Kilbirnie KA25 .149 A1
Garnock View KA13 .207 C2
Garnockside KA14 .170 A3
Garpel Way PA12 .129 A1
Garrallan KA13 .207 B1
Garraway Pl G84 .16 C1
Garraway Rd G84 .16 C1
Garrel Gr G65 .36 B1
Garrell Ave G65 .36 B1
Garrell Pl G65 .60 B4
Garrell Rd G65 .60 B4
Garrell Way
Cumbernauld G67 .61 C1
Kilsyth G65 .60 B4
Garrick Ave G77 .156 B1
Garrick Ct G77 .156 B1
Garrier Ct KA11 .220 C1
Garrier Pl KA1 .222 B1
Garrier Rd KA11 .220 C1
Garrioch Cres 3 G20 .96 B3
Garrioch Dr G20 .96 B3
Garrioch Gate 17 G20 .96 B3
Garrioch Quadrant 4
G20 .96 B3
Garrioch Rd G20 .96 B3
Garriochmill Rd G20 .96 C2
Garrion Bsns Pk ML2 .186 A4
Garrion Pl ML9 .185 C1
Garrion St ML2 .186 B3
Garrison Pl FK1 .42 A3
Garrowhill Dr G69 .119 C3
Garrowhill Halt G33 .119 C3
Garrowhill Prim Sch
G69 .120 A3
Garry Ave G61 .76 A1
Garry Dr PA2 .113 A1
Garry Pl Falkirk FK1 .42 B1
Kilmarnock KA1 .228 A3
Troon KA10 .229 D3
Garry St G44 .137 A4
Garry Way ML7 .146 C3
Garryhorn KA9 .236 B3
Garscadden Prim Sch
G13 .94 C4
Garscadden Rd G15 .75 A1
Garscadden Rd S
Glasgow G13 .95 A4
Glasgow G15 .94 C4
Garscadden Sta G14 .95 A3
Garscadden View G81 .74 B2
Garscube Cross G4 .97 A1
Garscube Mill G61 .76 A1
Garscube Rd G4, G20 .97 A1
Garshake Ave G82 .50 B3
Garshake Rd G82 .50 B3
Garshake Terr G82 .50 B3
Gartartan Rd PA1 .114 C3
Gartcarron Hill G68 .61 B2
Gartchaig Pl G33 .98 C1
Gartcloss Rd ML5 .101 B1
Gartclush Gdns FK7 .11 C4
Gartconnell Dr G61 .75 C3
Gartconnell Gdns G61 .75 C3
Gartconnell Rd G61 .75 C3
Gartconner Ave G66 .80 A4
Gartconner Prim Sch
G66 .80 A4
Gartcosh Prim Sch G69 .100 C2
Gartcosh Rd ML5 .101 A1
Gartcosh Wlk ML4 .141 C3
Gartcows Ave FK1 .42 A2
Gartcows Cres FK1 .42 A2
Gartcows Dr FK1 .42 A2
Gartcows Gdns FK1 .41 C2
Gartcows Pl FK1 .42 A2
Gartcows Rd FK1 .42 A2
Gartcraig Rd G33 .118 C4
Garten Dr ML7 .147 A2
Gartferry Ave G69 .80 C1
Gartferry Rd G69 .80 C1
Gartferry St G21 .98 A2
Gartfield St ML6 .123 A3
Gartgill Rd ML5 .101 C1
Garth St G1 .241 A2
Garthamlock Prim Sch
G33 .99 B1
Garthamlock Rd G33 .99 C1
Garthill Gdns FK1 .42 A2
Garthill La FK1 .42 A2
Garthland Dr
Ardrossan KA22 .205 B2
Glasgow G31 .118 A4
Garthland La PA1 .113 C3
Gartlea Ave ML6 .123 A4
Gartlea Rd ML6 .123 A4
Gartleahill ML6 .123 A3
Gartliston Rd ML5 .101 C2
Gartliston Terr G69 .121 A3
Gartloch Rd G69 .100 B2
Gartly St G44 .136 C2
Gartmore Gdns G71 .140 C4
Gartmore La G69 .81 A1
Gartmore Rd PA1 .114 B2
Gartmore Terr G72 .138 C2
Gartmorn Rd FK10 .5 B1
Gartnavel General Hospl
G12 .96 A2
Gartnavel Royal Hospl
G12 .96 A2
Gartness Dr ML6 .123 C3
Gartness Rd ML6 .124 A2
Gartocher Dr G32 .119 B3
Gartocher Rd G32 .119 B3
Gartocher Terr G32 .119 B3
Gartons Rd G21 .98 B2
Gartsherrie Ave ML5 .101 C3
Gartsherrie Ind Est ML5 .101 C1
Gartsherrie Prim Sch
ML5 .121 C4
Gartsherrie Rd ML5 .121 C4
Gartshore Cres G65 .59 C1
Gartshore Gdns G68 .60 C1
Garturk St
Coatbridge ML5 .122 A2
Glasgow G42 .117 A1
Garvald Ct G40 .118 A2
Garvald La FK6 .21 B1
Garvald Rd FK6 .39 B4
Garvald St Glasgow G40 .118 A2
Greenock PA15 .46 B2
Garvally Cres FK10 .10 A4
Garve Ave G44 .137 A3
Garvel Cres G33 .119 C3
Garvel Deaf Ctr PA16 .44 C3
Garvel Dr PA15 .45 B2
Garvel Pl G62 .54 B1
Garvel Rd Glasgow G33 .119 C3
Milngavie G62 .54 C1
Garven Ct KA1 .228 A4
Garven Rd KA20 .217 C3
Garvie Ave PA19 .44 C3
Garvin Lea ML4 .142 A4
Garvock Dr Glasgow G43 .136 A3
Greenock PA15 .45 C2
Garwhitter Dr G62 .55 A1
Gas St PA5 .112 A2
Gascoyne G75 .180 B4
Gask Pl G13 .94 C4
Gaskin Path G33 .99 C3
Gasworks Rd ML8 .187 B2
Gatehead Rd KA2 .221 C1
Gatehouse St G32 .119 B2
Gates Rd PA12 .129 B2
Gateshead Pl PA10 .111 A2
Gateside KA11 .219 C3
Gateside Ave
Bonnybridge FK4 .40 B3
Cambuslang G72 .139 B3
Greenock PA16 .45 A2
Kilsyth G65 .60 A4
Gateside Cres
Airdrie ML6 .123 A4
Barrhead G78 .134 A1
Gateside Gdns PA16 .45 A2
Gateside Gr PA16 .45 A2
Gateside Pk G65 .60 A4
Gateside Pl KA1 .227 C2
Gateside Prim Sch
KA15 .171 C4
Gateside Rd
Barrhead G78 .134 A1
Stirling FK7 .7 A2
Wishaw ML2 .164 C2
Gateside Sch for the Deaf
PA2 .133 B4
Gateside St Glasgow G31 .118 A3
Hamilton ML3 .162 C2
West Kilbride KA23 .190 B3
Gateway Ctr (Nat Pk Visitor Ctr)* G83 .19 B1
Gateway The G74 .160 A2
Gaughan Quadrant ML1 .163 B3
Gauldry Ave G52 .115 B2
Gauze St PA1 .113 C3
Gavell Rd G65 .60 A4
Gavin Hamilton Ct KA7 .239 B3
Gavin St ML1 .163 C3
Gavin's Mill Rd G62 .55 A1
Gavinburn Gdns G60 .73 A4
Gavinburn Pl G60 .73 A4
Gavinburn Prim Sch G60 .72 C4
Gavinburn St G60 .73 A4
Gavins Rd Alloa FK10 .4 C1
Clydebank G81 .74 A3
Gavinton St G44 .136 C3
Gayne Dr ML5 .101 B3
Gean Ct G67 .62 C2
Gean Rd FK10 .9 C4
Gearholm Rd KA7 .238 B2
Geary St 13 G23 .76 B1
Geddes Hill G74 .160 A2
Geddes Rd G21 .98 B4
Geelong Gdns G66 .33 B1
Geils Ave G82 .50 B1
Geils Quadrant G82 .50 B2
Geilsland Rd KA15 .171 B4
Geilsland Sch KA15 .171 B4
Geilston House & Gdns*
G82 .25 D1
Geilston Pk G82 .48 A4
Geirston Rd KA25 .148 C1
Gelston St G32 .119 A2
Gemini Gr ML1 .143 A3
Gemmel Pl G77 .156 B2
Gemmell Cres KA8 .236 B1
Gemmell Way ML9 .198 C1
General Roy Way ML8 .202 B4
Generals Gate G71 .140 C3
Gentle Row G81 .73 C3
George Aitken Ct KA22 .205 B2
George Ave G81 .74 B2
George Cres G81 .74 B2
George Ct Hamilton ML3 .162 A3
Paisley PA1 .113 B2
George Gray St G73 .138 B4
George La PA1 .113 C2
George Laing Ct FK5 .23 C1
George Mann Terr G73 .138 A2
George Pl PA1 .113 C2
George Rd PA19 .44 C3
George Reith Ave G12 .95 C3
George Sq Ayr KA8 .236 A1
Glasgow G2 .241 A2
Greenock PA15 .45 C3
George St Airdrie ML6 .122 C4
Alexandria G83 .27 C2
Alva FK12 .5 A3
6 Ayr KA8 .235 C1
Ayr KA8 .236 A1
Barrhead G78 .134 A2
Chapelhall ML6 .123 B2
Falkirk FK2 .42 A3
Glasgow G1 .241 B2
Glasgow, Biallieston G69 .120 A2
Hamilton ML3 .162 A3
Helensburgh G84 .16 C1
Howwood PA9 .130 C3
Johnstone PA5 .111 C2
Laurieston FK2 .42 C2
Motherwell ML1 .163 C2
Motherwell, New Stevenston
ML1 .143 A2
Paisley PA1 .113 B2
Stenhousemuir FK5 .23 B2
Stevenston KA20 .217 B4
George Street La G83 .27 C2
George Terr KA12 .219 B2
George Way 10 ML9 .185 A2
George's Ave KA8 .236 A2
Georgian Ct PA16 .45 C3
Gerald Terr FK5 .23 C2
Gerard Pl ML4 .142 A4
Germiston Cres G75 .180 A2
Germiston Ct G75 .180 A2
Gertrude Pl G78 .134 A1
Ghillies La ML1 .142 B1
Gibb Ct ML9 .198 C1
Gibb St Chapelhall ML6 .123 B1
Cleland ML1 .144 A1
Gibbdun Pl FK6 .39 C4
Gibbon Cres G74 .160 B2
Gibbshill Pl ML7 .127 B3
Gibshill Rd PA15 .46 C1
Gibson Ave G82 .50 A2
Gibson Cres PA5 .111 C1
Gibson La PA13 .69 B1
Gibson Quadrant ML1 .142 B1
Gibson Rd PA4 .94 A1
Gibson St Dumbarton G82 .50 A2
Glasgow G4 .241 C1
Glasgow, Kelvingrove G12 .96 C1
Greenock PA15 .46 C1
Kilmarnock KA1 .222 B1
Salsburgh ML7 .125 A1
Gibsongray St FK2 .42 A4
Giffen Rd KA21 .217 A4
Giffnock Park Ave G46 .136 B2
Giffnock Prim Sch G46 .136 B1
Giffnock Sta G46 .136 B2
Gifford Dr G52 .115 A3
Gifford Wynd PA2 .112 C1
Gigha Cres KA11 .220 A1
Gigha Gdns ML8 .202 A4
Gigha La KA11 .220 A1
Gigha Pl KA11 .220 A1
Gigha Quadrant ML2 .164 C1
Gigha Terr KA11 .220 A1
Gigha Wynd KA11 .220 A1
Gilbert St G3 .116 B4
Gilbertfield Path G33 .99 A1
Gilbertfield Pl
Glasgow G33 .99 A1
Irvine KA12 .219 B1
Gilbertfield Rd G72 .139 C2
Gilbertfield St G33 .99 A1
Gilburn Pl ML7 .146 C2
Gilchrist Dr FK1 .41 C2
Gilchrist St ML5 .122 A4
Gilchrist Way ML2 .165 B1
Gilderdale G74 .159 B1
Gilfillan Ave KA21 .206 A1
Gilfillan Pl Falkirk FK2 .24 B1
Overtown ML2 .186 B4
Gilfillan Way PA2 .132 C4
Gilhill St G20 .96 B4
Gill Pk FK6 .21 C1
Gill Rd ML2 .186 B3
Gillbank Ave ML8 .187 B1
Gillbank La 6 ML9 .185 B1
Gillburn Rd PA13 .89 B4
Gillburn St ML2 .186 B3
Gillespie Dr G84 .16 B2
Gillespie Pl FK7 .7 A1
Gillespie Terr FK7 .12 B1
Gillies Cres G74 .160 B3
Gillies Dr FK7 .7 B2
Gillies Hill FK7 .6 B3
Gillies La G69 .120 B2
Gillies St KA10 .229 C2
Gillsburn Gdns KA3 .223 A1
Gilmartin Rd PA3 .111 C3
Gilmerton St G32 .119 A2
Gilmour Ave
Clydebank G81 .74 A3
Thorntonhall G74 .158 A1
Gilmour Cres
Eaglesham G76 .178 C3
Rutherglen G73 .137 C4
Gilmour Dr ML3 .161 C1
Gilmour Pl Bellshill ML4 .141 C3
Coatbridge ML5 .121 C4
7 Glasgow G5 .117 B2
Gilmour St Alexandria G83 .27 B3
Clydebank G81 .74 B2
Eaglesham G76 .178 C3
Greenock PA15 .46 B1
Kilmarnock KA1 .228 A4
Paisley PA1 .113 C3
Stewarton KA3 .195 C1
Gilmourton Cres G77 .156 B2
Gilroy Cl ML11 .215 B3
Gilsay Ct FK1 .42 B1
Gilshochill Sta G23 .96 C4
Gimmerscroft Cres ML6 .123 C3
Girdle Gate KA11 .219 C3
Girdle Toll KA11 .220 A3
Girdons Way G71 .140 C3
Girthon St G32 .119 B2
Girvan Cres ML6 .123 B1
Girvan St G33 .118 B4
Glade The ML9 .185 A1
Gladney Ave G13 .94 C4
Gladsmuir Rd G52 .115 A3
Gladstone Ave
Barrhead G78 .134 A1
Johnstone PA5 .131 B4
Gladstone Ct ML3 .162 A3
Gladstone Pl FK8 .7 A3
Gladstone Rd
Saltcoats KA21 .217 A4
Stenhousemuir FK5 .23 B2
Gladstone St
Bellshill ML4 .142 A3
Clydebank G81 .73 C1
11 Glasgow G4 .97 A1
Glaive Ave FK7 .7 B2
Glaive Rd G13 .75 B1
Glamis Ave Carluke ML8 .187 C1
East Kilbride G74 .159 C2
Elderslie PA5 .112 A1
Newton Mearns G77 .156 C3
Glamis Ct ML1 .143 B1
Glamis Dr PA16 .45 A3
Glamis Gdns G64 .78 A2
Glamis Pl PA16 .45 A3
Glamis Rd G31 .118 B2
Glanderston Ave
Barrhead G78 .134 C1
Newton Mearns G77 .156 A3
Glanderston Ct G13 .95 A4
Glanderston Dr G13 .95 A4
Glanderston Gate G77 .156 A3
Glanderston Rd G77 .155 B3
Glasgow & Edinburgh Rd
Calderbank ML1,ML6 .123 A1
Coatbridge G69,ML5 .121 B2
Glasgow G69 .120 B3
Motherwell ML1 .144 A4
Glasgow Acad G12 .96 C2
Glasgow Bot Gdns* G12 .96 B2
Glasgow Caledonian Univ
G4 .241 A4
Glasgow Caledonian Univ Park Campus G3 .96 C1
Glasgow Coll of Building & Printing G5 .117 B3
Glasgow Coll of Building & Printing (Annexe) G31 .118 C3
Glasgow Coll of Building & Printing (David Dale Bldg)
G40 .117 C3
Glasgow Coll of Printing (Bridgeton Annexe)
G40 .117 C3
Glasgow Dental Hospl
G2 .240 B3
Glasgow Gaelic Sch G3 .240 A4
Glasgow Homeopathic Hospl
G12 .96 A2
Glasgow La KA22 .205 B1
Glasgow Prestwick Int Airport KA9 .233 C1
Glasgow Rd
Bannockburn FK7 .11 B4
Barrhead G53 .134 B2
Blantyre G72 .161 C4
Bonnybridge FK4 .39 B2
Cambuslang G72,G73 .138 C1
Cambuslang, Silverbank
G72 .138 C3
Clarkston G76 .157 B1
Clydebank G81 .94 B4
Clydebank, Hardgate G81 .74 B3
Coatbridge ML5 .121 B3
Cumbernauld G67 .82 B4
Cumbernauld, Kildrum G67 .62 A2
Denny FK6 .21 C1
Dumbarton G82 .50 B1
Eaglesham G76 .178 C4
East Kilbride G72,G74 .160 A4
Falkirk FK1 .41 B3
Glasgow G69 .120 A2
Kilmarnock KA3 .223 B3
Kilsyth G65 .60 A4
Kirkintilloch G66 .79 A4
Lanark ML11 .214 C2
Milngavie G62 .55 A1
Paisley PA1 .114 B2
Port Glasgow PA14 .47 C1
Renfrew PA4 .94 C1
Rutherglen G73 .117 C1
Stirling FK7 .7 A1
Strathblane G63 .31 A2

Glasgow Rd *continued*
Uddingston G71 ... 140 C4
Wishaw ML2 ... 164 C2
Glasgow Sch of Art G3 ... 240 B3
Glasgow St
Ardrossan KA22 ... 205 B1
Glasgow G12 ... 96 C1
Helensburgh G84 ... 16 B1
8 Kilbirnie KA25 ... 149 A1
Glasgow Univ (Annexe)
G13 ... 95 C4
Glasgow Vennel KA12 ... 219 B1
Glasgow Zoo* G71 ... 120 B1
Glassel Rd G34 ... 100 B1
Glasserton Pl G43 ... 136 C3
Glasserton Rd G43 ... 136 C3
Glassford Rd ML3,ML9 ... 198 B3
Glassford St Glasgow G1 ... 241 A2
Milngavie G62 ... 55 A1
Motherwell ML1 ... 164 A2
Glassford Twr ML1 ... 164 A2
Glasshouse Loan FK10 ... 10 A3
Glassock Rd KA3 ... 222 C3
Glaudhall Ave G69 ... 100 C4
Glazert Pl G66 ... 58 A3
Glebe Ave Bothwell G71 ... 141 A1
Carmunnock G76 ... 158 B4
Coatbridge ML5 ... 121 B2
Irvine KA11 ... 225 B4
Kilmarnock KA1 ... 228 A4
Stirling FK8 ... 7 A4
Glebe Cres Airdrie ML6 ... 123 B4
Alva FK12 ... 5 A4
Ayr KA8 ... 235 C1
East Kilbride G74 ... 159 C1
Hamilton ML3 ... 162 B1
Stirling FK8 ... 7 A4
Glebe Ct Beith KA15 ... 171 A4
Glasgow G4 ... 241 B3
Kilmacolm PA13 ... 89 B4
Glebe Dr ML11 ... 215 A2
Glebe Gdns
Alexandria G83 ... 27 C2
Houston PA6 ... 91 A1
Glebe Hollow G71 ... 141 A1
Glebe La G77 ... 156 B2
Glebe Pk G82 ... 50 A3
Glebe Pl Cambuslang G72 ... 139 A3
Rutherglen G73 ... 137 C4
Saltcoats KA21 ... 216 C4
Glebe Prim Sch KA12 ... 219 B1
Glebe Rd Ayr KA8 ... 235 C1
Beith KA15 ... 171 A4
Kilmacolm PA13 ... 89 B4
Kilmarnock KA1 ... 228 A4
Newton Mearns G77 ... 156 B2
Glebe St Bellshill ML4 ... 141 C3
Denny FK6 ... 21 C1
East Kilbride G74 ... 159 C1
Falkirk FK1 ... 42 A3
Glasgow G4 ... 241 B4
Glasgow G4 ... 241 C3
Hamilton ML3 ... 162 B1
Kilwinning KA13 ... 207 C2
Renfrew PA4 ... 94 B2
Saltcoats KA21 ... 216 C4
Stevenston KA20 ... 206 B1
Glebe Terr Alloa FK10 ... 10 A3
Fenwick KA3 ... 213 A2
Glebe The Alva FK12 ... 5 A4
Bothwell G71 ... 141 A1
Irvine KA11 ... 225 B4
Lanark ML11 ... 214 C2
Glebe Wynd G71 ... 141 A1
Glebefield Rd G84 ... 15 C3
Glebelands Way KA15 ... 171 A4
Gleddoch Rd G52 ... 114 C3
Gledstane Rd PA7 ... 72 A1
Glen Affric G74 ... 160 A1
Glen Affric Ave G53 ... 135 B2
Glen Affric Pl KA1 ... 227 B3
Glen Affric Way ML6 ... 123 B1
Glen Afton Ct KA1 ... 227 B3
Glen Alby Pl G53 ... 135 B2
Glen Almond G74 ... 160 B1
Glen Arroch G74 ... 160 A1
Glen Ave Balloch G83 ... 28 A4
Chryston G69 ... 80 C1
Glasgow G32 ... 119 A3
Gourock PA19 ... 44 C3
Neilston G78 ... 154 C4
Port Glasgow PA14 ... 47 A1
Glen Avon Dr ML6 ... 123 B1
Glen Bervie G74 ... 160 A1
Glen Brae
Bridge of W PA11 ... 110 B4
Falkirk FK1 ... 42 A2
Glen Cally G74 ... 160 A1
Glen Cannich G74 ... 160 A1
Glen Carron G74 ... 160 A1
Glen Clova G74 ... 160 A1
Glen Clova Dr G68 ... 61 B2
Glen Clunie G74 ... 160 B1
Glen Clunie Dr G53 ... 135 B2
Glen Clunie Pl G53 ... 135 B2
Glen Cona Dr G53 ... 135 B3
Glen Creran Cres G78 ... 154 B3
Glen Cres Falkirk FK1 ... 42 A1
Glasgow G13 ... 94 C4
Stevenston KA20 ... 206 B1
Glen Ct Coatbridge ML5 ... 121 B3
Motherwell ML1 ... 164 A2
Glen Dene Way G53 ... 135 B2
Glen Derry G74 ... 160 B2
Glen Dessary G74 ... 181 A4
Glen Devon G74 ... 160 B1
Glen Dewar Pl G53 ... 135 B2
Glen Dochart Dr G68 ... 61 B3
Glen Doll G74 ... 160 A1
Glen Doll Rd G78 ... 154 A3
Glen Douglas Dr G68 ... 61 B2
Glen Douglas Pl PA16 ... 45 B2
Glen Douglas Rd PA16 ... 45 B2
Glen Douglas Way PA16 ... 45 B2
Glen Dr Helensburgh G84 ... 16 B2
Motherwell ML1 ... 143 A3
Glen Dye G74 ... 160 A1
Glen Eagles G74 ... 160 B1
Glen Esk G74 ... 160 B1
Glen Esk Dr G53 ... 135 B2
Glen Etive Pl G73 ... 138 C1
Glen Falloch G74 ... 160 B1
Glen Falloch Cres G78 ... 154 B3
Glen Farg G74 ... 160 B1
Glen Farrar G74 ... 160 A1
Glen Farrar Wlk KA2 ... 227 B3
Glen Feshie G74 ... 181 A4
Glen Finlet Rd G78 ... 154 B3
Glen Fruin Dr 18 ML9 ... 185 B1
Glen Fruin Pl ML6 ... 123 B1
Glen Fruin Rd PA16 ... 45 B2
Glen Fyne Rd G68 ... 61 A2
Glen Gairn G74 ... 160 B1
Glen Gairn Cres G78 ... 154 B3
Glen Garrell Pl G65 ... 36 B1
Glen Garry G74 ... 181 A4
Glen Gdns Elderslie PA5 ... 112 B2
Falkirk FK1 ... 42 A2
Glen Gr East Kilbride G75 ... 180 B4
Kilsyth G65 ... 36 B1
Glen Isla G74 ... 160 B1
Glen Isla Ave G78 ... 154 B3
Glen Isla Quadrant ML1 ... 165 A4
Glen Kinchie FK10 ... 4 A1
Glen Kinglas Ave PA16 ... 45 B1
Glen Kinglas Rd PA16 ... 45 B1
Glen Kyle Dr G53 ... 135 B2
Glen La Paisley PA3 ... 113 C3
Uplawmoor G78 ... 153 A2
Glen Lednock Dr G68 ... 61 A2
Glen Lee G74 ... 160 B1
Glen Lethnot G74 ... 160 B1
Glen Livet Pl G53 ... 135 B2
Glen Lochay Gdns G68 ... 61 A2
Glen Loy Pl G53 ... 135 B2
Glen Luce Dr G32 ... 119 B2
Glen Luss Gdns G68 ... 61 A2
Glen Luss Pl
Coatbridge ML5 ... 122 B3
Glasgow G53 ... 135 B2
Glen Luss Rd PA16 ... 45 B1
Glen Luss Way PA16 ... 45 B1
Glen Lyon G74 ... 160 B1
Glen Lyon Cres KA2 ... 227 B3
Glen Lyon Ct G68 ... 61 A2
Glen Lyon Rd G78 ... 154 B3
Glen Mallie G74 ... 160 B1
Glen Mark G74 ... 160 B1
Glen Mark Rd G78 ... 154 B3
Glen More G74 ... 160 A1
Glen Moriston G74 ... 160 A1
Glen Moriston Rd
Cumbernauld G68 ... 61 A2
Glasgow G53 ... 135 B2
Glen Moy G74 ... 160 B1
Glen Muir Rd G78 ... 154 B3
Glen Nevis G74 ... 181 A4
Glen Nevis Pl
Kilmarnock KA2 ... 227 B3
Rutherglen G73 ... 138 B1
Glen Noble ML1 ... 165 A4
Glen Ochil Rd ML6 ... 123 B1
Glen Ogilvie G74 ... 160 B1
Glen Ogle St G32 ... 119 B2
Glen Orchy Ct G68 ... 61 A3
Glen Orchy Dr
Cumbernauld G68 ... 61 A2
Glasgow G53 ... 135 B2
Glen Orchy Gr G53 ... 135 B2
Glen Orchy Pl
Chapelhall ML6 ... 123 B1
Cumbernauld G68 ... 61 A2
Glasgow G53 ... 135 B2
Kilmarnock KA2 ... 227 B3
Glen Orchy Rd ML1 ... 165 A4
Glen Ord Rd ML1 ... 143 A1
Glen Orrin Ave KA2 ... 227 B3
Glen Pl G76 ... 157 B4
Glen Prosen G74 ... 160 B1
Glen Quoich G74 ... 160 B2
Glen Rannoch Dr ML6 ... 123 B1
Glen Rd Airdrie ML6 ... 123 C3
Bishopton PA7 ... 72 A2
Caldercruix ML6 ... 104 C2
East Kilbride G76 ... 158 C3
Glasgow G32 ... 119 A4
Lennoxtown G66 ... 33 A1
Motherwell ML1 ... 143 B4
Old Kilpatrick G60 ... 73 A3
Plean FK7 ... 12 B1
Shotts ML7 ... 146 C2
Torwood FK5,FK7 ... 22 B4
West Kilbride KA23 ... 190 B3
Wishaw ML2 ... 165 A2
Glen Rinnes Dr G78 ... 154 B3
Glen Rosa Gdns G68 ... 61 A2
Glen Roy Dr G78 ... 154 B3
Glen Sannox Dr G68 ... 61 B2
Glen Sannox Gr G68 ... 61 B2
Glen Sannox Loan G68 ... 61 B2
Glen Sannox View G68 ... 61 A2
Glen Sannox Way G68 ... 61 B2
Glen Sannox Wynd G68 ... 61 B2
Glen Sax Dr PA4 ... 94 C1
Glen Shee G74 ... 160 B1
Glen Shee Ave G78 ... 154 B3
Glen Shee Cres ML6 ... 123 B1
Glen Shiel Cres KA2 ... 227 B3
Glen Shirva Rd G65 ... 59 C2
Glen St Barrhead G78 ... 134 B2
Cambuslang G72 ... 139 B2
Greenock PA16 ... 45 B4
Motherwell ML1 ... 142 C1
Motherwell, Whittagreen
ML1 ... 143 B2
Paisley PA3 ... 113 C3
Glen Tanner G74 ... 160 B1
Glen Tarbert Dr G78 ... 154 B3
Glen Tennet G74 ... 160 B1
Glen Terr
Caldercruix ML6 ... 104 C2
Denny FK6 ... 21 B1
Glen The FK10 ... 4 B2
Glen Trool Wlk KA2 ... 227 B4
Glen Truim View KA2 ... 227 B3
Glen Turret G74 ... 160 B1
Glen Twr ML1 ... 164 A2
Glen Tye Rd FK7 ... 7 B3
Glen Urquhart G74 ... 160 A1
Glen View
Bonnybridge FK4 ... 39 B3
Cumbernauld G67 ... 62 B2
Hamilton ML3 ... 183 B4
Renton G82 ... 27 B1
Glenacre Cres G71 ... 140 C4
Glenacre Dr Airdrie ML6 ... 123 B3
Glasgow G45 ... 137 B2
Glenacre Gr G45 ... 137 C2
Glenacre Rd G67 ... 82 C4
Glenacre St G45 ... 137 B2
Glenacre Terr G45 ... 137 B2
Glenafeoch Rd ML8 ... 188 A1
Glenafton View ML3 ... 183 A4
Glenalla Cres KA7 ... 238 B1
Glenallan Terr ML1 ... 142 B1
Glenallan Way PA2 ... 132 C4
Glenalmond Rd G73 ... 138 B2
Glenalmond St G32 ... 119 A2
Glenalva Ct G65 ... 36 B1
Glenan Gdns G84 ... 16 B1
Glenapp Ave PA2 ... 114 A1
Glenapp Ct KA13 ... 207 B1
Glenapp Pl
Kilwinning KA13 ... 207 B1
Moodiesburn G69 ... 80 C2
Glenapp Quadrant KA1 ... 228 A4
Glenapp Rd PA2 ... 114 A1
Glenapp St G41 ... 116 C2
Glenarklet Dr PA2 ... 114 A1
Glenarn Rd G84 ... 15 C2
Glenartney PA6 ... 91 A1
Glenartney Rd G69 ... 80 B1
Glenashdale Way PA2 ... 114 A1
Glenavon Ct ML3 ... 162 A1
Glenavon Rd G20 ... 96 B4
Glenbank FK1 ... 42 A1
Glenbank Ave G66 ... 79 B2
Glenbank Ct G46 ... 135 C1
Glenbank Dr G46 ... 135 C1
Glenbank Rd G66 ... 79 B2
Glenbarr St G21 ... 97 C1
Glenbervie FK5 ... 23 B2
Glenbervie Ave FK5 ... 23 A2
Glenbervie Cres
Cumbernauld G68 ... 61 C3
Larbert FK5 ... 23 A2
Glenbervie Dr
Kilwinning KA13 ... 207 A2
Larbert FK5 ... 23 A2
Glenbervie Pl
17 Glasgow G23 ... 76 B1
Gourock PA19 ... 44 A3
Newton Mearns G77 ... 156 A3
Glenbervie Wynd KA11 ... 224 C4
Glenbo Dr FK6 ... 39 C4
Glenboig Farm Rd ML5 ... 101 C3
Glenboig New Rd ML5 ... 101 C3
Glenboig Prim Sch ML5 ... 101 C3
Glenboig Rd
Gartcosh G69 ... 101 A4
Glenboig ML5 ... 101 B3
Glenbrae Ct FK1 ... 42 A2
Glenbrae La PA15 ... 46 A1
Glenbrae Rd
Greenock PA15 ... 46 A1
Port Glasgow PA14 ... 68 B4
Glenbride Rd KA23 ... 190 B2
Glenbrittle Dr PA2 ... 114 A1
Glenbrittle Way PA2 ... 114 A1
Glenbuck Ave G33 ... 98 C3
Glenbuck Dr G33 ... 98 C3
Glenburn Ave
Cambuslang G72 ... 138 C3
Chryston G69 ... 80 C1
Glasgow G69 ... 120 B3
Motherwell ML1 ... 143 B2
Glenburn Cl KA13 ... 207 B3
Glenburn Cres
Milton of C G66 ... 58 B3
Paisley PA2 ... 133 B4
Uddingston G71 ... 141 B4
Glenburn Ct
East Kilbride G74 ... 159 A2
4 Kirkintilloch G66 ... 79 B4
Glenburn Dr PA13 ... 69 B1
Glenburn Gdns
Bishopbriggs G64 ... 77 C1
Glenboig ML5 ... 101 B3
Glenburn Ind Est KA9 ... 236 C4
Glenburn La Glasgow G20 ... 96 C4
Kilmacolm PA13 ... 69 B1
Glenburn Prim Sch KA9 ... 236 C4
Glenburn Rd
Bearsden G61 ... 75 C3
Glenburn Rd *continued*
East Kilbride G74 ... 159 A2
Falkirk FK1 ... 42 B1
Glasgow G46 ... 136 A1
Hamilton ML3 ... 162 A2
Kilmacolm PA13 ... 69 B1
Paisley PA2 ... 133 B4
Prestwick KA9 ... 236 C4
Glenburn Sch PA16 ... 44 C2
Glenburn St Glasgow G20 ... 96 C4
Port Glasgow PA14 ... 47 A1
Glenburn Terr
Carluke ML8 ... 201 C4
Motherwell ML1 ... 143 B1
Glenburn Way G74 ... 158 C2
Glenburn Wlk G69 ... 120 B3
Glenburn Wynd 3 ML9 ... 185 A2
Glenburnie Pl G34 ... 119 C4
Glencairn Ave ML2 ... 164 B2
Glencairn Dr
Chryston G69 ... 80 C1
Glasgow G41 ... 116 C1
Rutherglen G73 ... 137 C4
Glencairn Gdns
Cambuslang G72 ... 139 B3
Glasgow G41 ... 116 C1
Stevenston KA20 ... 206 B1
Glencairn Ind Est KA1 ... 227 C3
Glencairn La G41 ... 116 C1
Glencairn Prim Sch
Motherwell ML1 ... 163 C3
Stevenston KA20 ... 217 B4
Glencairn Rd Ayr KA7 ... 239 B3
Cumbernauld G67 ... 62 B1
Dumbarton G82 ... 49 B2
Greenock PA16 ... 44 C2
Kilmacolm PA13 ... 89 C4
Langbank PA14 ... 70 B4
Paisley PA3 ... 114 A4
Glencairn Ret Pk KA1 ... 227 C3
Glencairn Sq KA1 ... 227 C4
Glencairn St Falkirk FK1 ... 41 A3
11 Kirkintilloch G66 ... 79 B4
Motherwell ML1 ... 163 C3
Saltcoats KA21 ... 216 C4
Stevenston KA20 ... 206 C1
Stirling FK7 ... 7 A2
Glencairn Terr
Kilmaurs KA3 ... 222 A4
Stevenston KA20 ... 206 B1
Glencalder Cres ML4 ... 142 B2
Glencally Ave PA2 ... 114 A1
Glencart Gr PA10 ... 111 B1
Glencleland Rd ML2 ... 164 B2
Glenclora Dr PA2 ... 114 A1
Glenclova Gdns KA2 ... 227 B3
Glencloy St G20 ... 96 B4
Glenclune PA14 ... 47 C1
Glenclune Ct PA13 ... 89 B4
Glencoats Bsns Ctr PA3 ... 113 A3
Glencoats Dr PA3 ... 113 A2
Glencoe Dr ML1 ... 143 A3
Glencoe Pl Glasgow G13 ... 95 C4
Hamilton ML3 ... 183 A4
Glencoe Rd Carluke ML8 ... 202 A4
Rutherglen G73 ... 138 B2
Stirling FK8 ... 2 A1
Glencoe St G13 ... 95 C4
Glenconner Pl KA7 ... 239 A3
Glenconner Rd KA7 ... 239 A3
Glenconner Way G66 ... 59 A1
Glenconnor St ML9 ... 199 A4
Glencorse Rd PA2 ... 113 B1
Glencorse St G32 ... 118 C4
Glencraig St ML6 ... 122 C4
Glencraig Terr KA3 ... 213 A2
Glencraigs Dr KA3 ... 222 C3
Glencroft Ave G71 ... 140 C4
Glencroft Rd G44 ... 137 B3
Glencryan Rd G67 ... 62 A1
Glencryan Sch G67 ... 82 C4
Glendale Ave ML6 ... 123 B3
Glendale Cres Ayr KA7 ... 239 B2
Bishopbriggs G64 ... 98 B4
Glendale Dr G64 ... 98 B4
Glendale Gr ML5 ... 121 C2
Glendale Pl Ayr KA7 ... 239 A2
Bishopbriggs G64 ... 98 B4
Glasgow G31 ... 118 A3
Glendale Prim Sch G41 ... 116 C2
Glendale St G31 ... 118 A3
Glendaruel Ave G61 ... 76 A2
Glendaruel Rd G73 ... 138 C1
Glendarvel Gdns G22 ... 97 B2
Glendee Gdns PA4 ... 94 B1
Glendee Rd PA4 ... 94 B1
Glendentan Rd PA11 ... 110 B3
Glendermott Gdns ML8 ... 187 C2
Glendeveron Way ML1 ... 143 A1
Glendevon Dr FK8 ... 1 C1
Glendevon Pl
Clydebank G81 ... 73 C2
Hamilton ML3 ... 183 A4
Glendevon Sq G33 ... 99 A1
Glendinning Pl G76 ... 178 B2
Glendinning Rd G13 ... 75 C1
Glendoick Pl G77 ... 156 A3
Glendorch Ave ML2 ... 165 B4
Glendore St G14 ... 95 C1
Glendoune Rd G76 ... 157 C3
Glendower Way PA2 ... 132 C4
Glenduffhill Rd G69 ... 119 C3
Gleneagles Ave
Cumbernauld G68 ... 62 A3
Kilwinning KA13 ... 207 B2
Gleneagles Dr
Bishopbriggs G64 ... 78 A2
Gourock PA19 ... 44 A3
Gleneagles Dr *continued*
Newton Mearns G77 ... 157 A2
Gleneagles Gate G77 ... 157 A2
Gleneagles Gdns G64 ... 78 A2
Gleneagles La N G14 ... 95 B2
Gleneagles La S G14 ... 95 B2
Gleneagles Pk G72 ... 140 C1
Gleneagles Pl KA11 ... 224 C4
Glenelg Cres G66 ... 59 A1
Glenelg Path ML5 ... 101 B3
Glenelg Quadrant G34 ... 100 B1
Glenelm Pl ML4 ... 142 A3
Glenesk Cres G53 ... 135 B2
Glenesk Pl G53 ... 135 B2
Glenfarg Cres G61 ... 76 A2
Glenfarg Rd
Hamilton ML3 ... 183 A4
Rutherglen G73 ... 138 A2
Glenfarg St 12 G20 ... 97 A1
Glenfarm Rd ML1 ... 143 C2
Glenfield Ave PA2 ... 133 C4
Glenfield Cres PA2 ... 133 C3
Glenfield Gdns
Kilmarnock KA1 ... 227 C3
Paisley PA2 ... 133 B3
Glenfield Gr PA2 ... 133 B3
Glenfield Grange PA2 ... 133 C3
Glenfield Pl KA1 ... 227 C3
Glenfield Rd
East Kilbride G75 ... 181 A3
Paisley PA2 ... 133 B3
Glenfinlas St G84 ... 16 C1
Glenfinnan Dr
Bearsden G61 ... 76 B2
Glasgow G20 ... 96 B3
Glenfinnan Gr ML4 ... 142 B2
Glenfinnan Pl 12 G20 ... 96 B3
Glenfinnan Rd G20 ... 96 B3
Glenfruin Cres PA2 ... 114 A1
Glenfruin Rd G72 ... 161 B4
Glenfuir Rd FK1 ... 41 C3
Glenfuir St FK1 ... 41 B3
Glengarnock Prim Sch
KA14 ... 170 A4
Glengarnock Sta KA14 ... 170 B3
Glengarnock Workshops
KA14 ... 170 B4
Glengarriff Rd ML4 ... 142 A4
Glengarry Cres FK1 ... 41 C1
Glengarry Dr G52 ... 115 B3
Glengavel Cres G33 ... 98 C3
Glengavel Gdns ML2 ... 165 B4
Glengowan Prim Sch
Caldercruix ML6 ... 105 A2
Larkhall ML9 ... 185 A2
Glengowan Rd
Bridge of W PA11 ... 110 B4
Caldercruix ML6 ... 105 A2
Glengyre St G34 ... 100 B1
Glenhead Cres
Clydebank G81 ... 74 A4
Glasgow G22 ... 97 B3
Glenhead Dr ML1 ... 163 C2
Glenhead Prim Sch G67 ... 62 C3
Glenhead Rd
Clydebank G81 ... 74 A3
Kirkintilloch G66 ... 79 B2
Glenhead St G22 ... 97 B3
Glenholme Ave PA2 ... 113 A1
Glenhove Rd G67 ... 62 A1
Glenhuntly Rd PA14 ... 47 B1
Glenhuntly Terr PA14 ... 47 B1
Gleniffer Ave G13 ... 95 A3
Gleniffer Braes Ctry Pk*
PA2 ... 133 A3
Gleniffer Cres PA5 ... 112 B1
Gleniffer Dr G78 ... 134 A3
Gleniffer High Sch PA2 ... 133 A4
Gleniffer Rd
Paisley PA2,G78 ... 132 B2
Renfrew PA4 ... 114 A4
Uplawmoor G78 ... 152 B2
Gleniffer View
Clydebank G81 ... 74 B2
Neilston G78 ... 154 B4
Gleninver Rd PA16 ... 45 A2
Glenisla Ave G69 ... 81 A2
Glenisla St G31 ... 118 B2
Glenkirk Dr G15 ... 75 A1
Glenlee Prim Sch ML3 ... 162 A3
Glenlee St ML3 ... 161 C3
Glenleith Pl KA11 ... 220 B1
Glenlivet Pl KA3 ... 223 A2
Glenlivet Rd G78 ... 154 B3
Glenlora Dr G53 ... 135 A4
Glenlora Terr G53 ... 135 A4
Glenluce Gdns G69 ... 81 A2
Glenluce Terr G74 ... 159 B1
Glenluggie Rd G66 ... 80 A4
Glenlui Ave G73 ... 138 A3
Glenlyon Ct ML3 ... 183 A4
Glenlyon Gr KA11 ... 219 C3
Glenlyon Pl G73 ... 138 B2
Glenmalloch Pl PA5 ... 112 B2
Glenmanor Ave G69 ... 80 C1
Glenmanor Prim Sch
G69 ... 80 C1
Glenmanor Rd G69 ... 80 C1
Glenmare Ave G66 ... 80 A4
Glenmavis Cres ML8 ... 188 A1
Glenmavis Ct ML8 ... 188 A1
Glenmavis Rd ML6 ... 102 C1
Glenmavis St G4 ... 240 C4
Glenmore Ave
Alexandria G83 ... 27 B3

Glenmore Ave continued
Bellshill ML4 . . . . .142 A2
Glasgow G42 . . . . .137 C4
Glenmore Dr FK4 . . . . .39 C3
Glenmore Rd ML1 . . . . .143 B2
Glenmoss Ave PA8 . . . . .72 C1
Glenmosston Rd PA13 . . . . .29 C4
Glenmount Pl KA7 . . . . .238 A1
Glenmuir Ct KA8 . . . . .236 B1
Glenmuir Dr G53 . . . . .135 A3
Glenmuir Pl KA8 . . . . .236 B3
Glenmuir Rd KA8 . . . . .236 B1
Glenmuir Sq KA8 . . . . .236 B1
Glenochil Pk FK10 . . . . .4 C2
Glenochil Rd FK10 . . . . .42 A2
Glenochil Terr FK10 . . . . .4 C2
Glenoran La ■ ML9 . . . . . . .185 A2
Glenoran Rd KA8 . . . . .16 A2
Glenorchard Rd G64 . . . . . . .56 B1
Glenorrin Way G78 . . . . . . .154 B3
Glenpark ML6 . . . . .123 C3
Glenpark Ave
  Glasgow G46 . . . . .136 A1
  Prestwick KA9 . . . . .236 B3
Glenpark Dr PA14 . . . . .47 A1
Glenpark Gdns G72 . . . . . . .138 C4
Glenpark Pl KA7 . . . . .237 C2
Glenpark Rd PA12 . . . . .129 B2
Glenpark St
  Glasgow G31 . . . . .118 A3
  Wishaw ML2 . . . . .165 A2
Glenpark Terr G72 . . . . .138 C4
Glenpath G82 . . . . .50 B2
Glenpatrick Bldgs PA5 . .112 B1
Glenpatrick Rd PA5 . . . . . . .112 B1
Glenpath G33 . . . . .99 A2
Glenraith Rd G33 . . . . .99 A1
Glenraith Sq G33 . . . . .99 A2
Glenraith Wlk G33 . . . . .99 A2
Glenriddel Rd KA7 . . . . . . .239 A3
Glenriddet Ave KA25 . . . . .170 A4
Glenshee Ct G31 . . . . .118 B2
Glenshee Gdns G31 . . . . . . .118 C2
Glenshee St G31 . . . . .118 B2
Glenshee Terr ML3 . . . . . . .183 A4
Glenshiel Ave PA2 . . . . .114 A1
Glenshira Ave PA2 . . . . .114 A1
Glenside Ave G53 . . . . .115 A1
Glenside Cres KA23 . . . . . . .190 B3
Glenside Dr G73 . . . . .138 C3
Glenside Gr KA23 . . . . .190 B3
Glenside Rd
  Dumbarton G82 . . . . .50 B3
  Port Glasgow PA14 . . . . . . .68 B4
Glenspean Pl ML5 . . . . .122 B3
Glenspean St G43 . . . . .136 B3
Glentanar Dr G69 . . . . .81 A1
Glentanar Pl G22 . . . . .97 A4
Glentanar Rd G22 . . . . .97 A4
Glentarbert Rd G73 . . . . . . .138 B2
Glentore Quadrant ML6 . .103 A1
Glentrool Gdns
  Glasgow G22 . . . . .97 B2
  Moodiesburn G69 . . . . .81 A2
Glenturret St G32 . . . . .119 A2
Glentyan Ave PA10 . . . . . . .111 A2
Glentyan Dr G53 . . . . .135 A3
Glentye Gdns FK1 . . . . .41 C1
Glentynan Pl G53 . . . . .135 A4
Glenview Airdrie ML6 . . . . .123 B3
  Denny FK6 . . . . .21 A2
  ■ Kirkintilloch G66 . . . . . . .79 B4
  Larkhall ML9 . . . . .184 C2
  Menstrie FK11 . . . . .4 A3
  West Kilbride KA23 . . . . . .190 B2
Glenview Ave
  Banknock FK4 . . . . .38 C2
  Caldercruix ML6 . . . . .105 A4
Glenview Cres G69 . . . . .81 A2
Glenview Dr FK1 . . . . .41 C1
Glenview Pl G72 . . . . .140 B1
Glenview St ML6 . . . . .102 C2
Glenville Ave G46 . . . . .136 A2
Glenville Gate G78 . . . . .45 B2
Glenville Gate G76 . . . . . . .158 A3
Glenville Terr G76 . . . . .158 A3
Glenward Ave G66 . . . . .57 C4
Glenwell St ML6 . . . . .102 C2
Glenwinnel Rd FK12 . . . . . . .4 C4
Glenwood Ave ML6 . . . . . . .123 B2
Glenwood Bsns Ctr G45 . .137 C2
Glenwood Ct G66 . . . . .79 A3
Glenwood Dr G46 . . . . .135 C1
Glenwood Gdns G66 . . . . . .79 A3
Glenwood Path G45 . . . . . .137 C2
Glenwood Pl
  Glasgow G45 . . . . .137 C2
  Kirkintilloch G66 . . . . .79 A3
Glenwood Rd G66 . . . . .79 A3
Glenyards Rd FK4 . . . . .40 A1
Glidden Ct ML2 . . . . .186 B4
Glorat Ave G66 . . . . .57 C4
Gloucester Ave
  Clarkston G76 . . . . .157 B4
  Rutherglen G73 . . . . .138 B3
Gloucester St G1 . . . . .117 A2
Glowrorum Dr FK6 . . . . .39 C4
Glynwed Ct FK2 . . . . .42 B4
Goatfell View KA10 . . . . . . .229 C4
Gockston Rd PA3 . . . . .113 B4
Goddard Pl ML2 . . . . .166 A3
Godfrey Ave FK6 . . . . .21 B1
Godfrey Cres FK5 . . . . .23 B3
Gogar Loan FK9 . . . . .3 B3
Gogar Pl Glasgow G33 . . . . .118 C4

Gogar Pl continued
  Stirling FK7 . . . . .7 B1
Gogar St G33 . . . . .118 C4
Goil Ave ML4 . . . . .141 B3
Goil Way ML1 . . . . .143 C3
Goldberry Ave G14 . . . . .95 A3
Goldcraig Ct KA11 . . . . . . .220 A3
Goldenacre Pl ML6 . . . . . . .103 C2
Goldenberry Ave KA23 . . . .190 B2
Goldenhill Ct G81 . . . . .74 A3
Goldenhill Prim Sch G81 . .74 A3
Goldenlee View PA6 . . . . . .111 A4
Goldie Pl KA20 . . . . .206 B1
Goldie Rd G71 . . . . .141 A2
Golf Ave Bellshill ML4 . . . . .142 A2
  Stevenston KA20 . . . . .217 C3
Golf Course Rd
  Balmore G64 . . . . .77 A4
  Bridge of W PA11 . . . . . . .110 B4
Golf Cres KA10 . . . . .229 C1
Golf Ct G44 . . . . .136 C1
Golf Dr Clydebank G15 . . . . .74 C1
  Paisley PA1 . . . . .114 B2
Golf Gdns ML9 . . . . .185 B1
Golf Pl Bellshill ML4 . . . . . .142 A2
  Greenock PA16 . . . . .45 B4
  Helensburgh G84 . . . . .17 A1
  Irvine KA12 . . . . .219 B4
  Troon KA10 . . . . .229 C1
Golf Rd Bishopton PA7 . . . . .72 A2
  Clarkston G76 . . . . .157 B4
Gollan Ave ML6 . . . . .103 A1
Golspie Ave PA2 . . . . .114 A1
Golspie St G51 . . . . .116 A4
Good Shepherd Prim Sch
  KA8 . . . . .236 B3
Goodview Gdns ML9 . . . . . .185 B1
Goosecroft Rd FK8 . . . . .7 A4
Goosedubbs G1 . . . . .241 A2
Gooseholm Cres G82 . . . . . .50 A3
Gooseholm Rd G82 . . . . .50 A3
Gopher Ave G71 . . . . .141 A4
Gorbals Cross
  Glasgow G5 . . . . .117 B3
  Larkhall ML9 . . . . .185 A2
Gorbals St G1,G5 . . . . .117 B3
Gordon Ave Bishopton PA7 .72 A2
  Glasgow G69 . . . . .136 C1
  Glasgow, Netherlee G44 . .136 C1
  Paisley G52 . . . . .114 C4
Gordon Cres
  Bridge of A FK9 . . . . .2 A4
  Newton Mearns G77 . . . . .156 C3
  Stirling FK8 . . . . .1 C1
Gordon Ct ML6 . . . . .123 C4
Gordon Dr Alloa FK10 . . . . .10 B4
  East Kilbride G74 . . . . .160 A2
  Glasgow G44 . . . . .136 C2
Gordon La G1 . . . . .240 C2
Gordon Pl Bellshill ML4 . . . .141 C1
  Falkirk FK1 . . . . .42 A2
Gordon Rd Glasgow G44 . . .136 C1
  Hamilton ML3 . . . . .161 C2
Gordon Sq PA5 . . . . .111 C1
Gordon St Ayr KA8 . . . . . . .236 A2
  Glasgow G1 . . . . .240 C2
  Greenock PA15 . . . . .45 C2
  Paisley PA1 . . . . .113 C2
Gordon Terr Ayr KA8 . . . . . .239 A4
  Blantyre G72 . . . . .140 B1
  Hamilton ML3 . . . . .162 B2
Gorebridge St G32 . . . . .118 C4
Goremire Rd ML8 . . . . .202 A4
Gorget Ave G13 . . . . .75 B1
Gorget Pl G13 . . . . .75 B1
Gorget Quadrant G13 . . . . . .75 B1
Gorrie St FK6 . . . . .21 B1
Gorse Cres PA11 . . . . .110 C4
Gorse Pk KA7 . . . . .239 B2
Gorse Pl G71 . . . . .141 A4
Gorsehall St ML1 . . . . .144 A1
Gorsewood G64 . . . . .77 C1
Gorstan Pl G20 . . . . .96 B3
Gorstan St G23 . . . . .96 B4
Goschen Terr KA8 . . . . .236 A1
Gosford La G14 . . . . .95 A2
Gotterburn ML1 . . . . .89 C1
Gottries Pl KA12 . . . . .219 A1
Gottries Rd KA12 . . . . .219 A1
Goudie St PA3 . . . . .113 B4
Gough St G33 . . . . .118 B4
Goukscroft Pk KA7 . . . . . . .238 B2
Gould St KA8 . . . . .236 B1
Gourlay G74 . . . . .160 B3
Gourlay Dr ML2 . . . . .186 B3
Gourlay St Glasgow G21 . . . .97 B2
  ■ Glasgow, Springburn
  G21 . . . . .97 C2
Gourock High Sch G84 . . . . .44 B4
Gourock Prim Sch PA19 . . . .44 C4
Gourock St G5 . . . . .117 A2
Gourock Sta PA19 . . . . .44 C4

Govan Dr G83 . . . . .27 B3
Govan High Sch G51 . . . . . .115 C4
Govan Rd Glasgow G51 . . . .115 C4
  Glasgow, Plantation G51 . .116 B3
Govan Underground Sta
  G51 . . . . .116 A4
Govanhill St G42 . . . . .117 A1
Gowan Ave FK2 . . . . .42 A3
Gowan Brae ML6 . . . . .105 A3
Gowan La FK2 . . . . .42 A3
Gowanbank Gdns PA5 . . . .111 C1
Gowanbank Prim Sch
  G53 . . . . .135 A4
Gowanbank Rd KA7 . . . . . .239 A1
Gowanbrae G66 . . . . .79 B3
Gowanhill Gdns FK8 . . . . . . .1 C1
Gowanlea Ave G15 . . . . .75 A1
Gowanlea Dr
  Glasgow G46 . . . . .136 B2
  Slamannan FK1 . . . . .86 A3
Gowanlea Terr G71 . . . . . . .141 A4
Gowanside Pl ML8 . . . . . . .187 B1
Gower Pl KA7 . . . . .239 A2
Gower St G41 . . . . .116 B2
Gower Terr G41 . . . . .116 B3
Gowkhall Ave ML1 . . . . . . .143 C2
Gowkhouse Rd PA13 . . . . . .89 C4
Goyle Ave G15 . . . . .75 B2
Grace Ave G69 . . . . .120 C3
Grace St G3 . . . . .240 A2
Gracie Cres FK7 . . . . .8 B2
Gradlon Pl FK1 . . . . .42 A2
Graeme Ct ML1 . . . . .142 B1
Graeme High Sch FK1 . . . . .42 C2
Graeme Pl FK1 . . . . .41 C1
Graffham Ave G46 . . . . .136 C2
Grafton Pl G1 . . . . .241 A3
Graham Ave
  Cambuslang G72 . . . . .139 B3
  Clydebank G81 . . . . .74 A2
  East Kilbride G74 . . . . .159 C1
  Hamilton ML3 . . . . .183 B4
  Larbert FK5 . . . . .23 A2
Graham Cres G82 . . . . .48 A4
Graham Ct KA1 . . . . .228 C3
Graham Dr G62 . . . . .54 C1
Graham Ho G67 . . . . .61 C1
Graham Pl Ashgill ML9 . . . .185 C1
  Helensburgh G84 . . . . .17 A1
  Kilmarnock KA3 . . . . .223 B1
  Kilsyth G65 . . . . .36 B1
Graham Rd
  Crossford ML8 . . . . .201 A1
  Dumbarton G82 . . . . .49 B2
Graham Sq G31 . . . . .117 C3
Graham St Airdrie ML6 . . . .123 A4
  Barrhead G78 . . . . .134 A2
  Bridge of A FK9 . . . . .2 A4
  Greenock PA16 . . . . .45 B3
  Hamilton ML3 . . . . .162 C2
  Johnstone PA5 . . . . .111 C1
  Motherwell ML1 . . . . .143 A3
  Wishaw ML2 . . . . .165 A1
Graham Terr Airth FK2 . . . . .14 B2
  Bishopbriggs G64 . . . . .98 A4
  Stewarton KA3 . . . . .195 B1
Graham Wlk KA3 . . . . .223 B1
Grahamfield Pl KA15 . . . . .171 A4
Grahams Ave PA12 . . . . . . .129 B2
Grahamsdyke Ave FK4 . . . . .40 A2
Grahamsdyke Cres FK4 . . . .40 A2
Grahamsdyke Rd
  Bonnybridge FK4 . . . . .40 A2
  Kirkintilloch S66 . . . . .58 C1
Grahamsdyke St FK2 . . . . . .42 C2
Grahamshill Ave ML6 . . . . .123 B4
Grahamshill St ML6 . . . . . .123 B4
Grahamston Ave KA14 . . . .170 A4
Grahamston Cres PA2 . . . .134 B4
Grahamston Ct PA2 . . . . . . .134 B4
Grahamston Pk G78 . . . . . .134 A3
Grahamston Pl PA2 . . . . . . .134 B4
Grahamston Rd G78,
  PA2 . . . . .134 B3
Grahamston Sta FK1 . . . . . .42 A3
Graigleith View FK10 . . . . . . .4 B2
Graignestock Pl ■ G40 . . .117 C3
Graignestock St G40 . . . . . .117 C3
Graigside PJ G68 . . . . .81 C4
Grainger Rd G64 . . . . .78 C1
Grammar School Sq
  ML3 . . . . .162 C2
Grampian Ave PA2 . . . . . . .133 B4
Grampian Cres
  Chapelhall ML6 . . . . .123 C1
  Glasgow G32 . . . . .119 A2
Grampian Ct KA11 . . . . . . .220 A2
Grampian Dr G75 . . . . .180 A2
Grampian Pl G32 . . . . .119 A2
Grampian Rd
  Kilmarnock KA1 . . . . .228 A2
  Port Glasgow PA14 . . . . . . .69 A3
  Stirling FK7 . . . . .8 A3
  Wishaw ML2 . . . . .164 C2
Grampian St G32 . . . . .119 A2
Grampian Way
  Barrhead G78 . . . . .134 B1
  Bearsden G61 . . . . .75 A4
  Cumbernauld G68 . . . . .61 A1
Gran St G81 . . . . .94 C4
Granary Rd FK2 . . . . .42 A4
Granary Sq FK2 . . . . .42 A4
Granby La G12 . . . . .96 B2
Grandtuly Dr G12 . . . . .96 B3
Grange Acad KA1 . . . . .227 B4
Grange Ave Ayr KA7 . . . . . .239 A1
  Falkirk FK2 . . . . .42 B3

Grange Ave continued
  Milngavie G62 . . . . .55 A1
  Wishaw ML2 . . . . .164 C1
Grange Ct Lanark NL15 . . . .214 C3
  Stevenston KA20 . . . . .206 B1
Grange Dr FK2 . . . . .42 B3
Grange Gdns
  Bothwell G71 . . . . .141 A1
  Bridge of A FK9 . . . . .2 B4
Grange Pl Alexandria G83 . .27 C3
  Kilmarnock KA1 . . . . .227 C4
Grange Rd Alloa FK10 . . . . . .9 C3
  Bearsden G61 . . . . .75 C3
  Bridge of A FK9 . . . . .2 B3
  Glasgow G42 . . . . .137 A4
  Stevenston KA20 . . . . .206 B1
Grange St
  Motherwell ML1 . . . . .164 A2
Grange Terr KA1 . . . . .227 B4
Grange The KA11 . . . . .220 B3
Grange Twr ML1 . . . . .164 A2
Grangemouth Rd FK2 . . . . . .42 C3
Grangemuir Ct KA9 . . . . . .236 A4
Grangemuir Rd KA9 . . . . . .236 A4
Grangeneuk Gdns G68 . . . . .61 B1
Granger Rd Balloch G83 . . . .27 C4
Grangeview KA5 . . . . .23 C1
Grannoch Pl ML5 . . . . .122 B3
Grant Cres G82 . . . . .27 B1
Grant Ct Airdrie ML6 . . . . . .123 C4
  Hamilton ML3 . . . . .183 B4
Grant Pl Coatbridge ML5 . .122 B2
  Hamilton ML3 . . . . .183 B4
  Stirling FK9 . . . . .2 A2
Grant St Alloa FK10 . . . . .9 C3
  Glasgow G3 . . . . .240 A4
  Greenock PA15 . . . . .46 B2
  Helensburgh G84 . . . . .16 B1
Granthohm Ave ML1 . . . . . .143 A3
Grantlea Gr G32 . . . . .119 B2
Grantlea Terr G32 . . . . .119 B2
Grantley Gdns G41 . . . . . . .136 B4
Grantley St G41 . . . . .136 B4
Grantoften Path G75 . . . . . .180 C3
Granton St G5 . . . . .117 C1
Grantown Ave ML6 . . . . . . .123 C3
Grantown Gdns ML6 . . . . . .102 C2
Grants Ave PA2 . . . . .113 B1
Grants Cres PA2 . . . . .133 B4
Grants Pl PA2 . . . . .133 B4
Grants Way PA2 . . . . .113 B1
Granville St
  Clydebank G81 . . . . .74 A2
  Glasgow G3 . . . . .240 A3
  Helensburgh G84 . . . . .16 C1
Grasmere G75 . . . . .179 C3
Grasmere Ct ML3 . . . . .183 A4
Grassyards Intc KA3 . . . . . .223 B2
Grassyards Rd KA3 . . . . . . .223 B1
Grathellen Ct ML1 . . . . .164 A4
Gray Cres KA12 . . . . .224 C4
Gray Dr G61 . . . . .75 C2
Gray St Alexandria G83 . . . .27 C3
  Cleland ML1 . . . . .144 A1
Gray's Cl KA1 . . . . .241 B4
Glasgow G3 . . . . .240 A3
Greenock PA15 . . . . .46 A2
Kirkintilloch G66 . . . . .80 A4
Larkhall ML9 . . . . .185 A2
Prestwick KA9 . . . . .236 B4
Shotts ML7 . . . . .147 A2
Gray's Cl KA1 . . . . .214 B2
Gray's Rd G71 . . . . .141 A3
Grayshill Rd G68 . . . . .81 C3
Grayston Ave G40 . . . . .117 C2
Graystale Rd FK7 . . . . .7 B2
Graystonelee Rd ML7 . . . . .146 B3
Graystones KA13 . . . . .207 C3
Great Dovehill G1, G4 . . . . .241 B1
Great George La G12 . . . . . .96 B2
Great George St G12 . . . . . . .96 B2
Great Hamilton St PA2 . . . .113 C1
Great Kelvin La G12 . . . . . . .96 C1
Great Western Rd
  Clydebank G15,G81 . . . . . .74 B2
  Glasgow G12 . . . . .96 B2
Great Western Terr 33 . . . . . .96 B2
Great Western Terrace La 33
  G12 . . . . .96 B2
Green Ave KA12 . . . . .219 B2
Green Bank A24 . . . . .191 B4
Green Bank Rd G68 . . . . . . .61 B1
Green Dale ML2 . . . . .165 B3
Green Gdns ML1 . . . . .144 B1
Green Loan ML1 . . . . .143 A2
Green Pl Bothwell G71 . . . . .141 A1
  Calderbank ML6 . . . . .123 C1
Green Rd Paisley PA2 . . . . .113 A2
  Rutherglen G73 . . . . .138 A4
Green St Ayr KA8 . . . . .235 C1
  Bothwell G71 . . . . .141 A1
  Clydebank G81 . . . . .74 A2
  Glasgow G40 . . . . .117 C3
  Saltcoats KA21 . . . . .216 C4
  Stonehouse ML9 . . . . .198 C1
Green Street La KA8 . . . . . .235 C1
Green Street Lane Bsns Pk
  KA8 . . . . .235 C1
Green The Alva FK12 . . . . . . .5 A4
  Glasgow G40 . . . . .117 C2
Greenacre Cl FK7 . . . . .7 C1
Greenacre Pl FK7 . . . . .7 C1
Greenacres
  Ardrossan KA22 . . . . .205 C2
  Motherwell ML1 . . . . .163 B3
Greenacres Ct G53 . . . . . . .135 B2
Greenacres Dr G53 . . . . . . .135 B2

Greenacres View ML1 . . . .163 B3
Greenacres Way G53 . . . . . .135 B2
Greenan Ave G42 . . . . .137 C4
Greenan Gr KA7 . . . . .238 A2
Greenan Pk KA7 . . . . .238 A2
Greenan Rd Ayr KA7 . . . . . .238 B2
Greenan St KA3 . . . . .228 A4
Greenan Terr KA9 . . . . .236 B4
Greenan Way KA7 . . . . .238 A2
Greenbank G72 . . . . .161 B4
Greenbank Ave G46 . . . . . .157 A4
Greenbank Ct KA12 . . . . . .219 B1
Greenbank Dr PA2 . . . . . . .133 B4
Greenbank Gdns ■ G76 . . .157 B3
Greenbank Pl FK1 . . . . .41 B2
Greenbank Rd Falkirk FK1 . .41 B2
  Wishaw ML2 . . . . .165 B2
Greenbank St ■ G73 . . . . .138 A4
Greenbank Terr ML8 . . . . . .187 C1
Greencornhills Rdbt FK7 . .11 C4
Greencraig Ave FK1 . . . . . . .66 B3
Greendyke St G1 . . . . .241 B1
Greenend Ave PA5 . . . . . . .111 B1
Greenend Pl G32 . . . . .119 B4
Greenend View ML4 . . . . . .141 C3
Greenfarm Rd
  Linwood PA3 . . . . .112 A3
  Newton Mearns G77 . . . . .156 A3
Greenfaulds Cres G67 . . . . .83 A4
Greenfaulds Rd
  Cumbernauld G67 . . . . .83 A4
  Cumbernauld, Greenfaulds
  G67 . . . . .82 C4
Greenfaulds Sta G67 . . . . . .82 C4
Greenfield Ave Ayr KA7 . . .238 B1
  Glasgow G32 . . . . .119 A4
Greenfield Cres ML2 . . . . . .165 B2
Greenfield Dr
  Irvine KA12 . . . . .219 B1
  Wishaw ML2 . . . . .165 B2
Greenfield Pl G32 . . . . .119 A3
Greenfield Prim Sch
  G51 . . . . .115 C4
Greenfield Quadrant
  ML1 . . . . .143 C2
Greenfield Rd
  Carluke ML8 . . . . .187 C2
  Clarkston G76 . . . . .157 C3
  Glasgow G32 . . . . .119 B3
  Hamilton ML3 . . . . .162 A3
Greenfield St Alloa FK10 . . .10 A4
  Bonnybridge FK4 . . . . .40 A3
  Glasgow G51 . . . . .115 C4
  Wishaw ML2 . . . . .165 B2
Greenfields High Sch
  G67 . . . . .82 B4
Greenfoot ML1 . . . . .207 C2
Greengairs Ave G51 . . . . . .115 B4
Greengairs Prim Sch
  ML6 . . . . .83 C1
Greenhall Pl G72 . . . . .161 B3
Greenhead G84 . . . . .5 A3
Greenhead Ave
  Dumbarton G82 . . . . .50 A2
  Stevenston KA20 . . . . .206 C1
Greenhead Gdns G82 . . . . . .50 A2
Greenhead Rd
  Bearsden G61 . . . . .75 C2
  Dumbarton G82 . . . . .50 B2
  Inchinnan PA4 . . . . .93 B3
  Lennoxtown G66 . . . . .57 C4
  Wishaw ML2 . . . . .165 B1
Greenhead St G40 . . . . .117 C2
Greenhill G64 . . . . .98 B4
Greenhill Ave
  Gartcosh G69 . . . . .100 C4
  Glasgow G46 . . . . .136 B1
Greenhill Bsns Ctr ML5 . .102 A1
Greenhill Bsns Pk PA3 . . . .113 B3
Greenhill Cres
  Elderslie PA5,PA5 . . . . . . .112 B1
  Linwood PA3,PA5 . . . . . . .112 B3
Greenhill Ct Irvine KA11 . . .220 A3
  Rutherglen G73 . . . . .138 A4
Greenhill Dr PA3 . . . . .112 B3
Greenhill Ind Est ML5 . . . .122 A3
Greenhill Prim Sch ML5 . .122 A4
Greenhill Rd
  Blackridge EH48 . . . . .107 C2
  Bonnybridge FK4 . . . . .40 A2
  Cleland ML1 . . . . .144 C2
  Paisley PA3 . . . . .113 B3
  Rutherglen G73 . . . . .138 A3
Greenhill Smallholdings
  KA2 . . . . .222 A1
Greenhill St G73 . . . . .138 A4
Greenhill Terr KA22 . . . . . .221 C2
Greenhills KA15 . . . . .172 A1
Greenhills Cres G75 . . . . . .180 A3
Greenhills Prim Sch
  G75 . . . . .180 B3
Greenhills Rd G75 . . . . . . .180 B3
Greenhills Sq G75 . . . . . . .180 A3
Greenholm Ave
  Clarkston G76 . . . . .157 C4
  Uddingston G71 . . . . .140 C4
Greenholm St KA1 . . . . . . .227 C3
Greenholme Ct G44 . . . . . .137 A3
Greenholme St G44 . . . . . . .137 A3
Greenhorn's Well Ave
  FK1 . . . . .41 C2
Greenhorn's Well Cres
  FK1 . . . . .41 C2
Greenhorn's Well Dr FK1 . .41 C2
Greenknowe Pl ML8 . . . . . .186 C3

Greenknowe Pk KA9 233 B2
Greenknowe Rd G43 136 A3
Greenknowe St ML2 186 A3
Greenlady Wlk ML11 215 B2
Greenlaw Ave
Paisley PA1 114 A3
Wishaw ML2 165 B3
Greenlaw Cres PA1 114 A3
Greenlaw Dr
Newton Mearns G77 156 B3
Paisley PA1 114 A3
Greenlaw Ho PA1 114 A3
Greenlaw Ind Est PA3 113 C3
Greenlaw Rd Glasgow G14 94 C3
Newton Mearns G77 156 B3
Greenlea Rd G69 100 A4
Greenlea St G13 95 C3
Greenlees Ct KA24 191 A4
Greenlees Gdns G72 138 C2
Greenlees Gr ML5 122 B3
Greenlees Pk G72 139 A2
Greenlees Rd G72 139 A2
Greenloan Ave G51 115 B4
Greenloan View ML9 185 A1
Greenmoss Pl ML4 142 B3
Greenmount G22 97 A4
Greenmount Dr FK1 66 B3
Greenock Acad PA16 45 B4
Greenock Ave G44 137 A3
Greenock Central Sta
PA15 46 A2
Greenock High Sch PA16 44 B1
Greenock Rd
Bishopton PA7 71 B3
Greenock PA15 46 C1
Inchinnan PA4 93 B3
Langbank PA14 70 B4
Paisley PA3 113 B4
Port Glasgow PA14 47 B1
Greenock West Sta PA15 45 C3
Greenrig G71 140 C3
Greenrig Rd ML11 214 A1
Greenrig St G33 98 B2
Greenrigg Cotts ML7 127 C3
Greenrigg Prim Sch
ML7 127 C3
Greenrigg Rd G67 62 A1
Greenrigg St G71 140 C3
Greens Ave G66 79 B4
Greens Cres G66 79 B4
Greens Rd G67 82 C3
Greenshields Rd G69 120 A3
Greenside
Carmunnock G76 158 C4
Irvine KA11 220 A2
Greenside Ave
Kilbirnie KA25 170 A4
Prestwick KA9 236 B4
Springside KA11 221 A1
Greenside Cl ML11 215 A2
Greenside Cres G33 98 C2
Greenside La ML11 215 A2
Greenside Pl G61 75 B4
Greenside Rd
Clydebank G81 74 A4
Motherwell ML1 143 B4
Wishaw ML2 165 B1
Greenside St Alloa FK10 10 A3
Glasgow G33 98 C2
Motherwell ML1 143 C2
Greenside Terr KA11 221 A1
Greenside Way KA11 220 A2
Greentowers Rd ML11 214 C4
Greentree Dr G69 119 C2
Greentree Pk KA7 239 B2
Greenview St G43 136 B4
Greenway La G72 161 B3
Greenways Ave PA2 113 A1
Greenways Ct PA2 113 A1
Greenwood Acad KA11 220 A1
Greenwood Ave
Cambuslang G72 139 C3
Chryston G69 80 C1
Stirling FK8 7 A4
Greenwood Cres ML5 122 B3
Greenwood Ct G76 157 C3
Greenwood Dr
Bearsden G61 76 A2
Johnstone PA5 131 C4
Greenwood Intc KA11 224 D4
Greenwood Quadrant
G81 74 B1
Greenwood Rd
Clarkston G76 157 B4
Irvine KA11 220 B1
Greenwood St ML7 146 C3
Greenyards Intc G67 62 B1
Greer Quadrant G81 74 A2
Grenada Pl G75 159 A1
Grenadier Gdns ML1 163 B2
Grendon Ct FK8 7 A3
Grendon Gdns FK8 7 A3
Grenville Ct FK1 41 C2
Grenville Dr G72 138 C2
Grenville Rd PA19 44 C3
Gresham View ML1 164 A1
Greta Meek La G66 58 B3
Gretna St G40 118 A2
Grey Pl PA15 45 C3
Greyfriars Ct ML11 214 C2
Greyfriars Rd G71 140 B4
Greyfriars St G32 118 C4
Greygoran FK10 5 B1
Greystone Ave G73 138 B3
Greystone Bauks ML11 214 C2
Greywood St G13 95 C4
Grier Pl ML9 184 C1
Griers Wlk KA11 225 B3
Grierson Cres FK7 6 B3
Grierson La G33 118 B4
Grierson St G33 118 B4
Grieve Croft G72 140 C1
Grieve Rd
Cumbernauld G67 62 A2
Greenock PA16 45 A3
Griffen Ave PA1 112 C3
Griffin Dock Rd KA8 235 C1
Griffin Pl ML4 142 A4
Griffiths St FK1 42 A2
Griffiths Way ML8 186 C2
Griqua Terr G71 141 A1
Grodwell Dr FK12 4 C4
Grogarry Rd G15 75 A2
Grosvenor Cres 10 G12 96 B2
Grosvenor Crescent La 12
G12 96 B2
Grosvenor La
Glasgow G12 96 B2
Greenock PA15 46 B2
Grosvenor Rd PA15 46 B2
Grosvenor Terr 13 G12 96 B2
Grougar Dr KA3 223 A2
Grougar Gdns KA3 223 A2
Grougar Rd KA3 228 B4
Grove Cres Falkirk FK2 24 A1
Larkhall ML9 185 B1
Grove Park Gdns G20 97 A1
Grove Pk G66 79 B2
Grove St FK6 21 B1
Grove The Bishopton PA7 72 A2
Bridge of W PA11 110 C3
Kilbarchan PA10 111 A2
Neilston G78 154 B3
Rutherglen G46 157 A4
Grove Way ML4 141 C2
Grove Wood G71 121 B1
Grove Wynd ML1 143 A2
Groveburn Ave G46 136 A2
Grovepark Ct G20 97 A1
Grovepark Pl G20 97 A1
Grovepark St G20 97 A2
Groves The G64 98 B4
Grovewood Bsns Ctr
ML4 141 C4
Grudie St G34 120 A4
Gryfe Rd
Bridge of W PA11 110 B4
Port Glasgow PA14 68 C4
Gryfe St PA15 46 A1
Gryfebank Ave PA6 91 C1
Gryfebank Cl PA6 91 C1
Gryfebank Cres PA6 91 C1
Gryfebank Way PA6 91 C1
Gryfewood Cres PA6 91 C1
Gryfewood Way PA6 91 C1
Gryffe Ave PA11 90 B1
Gryffe Cres PA2 112 C1
Gryffe Gr PA11 110 B4
Gryffe High Sch PA6 91 A1
Gryffe Rd PA13 89 B4
Gryffe St G44 137 A4
Guildford St G33 99 B1
Guiltreehill KA7 239 A1
Gullane Cres G68 61 C3
Gullane Ct Hamilton ML3 183 A4
Irvine KA11 224 C4
Gullane Pl KA13 207 A2
Gullane St G11 96 A1
Gulliland Ave KA2 225 C1
Gulliland Pl KA12 219 B1
Gullin Dr KA9 236 C3
Gunn Quadrant ML4 141 C2
Gushet Ho ML6 122 C4
Guthrie Ct ML1 163 B3
Guthrie Dr G71 121 A1
Guthrie Pl
East Kilbride G74 159 C1
Rhu G84 15 B2
Torrance G64 57 B1
Guthrie Rd KA21 217 A4
Guthrie St Glasgow G20 96 B3
Hamilton ML3 162 B2
Guy Mannering Rd G84 25 B4
Gyle Pl ML2 165 C2

H

Habbieauld Rd KA3 222 A4
Haberlea Ave G53 135 B2
Haberlea Gdns G53 135 B1
Haddington Gdns KA11 220 A3
Haddington Way ML5 121 C2
Haddow Gr 6 G71 141 A4
Haddow St ML3 162 C2
Hadrian Terr ML1 163 B4
Hagart Rd PA6 91 A1
Hagen Dr ML1 143 C1
Hagg Cres PA5 111 C2
Hagg Pl PA5 111 C2
Hagg Rd PA5 111 C1
Haggs Castle* G41 116 B1
Haggs La G41 116 B1
Haggs Rd G41 116 B1
Haggswood Ave G41 116 B1
Haghill Prim Sch G31 118 A4
Haghill Rd G31 118 B4
Hagholm Rd ML11 215 C4
Hagmill Cres ML5 122 B1
Hagmill Rd ML5 122 A1
Hagthorn Ave KA25 170 A4
Haig Ave FK8 2 A1
Haig Dr G69 119 C2
Haig St Glasgow G21 98 A2
Greenock PA15 45 C3
Hailes Ave G32 119 B3
Haining Ave KA1 228 A3
Haining Rd PA4 94 B2
Haining The PA4 94 B1
Hairmyres Dr G75 179 C4
Hairmyres Hospl G75 179 C4
Hairmyres Pk G75 179 C4
Hairmyres Rdbt G75 158 C1
Hairmyres St G42 117 B1
Hairmyres Sta G75 158 C1
Hairst St PA4 94 B2
Halbeath Ave G15 74 C2
Halbert St G41 116 C1
Halberts Cres FK7 7 A1
Haldane Ave FK9 2 A3
Haldane Ct G83 27 C4
Haldane La 20 G14 95 B2
Haldane Pl G75 180 C4
Haldane Prim Sch G83 27 C4
Haldane St G14 95 B2
Haldane Terr G83 19 C1
Halfmerk N G74 160 A1
Halfmerk S G74 160 A1
Halfmerke Prim Sch
G74 160 A2
Halfway St KA23 190 B3
Halgreen Ave G15 74 C2
Halifax Way 7 PA4 94 B1
Halket Cres FK2 24 B1
Halkett Cres G83 27 C4
Hall Bar Gdns ML8 201 C2
Hall La KA10 230 A2
Hall Pl Lanark ML11 215 A2
Stepps G33 99 C3
Hall Rd Nemphlar ML11 214 A3
Rhu G84 15 B3
Hall St Alexandria G83 27 C2
Clydebank G81 74 A1
Hamilton ML3 162 B1
Motherwell ML1 143 A2
Renton G82 49 B4
Hallbrae St G33 98 C1
Hallcraig St ML6 123 A4
Halley Dr G13 94 C4
Halley Pl G13 94 C4
Halley Sq G13 94 C4
Halley St G13 94 C4
Hallforest St G33 99 A1
Hallglen Prim Sch FK1 42 A1
Hallglen Rd FK1 42 A1
Hallglen Terr FK1 42 A1
Hallgraig Pl ML8 187 B1
Hallhill Cres G33 119 C3
Hallhill Rd Glasgow G32 119 A3
Glasgow, Barlanark G33 119 C3
Glasgow, Garrowhill G69 120 A3
Johnstone PA5 131 B4
Halliburton Cres G34 119 C4
Halliburton Terr G34 120 A4
Hallidale Cres PA4 94 C1
Hallinan Gdns ML2 164 C1
Hallpark FK10 10 B4
Hallrule Dr G52 115 B3
Halls Vennal 3 KA8 235 C1
Hallside Ave G72 139 C3
Hallside Bvd G72 139 C2
Hallside Cres G72 139 C3
Hallside Dr G72 139 C3
Hallside Gdns ML2 165 C2
Hallside Pl G5 117 B2
Hallside Prim Sch G72 139 C2
Hallside Rd G72 139 C2
Hallside St PA9 130 C3
Hallydown Dr G13 95 B3
Halpin Cl ML4 141 B3
Halton Gdns G69 119 C2
Hamersley Pl G75 180 A4
Hamilcomb Rd ML4 142 A2
Hamill Dr G65 60 C4
Hamilton Ave
Glasgow G41 116 B2
Stenhousemuir FK5 23 C2
Hamilton Bsns Pk ML3 162 B3
Hamilton Coll ML3 162 B3
Hamilton Cres Ayr KA7 239 A4
Bearsden G61 75 C4
Bishopton PA7 71 C2
Cambuslang G72 139 B3
Coatbridge ML5 122 A3
Renfrew PA4 94 B3
Stevenston KA20 206 C1
Hamilton Ct KA3 222 A4
Hamilton Dr Airdrie ML6 103 A1
Blantyre G72 161 A3
Bothwell G71 141 A1
Cambuslang G72 139 A3
Erskine PA8 72 C2
Falkirk FK1 42 A2
Glasgow G12 96 C2
Glasgow, Giffnock G46 136 B1
Motherwell ML1 163 C2
Stirling FK9 2 B2
Hamilton Gate PA15 45 C3
Hamilton Gdns KA3 195 C1
Hamilton Gram Sch
ML3 162 B2
Hamilton Int Tech Pk
G72 161 B3
Hamilton Mauoleum*
ML3 162 C3
Hamilton Mus* ML3 162 C2
Hamilton Park Ave G12 96 C2
Hamilton Park N ML3 162 B3
Hamilton Park S ML3 162 B3
Hamilton Pl
East Kilbride G75 180 C4
Hamilton ML3 183 B3
Motherwell ML1 143 A2
Hamilton Pl *continued*
Motherwell, Whittagreen
ML1 143 B2
Hamilton Rd
Bellshill ML4 141 C2
Blantyre G72 161 A3
Bothwell G71 141 A1
Cambuslang G72 139 B2
East Kilbride G72,G74 160 B3
Glasgow G32 119 B1
Larkhall ML9 184 C3
Motherwell ML1 163 B3
Rutherglen G73 138 B4
Stenhousemuir FK2,FK5 23 B3
Hamilton Sch for the Deaf
ML3 162 A1
Hamilton St Carluke ML8 187 C1
Clydebank G81 94 B4
Dumbarton G82 50 A2
Falkirk FK1 41 B3
Glasgow G42 117 B1
Kilwinning KA13 207 C2
Larkhall ML9 185 A2
Paisley PA3 113 C3
Saltcoats KA21 216 C4
Hamilton Terr G81 94 B4
Hamilton View G71 141 A4
Hamilton Way
Greenock PA15 45 C3
Prestwick KA9 233 B1
Stonehouse ML9 198 C1
Hamiltonhill Cres G22 97 A2
Hamiltonhill Rd G22 97 A2
Hamlet G74 160 A3
Hampden Dr G42 137 A4
Hampden La G42 137 A4
Hampden Park Visitors Ctr*
G42 137 A4
Hampden Pk (Queen's Park
FC)* G42 137 A4
Hampden Terr G42 137 A4
Hampden Way 11 PA4 94 B1
Handel Pl 3 G5 117 B2
Hangingshaw Pl G42 137 B4
Hannah Pl G82 27 C1
Hanover Cl G42 137 A4
Hanover Ct Glasgow G1 241 A3
Paisley PA1 114 A3
Hanover Gdns
Bishopbriggs G64 78 A1
Paisley PA1 113 B2
Hanover St Glasgow G1 241 A2
Helensburgh G84 25 A4
Hanson St G31 117 C4
Hapland Ave G53 115 B1
Hapland Rd G53 115 B1
Happyhills KA23 190 B3
Haran Rd G83 19 C1
Harbour Ind Est KA22 205 B1
Harbour La PA3 113 C3
Harbour Pl KA22 205 A1
Harbour Rd
Ardrossan KA22 216 A4
Irvine KA12 219 A1
Paisley PA3 113 C3
Troon KA10 229 B2
Harbour St
Ardrossan KA22 216 A4
Irvine KA12 219 A1
Saltcoats KA21 216 C4
Harburn Pl G23 76 C1
Harbury Pl G14 94 C3
Harcourt Dr G31 118 A4
Hardacres ML11 215 A3
Hardgate Dr G51 115 B4
Hardgate Gdns G51 115 B4
Hardgate Pl G51 115 B4
Hardgate Rd G51 115 B4
Hardie Ave G73 138 B4
Hardie Cres FK7 8 B2
Hardie Ct FK7 7 B2
Hardie St Alexandria G83 27 B4
Blantyre G72 161 B4
Hamilton ML3 162 A1
Motherwell ML1 163 C4
Hardmuir Gdns 1 G66 58 C1
Hardmuir Rd G66 58 C1
Hardridge Ave G52 115 C1
Hardridge Pl G52 115 C1
Hardridge Rd G52 115 C1
Hardy Hill G84 17 A1
Harebell Pl KA7 239 A2
Harefield Dr G14 95 A3
Harelaw Ave
Barrhead G78 134 B1
Glasgow G44 136 C2
Neilston G78 154 B3
Port Glasgow PA14 68 B4
Harelaw Cres PA2 133 B4
Hareleeshill Prim Sch
ML9 185 B1
Hareleeshill Rd ML9 185 B1
Hareshaw Dr KA3 223 A3
Hareshaw Gdns KA3 223 A3
Hareshaw Rd ML1 144 B2
Harestanes Gdns G66 59 A1
Harestanes Ind Est ML8 201 C3
Harestanes Prim Sch
G66 59 A1
Harestanes Rd ML8 201 C2
Harestone Cres ML2 165 B1
Harestone Rd ML2 165 B1
Harfield Dr G33 119 C3
Harfield Gdns G33 119 C3
Harhill St G51 116 A4
Harkins Ave G72 161 B4
Harkness Ave G66 58 A3
Harland Cotts G14 95 B2
Harland St G14 95 B2
Harlands The FK10 9 C4
Harlaw Gdns G64 78 B1
Harley Ct FK2 42 A4
Harley Pl KA21 205 C1
Harley St G51 116 B3
Harling Dr KA10 229 C1
Harmetray St G22 97 B3
Harmony Ct G51 116 A4
Harmony Pl G51 116 A4
Harmony Row 1 G51 116 A4
Harmony Sq G51 116 A4
Harmsworth St G11 95 C1
Harper Cres ML2 165 C2
Harperland Dr KA1 227 B4
Harport St G46 135 C2
Harrier Wynd PA16 45 A2
Harriet Pl G43 136 A3
Harriet Rd KA3 223 A1
Harriet St G73 138 A4
Harrington Rd G74 159 C1
Harris Cl G77 156 A3
Harris Cres G60 73 A3
Harris Ct Alloa FK10 10 A3
Irvine KA11 225 B4
Harris Dr G60 73 A3
Harris Gdns G60 73 B3
Harris Pl Airdrie ML6 123 B3
Kilmarnock KA3 223 A3
Harris Quadrant ML2 165 C3
Harris Rd Glasgow G23 76 C1
Old Kilpatrick G60 73 B3
Port Glasgow PA14 69 A4
Harris Terr KA11 225 B4
Harrison Dr G51 116 A3
Harrison Pl Falkirk FK1 41 C3
Renton G82 27 B1
Harrow Ct G15 74 C2
Harrow Pl G15 74 C2
Hart St Clydebank G81 74 B4
Glasgow G31 118 C3
Linwood PA3 112 B3
Hart Wynd FK7 7 C1
Hartfield Cres G78 154 C4
Hartfield Ct G82 50 A2
Hartfield Gdns G82 50 A2
Hartfield Rd KA7 238 C3
Hartfield Terr
Paisley PA2 114 A1
Shotts ML7 167 A4
Harthall KA8 236 C1
Harthill Ind Est ML7 127 B3
Harthill Prim Sch ML7 127 C3
Harthill Rd EH48 107 B1
Hartlaw Cres G52 115 A3
Hartree Ave G13 94 C4
Hartstone Pl G53 135 A4
Hartstone Rd G53 135 A4
Hartstone Terr G53 135 A4
Hartwood Gdns
Hartwood ML7 146 A1
Newton Mearns G77 156 B1
Hartwood Hospl ML7 145 C2
Hartwood Rd ML7 145 C1
Hartwood Sta ML7 145 C2
Hartwoodhill Hospl
ML7 146 A2
Harvest Dr ML1 163 B2
Harvest St FK9 2 A2
Harvey Cotts PA12 129 B1
Harvey Ct PA12 129 B1
Harvey Gdns KA22 205 B2
Harvey Sq PA12 129 B1
Harvey St
Ardrossan KA22 205 B2
Glasgow G4 97 B1
Harvey Terr PA12 129 B1
Harvey Way ML4 142 B4
Harvey Wynd FK8 2 A1
Harvie Ave G77 156 B3
Harvie St G51 116 B3
Harvies L Ctr* KA21 217 A4
Harwood Gdns G69 81 A2
Harwood St G32 118 C4
Hastie St G3 96 B1
Hastings G75 180 A4
Hatfield Ct PA13 89 B4
Hatfield Dr G12 96 A3
Hathaway Dr G46 136 A1
Hathaway La G20 96 C3
Hathaway St G20 96 C3
Hathersage Ave G69 120 A3
Hathersage Dr G69 120 A3
Hathersage Gdns 15
G69 120 A3
Hatton Gdns G52 115 A2
Hatton Pl ML1 143 B1
Hatton Terr ML1 143 B1
Hattonhill ML1 143 B1
Hattonrigg Rd ML4 142 A4
Haugh Gdns FK2 24 A1
Haugh Pl ML3 162 C1
Haugh Rd Glasgow G3 116 B4
Kilsyth G65 60 B4
Stirling FK9 2 A1
Haugh St FK2 24 A1
Haughburn Pl G53 135 A4
Haughburn Rd G53 135 A4
Haughburn Terr G53 135 B4
Haughs Way FK6 21 C1
Haughton Ave G65 60 C4
Haughview Rd ML1 163 A3
Haupland Rd KA22 205 A3
Havelock La G11 96 B1
Havelock Pk G75 159 A1

Havelock Pl G84 ....16 C1
Havelock St Glasgow G11 ..96 B1
Helensburgh G84 ....16 C1
Haven Pk G75 ....179 C3
Haven The FK7 ....9 C2
Havoc Rd G82 ....49 B2
Hawbank Rd G14 ....159 A2
Hawbank Rdbt G75 ....159 A1
Hayward Ave ML8 ....202 B4
Hawick Ave PA2 ....113 A1
Hawick Cres ML9 ....185 A1
Hawick Dr ML5 ....122 B2
Hawick St Glasgow G13 ...165 B3
Wishaw ML2 ....165 B3
Hawkhead Ave PA2 ....114 A1
Hawkhead Hospl PA2 ......114 B1
Hawkhead Rd PA1,PA2 ....114 A2
Hawkhead Sta PA1 ....114 A2
Hawkhill Ave KA8 ....236 C1
Hawkhill Avenue La
KA8 ....236 A1
Hawkhill Dr KA20 ....206 C1
Hawkhill Pl KA20 ....206 C1
Hawkhill Rd FK10 ....10 B3
Hawkhill Ret Pk KA20 .....206 C1
Hawksland Wlk ML3 ....162 C1
Hawkwood G75 ....180 C3
Hawkwood Rd ML6 ....102 C2
Hawley Rd FK1 ....42 B2
Hawthorn Ave
Bearsden G61 ....76 A4
Bishopbriggs G64 ....98 A4
Dumbarton G82 ....49 A3
Erskine PA8 ....93 C4
Johnstone PA5 ....112 A1
Kirkintilloch G66 ....79 B3
Prestwick KA9 ....236 B4
Wishaw ML2 ....166 B3
Hawthorn Cres
Beith KA15 ....171 A4
Erskine PA8 ....93 C4
Fallin FK7 ....8 B2
Stirling FK8 ....1 C1
Hawthorn Ct
Clarkston G76 ....157 C3
Kilwinning KA13 ....207 C1
Hawthorn Dr Airdrie ML6 123 B3
Ayr KA7 ....239 B2
Banknock FK4 ....38 C1
Barrhead G78 ....155 B4
Denny FK6 ....42 B2
Falkirk FK1 ....41 C2
Harthill ML7 ....127 C3
Motherwell ML1 ....143 A2
Shotts ML7 ....147 B2
Stevenston KA20 ....206 C2
Wishaw ML2 ....166 B3
Hawthorn Gdns
Bellshill ML4 ....142 B2
Cambuslang G72 ....139 C2
Lenzie G66 ....157 C3
Larkhall ML9 ....185 B1
Prestwick KA9 ....236 B4
Hawthorn Gr ML3 ....186 C3
Hawthorn Pl
Blantyre G72 ....161 C4
Shotts ML7 ....167 A4
Troon KA10 ....229 C2
Hawthorn Prim Sch G72 ..97 B2
Hawthorn Quadrant G22 ..97 B3
Hawthorn Rd
Clarkston G76 ....157 C3
Cumbernauld G67 ....62 C2
Erskine PA8 ....93 C4
Hawthorn Sq KA1 ....227 B4
Hawthorn St
Clydebank G81 ....74 A2
Glasgow G22 ....97 B3
Torrance G64 ....57 B1
Hawthorn Terr
East Kilbride G75 ....180 A3
Uddingston G71 ....141 A4
Hawthorn Way
Dumbarton G82 ....49 A2
Erskine PA8 ....93 C4
Hamilton ML3 ....183 C2
Milton of Campsie 58 B3
Hawthorn Wlk G72 ....138 B3
Hawthornden Gdns G23 ...76 C1
Hawthorne Pl
Gourock PA17 ....44 A3
Stenhousemuir FK5 ....23 B1
Hawthornhill Rd G82 ....49 B3
Hay Ave PA7 ....72 B2
Hay Dr PA5 ....112 A2
Hay Hill KA8 ....236 C1
Hay St FK15 ....45 C2
Hayburn Cres G11 ....96 A2
Hayburn Gate G11 ....96 A1
Hayburn St G11 ....96 A1
Hayes Gr G83 ....27 C3
Hayfield FK2 ....42 B4
Hayfield Ct G5 ....117 B2
Hayfield Rd FK2 ....117 B2
Hayfield St G5 ....117 B2
Hayfield Terr FK6 ....39 C4
Hayford Mills KA3 ....6 B3
Hayford Pl FK7 ....6 B3
Hayhill Rd G74 ....179 B4
Hayle Gdns G69 ....80 C2
Haylie Sta G14 ....95 C1
Haymarket St G32 ....118 C4

Hayocks Prim Sch KA20 .206 C1
Hayocks Rd KA20 ....206 C1
Hayocks Rdbt KA20 ....206 C1
Haypark Rd FK6 ....39 B3
Haysholm Sch KA12 ......219 C2
Haystack Pl G66 ....79 C2
Hayston Cres G22 ....97 A3
Hayston Rd
Cumbernauld G68 ....61 C2
Kirkintilloch G66 ....79 A4
Hayston St G22 ....97 A3
Hayward Ave ML8 ....202 B4
Hayward Ct ML8 ....202 B4
Haywood St G22 ....97 B3
Hazel Ave
Ardrossan KA22 ....205 B2
Bearsden G61 ....76 A4
Dumbarton G82 ....49 A3
Glasgow G44 ....136 C2
Johnstone PA5 ....112 A1
Kilmarnock KA1 ....227 B4
Lenzie G66 ....79 B3
Hazel Bank G66 ....98 A4
Hazel Cres FK6 ....21 B2
Hazel Dene G64 ....98 A4
Hazel Gdns ML1 ....163 C2
Hazel Gr Falkirk FK2 ....42 B4
Kirkintilloch G66 ....79 B3
Law ML8 ....186 C3
Shotts ML7 ....147 A2
Hazel Path ML1 ....144 A1
Hazel Pk ML3 ....162 C1
Hazel Rd Banknock FK4 ...38 C1
Cumbernauld G67 ....62 B2
Hazel Terr Gourock PA19 ..44 B3
Uddingston G71 ....141 A4
Hazel Wood ML2 ....165 B3
Hazelbank
Motherwell ML1 ....143 A3
Plains ML6 ....103 C2
Hazelbank Gdns FK8 ....2 A1
Hazelbank Wlk ML6 ......122 B4
Hazeldean Cres ML2 ......165 B3
Hazeldene Pk KA13 ......207 C2
Hazelfield Gr ML6 ....123 C1
Hazelgrove KA13 ....208 A2
Hazella Dr G46 ....136 C2
Hazelmere Rd PA13 ....89 A4
Hazelton ML1 ....163 B3
Hazelwood Ave
Bridge of W PA11 ....110 C4
Newton Mearns G77 .....156 C2
Paisley PA2 ....133 C4
Hazelwood Dr G72 ....161 B4
Hazelwood Gdns G73 ....138 B2
Hazelwood La PA11 ......110 B4
Hazelwood Rd Ayr KA7 ..238 C3
Bridge of W PA11 ....110 B4
Glasgow G41 ....116 B2
Head of Muir Prim Sch
FK6 ....39 B3
Head St KA15 ....171 B4
Headhouse Ct G75 ....180 C4
Headhouse Gn G75 ......180 C4
Headlands Gr KA15 ......171 B4
Headlesscross Rd EH47 .147 C1
Headrigg Gdns KA23 .....190 B3
Headrigg Rd KA23 ....190 B3
Headsmuir Ave ML8 .....187 B1
Healthcare International
(HCI) G81 ....73 C1
Health Ave
Bishopbriggs G64 ....98 A4
Heath Rd ML9 ....185 A2
Heathcliffe Ave G72 .....140 B1
Heathcot Ave G15 ....74 C1
Heathcot Pl G15 ....74 C1
Heather Ave
Alexandria G83 ....27 C3
Barrhead G78 ....134 A3
Bearsden G61 ....75 C4
Clydebank G81 ....74 A4
Motherwell ML1 ....143 A3
Shieldhill FK1 ....83 B2
Heather Dr G66 ....79 A2
Heather Gdns G66 ....79 A2
Heather Gr G75 ....180 C4
Heather Pk ML7 ....239 B2
Heather Pl
Johnstone PA5 ....112 A1
Kilmarnock KA1 ....227 B4
Kirkintilloch G66 ....79 A2
Heather Row ML6 ....187 C2
Heather View G66 ....79 A2
Heather Way ML1 ....143 A2
Heatherbank Wlk ML6 ...122 B4
Heatherbrae G64 ....77 C3
Heatherdale Gdns FK6 ....39 C4
Heatherhouse Ind Est
KA12 ....224 B4
Heatherstone Bank
KA11 ....220 B1
Heatherstane Wlk KA11 .220 B1
Heatherstane Bank
KA11 ....220 B1
Heathery Knowe G75 ....180 C4

Heathery Knowe Prim Sch
G75 ....180 C4
Heathery Lea Ave ML5 ...122 B2
Heathery Rd ML2 ....164 C2
Heatheryknowe Rd
Coatbridge G69 ....120 C4
Glasgow G69 ....120 C4
Heathfield ML2 ....186 A4
Heathfield Ave G69 ....81 A1
Heathfield Dr G62 ....155 B2
Heathfield Ind Est KA8 ..236 B2
Heathfield Prim Sch
KA8 ....236 A3
Heathfield St G33 ....119 B4
Heathpark KA8 ....236 B2
Heathside Rd G46 ....156 A1
Heathwood Dr G46 ......136 A2
Hecla Ave G15 ....74 C2
Hecla Pl G15 ....74 C2
Hecla Sq G15 ....74 C2
Hector Rd G41 ....136 B4
Hedges The FK1 ....41 C3
Heggies Ave PA14 ....69 A4
Heights Rd G48 ....107 B2
Helen St G51 ....116 A3
Helen Way G83 ....27 C1
Helen Wynd ML9 ....185 A1
Helen's Terr KA13 ....207 C1
Helena Pl G76 ....156 C3
Helensburgh Central Sta
G84 ....16 B1
Helensburgh Dr G13 ......95 C3
Helensburgh Upper Sta
G84 ....16 B2
Helenslea G72 ....139 C2
Helenslea Pl ML4 ....141 C2
Helensburgh Cres G82 ...49 B2
Helenton Ct G31 ....118 B3
Helenvale St G31 ....118 B3
Helmsdale Ave G72 ......140 B2
Helmsdale Ct G72 ....139 B3
Helmsdale Dr PA2 ....112 C1
Hemlock St G13 ....95 C3
Hemmingen Ct ML8 .....187 C2
Hemphill View KA2 ....221 C2
Henderland Rd G61 ....75 C1
Henderson Ave
Alloa FK10 ....10 A4
Cambuslang G72 ....139 C3
Henderson Pl FK12 ....5 A4
Henderson Rd KA10 .....229 C1
Henderson St
Airdrie ML6 ....123 A4
Alloa FK10 ....10 A4
Clydebank G81 ....94 C4
Coatbridge ML5 ....121 C3
Glasgow G20 ....96 C2
Paisley PA1 ....113 B3
Henderson Terr PA19 .....44 C3
Hendry St FK2 ....42 A4
Hennings The FK10 ....5 B1
Henrietta St G14 ....95 B2
Henry Bell Gn □ G75 ....180 C4
Henry St Alva FK12 ....5 A3
Barrhead G78 ....134 A2
Hepburn Hill ML3 ....183 B4
Hepburn Rd G52 ....115 A4
Hepburn Way KA11 .....220 B4
Herald Ave G13 ....75 B1
Herald Gr ML1 ....163 B2
Herald St KA22 ....216 A4
Herald Way □ PA4 ....94 B1
Herbert St G20 ....96 C2
Herbertshire St FK6 ....21 C1
Herbertson Cres KA12 ..219 B2
Herbertson Gr G72 ......140 B1
Herbertson St
Blantyre G72 ....161 C4
Glasgow G5 ....117 A3
Herbison Ct ML9 ....185 A2
Hercules Way PA4 ....94 A4
Herdshill Ave FK1 ....66 B3
Heriot Ave PA2 ....132 C4
Heriot Cres G64 ....78 A2
Heriot Ct PA2 ....132 C4
Heriot Prim Sch PA2 ....132 C4
Heriot Rd G66 ....79 B2
Heriot Way PA2 ....132 C4
Heritage Ct G77 ....156 C3
Heritage Dr FK2 ....24 A2
Heritage View ML5 ......121 C4
Heritage Way ML5 ......121 C4
Herma St G23 ....96 C4
Hermes Way ML4 ....142 C3
Hermiston Ave G32 ......119 B3
Hermiston Pl
Glasgow G32 ....119 B3
Motherwell ML1 ....164 A4
Hermiston Rd G32 ....119 A3
Hermitage Acad G84 .....25 B4
Hermitage Ave G13 ....95 B3
Hermitage Cres ML5 ....122 A2
Hermitage Prim Sch G84 .16 B2
Hermitage Rd G84 ....16 B2
Herndon Ct G77 ....157 A3
Heron Ct G81 ....74 A3
Heron Pl PA5 ....131 B4
Heron Rd PA16 ....45 A2
Heron Way PA4 ....94 B1
Heronswood KA13 ....207 C3

Herries Rd G41 ....116 B1
Herriet St G41 ....116 C2
Herriot Ave KA25 ....149 A2
Herriot St ML5 ....121 C4
Herschell St G13 ....95 C3
Hertford Ave G12 ....96 A3
Hervey St FK10 ....10 A4
Heston Pl KA3 ....223 C3
Heugh St FK1 ....42 A2
Hewett Cres PA6 ....91 B1
Hexham Gdns G41 ....116 B1
Heys St G78 ....134 B1
Hibernia St FK6 ....45 B2
Hickman St G42 ....117 B1
Hickman Terr G42 ....117 B1
Hickory Cres G71 ....141 B4
Hickory St G22 ....97 C3
High Avon St ML9 ....184 C2
High Banton Rd G65 ......37 B2
High Barholm PA10 ......111 A2
High Barrwood Rd G65 ...60 C4
High Beeches G76 ....158 C4
High Blantyre Prim Sch
G72 ....161 C3
High Blantyre Rd G72,
ML3 ....161 C3
High Burnside Ave ML5 .121 C3
High Calside PA2 ....113 C2
High Carnegie Rd PA4 ...94 C1
High Coats ML5 ....122 A4
High Common Rd G74,
G75 ....181 A4
High Cotts G64 ....78 A3
High Craigends G65 ......60 C4
High Flender Rd G76 ....157 B3
High Glencairn St KA1 ..222 C4
High Graighall Rd G4 .....97 A1
High Kirk View PA5 ......111 C1
High Mains Ave G82 ......50 B2
High Mair PA4 ....94 B1
High Mdw ML8 ....188 B3
High Mill Rd ML8 ....188 B4
High Murray Gr G72 .....139 B3
High Overton St ML9 ....200 B2
High Parks Cres ML3 ....183 B3
High Parksail PA4 ....93 B4
High Patrick St ML3 .....162 C2
High Pleasance ML9 .....185 A2
High Rd Ayr KA8 ....236 C2
Motherwell ML1 ....163 C4
Paisley PA2 ....113 B2
Saltcoats KA20,KA21 ....206 A1
Stevenston KA20 ....206 B1
High Sch of Glasgow (Jun
Sch) G61 ....75 C3
High Sch of Glasgow The
G13 ....95 B2
High St Airdrie ML6 ......122 C4
Airth FK2 ....14 B2
Alloa FK10 ....10 A3
Bonnybridge FK4 ....40 A3
Carluke ML8 ....187 C1
Clackmannan FK10 ....10 C2
Dumbarton G82 ....49 C2
Falkirk FK1 ....42 A2
Glasgow G1 ....241 B2
Greenock PA15 ....45 C3
Irvine KA12 ....219 B1
Johnstone PA5 ....112 A1
Kilbirnie KA25 ....149 A2
Kilmacolm PA13 ....69 B1
Kilmarnock KA3 ....223 A1
Lanark ML11 ....215 A2
Lochwinnoch PA12 ....129 B1
Motherwell ML1 ....143 C2
Neilston G78 ....154 C4
Paisley PA1 ....113 C2
Renfrew PA4 ....94 C2
Rutherglen G73 ....138 A4
Shotts ML7 ....146 C2
Slamannan FK1 ....86 A4
Stewarton KA3 ....195 C1
High Station Ct FK1 ....42 A2
High Station Rd FK1 ......42 A2
High Street Sta □ 241 B2
High View Gr FK1 ....66 B2
High Whitehills Rd G75 .180 C3
High Wood Gdns ML4 ...141 C4
Highburgh Ave ML11 ...215 A2
Highburgh Ct ML11 .....215 A2
Highburgh Dr G73 ....138 B3
Highburgh Rd G12 ....96 B1
Highcraig Ave PA5 ....111 B1
Highcroft Ave G44 ....137 B3
Highcross Ave ML5 ......121 C3
Highdykes Prim Sch G83 28 A1
Higherness Way ML5 ...121 C2
Highet Gdns KA12 ....219 A2
Highet St KA3 ....222 C1
Highfield Ave
Kilmarnock KA3 ....223 A2
Kirkintilloch G66 ....58 C1
Paisley PA2 ....133 B4
Prestwick KA9 ....236 B4
Highfield Cres
Motherwell ML1 ....164 A4
Paisley PA2 ....133 B4
Kirkintilloch G66 ....58 C1
Highfield Dr
Clarkston G76 ....157 B4
Glasgow G12 ....96 A3
Glasgow G73 ....138 B2
Rutherglen G73 ....138 B2
Stevenston KA20 ....206 C1
Highfield Gr □ G66 ....58 C1
Highfield Pl
East Kilbride G74 ....159 C2
Glasgow G12 ....96 A3

Highfield Pl continued
Irvine KA11 ....219 C3
Highfield Rd Ayr KA8 ....236 C2
Ayr, Belmont KA7 ....239 A2
Kirkintilloch G66 ....58 C1
Larkhall ML9 ....185 A2
Highfield St KA13 ....207 C2
Highholm Ave PA14 ....47 A1
Highholm Prim Sch PA14 47 A1
Highholm St PA14 ....47 A1
Highland Ave G72 ....161 B4
Highland Dykes Cres
FK4 ....40 A3
Highland Dykes Dr FK4 ..40 A3
Highland La G51 ....116 B4
Highstonehall Rd ML3 ..162 A1
Highthorne Cres KA3 ....190 C3
Hilary Cres KA7 ....239 A3
Hilary Dr G69 ....119 C3
Hilda Cres G33 ....98 C2
Hill Ct Ayr KA7 ....156 B2
Hill Cres G76 ....157 C3
Hill Dr G76 ....178 C2
Hill House Rd FK6 ....39 C4
Hill House The* G84 .....16 C2
Hillcote KA11 ....219 C3
Highmill Prim Sch ML8 .187 C1
Hillcrest ML1 ....143 A2
Hillcrest Ave
Clydebank G81 ....74 A4
Coatbridge ML5 ....122 B3
Cumbernauld G67 ....62 B2
Glasgow G44 ....136 C2
Glasgow, Carmyle G32 ...139 A4
Paisley PA2 ....133 B3
Wishaw ML2 ....164 C2
Hillcrest Ct G67 ....61 C1
Hillcrest Dr Alloa FK10 ...10 B3
Newton Mearns G77 .....157 A3
Stevenston KA20 ....206 C1
Hillcrest Pl Denny FK6 ....21 C1
Kilwinning KA13 ....207 C2
Hillcrest Rd Bearsden G61 75 C2
Falkirk FK1 ....41 C1
Glasgow G32 ....139 B4
Queenzieburn G65 ....59 C4
Uddingston G71 ....141 A4
Hillcrest St G62 ....55 A1
Hillcrest Terr G71 ....141 B2
Hillcrest View ML9 ....185 A2
Hillcroft Terr □ G64 ......97 C4
Hillend Cres
Clarkston G76 ....157 B3
Clydebank G81 ....73 C4
Hillend Dr PA15 ....46 B2
Hillend Pl PA15 ....46 B2
Hillend Rd Clarkston G76 .157 B3
Glasgow G22 ....97 A4
Rutherglen G73 ....138 A3
Hillfoot Ave Bearsden G61 75 C2
Dumbarton G82 ....50 B2
Rutherglen G73 ....138 A4
Wishaw ML2 ....165 B4
Hillfoot Cres Ayr KA7 ...239 A3
Wishaw ML2 ....164 C2
Hillfoot Dr Bearsden G61 75 C3
Coatbridge ML5 ....121 B3

Hillfoot Dr *continued*
Howwood PA9 130 C3
Wishaw ML2 165 B4
Hillfoot Gdns
Uddingston G71 140 C4
Wishaw ML2 165 B4
Hillfoot Rd Airdrie ML6 123 A3
Ayr KA7 239 B3
Hillfoot St G31 118 A4
Hillfoot Sta G61 76 A3
Hillfoot Terr ML8 188 A1
Hillfoots Rd FK9 2 C2
Hillhead Ave
Banknock FK4 38 C2
Carluke ML8 188 A1
Chryston G69 80 C1
Motherwell ML1 143 A1
Rutherglen G73 138 A2
Hillhead Cres
Hamilton ML3 161 C2
Motherwell ML1 143 A1
Hillhead Dr Airdrie ML6 123 A3
Falkirk FK1 41 C1
Motherwell ML1 143 A1
Hillhead High Sch G12 96 C1
Hillhead Pl G73 138 A2
Hillhead Prim Sch
Glasgow G12 96 B2
Kilmarnock KA3 222 C2
Kirkintilloch G66 79 C4
Hillhead Rd Glasgow G21 98 B4
Kirkintilloch G66 58 C1
Stevenston KA20 206 C2
Hillhead Sq KA3 222 C2
Hillhead St Glasgow G12 96 B1
Milngavie G62 55 A1
Hillhead Terr ML3 161 C2
Hillhead Underground Sta G12 96 B2
Hillhouse Cres ML3 161 C2
Hillhouse Farm Gate ML11 214 C3
Hillhouse Farm Rd ML11 214 C2
Hillhouse Gate ML8 202 B4
Hillhouse Gdns KA10 229 C3
Hillhouse Pk Ind Est ML3 161 C2
Hillhouse Pl KA3 195 B1
Hillhouse Rd
Hamilton ML3 161 C2
Troon KA10 229 C3
Hillhouse St G21 98 A3
Hillhouse Terr ML3 161 C2
Hillhouseridge Rd ML7 146 B3
Hillington East Sta G52 115 A3
Hillington Gdns G52 115 B2
Hillington Ind Est
Glasgow G52 115 A4
Paisley PA3 114 C4
Hillington Park Cir G52 115 B3
Hillington Prim Sch G52 115 A3
Hillington Quadrant G52 115 A3
Hillington Rd
Glasgow G52 115 A4
Renfrew G52 94 C1
Hillington Rd S G52 115 A3
Hillington Terr G52 115 A3
Hillington West Sta G52 114 C4
Hillkirk Pl G21 97 C2
Hillkirk St G21 97 C2
Hillmoss KA3 222 A4
Hillneuk Ave G61 76 A3
Hillneuk Dr G61 76 A3
Hillocks Pl KA10 229 D4
Hillpark KA6 237 C3
Hillpark Ave PA2 113 B1
Hillpark Cres FK7 7 B1
Hillpark Dr
Bannockburn FK7 7 B1
Glasgow G43 136 B3
Kilmarnock KA3 222 C1
Hillpark Rise KA13 207 A2
Hillpark Sec Sch G43 136 B3
Hillrigg ML6 83 B1
Hillrigg Ave ML6 123 B4
Hillsborough Rd G69 119 C3
Hillshaw Foot KA11 220 B1
Hillshaw Gn KA11 220 B1
Hillside Alloa FK10 5 B1
Croy G65 60 C2
Houston PA6 111 C4
West Kilbride KA23 190 B2
Hillside Ave
Alexandria G83 27 B2
Bearsden G61 75 C3
Clarkston G76 157 B4
Kilmacolm PA13 69 B1
Hillside Cotts
Dalry KA24 191 C4
Glenboig ML5 101 C3
Hillside Cres
Coatbridge ML5 121 C2
Hamilton ML3 162 B1
Motherwell ML1 143 B2
Neilston G78 154 B4
Prestwick KA9 236 B4
Hillside Ct Glasgow G46 135 C2
Stevenston KA20 217 B4
Hillside Dr Barrhead G78 134 A2
Bearsden G61 76 A3
Bishopbriggs G64 78 A1
Blackridge EH48 107 B2
Port Glasgow PA14 47 A1
Hillside Gardens La 6 G11 96 A2
Hillside Gr G78 134 A1
Hillside Pk G81 74 A3
Hillside Pl
Blackridge EH48 107 B2
Motherwell ML1 143 B2
Hillside Quadrant G43 136 A3
Hillside Rd Barrhead G78 134 A2
Cardross G82 26 A1
Glasgow G43 136 A3
Gourock PA19 44 B4
Greenock PA15 46 A1
Neilston G78 154 B4
Paisley PA2 114 A1
Hillside St KA20 217 B4
Hillside Terr Alloa FK10 10 A4
Hamilton ML3 162 B1
Milton of C G66 58 A3
Hillswick Cres G22 97 A4
Hilltop Ave ML4 142 A4
Hilltop Cres PA19 44 C3
Hilltop Pl KA7 239 B3
Hilltop Rd Chryston G69 80 C1
Gourock PA19 44 C3
Hillview Banton G65 37 B2
Greengairs ML6 83 C1
Hillview Ave Kilsyth G65 60 B4
Lennoxtown G66 57 C4
Hillview Cotts G65 59 C2
Hillview Cres
Bellshill ML4 142 A4
Larkhall ML9 185 A1
Uddingston G71 140 C4
Hillview Dr Blantyre G72 140 B1
Bridge of A FK9 2 A3
Clarkston G76 157 C4
Helensburgh G84 16 B2
Hillview Gdns G64 98 B4
Hillview Pl Clarkston G76 157 C4
Fallin FK7 8 B2
Newton Mearns G77 156 B2
Hillview Rd
Bridge of W PA11 110 C4
Elderslie PA5 112 B1
High Bonnybridge FK4 40 B2
Stenhousemuir FK5 23 B2
Hillview St G32 118 C3
Hillview Terr FK10 10 B3
Hilton FK7 12 C4
Hilton Cres FK10 10 B4
Hilton Ct Ardrossan KA21 205 C2
Bishopbriggs G64 78 A2
Hilton Gdns G13 95 C4
Hilton Pk G64 77 C2
Hilton Rd Alloa FK10 10 B4
Bishopbriggs G64 78 A2
Milngavie G62 54 C1
Hilton Terr
Bishopbriggs G64 77 C2
Cambuslang G72 138 C2
Fallin FK7 8 B2
Glasgow G13 95 C4
Hiltonbank St ML3 162 A2
Hindog Pl KA24 191 A4
Hindsland Rd ML9 185 A1
Hinshaw St G20 97 A2
Hinshelwood Dr G51 116 A3
Hinshelwood Pl G51 116 A3
Hirsel Pl G71 141 A1
Hirst Cres FK7 8 B2
Hirst Ct FK7 8 B2
Hirst Gdns ML7 146 B3
Hirst Rd ML7 126 B2
Hirstrigg Cotts ML7 126 A2
Hobart Cres G81 73 B3
Hobart Quadrant ML2 165 C2
Hobart Rd G75 180 B4
Hobart St G22 97 A2
Hobden St G21 98 A2
Hoddam Ave G45 138 A2
Hoddam Terr G45 138 A2
Hodge St FK1 42 A2
Hoey Dr ML2 186 B4
Hogan Ct G81 73 C3
Hogan Way ML1 143 C1
Hogarth Ave
Glasgow G32 118 B4
Saltcoats KA21 205 C1
Hogarth Cres G32 118 B4
Hogarth Ct G83 27 C3
Hogarth Dr G32 118 B4
Hogarth Gdns G32 118 B4
Hogg Ave PA5 111 C1
Hogg Rd ML6 123 B2
Hogg St ML6 123 A4
Hogganfield St G33 98 B1
Holbourne Pl FK11 4 A4
Hole Farm Rd PA15,PA16 45 B2
Holeburn La G43 136 B3
Holeburn Rd G43 136 B3
Holehills Dr ML6 103 A1
Holehills Pl ML6 103 A1
Holehouse Brae G78 154 B4
Holehouse Dr
Glasgow G13 95 A3
Kilbirnie KA25 149 A2
Holehouse Rd
Eaglesham G76 178 C3
East Kilbride G74 179 A4
Kilmarnock KA3 228 A4
Holehouse Terr G78 154 B4
Holland St G2 240 B3
Hollandbush Ave FK4 38 C2
Hollandbush Cres FK4 38 C2
Hollandbush Gr ML3 183 B4
Hollandhurst Rd ML5 101 C1
Hollinwell Rd G23 76 B1
Hollow Pk KA7 239 A1
Hollowglen Rd G32 119 A3
Hollows Ave PA2 132 C4
Hollows Cres PA2 132 C4
Hollows The G46 136 A1
Holly Ave Milton of C G66 58 A3
Stenhousemuir FK5 23 C2
Holly Bank KA7 239 B3
Holly Dr Dumbarton G82 49 A3
Glasgow G21 98 A2
Holly Gr Banknock FK4 38 C1
Bellshill ML4 142 C3
Holly Pl Johnstone PA5 132 A4
Kilmarnock KA1 222 B1
Holly St Airdrie ML6 123 B3
Clydebank G81 74 A2
Hollybank Pl G72 139 A2
Hollybank St G21 98 A1
Hollybrook Pl 6 G42 117 A1
Hollybrook Sch G42 117 A1
Hollybrook St G42 117 A1
Hollybush Ave PA2 133 A4
Hollybush Pl KA3 223 A3
Hollybush Rd G52 114 C3
Hollymount G61 75 C1
Hollytree Gdns G66 57 B4
Holm Ave Paisley PA2 113 C1
Uddingston G71 140 C4
Holm Cres KA3 213 A2
Holm Ct ML8 201 A1
Holm Gdns ML4 142 B2
Holm La G74 159 C1
Holm Pl Larkhall ML9 184 C1
Linwood PA3 112 A4
Holm Rd ML8 201 A1
Holm St Carluke ML8 187 C1
Glasgow G2 240 C2
Motherwell ML1 143 A2
Stewarton KA3 211 C4
Holmbank Ave G41 136 B4
Holmbrae Ave G71 140 C4
Holmbrae Rd G71 140 C4
Holmbyne Ct G45 137 A1
Holmbyre Rd G45 137 A1
Holmbyre Terr G45 137 B1
Holmcrest ML8 201 A1
Holmes Ave PA4 94 B1
Holmes Cres KA1 227 B3
Holmes Farm Rd KA1 227 B3
Holmes Park Ave KA1 227 B3
Holmes Park Cres KA1 227 B3
Holmes Park Gdns KA1 227 B3
Holmes Park View KA1 227 B3
Holmes Park Wynd KA1 227 B3
Holmes Quadrant ML4 142 A2
Holmes Rd KA1 227 B3
Holmes Village KA1 227 B3
Holmfauld Rd G51 95 C1
Holmfauldhead Dr G51 115 C4
Holmfauldhead Pl 3 G51 115 C4
Holmfield G66 79 C4
Holmhead KA25 170 A4
Holmhead Cres G44 137 A3
Holmhead Pl G44 137 A3
Holmhead Rd G44 137 A3
Holmhill Ave G72 139 A2
Holmhills Dr G72 138 C2
Holmhills Gdns G72 138 C2
Holmhills Gr G72 138 C2
Holmhills Pl G72 138 C2
Holmhills Rd G72 138 C2
Holmhills Terr G72 138 C2
Holmlands Pl KA1 227 B3
Holmlea Dr KA1 227 C3
Holmlea Pl KA1 227 C3
Holmlea Prim Sch G44 137 A3
Holmlea Rd G42,G44 137 A4
Holmpark PA7 72 A2
Holmquarry Rd KA1 227 C3
Holms Ave KA11 220 B1
Holms Cres PA8 72 C1
Holms Pl G69 100 C4
Holms Rd KA14 170 A3
Holmscroft Ave PA15 45 C2
Holmscroft St PA15 45 C3
Holmscroft Way PA15 45 C2
Holmston Cres KA7 239 B4
Holmston Dr KA7 239 B3
Holmston Prim Sch KA7 239 A4
Holmston Rd KA7 239 B4
Holmston Rdbt KA7 239 C4
Holmswood Ave G72 140 B1
Holmwood Ave G71 140 C4
Holmwood Gdns G71 140 C3
Holmwood Ho* G44 137 A2
Holton Cres FK10 5 B1
Holton Sq FK10 5 B1
Holy Cross High Sch ML3 162 C2
Holy Cross Prim RC Sch G42 117 A1
Holy Cross Prim Sch G65 60 C2
Holy Cross RC Prim Sch PA16 45 A3
Holy Family Prim Sch
Kirkintilloch G66 79 A3
Port Glasgow PA14 69 A4
Holy Family RC Prim Sch ML4 142 B3
Holy Trinity Episcopal Prim Sch FK8 7 A4
Holy Trinity Prim Sch FK8 7 A4
Holyknowe Cres G66 57 C4
Holyknowe Rd G66 57 C4
Holyoake Ct KA1 228 C4
Holyrood Cres G20 96 C1
Holyrood Pl FK5 23 C2
Holyrood Quadrant 9 G20 96 C1
Holyrood Sec RC Sch G42 117 B1
Holyrood St ML3 162 A3
Holytown Prim Sch ML1 143 A3
Holytown Rd ML1,ML4 142 C3
Holytown Sta ML1 143 A2
Holywell St G31 118 A3
Home Farm Cotts FK6 39 C3
Home Farm Rd Ayr KA7 239 A1
Hartwood ML7 145 C2
Home St ML11 215 B2
Homeglen Ho G46 136 B1
Homer Pl ML4 142 C3
Homesteads The FK8 6 B4
Homeston Ave G71 141 A2
Honeybank Cres ML8 188 A2
Honeybog Rd G52 114 C3
Honeycomb Pl ML9 200 B2
Honeyman Cres ML11 215 B2
Honeysuckle La G83 27 C4
Honeysuckle Pk KA7 239 A1
Honeywell Cres ML6 123 C1
Hood Ct G84 16 A1
Hood St Clydebank G81 74 B1
Greenock PA15 45 C3
Hookney Terr FK6 21 B1
Hooper Pl ML4 142 A3
Hope Ave PA11 89 C1
Hope Cres ML9 185 A2
Hope St Ayr KA7 238 C4
Bellshill ML4 142 B3
Carluke ML8 188 A1
Falkirk FK1 42 A3
Glasgow G2 240 C3
Greenock PA15 45 C2
Hamilton ML3 162 C2
Helensburgh G84 25 A4
Lanark ML11 215 A2
Motherwell ML1 163 C4
Stirling FK8 1 C1
Wishaw ML2 166 A2
Hopefield Ave G12 96 B3
Hopehill Gdns G20 97 A2
Hopehill Rd G20 97 A2
Hopeman PA8 73 A2
Hopeman Ave G46 135 C2
Hopeman Dr G46 135 C2
Hopeman Path G46 135 C3
Hopeman Rd G46 135 C2
Hopeman St G46 135 C2
Hopepark Terr FK4 39 C3
Hopeton St PA19 44 C4
Hopetoun Bank KA11 220 B1
Hopetoun Dr FK9 2 A4
Hopetoun Pl G23 76 C1
Hopetoun Terr G21 98 A2
Hopkin's Brae 7 G66 58 B1
Horatius St ML1 142 A1
Hornal Rd G71 140 C2
Hornbeam Dr G81 74 A2
Hornbeam Rd
Cumbernauld G67 62 C3
Uddingston G71 141 A4
Horndean Ct G64 78 A2
Horne St G22 97 C3
Hornock Rd ML5 101 C1
Hornshill Dr ML1 144 A1
Hornshill Farm Rd G33 99 C3
Hornshill St G21 98 A2
Horsbrugh Ave G65 36 B1
Horsburgh St G33 99 B1
Horse Isle View KA22 205 A2
Horse Shoe KA23 190 B3
Horse Shoe Rd G61 75 C2
Horsewood Rd PA11 110 B4
Horslet St ML5 121 B2
Horslethill Rd G12 96 B2
Horsley Brae ML2 186 A2
Horton Pl G84 17 A2
Hospital Rd Wishaw ML2 186 A4
Wishaw ML2 165 B1
Hospital St ML5 122 A2
Hospitland Dr ML11 215 B2
Hotspur St G20 96 C2
Houldsworth Cres ML7 167 A4
Houldsworth La 7 G3 116 C4
Houldsworth St G3 240 A3
House O' Muir Rd ML7 126 A2
Househillmuir Cres G53 135 B4
Househillmuir La G53 135 B4
Househillmuir Pl G53 135 B4
Househillmuir Rd G53 135 A3
Househillmuir Sch G53 135 A3
Househillwood Cres G53 135 A4
Househillwood Rd G53 135 A3
Housel Ave G13 95 A4
Houston Cres KA24 191 A4
Houston Ct
Kilbirnie KA25 149 A1
Renfrew PA4 94 B2
Houston Pl Elderslie PA5 112 B1
Glasgow G5 116 C3
Houston Prim Sch PA6 91 A1
Houston Rd
Bridge of W PA11 90 B1
Houston PA6 91 A1
Inchinnan PA3,PA4,PA6 92 B2
Kilmacolm PA13 89 C4
Houston St Glasgow G5 116 C3
Greenock PA16 45 C3
Hamilton ML3 162 B1
Renfrew PA4 94 B2
Wishaw ML2 165 B1
Houston Terr G74 159 B1
Houstonfield Quadrant PA6 91 A1
Houstonfield Rd PA6 91 A1
Houstoun Ct PA5 111 C2
Houstoun Sq PA5 111 C2
Howacre ML11 214 C3
Howard Ave G74 160 A3
Howard Ct
East Kilbride G74 160 A3
Kilmarnock KA1 227 C4
Howard Park Dr KA1 227 C4
Howard St Falkirk FK1 41 C2
Glasgow G1 241 A1
Kilmarnock KA1 227 C4
Larkhall ML9 185 B1
Paisley PA1 114 A2
Howat Cres KA12 219 C2
Howat St G51 116 A4
Howatshaws Rd G82 50 A3
Howburn Cres ML7 127 C3
Howburn Rd ML7 127 B3
Howden Ave
Kilwinning KA13 207 C2
Motherwell ML1 143 B4
Howden Dr PA3 112 A3
Howden Pl ML1 143 A3
Howe Gdns G71 141 A4
Howe Rd G65 60 B4
Howe St PA1 112 C2
Howes St ML5 122 A2
Howetown FK10 5 B2
Howford Rd G52 115 A2
Howford Sch G53 115 A1
Howgate KA13 207 B2
Howgate Ave G15 74 C2
Howgate Rd ML3 183 B4
Howgate Sh Ctr 7 FK1 42 A2
Howie Bldgs G76 157 C4
Howie Cres G84 15 A2
Howie St ML9 185 A1
Howie's Pl FK1 41 A2
Howieshill Ave G72 139 A3
Howieshill Rd G72 139 A3
Howlands Rd FK7 7 A2
Howlet Pl ML3 162 C1
Howletnest Rd ML6 123 B3
Howson Lea ML1 164 A2
Howson View ML1 163 A4
Howth Dr G13 95 C4
Howth Terr G13 95 C4
Howwood Prim Sch PA9 131 A3
Howwood Sta PA9 130 C3
Hoylake Pk G72 140 C1
Hoylake Pl G23 76 C1
Hoylake Sq KA13 207 B2
Hozier Cres G71 140 C4
Hozier Loan 8 ML9 185 A2
Hozier Pl 16 G71 141 A2
Hozier St Carluke ML8 187 C1
Coatbridge ML5 122 A2
Hudson Pl KA9 233 B1
Hudson Terr G75 180 B4
Hudson Way G75 180 B4
Hudspeth Ct G83 27 B4
Hugh Watt Pl KA3 222 A4
Hughenden Ct G12 96 A2
Hughenden Dr G12 96 A2
Hughenden Gdns G12 96 A2
Hughenden La G12 96 A2
Hughenden Rd G12 96 A2
Hugo St G20 96 C3
Hulks Rd G67,ML6 83 B2
Humbie Ct G77 156 C1
Humbie Gate G77 156 C1
Humbie Gr G77 156 C2
Humbie Lawns G77 156 C1
Humbie Rd
Eaglesham G76 178 B4
Newton Mearns G77 156 C1
Hume Cres FK9 2 A3
Hume Ct FK9 2 A3
Hume Dr Bothwell G71 141 A2
Uddingston G71 140 C4
Hume Pl G75 180 B4
Hume Rd G67 62 A2
Hume St G81 74 A1
Hunt Hill G68 60 B1
Hunt Hill Rdbt G68 60 B1
Hunter Ave KA22 205 B1
Hunter Cres KA10 230 A1
Hunter Dr Irvine KA12 219 A3
Newton Mearns G77 156 A2
Hunter Gdns
Bonnybridge FK4 40 A3
Denny FK6 21 B1
Hunter High Sch G74 160 B1
Hunter House Mus* G74 160 B2
Hunter Pl
Kilbarchan PA10 111 A1
Kilwinning KA13 208 A2
Milngavie G62 54 C1
Shotts ML7 146 C3
Stenhousemuir FK2 24 A2
Hunter Prim Sch G74 160 B1
Hunter Rd
Crosshouse KA2 221 C1
Hamilton ML3 162 A3
Milngavie G62 54 C1
Rutherglen G73 118 B1
Hunter St Airdrie ML6 103 A1
Bellshill ML4 142 A3
East Kilbride G74 159 C1

Hunter St *continued*
Glasgow G4 241 C2
Paisley PA1 113 C3
Prestwick KA9 236 B4
Shotts ML7 146 B3
Hunter's Ave Ayr KA8 236 A2
Dumbarton G82 50 B2
Hunter's Cl ML11 215 A2
Hunterfield Dr G72 138 C3
Hunterhill Ave PA2 113 C2
Hunterhill Rd PA2 113 C2
Hunterian Mus* G12 96 B1
Hunterlees Rd ML10 198 A2
Hunters Hill Ct G21 97 C3
Hunters Pl PA15 45 C3
Huntersfield Rd PA5 111 B1
Huntershill Rd 3 G64 97 C4
Huntershill St G21 97 C3
Hunterston Rd KA23 190 B3
Hunthill La G72 161 A3
Hunthill Pl G76 158 A3
Hunthill Rd G72 161 A4
Hunting Lodge Gdns
ML3 163 A1
Huntingdon Rd G21 97 C1
Huntingdon Sq G21 97 C1
Huntingtower Rd G69 120 A2
Huntley Cres FK8 1 C1
Huntly Ave Bellshill ML4 142 A3
Glasgow G46 136 B1
Huntly Ct
Bishopbriggs G64 98 A4
Kilmarnock KA3 223 B2
Huntly Dr Bearsden G61 75 C4
Cambuslang G72 139 A2
Coatbridge ML5 121 B2
Greenock PA16 44 C2
Huntly Gdns G12 96 B2
Huntly Path G69 81 A1
Huntly Pl Kilmarnock KA3 223 B1
Port Glasgow PA14 47 A1
Huntly Quadrant ML2 165 A3
Huntly Rd Glasgow G12 96 B2
Paisley G52 114 C4
Huntly Terr Paisley PA2 114 A1
Port Glasgow PA14 47 A1
Shotts ML7 147 A2
Hurlawcrook Rd G75 180 C1
Hurlet Cotts G53 134 C3
Hurlet Rd PA2, G53 134 B4
Hurlford Ave G13 94 C4
Hurlford Prim Sch KA1 228 C3
Hurlford Rd KA1 228 A3
Hurly Hawkin G64 98 B4
Hurworth St FK1 41 C2
Hutcheson Rd G46 136 A1
Hutcheson St G1 241 A2
Hutchesons' Gram Sch
Glasgow G42 117 A1
Glasgow, Crossmyloof
G41 116 C1
Hutchinson Pl G72 139 C2
Hutchinson St ML2 186 B4
Hutchinson Town Ct 8
G5 117 B2
Hutchison Dr G61 76 A1
Hutchison Pl ML5 121 C3
Hutchison St ML3 162 B1
Hutton G12 96 A3
Hutton Ave PA6 111 B4
Hutton Dr
East Kilbride G74 159 C2
Glasgow G51 115 C4
Hutton Pk FK10 10 B4
Hyacinth Way ML8 201 C4
Hydepark St G3 240 A2
Hyndal Ave G53 115 B1
Hyndford Pl ML11 215 A2
Hyndford Rd ML11 215 B1
Hyndland Ave G11 96 A1
Hyndland Prim Sch G11 96 A1
Hyndland Rd G12 96 A2
Hyndland Sec Sch G12 96 A2
Hyndland St G11 96 B1
Hyndland Sta G12 96 A2
Hyndlee Dr G52 115 B3
Hyndman Rd KA23 190 B2
Hyndshaw Rd
Carluke ML8 188 A2
Law ML2 187 B4
Hyndshaw View ML8 187 A2
Hyslop Pl G81 74 A2
Hyslop Rd KA20 206 C1
Hyslop St ML6 122 C4

I

Iain Dr G61 75 B3
Iain Rd G61 75 B3
Ian Smith Ct G81 94 B4
IBM Sta PA16 44 B1
Ibrox Ind Est G51 116 B3
Ibrox Prim Sch G51 116 A3
Ibrox St G51 116 B3
Ibrox Sta G51 116 A3
Ibrox Stad (Rangers FC)
G51 116 A3
Ibrox Terr G51 116 A3
Ibroxholm Ave G51 116 A3
Ibroxholm Oval G51 116 A3
Ibroxholm Pl G51 116 A3
Ida Quadrant ML4 141 C3
Iddesleigh Ave G62 55 A1
Ilay Ave G61 96 A4
Ilay Ct G61 96 A4
Ilay Rd G61 96 A4
Imlach Pl ML1 163 B3
Imperial Dr ML6 122 C3
Inch Colm Ave FK5 23 B2
Inch Garve G74 160 B1
Inch Garvie Terr FK5 23 B2
Inch Keith G74 160 B1
Inch Marnock G74 160 B1
Inch Murrin G74 160 B1
Inchbrae Rd G52 115 B2
Inchcolm Gdns G69 81 A2
Inchcolm Pl G74 159 B1
Inchconnachan Ave G83 19 C1
Inchcruin G83 27 B4
Inchcruin Pl G15 74 C2
Inches Rd KA22 216 A4
Inchfad Cres G15 74 C2
Inchfad Dr G15 74 C2
Inchfad Pl G15 74 C2
Inchfad Rd G83 19 C1
Inchgotrick Rd KA1 227 C2
Inchgower Gr G84 15 B3
Inchgreen St PA14 46 C1
Inchholm La G11 95 C1
Inchholm St G11 95 C1
Inchinnan Bsns Pk PA4 93 A2
Inchinnan Dr PA4 93 B2
Inchinnan Ind Est PA4 93 A3
Inchinnan Prim Sch PA4 93 B4
Inchinnan Rd
Bellshill ML4 141 C4
Paisley PA3 113 C4
Renfrew PA4 94 A2
Inchkeith Pl Falkirk FK1 42 A1
Glasgow G32 119 A4
Inchlaggan Pl G15 74 C2
Inchlee St G14 95 C2
Inchlonaig Dr G83 19 C1
Inchmoan Pl G15 74 C2
Inchmurrin Ave G66 80 A4
Inchmurrin Cres G83 19 C1
Inchmurrin Dr
Kilmarnock KA3 223 A3
Rutherglen G73 138 B1
Inchmurrin Gdns G73 138 B1
Inchmurrin Pl G73 138 B1
Inchna FK11 4 A3
Inchneuk Path ML5 101 B3
Inchneuk Rd ML5 101 C3
Inchnock Ave G69 101 A3
Inchoch St G33 99 C1
Inchrory Pl G15 74 C2
Inchtavannach G83 27 B4
Inchwood Ct G68 82 A4
Inchwood Pl G68 81 C4
Inchwood Rd G68 82 A4
Incle St PA1 113 C3
Indale Ave KA9 236 C4
India Cotts G83 27 C3
India Dr PA4 93 B3
India St Alexandria G83 27 C3
Glasgow G2 240 B3
Industry St G66 79 B4
Inga St G20 96 C4
Ingerbreck Ave G73 138 B2
Ingleby Dr G31 118 A4
Ingleby Pl G78 154 C4
Inglefield Ct ML6 123 A4
Inglefield St G42 117 A1
Ingleneuk Ave G33 99 A3
Ingleside G66 79 B3
Ingleston Ave FK6 21 B3
Ingleston Pk PA15 46 A2
Ingleston St PA15 46 A2
Inglestone Ave G46 136 A1
Inglewood Cres
East Kilbride G75 180 A4
Paisley PA2 112 C1
Inglewood Gdns FK10 10 A4
Inglewood Rd FK10 9 C4
Inglis Ct ML9 198 C2
Inglis Dr FK2 24 B1
Inglis Pl G75 180 C4
Inglis St Glasgow G31 118 A3
Wishaw ML2 164 B1
Ingliston Dr PA7 71 C2
Ingram Pl KA3 223 A2
Ingram St G1 241 A2
Inishail Rd G33 99 B1
Inkerman Pl KA1 222 C1
Inkerman Rd G52 114 C3
Innellan Cres ML7 146 C3
Innellan Dr KA3 222 C2
Innellan Gdns G20 96 A4
Innellan Pl G20 96 A4
Inner City Trad Est G4 241 B4
Innerleithen Dr ML2 165 B3
Innermanse Quadrant
ML1 143 C3
Innerpeffray Dr FK2 24 A2
Innerwick Dr G52 115 A3
Innerwood Rd KA13 207 C3
Innes Ct 4 Airdrie ML6 123 C4
East Kilbride G74 159 C2
International Ave ML3 161 B2
Inver Ct FK2 24 B1
Inver Rd G33 119 C4
Inverallan Ct FK9 1 C4
Inverallan Dr FK9 1 C4
Inverallan Rd FK9 1 C4
Inverarish PA4 93 B4
Inverary Dr
Bishopbriggs G64 78 A2
Stenhousemuir FK5 23 C3
Inverary Gdns ML1 143 B1
Inveravon Dr ML1 163 B3
Inverbervie PA8 73 A1
Invercanny Dr G15 75 A2
Invercanny Pl G15 75 A2
Invercargill G75 180 A4
Invercloy Ct G75 180 A2
Invercloy Pl KA3 222 C2
Inverclyde Gdns G73 138 B2
Inverclyde Royal Hospl
PA16 44 C2
Invercree Wlk ML5 101 B3
Inveresk Pl ML5 122 A4
Inveresk Quadrant G32 119 A3
Inveresk St G32 119 A3
Inverewe Ave G46 135 B1
Inverewe Dr G46 135 B1
Inverewe Gdns G46 135 B1
Inverewe Pl G46 135 B2
Inverewe Way G77 156 A3
Invergarry Ave G46 135 B1
Invergarry Ct G46 135 C1
Invergarry Dr G46 135 C1
Invergarry Gdns G46 135 B1
Invergarry Gr G46 135 B1
Invergarry Pl G46 135 C1
Invergarry Quad G46 135 C1
Invergarry View G46 135 C1
Inverglas Ave PA4 94 C1
Invergordan Pl ML6 123 A3
Invergordon Ave G43 136 C4
Invergyle Dr G52 115 B3
Invergyle La G52 115 A3
Inverkar Dr PA2 113 A1
Inverkar Rd KA7 239 A3
Inverkip Dr ML7 146 C3
Inverkip Rd Gourock PA16 44 B1
Greenock PA16 45 B2
Inverkip St PA15 45 C3
Inverlair Ave G43 136 C3
Inverleith St G32 118 C4
Inverleven Pl KA11 219 C4
Inverlochy St G33 99 B1
Inverness St G51 115 B3
Inveroran Dr G61 76 A2
Invershiel Rd G23 76 C1
Invershin Dr 8 G20 96 B3
Inverurie St G21 97 B2
Invervale Ave ML6 123 C3
Inzievar Terr G32 119 A1
Iona ML6 123 B3
Iona Ave G74 160 A2
Iona Cres Gourock PA19 44 B3
Old Kilpatrick G60 73 B3
Iona Ct KA11 225 B4
Iona Dr PA2 133 B4
Iona Gdns G60 73 B3
Iona La G69 81 A1
Iona Path G72 161 B4
Iona Pl Coatbridge ML5 101 B1
Falkirk FK1 42 A1
Irvine KA11 225 B4
Kilmarnock KA3 223 A3
Old Kilpatrick G60 73 B3
Iona Quadrant ML2 165 C3
Iona Rd Port Glasgow PA14 69 A4
Renfrew PA4 94 B1
Rutherglen G73 138 C2
Wishaw ML2 165 C3
Iona Ridge ML3 161 C1
Iona St Glasgow G51 116 A4
Greenock PA16 45 B2
Motherwell ML1 142 B1
Iona Way Kirkintilloch G66 80 A4
Stepps G33 99 C2
Iona Wlk Coatbridge ML5 121 C2
Gourock PA19 44 B3
Iona Wynd G83 27 C1
Iris Ave G45 138 A2
Iris Ct KA7 239 B2
Irongray St G31 118 B4
Irvine Burns Club Mus*
KA12 219 B2
Irvine Cres ML5 122 B4
Irvine Ctr KA12 219 A1
Irvine Dr PA3 112 A4
Irvine Gdns G66 58 A3
Irvine Ind Est KA12 224 B4
Irvine Mains Cres KA12 219 B2
Irvine Pl Kilsyth G65 36 A1
Stirling FK8 7 A4
Irvine Rd Crosshouse KA2 221 C1
Irvine KA12 219 A4
Kilmarnock KA1 222 B1
Kilmaurs KA3 222 A4
Kilwinning KA13 207 C1
Irvine Royal Acad KA12 219 A3
Irvine St Glasgow G40 118 A2
Glenmavis ML6 102 C2
Irvine Sta KA12 219 A1
Irvine Terr ML3 183 B4
Irving Ave G81 74 A3
Irving Ct Clydebank G81 74 A3
Falkirk FK1 41 C3
Irving Quadrant G81 74 A3
Irwin St PA15 46 C1
Isabella Gdns ML3 163 B1
Isla Ave ML2 165 C3
Island Rd G67 82 B4
Island View KA22 205 A2
Islands Cres FK1 42 A1
Islay ML6 123 C3
Islay Ave
Port Glasgow PA14 69 A4
Rutherglen G73 138 C2
Islay Cres
Old Kilpatrick G60 73 B3
Paisley PA2 133 B4
Saltcoats KA21 205 C1
Islay Ct Hamilton ML3 161 C1
Irvine KA11 225 B4
Islay Dr
Newton Mearns G77 156 A3
Old Kilpatrick G60 73 B3
Islay Gdns Carluke ML8 202 A4
Larkhall ML9 185 A2
Islay Pl KA3 223 A3
Islay Quadrant ML2 164 C1
Islay Rd G66 80 A4
Islay Way ML5 121 B2
Isle Of Pin Rd KA10 230 A1
Isobel Mair Sch G76 136 B1
Ivanhoe G74 160 B2
Ivanhoe Cres ML2 165 B2
Ivanhoe Ct ML8 187 B1
Ivanhoe Dr
Kirkintilloch G66 79 C4
Saltcoats KA21 206 A1
Ivanhoe Pl
Motherwell ML1 143 A3
Stirling FK8 2 A1
Ivanhoe Rd
Cumbernauld G67 82 C4
Glasgow G13 95 B4
Paisley PA2 112 C1
Ivanhoe Way PA2 112 C1
Ivy Cres PA19 44 C3
Ivy Gr ML5 122 A3
Ivy Pl Ayr KA7 239 B3
Blantyre G72 161 B4
Motherwell ML1 143 A2
Ivy Rd G71 141 B4
Ivy Terr ML1 143 A3
Ivy Way ML6 123 C2
Ivybank Ave G72 139 B2
Ivybank Cres PA14 47 A1
Ivybank Rd PA14 47 A1
Izatt St FK10 10 A4

J

Jack St Hamilton ML3 183 B4
Motherwell ML1 164 A2
Jack's Rd Bothwell G71 141 A3
Saltcoats KA21 205 C1
Jacks View KA23 190 B3
Jackson Ct ML5 122 A3
Jackson Dr G33 100 A3
Jackson Pl Carluke ML8 187 C2
Renton G82 27 B1
Jackson St ML5 122 A4
Jackton Bsns Ctr G75 179 B4
Jackton Rd G75 179 B3
Jacob Pl FK1 42 A2
Jacob's Ladder Way
ML2 186 B3
Jacobite Pl ML4 142 B2
Jacobs Dr PA19 44 B3
Jagger Gdns G69 119 C2
Jail Wynd FK8 7 A4
Jamaica Dr G75 159 A1
Jamaica La PA15 45 C3
Jamaica St Glasgow G1 240 C1
Greenock PA15 45 C3
James Aiton Prim Sch
G72 139 A3
James Brown Ave KA8 236 C2
James Campbell Rd
KA8 239 B4
James Clements Cl
KA13 207 B2
James Cres KA12 219 B2
James Croft Dr FK1 41 C1
James Dempsey Ct ML5 121 C3
James Dempsey Gdns
ML5 121 C3
James Dunlop Gdns G64 98 A4
James Gray St G41 136 C4
James Hamilton Acad
KA3 223 B1
James Hamilton Dr
ML4 142 A3
James Hamilton Heritage
Pk* G74 159 B2
James Healy Dr ML3 183 B4
James Hemphill Ct G66 57 C4
James Johnston Pl KA3 223 A2
James Leeson Ct G66 58 B3
James Little St KA1 227 C4
James McFarlane Sch
KA22 205 B2
James Miller Cres KA21 217 A4
James Morrison St G1 241 B1
James Nisbet St G21 97 C1
James Reid Sch KA21 206 A1
James St Alexandria G83 27 C3
Alva FK12 5 A3
Ayr KA8 236 A1
Bannockburn FK7 7 B1
Bellshill ML4 141 C4
Carluke ML8 187 C1
Dalry KA24 191 A4
Falkirk FK2 42 A3
Glasgow G40 117 C2
Haggs FK4 39 A2
Helensburgh G84 16 B1
Laurieston FK2 42 C2
Motherwell ML1 163 B4
Prestwick KA9 236 A3
Stenhousemuir FK5 23 B1
Stirling FK8 2 A1
James Sym Cres KA1 227 C3
James View ML1 142 C2
James Watt Ave G75 181 A4
James Watt Coll
Greenock PA15 45 C3
Greenock PA15 46 A3
Kilwinning KA13 207 C2
James Watt Pl G74 159 A2
James Watt Rd G62 54 C2
James Watt St G2 240 B2
James Watt Way PA15 46 B2
James Wilson Pl ML8 201 A1
Jamestown Ind Est G83 27 C4
Jamestown Prim Sch
G83 27 C4
Jamieson Ave FK5 23 C2
Jamieson Ct
Clydebank G81 74 A4
5 Glasgow G42 117 A1
Jamieson Dr G74 160 A1
Jamieson Gdns ML7 146 C3
Jamieson Pl KA3 195 B1
Jamieson St G42 117 B1
Jamieson Way KA15 171 A4
Jane Ct ML9 185 A1
Jane Rae Gdns G81 94 B4
Jane's Brae G67 82 C4
Jane's Brae Intc G67 82 C4
Janebank Ave G72 139 B2
Janefield Ave PA5 111 C1
Janefield Pl Beith KA15 150 A1
Blantyre G72 161 B3
Lennoxtown G66 33 B1
Janefield St G31 118 A3
Janesmith St ML2 164 B2
Janetta St G81 74 A2
Jardine St G20 96 C2
Jardine Terr
Gartcosh G69 100 C3
Greenock PA16 45 C4
Jarvie Ave ML6 104 A1
Jarvie Cres G65 60 B4
Jarvie Pl FK2 42 A4
Jarvie Way PA2 132 C4
Jasmine Pl G67 82 A3
Jasmine Rd KA1 227 B4
Jasmine Way ML8 201 C4
Java St ML1 142 B1
Jean Armour Dr G81 74 B2
Jean Armour La PA16 44 C2
Jean Armour Pl KA21 206 A1
Jean Armour Terr PA16 44 C2
Jean Maclean Pl G64 78 A2
Jean St PA14 47 A1
Jeanette Ave ML3 183 B4
Jeanie Deans Dr G84 25 B4
Jedburgh Ave G73 138 A4
Jedburgh Dr PA2 113 A1
Jedburgh Gdns 2 G20 96 C2
Jedburgh Pl
Coatbridge ML5 121 C2
East Kilbride G74 159 C1
Jedburgh St
Blantyre G72 161 B4
Wishaw ML2 165 B3
Jedworth Ave G15 75 A2
Jedworth Ct G61 75 C3
Jedworth Rd G15 75 B2
Jeffrey Pl G65 36 B1
Jeffrey St KA1 227 C3
Jellicoe Pl G84 17 A1
Jellicoe St G81 73 C2
Jellyholm Rd FK10 10 C4
Jennie Lee Dr ML2 186 A4
Jennys Well Ct PA2 114 A1
Jennys Well Rd PA2 114 A1
Jermond Dr KA12 219 B3
Jervis Pl G84 17 A1
Jervis Terr G75 180 A4
Jerviston Ct ML1 143 A1
Jerviston Rd Glasgow G33 99 B1
Motherwell ML1 143 A1
Jerviston St
Motherwell ML1 163 C4
Motherwell, New Stevenston
ML1 143 A2
Jerviswood ML1 143 A1
Jerviswood Dr ML11 215 C4
Jerviswood Rd ML11 215 A2
Jessie St G42 117 B1
Jessiman Sq PA4 94 A1
Jimmy Sneddon Way
ML1 142 B1
Joanna Terr G72 161 B4
Jocelyn Sq G1 241 A1
Jocksthorn Terr KA3 222 B3
John Bassy Dr FK4 38 B2
John Bowman Gdns
ML4 142 A3
John Brannan Way ML4 141 B3
John Brogan Pl KA20 217 A4
John Brown Pl G69 100 B4
John Burnside Dr G81 74 B4
John Burtt Pl KA3 223 A2
John Campbell Ct PA19 44 C4
John Campbell St PA19 44 C4
John Cowane Row FK9 2 A2
John Davidson Dr FK6 21 B2
John Dickie St KA1 222 C1
John Ewing Gdns ML9 185 A2
John Finnie St KA1 227 C4
John Galt Prim Sch
KA12 219 B2
John Gregor Pl PA12 129 B1
John Hendry Rd G71 141 A2
John Jarvis Sq G65 36 B1
John Kennedy Pl KA3 223 A2
John Knox La ML3 161 B2
John Knox St
Clydebank G81 94 B4
Glasgow G4 241 C2
John Lang St PA5 112 A2
John Logie Baird Prim Sch
G84 17 A1
John Marshall Dr G64 97 C4

John McEwan Way G64 ....78 A4
John Murray Ct ML1 ....163 C2
John Murray Dr FK9 ......2 A4
John Ogilvie High Sch
  ML3 ....G51 C2
John Paul Acad G23 .....76 B1
John Rushforth Pl FK8 ...1 C1
John Smith Ct ML4 ......122 C4
John Smith Gdns G8 ....134 B2
John Smith Gdns ML5 ...122 B3
John Smith Way ML7 ...146 B3
John St Ayr KA8 ....239 A4
  Barrhead G78 ....134 A2
  Bellshill ML4 ....142 A3
  Blantyre G72 ....161 C4
  Carluke ML8 ....187 C1
  Falkirk FK2 ....42 A4
  Glasgow G1 ....241 A2
  Gourock PA15 ....44 C4
  Greenock PA15 ....46 A2
  Haggs FK4 ....39 A2
  Hamilton ML3 ....162 C2
  Helensburgh G84 ......16 B1
  Kirkintilloch G66 ......58 B1
  Larkhall ML9 ....185 A1
  Renton G82 ....49 B4
  Wishaw ML2 ....164 B2
John Street La G84 ....16 B1
John Wheatley Coll
  G32 ....119 A3
John Wheatley Coll
  (Easterhouse Campus)
  G34 ....120 A4
John Wilson Dr G65 ......36 A1
John Smith St PA15 ......46 B1
John Wood St PA14 ......47 B1
John Wright Sports Ctr The
  G74 ....160 A1
Johnsburn Dr G53 ......135 A3
Johnsburn Rd G53 ......135 A3
Johnshaven PA8 ....73 A1
Johnshaven St G43 .....136 B4
Johnshill PA12 ....129 B2
Johnson Ct G84 ....16 C1
Johnson Dr G72 ....139 A3
Johnston Ave
  Clydebank G81 ....94 B4
  Kilsyth G65 ....60 B4
  Stenhousemuir FK5 ....23 C2
  Stirling FK9 ....2 A2
Johnston Ct PA10 ......229 C3
Johnston Pl FK6 ....40 C2
Johnston Rd G69 ....101 A3
Johnston St Airdrie ML6 .123 A4
  Bannockburn FK7 ....7 B1
  Greenock PA16 ....45 B4
  Paisley PA1 ....113 C2
Johnston Terr PA16 ......45 B4
Johnstone Ave G52 ....115 A4
Johnstone Ct FK12 ....5 A3
Johnstone Dr
  Lochwinnoch PA12 ....129 B1
  Rutherglen G73 ....138 A4
Johnstone High Sch
  PA5 ....131 B4
Johnstone Hospl PA5 ...111 C2
Johnstone La ML8 ......188 A1
Johnstone Rd ML3 .....162 C1
Johnstone St Alva FK12 ...5 A3
  Bellshill ML4 ....142 B3
  Menstrie FK11 ....3 C3
Johnstone Sta PA5 .....112 A2
Johnstone Terr G65 .....59 C1
Joiners La KA3 ....195 A4
Jones Ave FK5 ....41 B4
Jones Wynd ML1 ....143 C1
Jonquil Way ML8 ....201 C4
Joppa St G13 ....118 C4
Jordan St G14 ....95 B1
Jordanhill Cres G13 .....95 B3
Jordanhill Dr G13 ....95 B3
Jordanhill La G13 ....95 B3
Jordanhill Sch G13 ......95 B3
Jordanhill Sta G11 ......95 B3
Jordanvale Ave G14 .....95 B1
Jowitt Ave G81 ....74 B1
Jubilee Bank G66 ....79 B2
Jubilee Ct G52 ....114 C4
Jubilee Dr KA3 ....195 C1
Jubilee Gdns G61 ....75 C2
Jubilee Pl KA3 ....195 C1
Jubilee Rd FK6 ....21 C2
Julian Ave G12 ....96 B2
Julian La G12 ....96 B2
Juniper Ave G75 ....180 B3
Juniper Ct G66 ....79 A3
Juniper Dr G66 ....58 A2
Juniper Gn KA7 ....239 B3
Juniper Pl ML3 ....162 C1
  Johnstone PA5 ....132 A4
  Uddingston G71 ......141 B4
Juniper Rd G71 ....141 B4
Juniper Terr G32 ....119 C2
Juniper Wynd ML1 .....143 A3
Juno La ML4 ....44 B2
Juno St ML1 ....142 B1
Juno Terr PA16 ....44 B2
Jupiter La PA16 ....44 B2
Jupiter Pl G84 ....15 B3
Jupiter St ML1 ....142 B1
Jupiter Terr PA16 ....44 B2
Jura G74 ....181 A4
Jura Ave PA4 ....94 B1
Jura Ct Glasgow G52 ...115 C3
  Irvine KA11 ....225 B4
Jura Dr Blantyre G72 ...140 B2

Jura Dr continued
  Kirkintilloch G66 ......80 A4
  Newton Mearns G77 ..156 A3
  Old Kilpatrick G60 .....73 B3
Jura Gdns Carluke ML8 .202 A4
  Hamilton ML3 ....162 A1
  Larkhall ML9 ....185 B2
  Old Kilpatrick G60 .....73 B3
Jura Pl Old Kilpatrick G60 .73 B3
  Troon KA10 ....229 D4
Jura Quadrant ML2 ....164 C1
Jura Rd Old Kilpatrick G60 .73 B3
  Paisley PA2 ....133 B4
Jura St Glasgow G52 ...115 C3
  Greenock PA16 ....45 B2
Jura Wynd ML5 ....101 B3
Jutland Ct G84 ....16 A2

K

Kaim Dr G53 ....135 B3
Kairnhill Ct ML11 ......214 C3
Kames Ct KA11 ....220 A3
Kames Rd ML7 ....146 C3
Kane Pl ML9 ....198 C1
Kane St G82 ....27 B1
Karadale Gdns ML9 ...185 A3
Karol Path G4 ....97 A1
Karries Ct PA4 ....39 B4
Katewell Ave G15 ....74 C2
Katewell Pl G15 ....74 C2
Katherine Pl G82 ....27 C1
Katherine St ML6 ......123 C4
Kathleen Pk G84 ....16 A2
Katrine Ave
  Bishopbriggs G64 ....78 A1
  Uddingston ML4 ....141 B3
Katrine Cres ML6 ....102 C1
Katrine Ct Alloa FK10 ...10 B3
  Kilmarnock KA1 ....228 A3
Katrine Dr
  Newton Mearns G77 ..157 A2
  Paisley PA2 ....113 A1
Katrine Pl
  Cambuslang G72 ......139 A3
  Coatbridge ML5 ....101 B1
  Denny FK6 ....39 B3
  Irvine KA12 ....225 B4
Katrine Rd Greenock PA15 .46 A2
  Shotts ML7 ....147 A1
Katrine Way G G71 ....141 A2
Katrine Wynd ML1 .....143 A3
Katriona Path G ML9 ...185 B1
Kay Gdns ML1 ....163 A3
Kay Park Cres KA3 ....223 A1
Kay Park Gr KA3 ......223 A1
Kay Park Terr KA3 ....223 A1
Kay St G21 ....97 C2
Kaystone Rd G15 ....75 A1
Keal Ave G15 ....95 A4
Keal Cres G15 ....95 A4
Keal Dr G15 ....95 A4
Keal Pl G15 ....95 A4
Keane Path ML1 ....164 A2
Kearn Ave G15 ....75 B1
Kearn Pl G15 ....75 B1
Keats Pk G71 ....141 A2
Keil Cres G82 ....49 B2
Keil St G82 ....49 B2
Keilarsbrae FK10 ....5 B1
Keir Ave FK6 ....2 A1
Keir Cres ML2 ....165 A2
Keir Dr G64 ....77 C1
Keir Gdns FK9 ....2 A4
Keir Hardie Ave KA13 .208 A2
Keir Hardie Ct G64 .....77 C1
Keir Hardie Dr
  Ardrossan KA22 ......205 A2
  Bellshill ML4 ....141 C2
  Kilbirnie KA25 ....149 A1
  G Kilsyth G65 ....60 B4
Keir Hardie Meml Prim Sch
  ML1 ....143 B2
Keir Hardie Pl
  Bellshill ML4 ....141 C2
  Saltcoats KA21 ....206 A1
Keir Hardie Rd Alva FK12 ...5 B4
  Larkhall ML9 ....185 B1
  Stevenston KA20 ......206 C1
Keir St Bridge of W FK9 ...2 C1
  Glasgow G41 ....116 C2
Keir's Wlk G72 ....139 A3
Keith Ave Glasgow G46 .136 B2
  Stirling FK7 ....7 B2
Keith Ct G11 ....96 B1
Keith Pl KA3 ....223 B1
Keith Quadrant ML2 ...165 A3
Keith St Bellshill ML4 ..142 A3
  Glasgow G11 ....96 B1
  Hamilton ML3 ....162 C2
Kelbourne Cres ML4 ...141 C3
Kelbourne St G20 ......96 C2
Kelburn Cres KA1 ......227 C2
Kelburn St G78 ....134 A1
Kelburn Terr PA14 ......48 A1
Kelburne Dr PA1 ....114 A3
Kelburne Gdns
  Glasgow G69 ....120 A2
  Paisley PA1 ....114 A3
Kelburne Oval PA1 .....114 A3
Kelhead Ave G52 ......114 C3

Kelhead Dr G52 ....114 C3
Kelhead Path G52 .....114 C3
Kelhead Pl G52 ....114 C3
Kellas St G51 ....116 A4
Kellie Gr G74 ....159 B2
Kellie Pl FK10 ....10 A4
Kelliebank FK10 ....9 C3
Kells Pl G15 ....74 C2
Kelly Ct FK8 ....7 A4
Kelly Dr FK6 ....21 C2
Kelly St PA16 ....45 B3
Kelly's La ML8 ....188 A1
Kelso Ave
  Bridge of W PA11 .....110 B4
  Paisley PA2 ....113 A1
  Rutherglen G73 ....138 A4
Kelso Cres ML2 ....165 A3
Kelso Dr Carluke ML8 ..188 B1
  East Kilbride G74 .....160 A2
Kelso Gdns G69 ....80 C2
Kelso Pl Glasgow G14 ..94 C3
  Renton G82 ....27 C1
Kelso Quadrant ML5 ...121 C4
Kelso St G13 ....94 C4
Kelton Rd G84 ....16 B3
Kelton St G32 ....119 A2
Kelvin Ave Glasgow G52 .115 A4
  Kilwinning KA13 ......207 C1
  Paisley PA2 ....114 C4
Kelvin Cres G61 ....75 C1
Kelvin Ct Glasgow G12 ..96 A3
  G Kirkintilloch G66 ....58 B1
Kelvin Dr Airdrie ML6 ..103 A1
  Barrhead G78 ....134 B1
  Bishopbriggs G64 .....97 C4
  Chryston G69 ....80 C1
  East Kilbride G75 .....180 C4
  Glasgow G20 ....96 B2
  Kirkintilloch G66 ......79 A4
  Shotts ML7 ....147 A2
Kelvin Gdns
  Hamilton ML3 ....161 C2
  Kilsyth G65 ....60 B4
Kelvin Hall Transport Mus*
  ....96 B1
Kelvin Park S G3 ......116 C4
Kelvin Pl G75 ....181 A4
Kelvin Rd Bellshill ML4 .142 A4
  Cumbernauld G67 ......83 A4
  East Kilbride G75 .....181 A4
  Milngavie G62 ....54 C2
  Uddingston G71 ......140 C4
Kelvin Rd N G67 ....83 A4
Kelvin Sch G3 ....96 B1
Kelvin South Bsns Pk
  G75 ....180 C2
Kelvin St ML5 ....122 B3
Kelvin Terr G65 ....59 C2
Kelvin View Torrance G64 .78 B4
  Twechar G65 ....59 C2
Kelvin Way
  G Bothwell G71 ....141 A2
  Glasgow G3,G12 ......96 C1
  Kilsyth G65 ....36 B1
  Kirkintilloch G66 ......79 A4
Kelvinbridge Rdbt G64 ..78 A4
Kelvinbridge Underground
  Sta G4 ....96 C1
Kelvindale Gdns G20 ...96 B3
Kelvindale Pl G G20 ....96 C3
Kelvindale Prim Sch G12 .96 B3
Kelvindale Rd G12 ......96 B3
Kelvingrove Mus & Art Gall*
  G3 ....96 C1
Kelvingrove St G3 .....116 C4
Kelvinhall Underground Sta
  G11 ....96 B1
Kelvinhaugh Gate G3 ..116 B4
Kelvinhaugh Pl G3 .....116 B4
Kelvinhaugh Prim Sch
  ....116 B4
Kelvinhaugh St G3 ....116 B4
Kelvinhead Rd G65 .....37 C2
Kelvinside Ave G20 .....96 C2
Kelvinside Cres G65 ....37 C2
Kelvinside Dr G20 ......96 C2
Kelvinside Gardens La G
  G20 ....96 C2
Kelvinside Gdns G20 ...96 C2
Kelvinside Gdns E G20 .96 C2
Kelvinside Terr S G G20 .96 C2
Kelvinside Terr W G G20
  ....96 C2
Kelvinvale G66 ....58 B1
Kelvinview Ave FK4 .....38 C1
Kemp Ave PA3 ....94 A3
Kemp Ct Ardrossan KA21 .205 C2
  Hamilton ML3 ....162 C2
Kemper Ave FK1 ....41 C3
Kempock Pk PA19 ......44 C4
Kempock St
  Glasgow G40 ....118 B2
  Gourock PA19 ....44 C4
Kempsthorn Cres G53 ..115 A3
Kempsthorn Rd G53 ...115 A3
Ken Rd KA1 ....228 A3
Kenbank Cres PA11 ....110 B4
Kenbank Rd PA11 ......110 B4
Kendal Ave Glasgow G46 .136 B2
  Glasgow,Giffnock G46 .136 B2
Kendal Dr G12 ....96 A3
Kendal Rd G75 ....179 C3
Kendon Ave G15 ....74 C2
Kenilburn Ave ML6 ....103 A1

Kenilburn Cres ML6 ...103 A1
Kenilworth G74 ....160 C2
Kenilworth Ave
  Glasgow G42 ....136 B4
  Helensburgh G84 ......25 B4
  Paisley PA2 ....132 C4
  Wishaw ML2 ....165 A2
Kenilworth Cres
  Bearsden G61 ....75 B3
  Bellshill ML4 ....142 A3
  Greenock PA16 ....45 B2
  Hamilton ML3 ....161 C2
Kenilworth Ct
  Bridge of A FK9 ....2 A4
  Carluke ML8 ....187 C1
  Cumbernauld G67 .....82 C4
  Motherwell ML1 ....143 A3
Kenilworth Dr
  Airdrie ML6 ....123 B4
  Irvine KA12 ....222 C4
  Lauriston KA21 ....206 A1
Kenilworth Rd
  Bridge of A FK9 ....2 A4
  Kirkintilloch G66 ......79 B4
  Lanark ML11 ....215 A2
Kenilworth Way PA2 ...112 C1
Kenmar Gdns G71 .....140 C4
Kenmar Rd ML3 ....162 A3
Kenmar Terr ML3 ......162 A3
Kenmore G74 ....181 A4
Kenmore KA10 ....229 C2
Kenmore Ave G84 .....236 B3
Kenmore Dr PA16 ......45 A2
Kenmore Gdns G61 ....76 A3
Kenmore Pl
  Greenock PA16 ....45 A2
  Shotts ML7 ....146 C3
Kenmore Rd
  Cumbernauld G67 ......62 A1
  Kilmacolm PA13 ....89 B4
  Uddingston G71 ......140 C4
Kenmore St G32 ....119 A3
Kenmore Way
  Carluke ML8 ....187 C2
  Coatbridge ML5 ....122 B2
Kenmuir Ave G32 .....119 C2
Kenmuir Rd G32 ......139 B4
Kenmuir St
  Coatbridge ML5 ....121 B2
  Falkirk FK1 ....41 A3
Kenmuiraid Pl ML4 ....141 C2
Kenmuirhill Gate G32 ..119 B1
Kenmuirhill Gdns G32 .119 B1
Kenmuirhill Rd G32 ...119 B1
Kennard St FK2 ....43 A4
Kennedy Ct Glasgow G46 .136 B2
  Kilmarnock KA3 ....223 B2
Kennedy Dr Airdrie ML6 .122 C4
  Helensburgh G84 ......16 C2
Kennedy Gdns ML2 ...186 A4
Kennedy Path G4 .....241 B3
Kennedy Rd
  Saltcoats KA21 ....205 C1
  Troon KA10 ....229 B1
Kennedy St Glasgow G4 .241 B3
Kennedy Way G42 ......14 C2
Kennedy's La PA15 .....46 A2
Kennelburn Rd ML6 ...123 B1
Kenneth Rd ML1 ....163 B3
Kennihill ML6 ....103 A1
Kennihill Quadrant ML6 .103 A1
Kenningknowes Rd FK7 ..6 C3
Kennishead Ave G46 ..135 C3
Kennishead Path G46 .135 C3
Kennishead Pl G46 ....135 C3
Kennishead Rd G53 ...135 C3
Kennishead Sta G46 ..135 C3
Kennisholm Ave G46 ..135 C3
Kennisholm Path G46 .135 C3
Kennisholm Pl G46 ....135 C3
Kennoway Dr G11 ......95 C1
Kennyhill Sq G31 ......118 A4
Kenshaw Ave ML9 .....199 A4
Kenshaw Pl ML9 ......199 A4
Kensington Dr G46 ....136 B2
Kensington Gate G21 ..96 B2
Kensington Gate La G
  G12 ....96 B2
Kensington Rd G12 ....96 B2
Kent Ct G84 ....17 A2
Kent Dr Helensburgh G84 .17 A2
  Rutherglen G73 ....138 B3
Kent Pl G75 ....179 C3
Kent Rd Alloa FK10 ....10 A2
  Glasgow G3 ....240 A3
  Stirling FK7 ....7 A3
Kent St G40 ....241 C1
Kentallen Rd G33 .....119 C3
Kentigern Terr G64 ....98 A4
Kentmere Cl G75 ......180 A3
Kentmere Dr G75 .....180 A3
Kentmere Pl G75 .....180 A3
Keppel Dr G44 ....137 C3
Keppoch St G21 ....97 B2

Keppochhill Dr G21 .....97 B2
Keppochhill Pl G21 .....97 B1
Keppochhill Rd G21 ....97 B2
Keppochhill Way G21 ...97 B1
Keppock Pl FK1 ....41 C1
Ker Rd G62 ....53 C3
Ker St PA15 ....45 C3
Kerelaw Ave KA20 ....206 C1
Kerelaw Rd KA20 .....206 B1
Kerelaw Sch KA20 ....206 B1
Kerfield Pl G15 ....74 B2
Kerr Ave KA21 ....217 A4
Kerr Cres Haggs FK4 ...39 A2
  Hamilton ML3 ....162 B1
Kerr Dr Glasgow G40 ..117 C3
  Irvine KA12 ....224 B1
  Motherwell ML1 ......163 B3
Kerr Gdns G71 ....141 A4
Kerr Grieve Ct G ML1 ..163 C3
Kerr Pl Denny FK6 ......21 B1
  Glasgow G40 ....117 C3
  Irvine KA12 ....219 B1
Kerr Rd KA3 ....223 B1
Kerr St Barrhead G78 ..134 A1
  Blantyre G72 ....161 C4
  Glasgow G40 ....117 C3
  Kirkintilloch G66 ......79 B4
  Paisley PA3 ....113 B3
Kerrera Pl G33 ....119 B3
Kerrera Rd G33 ....119 B3
Kerrix Rd KA1 ....231 A1
Kerrmuir Ave KA1 ....228 C3
Kerry La KA21 ....217 A4
Kerry Pl G15 ....74 C2
Kerrycroy Ave G42 ...137 B4
Kerrycroy Pl G42 .....137 B4
Kerrycroy St G42 .....137 B4
Kerrydale St G40 .....118 A2
Kerrylamont Ave G42 .137 C4
Kerse Ave KA24 ......191 C4
Kerse Gdns FK2 ....42 C3
Kerse La KA3 ....223 B1
Kerse Pl FK1 ....42 B3
Kerse Rd FK7 ....7 B3
Kersebonny Rd FK8 ....6 B4
Kersehill Cres FK2 .....42 B4
Kersepark KA7 ....239 A1
Kershaw St ML2 ......186 B4
Kersie Rd FK9 ....9 A2
Kersland Cres KA1 ....228 C3
Kersland Dr G62 ......53 C4
Kersland Foot KA11 ...219 C3
Kersland Gait KA11 ...211 C4
Kersland La
  G Glasgow G12 ......96 B2
  Milngavie G62 ....53 C4
Kersland Rd KA4 ......170 B3
Kersland Sch PA2 ....114 B1
Kersland St G12 ....96 B2
Kerswinning Ave KA25 .170 A4
Kessington Dr G61 ....76 A2
Kessington Rd G61 ....76 A2
Kessington Sq G61 ....76 A2
Kessock Dr G22 ....97 A2
Kessock Pl G22 ....97 A2
Kestrel Cres PA16 .....45 C1
Kestrel Ct G81 ....74 A3
Kestrel Pl Greenock PA16 .45 A3
  Johnstone PA5 ....131 B4
Kestrel Rd G13 ....95 B3
Kestrel View
  Bellshill ML4 ....141 C4
  Coatbridge ML4 ......121 C1
Keswick Dr ML3 ....183 B3
Keswick Rd G75 ......179 C3
Kethers La ML1 ....163 B4
Kethers St ML1 ....163 B3
Keverbae FK10 ....9 A2
Kevoc Cotts KA6 .....237 A3
Kew Gdns G71 ....141 A4
Kew La G12 ....96 B2
Kew Terr G12 ....96 B2
Keynes Sq ML4 ....142 B2
Keystone Ave G62 .....76 A4
Keystone Quadrant G62 .76 A4
Keystone Rd G62 ......76 A4
Kibble Sch The PA3 ...113 C4
Kibbleston Rd PA10 ...130 C4
Kidsneuk KA12 ....219 A3
Kidsneuk Gdns KA12 ..219 A3
Kidston Dr G84 ....16 A1
Kidston Pl G G65 .....117 B2
Kidston Terr G G65 ...117 B2
Kier Ct FK9 ....2 A4
Kier Hardie Ct KA15 ..171 A4
Kierhill Rd G68 ....61 B1
Kilallan Ave PA11 ......90 B1
Kilallan Rd PA11 ....90 B3
Kilbarchan Prim Sch
  PA10 ....111 A2
Kilbarchan Rd
  Johnstone PA5,PA10 ..130 C4
Kilbarchan St G G5 ...117 A3
Kilbean Dr FK1 ....41 C1
Kilberg Terr G46 ......135 B2
Kilberry St G21 ....98 A1
Kilbirnie Pl G5 ....117 A2
Kilbirnie St G5 ....117 A2
Kilbirnie Terr FK6 ......21 B2
Kilblain St PA15 ....45 C3
Kilbowie Pl ML6 ......123 B4
Kilbowie Prim Sch G81 .74 A2

Kilbowie Rd
Clydebank G81 ....74 A2
Cumbernauld G67 ....62 A1
Kilbrandon Cres KA7 ....238 A1
Kilbrandon Way KA7 ....238 A1
Kilbrannan Ave KA21 ....205 C1
Kilbrannan Dr PA16 ....45 A2
Kilbreck Gdns G61 ....75 B4
Kilbreck La ML1 ....143 B2
Kilbrennan Dr Falkirk FK1 ....41 A2
Motherwell ML1 ....163 A4
Kilbrennan Rd PA3 ....112 A3
Kilbride Dr G84 ....16 C2
Kilbride Rd KA3 ....195 B1
Kilbride St G5 ....117 B1
Kilbride View G71 ....141 A4
Kilburn Gr G72 ....140 B1
Kilburn Pl G13 ....95 A3
Kilchattan Dr G44 ....137 B4
Kilchoan Rd G33 ....99 B1
Kilcloy Ave G15 ....75 A2
Kilcreggan View PA15 ....46 B1
Kildale Rd PA12 ....129 A1
Kildale Way G73 ....137 C4
Kildare Dr ML11 ....215 A2
Kildare Pl ML11 ....215 A2
Kildare Rd ML11 ....215 A2
Kildary Ave G44 ....137 A3
Kildary Rd G44 ....137 A3
Kildean Hospl FK8 ....1 C1
Kildean Sch FK8 ....1 C1
Kildermorie Rd G34 ....120 A4
Kildonan Ct ML2 ....165 C4
Kildonan Dr Glasgow G11 ....96 A1
Helensburgh G84 ....16 C1
Kildonan Ho KA9 ....236 A3
Kildonan Pl
Motherwell ML1 ....163 B4
Saltcoats KA21 ....205 C1
Kildonan St ML5 ....122 A4
Kildrostan St G41 ....116 C1
Kildrum Prim Sch G67 ....62 B2
Kildrum Rd G67 ....62 B2
Kildrum South Rdbt G67 ....62 A1
Kildrummy Ave FK5 ....23 C2
Kildrummy Pl G74 ....159 B2
Kilearn Rd PA3 ....114 A4
Kilearn Sq PA3 ....114 A4
Kilearn Way PA3 ....114 A4
Kilfinan Rd ML7 ....146 B3
Kilfinan St G22 ....97 A4
Kilgarth St ML5 ....121 B2
Kilgraston Rd PA11 ....110 B3
Kilkerran KA13 ....207 A2
Kilkerran Ct G77 ....156 A2
Kilkerran Dr Glasgow G33 ....98 C3
Troon KA10 ....229 C4
Kilkerran Pk G77 ....156 A2
Kilkerran Way G77 ....156 A2
Killearn Dr PA1 ....114 C2
Killearn Rd PA15 ....46 A1
Killearn St G22 ....97 B2
Killermont Ave G61 ....76 A1
Killermont Ct G61 ....76 A2
Killermont Mdws G71 ....140 C1
Killermont Pl KA13 ....207 A2
Killermont Prim Sch G61 ....76 A2
Killermont Rd G61 ....76 A1
Killermont St G1 ....241 A3
Killermont View G61 ....76 A1
Killiegrew Rd G41 ....116 B1
Killin Ct ML5 ....122 A2
Killin Dr PA3 ....111 C3
Killin Pl Greenock PA16 ....45 A2
Troon KA10 ....229 D2
Killin St G32 ....119 A2
Killoch Ave PA3 ....113 A3
Killoch Dr Barrhead G78 ....134 B1
Glasgow G13 ....95 A3
Killoch La PA3 ....113 A3
Killoch Pl Ayr KA7 ....238 C4
Irvine KA11 ....219 C2
Killoch Rd PA3 ....113 A3
Killoch Way Irvine KA11 ....219 C2
Paisley PA3 ....113 A3
Kilmacolm Pl PA15 ....45 C2
Kilmacolm Prim Sch
PA13 ....89 B4
Kilmacolm Rd
Bridge of W PA11 ....90 A1
Greenock PA15 ....46 A1
Houston PA6 ....91 A2
Port Glasgow PA14 ....69 A3
Kilmahew Ave G82 ....26 A1
Kilmahew Ct
Ardrossan KA22 ....205 B1
Cardross G82 ....26 A1
Kilmahew Dr G82 ....26 A1
Kilmahew Gr G82 ....26 A1
Kilmahew St KA22 ....205 B1
Kilmailing Rd G44 ....137 A3
Kilmair Pl G20 ....96 B3
Kilmaluag Terr G46 ....135 B2
Kilmannan Gdns G62 ....54 C2
Kilmany Dr G32 ....118 C3
Kilmany Gdns G32 ....118 C3
Kilmardinny Ave G61 ....75 C3
Kilmardinny Cres G61 ....76 A3
Kilmardinny Dr G61 ....75 C3
Kilmardinny Gate G61 ....75 C3
Kilmardinny Gr G61 ....75 C3
Kilmari Gdns G15 ....74 C2
Kilmarnock Acad KA1 ....228 A4
Kilmarnock Coll KA3 ....228 A4

Kilmarnock Coll (Irvine Campus) KA12 ....219 B2
Kilmarnock Rd
Crosshouse KA2 ....222 A1
Dundonald KA2 ....225 C1
Glasgow G43 ....136 B4
Kilmaurs KA3 ....222 B3
Monkton KA9 ....233 C3
Springside KA11 ....221 A1
Symington KA1 ....231 B2
Troon KA10 ....229 D3
Kilmarnock Sta KA1 ....222 C1
Kilmartin La ML8 ....187 C2
Kilmartin Pl Airdrie ML6 ....123 B3
Glasgow G46 ....135 C2
Uddingston G71 ....121 A1
Kilmaurs Dr G46 ....136 C2
Kilmaurs Prim Sch KA3 ....222 A4
Kilmaurs Rd
Crosshouse KA2 ....221 C1
Fenwick KA3 ....212 C1
Kilmarnock KA3 ....222 C2
Kilmaurs St G51 ....115 C3
Kilmaurs Sta KA3 ....222 A4
Kilmeny Cres ML2 ....165 B3
Kilmeny Ct KA22 ....205 B1
Kilmeny Terr KA22 ....205 B1
Kilmichael Ave ML2 ....166 A3
Kilmore Cres G15 ....74 C2
Kilmore Dr G73 ....137 C4
Kilmory Ave G71 ....141 A4
Kilmory Ct
East Kilbride G75 ....180 B2
Falkirk FK1 ....41 B2
Kilmory Dr G77 ....156 C3
Kilmory Gdns ML8 ....188 A2
Kilmory Pl
Kilmarnock KA3 ....222 C2
Troon KA10 ....229 D3
Kilmory Rd Carluke ML8 ....2 A2
Saltcoats KA21 ....205 C1
Kilmory Terr PA14 ....47 B1
Kilmory Wlk KA3 ....195 B1
Kilmuir Cres G46 ....135 B2
Kilmuir Dr G46 ....135 C2
Kilmuir Rd Glasgow G46 ....135 C2
Uddingston G71 ....120 C1
Kilmun Rd PA15 ....46 A2
Kilmun St G20 ....96 B4
Kiln Ct KA12 ....219 B1
Kilnbank Cres KA7 ....239 B4
Kilnburn Rd ML1 ....163 B4
Kilncadzow Rd ML8 ....202 C4
Kilncraigs Ct FK10 ....10 B3
Kilncraigs Rd FK10 ....10 B3
Kilnford Cres KA2 ....225 B1
Kilnford Dr KA2 ....225 C1
Kilnknowe Cotts PA9 ....131 A3
Kilns Pl FK2 ....41 C3
Kilns Rd FK1 ....42 A3
Kilnside Rd PA1 ....114 A2
Kilnwell Quadrant ML1 ....163 B4
Kiloran Gr G77 ....156 A2
Kiloran Pl G77 ....156 A2
Kiloran St G46 ....135 C2
Kilpatrick Ave PA2 ....113 A1
Kilpatrick Cres PA2 ....133 B4
Kilpatrick Ct Irvine KA11 ....220 A2
Old Kilpatrick G60 ....73 A3
Kilpatrick Dr
Bearsden G61 ....75 B4
East Kilbride G75 ....180 A2
Erskine PA8 ....73 A2
Renfrew PA4 ....114 A4
Stepps G33 ....99 C3
Kilpatrick Gdns PG76 ....157 B4
Kilpatrick Pl KA11 ....220 A1
Kilpatrick Sta G60 ....73 A3
Kilpatrick View G82 ....50 A2
Kilrig Ave KA13 ....207 C2
Kilruskin Dr KA23 ....190 B2
Kilsyth Acad G65 ....36 B1
Kilsyth Cres KA11 ....220 A2
Kilsyth Gdns G75 ....180 A2
Kilsyth Prim Sch G65 ....60 B4
Kilsyth Rd Banknock FK4 ....38 B2
Kirkintilloch G66 ....58 C1
Queenzieburn G65 ....59 C4
Kilsyth Wlk KA11 ....220 A2
Kiltarie Cres ML6 ....123 C3
Kiltearn Rd G33 ....119 C4
Kiltongue Cotts ML6 ....122 B4
Kilvaxter Dr G46 ....135 C2
Kilwinning Abbey*
KA13 ....207 C2
Kilwinning Acad KA13 ....207 B2
Kilwinning Cres ML3 ....161 C1
Kilwinning Rd
Dalry KA24 ....191 A4
Irvine KA12 ....219 A3
Stevenston KA20 ....206 C1
Saltcoats KA21 ....211 B4
Kilwinning Sta KA13 ....207 B2
Kilwynet Way PA3 ....114 A4
Kimberley Gdns G75 ....180 B4
Kimberley St
Clydebank G81 ....73 C3
Wishaw ML2 ....164 B2
Kinalty Rd G44 ....137 A3
Kinarvie Cres G53 ....134 C4
Kinarvie Pl G53 ....134 C4
Kinarvie Rd G53 ....134 C4
Kinarvie Terr G53 ....134 C4
Kinbuck St G22 ....97 B2
Kincaid Dr G66 ....33 B1
Kincaid Field G66 ....58 B3
Kincaid Gdns G72 ....139 A3

Kincaid St PA16 ....45 A4
Kincaid Way G66 ....58 B3
Kincaidston Dr KA7 ....239 B2
Kincaidston Prim Sch
KA7 ....239 A2
Kincardine Dr G64 ....98 B4
Kincardine Pl
Bishopbriggs G64 ....98 B4
Paisley PA1 ....114 B2
Kincardine Rd FK2 ....24 B2
Kincardine Sq G33 ....99 B1
Kincath Ave G73 ....138 B2
Kinclaven Ave G15 ....75 A2
Kincraig St G51 ....115 B3
Kinellan Rd G61 ....75 C1
Kinellar Dr G14 ....95 A3
Kinfauns Dr Glasgow G15 ....75 A2
Newton Mearns G77 ....156 C3
King Edward La G13 ....95 C3
King Edward Rd G13 ....95 C3
King Edward St G83 ....27 C3
King George Ct PA4 ....94 C1
King George Gdns PA4 ....94 C1
King George Pl PA4 ....94 C1
King George Park Ave
PA4 ....94 C1
King George Way PA4 ....94 C1
King James Dr FK10 ....4 B1
King O' Muirs Ave FK10 ....4 C2
King O' Muirs Rd FK10 ....4 C2
King Pl G69 ....121 A3
King Robert Ct FK8 ....1 C1
King St Ayr KA8 ....236 A1
Clydebank G81 ....94 B4
Coatbridge ML5 ....121 C3
Paisley PA1 ....113 C2
Fallin FK7 ....8 B2
Glasgow G1 ....241 A1
Gourock PA19 ....44 C4
Greenock PA15 ....45 C3
Hamilton ML3 ....162 A2
Kilmarnock KA1 ....227 C4
Kilsyth G65 ....60 B4
Kilwinning KA13 ....207 C2
Larkhall ML9 ....185 A1
Paisley PA1 ....113 B3
Port Glasgow PA14 ....47 B1
Renton G82 ....27 B1
Rutherglen G73 ....138 A4
Shotts ML7 ....146 C2
Stenhousemuir FK5 ....23 C2
Stirling FK8 ....7 A4
Stonehouse ML9 ....198 C1
Wishaw ML2 ....165 A1
Wishaw, Newmains ML2 ....166 A3
King St E G84 ....16 C1
King Street La
Kilsyth G65 ....60 B4
Rutherglen G73 ....138 A4
King's Cres
Cambuslang G72 ....139 A3
Carluke ML8 ....188 A1
Helensburgh G84 ....16 C1
King's Ct KA15 ....150 A1
King's Dr Cumbernauld G68 ....61 C3
Glasgow G40 ....117 C2
Newton Mearns G77 ....157 A2
King's Gdns G77 ....157 A2
King's Glen Prim Sch
PA15 ....46 B1
King's Park Ave G44 ....94 C2
King's Park Prim Sch
G44 ....137 B3
King's Park Rd
Glasgow G44 ....137 A4
Stirling FK8 ....7 A4
King's Park Sec Sch
G44 ....137 C3
King's Park Sta G44 ....137 B3
King's Pk Rd FK6 ....6 C3
King's Pl G22 ....97 A2
King's Rd Beith KA15 ....150 A1
Elderslie PA5 ....112 A1
King's View G68 ....61 C3
King's Way G82 ....49 A1
Kingarth La G42 ....117 A1
Kingarth St Glasgow G42 ....117 A1
Hamilton ML3 ....183 B4
Kingcase Ave KA9 ....236 A3
Kingcase Prim Sch KA9 ....236 A3
Kingfisher Dr G13 ....94 C4
Kingfisher Gdns G13 ....95 A4
Kinghorn Dr G44 ....137 B4
Kinghorn La G44 ....137 B4
Kinglas Rd G61 ....75 B1
Kinglas Cres PA5 ....112 B2
Kings Ct Alloa FK10 ....10 A4
Ayr KA8 ....236 A1
Kings Dr ML1 ....142 C2
Kings Inch Dr PA4 ....94 B3
Kings Inch Pl PA4 ....95 A1
Kings Knot* FK8 ....6 C4
Kings Myre ML11 ....215 B2
Kings Pk KA7 ....238 C1
Kingsacre Rd G44 ....137 B4
Kingsbarns Dr G44 ....137 A4
Kingsborough Gate
G12 ....96 A2
Kingsborough Gdns G12 ....96 A2
Kingsborough La G12 ....96 A2
Kingsborough La E G12 ....96 A2
Kingsbrae Ave G44 ....137 B4
Kingsbridge Cres G44 ....137 B3
Kingsbridge Dr G44 ....137 B3

Kingsburgh Dr PA1 ....114 A3
Kingsburn Dr G73 ....138 A3
Kingsburn Gr G73 ....138 A3
Kingscliffe Ave G44 ....137 B3
Kingsdale Ave G44 ....137 B3
Kingscourt Ave G44 ....137 B3
Kingscroft Rd KA9 ....236 A4
Kingsdale Ave G44 ....137 B3
Kingsdyke Ave G44 ....137 B3
Kingseat Pl FK1 ....41 C2
Kingsford Ave G44 ....136 C2
Kingsford Ct G77 ....156 B3
Kingsford Pl KA3 ....223 A3
Kingsgate Ret Pk G74 ....160 A3
Kingsheath Ave G73 ....137 C3
Kingshill Ave G68 ....60 C1
Kingshill Dr G44 ....137 B3
Kingshill Rd ML7 ....167 A4
Kingshill View ML8 ....187 A2
Kingshouse Ave G44 ....137 B3
Kingsknowe Dr G44 ....137 B4
Kingsknowe Dr G73 ....137 C3
Kingsland Cres G52 ....115 A3
Kingsland Dr G52 ....115 A3
Kingslea Rd PA6 ....91 A1
Kingsley Ave
Glasgow G42 ....117 A1
Stenhousemuir FK5 ....23 C2
Kingsley Ct G71 ....141 A4
Kingslynn Dr G44 ....137 B3
Kingsmuir Dr G73 ....137 C3
Kingstables La FK8 ....7 A4
Kingston Ave
[1] Airdrie ML6 ....123 B4
Neilston G78 ....154 B3
Uddingston G71 ....141 A4
Kingston Flats G65 ....36 B1
Kingston Gr G64 ....78 A1
Kingston Ind Est G5 ....116 C3
Kingston Pl G81 ....73 B2
Kingston Rd
Bishopton PA7 ....72 A2
Kilsyth G65 ....36 B1
Neilston G78 ....154 B3
Kingston St G5 ....240 C2
Kingsway Dalry KA24 ....191 A4
East Kilbride G74 ....160 A2
Glasgow G14 ....95 A3
Gourock PA19 ....44 B3
Stepps G65 ....36 B1
Kingsway Ct G14 ....95 A3
Kingswell Ave KA3 ....223 A3
Kingswell Pk FK10 ....10 B4
Kingswood Dr G44 ....137 B4
Kingswood Rd PA7 ....71 C2
Kingussie Ave KA3 ....195 B1
Kingussie Dr G44 ....137 B4
Kiniver Dr G15 ....75 A1
Kinkell Gdns G66 ....59 A1
Kinloch Ave
Cambuslang G72 ....139 A2
Linwood PA3 ....112 A3
Stewarton KA3 ....195 B1
Kinloch Dr ML1 ....142 B1
Kinloch La PA16 ....44 C2
Kinloch Rd
Kilmarnock KA1 ....228 A3
Newton Mearns G77 ....156 B3
Renfrew PA4 ....94 A1
Kinloch St G40 ....118 B2
Kinloch Terr PA16 ....44 C2
Kinloch Pl G74 ....159 C1
Kinmount Ave G44 ....137 A4
Kinmount La G44 ....137 B4
Kinnaird Ave Falkirk FK2 ....24 A2
Newton Mearns G77 ....157 A2
Kinnaird Cres G61 ....76 A2
Kinnaird Dr Linwood PA3 ....112 A3
Stenhousemuir FK5 ....23 C2
Kinnaird Pl G64 ....98 A4
Kinnear Rd G40 ....118 A2
Kinneil Pl ML3 ....161 C1
Kinnell Ave G52 ....115 B2
Kinnell Cres G52 ....115 B2
Kinnell Path G52 ....115 B2
Kinnell Pl G52 ....115 B2
Kinnell Sq G52 ....115 B2
Kinnier Rd KA21 ....217 A4
Kinnin Brae KA23 ....190 B2
Kinning Park Ind Est
 ....116 C3
Kinning Park Underground
Sta G41 ....116 B3
Kinning St G5 ....117 A3
Kinnis Vennel KA13 ....207 B2
Kinnoul Gdns G61 ....75 B4
Kinnoull Pl G72 ....161 B4
Kinnoull Rd KA1 ....228 A2
Kinpurnie Rd PA1 ....114 B3
Kinross Ave
Glasgow G52 ....115 A2
Port Glasgow PA14 ....47 B1
Kinross Pk G74 ....160 B2
Kinsail Dr G52 ....114 C3
Kinstone Ave G14 ....95 A3
Kintail Gdns G66 ....59 A1
Kintessack Pl G64 ....78 B1
Kintillo Dr G13 ....95 A3
Kintore Pk ML3 ....183 A3
Kintore Rd G43 ....136 C3
Kintore Twr G72 ....138 C2
Kintra St G51 ....116 A4
Kintyre Ave PA5 ....111 C1
Kintyre Cres
Newton Mearns G77 ....156 B3
Plains ML6 ....104 A2
Kintyre Gdns G66 ....59 A1

Kintyre Pl FK1 ....41 B2
Kintyre Rd G72 ....161 B4
Kintyre St G21 ....98 A1
Kintyre Terr PA16 ....44 B2
Kintyre Wynd ML8 ....187 C2
Kinpland Wlk ML5 ....122 B3
Kippen Dr G76 ....158 A3
Kippen St Airdrie ML6 ....122 C4
Glasgow G22 ....97 B3
Kipperoch Rd G82 ....49 A4
Kippford Pl ML6 ....123 C1
Kippford St G32 ....119 B2
Kipps Ave ML6 ....122 C1
Kirk Ave FK5 ....23 C2
Kirk Cl KA24 ....191 B4
Kirk Cres G60 ....73 A4
Kirk Cl Way G3 ....198 C1
Kirk Glebe Neilston G78 ....154 C4
Stewarton KA3 ....211 B4
Kirk La Bearsden G61 ....75 C3
Glasgow G43 ....136 B4
Kirk O' Shotts Prim Sch
ML7 ....125 B2
Kirk Path ML7 ....167 A4
Kirk St Bearsden G61 ....75 C3
Cumbernauld G67 ....82 A4
Uddingston G71 ....140 C3
Kirk Port KA7 ....238 C4
Kirk Rd Bearsden G61 ....75 C3
Beith KA15 ....171 A4
Carluke ML8 ....187 C1
Carmunnock G76 ....158 B4
Dalserf ML9 ....186 A1
Houston PA6 ....91 B1
Motherwell ML1 ....143 B4
Motherwell ML1 ....146 C2
Wishaw ML2 ....165 B2
Kirk St Carluke ML8 ....187 C1
Coatbridge ML5 ....121 C3
Milngavie G62 ....55 A1
Motherwell ML1 ....163 C4
Prestwick KA9 ....233 B1
Stonehouse ML9 ....198 C1
Kirk Vennel KA12 ....219 B1
Kirk View KA15 ....171 A4
Kirk Wynd
[1] East Kilbride G74 ....159 C1
[2] Falkirk FK1 ....42 A2
Stirling FK7 ....7 A2
Kirkaig Ave PA4 ....94 C1
Kirkbean Ave G73 ....138 A2
Kirkbrae FK10 ....10 C2
Kirkbride Terr FK7 ....12 B2
Kirkbriggs Way G73 ....138 A3
Kirkburn Ave FK6 ....139 A2
Kirkburn Dr FK6 ....31 B2
Kirkburn Rd FK6 ....31 B2
Kirkcaldy Rd G41 ....116 B1
Kirkconnel Ave
Cumbernauld G68 ....60 C1
Glasgow G13 ....94 C3
Kirkconnel Dr G73 ....137 C3
Kirkcudbright Pl G74 ....160 B2
Kirkdale Dr G52 ....115 C2
Kirkdene Ave G77 ....157 A3
Kirkdene Bank G77 ....157 A3
Kirkdene Cres G77 ....157 A3
Kirkdene Gr G77 ....157 A3
Kirkdene Pl G77 ....157 A3
Kirkfield Bank Way
ML3 ....162 A2
Kirkfield Rd
Bothwell G71 ....141 A2
Kirkfieldbank ML11 ....214 B2
Kirkfield Wynd ML8 ....165 B2
Kirkfield Wynd PA9 ....130 C2
Kirkfieldbank Brae
ML11 ....214 B2
Kirkfieldbank Prim Sch
ML11 ....214 B2
Kirkford KA3 ....211 C4
Kirkford Rd G69 ....80 C1
Kirkgate Alloa FK10 ....10 A3
Irvine KA12 ....219 B1
Saltcoats KA21 ....216 A4
Wishaw ML2 ....165 C2
Kirkhall Gdns KA22 ....205 B1
Kirkhall Pl FK6 ....21 C1
Kirkhall Rd ML1 ....143 B2
Kirkhall KA13 ....207 B1
Kirkhill Ave G72 ....139 A2
Kirkhill Cres KA11 ....220 A1
Kirkhill Dr G20 ....96 B3
Kirkhill Gate G77 ....157 A2
Kirkhill Gdns G72 ....139 A2
Kirkhill Gr G72 ....139 A2
Kirkhill Pl Glasgow G20 ....96 B3
Wishaw ML2 ....164 B1
Kirkhill Prim Sch G77 ....157 A3
Kirkhill Rd Gartcosh G69 ....100 C3
Newton Mearns G77 ....157 A3
Uddingston G71 ....140 C4
Wishaw ML2 ....164 B1
Kirkhill Sta G72 ....139 A2
Kirkhill Terr G72 ....139 A2
Kirkholm Ave KA8 ....236 A2
Kirkhope Dr G15 ....75 A1
Kirkhouse Ave G63 ....31 B2
Kirkhouse Cres G63 ....31 B2
Kirkhouse Rd G63 ....31 B2
Kirkhouse St G22 ....119 B2
Kirkintilloch High Sch
G66 ....80 A4

Kirkintilloch Ind Est G66 .58 B1
Kirkintilloch Rd
Bishopbriggs G64 .78 B3
Kirkintilloch G66 .58 A1
Kirkintilloch, Waterside G66 .80 B4
Kirkland Ave
Kilmarnock KA3 .222 C2
Strathblane G63 .31 B2
Kirkland Cres KA24 .191 A4
Kirkland Dr FK6 .21 A1
Kirkland Gdns KA3 .222 B3
Kirkland Gr PA5 .111 C2
Kirkland La G83 .27 C2
Kirkland Rd Dunlop KA3 .195 A4
Glengarnock KA14,KA25 .170 A4
Kirkland St Glasgow G20 .96 C2
Motherwell ML1 .163 B4
Kirkland Terr KA11 .220 C1
Kirklandholm KA9 .236 B3
Kirklandneuk Cres PA4 .94 A2
Kirklandneuk Prim Sch
PA4 .94 A2
Kirklandneuk Rd PA4 .94 A2
Kirklands Cres
Bothwell G71 .141 A2
Kilsyth G65 .60 B4
Kirklands Dr G77 .156 B1
Kirklands Hospl G71 .141 A2
Kirklands Pl G77 .156 B1
Kirklands Rd
Lanark ML11 .215 A2
Newton Mearns G77 .156 B1
Kirklandside Hospl KA1 .228 B3
Kirkle Dr G77 .157 A3
Kirklea Gdns PA3 .113 A3
Kirklee Cir G12 .96 B2
Kirklee Gardens La G12 .96 B2
Kirklee Gate G12 .96 B2
Kirklee Gdns G12 .96 B2
Kirklee Pl G12 .96 B2
Kirklee Quadrant 42 G12 .96 B2
Kirklee Quadrant La G12 .96 B2
Kirklee Rd Glasgow G12 .96 B2
Motherwell ML1,ML4 .142 C2
Kirklee Terr G12 .96 B2
Kirklee Terrace La G12 .96 B2
Kirklee Terrace Rd 41
G12 .96 B2
Kirkliston St G32 .118 C3
Kirkmichael Ave 9 G11 .96 A2
Kirkmichael Gdns 8
G11 .96 A2
Kirkmichael Rd G84 .16 C1
Kirkmuir Dr
Rutherglen G73 .138 A2
Stewarton KA3 .195 B1
Kirkness St ML6 .123 A4
Kirknethan ML2 .164 B1
Kirknewton St G32 .119 A3
Kirkoswald G74 .160 B2
Kirkoswald Dr G81 .74 B2
Kirkoswald Rd
Glasgow G43 .136 B3
Motherwell ML1 .143 C2
Kirkpatrick Cres G83 .27 B4
Kirkpatrick St G40 .118 A3
Kirkriggs Ave G73 .138 A3
Kirkriggs Prim Sch G45 .138 A3
Kirkriggs View G73 .138 A3
Kirkshaw Ct PA5 .111 C2
Kirkshaws Ave ML5 .121 C2
Kirkshaws Pl ML5 .121 C2
Kirkshaws Prim Sch
ML5 .121 C2
Kirkshaws Rd ML5 .121 C2
Kirkside Cres FK7 .7 A3
Kirkslap FK6 .21 C1
Kirkstall Gdns G64 .78 A2
Kirkstone G77 .157 A3
Kirkstone Cl G75 .179 C3
Kirkstyle Ave ML8 .187 C1
Kirkstyle Cres
Airdrie ML6 .102 C1
Neilston G78 .154 B4
Kirkstyle Ct KA11 .220 A3
Kirkstyle La G78 .154 C4
Kirkstyle Pl ML6 .102 B2
Kirkstyle Prim Sch KA1 .228 A3
Kirksyde Ave G66 .79 C4
Kirkton
Erskine, North Barr PA8 .73 A2
Old Kilpatrick G60 .73 A4
Kirkton Ave
Barrhead G78 .134 A1
Blantyre G72 .161 B3
Carluke ML8 .187 C1
Glasgow G13 .95 A3
West Kilbride KA23 .190 B2
Kirkton Cres
Cardross G82 .26 A1
Coatbridge ML5 .122 B2
Glasgow G13 .95 A3
Milton of C G66 .58 B3
Kirkton Ct Carluke ML8 .187 C1
Eaglesham G76 .178 C2
Kirkton Dr G76 .178 C3
Kirkton Gate G74 .159 C1
Kirkton Moor Rd G76 .178 A2
Kirkton Pk G74 .159 C1
Kirkton Pl Blantyre G72 .161 B3
Coatbridge ML5 .122 B2
East Kilbride G74 .159 C1
Falkirk FK2 .24 B2
Fenwick KA3 .213 A2
Kirkton Prim Sch ML8 .187 C1
Kirkton Rd
Cambuslang G72 .139 A3
Cardross G82 .26 A1
Kirkton Rd *continued*
Dumbarton G82 .49 B2
Fenwick KA3 .213 A2
Kilmarnock KA3 .222 C3
Kilmaurs KA3 .222 B3
Neilston G78 .154 C3
Kirkton St ML8 .187 C1
Kirkton Terr G66 .32 C2
Kirktonfield Dr G78 .154 C4
Kirktonfield Pl G78 .154 C4
Kirktonfield Rd G78 .154 C4
Kirktonholm Pl 14 KA1 .227 C4
Kirktonholm St 12 KA1 .227 C4
Kirktonholme Cres G74 .159 B1
Kirktonholme Prim Sch
G74 .159 B1
Kirktonholme Rd G74 .159 B1
Kirktonside G78 .134 A1
Kirkvale Cres G77 .157 A3
Kirkvale Ct G77 .157 A3
Kirkvale Dr G77 .157 A3
Kirkview G67 .82 A3
Kirkview Ave ML7 .125 B1
Kirkview Cres G77 .156 C2
Kirkview Ct G67 .82 A3
Kirkview Gdns G71 .140 C4
Kirkville Pl G15 .75 A1
Kirkwall G67 .62 A3
Kirkwall Ave G72 .140 B2
Kirkwall Pl KA3 .223 A3
Kirkwall Rd PA16 .44 C2
Kirkway FK2 .14 B2
Kirkwell Rd G44 .137 A3
Kirkwood Ave
Clydebank G81 .74 C1
Stepps G33 .100 A3
Kirkwood Pl ML5 .121 C3
Kirkwood Quadrant G81 .74 B1
Kirkwood Rd G71 .140 C4
Kirkwood St
Coatbridge ML5 .121 C3
Glasgow G51 .116 B3
Rutherglen G73 .138 A4
Kirkwood Sta ML5 .121 B3
Kirn Dr PA19 .44 B3
Kirn Rd KA3 .222 C1
Kirn St G20 .96 B4
Kirriemuir G74 .160 B3
Kirriemuir Ave G52 .115 B2
Kirriemuir Gdns G64 .78 B1
Kirriemuir Pl G52 .115 B2
Kirriemuir Rd G64 .78 B1
Kirstie Pl G83 .27 C1
Kirtle Dr PA4 .94 C1
Kirtle Pl G75 .179 C4
Kishorn Pl G33 .99 B1
Kitchener St ML2 .165 A2
Kittoch Pl 4 G74 .159 C1
Kittoch Sch G75 .180 B4
Kittoch St G74 .159 C1
Kittochside Rd G76 .158 C3
Kittyshaw Rd KA24 .191 A4
Klondike Ct ML1 .143 A2
Knapdale St G22 .97 A4
Knights Gate G71 .140 C3
Knights Way FK6 .21 B1
Knightsbridge St G13 .95 B4
Knightscliffe Ave G13 .95 C4
Knightswood Ct G13 .95 B3
Knightswood Prim Sch
G13 .95 C4
Knightswood Rd G13 .95 B4
Knightswood Sec Sch
G13 .95 B3
Knightswood Sec Sch
(Annexe) G13 .95 B4
Knightswood Terr G72 .140 C1
Knivysbridge Pl ML4 .141 C2
Knock Jargon Ct KA21 .205 C2
Knock Way PA3 .114 A4
Knockbuckle Ave PA13 .69 A1
Knockbuckle Rd PA13 .89 B4
Knockburn Prim Sch
G21 .98 B4
Knockburnie Rd G71 .141 A2
Knockentiber Rd KA11 .221 A1
Knockhall St G33 .99 B1
Knockhill Dr G44 .137 A4
Knockhill Rd PA4 .94 A1
Knockinlaw Mount KA3 .222 C2
Knockinlaw Rd KA3 .222 C2
Knockmarloch Dr KA1 .227 C2
Knocknair St PA14 .68 C4
Knockrivoch Gdns KA22 .205 C2
Knockrivoch Pl KA22 .205 C2
Knockrivoch Wynd
KA22 .205 C2
Knockside Ave PA2 .133 B4
Knoll Croft Rd ML7 .147 A2
Knoll Pk KA7 .238 C2
Knollpark Dr G76 .157 B4
Knowe Cres ML1 .143 B2
Knowe Rd Chryston G69 .100 B4
Greenock PA15 .46 A2
Paisley PA3 .114 A4
Knowe St G62 .54 C1
Knowe The Alloa FK10 .5 B1
Troon KA10 .229 D4
Knowefaulds Rd FK10 .4 A2
Knowehead Dr G71 .140 C3
Knowehead Gdns G71 .140 C3
Knowehead Rd
Clachan of C G66 .32 C2
Hurlford KA1 .228 C3
Kilmarnock KA1 .227 C2
Wishaw ML2 .165 B1
Knoweholm KA7 .238 B1
Knowenoble St ML1 .144 A1
Knowes Ave G77 .156 C3
Knowes Rd G77 .156 C3
Knowetap St G20 .96 C4
Knowetop Ave ML1 .163 C2
Knowetop Cres G82 .49 B3
Knowetop Prim Sch
ML1 .163 C2
Knowhead Gdns 5 G41 .116 C2
Knowhead Terr 4 G41 .116 C2
Knox Ave PA11 .110 B4
Knox Pl
Newton Mearns G77 .156 A2
Saltcoats KA21 .206 A1
Knox St Airdrie ML6 .123 A4
Paisley PA1 .113 B2
Knoxland Prim Sch G82 .50 A2
Knoxland Sq G82 .50 A1
Knoxland St G82 .50 A1
Knoxville Rd KA25 .149 A1
Kronborg Way G75 .180 C3
Kyle Acad KA7 .239 B4
Kyle Ave Cowie FK7 .12 C4
Springside KA11 .220 C1
Kyle Cres KA10 .230 A2
Kyle Ct Ayr KA7 .239 A4
Cambuslang G72 .139 A3
Kyle Ctr KA7 .238 C4
Kyle Dr Glasgow G46 .136 C2
Troon KA10 .229 C3
Kyle Gr ML1 .143 A2
Kyle Quadrant
Motherwell ML1 .143 B2
Wishaw ML2 .164 C1
Kyle Rd Cumbernauld G67 .62 A2
Irvine KA12 .224 B4
Kyle Sq G73 .137 C3
Kyle St Ayr KA7 .238 C4
Glasgow G4 .241 A4
Motherwell ML1 .163 A4
Prestwick KA9 .236 B4
Kyle Terr G82 .49 A3
Kyleakin Dr G72 .140 A1
Kyleakin Rd G46 .135 B2
Kyleakin Terr G46 .135 B2
Kylemore Cres ML1 .142 B1
Kylemore La PA16 .44 C2
Kylemore Terr PA16 .44 C2
Kylepark Ave G71 .140 B3
Kylepark Cres G71 .140 B4
Kylepark Dr G71 .140 B4
Kylerhea Rd G46 .135 B2
Kyleshill KA21 .216 C4
Kyleswell St KA13 .207 C2

L

La Belle Allee 13 G3 .96 C1
La Belle Pl 12 G3 .96 C1
La Crosse Terr G12 .96 C2
Laberge Gdns ML1 .143 A2
Laburnum Ave
Beith KA15 .171 A4
Cambuslang G72 .139 C2
East Kilbride G75 .180 B3
Laburnum Cres ML2 .165 A3
Laburnum Ct G75 .180 B3
Laburnum Dr G66 .58 A3
Laburnum Gdns G66 .79 A3
Laburnum Gr
Coatbridge ML5 .122 A3
Kirkintilloch G66 .79 A3
Stirling FK8 .6 C3
Troon KA10 .229 C2
Laburnum Lea ML3 .162 C1
Laburnum Pl PA5 .132 A4
Laburnum Rd Ayr KA7 .239 B3
Banknock FK4 .38 C1
Cumbernauld G67 .62 B1
Glasgow G51 .116 B2
Kilmarnock KA1 .227 B4
Uddingston G71 .141 B4
Laburnum St PA15 .46 C1
Lachlan Cres PA8 .72 C1
Lacy St PA1 .114 A2
Ladder Ct G75 .180 A2
Lade Ct PA12 .129 B1
Lade Dr FK5 .41 B4
Lade Mill FK7 .7 B1
Lade Rd FK4 .40 A3
Lade Terr G52 .115 A2
Lade The G83 .27 C3
Ladeside KA3 .222 B4
Ladeside Cl G77 .156 B3
Ladeside Cres FK5 .23 C1
Ladeside Ct KA25 .170 A4
Ladeside Dr
Johnstone PA5 .111 B1
Kilsyth G65 .36 C1
Ladeside Gdns KA3 .222 B4
Ladeside Prim Sch FK5 .41 B4
Ladeside Rd KA3 .222 B4
Ladhope Pl G13 .94 C4
Lady Alice Prim Sch
PA16 .45 B2
Lady Ann Cres ML6 .123 B3
Lady Anne St G14 .94 C3
Lady Isle Cres G71 .140 C3
Lady Jane Gate G71 .140 C2
Lady La PA1 .113 B2
Lady Margaret Dr KA10 .230 A1
Lady Mary Wlk ML3 .162 C1
Lady Watson Gdns ML3 .162 A1
Lady Wilson St ML6 .123 A4
Lady's Gate G83 .27 C1
Ladyacre KA13 .207 C2
Ladyacre Rd ML11 .215 A2
Ladyacres PA4 .93 B3
Ladyacres Way PA4 .93 B3
Ladybank G68 .61 C3
Ladybank Ct 12 G74 .159 C1
Ladybank Dr G52 .115 C2
Ladybank Gdns G74 .159 C1
Ladybank Pl 11 G74 .159 C1
Ladyburn Ct KA11 .219 C3
Ladyburn St
Greenock PA15 .46 B2
Paisley PA1 .114 A2
Ladyford Ave KA13 .207 C2
Ladyha Ct KA11 .220 A3
Ladyhill Dr G69 .120 A2
Ladykirk Cres
Glasgow G52 .115 A3
Paisley PA2 .113 C2
Ladykirk Dr G52 .115 B3
Ladykirk Rd KA9 .236 B4
Ladyland Dr KA25 .149 A2
Ladyloan Ave G15 .74 C2
Ladyloan Ct G15 .74 C2
Ladyloan Gdns G15 .74 C2
Ladymuir Circ PA8 .72 C1
Ladymuir Cres G53 .115 B1
Ladysgate Ct FK2 .24 A2
Ladysmill FK2 .42 B3
Ladysmill Ind Est FK1 .42 B3
Ladysmith Ave PA10 .111 B1
Ladysmith Dr G75 .180 A2
Ladysmith Rd KA25 .149 A1
Ladysmith St ML2 .164 B2
Ladysneuk Rd FK9 .2 B1
Ladyton G83 .27 C2
Ladyton Prim Sch G83 .28 A2
Ladywell Ct FK5 .23 A2
Ladywell Dr FK10 .4 A2
Ladywell Pl FK10 .4 A2
Ladywell Prim Sch ML1 .163 B4
Ladywell Rd ML1 .163 B4
Ladywell St G4 .241 C2
Ladywood G62 .55 A1
Lagan Rd ML8 .188 A1
Laggan Ave ML7 .147 A2
Laggan Ho KA9 .236 A3
Laggan Path ML7 .146 C3
Laggan Quadrant ML6 .102 C1
Laggan Rd Airdrie ML6 .102 C1
Bishopbriggs G64 .78 A1
Glasgow G43 .136 C3
Newton Mearns G77 .156 B4
Laggan Terr PA4 .94 A2
Laggan Way ML2 .165 C4
Laggary Pk G84 .15 C3
Laggary Rd G84 .15 C3
Laidlaw Ave ML1 .142 C2
Laidlaw Gdns G71 .120 C1
Laidlaw St G5 .240 B1
Laidon Rd ML6 .102 C1
Laidon Wlk 3 ML2 .165 C3
Laigh Ct KA15 .150 A1
Laigh Milton Viaduct*
KA2 .226 B3
Laigh Mount KA7 .238 C1
Laigh Rd Beith KA15 .150 A1
Newton Mearns G77 .157 B3
Laighcartside St PA5 .112 A2
Laighdykes Rd KA21 .205 C1
Laighland KA9 .236 B3
Laighlands Rd G71 .141 A1
Laighmuir St G71 .140 C3
Laighpark Ave PA7 .72 A2
Laighpark View PA3 .113 C4
Laighstonehall Rd ML3 .162 A1
Laightoun Ct G67 .82 A3
Laightoun Dr G67 .82 A3
Laightoun Gdns G67 .82 A3
Lainshaw KA13 .207 B1
Lainshaw Ave KA1 .227 C2
Lainshaw Dr G45 .137 A1
Lainshaw Prim Sch KA3 .211 B4
Lainshaw St KA3 .211 B4
Laird Gr G71 .141 A4
Laird Pl G40 .117 C2
Laird St Coatbridge ML5 .122 A4
Greenock PA15 .45 C3
Laird Weir KA22 .205 B2
Laird's Hill Ct G65 .60 A4
Laird's Hill Pl G65 .60 A4
Lairds Gate G71 .140 B3
Lairds Hill G67 .61 C1
Lairdsland Prim Sch G66 .79 B4
Lairg Dr G72 .140 B1
Lairhills Rd G75 .180 C4
Lake Ave ML11 .215 B1
Lakefield Ct G72 .161 B3
Lamb St Glasgow G22 .97 A3
Hamilton ML3 .162 C2
Lambert Terr FK10 .10 B4
Lamberton Ave FK7 .7 B2
Lamberton Dr G52 .115 B3
Lamberton Gdns KA11 .220 B3
Lamberton Rd KA3 .195 B1
Lambhill Quadrant 5
G41 .116 C3
Lambhill St G41 .116 B3
Lambie Cres G77 .156 B3
Lambie Ct KA21 .216 C4
Lamerton Rd G67 .62 B1
Lamford Dr KA7 .238 B1
Lamington Rd G52 .115 A3
Lamlash Cres G33 .119 A4
Lamlash Pl
East Kilbride G75 .180 A2
Glasgow G33 .119 A4
Helensburgh G84 .16 C1
Motherwell ML1 .163 B4
Lamlash Prim Sch G33 .119 A4
Lamlash Sq G33 .119 B4
Lammer Wynd 16 ML9 .185 B1
Lammerknowes Rd G65 .37 C2
Lammermoor G74 .160 C2
Lammermoor Ave G52 .115 B2
Lammermoor Cres G66 .79 C4
Lammermoor Dr G67 .82 C4
Lammermoor Gdns G66 .79 C4
Lammermoor Prim Sch
ML2 .165 A3
Lammermoor Rd G66 .79 C4
Lammermoor Terr ML2 .165 A2
Lammermuir Ct KA11 .220 A2
Lammermuir Dr PA2 .133 C4
Lammermuir Gdns G61 .75 B4
Lammermuir Pl ML1 .143 A3
Lammermuir Rd KA1 .228 A2
Lammermuir Way ML6 .123 C1
Lammermuir Wynd
ML9 .184 C3
Lamond View FK5 .23 B1
Lamont Ave PA7 .72 B2
Lamont Cres Fallin FK7 .8 B3
Renton G82 .27 B1
Lamont Dr KA12 .224 C4
Lamont Pl KA12 .224 C4
Lamont Rd G21 .98 A3
Lanark Ave ML6 .123 A2
Lanark Gram Sch ML11 .215 A2
Lanark Ind Est ML11 .215 C3
Lanark Moor Ctry Pk*
ML11 .215 C2
Lanark Mus* ML11 .214 C2
Lanark Prim Sch ML11 .215 A3
Lanark Rd
Carluke ML8,ML11 .202 A2
Larkhall ML9 .185 B3
Netherburn ML8 .200 B4
Lanark St G1 .241 B1
Lanark Sta ML11 .215 A2
Lancaster Ave
Beith KA15 .171 A4
Chapelhall ML6 .143 C4
Lancaster Cres G12 .96 B2
Lancaster Crescent La
G12 .96 B2
Lancaster Rd G64 .78 A2
Lancaster Terr 31 G12 .96 B2
Lancaster Terrace La 30
G12 .96 B2
Lancaster Way 4 PA4 .94 B1
Lancefield Quay G3 .240 A2
Lancefield St G3 .240 A2
Landemer Dr G73 .138 A3
Landressy Pl G40 .117 C2
Landressy St G40 .117 C2
Landsborough Ct KA21 .205 C1
Landsborough Dr KA3 .223 A2
Landsborough Pl KA20 .206 C1
Landsdowne Gdns ML3 .162 C2
Landsdowne Rd ML9 .185 B1
Lane The G68 .61 B3
Lanfine Rd PA1 .114 B2
Lanfine Terr KA11 .219 C3
Lanfine Way KA11 .220 A3
Lang Ave Bishopton PA7 .72 B2
Renfrew PA4 .94 B1
Lang Pl PA5 .111 C2
Lang Rd KA10 .229 D4
Lang St PA1 .114 A2
Langa St G20 .96 C4
Langbank Dr PA13 .69 C1
Langbank Prim Sch
PA14 .70 A4
Langbank Rise PA13 .69 C1
Langbank St 1 G5 .117 A3
Langbank Sta PA14 .70 B4
Langbar Cres G33 .119 C4
Langbyres Rd ML1 .144 B1
Langcraig Rd KA1 .227 C1
Langcraigs Ct PA2 .133 B4
Langcraigs Dr PA2 .133 B3
Langcraigs Prim Sch
PA2 .133 B4
Langcraigs Terr PA2 .133 B3
Langcroft Ave KA9 .233 C1
Langcroft Dr G72 .139 B2
Langcroft Pl G51 .115 B4
Langcroft Rd G51 .115 B4
Langcroft Terr G51 .115 B4
Langdale
East Kilbride G74 .159 B2
Newton Mearns G77 .157 A3
Langdale Ave G33 .98 C2
Langdale Rd G69 .80 C1
Langdale St G33 .98 C2
Langdales Ave G68 .61 B1
Langfaulds Cres G81 .74 B3
Langfaulds Prim Sch
G15 .74 C2
Langford Dr G53 .135 A2
Langford Pl G53 .135 A2
Langhaul Rd G53 .114 C1
Langhill Dr G68 .61 B2
Langhill Pl FK6 .21 B1
Langholm G75 .179 C3
Langholm Cres ML2 .165 A3
Langholm Ct G69 .81 A1
Langholm Dr PA3 .112 B3
Langlands Ave
East Kilbride G75 .180 C2
Glasgow G51 .115 B4
Langlands Brae KA1 .222 C1
Langlands Ct
East Kilbride G75 .180 C2
Glasgow G51 .115 C4

Langlands Dr
East Kilbride G75 .....180 C2
Glasgow G51 ....115 B4
Langlands Gate G75 ...180 C2
Langlands Moss Nature
Reserve* G75 ....180 C2
Langlands Pl G75 ....180 C2
Langlands Rd
East Kilbride G75 .....180 C2
Glasgow G51 ....115 C4
Langlands Sch G51 ...115 C4
Langlands Sq G75 ....180 C2
Langlands St KA1 ....222 C1
Langlands Terr G82 ...50 A3
Langlands-Seafar Intc
G67 ....82 C4
Langlea Ave G72 .....138 B2
Langlea Ct G72 ......138 C2
Langlea Dr G72 ......138 C3
Langlea Gdns G72 ....138 C3
Langlea Gr G72,G73 ..138 C2
Langlea Way G72 .....138 C3
Langlees Ave G77 ....157 A3
Langlees Prim Sch FK2 .42 A4
Langlees St FK2 ......24 B1
Langley Ave G13 .....95 A4
Langloan Cres ML5 ...121 C3
Langloan Pl ML5 .....121 C3
Langloan Prim Sch ML5 .121 C3
Langloan St ML5 .....121 C3
Langmuir Ave
Kirkintilloch G66 ......58 C1
Perceton KA11 ....220 B3
Langmuir Ct KA11 ....220 B3
Langmuir Rd
Bargeddie G69 ......121 A3
Kirkintilloch G66 ......59 A1
Langmuir Way G69 ...121 A3
Langmuirhead Rd G66 ..79 B1
Langness Rd G33 ....119 A4
Langoreth Ave ML3 ...161 C1
Langrig Rd Glasgow G21 ..98 A2
Newton Mearns G77 ..156 B2
Langshaw Cres ML8 ..187 C1
Langshot St 4 G51 ..116 B3
Langside Ave
Glasgow G41 ....136 C4
Kilmarnock KA1 ......227 C2
Uddingston G71 .....141 B3
Langside Coll G42 ....137 A4
Langside Coll (Annexe)
G45 ....137 C2
Langside Coll Annexe
G73 ....138 A3
Langside Ct G71 .....141 A1
Langside Dr
Blackridge EH48 .....107 A2
Glasgow G43 ....136 C3
Kilbarchan PA10 .....111 A1
Langside Gdns G42 ..137 A4
Langside La G42 .....117 A1
Langside Pk PA10 ....111 A1
Langside Pl
Glasgow G41 ....136 C4
Kilbirnie KA25 ......149 A1
Langside Prim Sch G41 .136 C4
Langside Rd
Bothwell G71 ....141 A1
Glasgow G42 ....137 A4
Langside St G81 .....74 C3
Langside Sta PA14 ...68 B4
Langstile Pl G52 .....114 C3
Langstile Rd G52 ....114 C3
Langton Cres
Barrhead G78 ....134 B4
Glasgow G53 ....115 B1
Langton Gate G77 ...156 B3
Langton Gdns G69 ...119 C2
Langton Pl G77 .....156 B3
Langton Rd G53 .....115 B1
Langtree Ave G46 ...136 A1
Lanrig Pl G69 ....100 B4
Lanrig Rd G69 ......100 B4
Lansbury Gdns PA3 ..113 B4
Lansbury St
Alexandria G83 ......27 C4
Greenock PA15 .....185 B1
Lansbury Terr ML9 ...185 B1
Lansdowne Cres
Glasgow G20 ....96 C1
Shotts ML7 ....147 A2
Lansdowne Crescent La
G3 ....240 A4
Lansdowne Dr G68 ...61 C2
Lansdowne Rd KA8 ..236 A3
Lantana Gr ML1 .....163 B4
Lanton Dr G52 ......114 C3
Lanton Rd G43 ......136 C3
Lappin St G81 ....94 B4
Laputa Pl KA1 ......227 C2
Larbert High Sch FK5 ..23 C1
Larbert Rd FK4 ......40 A3
Larbert St G4 ....240 C4
Larbert Sta FK5 .....23 B1
Larbert Village Prim Sch
FK5 ....23 C1
Larch Ave
Bishopbriggs G64 ....98 A4
Kirkintilloch G66 ......79 B3
Larch Cres G66 .....79 B3
Larch Ct Blantyre G72 ..161 B4
Cumbernauld G67 ....62 C2
East Kilbride G75 ...180 A3

Larch Dr Banknock FK4 ...38 C1
East Kilbride G75 ...180 A3
Larch Gr Cumbernauld G67 ..62 C2
Hamilton ML3 ......162 C1
Milton of C G66 .....58 A3
Larch Ho KA9 ......236 A3
Larch Pl
East Kilbride G75 ...180 A3
Johnstone PA5 ......132 A4
Kilmarnock KA1 .....227 B4
Uddingston G71 .....141 B4
Larch Rd Cumbernauld G67 ..62 C2
Glasgow G41 ....116 A2
Larch Terr KA15 ....171 B4
Larch Way ML3 .....183 C2
Larches The G69 ....81 A2
Larchfield G84 ......16 B1
Larchfield Ave
Glasgow G14 ....95 A2
Newton Mearns G77 ..156 B3
Larchfield Cres ML2 ..165 B3
Larchfield Ct KA7 ...156 B2
Larchfield Dr G73 ...138 B2
Larchfield Gdns ML2 ..165 B3
Larchfield Gr ML2 ...165 B3
Larchfield Path ML7 ..147 A1
Larchfield Pl Glasgow G14 ..95 A2
Wishaw ML2 ....165 B3
Larchfield Rd G61 ...75 C1
Larchgrove Ave G32 ..119 B3
Larchgrove Pl G32 ..119 B4
Larchgrove Rd G32 ..119 B3
Larchwood Terr G78 ..155 B4
Larghill La KA7 .....239 A3
Largie Rd G43 ......136 C3
Largo Pl G51 ....115 C4
Largs Ave KA3 .....223 A2
Largs Rd KA25 .....148 B1
Lark Way ML4 ......141 C4
Larkfield Dr G72 ....161 B3
Larkfield Gr PA16 ...44 C2
Larkfield Ind Est PA16 ...44 B3
Larkfield Prim Sch PA16 ..44 C2
Larkfield Rd
Greenock PA16,PA19 ...44 C2
Kirkintilloch G66 ......79 C3
Gourock PA19 ......44 C3
Larkfield St 4 G42 ..117 A2
Larkhall Acad ML9 ..184 C1
Larkin Ind Est ML9 ..199 A4
Larkin Gdns 8 PA3 ..113 B4
Larkin Way ML4 ....141 C4
Larksfield Dr ML8 ...202 A4
Larkspur Dr KA7 ....159 B2
Larkspur Way KA13 ..207 C2
Lashley St G14 ......94 C3
Lasswade St G14 ....94 C3
Latherton Dr 7 G20 ...96 B3
Latimer Gdns G52 ...115 A2
Latta Ct KA9 ....236 B3
Latta St G82 ....50 A2
Lauchlan Way KA13 ..207 C2
Lauchlin Pl G66 .....80 A4
Lauchope Rd ML1 ...143 B4
Lauchope St ML6 ....123 C1
Laudedale La G12 ...96 A2
Lauder Cres ML2 ....165 A3
Lauder Ct KA3 ......223 B2
Lauder Dr Linwood PA3 ..112 A3
Rutherglen G73 .....138 C2
Lauder Gdns
Blantyre G72 ....140 B1
Coatbridge ML5 ....122 B2
Lauder Gn G74 .....160 A2
Lauder La ML3 .....161 C2
Lauder St 3 G5 .....117 A2
Lauderdale Dr G77 ..156 B2
Lauderdale Gdns G12 ..96 A2
Laudervale Gdns G83 ..27 B4
Laughland Dr ML1 ...143 B2
Laughlanglen Rd KA7 ..239 A2
Laundry La G33 .....99 B3
Lauranne Pl ML4 ....141 C3
Laurel Ave Clydebank G81 ..73 B2
Kirkintilloch G66 ......79 B3
Hamilton ML3 ......183 B4
Renfrew PA4 ....94 B1
Laurel Bank KA7 ....239 B2
Laurel Sq FK4 ......38 C1
Laurel St G11 ....96 A1
Laurel Way G78 ....134 A2
Laurel Wlk G73 ....138 C2
Laurel Wynd G72 ...139 C2
Laurelbank ML5 ....122 A4
Laurelbank Rd FK4 ..40 A2
Laurelbank Rd
Chryston G69 ....100 A4

Laurelbank Rd *continued*
Glasgow G32 ....139 B4
Laurelhill Gdns FK8 ..6 C3
Laurelhill Pl FK8 ....7 A3
Laurels The
Motherwell ML1 ....143 A1
Newton Mearns G77 ..156 B3
Tullibody FK10 ......4 A1
Lauren Ave ML6 ....122 C4
Lauren Way ML2 ....113 A1
Laurence Ct G15 ....74 C2
Laurence Dr
Bearsden G61 ......75 B3
Clydebank G15 .....74 C2
Laurence Gdns G15 ..74 C2
Laurencecroft Rd FK8 ..2 A1
Laurenstone Terr G74 ..160 A2
Laurie Ct G71 ......141 A4
Laurieland Ave KA2 ..221 C1
Laurieston Cres ML6 ..123 B1
Laurieston Ct KA2 ...225 C1
Laurieston Rd G5 ...117 B3
Laurieston Way G73 ..138 A2
Lauriston Ct KA22 ...205 B1
Lauriston Gr G77 ...156 A3
Lauriston Way KA3 ..223 A3
Lavelle Dr ML5 .....122 B4
Lavender Dr G75 ...180 B3
Lavender La ML8 ...201 C4
Laverock Ave
Greenock PA15 .....45 B2
Hamilton ML3 ......163 A1
Laverock Rd ML6 ...103 A2
Laverock Terr G69 ..100 A4
Laverockhall ML11 ..215 A3
Laverockhall St G21 ..97 C2
Law Brae KA23 .....190 B3
Law Dr ML1 ....143 C3
Law Pl G19 ....159 C3
Law Prim Sch ML8 ..187 A3
Law Rdbt G74 .....159 C2
Law St G40 ....118 A3
Law View ML2 .....186 B3
Lawers Cres KA1 ...228 A2
Lawers Dr G61 .....75 B4
Lawers La ML1 .....143 B2
Lawers Pl Greenock PA16 ..45 A2
Irvine KA11 ....220 A2
Lawers Rd Glasgow G43 ..136 A3
Kilmarnock KA1 ....228 A2
Renfrew PA4 ....94 B1
Lawfield Ave
Newton Mearns G77 ..157 A3
West Kilbride KA23 ..190 C2
Lawhill Ave G44 ....137 B3
Lawhill Rd Law ML8 ..187 A2
Symington KA1 .....231 B2
Lawhope Mill Rd ML6 ..123 B3
Lawmarnock Cres PA11 ..110 B4
Lawmarnock Rd PA11 ..110 B4
Lawmoor Ave G5 ...117 B2
Lawmoor Pl G5 ....117 B2
Lawmoor Rd G5 ....117 B2
Lawmoor St G5 ....117 B2
Lawmuir Cres G81 ..74 C4
Lawmuir Pl ML4 ....142 A1
Lawmuir Prim Sch ML4 ..142 A2
Lawmuir Rd Bellshill ML4 ..142 A2
Law ML8 ....186 C3
Lawn Pk G62 ......55 B1
Lawn St PA1 ....113 C3
Lawrence Ave
Glasgow G46 ......136 B1
Helensburgh G84 ....25 B4
Lawrence Dr G83 ...19 C1
Lawrence St G11 ...96 B1
Lawrie Pl ML1 .....143 C1
Lawrie St Glasgow G11 ..96 B1
Stonehouse ML9 ...198 C1
Lawrie Way ML9 ...185 B3
Lawson Ave 3 ML6 ..143 B2
Lawson Dr KA22 ...205 B2
Lawson St Ayr KA8 ..236 A1
Kilmarnock KA1 ....228 A4
Lawswell FK10 .....5 C4
Lawthorn Prim Sch
KA11 ....220 A3
Lawthorn Rd KA11 ..220 A3
Lawthorn Rdbt KA11 ..220 A3
Laxdale Dr FK6 .....39 B4
Laxford Ave G44 ...137 A2
Laxford Pl ML5 ....122 B2
Laxford Rd PA8 ....72 C1
Laxford Way ML1 ..143 B2
Laymoor Ave PA4 ..94 C3
Le Froy Gdns G75 ..180 B4
Le Froy La G75 ....180 B4
Lea Ave G78 ....154 C4
Leabank Ave PA2 ...133 C4
Leadburn Ave G52 ..118 B2
Leadburn Rd G21 ...98 B2
Leader St G33 .....98 B1
Leadhills Rd ML4 ...228 A2
Leaend Rd ML6 ....102 C1
Leander Cres
Bellshill ML4 ....142 C3
Renfrew PA4 ....94 C1
Learigg Rd ML6 ....104 A2
Learmont Pl G62 ...54 C2
Learmonth St FK1 ..42 A2
Leathem Pl ML2 ...164 B1
Leathen Pl PA8 ....72 C1
Leaveret Lea KA11 ..219 C3
Leckethill Ave G68 ..81 C4
Leckethill Ct G68 ...81 C4

Leckethill Pl G68 ....81 C4
Leckethill View G68 ..81 C4
Leckie Ct ML3 ......162 B2
Leckie Dr ML3 ......162 B2
Leckie St G41 ......136 B4
Ledaig St G31 ......118 B4
Ledard Rd G42 .....137 A4
Ledcameroch Cres G61 ..75 C2
Ledcameroch Pk G61 ..75 B2
Ledcameroch Rd G61 ..75 C2
Ledgate G66 ....58 B1
Ledgowan Pl G20 ...96 C4
Ledi Ave KA10 .....4 A1
Ledi Dr G61 ....75 A4
Ledi Path ML1 .....143 B2
Ledi Pl FK1 ....66 C4
Ledi Rd G43 ....136 B3
Ledi View FK9 .....2 A2
Ledmore Dr G15 ...74 C2
Ledmore Pl FK1 ...42 C1
Lednock Rd
Glasgow G52 ......115 A3
Stepps G33 ....99 B3
Ledrish Ave G83 ...19 C3
Lee Ave G33 ....98 C1
Lee Cres G64 ......98 A4
Lee Pl ML4 ....142 B2
Lee's Ct ML5 ......122 A3
Leebank Dr G44 ...136 C1
Leeburn Ave PA6 ...91 B1
Leeburn Gdns PA6 ..91 B1
Leechford ML11 ...215 A3
Leechee Rd ML3 ...162 C2
Leefield Dr G44 ...136 C1
Leehill Rd G21 ....97 C4
Leeman View ML8 ..202 A4
Leesburn Pl G74 ...159 C2
Leeside Rd G21 ...97 C4
Leesland G71 .....141 A4
Leeward Circ G75 ..159 A1
Leeward Pk KA7 ...239 A1
Leewood Dr G44 ...137 A1
Lefroy St ML5 .....121 C3
Legbrannock Ave ML1 ..143 B4
Legbrannock Cres ML1 ..143 C3
Legbrannock Rd ML1 ..143 C3
Leggatson Dr G33 ..135 B2
Leglen Wood Cres G21 ..98 B3
Leglen Wood Dr G21 ..98 B3
Leglen Wood Gdns G21 ..98 B3
Leglen Wood Rd G21 ..98 B3
Leicester Ave G12 ..96 A3
Leighton St Glasgow G20 ..96 C3
Leishman Ct EH48 ..107 B2
Leitch St PA15 .....45 A4
Leith Pl FK6 ....39 B4
Leith St G33 ....118 B4
Leithland Ave 5 G53 ..115 A1
Leithland Prim Sch G53 ..115 A1
Leithland Rd G53 ..115 A1
Leman Dr PA6 .....111 B4
Leman Gr PA6 .....111 B4
Lembert Dr G76 ...157 B4
Lemmon St PA15 ..45 B2
Lendal Pl G75 .....179 C3
Lendalfoot Gdns ML3 ..161 B3
Lendel Pl G51 .....116 B3
Lenihall Dr G45 ...137 C1
Lenihall Terr G45 ..137 C1
Lennox Ave Bishopton PA7 ..72 A2
Coatbridge ML5 ....121 C4
Glasgow G14 ......95 B2
Milngavie G62 .....55 A1
Stirling FK7 ....7 A2
Lennox Cres
Bishopbriggs G64 ..97 C4
Kilmarnock KA1 ....222 B1
Lennox Ct 2 G66 ..58 A4
Lennox Dr Bearsden G61 ..75 C3
Clydebank G81 .....74 B4
Newton Mearns G77 ..156 C1
Prestwick KA9 .....233 B4
Lennox Gdns G14 ..95 B2
Lennox La E
20 Glasgow G14 ..95 B2
9 Glasgow G14 ..95 B2
Lennox Pl G81 ....73 C2
Lennox Rd
Cumbernauld G67 ..61 C1
Dumbarton G82 ....50 A2
Milton G82 ....33 B1
Lennox St Alexandria G83 ..27 C3
Dumbarton G82 ....50 A2
Wishaw ML2 ......165 C2
Lennox Terr KA9 ...233 A4
Lennoxtown Prim Sch
G66 ....79 A3
Lentran St G34 ....120 B4
Lenwood Gdns G83 ..27 C2
Leny St G20 ....96 C2
Lenzie Acad G66 ...79 B3
Lenzie Moss Prim Sch
G66 ....79 A3
Lenzie Rd Kirkintilloch G66 ..79 B3
Stepps G33 ....99 B2
Lenzie St G21 .....97 C3
Lenzie Sta G66 ....79 B2

Lenzie Terr G21 ....97 C3
Lenzie Way G21 ....97 C3
Lenziemill Rd G67 ..83 A4
Leonard St ML1 ....143 C1
Leperstone Ave
Kilmacolm PA13 ....69 B1
Port Glasgow PA14 ..68 C4
Leperstone Rd PA13 ..69 B1
Lerwick Pl KA3 ....223 A3
Lesley Pl KA20 .....206 C1
Lesley Quadrant ML4 ..142 A1
Leslie Ave Bishopton PA7 ..72 A2
Newton Mearns G77 ..156 C4
Leslie Cres KA7 ....239 A3
Leslie Pl KA3 ......223 A1
Leslie Rd Glasgow G41 ..116 C2
Motherwell ML1 ....163 C4
Leslie Terr KA9 ....236 B4
Lesmahagow Rd ML11 ..214 A2
Lesmuir Dr G14 ....95 A3
Lesmuir Pl G14 ....94 C3
Lestrange Terr FK12 ..5 A4
Letham Cotts FK2 ..24 B4
Letham Ct G43 ....136 C3
Letham Dr
Bishopbriggs G64 ..98 B4
Glasgow G43 ......136 C3
Letham Grange G68 ..62 A3
Letham Oval G64 ..98 B4
Letham Terrs FK2 ..14 B1
Lethamhill Cres G33 ..98 C1
Lethamhill Pl G33 ..98 C1
Lethamhill Rd G33 ..98 C1
Lethbridge Pl 11 G75 ..180 B4
Letherby Dr G44 ...137 A4
Letheron Dr ML2 ..165 A3
Lethington Ave G41 ..136 C4
Lethington Rd G46 ..157 A4
Letterfaern Rd G23 ..76 C1
Letterickhills Cres G72 ..139 C2
Lettoch St 7 G51 ..116 A4
Levan Point PA19 ..43 C3
Levanne Gdns PA19 ..43 C3
Levanne Pl PA19 ...43 C3
Leven Ave
Bishopbriggs G64 ..78 A1
Kilmarnock KA3 ....223 A2
Leven Ct Alloa FK10 ..10 B3
Barrhead G78 .....134 A3
Hurlford KA1 ......228 C3
Leven Dr Bearsden G61 ..75 C2
Hamilton ML3 ......183 A4
Hurlford KA1 ......228 C3
Leven Path ML1 ...143 A3
Leven Pl Erskine PA8 ..72 C1
Irvine KA12 ....219 B3
Leven Quadrant ML6 ..102 C1
Leven Rd Coatbridge ML5 ..101 B1
Greenock PA15 .....46 B1
Troon KA10 ....229 B2
Leven Sq KA11 ....94 A2
Leven St Alexandria G83 ..27 C2
Dumbarton G82 ....50 A2
Falkirk FK2 ....42 A4
Glasgow G41 ......116 C2
Motherwell ML1 ...163 C2
Leven Terr ML1 ...163 C4
Leven Valley Ent Ctr G82 ..49 B2
Leven Way
East Kilbride G75 ..179 C3
Paisley PA2 ....112 C1
Levenbank Gdns G83 ..27 C4
Levenbank Terr G83 ..27 C4
Levencroft Mews G83 ..27 C2
Levenford Terr G82 ..49 C2
Levengrove Ct G82 ..49 C2
Levenhowe Pl G83 ..27 C4
Levenhowe Rd G83 ..27 C4
Levenvale Prim Sch G83 ..27 C4
Lever Rd G84 ......16 C2
Levern Bridge Ct G53 ..134 C3
Levern Bridge Gr G53 ..134 C3
Levern Bridge Way G53 ..134 C3
Levern Cres G78 ...134 A1
Levern Gdns G78 ..134 A2
Levern Prim Sch G53 ..135 A3
Levern Rd G53 ....134 C3
Leverndale Ct G53 ..114 C1
Leverndale Hospl G53 ..114 C1
Leverndale Rd G53 ..114 C1
Leverside
Barrhead G78 .....134 A1
Glasgow G53 ......135 B4
Levernside Ave G53 ..135 B4
Levernside Cres G53 ..135 B4
Levernside Rd G53 ..135 B4
Lewis Ave Renfrew PA4 ..94 C1
Wishaw ML2 ......165 C3
Lewis Cres Irvine KA11 ..219 C1
Johnstone PA10 ...111 B1
Lewis Ct Alloa FK10 ..10 A3
Falkirk FK1 ....42 A1
Lewis Dr Kilmarnock KA3 ..223 A3
Old Kilpatrick G60 ..73 A3
Lewis Gdns Bearsden G61 ..75 C3
Old Kilpatrick G60 ..73 A3
Lewis Gr G60 ......73 A3
Lewis Pl Airdrie ML6 ..123 B3
Newton Mearns G77 ..156 A3
Old Kilpatrick G60 ..73 B3

Lewis Rd Greenock PA16 ....45 B2
Port Glasgow PA14 ....69 A4
Lewis Rise KA11 ....220 A1
Lewis Terr KA11 ....220 A1
Lewis Wynd KA11 ....220 A1
Lewiston Dr 15 G23 ....76 B1
Lewiston Pl 16 G23 ....76 B1
Lewiston Rd G23 ....76 B1
Lexwell Ave PA5 ....112 B2
Leyden Gdns G20 ....96 C3
Leyden Ct G20 ....96 C3
Leyden St G20 ....96 C3
Leys Pk ML3 ....162 A2
Leys The G64 ....78 A1
Libary Gdns G72 ....138 C3
Libberton Way ML3 ....162 A2
Liberator Dr KA8 ....236 A2
Liberton St G33 ....118 C4
Liberty Ave G69 ....121 A3
Liberty Path G72 ....161 B4
Liberty Rd Bellshill ML4 ..142 A2
Caldercruix ML6 ....105 A3
Libo Ave Glasgow G53 ....115 B1
Uplawmoor G78 ....153 A2
Libo Pl PA6 ....72 C1
Library La G46 ....135 C2
Library Rd ML2 ....165 A2
Lichtenfels Gdns KA9 ....236 C4
Lickprivick Rd G75 ....180 A3
Liddel Rd G67 ....61 C1
Liddell Gr G75 ....180 B4
Liddell St G22 ....119 B1
Liddells Ct G64 ....98 A4
Liddesdale Pl G22 ....97 C4
Liddesdale Rd G22 ....97 B4
Liddesdale Sq G22 ....97 C4
Liddesdale Terr G22 ......97 C4
Liddesdale Ave PA2 ......132 B4
Liddesdale Pass G22 .....97 B4
Liddoch Way G73 ....137 C4
Liff Gdns G64 ....98 B4
Liff Pl G34 ....100 B1
Lifnock Ave KA1 ....228 C3
Lightburn Hospl G32 .....119 A4
Lightburn Pl G32 ....119 A4
Lightburn Rd G72 ....139 C2
Lilac Ave Duntocher G81 ..73 B3
Cumbernauld G67 ....62 C3
Lilac Cres G67 ....141 B4
Lilac Ct G67 ....62 C3
Lilac Gdns G64 ....98 A4
Lilac Hill Cumbernauld G67 .62 C3
Hamilton ML3 ....162 C1
Lilac Pl Cumbernauld G67 .62 C3
Kilmarnock KA1 ....227 C4
Lilac Way ML1 ....143 A3
Lilac Wynd G72 ....139 C2
Lilyburn Pl G15 ....74 C3
Lily St G40 ....119 A2
Lilybank Ave Airdrie ML6 .103 A1
Cambuslang G72 ....139 A2
Muirhead G69 ....100 B4
Lilybank Ct FK10 ....5 B1
Lilybank Gardens La G12 .96 B1
Lilybank Gdns G12 ......96 B1
Lilybank La G12 ....96 B1
Lilybank Rd
Port Glasgow PA14 ....47 A1
Prestwick KA9 ....236 A3
Lilybank Sch PA14 ....47 A1
Lilybank St ML3 ....162 B2
Lilybank Terr G12 ....96 B1
Lilybank Terrace La G12 ..96 B1
Lime Cres Airdrie ML6 ...123 B4
Cumbernauld G67 ....62 C2
Lime Gr Blantyre G72 ....140 B1
Kirkintilloch G66 ....79 B3
Motherwell ML1 ....163 C2
Stenhousemuir FK5 ......23 B1
Lime La 24 G14 ....95 B2
Lime Loan ML1 ....164 A3
Lime Pl KA1 ....227 B4
Lime Rd Dumbarton G82 ..49 C2
Falkirk FK1 ....41 A2
Lime St Glasgow G14 ....95 B2
Greenock PA15 ....45 C2
Limecraigs Ave PA2 .....133 B4
Limecraigs Cres PA2 ....133 B4
Limecraigs Rd PA2 ......133 B4
Limegrove St ML4 ....142 A4
Limekiln Rd Ayr KA8 ....236 A2
Stevenston KA20 ....217 C4
Limekilnburn Rd ML3 ....183 B2
Limekilns Rd G67 ....82 C3
Limekilns St G81 ....74 B4
Limelands Quadrant
ML6 ....104 C2
Limerigg Prim Sch FK1 ..36 B1
Limes The G44 ....137 A2
Limeside Ave G73 ....138 B4
Limeside Gdns G73 ......138 B4
Limetree Ave ML1 ....141 B4
Limetree Cres G77 ......156 B2
Limetree Ct ML3 ....162 A3
Limetree Dr G81 ....74 A2
Limetree Quadrant G71 ..141 A4
Limetree Wlk G66 ....58 A2
Limeview Ave PA2 ......133 A4
Limeview Cres PA2 .....133 A4
Limeview Rd PA2 ....133 A4
Limeview Way PA2 ......133 A4
Limonds Ct KA8 ....236 A1
Limonds Wynd KA8 .....236 A1
Limpetlaw ML11 ....215 A3
Linacre Dr G32 ....119 B3
Linacre Gdns G32 ....119 B3
Linburn Pl G52 ....115 A3
Linburn Rd Erskine PA8 ..72 C1

Linburn Rd continued
Glasgow G52 ....114 C4
Linburn Sch G52 ....114 C3
Linclive Intc PA3 ....112 B3
Linclive Terr PA3 ....112 B3
Lincluden Path 3 G41 ...116 C2
Lincoln Ave Glasgow G13 .95 B3
Uddingston G71 ....120 C1
Lincoln Rd PA16 ....44 B2
Lincuan Ave G46 ....157 B4
Lindams G71 ....140 C3
Linden Ave Denny FK6 ...21 B2
Stirling FK7 ....7 B3
Wishaw ML2 ....165 B3
Linden Dr Banknock FK4 .38 C1
Clydebank G81 ....74 A3
Linden Lea Hamilton ML3 .162 A2
Milton of C G66 ....58 A3
Linden Pl G13 ....95 C4
Linden St G13 ....95 C4
Linden Way G13 ....95 C4
Lindens The G71 ....141 A1
Lindores Ave G73 ....138 B4
Lindores Dr G74 ....159 B1
Lindores Pl G74 ....159 B1
Lindores St G42 ....137 A4
Lindrick Dr 4 G23 ......76 C1
Lindsay Ave
Kilbirnie KA25 ....149 A2
Saltcoats KA21 ....205 C1
Lindsay Dr Glasgow G12 .96 A3
Kilmarnock KA3 ....223 B2
Stirling FK9 ....2 A4
Lindsay Gdns G83 ......27 C3
Lindsay Gr G74 ....159 C1
Lindsay Loan ML11 .....215 B3
Lindsay Pl
East Kilbride G74 ....160 A1
Glasgow G12 ....96 A3
Johnstone PA5 ....112 A2
Kirkintilloch G66 ....79 B2
Lindsay Quadrant G83 ..28 A4
Lindsay Rd G74 ....159 C1
Lindsay St Ayr KA8 .....236 B1
Kilmarnock KA1 ....227 C4
Lindsay Terr G66 ....57 C4
Lindsaybeg Ct G69 ......100 B4
Lindsaybeg Rd G69 .....80 A1
Lindsayfield Ave G75 ....180 A2
Lindsayfield Rd G75 .....180 A2
Lindum Ct ML1 ....163 A4
Lindum Cres ML1 ....163 A4
Lindum St ML1 ....163 A4
Lineside Wlk G84 ....15 C3
Linfern Ave KA1 ....228 B4
Linfern Ave E KA1 ......228 B4
Linfern Ave W KA1 .....228 B4
Linfern Pl KA7 ....239 A2
Linfern Rd G12 ....96 B2
Linghope Pl ML2 ....185 C4
Lingley Ave ML6 ....123 A3
Linhope Pl G75 ....179 C4
Linister Cres PA9 ....130 C3
Links Cres KA10 ....229 C2
Links Rd Glasgow G44 ...137 B2
Glasgow, Mount Vernon
G32 ....120 B2
Prestwick KA9 ....233 A1
Saltcoats KA21 ....205 C1
Links The G68 ....62 A3
Links View ML9 ....185 B1
Linkview Rd ML1 ....143 A1
Linkwood Ave G15 ......74 C2
Linkwood Cres G15 .....75 A2
Linkwood Ct KA11 ......220 A3
Linkwood Gdns G15 ....75 A2
Linkwood Pl
Clydebank G15 ....74 C2
Irvine KA11 ....220 A3
Linlithgow Gdns G32 ....119 B3
Linlithgow Pl FK5 ....23 C2
Linn Cres
Kirkfieldbank ML11 ......214 A2
Paisley PA2 ....133 B4
Linn Dr G44 ....136 C2
Linn Pl FK2 ....14 C2
Linn Glen G66 ....57 C4
Linn Park Gdns PA5 .....112 A1
Linn Park Ind Est G45 ...137 A1
Linn Park Nature Trail*
G44 ....136 C2
Linnet Ave PA5 ....131 B4
Linnet Ct G13 ....94 C4
Linnet Pl G13 ....94 C4
Linnet Rd Bellshill ML4 ..142 A2
Greenock PA16 ....44 C1
Linnet Way ML4 ....141 C4
Linnhe Ave
Bishopbriggs G64 ....78 A1
Glasgow G44 ....137 A3
Hamilton ML3 ....162 A1
Linnhe Cres ML2 ....164 B1
Linnhe Ct ML9 ....184 C3
Linnhe Dr G78 ....114 B3
Linnhe Pl Blantyre G72 ..140 B1
Erskine PA8 ....72 C1
Linnhead Dr G53 ....135 B3
Linnhead Pl G14 ....95 A2
Linnpark Ave G44 ......136 C1
Linnpark Ct G44 ....136 C1
Linnpark Prim Sch G81 ..74 A1
Linnvale Way G68 ......61 A3
Linnwell Cres PA2 ....133 B4
Linrigg Rd ML1 ....144 B4

Linside Ave PA1 ....114 A2
Lint Brae KA3 ....195 C1
Lint Riggs FK1 ....42 A3
Lintfield Loan G71 ......141 A3
Linthaugh Rd G53 ......115 A2
Linthaugh Terr G53 .....115 B1
Linthill ML11 ....225 A3
Linthouse Bldgs 1 G51 .115 C4
Linthouse Rd G51 ....95 C1
Linthouse Vennel KA12 .219 A1
Lintie Rd ML1 ....143 B2
Lintlaw G72 ....140 B1
Lintlaw Dr G52 ....115 A3
Lintmill Terr G78 ....154 B3
Linton St ML5 ....121 C2
Linton St G33 ....118 C4
Lintview KA1 ....222 B1
Lintwhite Cres PA11 ....110 C4
Lintwhite Ct PA11 ......110 C4
Linwood Ave
Clarkston G76 ....157 C4
East Kilbride G74 ....159 A1
Linwood Ct G44 ....137 A3
Linwood High Sch PA3 ..111 C3
Linwood Ind Est PA3 ....111 C2
Linwood Rd PA1 ....112 C2
Linwood Terr ML3 ....162 A2
Lion Bank G66 ....58 B1
Lionthorn Rd FK1 ......41 C1
Lipney FK11 ....4 A2
Lisburn Rd KA8 ....236 A2
Lismore G74 ....181 B4
Lismore Ave
Motherwell ML1 ....163 A4
Port Glasgow PA14 ......69 A4
Lismore Dr
Coatbridge ML5 ....121 C2
Irvine KA11 ....225 A4
Linwood PA3 ....111 C3
Paisley PA2 ....133 B4
Lismore Gdns PA10 .....111 B1
Lismore Hill ML3 ....161 B2
Lismore Ho KA1 ....236 A3
Lismore Pl Airdrie ML6 ..123 A3
Moodiesburn G69 ....81 A2
Newton Mearns G77 ....156 A3
Lismore Rd G12 ....96 A3
Lismore Sch KA13 ......207 B3
Lister Cl FK9 ....4 A4
Lister Gdns G76 ....158 A3
Lister Pl 4 G52 ....115 A4
Lister Rd G52 ....115 A4
Lister St Crosshouse KA2 .222 A1
Glasgow G4 ....241 B4
Lister Wlk ML4 ....142 B4
Lithgow Ave
Kirkintilloch G66 ....79 C4
Langbank PA14 ....70 A4
Lithgow Cres PA2 ......114 A1
Lithgow Dr ML1 ....144 A1
Lithgow Pl G74 ....159 A1
Little Bellsland Rd KA1 ..227 C3
Little Corseford PA10 ...131 B4
Little Denny Rd FK6 .....21 B1
Little Dovehill G1 ....241 B1
Little John Gdns ML2 ...165 C2
Little St G3 ....240 A2
Littlehill Prim Sch G33 ..98 B2
Littlehill Cres G21 ......98 A2
Littleholm Pl G81 ....73 C3
Littlemill Ave G60 ......60 C1
Littlemill Cres G53 .....135 A4
Littlemill Dr G53 ....135 A4
Littlemill Gdns 10 G53 ..135 A4
Littlemill La G60 ....72 B4
Littlemill Way ML1 .....143 A1
Littlesdale Ave KA11 ...220 A3
Littlestane Rise KA11 ...220 A3
Littlestane Rd KA11 ....220 A3
Littleton Dr 4 G23 ......76 B1
Littleton St G23 ....76 B1
Livilands Ct FK8 ....7 A3
Livilands Gate FK8 ......7 A3
Livilands La FK8 ....7 A3
Livingston Dr ML6 ......123 B1
Livingston La 4 G71 ....141 A2
Livingstone Ave G52 ...95 A4
Livingstone Bvd G72 ...161 B2
Livingstone Cres
Blantyre G72 ....140 B1
East Kilbride G75 ....180 B4
Falkirk FK2 ....42 C3
Livingstone Ct G43 .....223 B2
Livingstone Dr
East Kilbride G75 ....180 C4
Laurieston FK2 ....42 C1
Livingstone Gdns ML9 ..185 A2
Livingstone Pk G65 .....36 B3
Livingstone Pl ML6 .....123 A4
Livingstone Quadrant
ML7 ....128 C2
Livingstone St
Clydebank G81 ....74 B1
Hamilton ML3 ....162 A1
Livingstone Terr KA12 ..219 A3
Lloyd Ave G32 ....119 A1
Lloyd Dr ML1 ....143 A1
Lloyd St Glasgow G31 ...118 A4
Motherwell ML1 ....143 A1
Rutherglen G73 ....118 A1
Lloyd Wlk KA3 ....211 B4
Lloyds St ML5 ....122 A2
Llynallan Rd ML7 ....127 A3

Loach Ave KA12 ....219 B1
Loadingbank KA25 .....170 A4
Loadingbank Ct KA25 ..170 A4
Loan Cres Lea ML9 ....185 A1
Loan Pl ML7 ....127 C3
Loan The G62 ....54 B2
Loanbank Pl G51 ....116 A4
Loanbank Quadrant
G51 ....115 C4
Loancroft Ave G69 .....120 B2
Loancroft Gate G71 ....140 C3
Loancroft Gdns G71 ....140 C2
Loancroft Pl G69 ......120 A2
Loanend Cotts G72 ....139 C1
Loanfoot Ave
Glasgow G13 ....95 A4
Kilmarnock KA1 ....222 B1
Loanfoot Gdns FK7 ....12 B2
Loanfoot Rd G72 ....161 B3
Loanhead Ave
Bonnybridge FK4 ....39 B3
Linwood PA3 ....112 A3
Motherwell ML1 ....143 B2
Renfrew PA4 ....94 B1
Loanhead Cres ML1 ....143 B2
Loanhead La PA3 ......112 A3
Loanhead Prim Sch
KA1 ....228 A4
Loanhead Rd
Ardrossan KA22 ....205 B1
Linwood PA3 ....112 A3
Motherwell ML1 ....143 B2
Loanhead St
Coatbridge ML5 ....121 C2
Glasgow G32 ....118 C4
Kilmarnock KA1 ....228 A4
Loaning 1 ML9 ....185 B1
Loaning The Ayr KA7 ...239 A1
Bearsden G61 ....79 B4
Kirkintilloch G66 ....79 B4
Motherwell ML1 ....163 B4
Rutherglen G46 ....157 A4
Loaninghead Dr G82 ...50 A3
Lobnitz Ave PA4 ....94 B2
Loccard Rd KA20 ......206 B1
Loch Achray Gdns G32 .119 B2
Loch Achray St G32 ....119 B2
Loch Ardinning Nature
Reserve* G63 ....55 B4
Loch Ardinning Nature
Trail* G63 ....55 B4
Loch Assynt G74 ....181 A4
Loch Awe ML8 ....201 C2
Loch Awe G74 ....181 A4
Loch Awe Pl ML5 ......121 C3
Loch Brora Cres ML5 ..121 C3
Loch Dr G84 ....160 A1
Loch Goil G74 ....160 A1
Loch Laidon St G32 ....119 B2
Loch Laxford G74 .....181 A4
Loch Lee G66 ....58 C1
Loch Lomond Factory Outlets
G83 ....27 B3
Loch Lomond YH* G83 .19 C1
Loch Long ML5 ....201 C2
Loch Loyal G74 ....181 A4
Loch Maree G74 ....181 A4
Loch Meadie G74 .....181 A4
Loch Park Ave ML8 ....201 C4
Loch Park Pl ML9 .....165 B2
Loch Pl PA11 ....110 B4
Loch Prim Sch G72 ....138 B2
Loch Rd
Bridge of W PA11 ......110 B4
Chapelhall ML6 ....123 B1
Kirkintilloch G66 ....58 C1
Milngavie G62 ....55 A2
Stepps G33 ....99 B2
Loch Shin G74 ....181 A4
Loch St ML6 ....123 A1
Loch Torridon G74 ....160 A1
Loch View
Calderbank ML6 ....123 A1
Chapelhall ML6 ....105 A3
Kilmarnock KA3 ....223 B1
Loch Voil St G32 ......119 B2
Lochaber Cres G66 ....58 B4
Lochaber Dr
Rutherglen G73 ....138 B2
Stenhousemuir FK5 ....23 C2
Lochaber Path G72 ....161 B4
Lochaber Pl G74 ......159 C2
Lochaber Rd G61 .....76 A1
Lochalsh Cres G66 ....58 B4
Lochalsh Dr PA2 ......113 A1
Lochalsh Pl G72 ......140 A1
Lochar Cres G53 ......115 B1
Lochard Dr PA2 ....113 A1
Lochay Pl KA10 ....229 D2
Lochay St G32 ....119 B2
Lochbrae Dr G73 .....138 B2
Lochbridge Rd G34 ...120 A4
Lochbroom Dr
Newton Mearns G77 ...156 C3
Paisley PA3 ....114 A1
Lochbuie La ML6 ......102 C2
Lochburn Cres G20 ....96 C4

Lochburn Pass G20 ....96 C4
Lochburn Rd G20 ......96 C4
Lochcraig Ct KA11 ....220 A2
Lochdochart Rd G34 ...120 B4
Lochearn Cres
Airdrie ML6 ....102 C1
Paisley PA2 ....113 A1
Lochearnhead Rd G33 ..99 B3
Lochend Ave G69 .....100 C4
Lochend Com High Sch
G34 ....120 B4
Lochend Cotts G83 ....20 C2
Lochend Cres G61 ....75 B2
Lochend Dr G61 .....75 C2
Lochend Pl KA10 .....229 D1
Lochend Rd Bearsden G61 .75 C2
Coatbridge ML5 ....101 C4
Glasgow G34,G69 .....100 B1
Glengarnock KA14 ....170 B4
Troon KA10 ....229 C1
Gartcosh G69 ....100 C3
Lochend St ML1 ......163 C3
Locher Ave PA6 ......91 C1
Locher Cres PA6 .....111 C4
Locher Gait PA6 ......111 C4
Locher Gdns PA6 .....111 C4
Locher Pl ML5 ....122 B2
Locher Rd PA10 ......110 C2
Locher Way PA6 .....111 C4
Locherburn Ave PA6 ..111 B4
Locherburn Gr PA6 ...111 B4
Locherburn Pl PA6 ...111 B4
Lochfauld Rd G23 ....77 A1
Lochfield Cres PA2 ...113 C1
Lochfield Dr PA2 .....114 A1
Lochfield Prim Sch
PA2 ....113 C1
Lochfield Rd PA2 .....114 A1
Lochgarry Way ML5 ..121 C2
Lochgilp St G20 ......96 B4
Lochgoin Ave G15 ....74 C2
Lochgoin Prim Sch G15 .74 C2
Lochgreen Ave KA10 ..229 D4
Lochgreen Ct
Coatbridge ML5 ....101 B3
Hamilton ML3 ....183 A4
Kilmarnock KA1 ......227 C2
Lochgreen Pl FK1 ....41 C4
Lochgreen St G33 ....98 C3
Lochhead Ave Denny FK6 .21 C1
Linwood PA3 ....112 A3
Lochiel Dr G66 ....58 B3
Lochiel La G73 ....138 B2
Lochiel Rd G46 ......135 C2
Lochinch Pl G77 .....156 A3
Lochinvar Rd G67 ....82 C4
Lochinver Cres PA2 ..113 A1
Lochinver Dr G44 ....137 A2
Lochinver Gr G72 ....139 A3
Lochknowe St ML8 ...201 C3
Lochlands Ind Est FK5 ..41 A4
Lochlea Ave
Clydebank G81 ....74 B2
Troon KA10 ....229 D2
Lochlea Dr KA7 ......239 A3
Lochlea Rd
Clarkston G76 ....157 C3
Cumbernauld G67 .....62 B2
Glasgow G43 ....137 C3
Rutherglen G73 ......137 C3
Saltcoats KA21 ....205 C1
Lochlea Loan 3 ML9 ..185 B1
Lochleven La G42 ....137 A4
Lochleven Rd G42 ...137 A4
Lochlibo Ave G13 ....94 C4
Lochlibo Cres G78 ...134 A1
Lochlibo Ct KA11 ....220 A3
Lochlibo Rd
Barrhead G78 ....134 A1
Burnhouse KA15 .....172 C2
Irvine KA11,KA13 .....209 B2
Lugton G78 ....154 C1
Neilston G78 ....154 C4
Lochlip Rd PA12 .....129 B1
Lochlea Pl KA20 .....206 C1
Lochlie Terr G78 .....154 C4
Lochmaben Cres KA3 .223 A3
Lochmaben Dr G52 ..114 C2
Lochmaben Rd
Glasgow G52 ....114 C2
Newton Mearns G77 ..156 C3
Lochmaben Wynd KA3 .223 A3
Lochmaddy Ave G44 .137 A2
Lochnagar Dr G61 ...75 A4
Lochnagar Rd
Kilmarnock KA1 ......228 A2
Motherwell ML1 .....143 B2
Lochnagar Way ML9 .199 B4
Lochore Ave PA3 ....114 A4
Lochpark Pl FK6 .....21 C1
Lochranza Ct KA3 ...223 A3
Lochranza Dr
East Kilbride G75 .....180 A2
Helensburgh G84 .....16 C1
Lochranza La G75 ...180 A2
Lochranza Pl KA21 ..206 A1
Lochranza St G34 ...100 A1
Lochridge Pl FK6 ....21 B1
Lochshore East Ind Est
KA14 ....170 B4
Lochshore South Ind Est
G69 ....236 A3
Lochside Bearsden G61 ..75 C2
Lochside Ct G69 ......100 C4
Lochside Rd Ayr KA8 ..236 A1

Lochside Rd continued
Slamannan KA1 ....86 B1
Lochside St 2 G41 ....116 C1
Lochview Ave PA15 ......45 A4
Lochview Cres G33 ......98 C2
Lochview Dr G33 ....98 C2
Lochview Gdns G33 .....98 C2
Lochview Pl G33 ....98 C2
Lochview Quadrant
ML4 ....141 C2
Lochview Rd
Bearsden G61 ....75 C2
Beith KA15 ....170 C4
Coatbridge ML5 ....101 B1
Port Glasgow PA14 ....47 A1
Lochview Terr G69 .....100 C3
Lochwinnoch Nature
Reserve ® PA12 ....129 C1
Lochwinnoch Prim Sch
PA12 ....129 B2
Lochwinnoch Rd PA13 ...89 B4
Lochwinnoch Sta PA12 .150 C4
Lochwood Cl KA13 .....207 B3
Lochwood Loan G69 ....81 A2
Lochwood Pl KA11 .....219 C3
Lochwood St G33 ....98 C1
Lochy Ave PA4 ....94 C1
Lochy Gdns G64 ....78 A1
Lochy Pl PA8 ....72 C1
Lochy St ML2 ....165 A1
Lock Sixteen FK1 ....41 B3
Locke Gr ML1 ....143 C1
Lockerbie Ave G43 .....136 C3
Locket Yett View ML4 .141 C3
Lockhart Ave G72 ....139 C3
Lockhart Ct G77 ....156 B1
Lockhart Dr
Cambuslang G72 ....139 B3
Lanark ML11 ....214 C3
Newton Mearns G77 .....156 B1
Lockhart Hospl ML11 ..215 B2
Lockhart Pl
Stonehouse ML9 ....198 C2
Wishaw ML2 ....165 C2
Lockhart St Carluke ML8 .187 C1
Glasgow G21 ....98 A1
Hamilton ML3 ....183 B3
Stonehouse ML9 ....199 A2
Lockhart Terr G74 ......160 A1
Locks St ML5 ....122 B3
Locksley Ave
Cumbernauld G67 ....82 C4
Glasgow G13 ....95 B4
Locksley Cres G67 ....82 C3
Locksley Ct G67 ....82 C3
Locksley Pl G67 ....82 C3
Locksley Rd
Cumbernauld G67 ....82 C3
Paisley PA2 ....112 C1
Lodge Cres PA13 ....89 C4
Lodge Dr FK5 ....23 C1
Lodge Gdns PA13 ....69 C1
Lodge Gr PA13 ....69 C1
Lodge Pk PA13 ....69 C1
Lodge Twr ML1 ....163 C2
Logan Ave G77 ....156 B3
Logan Ct Cumbernauld G68 .61 B2
Paisley PA3 ....113 B3
Troon KA10 ....229 C2
Logan Gdns ML1 ....161 C4
Logan St Blantyre G72 .161 C4
Glasgow G5 ....117 B2
Logan Twr G72 ....139 C3
Logandale Ave ML2 ....165 C3
Loganlea Dr ML1 ....143 A1
Logans Prim Sch ML1 ..163 A4
Logans Rd ML1 ....163 B4
Loganswell Dr G46 .....135 C1
Loganswell Gdns G46 ..135 C1
Loganswell Pl G46 ......135 C1
Loganswell Rd G46 .....135 C1
Logie Dr FK5 ....23 A2
Logie La FK9 ....2 B4
Logie Pk G74 ....160 A2
Logie Rd FK9 ....2 B2
Logie Sq G74 ....160 A2
Lomax St G33 ....118 B4
Lomond G75 ....180 C3
Lomond Ave
Hurlford KA1 ....228 C3
Port Glasgow PA14 ....68 C4
Renfrew PA4 ....94 A1
Lomond Cres
Alexandria G83 ....27 B4
Beith KA15 ....150 B1
Bridge of W PA11 ....110 B4
Cumbernauld G67 ....82 B4
Paisley PA2 ....133 B3
Stenhousemuir FK5 ....23 C2
Stirling FK9 ....2 A2
Lomond Ct Alloa FK10 ..10 B3
Barrhead G78 ....134 B1
Cumbernauld G67 ....82 B4
Lomond Dr Airdrie ML6 .102 C1
Alexandria G83 ....27 B4
Bannockburn FK7 ....7 C1
Barrhead G78 ....134 A2
Bishopbriggs G64 ....78 A2
Bothwell G71 ....141 A2
Cumbernauld G82 ....82 A4
Dumbarton G82 ....50 A3
Falkirk FK2 ....24 B1

Lomond Dr continued
Newton Mearns G77 .....156 B4
Wishaw ML2 ....165 A1
Lomond Gate G83 ....28 A4
Lomond Gdns PA5 ......112 B1
Lomond Gr G67 ....82 B4
Lomond Ind Est G83 ....27 C3
Lomond Jun Sch G84 ...16 B2

Lomond Pl
Coatbridge ML5 ....101 C1
Cumbernauld G67 ....82 A4
Erskine PA8 ....72 C1
Irvine KA12 ....219 B3
Stepps G33 ....99 C2
Lomond Rd
Alexandria G83 ....27 B4
Balloch G83 ....27 C4
Bearsden G61 ....75 C1
Coatbridge ML5 ....101 B1
Kilmarnock KA1 ....228 A2
Kirkintilloch G66 ....79 B3
Shotts ML7 ....146 C3
Uddingston G71 ....120 C1
Lomond Sec Sch G84 ....16 B2
Lomond Shores ® G83 .19 B1
Lomond St Alloa FK10 ....4 C1
Glasgow G22 ....97 A3
Helensburgh G84 ....16 C1
Lomond View
Cumbernauld G67 ....82 B4
Hamilton ML3 ....161 C1
Symington KA1 ....231 B2
Lomond Way Denny FK6 .39 B3
Irvine KA11 ....220 A2
Motherwell ML1 ....143 A3
Lomond Wlk
Z Larkhall ML9 ....185 A2
Motherwell ML1 ....143 B2
Lomondside Ave G76 ..157 B4
Lomondview Ind Est
PA5 ....111 C2
London Dr G1 ....118 B2
London Rd
Glasgow G31,G32,G40 ..118 B2
Kilmarnock KA3 ....228 A4
London Road Prim Sch
G40 ....118 A2
London St Larkhall ML9 ..185 A2
Renfrew PA4 ....94 B3
Lonend PA1 ....113 C2
Loney Cres FK6 ....39 C4
Long Calderwood Prim Sch
G74 ....160 B2
Long Crags View G82 ...50 B3
Long Dr East Kilbride G75 .181 A4
Irvine KA11, KA12 ....219 C3
Long Row Glasgow G69 .120 B3
Lanark ML11 ....214 C1
Menstrie FK11 ....4 A4
Longay Pl G22 ....97 B4
Longay St G22 ....97 B4
Longbank Dr KA7 ....239 A2
Longbank Rd KA7 ....239 A2
Longcroft Dr FK4 ....23 B4
Longcroft Holdings FK4 ..39 A2
Longdales Ave FK2 ....42 A4
Longdales Pl FK2 ....42 A4
Longdales Rd FK2 ....42 A4
Longdyke St G81 ....94 B4
Longfield Ave KA21 ....205 C3
Longfield Pl KA21 ....205 C3
Longford Ave KA13 .....207 C1
Longford St G33 ....119 A4
Longhill Ave KA7 ....238 B1
Longlands Pk KA7 ....238 C2
Longlands Prim Sch KA7 .82 C4
Longlee G69 ....120 A2
Longmeadow PA5 ......111 B1
Longmorn Pl ML1 ....143 A1
Longpark Ave KA3 ......222 C1
Longriggend Rd ML6 ....85 B1
Longrow Gdns KA11 ...219 C4
Longstone Pl G33 ....119 A4
Longstone Rd G33 ......119 A4
Longwill Terr G67 ....62 A2
Lonsdale Ave G46 ......136 B2
Loom Wlk PA10 ....111 A2
Lora Dr G52 ....115 C2
Lorenty Dr KA1 ....227 C1
Lorenty Ind Est KA1 ...227 C2
Loretto Pl G33 ....118 C4
Loretto St G33 ....118 C4
Lorien Ave KA8 ....236 B2
Lorimer Dr FK2 ....24 A1
Lorn Ave G69 ....100 B4
Lorn Dr G83 ....19 C1
Lorn Pl G66 ....59 B1
Lorne Arc KA7 ....238 C3
Lorne Cr PA8 ....78 B1
Lorne Dr Linwood PA3 .112 A3
Motherwell ML1 ....142 B1
Lorne Gdns
Laurieston FK2 ....42 C2
Salsburgh ML7 ....125 A1
Lorne Pl ML5 ....122 B3
Lorne Rd Paisley G52 ..114 C4
Stenhousemuir FK5 ....23 B1
Lorne St Glasgow G51 ..116 B3
Hamilton ML3 ....162 B2
Helensburgh G84 ....16 B4
Lorne Street Prim Sch
G51 ....116 B3
Lorne Terr G72 ....138 C2

Lornshill Acad FK10 ....4 C1
Lornshill Cres FK10 ....9 C4
Lorraine Gardens La ®
G12 ....96 B2
Lorraine Gdns ® G12 ...96 B2
Lorraine Rd ® G12 ......96 B2
Lorraine Way G83 ....27 C1
Loskin Dr G22 ....97 A4
Losshill FK11 ....4 A3
Lossie Cres PA4 ....94 C1
Lossie St G33 ....98 B1
Lothian Cres Paisley PA2 .113 B1
Stirling FK9 ....8 A3
Lothian Gdns ® G20 ....96 C2
Lothian Rd ® KA7 ......239 A4
Greenock PA16 ....44 B2
Stewarton KA3 ....211 B4
Lothian St G52 ....114 C4
Lothian Way G74 ....160 B2
Louden Hill Dr G33 ......98 C3
Louden Hill Pl G33 ....98 C3
Louden Hill Rd G33 ......98 C3
Louden Hill Way G33 ....98 C3
Louden St ML6 ....123 A4
Loudens Wlk FK6 ....21 B3
Loudon Gdns PA5 ....112 A2
Loudon Rd G33 ....99 A2
Loudon St ML2 ....165 A3
Loudon Terr G61 ....75 A2
Loudonhill Ave ML3 ....183 C4
Loudoun Ave KA1 ....228 A2
Loudoun Cres KA11 ....207 A2
Loudoun Pl
Crosshouse KA2 ....226 C4
Symington KA1 ....231 B2
Loudoun St KA3 ....211 C4
Loudoun Terr KA9 ......236 B4
Loudoun-Montgomery Prim
Sch KA9 ....236 B4
Louise Gdns ML1 ....142 C3
Louisville Ave ML2 .....165 B3
Lounsdale Ave PA2 .....113 A1
Lounsdale Cres PA2 ....113 A1
Lounsdale Dr PA2 ....113 A1
Lounsdale Gr PA2 ....113 A1
Lounsdale Ho PA2 ......113 A1
Lounsdale Pl G14 ....95 A2
Lounsdale Rd PA2 ....113 A1
Lounsdale Way PA2 ....113 A2
Lourdes Ave G52 ....115 B3
Lourdes Ct G52 ....115 B3
Lourdes Prim Sch G52 .115 B3
Lourdes Sec Sch G52 ..115 B2
Lovat Ave G61 ....75 C4
Lovat Dr G66 ....79 A4
Lovat Path 2 ML9 ......185 B1
Love Ave PA11 ....89 C1
Love Dr St Kilwinning KA13 .208 A2
Lovers WIk FK8 ....2 A1
Lovers Loan FK12 ....5 A4
Low Barholm PA10 ......111 A1
Low Broadlie Rd G78 ..154 B4
Low Church La ® KA1 ..227 C4
Low Craigends G65 ......60 C4
Low Cres G81 ....94 C4
Low Flender Rd G76 ....157 B3
Low Glencairn St KA1 ..227 C3
Low Green Rd KA12 ....219 A1
Low Moss Ind Est G64 ..78 A2
Low Parks ® ML3 ....162 C3
Low Parksail PA8 ....93 A4
Low Patrick St ML3 .....162 C2
Low Pleasance ML9 .....185 A2
Low Quarry Gdns ML3 .162 B1
Low Rd Ayr KA8 ....236 C2
Paisley PA2 ....113 B2
Low Waters Rd ML3 ....162 B1
Lower Auchingramont Rd
ML3 ....162 C2
Lower Bourtree Dr G73 .138 B2
Lower Bouverie St PA14 .47 B1
Lower Bridge St FK8 .....2 A1
Lower Castlehill FK8 ......2 A1
Lower Mill Rd G76 ....157 C3
Lower Millgate G71 .....140 C3
Lower Stoneymollan Rd
G83 ....16 A2
Lower Sutherland Cres
G84 ....16 A2
Lowndes St G78 ....134 B1
Lowther Ave G61 ....74 C4
Lowther Bank KA11 ....220 B1
Lowther Cres KA9 ....236 B4
Lowther Terr ® G12 ....96 C1
Loyal Ave PA8 ....72 C1
Loyal Gdns G61 ....74 C2
Loyal Pl PA8 ....72 C1
Loyne Dr PA4 ....94 C1
Luath St G51 ....116 A4
Lubas Ave G42 ....137 B4
Lubas Pl G42 ....137 B4
Lubnaig Dr PA8 ....72 C1
Lubnaig Gdns G61 ....75 B4
Lubnaig Pl ML6 ....102 C1
Lubnaig Rd G43 ....136 C2
Lubnaig Wlk ML1 ....143 A3
Luckenhill Dr ML6 ....84 B2
Luckiesfauld G78 ....154 B3
Luckingsford Ave PA4 ...93 B4
Luckingsford Dr PA4 .....93 B4
Luckingsford Rd PA4 ....93 B4

Lucy Brae G71 ....140 C4
Ludgate FK10 ....10 A3
Ludovic Sq PA5 ....111 C2
Luffness Gdns G32 .....119 A1
Lugar Ave KA11 ....220 A3
Lugar Cres KA9 ....236 A3
Lugar Dr G52 ....115 C2
Lugar Pl Glasgow G44 ..137 C3
Troon KA10 ....229 D3
Lugar St ML5 ....122 A4
Lugar Wynd KA3 ....223 A3
Luggie Rd ML8 ....187 C2
Luggie View G67 ....82 A4
Luggiebank Pl G69 .....121 A2
Luggiebank Rd
Kirkintilloch G66 ....79 B4
Kirkintilloch, Eastside G66 .58 C1
Lugton Ct KA3 ....219 B1
Lugton Rd KA3 ....195 A4
Luing ML6 ....123 C3
Luing Rd G52 ....115 C3
Luma Gdns G51 ....115 B4
Lumloch St G21 ....98 A2
Lumsden La G3 ....96 B3
Lumsden Pl KA20 ....206 C1
Lumsden St G3 ....96 B3
Lunan Dr G64 ....98 B4
Lunan Pl G51 ....115 C4
Lunar Path ML4 ....123 B1
Luncarty Pl G32 ....119 A2
Luncarty St G32 ....119 A2
Lunderston Cl G53 .....135 A3
Lunderston Dr G53 .....135 A4
Lunderston Gdns G53 ..135 A3
Lundholm Rd KA20 ....217 C4
Lundie Gdns G64 ....98 B4
Lundie St G32 ....118 C2
Lurg St PA14 ....68 B4
Luss Ave PA15 ....46 A1
Luss Brae ML3 ....161 C1
Luss Pl PA15 ....46 A1
Luss Rd Alexandria G83 ..27 B4
Glasgow G51 ....115 C4
Helensburgh G84 ....17 A3
Lusset Glen G60 ....73 A3
Lusset Rd G60 ....73 A3
Lusshill Terr G71 ....120 A1
Lybster Cres G73 ....138 B2
Lychgate Rd FK10 ....4 A1
Lye Brae G67 ....62 A1
Lyell Gr G74 ....159 C2
Lyell Pl G74 ....159 C2
Lyle Cres PA7 ....72 A2
Lyle Gr PA16 ....45 A4
Lyle Pl Greenock PA16 ...45 A4
Paisley PA2 ....113 C1
Lyle Rd Airdrie ML6 .....123 C4
Greenock PA16 ....45 A4
Kilmacolm PA13 ....69 A2
Lyle Sq G62 ....54 C1
Lyle St Greenock PA15 ...46 A2
Johnstone PA5 ....112 A2
Lyle's Land PA1 ....91 A2
Lylefoot Cres PA16 ......45 A4
Lylefoot Pl PA16 ....45 A4
Lylepen Rd PA2 ....113 C1
Lylestone Terr KA13 ...208 B4
Lyman Dr ML2 ....145 C4
Lymburn Pl KA8 ....239 A4
Lymburn St G3 ....116 B4
Lymekilns Rd G74 ....159 B2
Lyndale Pl G20 ....96 C4
Lyndale Rd G20 ....96 C4
Lyndhurst Gardens La
G20 ....96 C2
Lyndhurst Gdns G20 ....96 C2
Lyne Croft G64 ....78 A2
Lyne St ML2 ....165 A3
Lynebank Gr G77 ....156 B3
Lynebank Pl G77 ....156 B3
Lynedoch Cres G3 ......240 A4
Lynedoch Crescent La
G3 ....96 C1
Lynedoch Ind Est PA15 .46 A2
Lynedoch St Glasgow G3 .240 A4
Greenock PA15 ....45 C2
Lynedoch Terr G3 ....240 A4
Lynmouth Pl PA19 ....44 C3
Lynn Ave KA24 ....191 B4
Lynn Ct ML9 ....185 A1
Lynn Dr Eaglesham G76 .178 C3
Milngavie G62 ....55 B1
Lynn Wlk Balloch G83 ...27 C4
Bothwell G71 ....141 A4
Lynnburn Ave ML4 ......142 A3
Lynne Dr G23 ....76 C1
Lynnhurst G71 ....140 C4
Lynnwood Dr ML6 ......166 B3
Lyns Ave G46 ....136 A1
Lyon Cres FK9 ....2 A3
Lyon Rd Erskine PA8 .....72 C1
Johnstone PA5 ....112 A2
Linwood PA3 ....112 A2
Lyoncross Ave G78 .....134 B2
Lyoncross Cres G78 ....134 B2
Lyoncross Rd G53 ......115 A1
Lyons Quadrant ML2 ..164 B2
Lysa Vale PA14 ....141 C3
Lysander Way 9 PA4 ....94 B1
Lythe Gr G23 ....77 A2
Lytham Mdws G72 .....140 C1
Lytham Way ML1 ....173 B1
Lyttelton G75 ....180 A4

M

Mabel St ML1 ....163 C3
Maberry Cl KA3 ....195 B1
Maberry Pl KA10 ....229 D3
Mac Callum Dr G72 ....139 B3
Macadam Gdns ML4 ...142 A3
Macadam Pl Ayr KA8 ...236 A1
East Kilbride G75 ....180 C4
Falkirk FK1 ....41 B3
Irvine KA11 ....219 C1
Kilmarnock KA3 ....223 B1
Macadam Sq KA8 ....236 A1
Macallan Pl KA13 ....219 C4
Macallister Pl KA3 ......223 B1
Macalpine Pl KA3 ....223 B1
Macandrew Pl KA3 .....223 B1
Macara Dr KA12 ....219 C2
Macarthur Ave ML6 ....102 B2
Macarthur Cres G74 ...159 B2
Macarthur Ct G74 ......159 B2
Macarthur Dr
East Kilbride G74 ....159 B2
Macarthur Wynd G72 ..139 B3
Macaulay Pl G84 ....16 A1
Macbain Pl KA3 ....223 B1
Macbeth G74 ....160 A3
Macbeth Dr KA3 ....223 B1
Macbeth Pl G31 ....118 B2
Macbeth Rd
Greenock PA16 ....45 A3
Stewarton KA3 ....211 B4
Macbeth St G31 ....118 B2
Macbeth Wlk KA3 ......223 B1
Maccabe Gdns G66 .....57 C4
Maccallum Pl 4 ....KA13 B1
Maccrimmon Ps G74 ..185 A2
Macdairmid Dr ML3 ....183 A4
Macdonald Ave G74 ...159 A2
Macdonald Cres G65 ...60 A2
Macdonald Cts KA15 ..171 A4
Macdonald Dr
Kilmarnock KA3 ....223 B1
Stirling FK7 ....7 A2
Macdonald Gdns KA3 .223 B1
Macdonald Gr ML4 ....141 C1
Macdonald St
5 Motherwell ML1 ....163 C3
2 Rutherglen G73 ....138 A4
Macdonald Wlk G83 ...27 B4
Macdougal Dr G72 .....139 B3
Macdougall Quadrant
ML4 ....141 C1
Macdougall Dr KA3 ....223 B1
Macdougall St
Glasgow G43 ....136 B4
Greenock PA15 ....46 B2
Macduff PA8 ....73 A1
Macduff Pl G31 ....118 B2
Macduff St G31 ....118 B2
Mace Ct KA7 ....7 B2
Mace Rd G13 ....75 B1
Macewan Pl KA3 ....228 B4
Macfarlane Cres
Cambuslang G72 ....139 B3
Falkirk FK1 ....42 A3
Macfarlane Dr KA3 .....223 B1
Macfarlane Gr G61 ......76 A2
Macfie Pl G74 ....159 B3
Macgregor Ct G72 .....139 B3
Macgregor Dr KA3 .....223 B1
Machan Ave ML9 ....185 A2
Machan Rd ML9 ....185 A1
Machanhill ML9 ....185 A1
Machanhill Prim Sch
ML9 ....185 A1
Machanhill View ML9 ..185 A2
Machrie Ct FK1 ....41 B2
Machrie Dr
Helensburgh G84 ....16 A3
Newton Mearns G77 .....156 C3
Machrie Gr G75 ....180 A2
Machrie Rd Glasgow G45 .137 B2
Kilmarnock KA3 ....222 C2
Machrie St Glasgow G45 .137 B2
Motherwell ML1 ....163 A4
Machrihanish Pl KA3 ..223 B1
Macinnes Pl
East Kilbride G75 ....180 B4
Falkirk FK1 ....42 A1
Macintyre Pl KA3 ....223 B1
Macintyre Rd KA3 ......233 B1
Macivor Cres G74 ......159 A2
Macke Ave KA3 ....159 A2
Mackean St PA3 ....113 C3
Mackeith St G40 ....117 C2
Mackellar Pl KA3 ....223 B1
Mackendrick Pl KA3 ...228 B4
Mackenzie Dr
Johnstone PA10 ....111 A1
Kilmarnock KA3 ....223 A1
Mackenzie Gdns G74 ..159 A2
Mackenzie Pl G75 ....46 B2
Mackenzie Terr ML4 ...142 A3
Mackie Ave
Port Glasgow PA14 ....47 A1
Stewarton KA3 ....211 B4
Mackie Pl KA3 ....223 B1
Mackie St KA8 ....236 B3

Mackie's Mill Rd PA5 132 B4
Mackinlay Pl KA1 228 A4
Mackinlay St G5 117 A2
Mackinnon Dr KA3 228 B4
Mackinnon Terr KA12 219 C2
Mackintosh Pl KA11 219 C1
Maclachlan Ave FK6 21 B1
Maclachlan Pl G84 16 C2
Maclachlan Rd G84 16 C2
Maclaren Pl
Glasgow G44 136 C1
Kilmarnock KA3 228 B4
Maclaren Terr FK2 24 A1
Maclay Ave PA10 111 A1
Maclean Cres FK12 5 B4
Maclean Ct
East Kilbride G74 159 A2
Stirling FK7 7 B2
Maclean Dr KA3 223 A1
Maclean Gr G74 159 A2
Maclean Pl G74 159 A2
Maclean Sq G51 116 C3
Maclean St Clydebank G81 94 C4
Glasgow G51 116 B3
Maclean Terr EH48 107 B2
Maclehose Ct PA16 45 C4
Maclehose Rd G67 62 B2
Maclellan Rd G78 154 C3
Maclellan St G41 116 B3
Macleod Cres G84 16 A2
Macleod Dr
Helensburgh G84 16 B2
Kilmarnock KA3 228 B4
Macleod Pl
East Kilbride G74 160 A2
Kilmarnock KA3 228 B4
Macleod St G4 241 C2
Macmillan Dr
Gourock PA19 44 B3
Kilmarnock KA3 223 B1
Macmillan Gdns G71 121 A1
Macmillan Pl KA3 223 B1
Macmillan St ML9 184 C1
Macnab Pl KA3 223 A1
Macnaughton Dr KA3 223 B1
Macneil Pl KA3 223 A1
Macneill Dr G74 159 A2
Macneill Gdns G74 159 A2
Macneill St ML9 184 C2
Macneish Way G74 159 B2
Macnichol Gdns KA3 223 B1
Macnichol Pl KA3 223 B1
Macnicol Ct G74 159 A2
Macnicol Pk G74 159 A2
Macnicol Pl G74 159 A2
Macphail Dr KA3 223 B1
Macpherson Gdns KA3 223 B1
Macpherson Pk G74 159 B2
Macpherson Pl
Falkirk FK1 41 C1
Kilmarnock KA3 223 B1
Macpherson Wlk KA3 223 B1
Macphie Rd G82 50 B2
Macrae Dr KA9 233 B1
Macrae Gdns G74 159 B2
Macreadie Pl KA11 220 B3
Macrimmon Pl G75 180 C4
Macrobert Ave KA11 220 A1
Mactaggart Rd G67 82 C4
Madeira La PA16 45 B4
Madeira St PA16 45 B4
Madill Pl FK5 23 C2
Madison Ave G44 137 A3
Madison Path G72 161 B4
Madras Pl Glasgow G40 117 C2
Neilston G78 154 C4
Madras St G40 117 C2
Mafeking St
Glasgow G51 116 A3
Wishaw ML2 164 B2
Mafeking Terr G78 154 B4
Magdalen Way PA2 132 C4
Maggie Wood's Loan
FK1 41 C3
Magna St ML1 163 A4
Magnolia Dr G72 139 C2
Magnolia Gdns ML1 143 B2
Magnolia Pl G71 141 B4
Magnolia St ML2 165 A3
Magnum L Ctr* KA12 218 C1
Magnus Cres G44 137 A2
Magnus Rd PA6 111 B4
Mahon Ct G69 80 C1
Maid Morville Ave KA11 225 B4
Maidens G74 159 B2
Maidens Ave G77 157 A3
Maidland Rd G53 135 B4
Maidpath E G74 159 B1
Maidpath W G74 159 B1
Mailerbeg Gdns G69 80 C2
Mailie Wlk ML1 143 B2
Mailing Ave G64 78 B1
Mailings Rd G65 37 C2
Maimhor Rd KA23 190 B2
Main Rd Ayr KA8 236 C1
Cardross G82 48 A4
Crookedholm KA3 228 C4
Cumbernauld G67 82 A4
Elderslie PA5 112 B2
Fenwick KA3 213 A2
Gatehead KA2 226 C3
Kilbirnie KA25 149 A1
Langbank PA14 70 B4
Paisley PA2 113 B2
Rosneath G84 15 A2
Springside KA11 220 C1
Waterside KA3 213 C2
Main St Airth FK2 14 B2
Main St *continued*
Alexandria G83 27 C2
Alexandria, Dalmonach G83 27 C3
Alloa FK10 5 B1
Ayr KA8 235 C1
Balloch G83 19 C1
Bannockburn FK7 7 B1
Banton G65 37 B2
Barrhead G78 134 B1
Beith KA15 150 A1
Bellshill ML4 142 A3
Blackridge EH48 107 B2
Blantyre G72 161 B3
Bonnybridge FK4 40 A3
Bothwell G71 141 A1
Bridge of W PA11 110 B4
Calderbank ML6 123 B1
Caldercruix ML6 105 A2
California FK1 66 C3
Cambus FK10 9 A4
Cambuslang G72 139 A3
Chapelhall ML6 123 C2
Chryston G69 80 B1
Clarkston G76 157 C3
Cleland ML1 144 B1
Coatbridge ML5 122 A4
Coatbridge, Cliftonville
ML5 122 B3
Cowie FK7 12 B4
Cumbernauld G67 62 A3
Dalry KA24 191 B4
Drybridge KA11 225 C3
Drybridge, Dundonald
KA11,KA2 225 C1
Dunlop KA3 195 A4
East Kilbride G74 159 C1
Falkirk, Bainsford FK2 42 A4
Falkirk, Camelon FK1 41 C3
Falkirk, Carronshore FK2 24 B2
Fallin FK7 8 C2
Gateside KA15 171 C4
Glasgow G40 117 C2
Glasgow, Muirhead G69 120 B2
Glasgow, Thornliebank
G46 135 C2
Glenboig ML5 101 C3
Glengarnock KA14 170 A3
Greenock PA15 46 B2
Hamilton G72 161 C3
Houston PA6 91 A1
Howwood PA9 130 C3
Irvine KA11 220 B1
Kilmaurs KA3 222 B4
Kilsyth G65 60 B4
Kilwinning KA13 207 C2
Larbert FK5 23 B1
Lennoxtown G66 57 B4
Lochwinnoch PA12 129 B1
Longriggend ML6 85 A1
Milngavie G62 76 A4
Monkton KA9 233 B2
Motherwell ML1 143 A3
Neilston G78 154 B4
Overtown ML2 186 B3
Plains ML6 104 A1
Plean FK7 12 B2
Prestwick KA9 236 B4
Rutherglen G73 138 A4
Salsburgh ML7 125 A1
Shieldhill FK1 66 B3
Shotts ML7 147 A2
Slamannan FK1 86 A4
Stenhousemuir FK5 23 C1
Stevenston KA20 206 B1
Stewarton KA3 211 B4
Stirling FK7 6 B3
Stirling, St Ninians FK7 7 A2
Symington KA1 231 B2
Torrance G64 78 A4
Troon KA10 230 A2
Tullibody FK10 4 A1
Twechar G65 59 C2
Uddingston G71 140 C3
West Kilbride KA23 190 B3
Wishaw ML2 165 A2
Wishaw, Newmains ML2 166 A2
Main St E FK11 4 A3
Main St W FK11 3 C3
Mainhead Terr G67 62 A3
Mainhill Ave G69 120 B3
Mainhill Dr G69 120 B3
Mainhill Pl G69 120 B3
Mainhill Rd G69 120 C3
Mainholm Acad KA8 236 B1
Mainholm Cres KA8 236 B1
Mainholm Ct KA8 236 C1
Mainholm Rd Ayr KA8 239 C4
Ayr, Braehead KA8 236 B1
Mains Ave Beith KA15 150 A1
Glasgow G46 136 A1
Helensburgh G84 16 A2
Mains Ct ML11 215 B3
Mains Dr PA8 73 B1
Mains Hill PA8 73 A1
Mains Pl ML4 142 A2
Mains Rd Beith KA15 150 A1
East Kilbride G74 159 C3
Harthill ML7 127 C3
Mains River PA8 73 B1
Mains Wood PA8 73 B1
Mainscroft PA8 73 B1
Mainshill Ave PA8 73 A1
Mainshill Gdns PA8 73 A1
Mair Ave KA24 191 C4
Mair St G51 116 C3
Maitland Ave FK7 7 B1
Maitland Bank ML9 185 B2
Maitland Cres FK7 7 A2
Maitland Ct G84 16 B1
Maitland Dr G64 57 A1
Maitland Pl PA4 94 A1
Maitland St Glasgow G4 240 C4
Helensburgh G84 16 B1
Majors Loan FK1 42 A2
Majors Pl FK1 42 A2
Mal Fleming's Brae G65 60 C4
Malcolm Ct KA3 195 C1
Malcolm Dr FK5 23 C2
Malcolm Gdns
East Kilbride G74 159 B1
Irvine KA12 219 B1
Malcolm Pl G84 17 A1
Malcolm St ML1 163 B3
Malin Pl G33 118 C4
Mallaig Pl G51 115 B4
Mallaig Rd Glasgow G51 115 C4
Port Glasgow PA14 68 C4
Mallaig Terr PA16 44 C2
Mallard Cres
East Kilbride G75 180 A3
Greenock PA16 45 A3
Mallard La
14 Bothwell G71 141 A2
Greenock PA16 45 A3
Mallard Pl G75 180 A3
Mallard Rd G81 74 A3
Mallard Terr G75 180 A3
Mallard Way ML4 141 C4
Malleable Gdns ML1 142 B1
Malletsheugh Rd G77 156 A2
Malloch Cres PA5 112 A1
Malloch Pl G74 160 A1
Malloch St G20 96 C3
Mallots View G77 156 A2
Malov Ct G75 180 C3
Malplaquet Ct ML8 188 A1
Malta Terr G5 117 A2
Maltbarns St G20 97 A2
Malvaig La G72 161 B3
Malvern Ct G31 118 A3
Malvern Way 4 PA3 113 B4
Mambeg Dr G51 115 C4
Mamore Pl G43 136 B3
Mamore St G43 136 B3
Mamre Dr FK1 66 C3
Manchester Dr G12 96 A3
Mandela Ave FK2 42 B4
Mandora Ct ML8 188 A1
Manitoba Cres G75 159 A1
Mannering G74 160 B2
Mannering Ct G41 136 B4
Mannering Rd
Glasgow G41 136 B4
Paisley PA2 132 C4
Mannering Way PA2 112 C1
Mannfield Ave FK4 39 C2
Mannoch Pl ML5 122 B2
Mannofield G61 75 B2
Manor Ave KA3 223 A2
Manor Cres Gourock PA19 44 C4
Tullibody FK10 4 A1
Manor Dr ML6 122 C4
Manor Gate G77 156 C2
Manor Loan FK9 3 A3
Manor Park Ave PA2 113 A1
Manor Pk ML3 162 B1
Manor Powis Cotts FK9 3 A2
Manor Rd Clydebank G15 74 C1
Gartcosh G69 100 C3
Glasgow G14 95 C2
Paisley PA2 112 C1
Manor St FK1 42 A2
Manor View
Calderbank ML6 123 A1
Larkhall ML9 185 B1
Manor Way G73 138 B2
Manresa Pl 14 G4 97 A1
Mans field Dr G71 140 C3
Manse Ave Bearsden G61 75 C3
Bothwell G71 141 A1
Coatbridge ML5 121 B2
Manse Brae Dalserf ML9 200 A4
Glasgow G44 137 A3
Rhu G84 15 B3
Manse Cres Houston PA6 91 A1
Stirling FK7 7 A2
Manse Ct Barrhead G78 134 B2
Kilsyth G65 60 B4
Kilwinning KA13 207 C2
Law ML8 187 A2
Manse Dr G83 27 C4
Manse Gdns Balloch G83 27 C4
Glasgow G32 119 B2
Manse La G74 159 C2
Manse Mews ML2 166 A2
Manse Pl 6 Airdrie ML6 123 A4
Bannockburn FK7 7 C1
Falkirk FK1 42 A2
Rhu G84 15 B3
Slamannan FK1 86 A4
Manse Rd Bearsden G61 75 C3
Bowling G60 72 B4
Carmunnock G76 158 B4
Coatbridge G69 120 C3
Glasgow G32 119 B2
Kilsyth G65 60 C4
Lanark ML11 214 C2
Motherwell ML1 163 C2
Neilston G78 154 C4
Salsburgh ML7 125 B1
Shotts ML7 147 A2
Stonehouse ML9 198 B1
West Kilbride KA23 190 B3
Wishaw ML2 166 A2
Manse St Coatbridge ML5 121 C3
Kilmacolm PA13 89 C4
Manse St *continued*
Kilmarnock KA1 228 A4
Renfrew PA4 94 B2
Saltcoats KA21 216 C4
Manse View
Blantyre G72 161 A3
Motherwell ML1 143 C3
Mansefield Ave G72 139 A2
Mansefield Cres G60 73 A3
Mansefield Rd G76 157 B3
Mansefield Terr KA3 195 A4
Mansel St G21 98 A3
Manseview ML9 185 A1
Manseview Terr G76 178 C3
Mansewell Rd KA9 233 B1
Mansewood Ct G69 120 B2
Mansewood Dr G82 50 A3
Mansewood Rd G43 136 A3
Mansfield Ave FK10 5 B1
Mansfield Cres G76 157 B3
Mansfield Rd
Bellshill ML4 141 C2
Clarkston G76 157 C3
Lochwinnoch PA12 129 B2
Paisley G52 114 C4
Prestwick KA9 236 A3
Quarter ML3 183 C3
Mansfield St G11 96 B1
Mansfield Way KA11 220 A3
Mansion Ave PA14 69 A4
Mansion Ct G72 139 A3
Mansion St
Cambuslang G72 139 A3
Glasgow G22 97 B3
Mansionhouse Ave G32 139 B4
Mansionhouse Dr G32 119 B3
Mansionhouse Gdns
G41 136 C4
Mansionhouse Gr G32 119 C2
Mansionhouse Rd
Falkirk FK1 41 B3
Glasgow G32 119 C2
Glasgow, Langside G41 136 C4
Paisley PA1 114 A3
Manson Ave KA9 233 B1
Manson Pl G75 181 A3
Manson Rd KA12 219 C2
Manuel Ave KA15 171 A4
Manuel Ct Irvine KA11 225 B4
Kilbirnie KA25 170 A4
Manuel Terr KA11 225 B4
Manus Duddy Ct
Blantyre G72 140 B1
Hamilton G72 161 B4
Maple Ave Dumbarton G82 49 A3
Milton of C G66 58 A3
Newton Mearns G77 156 B2
Stenhousemuir FK5 23 C2
Maple Bank ML3 162 C1
Maple Cres G72 139 C2
Maple Ct 11 Alloa FK10 10 A3
Coatbridge ML5 121 C2
Cumbernauld G67 62 C3
Maple Dr Ayr KA7 239 B3
Barrhead G78 155 B4
Beith KA15 150 A1
Clydebank G81 74 A3
Johnstone PA5 132 A4
Kirkintilloch G66 79 A3
Larkhall ML9 185 A3
Maple Gr
East Kilbride G75 180 A3
Troon KA10 229 C2
Maple Pl Banknock FK4 38 C1
Denny FK6 21 B2
East Kilbride G75 180 A3
Kilmarnock KA1 227 B4
Uddingston G71 141 B4
Maple Quadrant ML6 123 B3
Maple Rd
Cumbernauld G67 62 C3
Glasgow G41 116 A2
Greenock PA16 45 A2
Motherwell ML1 143 A3
Maple Terr
East Kilbride G75 180 A3
Irvine KA12 219 B2
Maple Way G72 161 B4
Maplewood ML2 164 B1
Mar Ave PA7 72 A2
Mar Dr G61 75 C4
Mar Gdns G73 138 B2
Mar Pl Alloa FK10 10 A4
Alloa, New Sauchie FK10 5 B1
Stirling FK8 7 A4
Mar St FK10 10 A3
Marble Ave KA11 220 B1
March St G41 116 C1
Marchbank Gdns PA1 114 B2
Marchburn Ave KA9 236 C4
Marchdyke Cres KA1 227 C2
Marches The
Lanark ML11 215 A3
Stirling FK8 7 A4
Marchfield G64 77 C2
Marchfield Ave PA3 113 C4
Marchfield Quadrant
KA8 236 A3
Marchfield Rd KA8 236 A3
Marchglen FK13 5 C3
Marchglen Pl G51 115 B4
Marchmont Ct KA1 228 C4
Marchmont Gdns G64 77 C1
Marchmont Rd KA7 238 C3
Marchmont Road La
KA7 238 C4
Marchmont Terr 14 G12 96 B2
Marchside Ct FK10 5 B1
Mardale G74 159 B2
Maree Ct FK10 10 B3
Maree Dr
Cumbernauld G67 82 A4
Glasgow G52 115 C2
Maree Gdns G64 78 A1
Maree Pl KA12 219 B4
Maree Rd PA2 113 A1
Maree Way G72 161 B4
Maree Wlk 7 ML2 165 C3
Marfield St G32 118 C3
Margaret Ave Haggs FK4 39 A2
Salsburgh ML7 125 A1
Margaret Ct FK6 21 C1
Margaret Dr
Alexandria G83 27 B3
Bonnybridge FK4 40 A3
Margaret Pl ML4 141 C3
Margaret Rd
Bannockburn FK7 7 B1
Hamilton ML3 162 A3
Margaret St
Coatbridge ML5 122 A2
Gourock PA19 44 C4
Greenock PA16 45 B4
Margaret Terr FK5 23 C2
Margaret's Pl ML9 185 A2
Margaretta Bldgs G44 137 A3
Margaretvale Dr ML9 185 A1
Marguerite Ave G66 79 B3
Marguerite Dr G66 79 B3
Marguerite Gdns
Bothwell G71 141 A1
Kirkintilloch G66 79 B3
Marguerite Gr G66 79 B3
Marguerite Pl Ayr KA7 239 B2
Milton of C G66 58 A3
Marian Dr ML1 143 B1
Maric La ML6 104 A1
Marigold Ave ML1 163 C4
Marigold Sq KA7 239 A2
Marigold Way ML8 201 C4
Marina Ct ML4 141 C2
Marina Rd KA9 236 A4
Marine Cres G51 116 C3
Marine Dr KA11,KA12 224 B3
Marine Gdns G51 240 A1
Marine View Ct KA10 229 C1
Mariner Ave FK1 41 A3
Mariner Dr FK1 41 A3
Mariner Gdns FK1 41 B3
Mariner Rd FK1 41 B3
Mariner St FK1 41 A3
Marion St ML4 142 B3
Mariscat Rd G41 116 C1
Marius Cres ML1 142 B1
Marjory Dr PA3 114 A4
Marjory Rd PA4 94 A1
Markdow Ave G53 115 A1
Market Cl 7 G65 60 B4
Market End ML11 215 A2
Market Pl Carluke ML8 187 C1
Kilmacolm PA13 89 B4
5 Kilsyth G65 60 B4
Uddingston G71 141 B4
Market Rd Carluke ML8 187 C1
Kirkintilloch G66 80 A4
Uddingston G71 141 B4
Market Sq 6 G65 60 B4
Market St Airdrie ML6 123 A4
Kilsyth G65 60 B4
Uddingston G71 141 B4
Markethill Rd
East Kilbride G74 159 C3
East Kilbride, East Mains
G74 159 C2
Markethill Rdbt G74 159 C2
Markinch Rd PA14 68 C3
Marlach Pl 13 G53 135 A4
Marlborough Ave G11 95 C2
Marlborough Ct 15 KA7 235 C1
Marlborough Dr FK9 2 B2
Marlborough La N G11 95 C2
Marlborough La S G11 95 C2
Marlborough Pk G75 180 A4
Marldon La G11 95 C2
Marlepark KA7 239 A2
Marley Way G66 58 A3
Marlfield Gdns ML4 142 A4
Marloch Ave PA14 69 A3
Marlow St G41 116 C3
Marlow Terr G41 116 C2
Marmion Ave G84 25 B4
Marmion Cres ML1 142 B1
Marmion Ct PA2 132 C4
Marmion Dr G66 79 C4
Marmion Pl G67 82 C4
Marmion Rd
Cumbernauld G67 82 C4
Paisley PA2 132 C4
Marmion St FK2 42 A4
Marne St G31 118 A4
Marnoch Dr ML5 101 B3
Marnoch Way G69 80 C1
Marnock Terr PA2 114 A1
Marquis Ave ML3 162 A3
Marquis Gate G71 140 C3
Marr Coll KA10 229 D2
Marr Dr KA10 229 C2
Marr's Wynd ML11 215 B3
Marress Rd KA12 219 A2
Marress Rdbt KA12 219 A1
Marrswood Gn ML3 162 A2
Marrwood Ave G66 80 A3
Mars Rd PA16 44 B1

Marschal Ct FK7 . . . . .7 B2
Marshall Gr ML3 . . . . .162 A2
Marshall La ML2 . . . . .165 A2
Marshall St Larkhall ML9 .185 A1
 Wishaw ML2 . . . . .164 C1
Marshall Way FK10 . . . . .4 B2
Marshall's La PA1 . . . . .113 C2
Marshill FK10 . . . . .10 A3
Marsmount Rd KA9 . . . . . .233 C1
Mart St G1 . . . . .241 A1
Martha St G1 . . . . .241 A3
Martin Ave Balloch G83 . . . . .28 A4
 Irvine KA12 . . . . .219 B3
Martin Bannon Ct G82 . . . .49 B4
Martin Cres G69 . . . . .120 B3
Martin Ct ML3 . . . . .162 B2
Martin PI ML1 . . . . .143 B2
Martin Sq KA21 . . . . .206 A1
Martin St Coatbridge ML5 .122 B4
 Glasgow G40 . . . . .117 C2
Martinside G75 . . . . .180 C3
Martlet Dr PA5 . . . . .131 B3
Martyn St ML6 . . . . .122 C3
Martyrs PI G64 . . . . .98 A4
Marwick St G31 . . . . .118 A4
Mary Dr ML4 . . . . .141 C2
Mary Fisher Cres G82 . . . . .50 B1
Mary Glen ML2 . . . . .165 B3
Mary Love Rd KA20 . . . . . .206 A1
Mary Rae Rd ML4 . . . . .141 C2
Mary Russell Sch The
 PA2 . . . . .114 B1
Mary Sq G20 . . . . .120 C3
Mary St Greenock PA16 . . . .45 B2
 Hamilton ML3 . . . . .162 B1
 Johnstone PA5 . . . . .112 A2
 Laurieston FK2 . . . . .42 C2
 Paisley PA2 . . . . .113 C1
 Port Glasgow PA14 . . . . . . .47 A1
Mary Stevenson Dr FK10 .10 A4
Mary Street Rdbt FK2 . . . . .42 C2
Mary Young PI G76 . . . . . . .157 C3
Maryborough Ave KA9 . . .236 A3
Maryborough Rd KA9 . . . .236 A3
Maryfield PI Ayr KA8 . . . . .236 A2
 Falkirk FK1 . . . . .41 A2
Maryfield Rd KA8 . . . . .236 A2
Maryhill Prim Sch G20 . . . .96 B4
Maryhill Rd
 Bearsden G20,G61 . . . . .76 A1
 Glasgow G20 . . . . .96 B3
Maryhill Sta G20 . . . . .96 B4
Maryknowe Rd ML1 . . . . . .143 A1
Maryland Dr G52 . . . . .115 C3
Maryland Gdns G52 . . . . . .115 C3
Maryland Rd G82 . . . . .50 B3
Marypark Rd PA14 . . . . .70 A4
Maryston St G33 . . . . .118 B3
Maryville Ave G46 . . . . .136 B1
Maryville View G71 . . . . . . .120 B1
Marywood Sq G41 . . . . .116 C1
Mashock Path ML8 . . . . . . .201 A4
Mason La ML1 . . . . .163 C3
Mason St Larkhall ML9 . . . .185 B1
 Motherwell ML1 . . . . .163 C3
Masonfield Ave G68 . . . . . . .61 B1
Masonhill PI KA7 . . . . .239 B3
Masonhill Rd KA7 . . . . .239 B3
Masterton St G22 . . . . .97 B2
Masterton Way G71 . . . . . .121 A1
Mather Terr FK2 . . . . .42 C2
Matherton Ave G77 . . . . . .157 A3
Matheson Wlk G83 . . . . .27 C4
Mathew Smith Ave KA1 .227 C3
Mathie Cres PA19 . . . . .44 C3
Mathieson Rd G73 . . . . .118 B1
Mathieson St PA1 . . . . .114 A3
Matilda Rd G41 . . . . .116 C2
Matt PI G72 . . . . .161 B2
Matthew McWhirter PI
 ML9 . . . . .185 A2
Matthew PI KA13 . . . . .207 C3
Mauchline Ave G74 . . . . . . .160 C2
Mauchline Ave G66 . . . . .59 A1
Mauchline Ct
 Hamilton ML3 . . . . .161 B1
 Kilmarnock KA3 . . . . .223 A3
 Kirkintilloch G66 . . . . .59 A1
Mauchline La PA16 . . . . .44 C2
Mauchline Rd KA1 . . . . .228 C3
Mauchline St G5 . . . . .117 A2
Mauchline Terr PA1 . . . . . . .44 C2
Maukinfauld Ct G32 . . . . . .118 B2
Maukinfauld Gdns G31 .118 C2
Maukinfauld Rd G32 . . . . .118 C2
Mauldslie Dr ML8 . . . . .187 A3
Mauldslie PI ML9 . . . . .199 C4
Mauldslie Rd
 Carluke ML8 . . . . .187 A1
 ML8 . . . . .186 C1
Mauldslie St
 Bellshill ML4 . . . . .142 A2
 Coatbridge ML5 . . . . .122 A3
 Glasgow G40 . . . . .117 C3
Maule Dr G11 . . . . .96 A1
Maunsheugh Rd KA13 . . . .213 A2
Maurice Ave FK7 . . . . .7 B2
Mausoleum Dr ML3 . . . . . . .162 C3
Mavis Bank
 Bishopbriggs G64 . . . . .97 C4
 Blantyre G72 . . . . .161 B4
Mavis Rd PA16 . . . . .45 A2
Mavisbank Ave FK1 . . . . . . .66 B3

Mavisbank Gdns
 Bellshill ML4 . . . . .142 A3
 Glasgow G51 . . . . .116 C3
Mavisbank Rd G51 . . . . . . .116 B3
Mavisbank Sch ML6 . . . . . .122 C4
Mavisbank St
 Airdrie ML6 . . . . .122 C4
 Wishaw ML2 . . . . .166 B3
Mavisbank Terr
 Johnstone PA5 . . . . .111 C1
 Paisley PA1 . . . . .113 C2
Mavor Ave G74 . . . . .160 A2
Mavor Rdbt G74 . . . . .159 C2
Maxholm Rd KA1 . . . . .227 C3
Maxton Ave G78 . . . . .134 A2
Maxton Cres Alva FK12 . . . . .5 B4
 Wishaw ML2 . . . . .165 B3
Maxton Gr G78 . . . . .134 A2
Maxton Terr G72 . . . . .138 C2
Maxwell Ave
 Bearsden G61 . . . . .75 C1
 Glasgow G69 . . . . .120 A3
 G41 . . . . .116 C2
Maxwell Cres G72 . . . . .161 B3
Maxwell Ct Beith KA15 . . . .171 A4
 Coatbridge ML5 . . . . .122 A4
 Kilmarnock KA3 . . . . .223 B2
Maxwell Dr Erskine PA8 . . . .72 C2
 Glasgow G69 . . . . .120 A3
 G41 . . . . .116 C2
Maxwell Gdns
 Glasgow G41 . . . . .116 B2
 Hurlford KA1 . . . . .228 C3
Maxwell Gr G41 . . . . .116 B2
Maxwell Gr G41 . . . . .116 B2
Maxwell La G41 . . . . .116 C2
Maxwell Oval G41 . . . . .116 C2
Maxwell Park Sta G41 . . . .116 B1
Maxwell PI
 Bridge of W PA11 . . . . .110 B4
 Coatbridge ML5 . . . . .121 C3
 Glasgow G41 . . . . .117 A2
 Kilsyth G65 . . . . .36 B1
 Stevenston KA20 . . . . .206 C1
 Stirling FK8 . . . . .7 A4
 Uddingston G71 . . . . .141 A3
Maxwell Rd Bishopton PA7 .72 A2
 Glasgow G41 . . . . .116 C2
Maxwell St Clydebank G81 .73 C2
 Glasgow G1 . . . . .241 A1
 Glasgow, Bialliestoun G69 .120 A2
 Paisley PA3 . . . . .113 C3
Maxwell Terr G41 . . . . .116 C2
Maxwellton Ave G74 . . . . .160 A2
Maxwellton Ct G74 . . . . . . .159 C2
Maxwellton PI G74 . . . . . . .160 A2
Maxwellton Prim Sch
 G74 . . . . .160 A2
Maxwellton Rd
 East Kilbride G74 . . . . .160 B2
 Paisley PA1 . . . . .113 A2
 Port Glasgow PA14 . . . . . . .68 C3
Maxwellton St PA1 . . . . . . .113 B2
Maxwelton Rd G33 . . . . .98 B1
Maxwood PI KA11 . . . . .220 A3
May Gdns ML3 . . . . .162 B3
May Rd PA2 . . . . .133 C4
May St ML3 . . . . .162 B3
May Terr Glasgow G42 . . . .137 A4
 Glasgow, Merrylee G46 . . . .136 B2
Maybank La G42 . . . . .117 A1
Maybank St G42 . . . . .117 A1
Mayberry Cres G32 . . . . . . .119 B3
Mayberry Gdns G32 . . . . . .119 B3
Mayberry PI G32 . . . . .119 B3
Mayberry PI G72 . . . . .161 B4
Maybole Cres G77 . . . . .157 A2
Maybole Dr ML6 . . . . .123 A2
Maybole Gdns ML3 . . . . . . .161 B1
Maybole Gr G77 . . . . .157 A2
Maybole PI ML5 . . . . .122 B2
Maybole Rd Ayr KA7 . . . . .239 A2
Maybole St G53 . . . . .134 C3
Mayfield Ave
 Clarkston G76 . . . . .157 C4
 Hurlford KA1 . . . . .228 C3
Mayfield Cres
 Howwood PA9 . . . . .130 C3
 Stevenston KA20 . . . . .206 B1
Mayfield Ct
 Howwood PA9 . . . . .130 C3
 Stirling FK7 . . . . .7 A2
Mayfield Dr
 Howwood PA9 . . . . .130 C3
 Longcroft FK4 . . . . .39 A2
Mayfield Gdns ML8 . . . . . . .202 A4
Mayfield Mews FK1 . . . . . . .41 C2
Mayfield PI Carluke ML8 . .202 A4
 Coatbridge ML5 . . . . .122 A2
 Saltcoats KA21 . . . . .217 A4
Mayfield Prim Sch
 KA21 . . . . .206 A1
Mayfield Rd
 Hamilton ML3 . . . . .161 C2
 Saltcoats KA21 . . . . .217 A4
 Stevenston KA20 . . . . .206 B1
Mayfield St Glasgow G20 . . .96 C3
 Stirling FK7 . . . . .7 A2
Mayne Ave FK9 . . . . .2 A3
Mayville St KA20 . . . . .206 B1
McAdam Ct KA9 . . . . .236 B3
McAlister Rd G83 . . . . .27 C3

McAllister Ave ML6 . . . . . .123 B4
McAllister Ct KA7 . . . . .7 B1
McAlpine St Glasgow G2 . .240 B2
 Wishaw ML2 . . . . .165 A1
McArdle Ave ML1 . . . . .163 A4
McArthur Pk G66 . . . . .79 B4
McArthur St G43 . . . . .136 B4
McAslin Ct G4 . . . . .241 B3
McAslin St G4 . . . . .241 C3
McAuslan PI G84 . . . . .16 C1
McBride Ave G66 . . . . .79 B4
McCall's Ave KA8 . . . . .236 A1
McCallum Ave G73 . . . . . . .138 A4
McCallum Cres PA19 . . . . . .44 C4
McCallum Ct G74 . . . . .159 A2
McCallum Gdns ML4 . . . . .141 C1
McCallum Gr G74 . . . . .159 A2
McCallum PI G74 . . . . .159 A2
McCardel Way KA3 . . . . . . .211 C4
McCarrison Rd ML2 . . . . . .166 A3
McCash PI G66 . . . . .79 B4
McClue Ave PA4 . . . . .94 A2
McClue Rd PA4 . . . . .94 B2
McClue Gdns KA12 . . . . . . .219 B2
McClurg Ct G8 . . . . .163 C3
McColgan PI KA8 . . . . .236 B2
McColl Ave G83 . . . . .27 B3
McConnell Rd PA12 . . . . . .129 A1
McCormack Gdns ML1 . . .143 C2
McCourt Gdns ML4 . . . . . .142 B3
McCracken Ave PA4 . . . . . . .94 A1
McCreath Dr G71 . . . . .141 B4
McCreery St G81 . . . . .94 B4
McCrorie PI PA10 . . . . .111 A2
McCulloch Ave G71 . . . . . .141 B3
McCulloch La G83 . . . . .27 B4
McCulloch St G41 . . . . .116 C2
McDonald Ave PA5 . . . . . . .111 A1
McDonald Cres G81 . . . . . . .94 B4
McDonald PI Motherwell ML1 . . . . .143 A3
 Neilston G78 . . . . .154 C4
McDowall Ave KA22 . . . . . .205 B1
McDowall PI KA22 . . . . . . .205 B1
McEwan Dr G84 . . . . .16 C2
McEwan Gdns G74 . . . . . . .159 A2
McEwan Wlk G83 . . . . .27 C3
McEwan Way ML3 . . . . . . .198 B1
McFarlane Rd G83 . . . . .28 A4
McFarlane St
 Glasgow G4 . . . . .241 C1
 Paisley PA3 . . . . .113 B4
McGavin Ave KA13 . . . . . . .208 A2
McGavin Way KA13 . . . . . .207 B2
Mcghee PI FK1 . . . . .41 C1
McGhee St G81 . . . . .74 A2
McGibney Dr KA12 . . . . . . .219 B1
McGrigor PI ML1 . . . . .162 A3
McGowan St PA3 . . . . .113 B3
McGregor Ave
 Airdrie ML6 . . . . .123 B4
 Balloch G83 . . . . .28 A4
 Renfrew PA4 . . . . .94 A1
 Stevenston KA20 . . . . .206 B1
McGregor Dr G82 . . . . .50 B2
McGregor Path ML5 . . . . . .101 B3
McGregor Rd G67 . . . . .61 C1
McGregor St
 Clydebank G81 . . . . .94 B4
 Glasgow G51 . . . . .115 C3
 Wishaw ML2 . . . . .164 B2
McGregor Wlk G83 . . . . . . .27 B4
McGregor Rd
 Milngavie G62 . . . . .54 C2
 Stirling FK7 . . . . .7 A2
McHardy Cres KA15 . . . . . .171 C2
McInnes Ct ML2 . . . . .164 B1
McInnes Gdns ML9 . . . . . . .198 C1
McInnes PI ML9 . . . . .186 A4
McInnes St G83 . . . . .28 A4
McIntosh Ct G31 . . . . .117 C4
McIntosh Quadrant
 ML4 . . . . .141 C1
McIntosh St G31 . . . . .117 C4
McIntosh Way ML1 . . . . . . .163 B3
McIntyre Ave KA9 . . . . .233 B1
McIntyre PI PA2 . . . . .113 C1
McIntyre St G3 . . . . .240 A2
McIntyre Terr Balloch G83 . .27 C4
 Cambuslang G72 . . . . .139 A3
McInver St G72 . . . . .139 C3
McIsaac Rd KA21 . . . . .195 A4
McKay Cres PA5 . . . . .112 A1
McKay Ct G77 . . . . .156 B2
McKay Gr ML4 . . . . .141 C3
McKay PI
 East Kilbride G74 . . . . .159 A2
 Newton Mearns G77 . . . . . .156 B2
McKechnie St G51 . . . . .116 A4
McKell Ct FK1 . . . . .42 A2
McKellar Ave KA21 . . . . . . .205 B1
McKenna Dr ML6 . . . . .122 C4
McKenzie Ave G81 . . . . .74 A2
McKenzie Dr G83 . . . . .19 C1
McKenzie PI FK1 . . . . .42 A1
McKenzie St PA3 . . . . .113 B3
McKenzie's Cl ML15 . . . . . .215 A2
McKeown Gdns ML4 . . . . .142 B2
McKerrell St PA1 . . . . .114 A3
McKillop PI KA21 . . . . .205 C1
McKim Wlk G83 . . . . .49 B4
McKinlay Cres G83 . . . . .20 A1
McKinlay Cres Alloa FK10 . .10 B4

McKinlay Cres continued
 Irvine KA12 . . . . .219 A1
McKinnon PI KA21 . . . . . . .206 A1
McKnight Ave KA3 . . . . . . .213 C2
McLachlan Ave FK7 . . . . .7 A1
McLachlan St FK5 . . . . .23 B1
McLaren Ave PA4 . . . . .94 B1
McLaren Cres G20 . . . . .96 C4
McLaren Ct Glasgow G46 .136 A1
 Stenhousemuir FK5 . . . . . . .23 B1
McLaren Dr ML4 . . . . .142 B2
McLaren Gdns G20 . . . . . . .96 C4
McLaren Gr G74 . . . . .159 A2
McLaren PI G82 . . . . .27 C1
McLaren Terr FK7 . . . . .7 A2
McLauchlan View ML7 . . .127 C3
McLaurin Cres PA5 . . . . . . .111 B1
McLean Cres G83 . . . . .19 C1
McLean Dr Bellshill ML4 . . .141 C1
 Irvine KA11 . . . . .225 B4
McLean Gdns ML9 . . . . .198 C1
McLean Mus & Art Gall*
 PA16 . . . . .45 C3
McLean Pl PA3 . . . . .113 B4
 Plains ML6 . . . . .104 A1
McLennan St G42 . . . . .137 A4
McLeod Rd G82 . . . . .50 B2
McLeod St PA15 . . . . .46 B2
McLuckie Dr KA13 . . . . . . .207 B2
McLuckie Pk KA13 . . . . . . .207 B2
McLuskie Rd ML2 . . . . .166 A3
McMahon Gr ML4 . . . . .142 A3
McMillan Cres KA15 . . . . . .171 A4
McMillan Dr KA22 . . . . . . .205 A2
McMillan PI KA11 . . . . .224 D3
McMillan Way ML2 . . . . . . .166 C3
McMillan Way ML8 . . . . . . .186 C3
McNab Gdns FK6 . . . . .41 C1
McNair St G32 . . . . .119 A3
McNaught Pl
 Kilmaurs KA3 . . . . .222 A4
 Stewarton G82 . . . . .27 B1
McNay Cres KA21 . . . . .206 A1
McNee Rd KA9 . . . . .233 B2
McNeil Ave G81 . . . . .74 C1
McNeil Dr ML1 . . . . .143 A4
McNeil Gdns G5 . . . . .117 B2
McNeil St G5 . . . . .117 B2
McNeil Way G72 . . . . .186 A4
McNeill Ave G81 . . . . .74 C1
McNiven Ct ML9 . . . . .198 C1
McPhail Ave ML1 . . . . .143 C3
McPhail St Glasgow G40 . . .117 C2
 Greenock PA15 . . . . .46 B2
McPhater St G4 . . . . .240 C4
McPherson Dr
 Bothwell G71 . . . . .141 A2
 Gourock PA19 . . . . .44 B4
McPherson La G83 . . . . .27 B4
McPherson St
 Bellshill ML4 . . . . .142 B3
 Glasgow G1 . . . . .241 B1
McShannon Gr ML4 . . . . . .142 A2
McSparran Rd G65 . . . . .60 C2
McTaggart Ave FK6 . . . . . . .21 C1
McTaggart Rd FK4 . . . . .39 A2
Meadow Ave
 Blantyre G72 . . . . .161 B3
 Irvine KA12 . . . . .219 B2
Meadow Cl G75 . . . . .180 A2
Meadow Ct Carluke ML8 . .188 B1
 Dumbarton G82 . . . . .49 C3
Meadow Gn FK10 . . . . .5 A1
Meadow La Bothwell G71 . .141 A1
 Renfrew PA4 . . . . .94 B1
Meadow Park KA13 . . . . . .207 B3
Meadow Path ML6 . . . . . . .123 B1
Meadow Pk Alva FK12 . . . . .5 A3
Meadow PI FK8 . . . . .2 B1
Meadow Rd
 Braidwood ML8 . . . . .202 A2
 Dumbarton G82 . . . . .50 A2
 Glasgow G11 . . . . .96 A1
 Motherwell ML1 . . . . .164 A3
 Meadow Rise G77 . . . . .156 C3
Meadow St
 Coatbridge ML5 . . . . .122 A2
 Falkirk FK2 . . . . .42 B2
Meadow View
 Cumbernauld G67 . . . . .62 B2
 Irvine KA11 . . . . .225 B4
 Plains ML6 . . . . .104 A2
Meadow Way
 Kilwinning KA13 . . . . .207 B3
 Newton Mearns G77 . . . . . .156 B3
Meadowbank La KA13 . . . .155 C2
Meadowbank La
 Prestwick KA9 . . . . .236 A4
 Uddingston G71 . . . . .140 C3
Meadowburn PI G77 . . . . . .156 B3
Meadowburn
 Bishopbriggs G64 . . . . .78 A2
Meadowburn Ave
 Kirkintilloch G66 . . . . .79 C3
 Newton Mearns G77 . . . . . .156 B3
Meadowburn Prim Sch
 G64 .78 A2
Meadowburn Rd ML2 . . . . .165 B2
Meadowfield PI ML2 . . . . .166 B3
Meadowfoot Rd KA23 . . . .190 B2
Meadowforth Rd FK7 . . . . . .7 B4

Meadowhead Ave
 Chryston G69 . . . . .80 C1
 Irvine KA11 . . . . .224 D2
Meadowhead Ind Est
 KA11 . . . . .224 D3
Meadowhead Rd
 Irvine KA11 . . . . .224 D2
 Plains ML6 . . . . .103 C1
Meadowhead Rdbt
 KA11 . . . . .224 D1
Meadowhill G77 . . . . .156 B3
Meadowhill St ML9 . . . . . . .185 B2
Meadowhouse Rd FK9 . . . . .2 A3
Meadowpark Dr KA7 . . . . .239 A3
Meadowpark St G31 . . . . . .118 A4
Meadows Ave Erskine PA8 .73 B1
 Larkhall ML9 . . . . .185 A2
Meadows Dr PA8 . . . . .73 B1
Meadows The Falkirk FK2 . .24 A1
 Houston PA6 . . . . .91 C1
 Kilwinning KA13 . . . . .207 B2
Meadowside Beith KA15 . .171 A4
 Crookedholm KA3 . . . . .228 C4
 Hamilton ML3 . . . . .183 B3
 West Kilbride KA23 . . . . . . .190 B3
 Meadowside Gdns 🄳
 ML6 . . . . .123 B4
Meadowside Ind Est PA4 . .94 B3
Meadowside PI 🄳 ML6 . . .123 B4
Meadowside Rd G65 . . . . . .59 C4
Meadowside St
 Glasgow G11 . . . . .96 A1
 Renfrew PA4 . . . . .94 B3
Meadowvell St G32 . . . . . . .119 A3
Meadside Ave PA10 . . . . . .111 A2
Meadside Rd PA10 . . . . . . .111 A2
Mealkirk St G81 . . . . .74 B4
Mearns Castle High Sch
 G77 . . . . .157 A2
Mearns Ct ML3 . . . . .183 C4
Mearns Prim Sch G77 . . . .156 A2
Mearns Rd
 Motherwell ML1 . . . . .163 B4
 Newton Mearns G77 . . . . . .156 B1
Mearns St PA15 . . . . .45 C3
Mearns Way G64 . . . . .78 B1
Mearnscroft Gdns G77 . . .156 C2
Mearnscroft Rd G77 . . . . .156 C2
Mearnskirk Rd G77 . . . . . . .156 B1
Medine Ave KA15 . . . . .150 A1
Medine Ct KA15 . . . . .150 A1
Medlar Ct G72 . . . . .139 C2
Medlar Rd G67 . . . . .62 B3
Medrox Gdns G67 . . . . .81 C3
Medwin Ct G75 . . . . .179 C4
Medwin Gdns G75 . . . . . . .179 C3
Medwyn St G14 . . . . .95 B2
Medwyn PI FK10 . . . . .9 C3
Meek Pl G72 . . . . .139 A3
Meeks PI FK2 . . . . .42 A3
Meetinghouse La 🄶
 PA1 . . . . .113 C2
Megan St G40 . . . . .117 C2
Meigle Rd ML6 . . . . .122 C3
Meikle Ave PA4 . . . . .94 B1
Meikle Bin Brae G66 . . . . . .57 C4
Meikle Cres
 Greengairs ML6 . . . . .103 B4
 Hamilton ML3 . . . . .183 B4
Meikle Ct KA3 . . . . .195 C1
Meikle Drumgray Rd
 ML6 . . . . .103 C4
Meikle Earnock Rd ML3 .183 A4
Meikle PI KA11 . . . . .220 A3
Meikle Rd G53 . . . . .135 B4
Meiklehill Ct G66 . . . . .58 C1
Meiklehill Rd G66 . . . . .58 C1
Meiklerig Cres G53 . . . . . . .115 B1
Meiklewood Ave KA9 . . . .233 B1
Meiklewood Rd
 Glasgow G51 . . . . .115 B3
 Kilmarnock KA3 . . . . .222 C3
Melbourne Ave
 Clydebank G81 . . . . .73 B3
 East Kilbride G75 . . . . .180 B4
Melbourne Gr 🄷 G75 . . . . .180 B4
Melbourne Ct G46 . . . . . . .136 B2
Melbourne Gn G33 . . . . . . .117 C3
Melbourne St G31 . . . . .117 C4
Meldon PI G51 . . . . .115 B3
Meldrum Gdns G41 . . . . . . .116 B1
Meldrum Mains ML6 . . . . .102 C2
Meldrum St G81 . . . . .94 B4
Melford Ave
 Glasgow G46 . . . . .136 B1
 Kirkintilloch G66 . . . . .79 B1
 Shotts ML7 . . . . .147 A2
Melford Gdns PA10 . . . . . . .111 A1
Melford Rd ML4 . . . . .141 C4
Melford Way PA3 . . . . .114 A4
Melfort Ave
 Clydebank G81 . . . . .74 B2
 Glasgow G41 . . . . .116 A2
Melfort Ct G81 . . . . .74 B1
Melfort Dr FK7 . . . . .7 A2
Melfort Path ML2 . . . . .165 C4
Melfort Quadrant ML1 . . .143 B2
Melfort Rd ML3 . . . . .161 C1
Melfort Gr KA1 . . . . .228 A4
Mellerstain Dr G14 . . . . . . .94 C3
Mellock Gdns FK1 . . . . .41 C1
Melness PI G51 . . . . .115 B4
Melrose Ave
 Chapelhall ML6 . . . . .123 B1

Melrose Ave *continued*
Coatbridge G69 ....120 C3
Linwood PA3 ....112 A3
Motherwell ML1 ....143 A3
Paisley PA2 ....113 A1
Rutherglen G73 ....138 A4
Melrose Cres ML2 ....165 A3
Melrose Ct G73 ....138 A4
Melrose Gdns
Glasgow G20 ....96 C2
Twechar G65 ....59 C2
Uddingston G71 ....120 C1
Melrose Pl Blantyre G72 ...140 B1
Coatbridge ML5 ....121 C4
🔟 Falkirk FK1 ....42 A2
Larkhall ML9 ....185 A1
Melrose Prim Sch G67 ......82 C4
Melrose Rd
Cumbernauld G67 ....82 C4
Port Glasgow PA14 ....68 C4
Melrose St 🔟 Glasgow G4 ..97 A1
Hamilton ML3 ....162 A3
Melrose Terr
East Kilbride G74 ....159 C2
Hamilton ML3 ....162 A3
Melvaig Pl G20 ....96 B3
Melvick Pl G51 ....115 B4
Melville Cres ML1 ....163 C3
Melville Ct G1 ....241 A1
Melville Dr ML1 ....163 C3
Melville Gdns G64 ....78 A1
Melville Pk G74 ....160 A2
Melville Pl Bridge of A FK9 .2 A4
Carluke ML8 ....187 C1
Melville St Falkirk FK1 ....42 A2
Glasgow G41 ....116 C2
Kilmarnock KA3 ....228 A4
Melville Terr FK8 ....7 A3
Memel St G21 ....97 C3
Memus Ave G52 ....115 B2
Mennock Dr ML3 ....161 C1
Mennock Dr G64 ....78 A2
Mennock La G41 ....229 D3
Mennock St ML1 ....144 B1
Mennock Rd G44 ....137 B3
Menstrie Bsns Ctr FK11 ....3 C3
Menstrie Castle* FK11 .....3 C3
Menstrie Pl FK11 ....4 A3
Menstrie Prim Sch FK11 ....4 A3
Menteith Ave G64 ....78 A1
Menteith Ct G10 ....10 B3
Menteith Dr G73 ....138 B1
Menteith Gdns G61 ....75 B4
Menteith Loan ML1 ....143 A3
Menteith Pl G73 ....138 B1
Menteith Rd
Motherwell ML1 ....163 C4
Stirling FK9 ....2 A4
Menzies Dr Glasgow G21 ....98 A3
Stirling FK8 ....2 A1
Menzies Pl G21 ....98 A3
Menzies Rd G21 ....98 A3
Mercat Wynd 4️⃣ FK10 ......10 A3
Merchant La G1 ....241 A1
Merchants Cl PA10 ....111 A2
Merchiston Ave
Falkirk FK2 ....42 A4
Linwood PA3 ....112 A3
Merchiston Gdns FK2 ....42 A3
Merchiston Hosp! PA5 ......111 C3
Merchiston Ind Est FK2 ....42 B4
Merchiston Rd
Falkirk FK2 ....42 A3
Falkirk, Grahamston FK2 ...42 A3
Merchiston Sch G32 ....118 C4
Merchiston Terr FK2 ....42 A4
Mercury La PA16 ....44 B2
Meredith Dr FK5 ....23 C2
Merino Rd PA15 ....45 C2
Merkins Ave G82 ....50 A3
Merkland Ct Glasgow G11 ..96 A1
Kirkintilloch G66 ....59 A1
Merkland Dr PA5 ....80 A4
Merkland Rd Ayr KA7 ....239 A2
Coatbridge ML5 ....101 B1
Merkland Sch G11 ....96 A1
Merkland St G11 ....96 A1
Merksworth Ave KA24 ......191 B4
Merksworth High Sch
PA3 ....113 C4
Merksworth Way PA3 ......113 C4
Merlewood Rd KA23 ....190 A2
Merlin Ave Bellshill ML4 ...142 A4
Greenock PA16 ....45 A3
Merlin La PA16 ....44 B3
Merlin Way PA14 ....114 A4
Merlinford Ave PA4 ....94 C2
Merlinford Cres PA4 ....94 C2
Merlinford Dr PA4 ....94 C2
Merlinford Way PA4 ....94 C2
Merrick Ave
Prestwick KA9 ....233 B1
Troon KA10 ....229 D2
Merrick Ct ML6 ....103 A1
Merrick Gdns
Bearsden G61 ....75 B4
Glasgow G51 ....116 A3
Quarter ML3 ....183 C2
Merrick Pl Irvine KA11 ....220 A1
Symington KA1 ....231 B2
Merrick Rd KA1 ....228 A2
Merrick Terr G71 ....141 A4
Merrick View KA3 ....195 C1
Merrick Way G73 ....138 A2

Merry St ML1 ....163 C4
Merryburn Ave G46 ....136 B2
Merrycrest Ave G46 ....136 B2
Merrycroft Ave G46 ....136 B2
Merryflats G65 ....59 C2
Merrygreen Pl KA3 ....195 C1
Merryland Pl G51 ....116 B4
Merryland St G51 ....116 B4
Merrylee Ave PA14 ....68 C4
Merrylee Cres G46 ....136 A3
Merrylee Park Ave G46 ....136 B2
Merrylee Park Mews
G46 ....136 C3
Merrylee Prim Sch G44 ....136 C3
Merrylee Rd G43 ....136 C3
Merrylees Rd G72 ....161 B4
Merryston Ct ML5 ....121 C3
Merrystone St ML5 ....121 C4
Merryton Ave
Glasgow G15 ....75 B2
Glasgow, Merrylee G46 ....136 B2
Merryton Rd
Glasgow G15 ....75 B2
Merryton Pl G15 ....75 A2
Merryvale Ave
Larkhall ML9 ....184 C3
Motherwell ML1 ....164 B1
Merryton Twr ML1 ....164 A1
Merryvale Ave G46 ....136 B3
Merryvale Pl G46 ....136 B3
Merryvale Rd KA12 ....219 B1
Merryvale Rdbt KA12 ......219 B1
Merryvale Rd G52 ....115 A3
Merville Cres FK1 ....66 C3
Meryon Gdns G32 ....119 B1
Meryon Rd G32 ....119 B2
Metcalfe Pl KA11 ....224 D3
Methil Rd PA14 ....68 C3
Methil St G14 ....95 B2
Methlan Pk G82 ....49 B1
Methlick Ave ML6 ....122 C2
Methuen Rd Paisley PA3 ...114 A4
Renfrew PA3 ....93 C1
Methven Ave
Bearsden G61 ....76 A3
Kilmarnock KA1 ....227 C2
Methven Pl
East Kilbride G74 ....159 B1
Kilmarnock KA1 ....227 C2
Methven Rd G46 ....157 A4
Methven St Clydebank G81 .73 C2
Glasgow G31 ....118 B2
Methven Terr ML5 ....102 A1
Metropole La G1 ....241 A1
Mews La Ayr KA7 ....238 C4
Greenock PA16 ....45 B4
Kilmarnock KA1 ....227 C4
Mey Ct G77 ....156 A2
Mey Pl G77 ....156 A2
Mharie Pl G83 ....27 C2
Michael McParland Dr
G64 ....78 A4
Michael Terr ML6 ....123 A1
Micklehouse Oval 5️⃣
G69 ....120 A3
Micklehouse Pl 6️⃣ G69 ...120 A3
Micklehouse Rd G69 ......120 A3
Micklehouse Wynd 6️⃣
G69 ....120 A3
Mid Ave PA14 ....68 C4
Mid Barrwood Rd G65 .....60 C4
Mid Carbarns ML2 ....164 B1
Mid Dykes Rd KA21 ....205 C1
Mid Pk G75 ....180 C4
Mid Rd Beith KA15 ....150 A1
Middle Ward St G81 ....74 B4
Middlefield G75 ....180 C3
Middlefield Ind Est FK2 ...42 C4
Middlefield Sch G11 ....96 A2
Middlefield St ML8 ....187 A2
Middlemass Ct FK2 ....42 A3
Middlemass Dr KA1 ....228 A4
Middlemuir Ave G66 ......79 B3
Middlemuir Rd
Kirkintilloch G66 ....79 B3
Stirling FK7 ....7 B3
Middlepart KA20 ....206 B1
Middlepart Cres PA14 .....70 A4
Middlepenny Pl PA14 ......70 A4
Middlerigg Rd G68 ....61 B1
Middlesex Gdns 7️⃣ G41 ...116 C3
Middlesex St G41 ....116 C3
Middleton KA11 ....4 A3
Middleton Ave ML9 ....199 A4
Middleton Cres PA3 ....113 A3
Middleton Dr
Helensburgh G84 ....25 A4
Milngavie G62 ....55 B1
Middleton La G84 ....25 A4
Middleton Pk KA11 ....220 A2
Middleton Rd
Irvine KA11 ....220 A2
Linwood PA3 ....112 B4
Paisley PA3 ....113 A3
Middleton St
Alexandria G83 ....27 B3

Middleton St *continued*
Glasgow G51 ....116 B3
Midfaulds Ave PA4 ....94 C1
Midland St G1 ....240 C2
Midlem Dr G52 ....115 B3
Midlem Oval G52 ....115 B3
Midlock St G51 ....116 B3
Midlothian Dr G41 ....116 B1
Midthorn Cres FK2 ....42 C3
Midton Ave KA9 ....236 A4
Midton Rd Ayr KA7 ....238 C3
Howwood PA9 ....131 A3
Kilmarnock KA3 ....227 C1
Prestwick KA9 ....236 B4
Midton St G21 ....97 C2
Midtown FK11 ....3 C3
Migvie Pl G20 ....96 B3
Milford G75 ....180 A4
Milford St G33 ....119 A4
Milgarholm Ave KA12 .....219 B1
Milgarholm Rdbt KA12 ....219 B1
Mill Ave KA7 ....222 B4
Mill Brae Ayr KA7 ....239 A4
Mill Brae Ct KA1 ....121 B3
Mill Cres Glasgow G40 ....117 C2
Irvine KA12 ....219 C2
Torrance G64 ....57 B1
Mill Ct Falkirk FK2 ....24 A2
Hamilton ML3 ....162 B1
Kilbirnie KA25 ....149 A1
Kilmarnock KA1 ....228 A4
Rutherglen G73 ....138 A4
Mill Dr ML3 ....162 B1
Mill Hill FK7 ....6 B3
Mill Loan ML6 ....123 A4
Mill Of Airthrey Ct FK9 ...1 C4
Mill Of Gryffe Rd PA11 ...110 B4
Mill Pk Dalry KA24 ....191 B4
Mill Pl PA3 ....112 A3
Mill Rd Airdrie ML6 ....103 A1
Alloa FK10 ....10 A3
Banton G65 ....37 B2
Bothwell G71 ....141 A4
Cambusbarron FK7 ....6 B3
Cambuslang G72 ....139 B3
Cardross G82 ....26 A1
Carluke ML8 ....187 C1
Clydebank G81 ....94 B4
Falkirk FK2 ....24 A2
Hamilton ML3 ....162 B1
Harthill ML7 ....127 C3
Hartwood ML7 ....145 C1
Irvine KA12 ....219 C4
Kilbirnie KA25 ....149 A1
Motherwell ML1 ....163 C4
Queenzieburn G65 ....59 C4
Riggend ML6 ....83 A1
Shotts ML7,ML2 ....166 C3
Mill Rig G75 ....180 B3
Mill Rise G66 ....79 B2
Mill St Alloa FK10 ....10 A3
Ayr KA7 ....239 A4
Caldercriax ML6 ....104 C3
Glasgow G40 ....117 C2
Greenock PA15 ....45 C2
Kilmarnock KA1 ....227 C4
Paisley PA1 ....113 C2
Rutherglen G73 ....138 A3
Mill St Ind Est ML6 ....123 A4
Mill Vennel PA4 ....94 B2
Mill Waulk KA3 ....211 C4
Mill Way G66 ....80 A4
Mill Wynd KA7 ....238 C4
Millands Ave G72 ....140 B1
Millar Gr ML3 ....162 A2
Millar Pl
High Bonnybridge FK4 .....40 A2
Stenhousemuir FK2 ....24 A3
Stirling FK8 ....2 B1
Millar Rd KA21 ....205 C1
Millar St Greenock PA15 ..46 A1
🔟8 Paisley PA1 ....113 C3
Stonehouse ML9 ....198 C1
Millarbank St G21 ....97 C2
Millars Pl G66 ....79 B2
Millars Wynd FK10 ....5 B4
Millarston Ave PA1 ....113 A2
Millarston Dr PA1 ....113 A2
Millbank Ave ML4 ....142 B2
Millbank Rd
Port Glasgow PA14 ....68 B4
Wishaw ML2 ....164 C1
Millbeg Cres G33 ....119 C3
Millbeg Pl G33 ....119 C3
Millbrae Ave G69 ....100 B4
Millbrae Cres
Clydebank G81 ....94 B4
Glasgow G42 ....136 C4
Millbrae Ct Ayr KA7 ....239 A4
Glasgow G42 ....136 C4
Millbrae Gdns G42 ....136 C4
Millbrae Rd G42 ....136 C4
Millbrix Ave G14 ....95 A3
Millbrook G74 ....159 A1
Millbrook Pl FK11 ....3 C3
Millburn Ave
Clydebank G81 ....94 C4
Renfrew PA4 ....94 C2
Rutherglen G73 ....138 A3
Millburn Cres G82 ....50 A2
Millburn Ct G75 ....179 C4
Millburn Dr
Kilmacolm PA13 ....89 A4
Renfrew PA4 ....94 C2
Millburn Gdns G75 ....179 C4

Millburn La ML9 ....185 B1
Millburn Pl ML9 ....199 A4
Millburn Rd
Alexandria G83 ....27 B1
Ashgill ML9 ....186 A1
Dumbarton G82 ....50 A2
Port Glasgow PA14 ....68 B4
Renfrew PA4 ....94 B2
Millburn St Falkirk FK2 ...42 B3
Glasgow G21 ....98 A1
Lennoxtown G66 ....57 C4
Motherwell ML1 ....163 C4
Millburn Terr KA11 ....220 A3
Millburn Way
East Kilbride G75 ....179 C4
Renfrew PA4 ....94 C2
Millcroft Rd Airdrie ML6 ...83 A2
Cumbernauld G67 ....82 C2
Cumbernauld, Carbrain G67 .82 A1
Rutherglen G73 ....117 B3
Milldam Rd G81 ....74 B4
Milldown Pl KA11 ....220 B1
Millennium Ct G34 ....120 B4
Miller Ct G44 ....50 A2
Miller Field Pl ML3 ....162 C2
Miller Pl Airth FK2 ....14 C2
Ardrossan KA22 ....205 A2
Harthill ML7 ....127 C3
Miller Rd Ayr KA7 ....238 C4
Ardrossan KA22 ....205 A2
Balloch G83 ....27 C4
Miller Sq KA9 ....233 B1
Miller St Carluke ML8 ....188 A1
Clydebank G81 ....74 A1
Coatbridge ML5 ....122 A3
Dumbarton G82 ....50 A2
Glasgow G1 ....241 A2
Glasgow, Baillieston G69 ..120 A2
Hamilton ML3 ....162 C2
Harthill ML7 ....127 C3
Johnstone PA5 ....111 B2
Larkhall ML9 ....185 A2
Wishaw ML2 ....165 A2
Miller's Pl ML6 ....123 A4
Millerfield Pl G40 ....118 A2
Millerfield Rd G40 ....118 A2
Millersland G32 ....50 C1
Millerslea Gdns G84 ......16 C1
Millersneuk Ave G66 .....79 B2
Millersneuk Cres G33 ....99 C2
Millersneuk Dr G66 ......79 B2
Millersneuk Prim Sch
G66 ....79 C2
Millersneuk Rd G66 ......79 B2
Millerston St G31 ....118 A3
Millfield Ave Erskine PA8 .72 C1
Motherwell ML1 ....163 C4
Millfield Cres PA8 ....73 A1
Millfield Dr PA8 ....73 A1
Millfield Gdns PA8 ....73 A1
Millfield Hill PA8 ....72 C1
Millfield La PA8 ....72 C1
Millfield Mdws PA8 ....72 C1
Millfield Pl PA8 ....72 C1
Millfield Wlk PA8 ....73 A1
Millfield Wynd PA8 ....72 C1
Millflats St PA8 ....72 C1
Millford Dr PA3 ....112 A3
Millfore Ct KA11 ....220 A2
Millgate Ave G71 ....140 C4
Millgate Ct G71 ....140 C4
Millgate Rd ML3 ....162 B1
Millgate Ter ML3 ....162 B1
Millglen Pl KA22 ....205 B2
Millglen Rd KA22 ....205 B2
Millhall Rd
Caldercruix ML6 ....104 C3
Miliken Park Rd PA10 ....131 B1
Miliken Park Sta PA5 .....131 B1
Millersglen G32 ....50 C1
Milliken Rd PA10 ....131 A1
Millport Ave G44 ....137 B4
Millport Rd PA14 ....68 A4
Millroad Dr G40 ....241 C1
Millroad Gdns 2️⃣ G40 ....117 C3
Millroad St G40 ....241 C1
Millstream Cres ML6 .....105 A2
Millstream Ct PA1 ....114 A2
Millview G78 ....134 B2
Millview Mdws G78 ......154 B4
Millview Pl G53 ....135 A2
Millview Terr G78 ....154 B4
Millwood St G41 ....136 C3
Milnbank St G31 ....118 A4
Milncroft Pl G33 ....99 A1
Milncroft Rd G33 ....99 A1
Milncroft Sch G33 ....99 B1
Mindavie Rd G33 ....31 B1
Milne Ct ML2 ....165 C2
Milnepark Rd FK7 ....11 C4
Milner La G13 ....95 C3
Milner Rd G13 ....95 C3
Milngavie Prim Sch G62 ..55 A1

Milngavie Rd
Bearsden G61 ....76 A3
Strathblane G63 ....31 B1
Milngavie Sta G62 ....55 A1
Milnpark Gdns 1️⃣ G41 ...116 C3
Milnpark St G41 ....116 C3
Milnwood Dr
Bellshill ML4 ....142 B2
Motherwell ML1 ....142 B1
Milovaig Ave G23 ....76 B1
Milovaig St G23 ....76 B1
Milrig Rd G73 ....138 A4
Milroy Gdns ML4 ....142 A4
Milton Ave
Cambuslang G72 ....138 C3
Kilmarnock KA3 ....223 B1
Milton Brae Milton G82 ...50 C1
Stirling FK7 ....7 A1
Milton Cl FK6 ....21 B2
Milton Cres
Carluke ML8 ....187 C1
Irvine KA11 ....220 B1
Troon KA10 ....229 D3
Milton Ct Irvine KA11 .....220 B1
🔟 Kirkintilloch G66 ....58 C1
Milton G82 ....50 C1
Milton Douglas Rd G81 ...74 A3
Milton Dr
🔟 Bishopbriggs G64 ......97 C4
Kilmarnock KA3 ....223 B1
East Sq G83 ....27 C3
Milton Gdns
Bannockburn FK7 ....7 A1
Uddingston G71 ....140 C4
Milton Gr FK7 ....7 A1
Milton Hill G82 ....50 C1
Milton Mains Rd G81 .....74 A3
Milton Pk Ayr KA7 ....239 A2
Kilbirnie KA25 ....149 A1
Milton Prim Sch G22 .....97 A4
Milton Prim Sch G82 .....50 C1
Milton Quadrant KA25 ....149 A2
Milton Rd Bannockburn FK7 .7 B1
East Kilbride G74 ....159 A1
Irvine KA11 ....220 B1
Kilbirnie KA25 ....149 A2
Kilmarnock KA3 ....223 C1
Kirkintilloch G66 ....58 B1
Lennoxtown G66 ....57 C4
Port Glasgow PA14 ....68 C4
Milton Row FK6 ....21 C2
Milton Sec Sch G22 ......97 A4
Milton St Airdrie ML6 .....123 A4
Carluke ML8 ....187 C1
Glasgow G4 ....241 A4
Hamilton ML3 ....162 A2
Motherwell ML1 ....163 C4
Milton Terr
Bannockburn FK7 ....7 A1
Hamilton ML3 ....162 A3
Milton View KA2 ....226 C3
Miltonbank Prim Sch
G22 ....97 B4
Milverton Ave G46 ....75 B3
Milverton Rd G46 ....136 A1
Mimosa Rd PA11 ....110 B4
Minard Rd Glasgow G41 ..116 C1
Port Glasgow PA14 ....68 C4
Shotts ML7 ....146 B3
Minard Way G71 ....141 A4
Minch Way ML6 ....123 A3
Mincher Cres ML1 ....163 C2
Mine Rd FK9 ....2 A4
Minella Gdns ML4 ....142 A4
Minerva La PA16 ....44 B2
Minerva St G3 ....116 C4
Minerva Terr PA16 ....44 B2
Minerva Way G3 ....116 C4
Mingarry La G20 ....96 C2
Mingarry St G20 ....96 C2
Mingulay Cres G22 ......97 B4
Mingulay Pl G22 ....97 B4
Mingulay St G22 ....97 B4
Minmoir Rd G53 ....134 C4
Minster Wlk G69 ....120 C3
Minsters Pk G74 ....158 C2
Minstrel Rd G13 ....75 B3
Minthill Pl ML7 ....127 B3
Minto Ave G73 ....138 B2
Minto Cres G52 ....115 C3
Minto Ct FK12 ....5 A3
Minto Pk ML2 ....165 B3
Minto St Glasgow G52 ....115 C3
Mireton St 🔟 Greenock PA16 .45 B2
Mireton St G81 ....97 A3
Mirren Dr G81 ....73 C4
Mirren's Shore PA14 .....47 B1
Mirrlees Dr G12 ....96 C2
Mirrlees La G12 ....96 B2
Misk Knowes KA20 ....217 C3
Misk Rd KA20 ....218 B3
Mission Gdns ML2 ....165 A3
Mission La 🔟 FK1 ....42 A2
Mitchell Arc G73 ....138 A4
Mitchell Ave
Cambuslang G72 ....139 C3
Renfrew PA4 ....94 A1
Mitchell Cres FK10 ....9 C4
Mitchell Ct
East Kilbride G74 ....159 B1
Kilmarnock KA1 ....228 A4
Mitchell Dr Cardross G82 .48 A3

Mitchell Dr continued
Milngavie G62 55 B1
Rutherglen G73 138 A3
Mitchell Gr G74 159 B1
Mitchell Hill Rd G45 137 C1
Mitchell La G1 240 C2
Mitchell Pl Falkirk FK1 41 C1
Saltcoats KA21 205 C1
Mitchell Rd G67 62 A2
Mitchell St Airdrie ML6 122 C4
Beith KA15 150 B1
Coatbridge ML5 121 B3
Glasgow G1 240 C2
Greenock PA15 46 C1
Mitchell Way G83 27 C3
Mitchison Rd G67 62 A2
Mitre Ct G11 95 C2
Mitre Gate G11 95 C2
Mitre La G14 95 C2
Mitre La W G14 95 B2
Mitre Rd G14,G11 95 C2
Moat Ave G13 95 B4
Mochrum Ct KA9 236 B3
Mochrum Rd G43 136 C3
Modan Rd FK7 7 A2
Moffat Ave FK2 24 B2
Moffat Ct G75 179 C4
Moffat Gdns G75 179 C4
Moffat Pl Blantyre G72 140 B1
Coatbridge ML5 122 C2
East Kilbride G75 179 C4
Moffat Rd Airdrie ML6 123 C4
Prestwick KA9 233 B2
Moffat St Glasgow G5 117 B2
Greenock PA15 46 B2
Moffat View ML6 104 A2
Moffat Wynd KA21 205 C2
Moffathill ML6 123 C3
Mogarth Ave PA2 132 C4
Moidart Ave PA4 94 A2
Moidart Cres G52 115 C3
Moidart Ct G78 134 A2
Moidart Gdns
Kirkintilloch G66 59 A1
Newton Mearns G77 156 C3
Moidart Pl G52 115 C3
Moidart Rd Glasgow G52 115 C3
Port Glasgow PA14 68 C4
Moir St Alloa FK10 10 A4
Glasgow G1 241 B1
Molendinar St G1 241 B1
Molendinar Terr G78 154 B3
Mollanbowie Rd G83 19 C1
Mollins Ct G68 81 B3
Mollins Rd G68 81 B3
Mollinsburn Rd
Annathill G67,ML5 81 C1
Glenmavis ML5,ML6 102 B3
Mollinsburn St G21 97 C2
Mollison Ave ML7 127 C3
Monach Gdns KA11 225 A4
Monach Rd Glasgow G33 119 B4
Port Glasgow PA14 69 A4
Monaebrook Pl G84 25 A4
Monar Dr G22 97 A2
Monar Pl G22 97 A2
Monar St G22 97 A2
Monar Way 5 ML2 165 C3
Monart Pl G20 96 C2
Moncks Rd FK1 42 B2
Moncreiff Gdns G66 79 B3
Moncrieff Ave G66 79 B3
Moncrieff St 2 PA3 113 C3
Moncrieffe Rd ML6 123 B2
Moncur Ct KA13 207 B3
Moncur Rd KA13 208 A2
Moncur St G40 241 C1
Moness Dr G52 115 C2
Money Gr ML1 164 A2
Moniebrugh Cres G65 36 C1
Moniebrugh Rd G65 36 C1
Monifieth Ave G52 115 B2
Monikie Gdns G64 78 B1
Monkcastle Dr G72 139 A3
Monkland Ave G66 79 B3
Monkland La ML5 121 C2
Monkland St ML6 123 A4
Monkland Terr ML5 101 B3
Monkland View
Calderbank ML6 123 A1
Uddingston G71 121 A1
Monkland View Cres
G69 121 A3
Monklands KA10 229 D4
Monklands District General
Hospl ML5 122 B4
Monklands Ind Est ML5 121 C1
Monkreddan Cres KA13 207 B3
Monks La ML8 201 C2
Monks Rd ML6 123 B2
Monksbridge Ave G13 75 B1
Monkscourt Ave ML6 122 C4
Monkscroft Ave 7 G11 96 A2
Monkscroft Ct G11 96 A1
Monkscroft Gdns G11 96 A1
Monkton Ct KA9 233 B1
Monkton Dr G15 75 B1
Monkton Gdns G77 157 A2
Monkton Pl PA14 68 C4
Monkton Prim Sch KA9 233 B2
Monkton Rd KA9 233 B1
Monktonhill Rd KA9 233 A4
Monktonhill Rdbt KA9 233 B3
Monkwood Pl KA7 239 A1
Monmouth Ave G12 96 A3
Monreith Ave G61 75 B1
Monreith Rd G43 136 C3
Monreith Rd E G44 137 A3
Monroe Dr G71 120 C1
Monroe Pl G71 120 C1
Montague La G12 96 A2
Montague St G4 96 C1
Montalto Ave ML1 143 A1
Montclair Pl PA3 112 A3
Montego Gn 2 G75 159 A1
Monteith Dr G76 158 A4
Monteith Gdns G76 157 C4
Monteith Pl Blantyre G72 161 C4
10 Glasgow G40 117 C3
Monteith Row G40 117 C3
Monteith Wlk ML7 146 C3
Montfode Ct KA22 205 B2
Montfode Dr KA22 205 A2
Montford Ave G44 137 C4
Montfort Pl FK1 42 A2
Montgomerie Cres
KA21 216 C4
Montgomerie Ct KA22 205 B1
Montgomerie Pier Rd
KA22 205 A1
Montgomerie Rd
Prestwick KA9 233 A1
Saltcoats KA21 216 C4
Montgomerie St
Ardrossan KA22 205 B1
Port Glasgow PA14 47 B1
Montgomerie Terr
Ayr KA7 235 C1
Kilwinning KA13 208 A2
Montgomerieston Pl 5
KA25 149 A1
Montgomerieston St 6
KA25 149 A1
Montgomery Ave
Beith KA15 171 B4
Coatbridge ML5 121 C4
Paisley PA3 114 A4
Montgomery Cres
Falkirk FK2 24 A1
Wishaw ML2 185 C4
Montgomery Ct
Eaglesham G76 178 C2
Kilbirnie KA25 149 A1
Paisley PA3 114 A4
Montgomery Dr
Falkirk FK2 24 A1
Glasgow G46 136 B1
Kilbarchan PA10 111 A2
Montgomery Pl
9 East Kilbride G74 159 C1
Falkirk FK2 24 A1
Irvine KA12 219 A1
Kilmarnock KA3 222 C1
Larkhall ML9 185 A1
Montgomery Rd PA3 114 A4
Montgomery Sq G76 178 C2
Montgomery St
Cambuslang G72 139 C3
Eaglesham G76 178 C2
6 East Kilbride G74 159 C1
Falkirk FK2 42 C3
Glasgow G40 118 A2
Irvine KA12 219 A1
Kilmarnock KA3 222 C1
Larkhall ML9 185 A2
Montgomery Terr G66 58 B3
Montgomery Way FK9 2 A2
Montgomery Well FK2 24 A1
Montgomery Wynd 5
G74 159 C1
Montgomeryfield KA11 225 A4
Montgreenan View
KA13 207 C2
Montraive St G73 118 B1
Montrave St G52 115 B2
Montreal Pk G75 159 B1
Montrose Ave
Glasgow G32 119 B1
Paisley G52 114 C4
Port Glasgow PA14 68 C3
Montrose Cres ML3 162 B2
Montrose Ct PA2 132 C4
Montrose Dr G61 75 C4
Montrose Gdns
Blantyre G72 140 B1
Kilsyth G65 36 B1
Milngavie G62 55 A2
Montrose La ML3 162 B2
Montrose Pl PA3 112 A3
Montrose Rd
Paisley PA2 132 C4
Stirling FK9 2 B2
Montrose St
Clydebank G81 74 B1
Glasgow G1 241 B2
Motherwell ML1 142 B1
Montrose Terr
Bishopbriggs G64 98 B4
Bridge of W PA11 110 B4
Montrose Way
Bonnybridge FK4 39 B3
Paisley PA2 132 C4
Monument Cres KA9 233 C1
Monument Rd KA7 238 C2
Monument View FK8 2 A1
Monymusk Gdns G64 78 B1
Monymusk Pl G15 74 C3
Moodie Ct KA1 227 C3
Moodiesburn St G33 98 C1
Moor Park Cres KA9 236 B3
Moor Park Pl KA9 236 B3
Moor Pk KA9 236 B3
Moor Pl KA8 236 B2
Moor Rd Ayr KA8 236 B2
Cartland ML8,ML11 202 C1
Eaglesham G76 178 B2
Milngavie G62 55 A1
Strathblane G63 31 B1
Moorburn Ave G46 136 A2
Moorburn Pl PA3 111 C3
Moorcroft Dr ML6 123 C4
Moorcroft Rd G77 156 B2
Moore Dr Bearsden G61 75 C2
Helensburgh G84 25 B4
Moore Gdns ML3 183 C4
Moore St Glasgow G31 117 C3
Motherwell ML1 143 A2
Moorend Workshops
KA11 224 D4
Moorfield Ave
Kilmarnock KA1 227 B3
Port Glasgow PA14 68 B4
Moorfield Cres ML6 123 C4
Moorfield Ind Est KA2 227 A4
Moorfield La PA19 44 B3
Moorfield Pl KA2 226 B3
Moorfield Rd
Blantyre G72 161 B3
Gourock PA19 44 B4
Prestwick KA9 236 B4
Moorfield Rdbt KA1 227 A4
Moorfoot G64 78 B1
Moorfoot Ave
Glasgow G46 136 A2
Paisley PA2 113 B1
Moorfoot Dr
Gourock PA19 44 B3
Wishaw ML2 164 C2
Moorfoot Gdns G75 180 A2
Moorfoot Path PA2 133 B4
Moorfoot Pl KA11 220 A2
Moorfoot Prim Sch PA19 44 B3
Moorfoot St G32 118 C3
Moorfoot Way
Bearsden G61 75 B4
Irvine KA11 220 A2
Moorhill Cres G77 156 B2
Moorhill Rd G77 156 B2
Moorhouse Ave
Glasgow G13 94 C3
Paisley PA2 113 A1
Moorhouse St G78 134 B1
Moorland Dr ML6 123 C4
Moorpark Ave
8 Airdrie ML6 123 C4
Muirhead G69 100 B4
Moorpark Dr G52 115 A3
Moorpark Ind Est KA20 217 B4
Moorpark Pl
Glasgow G52 114 C3
Stevenston KA20 217 B4
Moorpark Prim Sch
Kilbirnie KA25 149 A2
Renfrew PA4 94 A1
Moorpark Rd E KA20 217 B4
Moorpark Rd W KA20 217 B4
Moorpark Sq PA4 94 A1
Moorside St ML8 188 A1
Morag Ave G72 140 B1
Moraine Ave G15 75 A1
Moraine Cir G15 75 A1
Moraine Dr
Clarkston G76 157 B4
Glasgow G15 75 A1
Moraine Pl G15 75 A1
Morar Ave G81 74 A2
Morar Cres Airdrie ML6 102 C1
Bishopbriggs G64 77 C1
Bishopton PA7 72 B1
Clydebank G81 74 A2
Coatbridge ML5 101 B1
Morar Ct Clydebank G81 74 A2
Cumbernauld G67 82 A4
Hamilton ML3 162 A1
Morar Dr Bearsden G61 76 A2
Clydebank G81 74 A2
Cumbernauld G67 82 A4
Falkirk FK2 24 B1
Linwood PA3 112 A3
Paisley PA2 113 A1
Rutherglen G73 138 A2
Morar Pl
East Kilbride G74 159 C2
Irvine KA12 219 B3
Newton Mearns G77 156 B4
Renfrew PA4 94 A2
Morar Rd Clydebank G81 74 A2
Glasgow G52 115 C3
Port Glasgow PA14 68 C4
Morar St ML2 165 A1
Morar Terr
Rutherglen G73 138 B2
Uddingston G71 141 A4
Morar Way
Motherwell ML1 143 B2
Shotts ML7 147 A2
Moravia Ave G71 141 A2
Moray Ave ML6 123 A3
Moray Ct G73 138 A4
Moray Dr Clarkston G76 157 C4
Torrance G64 57 A1
Moray Gate G71 140 C2
Moray Gdns
Clarkston G76 157 C4
Cumbernauld G68 61 C3
Uddingston G71 140 C4
Moray Pl Bishopbriggs G64 78 B1
Blantyre G72 161 B3
Chryston G69 100 B4
Glasgow G41 116 C1
Kirkintilloch G66 59 A1
Moray Pl continued
Linwood PA3 112 A3
Moray Quadrant ML4 142 A3
Moray Rd PA14 47 B1
Moray Way ML1 143 A3
Mordaunt St G40 118 A2
Moredun Cres G32 119 B4
Moredun Dr PA2 113 A1
Moredun St G32 119 B4
Morefield Rd G51 115 B4
Morgan Ct FK7 7 B2
Morgan Mews 17 G42 117 A2
Morgan St Hamilton ML3 162 B1
Larkhall ML9 184 C2
Morina Gdns G53 135 B2
Morion Rd G13 95 B4
Moriston Ct ML2 165 C3
Morland G74 160 B2
Morley Cres FK7 7 A2
Morley St G42 137 A4
Morna La G14 95 C1
Mornay Way ML7 146 B3
Morningside Prim Sch
ML2 166 A2
Morningside Rd ML2 166 B2
Morningside St G33 118 C4
Morrin Path G21 97 C2
Morrin St G21 97 C2
Morris Cres Blantyre G72 161 B4
Hurlford KA1 228 C3
Motherwell ML1 143 C1
Morris La KA3 223 A1
Morris Moodie Ave
KA20 217 C4
Morris Rd KA9 233 B1
Morris St Greenock PA15 46 B2
Hamilton ML3 162 B1
Larkhall ML9 185 B1
Morris Terr FK8 7 A4
Morrishall Rd G74 160 B2
Morrishill Dr KA15 171 A4
Morrison Ave
Bonnybridge FK4 39 C3
Stevenston KA20 206 C1
Morrison Ct KA20 206 C1
Morrison Dr
Bannockburn FK7 7 B1
Lennoxtown G66 57 C4
Morrison Gdns Ayr KA8 239 A4
Torrance G64 78 B4
Morrison Pl KA3 223 B1
Morrison Quadrant G81 74 C1
Morrison Rd KA9 233 B2
Morrison St
Clydebank G81 73 C3
Glasgow G5 240 B1
Morriston Cres PA4 94 C1
Morriston Park Dr G72 139 A3
Morriston St G72 139 A3
Morten Gdns G41 116 B1
Morton Ave KA7 239 A3
Morton Pl KA1 222 C1
Morton Rd Ayr KA7 239 A3
Stewarton KA3 211 B4
Morton St ML1 163 C4
Morven Ave
Bishopbriggs G64 78 B1
Blantyre G72 140 B1
Kilmarnock KA3 222 C2
Paisley PA2 133 B4
Morven Cres KA10 229 C1
Morven Ct FK1 42 B1
Morven Dr Clarkston G76 157 B4
Linwood PA3 112 A3
Troon KA10 229 C2
Morven Gait PA8 93 C4
Morven Gdns G71 140 C4
Morven La G72 140 B1
Morven Rd Bearsden G61 75 C3
Cambuslang G72 138 C2
Morven St
Coatbridge ML5 122 A4
Glasgow G52 115 C3
Morven Way 3 G71 141 A2
Morville Cres KA13 207 C3
Mosesfield St G21 97 C3
Mosque Ave G5 117 B3
Moss Ave
Caldercruix ML6 105 A3
Linwood PA3 112 A3
Moss Dr Barrhead G78 134 A3
Erskine PA8 93 A4
Irvine KA11 224 D3
Moss Heights Ave G52 115 B3
Moss Knowe G67 62 B1
Moss Path G69 119 C2
Moss Rd Airdrie ML6 123 A3
Bridge of W PA11 110 C4
Cumbernauld G67 62 C2
East Kilbride G75 180 B2
Fallin FK7 8 B2
Glasgow G51 115 B4
Helensburgh G82 25 C2
Kilmacolm PA13 89 B4
Kirkintilloch G66 80 A4
Kirkintilloch, High Gallowhill
G66 79 A3
Linwood PA3 112 B4
Muirhead G69 100 B4
Port Glasgow PA14 68 C4
Wishaw ML2 165 C2
Moss Side Ave ML6 122 C4
Moss St PA1 113 C3
Moss-Side Ave ML8 187 B1
Moss-Side Rd G41 116 C1
Mossacre Rd ML2 165 B2
Mossband La ML7 146 C3
Mossbank Blantyre G72 161 B3
Mossbank continued
East Kilbride G75 179 C4
Prestwick KA9 236 C4
Mossbank Ave G33 98 C2
Mossbank Cres ML1 143 C2
Mossbank Dr G33 98 C2
Mossbank Rd ML2 165 B2
Mossbell Rd ML4 141 C3
Mossblown St ML9 184 C2
Mossburn Ave
Balloch G83 19 C1
Harthill ML7 127 B3
Mossburn Rd ML2 165 B2
Mossburn St ML2 165 B1
Mosscastle Rd
Glasgow G33 99 B1
Slamannan FK1 86 A4
Mossdale G74 159 B2
Mossdale Ct ML4 142 B3
Mossdale Gdns ML3 161 C1
Mossedge Ind Est PA3 112 B3
Mossend Ave
Helensburgh G84 16 C1
Kilbirnie KA25 170 A4
Mossend La G33 119 B4
Mossend Pl G84 16 C1
Mossend Prim Sch ML4 142 B2
Mossend St G33 119 B4
Mossgiel G75 180 A4
Mossgiel Ave Cowie FK7 12 B4
Kilmarnock KA3 228 B4
Rutherglen G73 138 A3
Stirling FK8 2 A1
Troon KA10 229 D2
Mossgiel Cres G76 157 C3
Mossgiel Dr
Clydebank G81 74 B2
Irvine KA12 219 B2
Mossgiel Gdns
Kirkintilloch G66 58 C1
Uddingston G71 140 C4
Mossgiel La 10 ML9 185 B1
Mossgiel Pl Ayr KA7 239 A3
Rutherglen G73 138 A3
Stevenston KA20 206 C1
Mossgiel Rd
Ardrossan KA22 205 B2
Ayr KA7 239 A3
Cumbernauld G67 62 A1
Glasgow G43 136 B3
Saltcoats KA21 206 A2
Mossgiel St FK1 41 A3
Mossgiel Terr G72 140 B1
Mossgiel Way ML1 143 B2
Mosshall Gr ML1 143 C2
Mosshall Rd ML1 143 B4
Mosshall St ML1 143 C2
Mosshead Prim Sch G61 75 C4
Mosshead Rd
Bearsden G61 76 A4
Kilmarnock KA1 228 A2
Mosshill Rd ML4 142 A4
Mosshouse FK7 6 C2
Mosside Pl KA3 222 C2
Mosside Rd KA8 236 B2
Mossland Dr ML2 165 B2
Mossland Rd G52 114 C4
Mosslands Rd PA3 113 C4
Mosslingal G75 180 C3
Mossmulloch G75 180 C3
Mossneuk Ave G75 179 C4
Mossneuk Cres ML2 165 B2
Mossneuk Dr
East Kilbride G75 179 C4
Paisley PA2 133 B4
Wishaw ML2 165 B2
Mossneuk Pk ML2 165 B2
Mossneuk Prim Sch
G75 179 C4
Mossneuk Rd G75 180 A4
Mossneuk St ML5 121 C2
Mosspark Ave
Glasgow G52 115 C2
Milngavie G62 55 A2
Mosspark Bvd G52 115 C2
Mosspark Dr G52 115 C2
Mosspark La G52 115 C2
Mosspark Oval G52 115 C2
Mosspark Prim Sch
G52 115 C2
Mosspark Rd
Coatbridge ML5 121 B4
Milngavie G62 55 A2
Mosspark Sq G52 115 C2
Mosspark Sta G52 115 B2
Mossvale Cres G33 99 B1
Mossvale La PA3 113 B3
Mossvale Rd G33 99 B1
Mossvale Sq Glasgow G33 99 A1
Paisley PA3 113 B4
Mossvale St PA3 113 B4
Mossvale Terr G69 81 A2
Mossvale Way G33 99 B1
Mossvale Wlk G33 99 B1
Mossview Cres ML6 123 A3
Mossview La G52 115 B3
Mossview Quadrant
G52 115 B3
Mossview Rd G33 99 C3
Mosswell Rd G62 55 A2
Mossyde Ave PA14 69 A4
Mossywood Ct G68 81 C4
Mossywood Pl G68 81 C4
Mossywood Rd G68 81 C4
Mote Hill ML3 162 C3
Mote View KA2 221 B1
Motehill Rd PA3 114 A4
Motherwell Coll ML1 163 C2

Motherwell Heritage Ctr* ML1 163 B4
Motherwell Rd
Bellshill ML4 142 A2
Hamilton ML3 163 A2
Motherwell ML1 144 A3
Motherwell, Carfin ML1 143 B1
Motherwell St ML6 123 B4
Motherwell Sta ML1 163 B4
Motoring Heritage Ctr* G83 27 B3
Moulin Cir G52 115 A2
Moulin Pl G52 115 A2
Moulin Rd G52 115 A2
Moulin Terr G52 115 A2
Mount Annan Dr G44 137 A4
Mount Ave
Kilmarnock KA1 227 B3
Symington KA1 231 B2
Mount Bartholomew FK4 40 A3
Mount Cameron Dr N G74 181 A4
Mount Cameron Dr S G74 181 A4
Mount Cameron Prim Sch G74 181 A4
Mount Carmel Prim Sch KA3 222 C3
Mount Charles Cres KA7 238 B1
Mount Florida Prim Sch G42 137 A4
Mount Florida Sta G42 137 A4
Mount Harriet Ave G33 99 C3
Mount Harriet Dr G33 99 C3
Mount Hope FK9 2 A4
Mount Lockhart G71 120 A1
Mount Lockhart Gdns G71 120 A1
Mount Lockhart Pl G71 120 A1
Mount Oliphant FK7 12 B4
Mount Oliphant Cres KA7 239 A3
Mount Oliphant Pl KA7 239 A3
Mount Pl KA1 227 B3
Mount Pleasant KA20 206 B1
Mount Pleasant Cres G66 58 A3
Mount Pleasant Dr G60 73 A3
Mount Pleasant St PA15 45 C2
Mount St G20 96 C2
Mount Stewart St ML8 187 C1
Mount Stuart St G41 136 C4
Mount The Ayr KA7 239 A2
Motherwell ML1 163 B3
Mount Vernon Ave
Coatbridge ML5 121 C4
Glasgow G32 119 C2
Mount Vernon Prim Sch G32 119 B2
Mount Vernon Sta G32 119 C1
Mount View KA11 220 B1
Mount Village KA1 227 B4
Mount William FK10 5 C1
Mountainblue St G31 118 A3
Mountblow Ho G81 73 B3
Mountblow Rd G81 73 C3
Mountblow Sch G81 73 C3
Mountcharles KA7 238 B1
Mountgarrie Rd G51 115 B4
Mountherrick G75 180 C3
Mournian Way ML3 162 B1
Mousebank La ML11 214 C2
Mousebank Rd ML11 214 C3
Mousemill Rd ML11 214 B3
Mowbray G74 160 B2
Mowbray Ave G69 100 C3
Mowbray Cres FK7 7 B2
Moy Path 4 ML2 165 C3
Moy St G11 96 B1
Moyne Rd G53 115 A1
Muckcroft Rd G69 80 B2
Mudale Ct FK1 42 B1
Mugdock Ctry Pk* G62 55 A3
Mugdock Rd G62 55 A2
Muir Cl KA3 195 B1
Muir Cres G83 27 B4
Muir Dr Irvine KA12 219 B2
Stevenston KA20 217 B4
Troon KA10 229 C3
Muir Drive Cotts KA20 217 B4
Muir Glen ML11 215 B2
Muir Rd G82 50 B3
Muir St Alexandria G83 27 B4
Bishopbriggs G64 78 A1
Blantyre G72 161 B3
Coatbridge ML5 121 C4
Hamilton ML3 162 C2
Larkhall ML9 185 A2
Law ML8 186 C3
Motherwell ML1 163 B4
Renfrew PA4 94 B2
Stenhousemuir FK5 23 B1
Muir Street Prim Sch ML1 163 B4
Muir Terr PA3 114 A4
Muiralehouse Rd FK7 11 C4
Muirbank Ave G73 137 C4
Muirbank Gdns G73 137 C4
Muirbrae Rd G73 138 A2
Muirbrae Way G73 138 A2
Muirburn Ave G44 136 C2
Muirburn Rd Beith KA15 150 A2
Stonehouse ML10 198 A1
Muircroft Dr ML1 144 A1
Muirdrum Ave G52 115 B2
Muirdyke Ave FK2 24 B2
Muirdyke Rd
Coatbridge ML5,ML6 102 A3
Coatbridge, Drumpellier ML5 121 B4
Muirdykes Ave
Glasgow G52 115 A3
Port Glasgow PA14 68 B4
Muirdykes Rd
Glasgow G52 115 A3
Paisley PA3 113 A3
Muiredge & Jersy Rd
Cleland ML1 145 A1
Shotts ML7,ML1 145 B4
Muiredge Ct G71 140 C3
Muiredge Prim Sch G71 141 A3
Muiredge Terr G69 120 A2
Muirend Ave G44 136 C3
Muirend Rd Cardross G82 48 A4
Glasgow G44 136 C2
Kilmarnock KA3 222 C3
Stirling FK7 7 A3
Muirend St KA25 149 A1
Muirend Sta G44 136 C2
Muirfield Cres 6 G23 76 C1
Muirfield Ct
Glasgow G44 136 C2
Irvine KA11 224 D4
Muirfield Mdws G72 140 C1
Muirfield Pl KA13 207 B2
Muirfield Rd
Cumbernauld G68 62 A3
Stenhousemuir FK5 23 C1
Muirhall Pl FK5 23 B2
Muirhall Rd FK5 23 B2
Muirhall Terr ML7 125 A1
Muirhead Ave FK2 42 A4
Muirhead Cotts G66 80 A4
Muirhead Dr Law ML8 187 A3
Linwood PA3 112 A3
Motherwell ML1 143 C2
Muirhead Gate 4 G71 141 A4
Muirhead Gdns
Glasgow G69 120 B2
Salsburgh ML7 125 A1
Muirhead Pl ML7 127 B2
Muirhead Prim Sch KA10 229 D2
Muirhead Rd
Glasgow G69 120 A2
Stenhousemuir FK5 23 C2
Muirhead St
10 Kirkintilloch G66 79 B4
Lochwinnoch PA12 129 B1
Muirhead Terr ML1 163 C2
Muirhead Way G64 78 B1
Muirhead-Braehead Rdbt G67 62 A2
Muirhill Ave G44 136 C3
Muirhill Cres G13 95 A4
Muirhouse Ave
Motherwell ML1 164 A2
Wishaw ML2 166 A3
Muirhouse Dr ML1 164 B1
Muirhouse La 7 G75 180 C4
Muirhouse Pk G61 75 B4
Muirhouse Prim Sch ML1 164 A1
Muirhouse Rd ML1 164 A1
Muirhouse St 12 G41 117 A2
Muirhouse Twr ML1 164 A2
Muirkirk Dr Glasgow G13 95 C4
Hamilton ML3 161 B1
Muirlee Rd ML8 188 A1
Muirlees Cres G62 54 C1
Muirmadkin Rd ML4 142 A3
Muirmaillen Ave ML1 144 B1
Muirpark Ave PA4 94 B1
Muirpark Dr
Bishopbriggs G64 98 A4
Shieldhill FK1 66 B3
Muirpark Gdns FK10 4 C2
Muirpark Rd KA15 150 A1
Muirpark St G11 96 A1
Muirs The FK10 4 B2
Muirshiel Ave G53 135 B3
Muirshiel Cres G53 135 B3
Muirshiel Ctry Pk & Visitor Ctr* PA12 108 A2
Muirshiel La PA14 68 B4
Muirshiel Rd PA14 68 B4
Muirshot Rd ML9 185 A2
Muirside Ave
Glasgow G32 119 C2
Kirkintilloch G66 80 A4
Tullibody FK10 4 B2
Muirside Ct KA13 207 B1
Muirside Pl
Kilwinning KA13 207 B1
21 Wishaw ML2 165 C3
Muirside Rd
Glasgow G69 120 A2
Kilwinning KA13 207 B1
Tullibody FK10 4 B2
Muirside St G69 120 A2
Muirskeith Cres G44 137 A3
Muirskeith Pl G43 136 C3
Muirskeith Rd G43 136 C3
Muirton Dr G64 77 C2
Muirton Rd FK7 7 C3
Muirton Rdbt FK7 7 C4
Muiryfauld Dr G31 118 C3
Muiryhall St ML5 122 A4
Muiryhall St E ML5 122 B4
Mulben Cres G53 134 C4
Mulben Pl G53 134 C4
Mulben Terr G53 134 C4
Mulberry Cres ML6 123 C2
Mulberry Dr G75 180 B3
Mulberry Rd
Glasgow G43 136 B3
Uddingston G71 121 B1
Mulberry Way G75 180 B3
Mulberry Wynd G72 139 C2
Muldron Terr ML7 147 A1
Mulgrew Ave KA21 206 A1
Mull Airdrie ML6 123 B3
East Kilbride G74 181 B4
Mull Ave Paisley PA2 133 C4
Port Glasgow PA14 69 A4
Renfrew PA4 94 B1
Mull Cres KA11 220 A1
Mull Ct Alloa FK10 10 A3
Hamilton ML3 161 C1
Irvine KA11 220 A1
Mull Pl KA11 220 A1
Mull Quadrant ML2 165 C3
Mull St G21 98 A1
Mull Terr KA11 220 A1
Mullardoch St 8 G23 76 B1
Mulvey Cres ML6 122 C4
Mungalend FK2 42 A4
Mungalend Ct FK2 42 A4
Mungalhead Rd FK2 42 A4
Mungo Pk G75 180 B4
Mungo Pl G71 121 A1
Munlochy Rd G51 115 B4
Munnoch Cres KA22 205 A3
Munro Ave
Kilmarnock KA1 222 B1
Stirling FK9 2 A2
Munro Ct G81 73 C3
Munro Dr Kilbirnie KA25 170 A4
Milton of C G66 58 A3
Munro Dr E G84 16 C2
Munro Dr W G84 16 B2
Munro Gdns FK2 42 C2
Munro La G13 95 C3
Munro La E G13 95 C3
Munro Pl Alloa FK10 9 C3
East Kilbride G74 160 A2
Glasgow G13 95 C3
Kilmarnock KA1 222 C1
Saltcoats KA21 206 A1
Munro Rd Glasgow G13 95 C3
Stirling FK7 7 C3
Munro St Alexandria G83 27 C3
Greenock PA16 45 A2
Stenhousemuir FK5 23 C2
Munro Wlk KA21 206 A1
Murano St G20 96 C2
Murchie Dr KA9 236 B3
Murchison G12 96 A3
Murchison Dr G75 180 A4
Murchison Rd PA6 91 B1
Murchland Ave KA3 213 A2
Murchland Way KA12 219 B2
Murdieston St PA15 45 B2
Murdoch Cres KA20 217 B4
Murdoch Ct KA21 205 C2
Murdoch Dr G62 76 B4
Murdoch Pl Irvine KA11 224 D3
Motherwell ML1 142 C2
Murdoch Rd G75 180 C4
Murdoch Sq ML4 142 B4
Murdoch's Lone KA7 238 C1
Murdostoun Cres ML7 127 C3
Murdostoun Gdns ML2 165 A3
Murdostoun Terr ML1 144 C1
Murdostoun View ML2 165 C3
Mure Ave KA3 223 A3
Mure Pl G78 153 A2
Muriel La G78 134 B2
Muriel St G78 134 B2
Muriel Street Ind Est G78 134 B2
Murnin Ct FK7 7 B2
Murnin Rd FK4 40 A2
Murnin Road Ind Est FK4 40 A2
Murray Ave Kilsyth G65 60 B4
Saltcoats KA21 205 C1
Murray Bsns Area PA3 113 B3
Murray Cres ML2 166 A4
Murray Ct ML3 162 A2
Murray Dr ML9 198 C1
Murray Gdns G66 58 B3
Murray Gr G61 75 A4
Murray Path G71 140 C3
Murray Pl Ayr KA8 236 B2
Barrhead G78 134 B2
Bellshill ML4 141 C4
Cambusbarron FK7 6 B3
Dumbarton G82 50 B2
Gourock PA19 44 C3
Kilmarnock KA3 223 B1
Stirling FK8 7 A4
Murray Prim Sch G75 180 C4
Murray Rd Bothwell G71 141 A2
Law ML8 186 C2
Murray Rd The G75 180 C4
Murray Rdbt The G75 180 C4
Murray Sq The 17 G75 180 C4
Murray St Ayr KA8 236 B1
Greenock PA16 45 B3
Paisley PA3 113 B3
Renfrew PA4 94 B2
Murray Terr ML1 163 A4
Murrayfield G64 78 A2
Murrayfield Dr G61 75 C1
Murrayfield Pl FK7 7 B1
Murrayfield St G32 118 C4
Murrayfield Terr FK7 7 B1
Murrayhill G75 180 B4
Murrayshall Rd FK7 7 A2
Murrayside ML9 198 B1
Murrin Ave G64 78 B1
Murroch Ave G82 50 B3
Murroch Cres G83 28 A1
Murroes Rd G51 115 B4
Mus of Modern Art* G5 241 A2
Mus of Transport* G3 96 B1
Museum of Scottish Country Life The G76 158 C2
Musgrove Pl G75 180 B4
Muslin St G40 117 C2
Muttonhole Rd ML3 182 C4
Mybster Pl G51 115 B4
Myers Cres G71 141 A3
Myles Ho FK8 7 A4
Mylne Pl FK2 24 A1
Myothill Rd FK6 39 B4
Myres Rd G53 135 B4
Myreside Pl G32 118 B3
Myreside St G32 118 C3
Myreton FK11 4 A3
Myreton Ave PA13 89 B4
Myreton Dr FK7 11 C4
Myreton Way FK1 41 C2
Myretoungate FK12 4 C3
Myrie Gdns G64 78 A1
Myroch Pl G34 100 B1
Myrtle Ave G66 79 B3
Myrtle Bank KA15 171 A4
Myrtle Dr
Motherwell ML1 143 A3
Wishaw ML2 164 B2
Myrtle Hill La G42 137 B4
Myrtle La ML9 185 B1
Myrtle Pk G42 117 B1
Myrtle Pl G42 137 B4
Myrtle Rd Clydebank G81 73 B2
Uddingston G71 141 A4
Myrtle Sq G64 98 A4
Myrtle St G72 140 B1
Myrtle View Rd G42 137 B4
Myrtle Wlk G72 138 C3
Myvot Ave G67 82 A3
Myvot Rd G67 82 A3

N

Nable Gdns ML1 164 C4
Naburn Gate 6 G5 117 B2
Nailer Rd Falkirk FK1 41 C3
Stirling FK7 7 A1
Nairn Ave Bellshill ML4 142 A3
Blantyre G72 140 B1
Nairn Cl KA3 195 B1
Nairn Cres ML6 123 A3
Nairn Ct Falkirk FK1 42 B1
Kilwinning KA13 207 A2
Nairn Dr PA16 44 B3
Nairn Pl Clydebank G81 73 C2
East Kilbride G74 160 B2
Nairn Quadrant ML2 165 A3
Nairn Rd PA16 44 B2
Nairn St Blantyre G72 161 B3
Clydebank G81 73 C2
Glasgow G3 96 B1
Larkhall ML9 184 C1
Nairn Way G68 62 A3
Nairnside Rd G21 98 B4
Naismith Ct ML9 198 C1
Naismith St G32 139 B4
Naismith Wlk ML4 142 B4
Nansen St G20 97 A2
Napier Ave G82 48 A4
Napier Cres
Dumbarton G82 49 B2
Falkirk FK2 42 A4
Napier Ct Cardross G82 48 A4
Cumbernauld G68 62 B4
Old Kilpatrick G60 73 B3
Napier Dr G51 116 A4
Napier Gdns PA3 112 B3
Napier Hill G75 180 C4
Napier La G75 180 C4
Napier Pk G68 62 B4
Napier Pl
Cumbernauld G68 62 B4
Falkirk FK2 42 A4
Glasgow G51 116 A4
Old Kilpatrick G60 73 B3
Napier Rd
Cumbernauld G68 62 B4
Glasgow G51 116 A4
Paisley G52 114 C4
Napier Sq ML4 142 B4
Napier St Clydebank G81 94 B4
Glasgow G51 116 A4
Johnstone PA5 111 C2
Linwood PA3 112 B3
Napier Terr G51 116 A4
Napier Way G68 62 B4
Napiershall La G20 96 C1
Napiershall Pl 10 G20 96 C1
Napiershall St G20 96 C1
Napierston Rd G83 27 C3
Naproch Pl G77 157 B3
Naseby Ave G11 95 C2
Naseby La G11 95 C2
Nasmyth Ave
Bearsden G61 75 A4
East Kilbride G75 181 A4
Nasmyth Pl G75 180 C4
Nasmyth Rd G52 115 A4
Nasmyth Rd N G52 115 A4
Nasmyth Rd S G52 115 A4
Nassau Pl 1 G75 159 A1
Navar Ct ML7 147 A2
Navar Pl PA2 114 A1
Naver St G33 98 C1
Navy Way G84 15 A2
Naylor La ML6 123 A4
Naysmyth Bank G75 180 C4
Nebit The FK12 4 C3
Needle Gn ML8 187 C1
Neidpath G69 120 A2
Neidpath Ave ML5 122 A2
Neidpath Dr FK5 23 C2
Neidpath Pl ML5 122 A2
Neidpath Rd ML8 187 C2
Neidpath Rd E G46 157 A3
Neidpath Rd W G46 157 A4
Neil Ave KA12 219 B3
Neil St Greenock PA16 45 A2
Renfrew PA4 94 B3
Neilsland Dr
Hamilton ML3 183 B4
Motherwell ML1 163 A3
Neilsland Oval G53 115 B1
Neilsland Prim Sch ML3 162 A1
Neilsland Rd ML3 183 B4
Neilsland Sq
Glasgow G53 115 B1
Hamilton ML3 162 B1
Neilsland St ML3 162 B1
Neilson Ct ML3 162 C1
Neilson St Bellshill ML4 142 A3
Falkirk FK1 42 A2
Neilston Ave G53 135 B3
Neilston Pl G65 36 A1
Neilston Prim Sch G78 154 C4
Neilston Rd Neilston G78 154 C4
Paisley PA2 113 C1
Uplawmoor G78 153 A2
Neilston Sta G78 154 B4
Neilston Wlk G65 36 B1
Neilvaig Dr G73 138 B2
Neistpoint Dr G33 119 A4
Nelson Ave ML5 121 C2
Nelson Cres ML1 164 A2
Nelson Mandela Pl G2 241 A3
Nelson Pl Ayr KA8 236 A1
Glasgow G69 120 A2
Helensburgh G84 17 A1
Stirling FK7 7 B3
Nelson Rd Gourock PA19 44 C3
Saltcoats KA21 217 A4
Nelson St Glasgow G5 117 A3
Glasgow, Baillieston G69 120 A2
Greenock PA15 45 C3
Kilmarnock KA1 227 C4
Nelson Terr G74 181 A4
Nemphlar Moor Rd
Crossford ML8,ML11 201 B1
Nemphlar ML11 214 A4
Nemphlar Rd ML11 214 A3
Nemphlat Hill ML11 214 C3
Neptune St G51 116 A4
Neptune Way ML4 142 C3
Nerston Rd G74 159 C3
Ness Ave PA5 131 B4
Ness Dr Blantyre G72 140 C1
East Kilbride G74 160 A1
Ness Gdns
Bishopbriggs G64 78 A1
Larkhall ML9 199 A4
Ness Pl KA10 229 D3
Ness Rd Greenock PA16 45 B3
Renfrew PA4 94 A2
Ness St Glasgow G33 98 C1
Wishaw ML2 186 A4
Ness Terr ML3 162 A1
Ness Way ML1 143 A3
Nethan Ave ML2 164 B1
Nethan Gate ML3 162 B2
Nethan Glen ML8 201 A1
Nethan Path ML9 199 A4
Nethan Pl ML3 183 B3
Nethan St Glasgow G51 116 A4
Motherwell ML1 142 B1
Nethanfoot Brig Rd ML8 201 A1
Nether Auldhouse Rd G43 136 B3
Nether Robertland Prim Sch KA3 195 C1
Netherbank Rd ML2 164 B1
Netherblane G63 31 A2
Netherbog Ave G82 50 A2
Netherbog Rd G82 50 A2
Netherburn Ave
Glasgow G44 136 C1
Houston PA6 111 C4
Netherburn Gdns PA6 111 C4
Netherburn Prim Sch ML9 200 A2
Netherburn Rd ML9 200 A4
Netherby Dr G41 116 B2
Netherby Rd FK2 14 B2
Nethercairn Pl G77 157 B3
Nethercairn Rd G43 136 B2
Nethercliffe Ave G44 136 C1
Nethercraigs Dr PA2 133 B4
Nethercraigs Rd PA2 133 A4
Nethercroy Rd G65 60 C3
Netherdale G77 157 A3
Netherdale Cres ML2 164 B1
Netherdale Dr PA1 114 C2
Netherdale Rd ML2 164 C1
Netherfield St G31 118 B3
Nethergate The FK12 4 C3
Nethergreen Cres PA4 94 A2
Nethergreen Wynd PA4 94 A2
Netherhall Rd ML2 164 B1

Netherhill Ave G44 . . . . **137** A3
Netherhill Cotts PA3 . . . .**114** A4
Netherhill Cres PA3 . . . .**114** A3
Netherhill Rd
Moodiesburn G69 . . . . .80 C1
Paisley PA3 . . . .**114** A4
Netherhill Way PA3 . . . .**114** A4
Netherhouse Ave
Coatbridge ML5 . . . .**121** C2
Kirkintilloch G66 . . . . .79 C2
Netherhouse Pl G34 . . . .**120** C4
Netherhouse Rd G69 . . . .**120** C4
Netherland Rd KA3 . . . .**211** C4
Netherlee Cres KA24 . . . .**169** A1
Netherlee Pl G44 . . . .**137** A2
Netherlee Prim Sch
G44 . . . .**136** C1
Netherlee Rd G44 . . . .**137** A2
Nethermains Prim Sch
FK6 . . . . .21 B1
Nethermains Rd
Denny FK6 . . . . .21 B1
Kilwinning KA13 . . . .**207** C1
Milngavie G62 . . . . .76 A4
Nethermiln Rd KA23 . . . .**190** B2
Netherpark Ave G44 . . . .**137** A1
Netherplace Cres
Glasgow G53 . . . .**135** A4
Newton Mearns G77 . . . .**156** B2
Netherplace Rd
Glasgow G53 . . . .**135** A3
Newton Mearns G77 . . . .**156** A2
Netherton Ave PA14 . . . . .69 A4
Netherton Ct
Glasgow G45 . . . .**137** C1
Newton Mearns G77 . . . .**157** A4
Netherton Dr G78 . . . .**134** C1
Netherton Hill G66 . . . . .57 A4
Netherton Ind Est ML2 . . . . . .**164** C1
Netherton Oval G66 . . . . .33 A1
Netherton Prim Sch
Glasgow G45 . . . .**137** B1
Wishaw ML2 . . . .**164** C1
Netherton Rd
East Kilbride G75 . . . .**180** A2
East Kilbride, The Murray
G75 . . . .**180** B4
Glasgow G13 . . . . .95 C4
Newton Mearns G77 . . . .**156** C3
Wishaw ML2 . . . .**164** C1
Netherton St
Harthill ML7 . . . .**127** B3
Wishaw ML2 . . . .**164** C1
Nethervale Ave G44 . . . .**136** C1
Netherview Rd G44 . . . .**137** A1
Netherway G44 . . . .**136** C1
Netherwood Ave G68 . . . . .81 C4
Netherwood Ct
Cumbernauld G68 . . . . .82 A4
Motherwell ML1 . . . .**164** A1
Netherwood Gr G68 . . . . .82 A4
Netherwood Pl G68 . . . . .81 C4
Netherwood Rd
Cumbernauld G68 . . . . .82 A4
Motherwell ML1 . . . .**164** B2
Netherwood Twr ML1 . . . .**164** A1
Netherwood Way G68 . . . . .82 A4
Nethy Way PA4 . . . . .94 C1
Neucks The FK1 . . . . .87 A3
Neuk Ave Houston PA6 . . . . .91 B1
Neuk Cres PA6 . . . .**100** B4
Neuk The ML2 . . . .**164** C2
Neuk Way G32 . . . .**139** B4
Neukfoot La G78 . . . .**153** A2
Nevan Rd KA10 . . . .**229** D3
Neville G74 . . . .**160** B2
Nevis Ave ML3 . . . .**162** A1
Nevis Cres FK10 . . . . .10 A4
Nevis Ct Barrhead G78 . . . .**134** B1
Coatbridge ML5 . . . .**122** B2
Motherwell ML1 . . . .**163** C2
Nevis Dr G64 . . . . .57 A1
Nevis Pl Falkirk FK1 . . . . .42 B1
Kilmarnock KA1 . . . .**228** A2
Shotts ML7 . . . .**147** A2
Nevis Rd Bearsden G61 . . . . . . .75 A4
Glasgow G43 . . . .**136** A3
Renfrew PA3 . . . . .93 C1
Nevis Way Irvine KA11 . . . .**220** A2
Renfrew PA3 . . . . .93 C1
Nevison St ML9 . . . .**185** A1
New Ashtree St ML2 . . . .**164** C2
New Ave PA9 . . . .**130** C3
New Bldgs ML11 . . . .**215** A1
New Bridge St KA7 . . . .**235** C1
New Carron Rd FK5 . . . . .24 A2
New Century Dr ML7 . . . .**146** C2
New City Row
Glasgow G4 . . . .**240** C4
New City Row G61 . . . . .31 A2
New Cordale Rd G82 . . . . .27 B1
New Cross ML3 . . . .**162** C2
New Dock La PA15 . . . . .46 A3
New Edinburgh Rd
ML4 . . . .**141** B3
New England Rd KA21 . . . .**206** A1
New Hallglen Rd FK1 . . . . .42 B1
New Hill Rd KA20 . . . .**218** B2
New Inchinnan Rd PA3 . . . .**113** C4
New Inchinnan Way
PA3 . . . .**113** C4
New Kirk Rd G61 . . . . .75 C3
New La ML6 . . . .**123** C2
New Lairdsland Rd G66 . . . . . . .79 B4

New Lanark (YH)*
ML11 . . . .**214** C1
New Lanark Heritage Trail*
ML11 . . . .**215** A1
New Lanark Prim Sch
ML11 . . . .**215** A1
New Lanark Rd ML11 . . . .**214** C1
New Lanark World Heritage
Village* ML11 . . . .**215** A1
New Line Pend 3 G74 . . . .**159** C1
New Line Rd FK7 . . . . .11 A4
New Luce Dr G32 . . . .**119** B2
New Mill Rd KA1 . . . .**228** A4
New Monkland Prim Sch
ML6 . . . .**102** C2
New Park St ML3 . . . .**162** B3
New Plymouth G75 . . . .**180** A4
New Rd Ayr KA8 . . . .**235** C1
Bannockburn FK7 . . . . .7 B1
Cambuslang G72 . . . .**139** C2
New Sneddon St PA3 . . . .**113** C3
New St Beith KA15 . . . .**171** A4
Blantyre G72 . . . .**161** B4
Bridge of A FK9 . . . . .1 C4
Clydebank G81 . . . . .74 A3
Dalry KA24 . . . .**191** B4
Irvine KA12 . . . .**219** A1
Kilbarchan PA10 . . . .**111** A2
Kilmarnock KA1 . . . .**227** C3
Lochwinnoch PA12 . . . .**129** B1
Paisley PA1 . . . .**113** C2
Slamannan FK1 . . . . .86 A4
Stevenston KA20 . . . .**217** B4
Stewarton KA3 . . . .**195** B1
Stonehouse ML9 . . . .**198** C1
New Stevenston Prim Sch
ML1 . . . .**142** C2
New Stevenston Rd
ML1 . . . .**143** A1
New View Cres ML4 . . . .**142** A2
New View Dr ML4 . . . .**142** A2
New View Pl ML4 . . . .**142** A2
New Wynd G1 . . . .**241** A1
Newark Cres G64 . . . .**236** B3
Newark KA13 . . . .**207** B1
Newark Ave PA16 . . . . .45 B4
Newark Castle* PA14 . . . . .47 B1
Newark Cres KA7 . . . .**238** A1
Newark Dr Glasgow G41 . . . . .**116** C2
Paisley PA2 . . . .**133** B4
Wishaw ML2 . . . .**165** B3
Newark Pl
Port Glasgow PA14 . . . . .47 B1
Wishaw ML2 . . . .**165** B3
Newark St Greenock PA16 . . . . .45 B4
Port Glasgow PA14 . . . . .47 B1
Newark Terr KA9 . . . .**236** B4
Newarthill Prim Sch
ML1 . . . .**143** C2
Newbank Ct G31 . . . .**118** C2
Newbank Gdns G31 . . . .**118** B2
Newbank Rd G31 . . . .**118** C2
Newbarns St ML8 . . . .**187** C2
Newbattle Ave ML6 . . . .**123** A1
Newbattle Ct G32 . . . .**119** A1
Newbattle Gdns G32 . . . .**119** A1
Newbattle Pl G32 . . . .**119** A1
Newbattle Rd G32 . . . .**119** A1
Newbiggin Cres FK10 . . . . .4 B1
Newbold Ave 11 G21 . . . . .97 C4
New Burgh 8 PA8 . . . . .73 A2
Newburgh St G43 . . . .**136** B4
Newcarron Ct FK2 . . . . .42 A4
Newcastleton Dr 9 G23 . . . . . . .76 C1
Newcraigs Dr G76 . . . .**158** B4
Newcroft Dr G44 . . . .**137** B3
Newdyke Ave G66 . . . . .79 C4
Newdykes Rd KA9 . . . .**233** B1
Newfield Cres ML3 . . . .**162** A2
Newfield Dr KA2 . . . .**225** C1
Newfield La 8 G71 . . . .**141** A1
Newfield Pl
Dundonald KA2 . . . .**225** C1
Glasgow G46 . . . .**135** C1
Irvine KA11 . . . .**220** A3
Rutherglen G73 . . . .**137** C4
Newfield Rd ML3 . . . .**198** C1
Newfield Sq G53 . . . .**135** A3
Newford Gr G76 . . . .**157** C3
Newgrove Gdns G72 . . . .**139** B3
Newhall St G40 . . . .**117** C2
Newhaven Rd G33 . . . .**119** A4
Newhaven St G32 . . . .**119** A4
Newhills Rd G33 . . . .**119** C4
Newhouse FK8 . . . . .7 A3
Newhouse Dr Falkirk FK1 . . . . . .41 C1
Kilbirnie KA25 . . . .**169** C4
Newhouse Ind Est ML1 . . . . . .**143** B4
Newhouse Int KA11 . . . .**220** D3
Newhousemill Cotts
G74 . . . .**181** B4
Newhousemill Rd
East Kilbride G74,G72 . . . .**181** B4
Hamilton G72,ML3 . . . .**161** B1
Newhouses Rd G68 . . . . .61 A2
Newhut Rd ML1 . . . .**142** B1
Newington La FK5 . . . . .22 B3
Newington St G32 . . . .**118** C3
Newlands Dr
Hamilton ML3 . . . .**183** B4
Kilmarnock KA3 . . . .**222** C3
Newlands Gdns PA5 . . . .**112** B1
Newlands Pl
East Kilbride G75 . . . .**159** C1
Kilmarnock KA3 . . . .**222** C2

Newlands Pl continued
Tullibody FK10 . . . . .4 B2
Newlands Rd
Bannockburn FK7 . . . . .11 B4
East Kilbride G75 . . . .**179** C3
East Kilbride, Newlandsmuir
G75 . . . .**180** A4
Uddingston G71 . . . .**140** C4
Glasgow G43 . . . .**136** C3
Newlands Terr
Carluke ML8 . . . .**187** C1
Milton of C G66 . . . . .58 B3
Newlandsfield Rd G43 . . . .**136** B4
Newlandsmuir Rd G75 . . . .**180** A3
Newmains Ave PA4 . . . . .93 A3
Newmains Prim Sch
Renfrew PA4 . . . . .94 B1
Wishaw ML2 . . . .**166** A2
Newmains Rd PA4 . . . . .94 B1
Newmarket FK7 . . . . .7 A1
Newmarket Ctr FK1 . . . . .42 A3
Newmarket St Ayr KA7 . . . . . .**238** C4
Falkirk FK1 . . . . .42 A3
Newmill & Canthill Rd
ML7 . . . .**146** A3
Newmill Gdns ML7 . . . .**145** C2
Newmill Rd Dunlop KA3 . . . . . .**195** B4
Glasgow G21 . . . . .98 B3
Newmilns FK10 . . . . .4 A2
Newmilns Gdn KA3 . . . .**223** A3
Newmoor Intc KA11 . . . .**219** C1
Newnham Rd PA1 . . . .**114** C2
Newpark Cres
Cambuslang G72 . . . .**139** A4
Stirling FK7 . . . . .7 A1
Newpark Rd FK7 . . . . .7 A1
Newshot Ave ML4 . . . .**142** B4
Newshot Dr PA8 . . . . .73 B1
Newstead Gdns G23 . . . . .76 C1
Newton Ave
Cambuslang G72 . . . .**139** B3
Elderslie PA5 . . . .**112** C2
Skinflats FK2 . . . . .24 C2
Newton Brae G72 . . . .**139** C3
Newton Ct G77 . . . .**156** B2
Newton Dr Elderslie PA5 . . . . .**112** C2
Uddingston G71 . . . .**141** A4
Newton Farm Rd G72 . . . .**140** B3
Newton Gr G77 . . . .**156** C2
Newton of Barr PA12 . . . .**129** A1
Newton Pk KA11 . . . .**220** A3
Newton on Ayr Sta KA8 . . . . . .**236** A1
Newton Park Ct KA8 . . . .**236** A1
Newton Pl Glasgow G3 . . . .**240** A4
Newton Mearns G77 . . . .**156** C2
Newton Prim Sch KA8 . . . . . .**236** A1
Newton Rd Bishopton PA7 . . .72 A2
Kirkintilloch G66 . . . . .79 C2
Newton St
Coatbridge ML5 . . . .**121** C2
Glasgow G3 . . . .**240** B3
Greenock PA16 . . . . .45 B3
Kilbirnie KA25 . . . .**149** A1
Paisley PA1 . . . .**113** B2
Newton Sta G72 . . . .**139** C3
Newton Station Rd G72 . . . . . .**139** C3
Newton Terr
Elderslie PA3 . . . .**112** C2
Glasgow G3 . . . .**240** A3
Greenock PA16 . . . . .45 B3
Newton Terrace La G3 . . . .**240** A3
Newton Way PA1 . . . .**114** A4
Newton Wlk KA1 . . . .**228** A4
Newtongrange Ave G32 . . . . . .**119** A1
Newtongrange Gdns
G32 . . . .**119** A2
Newtonhead KA11 . . . .**220** B3
Newtonhill Ave G72 . . . .**156** C2
Newtonshaw FK10 . . . . .5 B1
Newtown St G65 . . . . .60 B4
Newtyle Dr G53 . . . .**114** B2
Newtyle Pl
Bishopbriggs G64 . . . . .78 B1
Glasgow G53 . . . .**114** C1
Newtyle Rd Paisley PA1 . . . . . .**114** B2
Nicholas St G1 . . . .**241** B2
Nicholson Pl FK1 . . . . .41 C1
Nicholson St G5 . . . .**117** B3
Nickinas Way ML1 . . . .**143** C4
Nicol Dr PA16 . . . . .45 A3
Nicol St Airdrie ML6 . . . .**103** B1
Greenock PA16 . . . . .45 A2
Nicolson Ct G33 . . . . .99 C3
Nicolson St G5 . . . .**117** B3
Niddrie Rd G42 . . . .**117** A1
Niddrie Sq 6 G42 . . . .**116** C1
Niddry St G73 . . . .**113** C3
Nigel Gdns G41 . . . .**116** B1
Nigel St ML1 . . . .**163** B3
Nigg Pl G34 . . . .**120** A4
Nightingale Pl PA5 . . . .**131** B3
Nikitas Ave ML9 . . . .**199** A4
Nile Ct KA7 . . . .**238** C4
Nile St PA15 . . . . .46 B1
Nimmo Dr G51 . . . .**115** C4
Nimmo Pl Carluke ML8 . . . . . .**187** C2
Wishaw ML2 . . . .**165** B2
Nimmo St PA16 . . . . .45 B2
Nimmo St ML9 . . . .**185** A1
Nineyard St KA21 . . . .**216** C4
Ninian Ave PA6 . . . .**111** B4
Ninian Rd ML6 . . . .**123** B3
Ninian's Rise G66 . . . . .79 C4
Ninian's Terr KA13 . . . .**207** C1

Niph Ct PA4 . . . . .93 B4
Nisbet Dr Denny FK6 . . . . .21 B1
Prestwick KA9 . . . .**236** B3
Nisbet St G31 . . . .**118** B3
Nisbet Pl ML6 . . . .**123** C1
Nisbet St ML6 . . . .**123** C1
Nith Ave PA2 . . . .**112** C1
Nith Dr Hamilton ML3 . . . .**183** A4
Renfrew PA4 . . . . .94 C1
Nith La 2 ML2 . . . .**165** C3
Nith Path ML1 . . . .**144** B1
Nith Pl KA1 . . . .**228** A3
Nith Quadrant ML1 . . . .**143** B2
Nith St G33 . . . . .98 B1
Nithsdale G74 . . . .**160** B2
Nithsdale Cres G61 . . . . .75 B3
Nithsdale Cres G41 . . . .**116** B2
Nithsdale Dr G41 . . . .**116** C1
Nithsdale Pl G41 . . . .**116** C2
Nithsdale Rd
Ardrossan KA22 . . . .**205** B2
Glasgow G41 . . . .**116** B2
Nithsdale St
Carluke ML8 . . . .**116** C1
Shotts ML7 . . . .**146** B3
Nitshill Prim Sch G53 . . . .**135** A2
Nitshill Rd G53 . . . .**135** A3
Nitshill Sta G53 . . . .**135** A3
Niven Ct KA3 . . . .**222** B3
Niven St G20 . . . . .96 B3
Noble Dr ML4 . . . .**142** A3
Noble Rd ML4 . . . .**142** A3
Nobles Pl ML4 . . . .**141** C2
Nobles View ML4 . . . .**141** C2
Nobleston G83 . . . . .27 C1
Noldrum Ave G32 . . . .**139** B4
Noldrum Gdns G32 . . . .**139** B4
Noltmire Rd KA8 . . . .**236** B2
Noran Cres KA10 . . . .**229** D3
Norbreck Dr G46 . . . .**136** B2
Norby Rd G11 . . . . .95 C2
Norfield Dr G44 . . . .**137** A4
Norfolk Cres G64 . . . . .77 C2
Norfolk Ct G5 . . . .**117** A3
Norfolk Ho 8 G74 . . . .**159** C1
Norfolk Rd PA16 . . . . .44 C2
Norfolk St G5 . . . .**117** A3
Norham St G41 . . . .**116** C1
Norman Cres KA12 . . . .**219** A3
Norman St G40 . . . .**117** C2
Norse La N G14 . . . . .95 B2
Norse La S 6 G14 . . . . .95 B2
Norse Pl G14 . . . . .95 B2
Norse Rd G14 . . . . .95 B2
North & South Rd ML1 . . . .**144** C1
North Ayrshire Mus*
KA21 . . . .**216** C4
North Ave
Cambuslang G72 . . . .**138** C3
Carluke ML8 . . . .**187** B1
Clydebank G81 . . . . .74 A1
Motherwell ML1 . . . .**143** A1
North Bank Pl G81 . . . . .94 B4
North Bank St G81 . . . . .94 B4
North Barr PA8 . . . . .73 A2
North Barr Ave PA8 . . . . .73 A1
North Berwick Ave G68 . . . . . . .61 C3
North Berwick Cres
G75 . . . .**180** A3
North Berwick Gdns G68 . . . . . .61 C2
North Biggar Rd ML6 . . . .**123** A4
North Birbiston Rd G66 . . . . . . .57 C4
North Bridge St ML6 . . . .**122** C4
North British Rd G71 . . . .**140** C3
North Broomage Rdbt
FK5 . . . . .23 A2
North Bute St ML5 . . . .**122** A2
North Caldeen Rd ML5 . . . . . .**122** B3
North Calder Dr G71 . . . .**120** A1
North Calder Pl G71 . . . .**120** A1
North Calder Rd G71 . . . .**121** B1
North Campbell Ave G62 . . . . . .54 C1
North Canal Bank G4 . . . . .97 B1
North Canal Bank St G4 . . . . . . .97 B1
North Carbrain Rd G67 . . . . . . .61 C1
North Castle St G14 . . . . .10 A3
North Claremont La G62 . . . . . .55 A1
North Claremont St 14
G3 . . . . .96 C1
North Corsebar Rd PA2 . . . . . .**113** B1
North Court La G1 . . . .**241** A2
North Crescent Ave
KA22 . . . .**205** B2
North Crescent Rd
KA22 . . . .**205** A2
North Croft St PA3 . . . .**113** C3
North Ct G1 . . . .**241** A2
North Dean Park Ave
G71 . . . .**141** A1
North Douglas St G81 . . . . .94 B4
North Dr Carluke KA25 . . . .**170** A4
Lennoxtown G66 . . . . .57 B3
Linwood PA3 . . . .**112** A3
North Dryburgh Rd ML2 . . . . .**165** A3
North Dumgoyne Ave
G62 . . . . .54 C2
North Elgin Pl G81 . . . . .94 B4
North Elgin St G81 . . . . .94 B4
North Erskine Pk G61 . . . . .75 B3
North Faulds Rd ML11 . . . .**215** C3
North Frederick St G1 . . . .**241** A3
North Gardner St G11 . . . . .96 A2
North Gargieston Rd
KA1 . . . .**227** B3
North Glasgow Coll
Glasgow G21 . . . . .98 B3

North Glasgow Coll continued
Glasgow, Springburn G21 . . . . .97 C2
North Gower St 8 G51 . . . .**116** B3
North Grange Rd G61 . . . . .75 C3
North Green Dr FK2 . . . . .14 B2
North Hamilton Pl KA1 . . . . . .**222** C1
North Hamilton St KA1 . . . . . .**222** C1
North Hanover St G1,
G4 . . . .**241** A3
North Harbour Ind Est
KA8 . . . .**235** C1
North Harbour St KA8 . . . .**235** C1
North Iverton Park Rd
PA5 . . . .**112** A2
North Kilmeny Cres
ML2 . . . .**165** B3
North La PA3 . . . .**112** B3
North Lodge Ave ML1 . . . .**163** C2
North Lodge Rd PA4 . . . . .94 B2
North Main St
Alexandria G83 . . . . .27 B3
Falkirk FK2 . . . . .24 B2
North Moraine La G15 . . . . .75 B1
North Neuk KA10 . . . .**229** D4
North Newmoor Ind Est
KA11 . . . .**219** C1
North Orchard St ML1 . . . .**163** B4
North Park Ave KA8 . . . .**236** A2
Barrhead G78 . . . .**134** A2
Glasgow G46 . . . .**135** C2
North Portland St G1,
G4 . . . .**241** B2
North Rd Bellshill ML4 . . . .**142** A4
Coatbridge ML5 . . . .**122** A1
Cumbernauld G68 . . . . .82 A4
Johnstone PA5 . . . .**111** C1
Port Glasgow PA14 . . . . .68 A4
West Kilbride KA23 . . . .**190** B3
North Ring Rd KA20 . . . .**218** A3
North Shore Rd KA10 . . . .**229** C2
North Sq ML5 . . . .**121** C4
North St Alexandria G83 . . . . . .27 C3
North Rd
Alloa FK10 . . . . .10 A4
Dalry KA24 . . . .**191** B4
Falkirk FK2 . . . . .42 A4
Glasgow G3 . . . .**240** A3
Greenock PA16 . . . . .45 B4
Houston PA6 . . . . .91 A2
Larkhall ML9 . . . .**185** A2
Motherwell ML1 . . . .**163** C4
Paisley PA3 . . . .**113** C3
Stirling FK9 . . . . .2 B1
North Street Ind Est G83 . . .27 C3
North Vennel
Irvine KA11 . . . .**220** A2
Lanark ML11 . . . .**215** A2
North View G61 . . . . .75 B1
North View Rd PA11 . . . .**110** C3
North Wallace St G4 . . . .**241** B4
North Woodside Rd G20 . . . . .96 C2
Northacre KA13 . . . .**207** C3
Northacre Gr KA13 . . . .**207** B3
Northall Quadrant ML1 . . . . . .**143** A1
Northampton Dr G12 . . . . .96 A3
Northampton La G12 . . . . .96 A3
Northbank Ave
Cambuslang G72 . . . .**139** B3
Kirkintilloch G66 . . . . .79 B4
Northbank St G72 . . . .**139** B3
Northbrae Pl G13 . . . . .95 A3
Northburn Ave ML6 . . . .**103** A1
Northburn Pl ML6 . . . .**103** A1
Northburn Rd ML5 . . . .**102** B1
Northburn St ML6 . . . .**100** A1
Northcraig Rd KA3 . . . .**223** A2
Northcroft Rd G69 . . . . .80 C1
Northdoon Pl KA7 . . . .**238** B2
Northend FK7 . . . . .6 B3
Northfield G75 . . . .**179** C4
Northfield Dr Ayr KA8 . . . .**236** A2
Port Glasgow PA14 . . . . .68 A4
Shotts ML7 . . . .**147** A1
Northfield St ML1 . . . .**163** C4
Northfield Dr G83 . . . . .27 C3
Northfield Pl KA8 . . . .**236** A2
Northfield Rd
Alexandria G83 . . . . .28 A3
Bonhill G83 . . . . .21 B2
Kilsyth G65 . . . . .59 C4
Northflat Pl ML8 . . . .**163** C4
Northflat Pl ML8 . . . .**202** B4
Northgate Quadrant G21 . . . . . .98 B3
Northgate Rd G21 . . . . .98 B4
Northinch Ct G14 . . . . .95 B1
Northinch St G14 . . . . .95 B1
Northland Dr G14 . . . . .95 B3
Northland Gdns G14 . . . . .95 B3
Northland La G14 . . . . .95 B3
Northmuir Dr ML2 . . . .**165** B2
Northmuir Rd G15 . . . . .75 C2
Northpark St G20 . . . . .96 C2
Northumberland St G20 . . . . . . .96 C2
Northway G72 . . . .**140** B1
Northwood Dr ML2 . . . .**166** A3
Norton St FK12 . . . . .5 A4
Norval St G11 . . . . .96 A1
Norval Terr KA10 . . . .**229** C3
Norwood Ave Alloa FK10 . . . . . . .9 C4
Bonnybridge FK4 . . . . .40 A4
Kirkintilloch G66 . . . . .79 A4
Norwood Cres FK10 . . . . .9 C4
Norwood Ct G44 . . . .**137** A4
Norwood Dr G46 . . . .**136** A1
Norwood Gr FK10 . . . . .9 C4
Norwood Pk G61 . . . . .75 C2
Norwood Pl FK4 . . . . .40 A4

Norwood Terr G71 ......141 A4
Notre Dame High RC Sch G12 ......96 B2
Notre Dame High Sch PA16 ......45 B2
Notre Dame Prim RC Sch G12 ......96 B2
Nottingham Ave G12 ......96 A3
Nottingham La G12 ......96 A3
Novar Dr G12 ......96 A2
Novar Gdns G64 ......77 C1
Novar St ML3 ......162 B1
Nuneaton St G40 ......118 A2
Nuneaton Street Ind Est G40 ......118 A2
Nurseries Rd G69 ......119 C3
Nursery Ave Erskine PA7 ......72 C2
Kilmarnock KA1 ......228 A4
Prestwick KA9 ......236 A3
Nursery Bldgs ML11 ......215 A1
Nursery Ct Carluke ML8 ......187 C2
Lanark ML11 ......214 C2
Nursery Dr ML9 ......200 A4
Nursery Gdns
Kilmarnock KA1 ......228 A4
Springside KA11 ......221 A1
Nursery Gr Ayr KA7 ......239 A3
Kilmacolm PA13 ......69 B1
Nursery La Glasgow G41 ......116 C1
Kilmacolm PA13 ......69 B1
Nursery Pk ML8 ......187 C1
Nursery Pl
Ardrossan KA22 ......205 B1
Blantyre G72 ......161 B3
Nursery Rd Ayr KA7 ......239 A3
Falkirk FK1 ......41 C2
Nursery St Glasgow G41 ......117 A2
Helensburgh G84 ......25 A4
Kilmarnock KA1 ......227 C4
Nursery Wynd KA7 ......239 A3
Nutberry Ct G42 ......117 A1

O

O'Connor Ct KA21 ......216 C4
O'Hanlon Way FK8 ......1 C1
O'Hare G83 ......28 A2
O'Neil Ave G64 ......98 A4
O'Neil Terr G83 ......27 C2
O'Wood Ave ML1 ......143 A3
Oak Ave Bearsden G62 ......75 C4
East Kilbride G75 ......180 A3
Oak Cres Glasgow G69 ......120 A2
Plean FK7 ......12 B2
Oak Dr Cambuslang G72 ......139 B2
Fallin FK7 ......8 B2
Kirkintilloch G66 ......79 A3
Stenhousemuir FK5 ......23 B1
Oak Fern Dr G74 ......159 B2
Oak Fern Gr G74 ......159 B2
Oak Gr ML6 ......123 C2
Oak Lea ML3 ......162 C1
Oak Mall The PA15 ......45 C3
Oak Path ML1 ......143 A3
Oak Pk Bishopbriggs G64 ......78 A1
Motherwell ML1 ......163 B2
Oak Pl Coatbridge ML5 ......122 B3
East Kilbride G75 ......180 A3
Kilmarnock KA1 ......227 B4
Uddingston G71 ......141 B4
Oak Rd Ardrossan KA22 ......205 B2
Clydebank G81 ......73 C3
Cumbernauld G67 ......62 C2
Paisley PA2 ......114 A1
Oak St Glasgow G2 ......240 B2
Stirling FK8 ......1 C1
Oak Wynd G72 ......139 C2
Oakbank Ave ML2 ......164 C1
Oakbank Dr G78 ......155 C4
Oakbank Ind Est G20 ......97 A2
Oakbank Rd PA14 ......68 C4
Oakbank St ML6 ......123 B4
Oakburn Ave G62 ......54 C1
Oakburn Cres G62 ......54 C1
Oakdene Ave
Bellshill ML4 ......142 A4
Uddingston G71 ......141 A4
Oakdene Cres ML1 ......143 B2
Oakfield Ave G12 ......96 C1
Oakfield Dr 2 ML1 ......163 C3
Oakfield La 2 G12 ......96 C1
Oakfield Prim Sch PA15 ......46 B2
Oakfield Rd ML1 ......163 C3
Oakgrove Prim Sch G4 ......97 A1
Oakhill Ave G69 ......119 C2
Oakland Dr KA20 ......206 C1
Oaklands Ave KA12 ......219 B2
Oaklea Cres G72 ......161 B4
Oakleigh Dr PA16 ......45 B4
Oakley Dr G44 ......136 C2
Oakley Terr 4 G31 ......117 C4
Oakridge Cres PA3 ......113 A3
Oakridge Rd G69 ......121 A3
Oaks The Glasgow G44 ......137 A2
Johnstone PA5 ......111 C1
Oakshaw Brae PA1 ......113 B3
Oakshaw St E PA1 ......113 C3
Oakshaw St W PA1 ......113 B3
Oakshawhead PA1 ......113 B3
Oakside Pl ML3 ......183 B4
Oaktree Gdns
Dumbarton G82 ......50 B1
Glasgow G45 ......137 C2
Oakwood Ave Ayr KA8 ......236 C1
Paisley PA2 ......113 A1
Oakwood Cres G34 ......100 B1
Oakwood Dr Beith KA15 ......171 A4
Oakwood Dr *continued*
Coatbridge ML5 ......121 B3
Glasgow G34 ......100 B1
Newton Mearns G77 ......156 C2
Oates Gdns ML1 ......164 A2
Oatfield St G21 ......98 A2
Oban Ct 5 G20 ......96 C2
Oban Dr G20 ......96 C2
Oban La G20 ......96 C2
Oban Terr PA16 ......44 C2
Oberon FK10 ......9 C4
Obiston Gdns G32 ......119 A3
Obree Ave KA9 ......236 C3
Observatory La 11 G12 ......96 B2
Observatory Rd G12 ......96 B2
Ochel Path ML6 ......123 C1
Ochil Cres FK8 ......2 A1
Ochil Ct East Kilbride G75 ......180 A2
Irvine KA11 ......220 A2
Tullibody FK10 ......4 B2
Ochil Dr Barrhead G78 ......134 B1
Paisley PA2 ......133 C4
Stenhousemuir FK5 ......23 C2
Ochil Pl Glasgow G32 ......119 A2
Kilmarnock KA1 ......228 A2
Ochil Rd Alva FK12 ......5 A4
Bearsden G61 ......75 A4
Bishopbriggs G64 ......78 B1
Menstrie FK11 ......4 A4
Renfrew PA4 ......94 A1
Stirling FK9 ......2 B2
Ochil St Alloa FK10 ......10 A4
Fallin FK7 ......8 B2
Glasgow G32 ......119 A2
Tullibody FK10 ......4 A2
Wishaw ML2 ......164 C2
Ochil Terr FK2 ......24 A1
Ochil View Denny FK6 ......39 B4
Shieldhill FK1 ......66 B4
8 Uddingston G71 ......141 A4
Ochil View Ct FK5 ......23 B3
Ochilmount FK7 ......7 C1
Ochiltree Ave G13 ......95 C4
Ochiltree Dr ML3 ......161 C1
Ochiltree Pl KA3 ......223 A3
Ochiltree Terr FK1 ......41 A3
Ochilvale Terr FK10 ......5 B2
Ochilview Alva FK12 ......5 A4
Cowie FK7 ......12 C3
Ochilview Pk (Stenhousemuir FC) FK5 ......23 B2
Ochre Cres FK7 ......12 B4
Octavia Terr PA16 ......45 B4
Odense Ct G75 ......180 C3
Ogilface Cres EH48 ......107 B1
Ogilvie Ct 2 ML6 ......123 C4
Ogilvie Pl Bridge of A FK9 ......2 A3
Glasgow G31 ......118 B2
Kilmarnock KA3 ......223 B1
Ogilvie Prim RC Sch G33 ......119 C4
Ogilvie Rd FK8 ......7 A3
Ogilvie St G31 ......118 B2
Old Airbles Rd ML1 ......163 B3
Old Aisle Rd G66 ......79 C4
Old Auchans View KA2 ......225 C1
Old Avon Rd ML3 ......163 A1
Old Balmore Rd G64 ......77 C4
Old Bellsdyke Rd FK5 ......23 A2
Old Biggar Rd ML6 ......83 A1
Old Bore Rd ML6 ......123 C4
Old Bothwell Rd G71 ......162 A4
Old Bridge of Weir Rd PA6 ......91 A1
Old Bridge Rd KA8 ......236 C2
Old Bridge St
9 Alloa FK10 ......10 A3
Ayr KA7 ......235 C1
Old Bridge Wynd FK9 ......2 A2
Old Bridgend ML8 ......187 C1
Old Caley Rd KA12 ......219 B2
Old Castle Gdns G44 ......137 A3
Old Castle Rd G44 ......137 A3
Old Church Gdns G69 ......121 A3
Old Coach Rd G74 ......159 C2
Old Cross 4 Airdrie ML6 ......123 A4
Hamilton ML3 ......162 C2
Old Dalmarnock Rd G40 ......117 C2
Old Dalnottar Rd G60 ......73 B3
Old Denny Rd FK5 ......23 A2
Old Drove Rd FK7 ......6 B3
Old Dulatur Rd G68 ......61 B3
Old Dumbarton Rd G3 ......96 B1
Old Eastfield St ML7 ......127 B3
Old Edinburgh Rd G71 ......141 B4
Old Farm Rd KA8 ......236 B2
Old Gartloch Rd G34 ......100 B3
Old Glasgow Rd
Cumbernauld G67 ......62 A2
Stewarton KA3 ......195 C1
Uddingston G71 ......140 C3
Uddingston, Kylepark G71 ......140 B4
Old Govan Rd PA4 ......94 C2
Old Greenock Rd
Bishopton PA7 ......71 B3
Bishopton, Kingston PA7, PA8 ......72 B1
Langbank PA14 ......70 B3
Old Hillfoot Rd KA7 ......239 A3
Old Humbie Rd G77 ......156 C1
Old Inns Int G67 ......62 B3
Old Inns Rdbt G68 ......62 A3
Old Inverkip Rd PA16 ......45 A2
Old Irvine Rd KA1 ......227 C4
Old Lanark Rd
Carluke ML8 ......202 A4
Old Lanark Rd *continued*
Carluke, Braidwood ML8, ML11 ......202 A2
Old Largs Rd PA16 ......45 C1
Old Loans Rd KA10 ......230 A2
Old Luss Rd Balloch G83 ......19 A1
Helensburgh G84 ......16 C1
Old Manse Gdns ML5 ......122 A4
Old Manse Rd
Glasgow G32 ......119 B3
Wishaw ML2 ......164 C1
Old McDonalds Clyde Valley Farm Pk* ML9 ......186 A1
Old Military Rd G83 ......20 C4
Old Mill Ct G81 ......74 A3
Old Mill Gate G73 ......138 A3
Old Mill Park Ind Est G66 ......58 B1
Old Mill Rd Bothwell G71 ......141 A1
Cambuslang G72 ......139 B3
Clydebank G81 ......74 A3
East Kilbride G74 ......159 C1
Hartwood ML7 ......146 A1
Kilmarnock KA1 ......228 A4
Paisley PA2 ......113 A2
Uddingston G71 ......140 C3
Old Mill View G65 ......60 C2
Old Mill Wlk G83 ......27 C4
Old Monkland Prim Sch ML5 ......121 B2
Old Monkland Rd ML5 ......121 C2
Old Mugdock Rd G63 ......31 B1
Old Playfield Rd G76 ......158 B4
Old Quarry Rd
Cumbernauld G68 ......81 B3
Stevenston KA20 ......217 B4
Old Raise Rd KA21 ......206 A1
Old Rd PA5 ......112 B2
Old Redding Rd FK2 ......42 C2
Old Rome Way KA2 ......226 C3
Old School Ct FK10 ......4 A1
Old Schoolhouse La PA6 ......91 A2
Old Shettleston Rd G32 ......119 A3
Old Sneddon St PA3 ......113 C3
Old St Clydebank G81 ......73 C3
Kilmarnock KA1 ......227 C3
Old Stable Row ML5 ......122 A4
Old Station Ct G71 ......141 A1
Old Station Wynd KA10 ......229 D2
Old Town FK7 ......7 B1
Old Union St ML6 ......123 A4
Old Willowyard Rd KA15 ......171 A4
Old Wishaw Rd ML8 ......187 C2
Old Wood Rd G69 ......120 A2
Old Woodwynd Rd KA13 ......207 C2
Old Wynd G1 ......241 A1
Oldbarhills TP Site PA2 ......134 B4
Oldhall Dr PA13 ......69 B1
Oldhall Rd PA1 ......114 B3
Oldhall Rdbt KA11 ......224 D3
Oldhall West Ind Est KA11 ......224 D3
Olifard Ave G71 ......141 A2
Oliphant Cres
Clarkston G76 ......157 C3
Paisley PA2 ......132 C4
Oliphant Ct Paisley PA2 ......132 C4
Stirling FK8 ......2 A1
Oliphant Dr KA3 ......228 B4
Oliphant Oval PA2 ......132 C4
Olive Bank G71 ......121 B1
Olive Ct ML1 ......143 A3
Olive Rd KA1 ......227 B4
Olive St G33 ......98 B2
Oliver Rd FK1 ......42 B2
Olympia Arc 4 G74 ......180 C4
Olympia Ct G74 ......180 C4
Olympia St 5 G40 ......117 C3
Olympia The 3 G74 ......180 C4
Omoa Rd ML1 ......144 A1
Onich Pl ML7 ......147 A2
Onslow G75 ......180 B4
Onslow Dr G31 ......118 A4
Onslow Rd G81 ......74 B1
Onslow Sq G31 ......118 A4
Ontario Pk G75 ......159 A1
Ontario Pl G75 ......159 A1
Onthank Dr KA3 ......222 C2
Onthank Prim Sch KA3 ......222 C3
Onyx St ML4 ......142 A2
Open Shore PA15 ......46 A3
Oran Gate G20 ......96 C3
Oran Gdns G20 ......96 C3
Oran Pl G20 ......96 C2
Oran St G20 ......96 C2
Orangefield PA15 ......45 C3
Orangefield Dr KA9 ......233 B1
Orangefield Ind Est KA9 ......233 B1
Orangefield La PA15 ......45 C3
Orbiston Ct ML1 ......164 A3
Orbiston Dr Bellshill ML4 ......142 B2
Clydebank G81 ......74 B4
Orbiston Pl G81 ......74 B4
Orbiston Rd Bellshill ML4 ......141 C2
Bellshill ML4 ......142 A1
Orbiston Sq ML4 ......141 C2
Orbiston St ML1 ......163 C3
Orcades Dr G44 ......137 B2
Orchard Ave Ayr KA7 ......239 A3
Bothwell G71 ......141 A1
Orchard Brae
Hamilton ML3 ......162 B2
Kirkintilloch G66 ......79 C2
Orchard Ct Glasgow G32 ......139 A4
Glasgow, Orchard Pk G46 ......136 A2
Orchard Dr Blantyre G72 ......161 B4
Orchard Dr *continued*
Glasgow G46 ......136 A2
Rutherglen G73 ......137 C4
Orchard Field G66 ......79 C2
Orchard Gate ML9 ......185 A1
Orchard Gn G74 ......160 A2
Orchard Gr
Coatbridge ML5 ......122 A3
Glasgow G46 ......136 A2
Kilmacolm PA13 ......89 B4
Kilwinning KA13 ......207 C2
Orchard House Hospl FK8 ......2 A1
Orchard Park Ave G46 ......136 A2
Orchard Pk G46 ......136 B2
Orchard Pl Ayr KA7 ......239 A3
Bellshill ML4 ......141 C2
Hamilton ML3 ......162 B2
Kilwinning KA13 ......207 B2
Kirkintilloch G66 ......80 A4
Orchard Rd FK9 ......2 A3
Orchard St Carluke ML8 ......187 C1
Falkirk FK1 ......42 A3
Glasgow G69 ......119 C2
Greenock PA15 ......46 A2
Hamilton ML3 ......162 C2
Kilmarnock KA3 ......222 C1
Motherwell ML1 ......163 B4
Paisley PA1 ......113 C2
Renfrew PA4 ......94 B2
West Kilbride KA23 ......190 B3
Wishaw ML2 ......186 A3
Orchard The FK10 ......4 A1
Orchard View Dr ML11 ......214 A2
Orchardcroft FK8 ......7 A4
Orchardton Rd G68 ......81 B4
Orchardton Woods Ind Pk G68 ......81 B4
Orchid Pl G66 ......57 B4
Orchy Ave G76 ......136 C1
Orchy Cres Airdrie ML6 ......123 B2
Bearsden G61 ......75 B1
Paisley PA2 ......112 C1
Orchy Ct G81 ......74 B3
Orchy Dr G44 ......136 C1
Orchy Gdns G76 ......136 C1
Orchy St G44 ......137 A3
Orchy Terr G74 ......160 A1
Orefield Pl G74 ......159 C2
Oregon Pl G5 ......117 B2
Orion Pl ML4 ......142 C3
Orion Way
Cambuslang G72 ......139 A3
Carluke ML8 ......187 B1
Orkney Ct FK10 ......10 A3
Orkney Dr KA3 ......223 A3
Orkney Pl Falkirk FK1 ......42 A1
6 Glasgow G51 ......116 A4
Orkney Quadrant ML2 ......165 B2
Orkney St G51 ......116 A4
Orlando G74 ......160 B3
Orleans Ave G14 ......95 C2
Orleans La G14 ......95 C2
Orlington Ct ML5 ......121 C4
Ormiston Ave G14 ......95 B2
Ormiston Dr Alloa FK10 ......4 C1
Hamilton ML3 ......183 B4
Ormiston La 12 G14 ......95 B2
Ormiston La N 6 G14 ......95 B2
Ormiston La S 14 G14 ......95 B2
Ormiston Pl KA11 ......220 B4
Ormond Ct FK5 ......23 A2
Ormonde Ave G44 ......136 C2
Ormonde Cres G44 ......136 C2
Ormonde Ct G44 ......136 C2
Ormonde Dr G44 ......136 C2
Ornsay St G22 ......97 B4
Oronsay Ave PA14 ......69 A3
Oronsay Cres
Bearsden G61 ......76 A2
Old Kilpatrick G60 ......73 B3
Oronsay Ct G60 ......73 B3
Oronsay Gdns G60 ......73 B3
Oronsay Pl
Old Kilpatrick G60 ......73 B3
Wishaw ML2 ......165 A1
Oronsay Sq G60 ......73 B3
Orr Sq PA1 ......113 C3
Orr Square Church PA1 ......113 B3
Orr St Glasgow G40 ......117 C3
Paisley PA2 ......113 C2
Paisley, Castlehead PA1 ......113 C3
Orr Terr Harthill ML7 ......127 B2
Neilston G78 ......154 B3
Orton Pl G51 ......116 A3
Osborne Cres G74 ......158 A2
Osborne Gdns FK1 ......41 C2
Osborne St Clydebank G81 ......74 A2
Falkirk FK1 ......41 C2
Glasgow G1 ......241 A1
Oslie View KA3 ......195 C1
Osprey Cres ML2 ......165 A2
Osprey Dr
Kilmarnock KA1 ......228 B4
Uddingston G71 ......141 A4
Osprey Rd PA16 ......45 A2
Ossian Ave PA1 ......114 C3
Ossian Rd G43 ......136 C3
Oswald Ct KA8 ......236 A2
Oswald Dr KA9 ......233 B1
Oswald Gdns ML8 ......201 C2
Oswald La KA8 ......235 C1
Oswald Pl KA8 ......236 A3
Oswald Rd KA8 ......236 A2
Oswald St Falkirk FK1 ......42 A2
Glasgow G1 ......240 C2
Oswald Wlk G62 ......76 B4
Otago La G12 ......96 C1
Otago La N G12 ......96 C1
Otago Pk G75 ......159 A1
Otago Pl G82 ......50 B1
Otago St G12 ......96 C1
Othello G74 ......160 A3
Ottawa Cres G81 ......73 B2
Otterburn Ave KA3 ......223 A2
Otterburn Dr G46 ......136 B1
Otterswick Pl G33 ......99 B1
Ottoline Dr KA10 ......229 D1
Oudenarde Ct ML8 ......188 A1
Our Holy Redeemer's RC Prim Sch G81 ......94 B4
Our Lady & St Francis RC Prim Sch ML1 ......143 B1
Our Lady & St Patricks High Sch G82 ......49 B2
Our Lady of Loretto Prim Sch G81 ......73 C2
Our Lady of Lourdes RC Prim Sch G75 ......180 B4
Our Lady of Peace Prim Sch PA3 ......112 A3
Our Lady of the Annunciation Prim RC Sch G43 ......136 C3
Our Lady of the Assumption Prim RC Sch G20 ......97 A3
Our Lady of the Missions Prim Sch G46 ......136 A1
Our Lady of the Rosary Sch G52 ......115 B2
Our Lady's High Sch G67 ......61 B1
Our Lady's RC High Sch ML1 ......164 A2
Outdale Ave KA9 ......236 C4
Oval The Glasgow G76 ......136 C1
Glenboig ML5 ......101 B3
Overbrae Gdns G15 ......74 C3
Overbrae Pl G15 ......74 C3
Overburn Ave G82 ......49 C2
Overburn Cres G82 ......49 C3
Overburn Terr G82 ......50 A3
Overdale Ave G42 ......136 C4
Overdale Cres KA9 ......236 B3
Overdale Gdns G42 ......136 C4
Overdale Pl ML2 ......186 B3
Overdale St G42 ......136 C4
Overjohnstone Dr ML2 ......164 B2
Overlea Ave G73 ......138 B3
Overlee Ho G76 ......157 C4
Overlee Rd G76 ......157 C4
Overmills Cres KA7 ......239 B4
Overmills Rd KA7 ......239 B4
Overnewton Pl G3 ......116 B4
Overnewton Sq G3 ......96 B1
Overnewton St G3 ......96 B1
Overton Cres Denny FK6 ......21 B1
Greenock PA15 ......45 B2
Johnstone PA5 ......112 A2
West Kilbride KA23 ......190 B3
Overton Ct KA23 ......190 B3
Overton Dr KA23 ......190 B3
Overton Gdns PA13 ......69 C1
Overton Gr PA13 ......69 C1
Overton Pl KA11 ......220 A3
Overton Prim Sch PA16 ......45 B2
Overton Rd Alexandria G83 ......27 B2
Cambuslang G72 ......139 B3
Johnstone PA5 ......112 A1
Netherburn ML9 ......200 B3
Springside KA11 ......220 C2
Overton St Alexandria G83 ......27 C3
Cambuslang G72 ......139 B2
Overton Terr FK6 ......21 B1
Overtoun Ave G82 ......50 A2
Overtoun Ct KA11 ......221 A1
Overtoun Dr
Clydebank G81 ......73 C2
Rutherglen G73 ......138 A4
Overtoun Est* G82 ......50 C3
Overtoun Rd G81 ......73 C2
Overtown Ave G53 ......135 A3
Overtown Prim Sch ML2 ......186 B4
Overtown Rd ML2 ......165 C1
Overtown St G31 ......118 A3
Overwood Dr
Dumbarton G82 ......50 A2
Glasgow G44 ......137 B3
Overwood Gr G82 ......50 A2
Owen Ave G75 ......180 A4
Owen Kelly Pl KA21 ......205 C1
Owen Pk G75 ......180 B4
Owen St ML1 ......163 C4
Owendale Ave ML4 ......142 A4
Oxford Ave PA19 ......45 A3
Oxford Dr PA3 ......112 A3
Oxford La Glasgow G5 ......117 A3
Renfrew PA4 ......94 B2
Oxford Rd Greenock PA16 ......44 B2
Renfrew PA4 ......94 B2
Oxford St Coatbridge ML5 ......121 C3
Glasgow G5 ......240 C1
Kirkintilloch G66 ......79 B4
Oxgang Pl G66 ......79 C4
Oxgang Prim Sch G66 ......79 C4
Oxgang Smallholdings G66 ......79 C4
Oxhill Pl G82 ......49 B2
Oxhill Rd G82 ......49 B2
Oxton Dr G52 ......115 A3

P

Pacemuir La PA13 ......89 A4

Pacemuir Rd PA13 ....89 A4
Paddock St ML5,ML6 ....122 B2
Paddock The
 Clarkston G76 ....158 A3
 Hamilton ML3 ....162 B3
 Perceton KA11 ....220 B3
Paddock View KA2 ......221 B1
Paddockholm North Ind Est
 KA25 ....149 A1
Paddockholm South Ind Est
 KA25 ....149 A1
Paduff Pl KA25 ....149 A1
Paidmyre Cres G77 ....156 B2
Paidmyre Gdns G77 ....156 B2
Paidmyre Rd G77 ....156 B2
Paisley (Gilmour St) Sta
 PA3 ....113 C3
Paisley Abbey* PA1 ....113 C2
Paisley Canal Sta PA1 ..113 C2
Paisley Gram Sch PA1 ..114 A3
Paisley Maternity Hospl
 PA2 ....113 B1
Paisley Mus & Art Gallery*
 PA1 ....113 C3
Paisley Rd Barrhead G78 ..134 A2
 Glasgow G5 ....240 B1
 Renfrew PA4 ....94 B1
Paisley Rd W G52 ....115 B2
Paisley St James Sta
 PA1 ....113 B3
Palace Grounds Rd
 ML3 ....162 C2
Palace of Art G52 ....115 C2
Palacecraig St ML5 ....122 A2
Palacerigg Country Pk*
 G67 ....83 C4
Paladin Ave G13 ....95 A4
Palermo St ☒ G21 ....97 C2
Palladium Pl G14 ....95 B2
Palm Pl G71 ....121 B1
Palmer Ave G13 ....75 B1
Palmerston G75 ....180 A4
Palmerston Pl
 Glasgow G3 ....116 B4
 Johnstone PA5 ....131 B4
Pandora Way G71 ....141 A4
Pankhurst Pl G74 ....159 C1
Panmure St G20 ....97 A3
Panrock Ct KA10 ....229 C2
Pantonville Rd KA23 ..198 B2
Papermill Rd PA15,PA16 ..45 B1
Papingo Ct KA13 ....207 B3
Pappert G83 ....28 A2
Pardovan Pl FK1 ....41 C3
Parilament Rd G66 ....79 B4
Paris Ave FK6 ....21 C4
Park Ave Balloch G83 ....19 C1
 Barrhead G78 ....134 A1
 Beith KA15 ....150 A1
 Bishopbriggs G64 ....78 A2
 Carluke ML8 ....187 C2
 Denny FK4 ....39 C3
 Dumbarton G82 ....50 A2
 Eldersfie PA5 ....112 B1
 Glasgow G3 ....96 C1
 Greenock PA16 ....45 A4
 Kilwinning KA13 ....207 C2
 Kirkintilloch G66 ....79 B4
 Laurieston FK2 ....42 C2
 Milngavie G62 ....55 A1
 Motherwell ML1 ....143 A3
 Paisley PA2 ....113 B1
 Prestwick KA9 ....236 A4
 Stenhousemuir FK5 ......23 B1
 Stirling FK8 ....7 A3
 Twechar G65 ....59 C2
Park Bank PA8 ....73 A1
Park Brae PA8 ....93 B4
Park Burn St ML3 ....162 A3
Park Burn Ind Est ML3 ..162 A3
Park Cir Ayr KA7 ....238 C4
 Carluke ML8 ....187 C2
 Glasgow G3 ....240 A4
Park Circus La Ayr KA7 ..238 C4
 Glasgow G3 ....240 A4
Park Circus Pl G3 ....240 A4
Park Cres Airdrie ML6 ..122 C4
 Alloa FK10 ....5 B1
 Bannockburn FK7 ....7 B1
 Bearsden G61 ....75 B3
 Bishopbriggs G64 ....78 A1
 Blantyre G72 ....140 B1
 Dumbarton G82 ....49 C3
 Eaglesham G76 ....178 C3
 Falkirk FK2 ....24 A1
 Inchinnan PA4 ....93 B4
 Stewarton KA3 ....17 B1
 Torrance G64 ....57 B1
Park Ct Beith KA15 ......171 B4
 Bishopbriggs G64 ....78 A2
 Clydebank G81 ....73 C2
 Glasgow G46 ....136 A2
 Shotts ML7 ....146 C3
Park Dr Bannockburn FK7 ..7 B1
 Bellshill ML4 ....142 A2
 Erskine PA8 ....93 A4
 Erskine, Park Mains PA8 ..93 B4
 Glasgow G3 ....240 A4
 Hamilton ML3 ....163 B1
 Lanark ML11 ....214 C2
 Rutherglen G73 ....138 A4
 Stenhousemuir FK5 ......23 B1
 Thorntonhall G74 ......158 B2

Park Dr continued
 Wishaw ML2 ....166 A3
Park Gardens La G3 ......96 C1
Park Gate Erskine PA8 ..93 A4
Park Gate La G3 ....96 C1
Park Gate Pl ML4 ....141 C3
Park Gdns Bannockburn FK7 ..7 B1
 Glasgow G3 ....96 C1
 Kilbarchan PA10 ....111 A2
Park Glade PA8 ....93 A4
Park Gn PA8 ....93 A4
Park Gr Cardross G82 ....48 A4
 Erskine PA8 ....93 B4
Park Hill PA8 ....73 A1
Park La Ardrossan KA22 ..205 B2
 Blantyre G72 ....161 C4
 Carluke ML8 ....187 C1
 Glasgow G40 ....117 C3
 Kilsyth G65 ....60 B4
 Kilwinning KA13 ....207 B3
 Stirling FK8 ....7 A4
Park Lea ML6 ....105 A2
Park Moor PA8 ....93 A4
Park Pl Alloa FK10 ....10 B4
 Bellshill ML4 ....141 C2
 Irvine KA12 ....219 A3
 Johnstone PA5 ....111 C1
 Lanark ML11 ....214 C2
 Stirling FK7 ....6 C3
 Strathblane G63 ....31 A2
 Thorntonhall G74 ......158 B2
 Park Prim Sch FK10 ....10 B4
Park Quadrant
 Glasgow G3 ....240 A4
 Wishaw ML2 ....164 C1
Park Rd Ardrossan KA22 ..205 B1
 Bargeddie G69 ....121 A3
 Bellshill ML4 ....142 A2
 Bishopbriggs G64 ....78 A1
 Blackridge EH48 ....107 C2
 Bridge of W PA11 ....90 B1
 Calderbank ML6 ....123 A2
 Chryston G69 ....100 B4
 Clydebank G81 ....73 C2
 Falkirk FK2 ....24 A1
 Glasgow G4 ....96 C1
 Glasgow, Carmyle G32 ..139 B4
 Glasgow, Giffnock G46 ..136 B1
 Hamilton ML3 ....162 B2
 Inchinnan PA4 ....93 B4
 Johnstone PA5 ....111 C1
 Kilmacolm PA13 ....89 B4
 Menstrie FK11 ....4 A3
 Motherwell ML1 ....143 A1
 Paisley PA2 ....113 B1
 Saltcoats KA21 ....216 C4
 Shotts ML7 ....146 B3
Park Ridge PA8 ....93 B4
Park Sch KA3 ....223 A1
 Alexandria G83 ....27 B3
 Alva FK12 ....5 A4
 Carluke ML8 ....187 C1
 Cleland ML1 ....144 A2
 Coatbridge ML5 ....122 A4
 Cowie FK7 ....12 C4
 Dumbarton G82 ....50 A2
 High Bonnybridge FK4 ..40 A2
 Kilmarnock KA1 ....222 C1
 Kirkintilloch G66 ....80 A4
 Motherwell ML1 ....163 C3
 New Stevenston
 ML1 ....143 A2
Park St S G3 ....96 C1
Park Terr Ayr KA2 ......238 C4
 Cardross G82 ....48 A4
 East Kilbride G74 ......159 C1
 Glasgow G3 ....96 C1
 Gourock PA19 ....44 C4
 Stirling FK8 ....7 A4
 Tullibody FK10 ....4 A1
Park Terrace East La
 G3 ....240 A4
Park Terrace La G3 ......96 C1
Park Top PA8 ....73 B1
Park View
 Ardrossan KA22 ....205 B2
 Caldercruix ML6 ....105 A3
 Kilbarchan PA10 ....111 A2
 Kilbirnie KA25 ....149 A1
 Paisley PA2 ....113 B1
Paterson Dr
 Helensburgh G84 ....16 A2
 Shieldhill FK1 ....66 B3
Paterson Pl Bearsden G61 ..75 B4
 Bonnybridge FK4 ....40 B3
 Bridge of A FK9 ....2 A2
Paterson St Ayr KA8 ..236 A2
 Glasgow G5 ....240 B1
 Motherwell ML1 ....163 C4
Paterson Terr G75 ......180 B4
Paterson's Laun G64 ....77 C4
Path The FK7 ....7 B1
Pathfoot Ave FK9 ....2 C3
Pathhot KA13 ....207 C2
Pathfoot Ave FK9 ....2 B3
Pathfoot Dr FK9 ....2 B4
Pathfoot Rd FK9 ....2 B3
Parker Pl ☑ Kilsyth G65 ..60 B4
 Larkhall ML9 ....185 A2
Parkfield G75 ....180 C3
Parkfoot Ct FK1 ....42 A2
Parkfoot St G65 ....36 B1
Parkgate FK12 ....4 C3

Parkgrove Ave G46 ....136 B2
Parkgrove Terr ☒ G3 ..96 C1
Parkgrove Terrace La
 ☒ 96 C1
Parkhall Rd G81 ....73 C2
Parkhall St G74 ....159 C1
Parkhall Terr G81 ....73 C3
Parkhead Ave KA13 ....207 C2
Parkhead Cross G31 ..118 B3
Parkhead Ct FK10 ....10 B4
Parkhead La ☒ ML6 ....123 A4
Parkhead Rd Alloa FK10 ..10 B4
 Falkirk FK1 ....42 A1
Parkhead St Airdrie ML6 ..123 A4
 Motherwell ML1 ....163 C3
Parkhill Ave
 Crosshouse KA2 ....226 C4
 Port Glasgow PA14 ......69 A4
Parkhill Dr Dalry KA24 ..191 B4
 Rutherglen G73 ....138 A4
Parkhill Rd G43 ....136 B4
Parkholm La G5 ....116 C3
Parkhouse KA25 ....205 B1
Parkhouse Gdns KA22 ..205 B1
Parkhouse Rd
 Ardrossan KA22 ....205 B1
 Glasgow G53 ....135 A2
Parkhouse Sch G22 ......97 B3
Parkhouse St KA7 ......238 C4
Parkinch ML3 ....93 B4
Parklands L Ctr G77 ..156 C3
Parklands Rd G44 ......136 C2
Parklands Sch G84 ......16 C1
Parklands View G53 ..114 C1
Parkle G64 ....77 C2
Parklee Dr G76 ....158 C4
Parkneuk Rd
 Blantyre ML6 ....161 A1
 Glasgow G43 ....156 B2
Parknook St ML1 ....163 B4
Parknook Way ☒ ML6 ..185 A2
Parks View ML3 ....183 B3
Parksail Dr PA8 ....93 B4
Parkside KA11 ....220 A2
Parkside Ct FK7 ....12 B2
Parkside Gdns G20 ......97 A3
Parkside Pl G20 ....97 A3
Parkside Rd
 Motherwell ML1 ....163 A3
 Shotts ML7 ....146 B2
Parkthorn View KA2 ..225 C1
Parkvale Ave PA8 ....93 B4
Parkvale Cres PA8 ......93 C4
Parkvale Dr PA8 ....93 B4
Parkvale Gdns PA8 ......93 B4
Parkvale Pl PA8 ....93 B4
Parkvale Way PA8 ......93 B4
Parkview Ave Falkirk FK1 ..41 C1
 Kirkintilloch G66 ....79 B4
Parkview Cres ML2 ....166 A2
Parkview Ct G66 ....79 B4
Parkview Dr
 Coatbridge ML5 ....121 C4
 Stepps G33 ....99 C3
Parkview Prim Sch G23 ..96 B4
Parkville Dr G72 ....161 C3
Parkville Rd ML4 ....142 A2
Parkway Alloa FK10 ......10 A4
 Erskine PA8 ....93 A4
 Glasgow G32 ....139 B4
Parkway Ct
 Coatbridge ML5 ....121 C3
 Glasgow G32 ....120 A4
Parkway Pl ML5 ....121 C3
Parnell St ML6 ....122 C3
Parnie St G1 ....241 A1
Parry Terr G75 ....180 B4
Parsonage Row G1 ....241 B2
Parsonage Sq G4 ......241 B2
Parterre KA21 ....219 B1
Partick Bridge St G11 ..96 B1
Partick St ML5 ....122 B3
Partick Sta (Underground)
 G11 ....96 A1
Partickhill Ave G11 ......96 A2
Partickhill Ct G11 ....96 A2
Partickhill Rd G11 ....96 A1
Partridge Rd PA16 ......45 A3
Pate Pk ML9 ....199 A4
Paterson Ave KA12 ....219 C3
Paterson Cres KA12 ..219 B3
Paterson Dr

Paton St Alloa FK10 ......10 A4
 Glasgow G31 ....118 A4
 Greenock PA16 ....45 B3
Patrick Ave KA20 ....206 B1
Patrick Dr FK1 ....66 C4
Patrick St Greenock PA16 ..45 C3
 Paisley PA2 ....113 C2
Patterson Dr ML8 ......187 A3
Patterton Dr G78 ....134 B1
Patterton Sta G77 ......156 B4
Pattison St G81 ....73 C2
Pattle Pl KA7 ....238 C1
Paul Dr FK2 ....14 C2
Pavilion Pl KA22 ....205 B1
Pavilion Rd KA7 ....238 C4
Pavilion View FK10 ....9 C4
Pavilions The FK10 ....9 C4
Paxstone Cres ML7 ....127 C3
Paxstone Dr ML7 ....127 C3
Paxton Cres G74 ....159 C2
Paxton Ct G74 ....159 C2
Paxton Pl KA1 ....228 A4
Payne St G4 ....97 B1
Peace Ave
 Kilmarnock KA1 ....222 B1
 Quarriers Village PA11 ..89 C1
Peacock Ave PA2 ....112 C1
Peacock Cross ML3 ....162 B2
Peacock Cross Ind Est
 ML3 ....162 B2
Peacock Dr
 Hamilton ML3 ....162 B2
 Paisley PA2 ....112 C1
Peacock Loan ML8 ....187 C2
Pearce La G51 ....116 A4
Pearce St G51 ....116 A4
Pearl St ML4 ....142 A2
Pearson Dr PA4 ....93 B3
Pearson Dr PA4 ....94 B2
Peat Pl G53 ....135 A3
Peat Rd Bridge of W PA11 ..110 C4
 Glasgow G53 ....135 A3
 Glasgow G53 ....155 B2
Peathill Ave G69 ....100 A4
Peathill Rd FK4 ....40 A3
Peathill St G21 ....97 B2
Peatland Quadrant KA1 ..228 A2
Peatland Rd KA1 ....228 A2
Pebbles Dr G73 ....138 B4
Peden Ave KA24 ....191 A4
Peden Pl KA22 ....219 B1
Pedmyre La G76 ....158 B4
Peebles Path ML5 ......122 B2
Peebles St KA8 ....235 C1
Peel Ave ML1 ....163 C2
Peel Brae G66 ....58 B1
Peel Glen Rd G15,G61 ..75 A3
Peel La G11 ....96 A1
Peel Pk Cvn Pk G74 ....158 C1
Peel Pl Bothwell G71 ..141 A3
Peel Rd G74 ....158 A1
Peel St Cardross G82 ..48 A4
 Glasgow G11 ....96 A1
Peel View G81 ....74 B2
Pegasus Ave
 Carluke ML8 ....187 C1
 Paisley PA1 ....112 C3
Pegasus Rd ML4 ....142 C3
Peggieshill Pl KA7 ......239 A3
Peggieshill Rd KA7 ....239 A3
Peile La PA16 ....45 B3
Peile St PA16 ....45 B3
Peiter Pl G72 ....161 B4
Pelstream Ave FK7 ....7 A2
Pemberton Valley KA7 ..239 A1
Pembroke G74 ....160 B2
Pembroke Rd PA16 ......44 B2
Pembroke St
 Glasgow G3 ....240 A3
 Stenhousemuir FK5 ......23 B2
Pembrock Ct KA11 ......220 B3
Pencaitland Dr G32 ....119 A2
Pencaitland Gr G32 ....119 A2
Pencaitland Pl G23 ......76 C1
Pendale Rise G45 ......137 B2
Pendeen Cres G33 ....119 C3
Pendeen Pl G33 ....119 C3
Pendeen Rd G33 ....119 C3
Penders La FK1 ....42 A3
Pendicle Cres G61 ......75 B2
Pendicle Rd G61 ....75 C2
Pendreich Ave G78 ....134 B1
Pendreich Way FK9 ......2 B2
Penfold Cres G75 ......180 B4
Penicuik St G32 ....118 B3
Penilee Rd PA1,G52 ..114 C3
Penilee Sch G52 ....114 C3
Penilee Sec Sch (Crookston
 Building) G53 ....115 A1
Penilee Terr G52 ....115 C4
Peninver Dr G51 ....115 C4
Penman Ave G73 ......137 C4
Pennan PA8 ....73 A2
Pennan Pl G14 ....95 C4
Penneld Rd G52 ....114 C3
Penniecroft Ave G82 ..50 B3
Pennine Gr G69 ....100 C1
Pennyburn Prim Sch
 KA13 ....207 B1
Pennyburn Rd KA20 ..206 B1
Pennyburn Rdbt KA20 ..207 A1
Pennyfern Dr PA16 ......45 A2

Pennyfern Rd PA16 ......45 A2
Pennyroyal Ct G74 ....159 B2
Pennyvenie Way KA11 ..220 A3
Penrioch Dr G75 ....180 B2
Penrith Ave G46 ....136 B1
Penrith Dr G12 ....96 A3
Penrith Pl G75 ....179 C3
Penryn Gdns G32 ......119 B2
Penston Rd G33 ....119 B4
Pentland Ave
 Linwood PA3 ....112 A3
 Port Glasgow PA14 ......68 C3
Pentland Cres
 Larkhall ML9 ....184 C3
 Paisley PA2 ....133 B4
Pentland Ct Airdrie ML6 ..103 A1
 Barrhead G78 ....134 B1
 Coatbridge ML5 ....122 B2
Pentland Dr
 Barrhead G78 ....134 B1
 Bishopbriggs G64 ....78 B1
 Prestwick KA9 ....236 B3
 Renfrew PA4 ....114 A4
Pentland Pl Bearsden G61 ..75 A4
 Irvine KA11 ....220 A2
Pentland Rd
 Chryston G69 ....100 B4
 East Kilbride G75 ....180 A2
 Glasgow G43 ....136 B3
 Kilmarnock KA1 ....228 A2
 Wishaw ML2 ....164 C2
Pentland Way ML3 ......183 A4
Penzance Way G69 ......80 C1
Peockland Gdns PA5 ..112 A2
Peockland Pl PA5 ....112 A2
People's Palace (Mus)*
 G40 ....117 C3
Peploe Dr G74 ....160 B3
Perceton Rdbt KA11 ..220 A3
Perceton Row KA11 ..220 B2
Perchy View ML2 ....165 B1
Percy Dr G46 ....136 B1
Percy Rd PA4 ....94 A1
Percy St Glasgow G51 ..116 B3
 Larkhall ML9 ....185 A2
Perran Gdns G69 ....80 C1
Perray Ave G32 ....49 A3
Perrays Cres G82 ....49 A3
Perrays Dr G82 ....49 A3
Perrays Gr G82 ....49 A3
Perth Ave ML6 ....123 A2
Perth Cres G81 ....73 B3
Perth St G3 ....240 A2
Peter Coats Building
 PA2 ....113 C2
Peter DStirling Rd ☒
 G66 ....58 B1
Peters Ave KA12 ....219 A1
Peters Ct G61 ....75 B2
Petersburn Prim Sch
 ML6 ....123 B3
Petersburn Rd ML6 ....123 B3
Petershill Ct G21 ....98 B2
Petershill Dr G21 ....98 B2
Petershill Pl G21 ....98 B2
Petershill Rd G21 ....98 A3
Peterson Dr G13 ....94 C4
Peterson Gdns G13 ......94 C4
Peterwell Brae FK7 ......7 C1
Petition Pl G71 ....141 A3
Pettigrew St G32 ......119 A3
Peveril Ave Glasgow G41 ..116 B1
 Rutherglen G73 ....138 B3
Peveril Ct G73 ....138 B3
Pharonhill St G31 ......118 B3
Philip Dr FK5 ....23 B1
Philip Murray Rd ML4 ..141 B3
Philip Sq KA8 ....236 A3
Philip St FK2 ....42 A4
Philiphill Gate G74 ....158 C2
Philipshill Rd G74,G76 ..158 C2
Phoenix Bsns Pk The
 PA3 ....112 C3
Phoenix Cres ML4 ......141 C4
Phoenix Ind Est
 Paisley PA3 ....113 C4
 Stirling FK7 ....7 B4
Phoenix Pl
 Elderslie PA5 ....112 B2
 Motherwell ML1 ....143 A2
Phoenix Rd ML4 ....142 C3
Phoenix Ret Pk The
 PA3 ....113 C3
Piazza Sh Ctr PA1 ......113 C3
Piccadilly St G3 ....240 A2
Picken St KA1 ....227 C3
Pickerstonhill ML1 ....143 C2
Picketlaw Dr G76 ......158 B4
Picketlaw Farm Rd G76 ..158 B4
Pienchorran PA4 ....93 B4
Pier Rd Balloch G83 ....19 B1
 Rhu G84 ....15 C2
Piershill St G32 ....118 C4
Piersland Pl KA11 ......220 A3
Pike Rd FK7 ....7 B2
Pikeman Rd G13 ....95 B4
Pillang Ct ML3 ....162 A4
Pilmuir Ave G44 ....136 C2
Pilrig St G32 ....118 C4
Pilton Rd G15 ....75 A2
Pine Ave G72 ....139 C2
Pine Brae KA7 ....239 B3
Pine Cl G67 ....62 C2
Pine Cres
 Cumbernauld G67 ....62 C2

Pine Cres continued
East Kilbride G75 . . . . .180 A3
Johnstone PA5 . . . . .112 A1
Pine Ct Coatbridge ML5 . . .121 C2
Cumbernauld G67 . . . . .62 C2
East Kilbride G75 . . . . .180 B3
Pine Gr Alloa FK10 . . . . .10 B3
Calderbank ML6 . . . . .123 A1
Cumbernauld G67 . . . . .62 C2
Motherwell ML1 . . . . .143 A3
Uddingston G71 . . . . .141 A4
Pine Ho K9 . . . . .236 A3
Pine Lawn ML2 . . . . .165 B3
Pine Pk ML3 . . . . .162 C1
Pine Pl Cumbernauld G67 . .62 C2
Glasgow G5 . . . . .117 B2
Pine Quadrant ML6 . . . . . .123 C2
Pine Rd Clydebank G81 . . . .73 B2
Cumbernauld G67 . . . . .62 C2
Dumbarton G82 . . . . .49 C2
Kilmarnock KA1 . . . . .227 B4
Pine St Airdrie ML6 . . . . . .123 B4
Greenock PA15 . . . . .45 C2
Lennoxtown G66 . . . . .57 C4
Paisley PA2 . . . . .114 A1
Pine Wlk FK5 . . . . .23 B1
Pineapple The* FK2 . . . . . . .14 A3
Pinelands G64 . . . . .78 A2
Pines The G44 . . . . .137 A2
Pineview Ct G15 . . . . .75 A2
Pinewood G61 . . . . .75 C2
Pinewood Ave G66 . . . . .79 A3
Pinewood Ct
Dumbarton G82 . . . . .50 B3
Kirkintilloch G66 . . . . .79 A3
Pinewood Pl G66 . . . . .79 A3
Pinewood Prim Sch G15 . . .75 B2
Pinkerton Ave G73 . . . . . . .137 C4
Pinkerton La PA4 . . . . .94 B1
Pinkston Dr G21 . . . . .97 C1
Pinkston Rd G21, G4 . . . . . .241 B4
Pinmore KA13 . . . . .207 B1
Pinmore Pl G53 . . . . .134 C3
Pinmore St G53 . . . . .134 C3
Pinwherry Dr G33 . . . . .98 C3
Pinwherry Pl G71 . . . . .141 A2
Pioneer Pk G82 . . . . .50 A1
Piper Ave PA6 . . . . .111 B4
Piper Rd Airdrie ML6 . . . . .123 C2
Houston PA6 . . . . .111 B4
Piperhill KA7 . . . . .239 A1
Piping Ctr The G4 . . . . . . .240 C4
Pirleyhill Dr FK1 . . . . .66 B3
Pirnhall Rd FK7 . . . . .11 B4
Pirnie Pl G65 . . . . .60 B4
Pirnmill Ave
East Kilbride G75 . . . . .180 A3
Motherwell ML1 . . . . .163 A4
Pirnmill Pl G84 . . . . .16 C1
Pirnmill Rd KA21 . . . . .205 C1
Pit Rd Bellshill ML4 . . . . . .141 C3
Kirkintilloch G66 . . . . .80 B4
Pitcairn Cres G75 . . . . . . .179 C4
Pitcairn Dr G75 . . . . .180 A4
Pitcairn Pl G75 . . . . .179 C4
Pitcairn St G31 . . . . .118 C2
Pitcairn Terr ML3 . . . . .162 A2
Pitcaple Dr G43 . . . . .136 A3
Pitfairn Rd FK10 . . . . .5 C2
Pitlochry Dr
Glasgow G52 . . . . .115 B2
Larkhall ML9 . . . . .185 B1
Pitmedden Rd G64 . . . . .78 B1
Pitmilly Rd G15 . . . . .75 B2
Pitreavie Ct ML3 . . . . .183 A4
Pitreavie Pl G33 . . . . .99 B1
Pitt St G2 . . . . .240 B3
Pitt Terr FK8 . . . . .7 A1
Place Of Bonhill G82 . . . . . .27 B2
Place View KA25 . . . . .149 A1
Pladda Ave Irvine KA11 . . .220 A2
Port Glasgow PA14 . . . . .69 A4
Pladda Cres KA11 . . . . .220 A1
Pladda Ct KA11 . . . . .220 A1
Pladda Dr KA9 . . . . .236 B3
Pladda Rd Renfrew PA4 . . . .94 B1
Saltcoats KA21 . . . . .205 C1
Pladda St ML1 . . . . .163 A4
Pladda Terr KA11 . . . . .220 A1
Pladda Way G84 . . . . .16 C1
Pladda Wynd KA11 . . . . . . .220 A1
Plains Prim Sch ML6 . . . . .104 A1
Plaintrees Ct PA2 . . . . .113 C1
Plan View KA25 . . . . .149 A2
Plane Pl G71 . . . . .121 B1
Planetree Pl PA5 . . . . .112 A1
Planetree Rd G81 . . . . .74 A3
Plann Ho KA2 . . . . .221 C2
Plant St G31 . . . . .118 B3
Plantation Ave ML1 . . . . . .143 A3
Plantation Park Gdns
G51 . . . . .116 B3
Plantation Sq G51 . . . . . . .116 C3
Plateau Dr KA10 . . . . .229 D4
Platthorn Dr G74 . . . . .159 C1
Platthorn Rd G74 . . . . .159 C1
Players Rd FK7 . . . . .7 B4
Playfair St G40 . . . . .118 A2
Playingfield Cres KA2 . . . .221 C1
Playingfield Rd KA22 . . . . .221 C1
Plaza The G74 . . . . .159 C1
Pleaknowe Cres G69 . . . . . .80 C1
Pleamuir Pl G68 . . . . .61 B1
Plean Gry Plk* FK2 . . . . .12 A1
Plean Ind Est FK7 . . . . .12 B1
Plean St G14 . . . . .95 A3
Pleasance FK1 . . . . .42 A2

Pleasance Ct 13 FK2 . . . . . .42 A2
Pleasance Gdns FK1 . . . . . .42 A2
Pleasance Rd FK2 . . . . .42 A2
Pleasance Sq 12 FK1 . . . . . .42 A2
Pleasance St G43 . . . . .136 B4
Pleasantfield Rd KA9 . . . . .236 A3
Pleasantside Ave PA14 . . . .69 A4
Pleasures The FK10 . . . . .9 C4
Plotcock Rd ML3 . . . . .198 B4
Plover Dr G75 . . . . .180 A3
Plover Pl PA5 . . . . .131 B4
Plusgarten Loan ML2 . . . . .165 C4
Plymouth Ave PA19 . . . . . . .44 C3
Pochard Way ML4 . . . . .141 C4
Poet's View G66 . . . . .79 C4
Poindlandt Terr G82 . . . . . . .50 A2
Pointhouse Rd G3 . . . . .116 B4
Pokelly Pl KA3 . . . . .195 C1
Polbae Cres G76 . . . . .178 C3
Poldean Ave G75 . . . . .180 A2
Poles Rd KA3 . . . . .213 A2
Polkemmet Dr ML7 . . . . . . .127 C3
Polkemmet La ML7 . . . . . . .127 C3
Polkemmet Rd ML7 . . . . . . .127 C3
Pollick Ave G78 . . . . .153 A2
Pollock Farm La G78 . . . . .153 A1
Pollock Ave
Eaglesham G76 . . . . .178 C3
Hamilton ML3 . . . . .162 A2
Pollock Cres KA13 . . . . . . .207 C1
Pollock Rd Bearsden G61 . . .76 A2
Newton Mearns G77 . . . . . .156 B2
Pollock St Bellshill ML4 . . .142 B3
Motherwell ML1 . . . . .163 C4
Pollok Country Ho*
G43 . . . . .116 A1
Pollok City Pk G43 . . . . . . .116 A1
Pollok Dr G64 . . . . .77 C1
Pollok Ho* G43 . . . . .135 C4
Pollok La G74 . . . . .160 A2
Pollok Pl G74 . . . . .160 A2
Pollokshaws East Sta
G43 . . . . .136 A4
Pollokshaws Rd G41 . . . . . .117 A2
Pollokshaws West Sta
G43 . . . . .136 A4
Pollokshield Sq G41 . . . . . .116 C1
Pollokshields East Sta
G41 . . . . .117 A2
Pollokshields Prim Sch
Annexe (Infs) G41 . . . . . . .116 C2
Pollokshields West Sta
G41 . . . . .116 C1
Polmadie Ave G5 . . . . .117 B1
Polmadie Ind Est G5,
G73 . . . . .117 B1
Polmadie Rd G42,G5 . . . . .117 B1
Polmadie St G42 . . . . .117 B1
Polmaise Ave FK7 . . . . .7 A2
Polmaise Cres FK7 . . . . .8 B3
Polmaise Ct FK7 . . . . .7 A2
Polmaise Rd FK7,FK8 . . . . . . .6 C2
Polnoon Ave G13 . . . . .95 A3
Polnoon Dr G76 . . . . .178 C3
Polnoon Mews G76 . . . . . . .178 C3
Polnoon St G76 . . . . .178 B2
Polo Ave KA10 . . . . .229 D1
Polo Gdns KA10 . . . . .229 D1
Polquhap Ct 4 G53 . . . . . .135 A4
Polquhap Gdns G53 . . . . . .135 A4
Polquhap Pl 5 G53 . . . . . .135 A4
Polson Dr PA5 . . . . .111 C1
Polsons Cres PA2 . . . . .113 B1
Polwarth La G12 . . . . .96 A2
Pomona Pl ML3 . . . . .161 C1
Pompee Rd G69 . . . . .99 B4
Poplar Ave Bishopton PA7 . .72 A1
Glasgow G11 . . . . .95 C2
Johnstone PA5 . . . . .112 A1
Newton Mearns G77 . . . . . .156 C2
Poplar Cres
Bishopton PA7 . . . . .72 A1
Hamilton ML3 . . . . .183 C2
Poplar Ct ML5 . . . . .121 C2
Poplar Dr Clydebank G81 . . .73 C3
Kirkintilloch G66 . . . . .79 A3
Milton of C G66 . . . . .58 B3
Poplar Gdns G75 . . . . .180 B3
Poplar Pl Blantyre G72 . . . .140 B1
Gourock PA19 . . . . .44 B4
Motherwell ML1 . . . . .143 A2
Uddingston G71 . . . . .141 B4
Poplar Rd G82 . . . . .49 C2
Poplar St Airdrie ML6 . . . . .123 B4
Greenock PA15 . . . . .46 C2
Poplar Way Ayr KA7 . . . . . .239 B3
Cambuslang G72 . . . . .139 C4
Poplars The Bearsden G61 . .75 B4
Tullibody FK10 . . . . .4 B2
Poplin St G40 . . . . .118 A2
Porchester St G33 . . . . .99 B1
Port Dundas Ind Est G4 . . .97 B1
Port Dundas Pl G2 . . . . . . .241 A3
Port Dundas Rd G4 . . . . . . .241 A4
Port Glasgow High Sch
PA14 . . . . .69 A3
Port Glasgow Ind Est
PA14 . . . . .68 C4
Port Glasgow Rd
Greenock PA15 . . . . .46 C2
Kilmacolm PA13 . . . . .69 A1
Port Ranald dr KA10 . . . . . .229 B2
Port St Glasgow G3 . . . . . . .240 A2

Port St continued
Stirling FK8 . . . . .7 A4
Portal Rd G13 . . . . .95 B4
Portdownie FK1 . . . . .41 B3
Portencross Rd KA23 . . . . .190 B3
Porter Dr KA2 . . . . .227 A3
Porter St 1 G51 . . . . .116 B3
Porterfield Rd
Kilmacolm PA13 . . . . .89 C4
Renfrew PA4 . . . . .94 A2
Porters La ML6 . . . . .123 B1
Porters Well G71 . . . . .140 C3
Portessie PA8 . . . . .73 A1
Porthlenthen PA8 . . . . .73 A1
Porting Cross Pl KA23 . . . .223 A3
Portland Ave KA12 . . . . . . .224 B4
Portland Brae KA11 . . . . . .228 C3
Portland Ct KA1 . . . . .228 C3
Portland Pk ML3 . . . . .162 C1
Portland Pl
Hamilton ML3 . . . . .162 C1
Irvine KA12 . . . . .224 B4
Kilmarnock KA1 . . . . .227 C4
Lanark ML11 . . . . .215 A2
Stevenston KA20 . . . . .217 B4
Portland Place Ind Est
KA20 . . . . .217 B4
Portland Rd
Cumbernauld G68 . . . . .61 C3
Irvine KA12 . . . . .224 B4
Kilmarnock KA1 . . . . .227 C4
Paisley PA2 . . . . .114 A2
Portland Rdbt KA12 . . . . . .219 A1
Portland Sq ML3 . . . . .162 C1
Portland St
Coatbridge ML5 . . . . .122 A4
Kilmarnock KA1 . . . . .222 C1
Troon KA10 . . . . .229 C2
Portland Terr KA10 . . . . . . .229 B1
Portland Wynd 4 ML9 . . . .185 A2
Portmarnock Dr G23 . . . . . .96 C4
Porton Pl PA7 . . . . .72 A2
Portpatrick Rd G60 . . . . . . .72 C4
Portreath Rd G69 . . . . .80 C2
Portree Ave
Coatbridge ML5 . . . . .121 C2
Kilmarnock KA3 . . . . .223 A3
Portree Pl G15 . . . . .74 C2
Portree Terr PA16 . . . . .44 C2
Portsmouth Dr PA19 . . . . . .44 C3
Portsoy PA8 . . . . .73 A1
Portsoy Ave G13 . . . . .94 C4
Portsoy Pl G13 . . . . .94 C4
Portugal St G5 . . . . .117 A3
Portwell ML3 . . . . .162 C1
Possil Cross G22 . . . . .97 B2
Possil Rd G4 . . . . .97 A2
Possilpark & Parkhouse Sta
G22 . . . . .97 A3
Postgate ML3 . . . . .162 C2
Posthill FK10 . . . . .4 B2
Potassels Rd G69 . . . . .100 B4
Potrail Pl ML3 . . . . .162 A2
Potter Cl G32 . . . . .118 C2
Potter Gr G32 . . . . .118 C2
Potter Pl Glasgow G32 . . . .118 C2
Skinflats FK2 . . . . .2 B2
Potter St G32 . . . . .118 C2
Potterhill Ave PA2 . . . . . . .133 C4
Potterhill Rd G53 . . . . .115 A1
Potters Wynd ML11 . . . . . .215 A3
Pottery Pl ML11 . . . . .222 C1
Pottery Pl PA15 . . . . .46 C2
Potts Way ML1 . . . . .142 B4
Powbrone G75 . . . . .180 C3
Powburn Cres G71 . . . . . . .140 B4
Power Plant Rd KA20 . . . . .218 A4
Powfoot St G31 . . . . .118 B3
Powforth Cl ML9 . . . . .184 C2
Powgree Cres KA15 . . . . . .171 B3
Powmill Gdns KA9 . . . . . . .233 B1
Powmill Rd KA9 . . . . .233 B1
Powrie St G33 . . . . .99 B2
Prentice La 5 G71 . . . . . . .141 A4
Prentice Rd ML1 . . . . .163 A1
President Kennedy Dr
FK7 . . . . .12 B2
Preston Pl Glasgow G42 . . .117 A1
Prestondene G66 . . . . .79 A3
Prestonfield G62 . . . . .54 C1
Prestonfield Ave KA9 . . . . .233 B1
Prestwick Acad KA9 . . . . . .233 B1
Prestwick Ct G68 . . . . .61 C2
Prestwick Int Airport Sta
KA9 . . . . .233 B2
Prestwick Pl G77 . . . . .157 A2
Prestwick Rd KA8 . . . . .236 A2
Prestwick Sta KA9 . . . . . . .233 A1
Pretoria Ct G75 . . . . .180 A3
Pretoria Rd FK5 . . . . .23 A1
Priesthill Ind Est G72 . . . .161 B3
Priestfield St G72 . . . . .161 B3
Priesthill & Darnley Sta
G53 . . . . .135 B3
Priesthill Ave G53 . . . . . . .135 B3
Priesthill Cres G53 . . . . . . .135 B3
Priesthill Rd G53 . . . . .135 B3
Priestknowe Rdbt G74 . . . .159 C1
Priestland Ct KA3 . . . . .223 A3
Prieston Rd PA11 . . . . .110 B4
Primrose Ave
Bellshill ML4 . . . . .142 A4
Larkhall ML9 . . . . .199 A4

Primrose Cres ML1 . . . . . . .163 C3
Primrose Ct 13 G14 . . . . . . .95 B2
Primrose Pk KA7 . . . . .239 B2
Primrose Pl Alloa FK10 . . . . .10 A3
Cumbernauld G67 . . . . .82 A3
Kilmarnock KA1 . . . . .222 B1
Saltcoats KA21 . . . . .206 A1
Uddingston G71 . . . . .141 B4
Primrose St Alloa FK10 . . . . .10 A4
Bonnybridge FK4 . . . . .40 A3
Glasgow G14 . . . . .95 B2
Primrose Way ML8 . . . . . . .201 C4
Prince Albert Rd G12 . . . . . .96 B2
Prince Albert Terr G84 . . . . .16 B1
Prince Edward St 2
G42 . . . . .117 A1
Prince of Wales Gdns
G20 . . . . .96 B4
Prince Pl ML2 . . . . .166 A3
Prince's Gdns G12 . . . . .96 A2
Prince's Pl 23 G12 . . . . .96 B2
Prince's Terr G12 . . . . .96 B2
Princes Ct KA8 . . . . .236 A1
Princes Gardens La G12 . . .96 A2
Princes Mall G74 . . . . .159 C1
Princes Pk KA7 . . . . .239 C2
Princes Pl KA22 . . . . .205 A1
Princes Sq Barrhead G78 . .134 B2
14 East Kilbride G74 . . . . .159 C1
Troon KA10 . . . . .229 C2
Princes Square Shop Ctr
G1 . . . . .241 A2
Princes St
Ardrossan KA22 . . . . .205 A1
Caldercruix ML6 . . . . .105 A3
California FK1 . . . . .66 C3
Falkirk FK1 . . . . .42 A3
Greenock PA15 . . . . .45 C3
Kilmarnock KA1 . . . . .227 C4
Motherwell ML1 . . . . .163 C4
Port Glasgow PA14 . . . . .47 B1
Stirling FK8 . . . . .7 A4
Princess Anne Quadrant
ML1 . . . . .142 C3
Princess Cres PA1 . . . . .114 A3
Princess Ct
Helensburgh G84 . . . . .16 B1
Kilmarnock KA1 . . . . .228 A2
Princess Dr G69 . . . . .121 A3
Princess Rd ML1 . . . . .142 C2
Princess Sq 22 ML2 . . . . . .165 C3
Princess St FK4 . . . . .40 A3
Princess Way G84 . . . . .15 A2
Printers Land G76 . . . . .158 A3
Printers Lea G66 . . . . .57 B4
Priorwood Ct G13 . . . . .95 B3
Priorwood Gate G77 . . . . . .156 A2
Priorwood Way G77 . . . . . .156 A2
Priory Ave PA3 . . . . .114 A4
Priory Dr G71 . . . . .140 B4
Priory Gate ML2 . . . . .186 A4
Priory Pl Cumbernauld G68 . .60 C1
Glasgow G13 . . . . .95 B4
Priory Rd G13 . . . . .95 B4
Priory St G72 . . . . .161 B4
Priory Terr ML2 . . . . .164 B3
Priory Wynd KA13 . . . . .207 B3
Procession Rd PA2 . . . . . . .133 B3
Professors' Sq G12 . . . . .96 B1
Progress Dr ML6 . . . . .105 A3
Promenade KA8 . . . . .236 A2
Propulsives Rd KA20 . . . . .218 A2
Prosen St G32 . . . . .118 C2
Prospect Ave
Cambuslang G72 . . . . .138 C3
Uddingston G71 . . . . .140 C4
Prospect Ct G72 . . . . .161 B3
Prospect Dr ML7 . . . . .199 C4
Prospect Rd Dullatur G68 . .61 B3
Glasgow G41 . . . . .136 B4
Prospect St FK1 . . . . .41 C3
Prospecthill Cir G42 . . . . . .117 C1
Prospecthill Cres G42 . . . . .117 C1
Prospecthill Ct G42 . . . . . .137 B4
Prospecthill Pl
Glasgow G42 . . . . .137 C4
Greenock PA15 . . . . .45 C2
Prospecthill Rd
Falkirk FK1 . . . . .42 A1
Glasgow G42 . . . . .137 B4
Saltcoats KA21 . . . . .206 A1
Prospecthill Sq G42 . . . . . .137 C4
Provan Hall* G34 . . . . .99 C1
Provan Rd G33 . . . . .98 B1
Provand Hall Cres G69 . . . .120 A2
Provand's Lordship Ho*
G4 . . . . .241 C3
Provanhall Prim Sch
G34 . . . . .100 A1
Provanhill St G21 . . . . .97 C1
Provanmill Rd G33 . . . . .98 A1
Provost Ct PA5 . . . . .111 C2
Provost Driver Ct PA4 . . . . .94 C1
Provost Gate ML9 . . . . .185 A2
Provost Hunter Ave FK12 . . .5 B4
Pullar Ave FK9 . . . . .2 A2
Pullar Ct FK9 . . . . .2 A2
Pundeavon Ave KA25 . . . . .149 A2
Purdie G75 . . . . .160 B3
Purdie St ML3 . . . . .162 A3
Purdon St G11 . . . . .96 A1

Primrose Cres ML1 . . . . . . .163 C3

Putyan Ave KA24 . . . . .191 A4
Pyatshaw Rd ML9 . . . . .185 A1

Q

Quadrant Rd G43 . . . . .136 C3
Quadrant The G76 . . . . . . .157 C4
Quail Rd KA8 . . . . .236 A2
Quakerfield FK7 . . . . .7 C1
Quantock Dr G75 . . . . .180 A2
Quarrelton Rd PA5 . . . . . . .111 B2
Quarrier St PA15 . . . . .46 B2
Quarrolhall Cres FK2 . . . . . .24 A2
Quarry Ave G72 . . . . .139 C2
Quarry Dr Kilmacolm PA13 . .69 B1
Kirkintilloch G66 . . . . .79 C4
Quarry Knowe
Bannockburn FK7 . . . . .11 C4
Dumbarton G82 . . . . .49 B3
Rhu G84 . . . . .15 A3
Quarry La Dumbarton G82 . .49 C2
Eaglesham G76 . . . . .178 B2
Lennoxtown G66 . . . . .33 B1
Quarry Pk G75 . . . . .180 C4
Quarry Pl Alloa FK10 . . . . . .10 B4
Cambuslang G72 . . . . .138 C3
Dumbarton G82 . . . . .49 B3
Hamilton ML3 . . . . .162 C2
Shotts ML7 . . . . .146 B3
Quarry Rd Airdrie ML6 . . . .103 A1
Barrhead G78 . . . . .134 A2
Cambusbarron FK7 . . . . .6 B3
East Kilbride G75 . . . . .180 B3
Larkhall ML9 . . . . .185 A1
Paisley PA2 . . . . .113 C1
Port Glasgow PA14 . . . . .48 A3
Shotts ML7 . . . . .146 B3
Quarry St Coatbridge ML5 . .122 B4
Hamilton ML3 . . . . .162 C2
Johnstone PA5 . . . . .111 C1
Larkhall ML9 . . . . .185 A1
Motherwell ML1 . . . . .143 A2
Shotts ML7 . . . . .147 B3
Wishaw ML2 . . . . .165 A2
Quarrybank PA10 . . . . .111 B1
Quarrybrae Gdns G71 . . . . .141 B3
Quarrybrae Prim Sch
G31 . . . . .118 B3
Quarrybrae St G31 . . . . . . .118 C3
Quarryknowe
Lanark ML11 . . . . .215 A2
Rutherglen G73 . . . . .137 C4
Quarryknowe Pl ML4 . . . . .141 C2
Quarryknowe St
Clydebank G81 . . . . .74 C4
Glasgow G31 . . . . .118 C3
Quarryside St ML6 . . . . . . .102 C2
Quarrywood Ave G21 . . . . . .98 B2
Quarrywood Rd G21 . . . . . . .98 B2
Quarter Prim Sch ML3 . . . .183 C2
Quay (Leisure Complex) The
G5 . . . . .240 C1
Quay Pend G82 . . . . .49 C2
Quay Rd G73 . . . . .118 A1
Quay Road N G73 . . . . .118 A1
Quay St Dumbarton G82 . . . .49 C2
Saltcoats KA21 . . . . .216 C4
Quebec Dr G75 . . . . .159 B1
Quebec Gn G75 . . . . .159 B1
Quebec Wynd G32 . . . . .139 B4
Queen Elizabeth Ave
G52 . . . . .114 C4
Queen Elizabeth Ct
Clydebank G81 . . . . .74 A2
Motherwell ML1 . . . . .163 B4
Queen Elizabeth Gdns
G81 . . . . .74 A2
Queen Elizabeth Sq 11
G5 . . . . .117 B2
Queen Margaret Acad
KA7 . . . . .239 B2
Queen Margaret Ct 6
G20 . . . . .96 C2
Queen Margaret Dr
Glasgow G20 . . . . .96 C2
Glasgow G20 . . . . .96 B2
Queen Mary Ave
Clydebank G81 . . . . .74 B1
Glasgow G42 . . . . .117 A1
Queen Mary Gdns G81 . . . . .74 A2
Queen Mary St G40 . . . . . .118 A2
Queen Mother's Hospl The
G3 .96 B1
Queen Sq G41 . . . . .116 C2
Queen Rd KA12 . . . . .219 B3
Queen Sq G41 . . . . .116 C1
Queen St Alexandria G83 . . .27 B2
Alloa FK10 . . . . .10 A4
Alva FK12 . . . . .5 A4
Ayr KA8 . . . . .236 A1
Bannockburn FK7 . . . . .7 B1
Falkirk FK2 . . . . .42 B3
Fallin FK7 . . . . .8 B2
Glasgow G1 . . . . .241 A2
Helensburgh G84 . . . . .16 B2
11 Kilmarnock KA1 . . . . . .227 C4
Kilwinning KA13 . . . . .208 A2
Kirkintilloch G66 . . . . .79 B4
Motherwell ML1 . . . . .163 C4
Paisley PA1 . . . . .113 B2
Port Glasgow PA14 . . . . .47 B1
Renfrew PA4 . . . . .94 B2
Rutherglen G73 . . . . .138 A4

Queen St continued
Stirling FK8 . . . . 7 A4
Stonehouse ML9 . . . . .198 C1
Wishaw ML2 . . . . .165 C3
Queen Street Sta G1 . . . . .241 A3
Queen Victoria Ct G14 . . . . .95 B2
Queen Victoria Dr G14 . . . . .95 B2
Queen Victoria Dr G4 . . . . .95 B2
Queen Victoria Gate G13 . . . . . .95 B3
Queen Victoria St ML6 . . . . . . .122 C4
Queen's Ave Bridge of d FK9 . .2 A3
Cambuslang G72 . . . . .139 A3
Queen's Cres
Carluke ML8 . . . . .188 A1
Chapelhall ML6 . . . . .123 B2
Coatbridge G69 . . . . .120 C3
Falkirk FK1 . . . . .41 C3
7 Glasgow G4 . . . . .97 A1
Queen's Ct FK9 . . . . .1 C4
Queen's Ct G84 . . . . .25 A4
Queen's Ct G62 . . . . .76 A4
Queen's Dr Alexandria G83 . . .27 B2
Ardrossan KA22 . . . . .205 B2
Cumbernauld G68 . . . . .61 C3
Glasgow G42 . . . . .117 A1
Kilmarnock KA1 . . . . .228 A3
Monkton KA9 . . . . .233 B3
Stenhousemuir FK5 . . . . .23 B1
Troon KA10 . . . . .229 C3
Queen's Drive La G42 . . . . . . .117 A1
Queen's Gate G76 . . . . .157 C4
Queen's Gdns G12 . . . . .96 B2
Queen's La FK9 . . . . .2 A4
Queen's Park Ave G42 . . . . . . .117 A1
Queen's Park Sta G42 . . . . . . .117 A1
Queen's Pl Glasgow G12 . . . . . .96 B2
Kilwinning KA13 . . . . .208 A2
Queen's Quadrant KA8 . . . . . .236 A1
Queen's Rd Elderslie PA5 . . . . .112 B1
Stirling FK8 . . . . .6 C3
Queen's St California FK1 . . . . .66 C3
Cleland ML1 . . . . .144 A1
Queen's Terr KA7 . . . . .238 C4
Queen's Terrace La KA7 .238 C4
Queens Cres
Bellshill ML4 . . . . .141 C2
Motherwell ML1 . . . . .142 C2
Queens Ct Ayr KA7 . . . . .238 C4
Irvine KA12 . . . . .219 B1
Stenhousemuir FK5 . . . . .23 B2
Queens Dr Bishopton PA7 . . . .72 B2
Denny FK6 . . . . .21 C2
Falkirk FK1 . . . . .41 B3
Hamilton ML3 . . . . .183 B3
Queens Point G84 . . . . .15 A4
Queens Terr KA9 . . . . .233 A1
Queens Way
Alexandria G83 . . . . .27 B2
Torrance G64 . . . . .78 A4
Queensbank Ave G69 . .100 C4
Queensberry Ave
Bearsden G61 . . . . .75 C4
Clarkston G76 . . . . .157 C4
Queensborough Gdns
G12 .96 A2
Queensby Ave 10 G69 . . . . . . .120 A3
Queensby Dr G69 . . . . .120 A3
Queensby Pl G69 . . . . .120 B3
Queensby Rd G69 . . . . .120 B3
Queensdale Ave ML9 . . . . . . .199 A4
Queensdale Rd ML9 . . . . .199 A4
Queensferry St G5 . . . . .117 C1
Queenshaugh Dr FK8 . . . . .2 B1
Queenside Cres PA8 . . . . .72 C1
Queensland Ct G52 . . . . .115 B3
Queensland Dr G52 . . . . .115 B3
Queensland Gdns G52 . . . . . .115 B3
Queensland La E G52 . . . . . . .115 B3
Queensland La W G52 . . . . . .115 B3
Queensle Ind Est G33 . . . . . . .119 B4
Queenslie St G33 . . . . .98 B1
Queensway
East Kilbride G74 . . . . .159 B1
Gourock PA19 . . . . .44 B3
Queenzieburn Ind Est
G65 . . . . .59 C4
Quendale Dr G32 . . . . .118 C2
Quentin St G41 . . . . .116 C1
Quinton Gdns G69 . . . . .120 A3

R

Raasay Cres ML6 . . . . .123 C3
Raasay Dr PA2 . . . . .133 B4
Raasay Gdns G77 . . . . .156 A3
Raasay Pl Glasgow G22 . . . . . .97 B4
Kilmarnock KA3 . . . . .223 A3
Raasay St G22 . . . . .97 B4
Racecourse Rd KA7 . .238 C3
Racecourse View
Ayr KA7 . . . . .238 C3
Hamilton ML3 . . . . .162 C3
Rachan St G34 . . . . .100 B1
Radleigh Sch G76 . . . . .157 B4
Radnor St Clydebank G81 . . . . .74 A2
Glasgow G3 . . . . .96 B1
Rae Ct FK2 . . . . .24 B2
Rae St FK5 . . . . .23 B2
Raeberry St G20 . . . . .96 C2
Raeburn Cres ML6 . . . . .102 C2
Raeburn Pl G74 . . . . .160 A2
Raeburn Cres ML3 . . . . .161 C2
Raeburn Pl G74 . . . . .160 A2
Raeburn Wlk ML4 . . . . .142 A4

Raes Rd ML8 . . . . .201 A4
Raeside Ave G77 . . . . .156 B2
Raeswood Dr G53 . . . . .134 C4
Raeswood Pl 3 G53 . . . . .135 A4
Raeswood Rd G53 . . . . .134 C4
Raewell Cres ML4 . . . . .141 C2
Rafford St G51 . . . . .116 A4
Raggithill Ave KA6 . . . . .237 C3
Raglan St Glasgow G83 . . . . . . .27 C2
Glasgow G4 . . . . .97 A1
Raglan Street La G83 . . . . .27 C2
Railway Rd ML6 . . . . .122 B4
Raise St KA21 . . . . .216 C4
Raith Ave Glasgow G45 . . . . . .137 B2
Prestwick KA9 . . . . .236 C4
Raith Dr Bellshill ML4 . . . . .142 A2
Cumbernauld G68 . . . . .60 B1
Raith Rd KA3 . . . . .213 A2
Raith Terr KA9 . . . . .236 C4
Raithburn Ave
Glasgow G45 . . . . .137 B2
Kilmarnock KA3 . . . . .222 C2
Raithburn Rd G45 . . . . .137 B2
Raithhill KA7 . . . . .239 A1
Raleigh Ct FK1 . . . . .41 C3
Ralston Ave PA1,G52 . . . . .114 C2
Ralston Ct G52 . . . . .114 C2
Ralston Dr
Crookedholm KA3 . . . . .228 B4
Glasgow G52 . . . . .114 C2
Ralston Path G52 . . . . .114 C2
Ralston Pl G52 . . . . .114 C2
Ralston Prim Sch G52 . . . . . . .114 C2
Ralston Rd Barrhead G78 . . . .134 B1
Bearsden G61 . . . . .75 C3
Ralston St Airdrie ML6 . . . . . . .122 C4
Paisley PA1 . . . . .114 A2
Ralstonyards Rd KA3 . . . . . . .228 C4
Ram St G32 . . . . .118 C3
Ramage Rd ML8 . . . . .188 A1
Ramillies Ct ML8 . . . . .188 A1
Ramoth ML11 . . . . .214 B2
Rampart Ave G13 . . . . .95 A4
Ramsay Ave
Johnstone PA5 . . . . .111 C1
Laurieston PA2 . . . . .42 C2
Ramsay Cres PA10 . . . . .111 A1
Ramsay Ct G77 . . . . .156 C2
Ramsay Hill G74 . . . . .160 A2
Ramsay Pl
Coatbridge ML5 . . . . .121 B3
Johnstone PA5 . . . . .111 C1
Stirling FK8 . . . . .2 A1
Ramsay St G81 . . . . .73 C2
Ramsey Ind Est G66 . . . . .58 A1
Ramsey Tullis Ave FK10 . . . . . .4 B1
Ramsey Tullis Dr FK10 . . . . . . .4 B1
Ramsey Wynd ML4 . . . . .142 A4
Ramstane Pl KA11 . . . . .220 B3
Ranald Gdns G73 . . . . .138 B2
Randolph Ave G76 . . . . .137 A1
Randolph Cres FK7 . . . . .7 B1
Randolph Ct FK8 . . . . .7 A3
Randolph Dr G76 . . . . .136 C1
Randolph Gate G11 . . . . .95 C2
Randolph Gdns
Denny FK6 . . . . .21 B1
Glasgow G76 . . . . .136 C1
Randolph La G11 . . . . .95 C2
Randolph Pl FK7 . . . . .7 B1
Randolph Rd Glasgow G11 . . . .95 C2
Stirling FK8 . . . . .7 A2
Randolph Terr FK7 . . . . .7 A2
Randyford St FK2 . . . . .42 B3
Ranfurly Ct PA11 . . . . .110 B4
Ranfurly Dr G68 . . . . .61 C2
Ranfurly Pl PA11 . . . . .110 B4
Ranfurly Rd
Bridge of W PA11 . . . . .110 C3
Glasgow G52 . . . . .114 C3
Range Ave ML1 . . . . .164 B2
Range Rd ML1 . . . . .164 A2
Range Road Ind Est
ML2 . . . . .164 B2
Range St ML1 . . . . .164 A2
Rangerhouse Rd G75 . . . . . . .180 C3
Ranken Cres KA12 . . . . .219 B2
Rankin Cres
Bonnybridge FK4 . . . . .39 B3
Greengairs ML6 . . . . .83 C1
Rankin Ct Chryston G69 . . . . .100 B4
Kilmarnock KA3 . . . . .223 B2
Rankin Dr G77 . . . . .156 B3
Rankin Rd ML2 . . . . .165 C2
Rankin St Carluke ML8 . . . . . .187 C1
Greenock PA16 . . . . .45 B2
Rankin Way G78 . . . . .134 C2
Rankine Ave G75 . . . . .181 A4
Rankine Pl
East Kilbride G75 . . . . .181 A4
Johnstone PA5 . . . . .111 C2
Rankine St PA5 . . . . .111 C2
Rankine Wynd FK10 . . . . .4 B1
Rannoch Ave
Bishopbriggs G64 . . . . .78 A1
Coatbridge ML5 . . . . .101 B1
Hamilton ML3 . . . . .162 A1
Newton Mearns G77 . . . . .156 B4
Rannoch Cl KA3 . . . . .195 B1
Rannoch Ct Alloa FK10 . . . . .3 A3
Cumbernauld G67 . . . . .82 A3
Hamilton G72 . . . . .161 C3
Rannoch Dr Bearsden G61 . . .76 A2
Cumbernauld G67 . . . . .82 A3
Kirkintilloch G66 . . . . .59 A1
Renfrew PA4 . . . . .94 B2

Rannoch Dr continued
Wishaw ML2 . . . . .165 A1
Rannoch Gdns G64 . . . . .78 B1
Rannoch Gn G74 . . . . .159 C2
Rannoch Pl Irvine KA12 . . . . . .219 B3
Paisley PA2 . . . . .114 A2
Shieldhill FK1 . . . . .66 C4
Shotts ML7 . . . . .146 C3
Stenhousemuir FK5 . . . . .23 C2
Rannoch Rd Airdrie ML6 . . . . .102 C1
Johnstone PA5 . . . . .131 C4
Kilmacolm PA13 . . . . .89 B4
Uddingston G71 . . . . .120 C1
Rannoch St G44 . . . . .137 A3
Rannoch Terr ML9 . . . . .185 B1
Rannoch Way 7 G71 . . . . . . .141 A2
Rannoch La G69 . . . . .81 A1
Raploch Ave G14 . . . . .95 A2
Raploch Cres G81 . . . . .74 B4
Raploch La G14 . . . . .95 A2
Raploch Prim Sch FK8 . . . . . . .1 C1
Raploch Rd Larkhall ML9 . .184 C2
Stirling FK8 . . . . .1 C1
Raploch St ML9 . . . . .184 C2
Rashieburn PA8 . . . . .73 A1
Rashieglen PA8 . . . . .73 A1
Rashiehill Rd FK1 . . . . .86 A3
Rashielee Ave PA8 . . . . .73 A1
Rashielee Prim Sch PA8 . . .73 A1
Rashielee Rd PA8 . . . . .73 A1
Rashiewood PA8 . . . . .73 A1
Rashley Sq KA22 . . . . .205 B2
Rathlin Ave KA1 . . . . .227 C2
Rathlin Ho KA9 . . . . .236 A3
Rathlin St G51 . . . . .116 A4
Rathlin Terr G82 . . . . .49 B3
Ratho Dr Cumbernauld G68 . .61 C3
Glasgow G21 . . . . .97 C2
Ratho Pk ML3 . . . . .183 A4
Ratho St PA15 . . . . .46 B2
Rattray PA8 . . . . .73 A2
Rattray St G32 . . . . .118 C2
Ravel Row G31 . . . . .118 B3
Ravel Wynd G71 . . . . .141 A4
Ravelston Rd G61 . . . . .75 C1
Ravelston St G32 . . . . .118 C3
Raven Rd PA16 . . . . .45 A3
Raven Wynd ML2 . . . . .165 A2
Ravens Ct 8 G64 . . . . .97 C4
Ravenscliffe Dr G46 . . . . .136 A2
Ravenscourt C74 . . . . .158 B1
Ravenscraig Ave PA2 . . . . . . .113 B1
Ravenscraig Ct ML4 . . . . .142 A3
Ravenscraig Dr G53 . . . . .135 B3
Ravenscraig Hospl PA16 . .45 C2
Ravenscraig Prim Sch
PA16 .44 C2
Ravenscraig Terr G53 . . . . . . .135 B3
Ravenscroft KA12 . . . . .219 A3
Ravenshall ML1 . . . . .165 A4
Ravenshall Rd G41 . . . . .136 B4
Ravenshill Dr ML1 . . . . .144 B1
Ravenstone Dr G46 . . . . .136 A2
Ravenswood Ave ML6 . . . . . . .103 A1
Ravenswood Dr G41 . . . . .116 B1
Ravenswood Rd G69 . . . . .100 C3
Raymond Pl G75 . . . . .159 B1
Rayne Pl G15 . . . . .75 A2
Ream Ave ML6 . . . . .123 C3
Reay Ave Cardross G82 . . . . . .48 A4
Reay Ave G74 . . . . .159 A1
Reay Gdns G74 . . . . .159 A1
Recawr Pk KA7 . . . . .239 A2
Red Bridge Ct ML5 . . . . .122 A4
Red Deer Rd G81 . . . . .180 B4
Red Fox Ct G83 . . . . .27 C4
Red Fox Terr G83 . . . . .27 C4
Red Gables Sq KA22 . . . . . . .205 A2
Red Road G21 . . . . .98 A2
Red Road Ct G21 . . . . .98 A2
Red Row G82 . . . . .27 B1
Redan St 6 G40 . . . . .117 C3
Redburn Ave G46 . . . . .157 A4
Redburn Ct G67 . . . . .62 C3
Redburn Ind Est KA12 . . .219 B4
Redburn Pl G67 . . . . .62 C3
Redburn Rd
Blackridge EH48 . . . . .107 A1
Cumbernauld G67 . . . . .62 C3
Irvine KA12 . . . . .219 A3
Redburn Rdbt KA12 . . . . . . .219 A4
Redburn Sch G67 . . . . .62 B1
Redcastle Sq G33 . . . . .99 B1
Redcliffe Dr G75 . . . . .180 A4
Redclyffe Gdns G84 . . . . .16 B2
Reddance Terr KA24 . . . . .191 A4
Reddans Pk KA3 . . . . .195 B1
Redding Ave KA3 . . . . .222 C2
Redding Rd FK2 . . . . .42 C2
Rederech Cres ML3 . . . . .161 C1
Redford St G33 . . . . .118 B4
Redgate Pl G14 . . . . .95 A2
Redgauntlet Rd G84 . . . . .25 B4
Redgrave G71 . . . . .140 B4
Redhaws Rd ML7 . . . . .147 A2
Redhill Rd G68 . . . . .61 B2

Redhills View G66 . . . . .57 C4
Redholme ML9 . . . . .185 A1
Redhouse La ML8 . . . . .187 C2
Redhurst Cres PA2 . . . . .133 B4
Redhurst La PA2 . . . . .133 B4
Redhurst Way PA2 . . . . .133 B4
Redlands La G12 . . . . .96 B2
Redlands Rd
46 Glasgow G12 . . . . .96 B2
Tullibody FK10 . . . . .4 A2
Redlands Terr 34 G12 . . . . . . .96 B2
Redlands Terrace La 44
G12 .96 B2
Redlawood Pl G72 . . . . .140 A3
Redlawood Rd G72 . . . . .140 A3
Redmire Cres ML7 . . . . .167 A4
Redmoss Rd
Clydebank G81 . . . . .73 C4
Milton of C G66 . . . . .58 B1
Redmoss St G22 . . . . .97 A3
Redmoss St G22 . . . . .97 B2
Rednock St Glasgow G22 . .115 B3
Stenhousemuir FK2 . . . . .24 A2
Redpath Dr Glasgow G52 . . . .115 B3
Stenhousemuir FK2 . . . . .24 A2
Redwell Pl FK10 . . . . .9 C4
Redwing Gdns ML2 . . . . .165 A1
Redwood Ave G74 . . . . .158 C1
Redwood Cres
Bishopton PA7 . . . . .72 B2
Cambuslang G72 . . . . .139 C2
East Kilbride G74 . . . . .158 C1
Uddingston G71 . . . . .141 B4
Redwood Ct G74 . . . . .179 C4
Redwood Dr
East Kilbride G74 . . . . .158 C1
Glasgow G21 . . . . .98 A2
Redwood Gr ML5 . . . . .122 A3
Redwood Pl
East Kilbride G74 . . . . .158 C1
Kirkintilloch G66 . . . . .79 A3
Uddingston G71 . . . . .141 B4
Redwood Rd
Cumbernauld G67 . . . . .62 C2
Motherwell ML1 . . . . .143 A3
Redwood Way G72 . . . . .139 C2
Reedlands Dr FK6 . . . . .39 B4
Reedloch Dr KA10 . . . . .229 D4
Reek St KA15 . . . . .171 C4
Reelick Ave G13 . . . . .94 C4
Reelick Quadrant G13 . . . . . . .94 C4
Reema Rd ML4 . . . . .142 A3
Reen Pf G71 . . . . .141 A2
Reform St KA15 . . . . .150 A1
Regal Ct G44 . . . . .191 B4
Regal Gr ML7 . . . . .146 C2
Regency Way
Hamilton ML3 . . . . .183 A4
Motherwell ML1 . . . . .142 C2
Regent G73 . . . . .138 A4
Regent Moray St G3 . . . . .96 B1
Regent Park Sq G41 . . . . .116 C1
Regent Pk G49 . . . . .233 B1
Regent Pl G81 . . . . .73 C2
Regent Sq G66 . . . . .79 B2
Regent St Clydebank G81 . . . . .73 C2
Greenock PA15 . . . . .45 C2
Kirkintilloch G66 . . . . .79 B4
Paisley PA1 . . . . .114 A3
Regents Gate G72 . . . . .140 B2
Register Ave ML4 . . . . .142 A2
Register Rd G65 . . . . .60 B4
Reid Ave Bearsden G61 . . . . . .76 A3
Reid Gr ML1 . . . . .143 C4
Reid Kerr Coll PA3 . . . . .113 C4
Reid Rd G40 . . . . .117 C2
Reid St Airdrie ML6 . . . . .103 A1
Coatbridge ML5 . . . . .122 A4
Glasgow G40 . . . . .117 C2
Hamilton ML3 . . . . .161 C1
Rutherglen G73 . . . . .138 A4
Salsburgh ML7 . . . . .125 A1
Reid Terr KA21 . . . . .217 A4
Reidhouse St G21 . . . . .98 A2
Reidvale St G31 . . . . .118 A3
Reilly Gdns FK4 . . . . .40 A3
Reilly Rd
High Bonnybridge FK4 . . . . . . .40 A2
Houston PA6 . . . . .91 B4
Reith Dr G75 . . . . .180 B4
Remus Pl ML4 . . . . .142 C3
Renfield La G2 . . . . .240 C2
Renfield St Glasgow G2 . . . . .240 C2
Renfrew PA4 . . . . .94 B2
Renfrew Ct G2 . . . . .241 A3
Renfrew High Sch PA4 . . . . . . .94 B1
Renfrew La G2 . . . . .240 C2
Renfrew Rd
Glasgow PA4,G51 . . . . .95 A1
Paisley PA3 . . . . .113 C4
Renfrew St
Coatbridge ML5 . . . . .122 A2
Glasgow G3 . . . . .240 C3
Rennie Bsns Units KA21 .217 A4
Rennie Pl
East Kilbride G74 . . . . .159 A2
Saltcoats KA21 . . . . .216 C4
Rennie Rd G65 . . . . .36 A1
Rennie St ML1 . . . . .143 B4
Renshaw Dr G52 . . . . .115 A3
Renshaw Rd
Bishopton PA7 . . . . .72 A2
Elderslie PA5 . . . . .112 B1

Renton Pk KA11 . . . . .220 B4
Renton Prim Sch G82 . . . . .27 B1
Renton Rd Dumbarton G82 . .49 B3
Greenock PA15 . . . . .46 B3
Renton St G4 . . . . .241 A4
Renton Sta G82 . . . . .27 B1
Renwick Pl ML11 . . . . .215 B3
Renwick Way KA9 . . . . .236 B3
Reservoir Rd PA19 . . . . .44 C3
Resipol Rd G33 . . . . .99 C3
Reston Dr G52 . . . . .115 A3
Reuther Ave G73 . . . . .138 A4
Revoch Dr G13 . . . . .95 A4
Reynolds Ave G75 . . . . .181 A3
Reynolds Dr G33 . . . . .99 C3
Reynolds Path ML2 . . . . .165 B1
Rhannan Rd G44 . . . . .137 A3
Rhannan Terr G44 . . . . .137 A3
Rhindhouse Pl G69 . . . . .120 B3
Rhindhouse Rd G69 . . . . .120 B3
Rhindmuir Ave G69 . . . . .120 B3
Rhindmuir Cres G69 . . . . .120 B3
Rhindmuir Dr G69 . . . . .120 B3
Rhindmuir Gdns G69 . . . . . . .120 B3
Rhindmuir Gr G69 . . . . .120 B3
Rhindmuir Path G69 . . . . .120 B3
Rhindmuir Pl G69 . . . . .120 B3
Rhindmuir Rd G69 . . . . .120 B3
Rhindmuir View G69 . . . . .120 B3
Rhindmuir Wynd G69 . . . . . . .120 B3
Rhinds St ML5 . . . . .121 B2
Rhinsdale Cres G69 . . . . .120 B3
Rhodders Gr FK12 . . . . .5 A4
Rhu Prim Sch G84 . . . . .15 A3
Rhu Quad ML7 . . . . .186 B3
Rhu Rd Lower
Helensburgh G84 . . . . .16 A1
Rhu G84 . . . . .15 C2
Rhu Road Higher G84 . . . . . . .16 A2
Rhu-Ellen Ct G84 . . . . .15 B2
Rhumhor Gdns PA5 . . . . .111 B1
Rhyber Ave ML11 . . . . .215 A3
Rhymer St G21 . . . . .97 C1
Rhymie Rd G32 . . . . .119 B2
Rhymnhaugh ML9 . . . . .198 B1
Rhynie Dr G51 . . . . .116 A3
Riach Gdns ML1 . . . . .142 B1
Ribblesdale G74 . . . . .159 B2
Riccarton G75 . . . . .180 A4
Riccarton Rd KA1 . . . . .228 B3
Riccarton St G42 . . . . .117 B1
Riccartsbar Ave PA2 . . . . .113 B2
Rice Way ML1 . . . . .164 A2
Richard Pl KA10 . . . . .229 C2
Richard Quinn St FK7 . . . . .7 B4
Richard St G2 . . . . .240 B2
Richardland Pl KA1 . . . . .228 A4
Richardland Rd 10 KA1 . .227 C4
Richardson Ave KA1 . . . . .228 C3
Richie Ave G82 . . . . .48 A4
Richmond Ave G76 . . . . .157 C4
Richmond Ct
Bishopbriggs 78 A2
Greenock PA15 . . . . .46 A3
Rutherglen G73 . . . . .138 B4
Rutherglen, Cambuslang
G72 .138 C3
Richmond Gdns G69 . . . . .100 A4
Richmond Gr G73 . . . . .138 B4
Richmond Park Sch G5 . . .117 B2
Richmond Pl G73 . . . . .138 B4
Richmond St
Clydebank G81 . . . . .74 B1
Glasgow G1 . . . . .241 B2
Richmond Terr KA2 . . . . .225 C1
Riddell St Clydebank G81 . . . . .74 B2
Coatbridge ML5 . . . . .122 B4
Riddon Ave G13,G81 . . . . .94 C4
Riddon Pl G13 . . . . .94 C4
Riddrie Cres G33 . . . . .118 C4
Riddrie Knowes G33 . . . . .118 C4
Riddrievale Ct G33 . . . . .98 C1
Riddrievale St G33 . . . . .98 C1
Ridgepark Dr ML11 . . . . .214 C3
Ridgepark Sch ML11 . . . . . . .214 C3
Rig St KA3 . . . . .211 B4
Rigby St G32 . . . . .118 C3
Rigfoot KA11 . . . . .220 A3
Rigg Pl G33 . . . . .119 C4
Rigghead KA3 . . . . .211 B4
Righead Gdns G75 . . . . .233 B1
Riggside Rd G33 . . . . .99 B1
Righead Gate G74 . . . . .159 C1
Righead Ind Est ML4 . . . . . . .141 B1
Righead Rdbt G75 . . . . .159 B1
Riglands Gate PA4 . . . . .94 B2
Riglands Way PA4 . . . . .94 B2
Riglaw Pl G13 . . . . .95 A3
Rigmuir Rd G51 . . . . .115 B4
Rigwoodie Pl KA7 . . . . .238 C1
Rimmon Cres ML7 . . . . .146 C3
Rimsdale St G40 . . . . .117 C3
Ring Rd FK10 . . . . .4 A1
Ringford St G21 . . . . .97 C2
Ripon Dr G12 . . . . .96 A3
Risk St Clydebank G81 . . . . . . .73 C2
Dumbarton G82 . . . . .49 C2
Ritchie Ct G53 . . . . .95 A3
Ritchie Cres PA5 . . . . .112 B3
Ritchie Cr ML11 . . . . .223 B1
Ritchie Pk PA5 . . . . .112 B3
Ritchie Pl G77 . . . . .156 B2
Ritchie St 5 Glasgow G5 . . . .117 A2

Ritchie St *continued*
West Kilbride KA23 190 B3
Wishaw ML2 164 B2
Ritchie's Cl ML11 215 A2
River Ct G76 157 C3
River Dr PA4 93 B2
River Pl KA25 149 A1
River Rd G32 139 A4
River St Ayr KA8 235 C1
Falkirk FK2 24 A1
River Terr KA8 235 C1
River View Cres G82 48 A4
River Wlk KA13 207 C3
Riverbank Dr ML4 142 B2
Riverbank Pl KA1 228 A4
Riverbank St G43 136 B4
Riverbank View FK8 7 B4
Riverdale Gdns ML3 162 C1
Riverford Rd
Glasgow G43 136 B4
Rutherglen G73 118 B1
Riversdale La G14 95 A2
Riverside Balloch G83 27 C4
Houston PA6 91 B1
Milngavie G62 55 A1
Riverside Bsns Pk KA11 224 D4
Riverside Ct G76 157 C1
Riverside Dr FK8 2 B1
Riverside Gdns
Balloch G83 27 C4
Clarkston G76 157 C3
Gourock PA19 44 C4
Riverside La G82 49 C2
Riverside Pk G44 137 A1
Riverside Pl Ayr KA8 239 A4
Cambuslang G72 139 C3
Irvine KA11 225 A4
Kilbirnie KA25 149 A1
Riverside Prim Sch FK8 2 A1
Riverside Rd
Eaglesham G76 178 C4
Glasgow G43 136 C4
Greenock PA15 46 A2
Irvine KA11 220 B1
Kilbirnie KA25 149 A1
Kirkfieldbank ML11 214 B2
Larkhall ML9 199 A4
Stewarton KA3 211 C4
Riverside Rdbt KA11 225 A4
Riverside Ret Pk KA12 219 A1
Riverside Terr G76 157 C3
Riverside View FK10 10 A2
Riverside Way KA11 224 D4
Riverside Wlk ML1 163 C4
Riverton Dr G75 180 A4
Riverview Dr G5 240 B1
Riverview Gdns G5 240 B1
Riverview Pl G5 240 B1
Riverway KA12 219 A1
Riverway Ret Pk KA12 219 A1
Roaden Ave PA2 132 C4
Roaden Rd PA2 132 C4
Roadhead PA12 150 C4
Roadmeetings Hospl
ML8 202 B4
Roadside G67 62 A3
Roadside Pl ML6 103 B4
Robb Terr G66 80 A3
Robert Bruce Ct FK5 23 A1
Robert Burns Ave
Clydebank G81 74 B2
Motherwell ML1 143 C2
Robert Burns Ct KA15 150 A1
Robert Burns Quadrant
ML4 141 C3
Robert Creighton Pl
KA3 222 C1
Robert Dick Ct FK10 4 B1
Robert Dr G51 116 A4
Robert Gilson Gdns
ML5 122 A3
Robert Hardie Ct FK5 23 B1
Robert Kinmond Ave FK10 4 B1
Robert Knox Ave FK10 4 B1
Robert Noble Pl KA1 222 B1
Robert Owen Meml Prim Sch
ML11 215 B2
Robert Smillie Cres
ML9 185 A1
Robert Smillie Meml Prim
Sch ML9 185 A1
Robert St Glasgow G51 116 A4
Port Glasgow PA14 47 C1
Shotts ML7 146 C2
Robert Stewart Pl KA1 222 C1
Robert Templeton Dr
G72 139 A3
Robert W Service Ct
KA13 207 C1
Robert Wynd ML2 166 A3
Robertland Rigg KA3 195 C1
Robertland Sq KA3 211 C4
Roberton Ave G41 116 B1
Roberton St ML6 123 C2
Roberts Quadrant ML4 142 A2
Roberts St Clydebank G81 73 C2
Wishaw ML2 165 A2
Robertson Ave
Bonnybridge FK4 40 A3
Renfrew PA4 94 A2
Robertson Cl PA4 94 B2
Robertson Cres Ayr KA8 236 B1
Neilston G78 154 B4
Saltcoats KA21 217 A4
Robertson Ct FK5 23 B1
Robertson Dr
Bellshill ML4 142 A2
East Kilbride G74 160 A1

Robertson Dr *continued*
Renfrew PA4 94 A2
Robertson La G2 240 C2
Robertson Pl
Kilmarnock KA1 228 A4
Stirling FK7 7 A2
Robertson Rd KA9 233 B2
Robertson St
Airdrie ML6 122 C4
Alva FK12 5 A4
Barrhead G78 134 A1
Glasgow G1, G2 240 C2
Greenock PA16 45 C3
Hamilton ML3 161 C3
Robertson Terr G69 120 B3
Robin Pl ML2 165 A2
Robin Rd PA16 45 A3
Robin Way G32 139 B4
Robroyston Ave G33 98 C2
Robroyston Rd
Bishopbriggs G64 78 C1
Glasgow, Barmulloch G33 98 B2
Glasgow, Blackhill G33 98 C2
Glasgow, Robroyston G33 98 C3
Kirkintilloch G66 79 A2
Robshill Ct G77 156 B2
Robsland Ave KA7 238 C3
Robslee Cres G46 136 A2
Robslee Dr G46 136 A2
Robslee Prim Sch G46 136 A1
Robslee Rd G46 136 A2
Robson Gr 16 G42 117 A2
Rocep Dr PA4 94 C1
Rochdale Pl 1 G66 79 B4
Roche Way KA24 191 B4
Rochsoles Cres ML6 103 A1
Rochsoles Dr ML6 103 A1
Rochsolloch Farm Cotts
ML6 122 C4
Rochsolloch Prim Sch
ML6 122 C3
Rochsolloch Rd ML6 122 B3
Rock Dr PA10 111 A1
Rock St G4 97 A2
Rockall Dr G44 137 B2
Rockbank Pl
Clydebank G81 74 B3
Glasgow G40 118 A3
Rockbank St G40 118 A3
Rockburn Cres ML4 142 A4
Rockburn Dr G76 157 B4
Rockcliffe St G40 117 C2
Rockfield Pl G21 98 B3
Rockfield Rd G21 98 B3
Rockhampton Ave G75 180 A4
Rockliffe Path ML6 123 C1
Rockmount Ave
Barrhead G78 134 B1
Glasgow G46 136 A2
Rockrose Pk KA7 239 A2
Rockwell Ave PA2 133 B4
Rodding The ML11 215 A3
Roddinghead Rd G46 157 A3
Rodger Ave G77 156 B3
Rodger Dr G73 138 A3
Rodger Pl G73 138 A3
Rodil Ave G44 137 B2
Rodney Pl G84 17 A1
Rodney Rd PA19 44 C3
Rodney St G4 97 A1
Roebank Dr G78 134 B1
Roebank Rd KA15 150 B1
Roebank St G31 118 A4
Roffey Park Rd PA1 114 B3
Rogart St G40 117 C3
Rogerfield Prim Sch
G34 120 B4
Rogerfield Rd G34 120 B4
Rogers Ct ML9 198 B1
Rokeby La G12 96 C2
Roland Cres G77 156 C2
Roman Ave Bearsden G61 75 C3
Glasgow G15 75 A1
Roman Cres
Old Kilpatrick G60 72 C4
Shotts ML7 147 A2
Roman Ct Bearsden G61 75 C3
Cleghorn ML11 215 C4
Clydebank G81 74 A3
Roman Dr Bearsden G61 75 C3
Bellshill ML4 142 A2
Falkirk FK1 41 B3
Roman Gdns G61 75 C3
Roman Hill Rd G81 74 A4
Roman Pl ML4 141 C2
Roman Rd Ayr KA7 239 B3
Bearsden G61 75 C3
Bonnybridge FK4 40 A2
Clydebank G81 74 A3
Kirkintilloch G66 79 A4
Motherwell ML1 163 C4
Roman Way G71 141 B3
Romney Ave G44 137 B3
Romulus Ct ML1 142 B1
Rona Ave PA14 69 A4
Rona Pl KA3 223 A3
Rona St G21 98 A1
Rona Terr G72 138 C2
Ronades Rd FK2 42 A4
Ronald Cres FK5 23 A1
Ronald Pl FK8 7 A4
Ronaldsay Ct KA11 225 A4
Ronaldsay Dr G64 78 B1
Ronaldsay Pl G67 82 B4
Ronaldsay St G22 97 B4
Ronaldshaw Pk KA7 238 C3
Ronay St Glasgow G22 97 B4
Wishaw ML2 165 C3

Rook Rd PA16 45 A3
Rooksdell Ave PA2 113 B1
Ropework La G1 241 A1
Rorison Pl ML9 185 C1
Rosa Burn Ave G75 180 A2
Rosa Pl KA21 206 A1
Rose Cres Gourock PA19 44 B3
Hamilton ML3 161 C2
Rose Dale G64 98 A4
Rose Knowe Rd G42 137 B4
Rose Mount Ct ML6 123 B4
Rose Pl G74 160 B2
Rose St Alloa FK10 4 C1
Bonnybridge FK4 40 A3
Cumbernauld G67 82 A3
Glasgow G3 240 C4
Greenock PA16 45 B2
Kirkintilloch G66 79 B4
Motherwell ML1 164 A3
Rose Terr Denny FK6 21 B1
Stenhousemuir FK5 23 C2
Rosebank FK10 5 B1
Rosebank Ave
Blantyre G72 140 C1
Falkirk FK1 41 C3
Kirkintilloch G66 79 C4
Rosebank Cres KA7 238 C3
Rosebank Dr
Cambuslang G72 139 B2
Uddingston G71 141 B4
Rosebank Gdns
Alloa FK10 10 B4
Glasgow G71 120 A1
Irvine KA11 219 C4
Rosebank La 10 G71 141 A2
Rosebank Pl Dullatur G68 61 B3
Falkirk FK1 41 C3
Glasgow G71 120 A1
Hamilton ML3 162 A2
Kilmarnock KA3 222 C1
Rosebank Rd
Bellshill ML4 142 A4
Wishaw ML2 186 B3
Rosebank Sch KA7 239 A3
Rosebank St ML6 123 C4
Rosebank Terr
Bargeddie G69 121 A2
Kilmacolm PA13 89 B4
Rosebay Pk KA7 239 A1
Roseberry La ML6 123 C2
Roseberry Pl ML3 162 A2
Roseberry Rd ML6 123 C2
Roseberry St G5 117 C1
Rosebery Ct KA25 149 A1
Rosebery Pl FK8 2 A1
Roseburn Ct G67 62 C3
Rosedale G74 159 B2
Rosedale Ave PA2 132 B4
Rosedale Dr G69 120 A2
Rosedale Gdns
Glasgow G20 96 B4
Helensburgh G84 16 C1
Rosedale St ML11 214 C1
Rosedene Terr ML4 142 A3
Rosefield Gdns G71 140 C4
Rosegreen Cres ML4 142 A4
Rosehall Ave ML5 122 A2
Rosehall High Sch ML5 121 C2
Rosehall Ind Est ML5 122 A2
Rosehall Rd Bellshill ML4 141 C3
Shotts ML7 146 B2
Rosehall Terr Falkirk FK1 42 A2
Wishaw ML2 164 C1
Rosehill Dr G67 82 A3
Rosehill Rd G64 78 B4
Roseholm Ave KA12 219 C1
Roselea ML6 104 C2
Roselea Dr G62 55 A2
Roselea Gdns G13 95 C4
Roselea Pl G72 140 B1
Roselea Rd G71 140 C4
Roselea St ML9 185 A2
Rosemary Cres G74 159 B2
Rosemary Ct FK6 21 B1
Rosemary Pl G74 159 B2
Rosemead Terr FK1 66 C3
Rosemount
Cumbernauld G68 61 C3
Kilwinning KA13 207 B1
Rosemount Ave G77 156 B1
Rosemount Ct G77 156 B1
Rosemount Dr KA10 229 C4
Rosemount Gdns
Prestwick KA9 236 B3
Shieldhill FK1 66 B3
Rosemount La
Bridge of W PA11 110 A3
13 Larkhall ML9 185 B1
Rosemount Mdws G72 140 C1
Rosemount Pl PA19 44 A3
Rosemount St G21 97 C1
Rosendale Way G72 161 C4
Roseneath Dr G84 16 A1
Roseneath Gate G74 159 B1
Roseneath Prim Sch G84 15 A2
Roseneath St PA16 45 B4
Roseness Pl G33 119 A4
Rosepark Ave G71 141 B3
Rosepark Cotts ML5 121 C2
Rosevale Cres
Bellshill ML4 142 B2
Hamilton ML3 162 A1
Rosevale Rd G61 75 C2
Rosevale Sch G22 97 B4
Rosevale St G11 96 A1
Rosewood Ave
Bellshill ML4 142 A4
Paisley PA2 113 A1

Rosewood Path ML4 141 C3
Rosewood St G13 95 C4
Roseyard Pl PA14 47 B1
Roslea Dr G31 118 A4
Roslin Ct PA13 89 B4
Roslin St PA15 45 C3
Roslin Twr G72 138 C2
Roslyn Dr G69 120 C3
Rosneath Rd
Port Glasgow PA14 68 B4
Rosneath G84 15 A1
Rosneath St G51 116 A4
Ross Ave Kirkintilloch G66 79 C4
Renfrew PA4 94 A1
Ross Cres Falkirk FK1 41 B3
Motherwell ML1 163 B3
Ross Ct FK7 7 A2
Ross Dr Airdrie ML6 122 C2
Motherwell ML1 163 B3
Uddingston G71 121 B1
Ross Gdns ML1 163 B3
Ross Hall Hospl G52 115 A2
Ross Hall Pl PA4 94 B2
Ross Pl G73 138 B2
Ross Rd KA21 205 C1
Ross St Ayr KA8 236 B1
Coatbridge ML5 122 A4
Glasgow G40 241 B1
Paisley PA1 114 A2
Ross Terr ML3 163 B1
Ross Wlk KA3 223 A1
Rossbank Rd PA14 47 A1
Rossendale Ct G43 136 B4
Rossendale Rd G43 136 B4
Rosshall Ave PA1 114 B2
Rosshall Sec Sch G52 115 A2
Rosshill Ave G52 114 C3
Rosshill Rd G52 114 C3
Rossie Cres G64 98 B4
Rossie Gr G77 156 A3
Rossland Cres PA7 72 A2
Rossland Pl PA7 72 A1
Rossland View PA7 72 A2
Rosslea Dr G46 136 B1
Rosslyn Ave
East Kilbride G74 160 A2
Rutherglen G73 138 B4
Rosslyn Ct ML3 162 A2
Rosslyn Pl KA8 236 A4
Rosslyn Rd Ashgill ML9 199 C4
Bearsden G61 75 A3
Rosslyn Terr 38 G12 96 B2
Rossvail Sch FK1 41 B3
Rostan Rd G43 136 B3
Rosyth Rd G5 117 C1
Rosyth St G5 117 C1
Rotherwick Dr PA1 114 C2
Rotherwood Ave
Glasgow G13 75 B1
Paisley PA2 132 C4
Rotherwood La G13 75 B1
Rotherwood Pl G13 95 B4
Rotherwood Way PA2 132 C4
Rothes Dr G23 96 B4
Rothes Pl 3 G23 76 B1
Rothesay Cres ML5 122 A2
Rothesay Pl
Coatbridge ML5 122 A2
East Kilbride G74 159 C1
Kilmarnock KA3 222 C2
Rothesay Rd PA16 44 C2
Rothesay St G74 180 C4
Rottenrow Glasgow G4 241 B3
Glasgow G4 241 C2
Rottenrow E G4 241 B2
Roughburn Rd FK9 2 A3
Roughcraig St ML6 103 A1
Roughlands Cres FK2 24 A2
Roughlands Dr FK2 24 A2
Roughlea Pl KA10 229 D3
Roughrigg Rd ML6 124 B3
Rouken Glen Pk* G46 135 C1
Rouken Glen Rd G46 136 A1
Roukenburn St G46 135 C2
Round Riding Rd G82 50 A2
Roundel The Falkirk FK2 42 B4
Wishaw ML2 165 B1
Roundelwood FK10 5 A1
Roundhill Dr PA5 112 C2
Roundhouse FK7 12 B4
Roundknowe Rd G71 120 B1
Rousay Wynd KA3 223 A3
Rowallan KA13 207 B1
Rowallan Cres KA9 236 B4
Rowallan Ct 17 KA7 235 C1
Rowallan Dr
Bannockburn FK7 11 C4
Kilmarnock KA3 223 A2
Rowallan Gdns G11 96 A2
Rowallan La
Clarkston G76 157 C4
Glasgow G11 96 A2
Rowallan Rd G46 135 C1
Rowallan St G84 16 A2
Rowallan Terr G33 99 A2
Rowan Ave Beith KA15 171 B4
Milton of C G66 58 B3
Renfrew PA4 94 B2
Rowan Cres Ayr KA7 239 B3
Chapelhall ML6 123 C2
Falkirk FK1 41 A2
Kirkintilloch G66 79 B3
Rowan Ct Bannockburn FK7 7 C1
Cambuslang G72 139 C2
Wishaw ML2 164 B1
Rowan Dr Banknock FK4 38 C1
Bearsden G61 76 A4
Clydebank G81 73 C2

Rowan Dr *continued*
Dumbarton G82 49 A2
Rowan Gate PA2 113 C1
Rowan Gdns G41 116 A2
Rowan Gr ML3 183 C2
Rowan Ho KA9 236 A3
Rowan La ML1 143 A1
Rowan Pl Beith KA15 171 B4
Blantyre G72 161 B4
Cambuslang G72 139 B3
Coatbridge ML5 121 C2
Kilmarnock KA1 227 B4
Troon KA10 229 C2
Rowan Rd
Cumbernauld G67 62 B2
Glasgow G41 116 A2
Linwood PA3 111 C4
Rowan Rise ML3 162 C1
Rowan St Greenock PA16 45 B3
Paisley PA2 113 C1
Wishaw ML2 165 A3
Rowan Terr KA12 219 B2
Rowanbank Pl ML6 122 B4
Rowanbank Rd KA9 236 C4
Rowand Ave G46 136 B2
Rowandale Ave G69 120 A2
Rowanden Ave ML4 142 A3
Rowanhill Pl KA1 227 B4
Rowanlea ML6 103 C2
Rowanlea Ave PA2 132 C4
Rowanlea Dr G46 136 B2
Rowanpark Dr G78 134 A3
Rowans Gdns G71 141 A2
Rowans The Alloa FK10 5 B1
Bishopbriggs G64 77 C1
Rowanside Terr KA22 205 B2
Rowantree Ave
Motherwell ML1 143 B4
Rutherglen G73 138 A3
Uddingston G71 141 B4
Rowantree Gdns
Irvine KA11 220 A3
Rutherglen G73 138 A3
Rowantree Gr G83 27 C2
Rowantree Pl
Johnstone PA5 111 C1
Larkhall ML9 185 B1
Lennoxtown G66 57 C4
Rowantree Rd PA5 112 A1
Rowantree Terr
Lennoxtown G66 57 C4
Motherwell ML1 143 A3
Rowantree Wlk FK5 23 B2
Rowantreehill Rd PA13 89 C4
Rowanwood Cres ML5 121 B3
Rowena Ave G13 75 B1
Rowmore Quays G84 15 C2
Roxburgh Ave PA15 45 C2
Roxburgh Dr
Bearsden G61 75 C4
Coatbridge ML5 122 B2
Roxburgh Pk G74 159 C1
Roxburgh Pl
Blantyre G72 161 B4
Stenhousemuir FK5 23 C2
Roxburgh Rd
Hurlford KA1 228 C3
Paisley PA2 132 B4
Roxburgh St Glasgow G12 96 B2
Greenock PA15 45 C2
Roxburgh Way PA15 45 C2
Roy St G21 97 B2
Roy Young Ave G83 28 A4
Royal Alexandra Hospl
PA2 113 B1
Royal Bank Pl G1 241 A2
Royal Cres G3 116 C4
Royal Dr ML3 163 A1
Royal Exchange Ct G1 241 A2
Royal Exchange Sq G1 241 A2
Royal Gdns Bothwell G71 140 C1
Stirling FK8 7 A4
Royal Hospl (For Sick
Children) G3 96 B1
Royal Inch Cres PA4 94 B3
Royal Infmy G4 241 C3
Royal Scottish Acad of Music
& Drama G3 240 C3
Royal Scottish National Hospl
The FK5 22 C2
Royal St PA19 44 C4
Royal Terr Glasgow G3 96 C1
Wishaw ML2 165 B4
Royal Terrace La G3 96 C1
Royal Troon Golf Club*
KA10 232 B4
Royellen Ave ML3 161 C1
Royston Rd G21,G33 98 B2
Royston Sq G21 241 C4
Roystonhill G21 97 C1
Rozelle* KA7 238 C1
Rozelle Ave Glasgow G15 75 A2
Newton Mearns G77 156 A2
Rozelle Dr G77 156 A2
Rozelle Pl G77 156 A2
Rozelle Terr KA7 239 A1
Rubie Cres KA12 219 B1
Rubislaw Dr G61 75 C2
Ruby St G40 118 A2
Ruchazie Pl G33 118 C4
Ruchazie Prim Sch G33 99 A1
Ruchazie Rd G32 118 C4
Ruchill Pl G20 96 C3
Ruchill Prim Sch G20 96 C3
Ruchill St G20 96 C3

Rue End St PA15 ....46 A2
Ruel St G44 ....137 A4
Rufflees Ave G78 ....134 B2
Rugby Ave G13 ....95 A4
Rugby Cres KA1 ....227 B4
Rugby Pk (Kilmarnock FC)
KA1 ....227 C4
Rugby Rd KA1 ....227 B4
Rulley View FK6 ....21 B2
Rullion Pl G33 ....118 C4
Rumford Pl KA3 ....223 B3
Rumford St G40 ....117 C2
Rumlie The FK1 ....86 A3
Runciman Pl G74 ....160 A2
Rundell Dr G66 ....58 B3
Rupert St G4 ....96 C1
Rushyhill St G21 ....98 A2
Ruskie Rd FK9 ....2 A2
Ruskin La G12 ....96 C2
Ruskin Pl Glasgow G12 ....96 C2
Kilsyth G65 ....60 B4
Ruskin Sq G64 ....78 A1
Ruskin Terr Glasgow G12 ....96 C2
Rutherglen G73 ....118 A1
Russel St FK2 ....42 A3
Russell Colt St ML5 ....122 A4
Russell Ct KA3 ....223 B2
Russell Dr Alexandria G83 ....27 B4
Ayr KA8 ....236 A1
Bearsden G61 ....75 C3
Dalry KA24 ....191 B4
Russell Gdns
Newton Mearns G77 ....156 B2
10 Uddingston G71 ....141 A4
Russell Hill Ct FK5 ....23 A1
Russell La ML2 ....165 A1
Russell Pl Bonnybridge FK4 .39 B3
Clarkston G76 ....158 A3
East Kilbride G75 ....180 B4
Linwood PA3 ....111 C3
Russell Rd Clydebank G81 ..73 C4
Lanark ML11 ....215 A3
Russell St Ayr KA8 ....236 A1
Bellshill ML4 ....142 B3
Chapelhall ML6 ....123 C1
Hamilton ML3 ....161 C3
Johnstone PA5 ....112 A2
Paisley PA3 ....113 B4
Port Glasgow PA14 ....47 A1
Wishaw ML2 ....165 A1
Rutherford Ave
Bearsden G61 ....75 A4
Kirkintilloch G66 ....80 A3
Rutherford Ct
Bridge of A FK9 ....2 A4
Clydebank G81 ....74 A1
Rutherford Grange G66 ..79 B3
Rutherford La G75 ....180 C4
Rutherford Sq G75 ....180 C4
Rutherglen Ind Est G73 .118 A1
Rutherglen Rd G5 ....117 C1
Rutherglen Sta G73 ....138 A4
Ruthven Ave G46 ....136 B1
Ruthven La
8 Glasgow G12 ....96 B2
Glenboig ML5 ....101 B3
Ruthven Pl
Bishopbriggs G64 ....98 B4
Troon KA10 ....229 D2
Ruthven St G12 ....96 B2
Rutland Cres G51 ....116 C3
Rutland Ct G51 ....116 C3
Rutland Pl G51 ....116 C3
Ryan Rd G64 ....78 A1
Ryan Way G73 ....138 B2
Ryat Dr G77 ....156 B3
Ryat Gn G77 ....156 B3
Ryatt Linn PA8 ....72 C1
Rydal Gr G75 ....179 C3
Rydal Pl G75 ....179 C3
Ryde Rd ML2 ....165 B2
Ryden Mains Rd ML6 ....102 B2
Rye Cres G21 ....98 A3
Rye Rd G21 ....98 B3
Rye Way PA2 ....112 C1
Ryebank Rd G21 ....98 B3
Ryecroft Dr G69 ....120 A3
Ryedale Pl G15 ....75 A2
Ryefield Ave
Coatbridge ML5 ....121 B4
Johnstone PA5 ....111 B1
Ryefield Ho KA24 ....169 A1
Ryefield Pl PA5 ....111 B1
Ryefield Rd G21 ....98 A3
Ryehill Pl G21 ....98 B3
Ryehill Rd G21 ....98 B2
Ryemount Rd G21 ....98 B3
Ryeside Pl KA24 ....169 B1
Ryeside Rd G21 ....98 A2
Ryewraes Rd PA3 ....112 A3
Rylands KA9 ....236 B3
Rylands Dr G32 ....119 B2
Rylands Gdns G32 ....119 C2
Rylees Cres G52 ....114 C3
Rylees Pl G52 ....114 C3
Rylees Rd G52 ....114 C3
Rysland Ave G77 ....156 C3
Rysland Cres G77 ....156 C3
Ryeland Dr KA3 ....213 A2
Ryvra Rd G13 ....95 B3

S

Sachelcourt Ave PA7 ....72 A1
Sackville Ave G13 ....95 C3
Sackville La G13 ....95 C3
Sacred Heart Prim Sch
Cumbernauld G67 ....62 A1
Gourock PA16 ....44 C2
Sacred Heart RC Prim Sch
Bellshill ML4 ....142 A2
Glasgow G40 ....117 C2
Saddell Rd G15 ....75 A2
Saffron Cres ML2 ....164 B1
Saffronhall Cres ML3 ....162 B2
Saffronhall La ML3 ....162 B2
Sainford Cres FK2 ....24 A1
St Abb's Dr PA2 ....113 A1
St Agatha's Prim Sch
G66 ....80 A4
St Agnes' Prim Sch G23 ..96 C4
St Aidan's High Sch
ML2 ....165 A2
St Aidan's Path ML2 ....165 B3
St Aidan's RC Prim Sch
ML2 ....165 B3
St Aidan's RC Sch G31 ..118 B3
St Albert's RC Prim Sch
G41 ....116 C2
St Aloysius Coll G3 ....240 B4
St Aloysius RC Prim Sch
ML6 ....123 C1
St Aloysius' Prim Sch
G22 ....97 C3
St Ambrose High Sch
ML5 ....121 C4
St Ambrose's Prim RC Sch
G22 ....97 C4
St Andrew St PA15 ....46 A2
St Andrew's Acad PA2 ..114 B1
St Andrew's Acad
KA21 ....205 C1
St Andrew's Ave
Bishopbriggs G64 ....77 C1
Prestwick KA9 ....236 B3
St Andrew's Brae G82 ....50 A3
St Andrew's Cres
Dumbarton G82 ....50 A3
Paisley PA3 ....113 B4
St Andrew's Cross G41 ..117 A2
St Andrew's Ct ML8 ....187 C1
St Andrew's Ct FK5 ....23 A2
St Andrew's Dr Airth FK2 ..14 A4
Glasgow G41 ....116 B2
Hamilton ML3 ....161 B2
Paisley PA3 ....113 B4
St Andrew's Dr W PA3 ....93 B1
St Andrew's Gdns
10 Airdrie ML6 ....123 A4
Dalry KA24 ....191 A3
St Andrew's High Sch
Clydebank G81 ....94 B4
East Kilbride G75 ....180 B3
St Andrew's La G1 ....241 B1
St Andrew's Pl KA20 ....206 C1
St Andrew's Prim Sch
ML6 ....102 C1
St Andrew's RC Cath*
G1 ....241 A1
St Andrew's RC Prim Sch
G61 ....75 B3
St Andrew's RC Prim Sch
FK1 ....42 C2
St Andrew's Rd
Ardrossan KA22 ....205 B2
Glasgow G41 ....116 C2
Renfrew PA4 ....94 B1
St Andrew's Sec Sch
G32 ....119 A4
St Andrew's Sq G1 ....241 B1
St Andrew's St Ayr KA7 ..239 A4
Glasgow G1 ....241 B1
Kilmarnock KA1 ....227 C4
St Andrew's Way ML2 ....165 B3
St Andrew's Wlk 15
KA1 ....227 C4
St Andrews Ave G71 ....141 A1
St Andrews Cres G41 ....116 C2
St Andrews Ct
East Kilbride G75 ....180 B3
Motherwell ML1 ....143 A3
St Andrews Dr
Bridge of W PA11 ....110 B3
Coatbridge ML5 ....121 C3
Cumbernauld G68 ....62 A3
Gourock PA19 ....44 A3
St Andrews Gate ML4 ....141 C3
St Andrews La
Alexandria G83 ....27 C2
Gourock PA19 ....44 A3
St Andrews Path 19
ML9 ....185 B1
St Andrews Pl
Beith KA15 ....171 A4
11 Falkirk FK1 ....42 A2
Kilsyth G65 ....36 B1
St Andrews St ML1 ....143 A3
St Andrews Way KA11 ..224 D4
St Andrews Wynd G84 ....16 C2
St Angela's Prim Sch
G53 ....135 B2
St Ann's Dr G46 ....136 B1
St Anne's Cres FK7 ....7 C1
St Anne's Prim Sch PA8 ..93 B4
St Anne's RC Prim Sch
G40 ....118 A3
St Annes Ave PA8 ....93 B4
St Annes Wynd PA8 ....93 B4
St Anthony's Prim Sch
Glasgow G51 ....115 C4
Johnstone PA5 ....131 B4
Rutherglen G73 ....138 B2
St Anthony's Prim Sch
KA21 ....205 C1
St Athanasius' Prim Sch
ML8 ....187 C1
St Augustine's Prim RC Sch
G22 ....97 B4
St Augustine's RC Prim Sch
ML5 ....121 C3
St Barbara's Prim Sch
G69 ....100 B4
St Barchan's Rd PA10 ....111 A1
St Bartholomew's RC Prim Sch
Coatbridge ML5 ....101 B1
Glasgow G45 ....137 C2
St Benedict's RC Prim Sch
G34 ....100 A1
St Bernadette's RC Prim Sch
Motherwell ML1 ....163 A4
Tullibody FK10 ....4 A1
St Bernard's RC Prim Sch
ML5 ....122 A2
St Bernards Prim RC Sch
G53 ....135 A3
St Blane's Dr G73 ....137 C3
St Blane's Prim Sch
G72 ....161 B4
St Blanes Prim Sch G23 ..76 B1
St Boswell's Cres PA2 ..113 A1
St Boswells Dr ML5 ....122 B2
St Brendan's High Sch
PA3 ....112 B3
St Brendan's Prim Sch
G13 ....94 C4
St Brendan's RC Prim Sch
ML1 ....164 A1
St Brennans Ct KA25 ....170 A4
St Bride's Ave G71 ....141 B4
St Bride's Dr KA23 ....190 B3
St Bride's Pl KA12 ....219 B3
St Bride's RC High Sch
G74 ....160 A1
St Bride's RC Prim Sch
G71 ....141 A2
St Bride's Rd
Glasgow G43 ....136 B3
West Kilbride KA23 ....190 B3
St Bride's Sec Sch G72 ..139 A3
St Brides Way G71 ....141 A2
St Bridget's Prim Sch
Glasgow G69 ....120 A3
Kilbirnie KA25 ....170 A4
St Brigid's RC Prim Sch
Glasgow G42 ....137 B4
Wishaw ML2 ....166 A3
St Bryde St G74 ....159 C1
St Cadoc's Prim Sch
G77 ....156 B3
St Cadoc's Sch G72 ....139 B2
St Catherine's Prim Sch
PA3 ....113 C3
St Catherine's RC Prim Sch
G21 ....98 B3
St Catherine's Rd G46 ..136 B1
St Catherines Cres ML7 .146 C3
St Catherines Rd KA8 ..236 C1
St Charles Prim Sch
Cambuslang G72 ....139 C3
Paisley PA2 ....113 C1
St Charles's Prim Sch
G20 ....96 C2
St Clair Ave G46 ....136 B2
St Clair Terr KA10 ....229 B1
St Clare's Prim RC Sch
G15 ....75 A2
St Clare's RC Prim Sch
G34 ....120 B4
St Columba Dr G66 ....79 C4
St Columba Pl KA20 ....206 C1
St Columba's High Sch
G81 ....74 B2
St Columba's High Sch
PA16 ....45 A3
St Columba's Prim Sch
Kilmacolm PA13 ....89 B4
Kilmarnock KA1 ....228 A4
St Columba's RC Prim Sch
G71 ....141 B4
St Columba's Sch PA13 ..89 B4
St Columbkille's Prim Sch
G73 ....138 A4
St Conval's Prim RC Sch
G43 ....136 B4
St Crispin's Pl FK1 ....42 A2
St Cuthbert's Cres KA9 ..236 B3
St Cuthbert's Prim RC Sch
G22 ....97 A2
St Cuthbert's RC Prim Sch
ML3 ....162 A3
St Cuthbert's Rd KA9 ..236 B3
St Cuthberts High Sch
PA5 ....131 B4
St Cyrus Gdns G64 ....78 B1
St Cyrus Rd G64 ....78 B1
St David's Ct FK5 ....23 A1
St David's Pl ML9 ....185 A2
St David's RC Prim Sch
PA5 ....111 B1
St David's RC Sec Sch
ML6 ....103 C1
St Davids Dr ML6 ....123 B2
St Denis Way ML5 ....121 C4
St Denis' RC Prim Sch
G31 ....118 A4
St Dominic's RC Prim Sch
Airdrie ML6 ....123 B3
Glasgow G45 ....137 C1
St Edmunds Gr G62 ....55 A2
St Edmunds Prim Sch
G53 ....115 B1
St Edward's Prim Sch
ML6 ....123 B4
St Elizabeth Seton RC Prim Sch G33 ....119 B4
St Elizabeth's Prim Sch
ML3 ....183 B4
St Enoch Ave G71 ....141 B4
St Enoch Pl G1 ....240 C2
St Enoch Sh Ctr G1 ....241 A1
St Enoch Sq G1 ....240 C1
St Enoch Underground Sta
G1 ....240 C2
St Eunan's Prim Sch G81 .74 B1
St Fergus's RC Prim Sch
PA3 ....113 A3
St Fillan's Prim Sch
G44 ....137 A3
St Fillan's Prim Sch
PA6 ....91 A1
St Fillans Dr PA6 ....91 A1
St Fillans Rd G33 ....99 B3
St Flanan Rd G66 ....59 B1
St Flannan's Prim Sch
G66 ....58 C1
St Francis of Assisi Prim Sch
Cumbernauld G68 ....82 A4
Glasgow G69 ....119 C2
St Francis Prim RC Sch
G5 ....117 B2
St Francis Prim Sch
PA14 ....68 C4
St Francis Private Prim Sch
G43 ....136 B3
St Francis Xavier Coll
ML5 ....122 B2
St Francis Xavier's RC Prim Sch FK2 ....42 A3
St Gabriel's Prim Sch
Gourock PA16 ....44 B2
Uddingston G71 ....141 B4
St George's Cross 10
G3 ....97 A1
St George's Cross Underground Sta G3 ....97 A1
St George's Ct FK5 ....23 A1
St George's Pl 8 G20 ....97 A1
St George's Prim Sch
G52 ....114 C3
St George's RC Prim Sch
ML4 ....142 A4
St George's Rd Ayr KA8 ..236 A2
Glasgow G3 ....240 B4
St Gerard's Sec Sch
G51 ....116 A4
St Germains G61 ....75 C2
St Gilbert's RC Prim Sch
G21 ....98 B2
St Giles Pk ML3 ....162 A1
St Giles Sq FK1 ....41 A3
St Giles Way Falkirk FK1 ....41 A3
Hamilton ML3 ....162 A1
St Gregory's Prim RC Sch
G20 ....96 B3
St Helen's Prim Sch
Bishopbriggs G64 ....78 B1
Cumbernauld G67 ....82 A4
St Helena Cres G81 ....74 B3
St Hilary's Prim Sch
G74 ....181 A4
St Ignatius's RC Prim Sch
ML2 ....165 A2
St Inan Ave KA12 ....219 C2
St Inan's Dr KA15 ....150 B1
St Ives Rd G69 ....80 C2
St Jame's RC Prim Sch
ML5 ....121 C2
St James Ave PA3 ....113 A4
St James Bsns Ctr PA1 ..112 C2
St James Ct ML5 ....121 C2
St James Prim Sch PA3 .113 B4
St James Rd G4 ....241 B3
St James Terr PA13 ....89 B4
St James Way ML5 ....121 C2
St James' Orch FK9 ....2 B1
St James' Pl KA20 ....206 C1
St James' Prim Sch
Glasgow G40 ....117 C3
Renfrew PA4 ....94 B2
St James' St PA3 ....113 C3
St Jerome's Prim Sch
G51 ....115 C4
St Joachim's RC Prim Sch
G32 ....119 B1
St Joan of Arc RC Sch
G22 ....97 A4
St Joan's Cres KA13 ....207 C1
St John Bosco Prim Sch
PA8 ....72 C1
St John Ogilvie Prim Sch
Irvine KA11 ....220 A2
Paisley PA1 ....114 A2
St John St 9 Ayr KA7 ....235 C1
Coatbridge ML5 ....122 A4
Prestwick KA9 ....236 B4
Stirling FK8 ....7 A4
St John The Baptist Prim Sch
G71 ....141 A3
St John's Ave FK2 ....42 B3
St John's Ct G41 ....116 C2
St John's Gate FK6 ....21 B1
St John's Gdns FK6 ....21 B1
St John's Gr FK6 ....21 B1
St John's Manor PA19 ....44 C4
St John's Pl KA22 ....205 B1
St John's Pl KA20 ....206 C1
St John's Prim RC Sch
G5 ....117 A3
St John's Prim Sch
Alloa FK10 ....9 C3
Barrhead G78 ....134 B2
Hamilton ML3 ....162 B2
St John's Quadrant 1
G41 ....116 C2
St John's RC Prim Sch
PA14 ....47 A1
St John's RC Prim Sch
KA20 ....206 C1
St John's Rd
Glasgow G41 ....116 C2
Gourock PA19 ....44 C4
St John's Sch KA8 ....236 A1
St Joseph's Acad (Kilmarnock Campus)
KA3 ....223 A1
St Joseph's Ct G21 ....97 C1
St Joseph's Pl G21 ....97 C1
St Joseph's Prim Sch
Blantyre G72 ....161 B4
Clarkston G76 ....157 C3
Clydebank G81 ....74 B4
Glasgow G4 ....97 A1
Milngavie G62 ....54 C1
St Joseph's Prim Sch
G33 ....99 C3
St Joseph's RC Prim Sch
Bonnybridge FK4 ....40 A2
Cumbernauld G67 ....82 C4
St Joseph's RC Prim Sch
PA16 ....45 A2
St Joseph's Sch ML5 ....101 B4
St Joseph's View G21 ....97 C1
St Josephs Prim Sch
G84 ....16 C1
St Jude's Prim RC Sch
G33 ....119 C3
St Julie's RC Prim Sch
G45 ....137 B2
St Kenneth Dr G51 ....115 C4
St Kenneth's RC Prim Sch
G74 ....159 C1
St Kenneth's RC Prim Sch
PA15 ....46 B1
St Kentigerns Rd ML11 ..215 A3
St Kessogs RC Prim Sch
G83 ....27 C4
St Kevin's RC Prim Sch
G69 ....121 A3
St Kevin's Sch G21 ....97 C1
St Kilda Bank KA11 ....220 A1
St Kilda Ct KA11 ....220 A1
St Kilda Dr G14 ....95 C2
St Kilda Pl KA11 ....220 A1
St Kilda Way ML2 ....165 C3
St Laurence Cres FK1 ....86 A3
St Lawrence Pk G75 ....159 B1
St Lawrence Pl KA21 ....206 A1
St Lawrence Prim Sch
PA15 ....46 A2
St Lawrence St PA15 ....46 A2
St Leonard St ML11 ....215 A3
St Leonard's Dr G46 ....136 B2
St Leonard's Prim Sch
G74 ....160 B2
St Leonard's Rd Ayr KA7 .239 A3
Lanark ML11 ....215 A2
St Leonard's Sq G74 ....160 B1
St Leonards Ct KA7 ....239 A3
St Leonards Rd G74 ....160 B1
St Leonards Wlk ML5 ....122 B2
St Leonards Wynd KA7 ..239 A3
St Louise Prim Sch G46 .135 B2
St Louise's Prim Sch
G75 ....180 C3
St Lucy's Prim Sch G67 ..62 C2
St Luke's Ave ML8 ....201 C4
St Luke's Prim Sch
KA13 ....207 A1
St Lukes High Sch G78 ..155 B4
St Lukes Pl G5 ....117 B3
St Lukes Terr G5 ....117 B3
St Machan's Prim Sch
G66 ....33 B1
St Machan's Way G66 ....33 B1
St Machars Rd PA11 ....110 C4
St Margaret Ave KA24 ....191 A4
St Margaret Mary RC Sec Sch
G45 ....137 B1
St Margaret Mary's RC Prim Sch G45 ....137 B1
St Margaret's Ave G65 ....37 C2
St Margaret's Ct PA3 ....113 C4
St Margaret's Dr ML2 ....164 C1
St Margaret's High Sch
ML6 ....123 A4
St Margaret's Pl G1 ....241 A1
St Margaret's Prim Sch
PA5 ....111 C1
St Margaret's RC Prim Sch
FK7 ....12 B4
St Margarets Rd KA22 ....205 B2
St Mark Gdns G32 ....118 C3
St Mark St G32 ....118 C3
St Mark's Ct ML2 ....165 B3
St Mark's Prim Sch
Barrhead G78 ....134 B1
Glasgow G73 ....138 A3
Hamilton ML3 ....161 C1
Irvine KA12 ....219 C2
St Mark's RC Prim Sch
G31 ....118 C3
St Marnock Pl 10 KA1 ....227 C4
St Marnock St
Glasgow G40 ....118 A3

St Marnock St *continued*
Kilmarnock KA1 227 C4
St Marnock's Prim Sch G53 115 B1
St Marnock's Prim Sch Annexe G53 115 B1
St Martha's RC Prim Sch G21 98 A3
St Martin's Prim Sch G83 27 C2
St Martin's RC Prim Sch G45 137 C1
St Martins Gate ML5 122 A2
St Mary's Cres G78 134 B1
St Mary's Ct ML2 165 A1
St Mary's La G2 240 C2
St Mary's Pl KA21 205 C1
St Mary's Prim RC Sch G20 96 B4
St Mary's Prim Sch
Clydebank G81 74 A3
Cumbernauld G67 61 C1
Hamilton ML3 162 B2
Lanark ML11 215 B2
St Mary's Prim Sch ML9 184 C1
St Mary's Prim Sch PA1 113 B2
St Mary's RC Prim Sch
Alexandria G83 27 C3
Bannockburn FK7 7 B1
St Mary's RC Prim Sch ML6 104 C3
St Mary's RC Prim Sch
Cleland ML1 144 A1
Coatbridge ML5 122 A3
Stirling FK8 1 C1
St Mary's RC Sec Sch PA16 45 C3
St Mary's Rd
Bellshill ML4 141 C3
Bishopbriggs G64 77 C1
St Mary's Way G82 49 C2
St Mary's Wynd FK8 7 A4
St Marys Ct ML11 215 B2
St Marys Gdns G78 134 B1
St Matthew's Prim Sch
Bishopbriggs G64 78 A1
Kilmarnock KA3 223 B1
St Matthew's RC Prim Sch ML2 164 C2
St Maur's Cres KA3 222 C2
St Maur's Pl KA3 222 C2
St Maurice's Rdbt G68 61 A1
St Maurices High Sch G68 82 A4
St Maurs Gdns KA3 222 B4
St Medan's Pl KA21 205 C1
St Meddans Cres KA10 229 C2
St Meddans Ct KA10 229 C1
St Meddans St KA10 229 C1
St Michael Dr G84 16 C1
St Michael Rd ML2 164 B1
St Michael's Acad KA13 207 B2
St Michael's Ct G31 118 B3
St Michael's La G31 118 B3
St Michael's Prim Sch
Moodiesburn G69 81 A1
Port Glasgow PA14 68 C4
St Michael's RC Prim Sch
Dumbarton G82 49 B2
Glasgow G31 118 B3
St Mirin's Prim Sch G44 137 B3
St Mirin's RC Cath PA1 113 C3
St Mirren Pk (St Mirren FC) PA3 113 C3
St Mirren St PA1 113 C2
St Mirren's Rd G65 60 C4
St Modan's High Sch FK7 7 A2
St Modan's RC Prim Sch G33 119 A4
St Modan's Way G84 15 A2
St Modans Ct 14 FK1 42 A2
St Monach's Pl KA20 206 C1
St Monance St G21 97 C3
St Monica's Prim Sch G53 115 A1
St Monica's RC Prim Sch ML5 121 B2
St Monicas Way ML5 121 B2
St Mungo Ave G4 241 B3
St Mungo Ct PA11 110 C4
St Mungo Mus* G4 241 C3
St Mungo Pl Glasgow G4 241 B3
Hamilton ML3 161 B2
St Mungo St G64 97 C4
St Mungo's ML11 215 A2
St Mungo's Acad G40 118 A3
St Mungo's High Sch FK2 42 A3
St Mungo's Prim Sch PA15 46 B2
St Mungo's RC Prim Sch
Alloa FK10 10 B3
Glasgow G4 241 C3
St Mungo's Rd G67 61 C1
St Mungo's Wynd FK10 10 A3
St Mungos Cres ML1 143 A1
St Nicholas Rd
Lanark ML11 215 A3
Prestwick KA9 236 A4
St Ninian Terr G5 117 B3
St Ninian's ML11 215 A3
St Ninian's Cres PA2 113 C1
St Ninian's Dr KA22 205 B2
St Ninian's High Sch
Glasgow G46 136 A1
Kirkintilloch G66 79 A4
St Ninian's Pl ML3 161 C2
St Ninian's Prim Sch G13 75 B1
St Ninian's Prim Sch PA19 44 B3
St Ninian's RC Prim Sch KA9 236 C4
St Ninian's Rd
Hamilton ML3 161 C2
Prestwick KA9 236 A4
St Ninians Gr ML2 165 B3
St Ninians Pl ML9 198 C1
St Ninians Prim Sch FK7 7 A2
St Ninians Rd
Cambusbarron FK7 6 C3
Paisley PA2 113 C1
Stirling FK8 7 A3
St Ninien's Prim Sch ML3 161 C2
St Oswold's Sch G44 137 A3
St Palladius Terr KA24 191 B4
St Palladius' Prim Sch KA24 191 B4
St Patrick's Ct ML11 214 C2
St Patrick's High Sch ML5 122 A4
St Patrick's Prim Sch PA15 45 C2
St Patrick's Prim Sch
Kilsyth G65 60 B4
Motherwell ML1 142 C2
Troon KA10 229 C1
St Patrick's RC Prim Sch
Coatbridge ML5 122 A4
Denny FK6 21 C2
Dumbarton G82 50 A2
Glasgow G3 240 A2
Shotts ML7 146 C2
St Patrick's Rd ML11 214 C2
St Paul's High Sch G53 135 B4
St Paul's Prim Sch G14 95 B2
St Paul's Prim Sch PA2 112 C1
St Paul's RC Prim Sch
Glasgow G32 119 A2
Hamilton ML3 162 A3
St Peter's La G2 240 B2
St Peter's Path 13 G4 97 A1
St Peter's Prim RC Sch (Girls & Infs) G11 96 B1
St Peter's Prim Sch KA22 205 B2
St Peter's Prim Sch PA2 133 B4
St Peter's RC Prim Sch
Dumbarton G82 50 A3
Hamilton ML3 162 A1
St Peter's St G4 97 A1
St Philip's RC Prim Sch G33 99 A1
St Philip's Sch ML6 103 C1
St Phillans Ave KA7 239 A3
St Philomena's RC Prim Sch G33 98 B2
St Pius' Prim Sch G15 75 A2
St Quivox Rd KA9 236 B4
St Raymond's Sch G45 137 A1
St Rhonans La G83 27 C2
St Robert's RC Prim Sch G53 135 B3
St Roch's RC Prim Sch G21 98 A1
St Roch's Sec Sch G21 241 C4
St Rollox Brae G21 97 C1
St Ronan's Dr
Glasgow G41 136 B4
Hamilton ML3 183 B4
St Ronan's RC Prim Sch G83 28 A2
St Ronans Dr G73 138 B3
St Rose of Lima Prim Sch G33 99 B1
St Saviour's Sch G51 116 A4
St Serf's Pl FK10 4 A2
St Serf's Prim Sch FK10 4 A2
St Serf's RC Prim Sch ML6 103 A1
St Serf's Rd FK10 4 A2
St Serf's Wlk FK12 4 C3
St Stephen's Cres G73 138 C2
St Stephen's High Sch PA14 69 A4
St Stephen's Pl KA20 206 C1
St Stephen's Prim Sch G81 73 C2
St Stephen's RC Prim Sch ML5 122 B3
St Stephen's RC Prim Sch G21 97 C1
St Stephens Ave G73 138 B2
St Teiling ML11 215 A3
St Teresa's Prim RC Sch G21 97 B2
St Theresa's RC Prim Sch ML1 143 B2
St Thomas Aquinas RC Sec Sch G14 95 C2
St Thomas RC Prim Sch G78 154 B4
St Thomas' RC Prim Sch
Glasgow G33 118 B4
Wishaw ML2 165 A1
St Thomas's Pl FK7 6 C3
St Thomas's Well FK7 6 B4
St Timothy's RC Prim Sch ML5 121 C2
St Timothy's RC Prim Sch G32 119 A3
St Valery Dr FK7 7 A2
St Vigeans Ave G77 156 B2
St Vigeans Pl G77 156 B2
St Vincent Cres Ayr KA7 239 A1
Glasgow G3 116 C4
St Vincent Crescent La G3 116 C4
St Vincent La G2 240 C2
St Vincent Pl
East Kilbride G75 180 A4
Glasgow G1 241 A2
Lanark ML11 215 A2
Motherwell ML1 163 C4
St Vincent RC Prim Sch G46 135 C2
St Vincent St G2 240 B3
St Vincent Terr G3 240 A3
St Vincent's Prim Sch G75 180 A3
St Vincent's Sch for the Blind & Deaf G32 119 A1
St Winifred's Way ML2 165 A2
St Winning's La KA13 207 B2
St Winning's RC Prim Sch KA13 207 B2
St Winning's Rd
Kilwinning KA13 207 B2
Kilwinning KA13 207 C2
St Winning's Well KA13 207 B2
St Winnoc Rd PA12 129 B2
Salamanca St G31 118 B3
Salasaig Ct G33 119 A4
Salen Loan ML7 147 A2
Salen St G52 115 C3
Saline St ML6 122 B3
Salisbury G74 160 B2
Salisbury Ave KA1 228 C3
Salisbury Cres ML1 163 A4
Salisbury Pl
Clydebank G81 73 B3
Prestwick KA9 236 B4
Salisbury St 2 G5 117 A2
Salkeld St G5 117 A3
Salmon Dr FK1 41 C1
Salmon St PA15 45 C3
Salmona St G22 97 A2
Saltaire Ave G71 141 A3
Saltcoats Rd KA20 217 A4
Saltcoats Sta KA21 216 C4
Salterland Rd G78 134 C2
Saltfield La 2 KA8 235 C1
Saltire Cres ML9 185 B1
Saltmarket G1 241 B1
Saltmarket Pl G1 241 A1
Saltoun La 9 G12 96 B2
Saltoun St G12 96 B2
Saltpans Rd KA8 235 C2
Salvia St G72 138 C3
Samrt Village Bsns Campus FK10 9 C4
Samson Ave KA1 228 A4
Samson Cres ML8 202 B4
Samson La ML8 202 B4
Sanda Pl Kilmarnock KA3 223 A3
Saltcoats KA21 205 C1
Sanda St G20 96 C2
Sandaig Prim Sch G33 119 C3
Sandaig Rd G33 119 C3
Sandale Path G72 161 B3
Sandalwood Ave G74 159 B2
Sandalwood Ct G74 159 B2
Sandbank Ave G20 96 B3
Sandbank Cres
Alexandria G83 27 C3
Glasgow G20 96 B3
Sandbank Dr G20 96 B4
Sandbank St G20 96 B4
Sandbank Terr G20 96 B4
Sandbed La 7 KA1 227 C4
Sandbed St KA1 227 C4
Sandend PA8 73 A2
Sandend Rd G53 135 A4
Sanderling Pl
East Kilbride G75 180 A3
Johnstone PA5 131 B3
Sanderling Rd PA3 113 C4
Sanderson Ave
Irvine KA12 219 A1
Uddingston G71 141 B3
Sanderson High Sch G74 181 B4
Sandfield Ave G62 55 A2
Sandfield Rd KA9 236 B4
Sandfield St G20 96 C3
Sandford Gdns G69 120 A3
Sandgate KA7 238 C4
Sandgate Ave G32 119 B2
Sandhaven Pl G53 135 A4
Sandhaven Rd G53 135 A4
Sandhead Cres ML6 123 C1
Sandhill Gdns KA10 229 D2
Sandholes Rd PA5 111 B3
Sandholes St PA1 113 B2
Sandholm Pl G14 94 C3
Sandholm Terr G14 94 C3
Sandiefield Rd
Glasgow G5 117 B2
1 Glasgow G5 117 B2
Sandielands Ave PA8 93 B4
Sandilands KA10 229 C1
Sandilands Cres ML1 163 A3
Sandilands St G32 119 B3
Sandmill St G21 98 A1
Sandpiper Dr G75 180 A3
Sandpiper Pl G75 180 A3
Sandpiper Rd PA12 129 B1
Sandra Rd G64 78 B1
Sandray Ave PA14 69 A4
Sandringham Ave G77 157 A3
Sandringham Ct G77 157 A3
Sandringham Dr PA5 112 A1
Sandringham La 2 G12 96 B2
Sandringham Terr PA16 45 C4
Sandwood Cres G52 115 A3
Sandwood Prim Sch G52 115 A3
Sandwood Rd G52 115 A3
Sandy Ct KA23 190 B2
Sandy Rd Carluke ML8 187 C1
Glasgow G11 96 A1
Irvine KA12 219 A3
Renfrew PA4 94 B1
Seamill KA23 190 B2
Sandyfaulds Sq 10 G5 117 B2
Sandyfaulds St 12 G5 117 B2
Sandyford Ave ML1 143 B4
Sandyford Pl
Glasgow G3 240 A3
Motherwell ML1 143 B4
Sandyford Place La G3 240 A3
Sandyford Rd
Motherwell ML1 143 B4
Paisley PA3 114 A4
Prestwick KA9 234 A1
Sandyford St G3 116 B4
Sandyhill Ave ML7 147 A2
Sandyhill Terr KA6 239 C3
Sandyhills Cres G32 119 A2
Sandyhills Dr G32 119 A2
Sandyhills Gr G32 119 A1
Sandyhills Pl G32 119 A2
Sandyhills Rd G32 119 B2
Sandyknowes Rd G67 83 A4
Sandylands Prom KA21 217 A4
Sandyvale Pl ML7 147 A2
Sannox Dr
Motherwell ML1 163 A4
Saltcoats KA21 206 A1
Sannox Gdns G31 118 A4
Sannox Pl Ayr KA8 236 B1
East Kilbride G75 180 A2
Helensburgh G84 16 C2
Sannox Rd KA1 222 B1
Sannox View KA8 236 C1
Sanquhar Ave KA9 236 B4
Sanquhar Dr G53 135 A4
Sanquhar Farm Rd KA8 236 B2
Sanquhar Gdns
Cambuslang G72 140 A1
1 Glasgow G53 135 A4
Sanquhar Pl 2 G53 135 A4
Sanquhar Rd G53 115 A1
Sapphire Rd ML4 142 A2
Saracen Head Rd G1 241 C1
Saracen Prim Sch G22 97 A2
Saracen St G22 97 B2
Sarazen Ct ML1 164 C4
Sardinia La G12 96 B2
Sark Dr KA10 229 D3
Saskatoon Pl G75 159 A1
Saturn Ave PA1 112 C3
Saucel Hill Terr PA2 113 C2
Saucel St PA1 113 C2
Sauchie Ct FK7 7 C1
Sauchie Hospl FK10 10 B4
Sauchie St FK7 7 A1
Sauchiehall La
Glasgow G2 240 B3
Glasgow G2 240 C3
Sauchiehall St G2 240 B3
Sauchiesmoor Rd ML8 202 A4
Saugh Ave KA3 173 B4
Saughs Ave G33 98 C3
Saughs Dr G33 98 C3
Saughs Gate G33 98 C3
Saughs Pl G33 98 C3
Saughs Rd G33 98 C3
Saughton St G32 118 C4
Saughtree Ave KA21 205 C1
Saunders Ct G78 134 A2
Saunterne Rd KA9 233 B1
Savoy Ct KA7 238 C4
Savoy Pk KA7 238 C4
Savoy St G40 117 C2
Sawers Ave FK6 21 B1
Sawmill Rd G11 95 C1
Sawmillfield St G4 97 A1
Saxon Rd G13 95 B4
Scadlock Rd PA3 113 A3
Scalpay G74 160 B1
Scalpay Pass G22 97 B4
Scalpay Pl Glasgow G22 97 B4
Kilmarnock KA3 223 A3
Scalpay St G22 97 B4
Scamadale Rd ML6 84 B2
Scapa St G23 96 C4
Scaraway Dr G22 97 B4
Scaraway Pl G22 97 B4
Scaraway St G22 97 B4
Scaraway Terr G22 97 B4
Scarba Dr G43 136 A3
Scarba Quadrant ML2 164 C1
Scarffe Ave PA3 111 C3
Scargie Rd KA1 227 C2
Scarhill Ave ML6 122 C3
Scarhill La ML6 123 A3
Scarhill St Cleland ML1 144 A1
Coatbridge ML5 121 C2
Scarletmuir ML11 214 C3
Scarlow St PA14 47 B1
Scarrel Dr G45 138 A2
Scarrel Gdns G45 138 A2
Scarrel Rd G45 138 A2
Scarrel Terr G45 138 A2
Scaur O' Doon Rd KA7 238 B2
Scavaig Cres G15 74 C2
Sch of Art G3 240 B4
Sch of Art (Annexe) G3 240 C4
Schaw Ct Alloa FK10 5 B1
Bearsden G61 75 C3
Schaw Dr Bearsden G61 75 C3
Clydebank G81 74 C4
Schaw Rd PA3 114 A3
Schawpark Ave FK10 5 B1
Schiltron Way FK7 7 B2
Scholar's Gate G75 180 B3
School Ave G72 139 A3
School Ho PA11 89 C2
School La
Cambuslang G72 139 C2
Carluke ML8 187 C1
Dumbarton G82 49 B2
Irvine KA12 219 B1
Lennoxtown G66 57 B4
Menstrie FK11 4 A4
Milton of C G66 58 B3
Shotts ML7 167 A4
School Mews FK11 4 A4
School Pl KA22 205 B1
School Quadrant ML6 102 C1
School Rd Kilbirnie KA25 149 A1
Newton Mearns G77 156 B2
Paisley PA1 114 C3
Rhu G84 15 B3
Salsburgh ML7 125 B2
Stepps G33 99 C3
Torrance G64 57 B1
Tullibody FK10 4 A1
Wishaw ML2 166 A2
School St Chapelhall ML6 123 B1
Coatbridge ML5 122 A2
Hamilton ML3 162 B1
Shotts ML7 146 C2
School View ML1 163 C3
School Wlk FK5 23 B2
School Wynd
Kilbirnie KA25 149 A1
Paisley PA1 113 C3
Quarriers Village PA11 89 C2
Schoolhouse La G72 161 B3
Schoolwell St KA20 206 B1
Scioncroft Ave G73 138 B4
Sclandersburn Rd FK6 39 B4
Scone Pl
East Kilbride G74 159 B2
Newton Mearns G77 157 A2
Scone St G21 97 B2
Sconser PA4 93 B4
Sconser St G23 76 C1
Scorton Gdns G69 119 C2
Scotas Coll G61 75 B2
Scotia Cres ML9 185 A1
Scotia Gdns ML3 183 B4
Scotia Pl FK2 42 B3
Scotia St ML1 163 B4
Scotland St G5 116 C3
Scotland St W G41 116 C3
Scotland Street School Mus* G5 116 C3
Scotland Theme Pk* ML1 141 C1
Scotsblair Ave G66 79 B4
Scotsburn Rd G21 98 B2
Scotstoun Prim Sch G14 95 B2
Scotstoun Rd FK7 12 C4
Scotstoun St G14 95 B2
Scotstoun Way ML5 122 B3
Scotstounhill Sta G13 95 A3
Scott Ave Bowling G60 72 B4
Johnstone PA5 131 C4
Milton of C G66 58 B3
Scott Cres Alloa FK10 10 A3
Cumbernauld G67 82 B4
Kilmarnock KA1 227 C4
Troon KA10 229 D2
Scott Ct Alva FK12 5 A3
Helensburgh G84 16 B1
Scott Dr Bearsden G61 75 B3
Cumbernauld G67 82 B4
Scott Gr ML3 162 B1
Scott Hill G74 160 A2
Scott Ho G67 62 A2
Scott Pl Bellshill ML4 142 A4
Johnstone PA5 131 C4
Saltcoats KA21 205 C1
Troon KA10 229 C3
Scott Rd Irvine KA12 219 B1
Kilmarnock KA1 227 C4
Paisley G52 114 C4
Scott St Alexandria G83 27 C2
Clydebank G81 73 C2
Glasgow G69 120 A2
Glasgow, Garnethill G3 240 B4
Greenock PA15 46 A2
Hamilton ML3 162 B1
Larkhall ML9 185 A1
Motherwell ML1 163 C4
Stirling FK8 2 A1
Scott's Pl ML6 123 A4
Scott's Rd PA2 114 B2
Scottish Exhibition & Conference Ctr G3 116 B4
Scottish Maritime Mus* KA12 219 A1
Scottish National Science Mus* G3 116 B4
Sea Twr Ct KA7 238 C3
Seabank Rd Ayr KA7 235 C1
Prestwick KA9 233 A1
Seabank St KA21 217 A4
Seabegs Cres FK4 40 A2
Seabegs Pl FK4 39 C2
Seabegs Rd FK4 39 C2

Seafar Rd G67 ....61 C1
Seafield Ave G61 ....75 C4
Seafield Cottage La
PA16 ....45 B4
Seafield Cres Ayr KA7 ..238 C3
Cumbernauld G68 ....60 C1
Seafield Ct
Ardrossan KA22 ....205 A2
Falkirk FK1 ....41 C1
Seafield Dr
Ardrossan KA22 ....205 B2
Ayr KA7 ....238 B3
Rutherglen G73 ....138 B2
Seafield Rd KA7 ....238 C3
Seafield Sch KA22 ....205 A2
Seaford St KA1 ....227 C4
Seaforth Ave Ayr KA8 ..236 A2
Barrhead G78 ....134 A2
Seaforth PI Bellshill ML4 .141 C2
Stirling FK8 ....7 A4
Seaforth Rd Ayr KA8 ...236 A2
Clydebank G81 ....74 A1
Falkirk FK2 ....24 B1
3 Glasgow G52 ....115 A4
Seaforth Rd N G52 ......115 A4
Seaforth Rd S G52 ......115 A4
Seagate Irvine KA12 ....219 A2
Prestwick KA9 ....233 B1
Seagrove St G32 ....118 B3
Seamill Gdns G74 ....159 B1
Seamill Path G53 ....134 C3
Seamill St G53 ....134 C3
Seamore St 3 G20 ....97 A1
Seath Ave Airdrie ML6 ..122 C4
Langbank PA14 ....70 B3
Seath Rd G73 ....118 A1
Seath St G42 ....117 B1
Seaton PI FK1 ....42 B2
Seaton Terr
Hamilton ML3 ....162 A2
Irvine KA12 ....219 B3
Seaview Rd KA21 ....216 C4
Seaview Terr KA10 ....230 A2
Seaward La G41 ....116 C3
Seaward St 6 G41 ....116 C3
Second Ave
Alexandria G83 ....27 C3
Bearsden G61 ....76 A2
Clydebank G81 ....74 A2
Dumbarton G82 ....50 B1
Glasgow G44 ....137 A3
Irvine KA12 ....224 C4
Kirkintilloch G66 ....79 B1
Millerston G33 ....99 A3
Renfrew PA4 ....94 B1
Uddingston G71 ....120 C1
Second Ave La G44 ......137 A4
Second Gdns G41 ....116 A2
Second Rd G72 ....161 C3
Second St G71 ....140 C4
Seedhill ML1 ....113 C2
Seedhill Rd PA1 ....114 A2
Seggielea La G13 ....95 B3
Seggielea Rd G13 ....95 B3
Segton Ave KA13 ....207 C2
Seil Dr G44 ....137 B2
Selborne PI 5 G13 ....95 C3
Selborne Place La 4
G13 ....95 C3
Selborne Rd G13 ....95 C3
Selby Gdns G32 ....119 B3
Selby PI ML5 ....101 B1
Selby St ML5 ....101 B1
Selkirk Ave Glasgow G52 .115 B2
Paisley PA2 ....133 A4
Selkirk Dr G73 ....138 B4
Selkirk PI
East Kilbride G74 ....160 B2
Hamilton ML3 ....162 C1
Selkirk Rd PA4 ....68 B4
Selkirk St Blantyre G72 ..161 B4
Hamilton ML3 ....162 B1
Wishaw ML2 ....165 B3
Selkirk Way Bellshill ML4 .142 A4
Coatbridge ML5 ....122 C2
Sella Rd G64 ....78 B1
Selvieland Rd G52 ....114 C3
Semphill Gdns G74 ......160 A1
Sempie St ML3 ....161 C2
Sempill Ave PA8 ....72 C1
Semple Ave
Bishopton PA7 ....72 A2
Lochwinnoch PA12 ......129 B2
Semple PI PA3 ....112 A4
Semple Rd KA9 ....236 B3
Semple View PA9 ....130 C3
Senate PI ML1 ....142 B1
Senga Cres ML4 ....142 A4
Seres Rd G76 ....157 B4
Sergeant Law Rd
Paisley PA2,G78 ....132 C2
Uplawmoor G78 ....153 A4
Seright Cres KA3 ....228 B4
Seright Sq KA3 ....228 B4
Serpentine Wlk PA15 .....46 B2
Sersley Dr KA25 ....148 C1
Service St G66 ....33 B1
Seton Dr FK7 ....7 B2
Seton La KA22 ....205 B1
Seton St KA22 ....205 B1
Seton Terr 3 G31 ....117 C4
Settle Gdns G64 ....119 C2
Seven Sisters G66 ....79 C3
Seventh Ave G71 ....140 C4

Seventh Rd G72 ....161 C3
Severn Rd G75 ....179 C4
Seward PI G41 ....116 C3
Seymour Ave KA13 ......207 C1
Seymour Gn G75 ....180 A4
Seyton Ave G46 ....136 B1
Seyton La G46 ....136 B1
Seyton La G74 ....159 C2
Shaftesbury St Alloa FK10 .10 A4
Glasgow G3 ....240 A3
Shafton PI G13 ....95 C4
Shafton Rd G13 ....95 C4
Shaftsbury Ave G81 ....73 C1
Shaftsbury Cres ML1 ...143 B2
Shakespeare Ave G81 ....73 C2
Shakespeare St G20 ......96 C3
Shalloch Pk KA7 ....238 B1
Shalloch PI KA11 ....220 A1
Shamrock St
Glasgow G4 ....240 B4
Kirkintilloch G66 ....79 B4
Shand La ML8 ....187 C2
Shand St ML1 ....165 B1
Shandon Brae G83 ....27 C4
Shandon Cres Balloch G83 .27 C4
Bellshill ML4 ....142 A4
Shandon PI PA15 ....46 B1
Shandon Terr ML3 ....161 C2
Shandwick St G34 ....120 A4
Shangill St ML8 ....186 C2
Shankland Gr PA15 ....46 C1
Shankland Rd PA15 ....46 C1
Shanks Ave
Barrhead G78 ....134 B1
Denny FK6 ....39 C4
Shanks Cres PA5 ....111 C1
Shanks Ct KA3 ....222 C1
Shanks Ind Pk G78 ......134 B2
Shanks St Airdrie ML6 ..103 A1
Glasgow G20 ....96 C3
Shanks Way G78 ....134 B3
Shannon Dr FK1 ....41 C2
Shannon St G20 ....96 C3
Shanter PI Ayr KA7 ......238 C1
Shanter Way KA7 ....238 C1
Shanter Wynd KA7 ......238 C1
Shantron Rd G83 ....27 C3
Shapinsay St G22 ....97 B4
Sharon St KA24 ....191 A4
Sharp Ave ML5 ....121 B2
Sharp St Gourock PA19 ..44 C4
Motherwell ML1 ....144 A1
Sharpe Ave KA11 ....220 B1
Sharphill Ind Est KA21 .206 A2
Shavian Terr G81 ....207 C1
Shavin Brae KA7 ....239 B3
Shaw Ave PA7 ....72 B2
Shaw Cres ML2 ....144 B3
Shaw Ct PA8 ....72 C2
Shaw Farm Ind Est KA9 .233 C1
Shaw PI Dalry KA24 .....191 A4
Greenock PA15 ....45 C3
Linwood PA3 ....112 A3
Saltcoats KA21 ....206 A1
Shaw Rd Milngavie G62 ..76 A4
Newton Mearns G77 .....156 C2
Prestwick KA9 ....233 C1
Shaw St Glasgow G51 ..116 A4
Larkhall ML9 ....199 A4
Shawbank PI KA1 ....228 A4
Shawbridge Arc G43 ...136 B4
Shawbridge Ind Est
G43 ....136 A4
Shawbridge St G43 .....136 A4
Shawburn Cres ML3 ....162 A2
Shawburn St ML3 ....162 A2
Shawfarm Ct KA9 ....233 B1
Shawfarm PI KA9 ....233 B1
Shawfield Ave KA7 ......239 A2
Shawfield Cres ML8 ....186 C3
Shawfield Dr G5 ....117 C1
Shawfield Ind Est G73 .117 C1
Shawfield Rd G73 ....117 C1
Shawhead Ave ML5 .....122 A2
Shawhead Cotts ML5 ...122 A2
Shawhead Prim Sch
ML5 ....122 A2
Shawhill Cres ML7 ......156 C2
Shawhill Rd G43 ....136 B4
Shawholm Cres G43 ....136 A4
Shawlands Acad G41 ...116 C1
Shawlands Arc G41 .....136 C4
Shawlands Cross 5
G41 ....116 C1
Shawlands Prim Sch
G41 ....136 B4
Shawlands Sta G41 .....136 B4
Shawmoss Rd G41 ......116 B1
Shawpark St G20 ....96 C2
Shawrigg Rd ML9 ....185 B1
Shaws Rd ML9 ....199 B4
Shawstonfoot Rd ML1 .145 A1
Shawwood Cres G77 ...156 C2
Shearer Dr ML3 ....183 B4
Shearer Quadrant G83 ..28 A4
Sheddens PI G12 ....118 C3
Sheena Dr G83 ....27 C1
Sheepburn Rd G71 ......140 C4
Sheila St G33 ....98 C2
Sheil Ave ML9 ....185 B1
Sheila Hill ML1 ....162 C2
Sheldaig Rd G22 ....97 A4
Sheldrake PI PA5 ....131 B3
Shellbridge Way KA22 .205 B1
Shelley Cl G12 ....96 A3
Shelley Dr Bothwell G71 .141 A1
Clydebank G81 ....74 A2

Shelley Rd G12 ....96 A3
Shells Rd G66 ....58 C1
Sherbrooke Ave G41 ...116 B2
Sherbrooke Dr G41 .....116 B2
Sherbrooke Gdns G41 ..116 B2
Sherbrooke PI G75 ......159 B1
Sherburn Gdns G69 ....119 C2
Sherdale Ave ML6 ....123 B1
Sheriff Park Ave G73 ...138 A4
Sheriffmuir Rd FK9 ....2 B4
Sheriffmuirlands PI FK9 ..2 B2
Sherriff La FK5 ....23 C2
Sherry Dr ML3 ....162 A1
Sherwood Ave
Paisley PA1 ....114 A3
Uddingston G71 ....141 A3
Sherwood Dr G46 ....136 A2
Sherwood PI G15 ....75 A2
Sherwood Rd
Hurlford KA1 ....228 C3
Prestwick KA9 ....236 C4
Larkhall ML9 ....184 C3
Sidney St KA21 ....216 C4
Siela PI G34 ....120 A4
Siemens PI G21 ....98 A1
Siemens St G21 ....98 A1
Sievewright St G73 .....118 B1
Sighthill Loan 8 ML9 ...185 A2
Sighthill Prim Sch G21 ..97 B2
Sighthill Terr ML7 ....125 A1
Sikeside PI ML5 ....122 B3
Sikeside Prim Sch ML5 .122 B3
Silk Ho FK1 ....42 A3
Silk St PA1 ....113 C3
Silkin Ave G81 ....74 B1
Sillars Mdw KA12 ....219 C1
Silvan PI G76 ....158 A3
Silver Birch Dr G51 .....115 B4
Silver Birch Gdns G51 ..115 B4
Silver Firs ML1 ....143 B2
Silver Glade G52 ....115 A2
Silverbirch Gdns ML3 ..183 C2
Silverburch Gr ML3 .....183 C2
Silverburn Cres ML1 ....143 B2
Silverburn Gdns FK12 ....5 B4
Silverburn St G33 ....118 C4
Silverdale G74 ....159 B2
Silverdale Cres ML11 ...214 C2
Silverdale Ct ML11 ......214 C2
Silverdale St G31 ....118 B2
Silverdale Terr ML6 .....103 C2
Silverfir St G5 ....117 B2
Silvergrove St G40 ......117 C3
Silvermuir Ave ML11 ...215 C4
Silverton Ave G82 ....50 A2
Silvertonhill Ave ML3 ..162 C1
Silvertonhill La G82 ....50 A2
Silverwells Cres G71 ...141 A1
Silverwells Ct G71 ......141 A1
Silverwood Prim Sch
KA1 ....223 B2
Sim St KA1 ....211 B4
Simons Cres
Kilmarnock KA3 ....227 C2
Renfrew PA4 ....94 B3
Simonsburn Rd KA1 ....227 C2
Simpson Ct Clydebank G81 .74 A1
Uddingston G71 ....140 C3
Simpson Dr
East Kilbride G75 ....180 B4
Saltcoats KA21 ....205 C2
Simpson Gdns G78 .....134 A1
Simpson PI
East Kilbride G75 ....180 B4
Kilwinning KA13 ....207 C1
Simpson Quadrant G83 ..28 A4
Simpson St
Crosshouse KA2 ....222 A1
Falkirk FK1 ....41 C3
Glasgow G20 ....96 C2
Simpson Way ML4 ......142 B4
Simshill Prim Sch G44 ..137 A2
Simshill Rd G44 ....137 A2
Simson Ave KA23 ....190 C2
Sinclair Ave G61 ....75 C3
Sinclair Cres FK6 ....21 B1
Sinclair Dr
Coatbridge ML5 ....121 B4
Fallin FK7 ....8 B2
Glasgow G42 ....136 C4
Helensburgh G84 ....16 C2
Sinclair Gdns G64 ....98 A4
Sinclair La G84 ....141 C1
Sinclair PI 6 G75 ....180 C4
Sinclair St
East Kilbride G75 ....180 C4
Greenock PA15 ....46 B2
Helensburgh G84 ....16 B1
Milngavie G62 ....55 A1
Stevenston KA20 ....206 B1
Singer Rd Clydebank G81 ..73 C2
East Kilbride G75 ....181 A3
Singer St G81 ....74 A2
Singer Sta G81 ....74 A1
Sir John Graham Ct FK5 ..23 A1
Sir John Maxwell Prim Sch
G43 ....136 B4
Sir Michael PI
Greenock PA15 ....45 C3

Sir Michael PI continued
Paisley PA1 ....113 B2
Sir Michael St PA15 ......45 C3
Sir William Wallace Ct
FK5 ....23 A2
Sixth Ave PA4 ....94 B1
Sixth St G71 ....120 C1
Skaethorn Rd G20 ....96 A4
Skaithmuir Ave FK2 .....24 A2
Skaithmuir Cres FK2 ....24 A2
Skara Wlk ML8 ....165 C4
Skaterigg Dr G13 ....95 C3
Skaterigg Gdns G13 .....95 C3
Skaterigg La G13 ....95 C3
Skelbo Path G34 ....100 B1
Skelbo PI G34 ....100 B1
Skellyton Cres ML9 .....185 A1
Skelmorlie PI
Kilwinning KA13 ....207 B2
Stenhousemuir FK5 ....23 C2
Skene Rd Glasgow G51 .116 A3
Kilmarnock KA3 ....223 B2
Skene St FK4 ....40 A3
Skerne Gr G75 ....179 C3
Skerneland Rd KA3 ......213 A2
Skerray Quadrant G22 ..97 B4
Skerray St G22 ....97 B4
Skerryvore PI G33 ......119 A4
Skerryvore Rd G33 .....119 A4
Skibo La G66 ....135 C2
Skipness Ave ML8 ....202 A4
Skipness Dr G51 ....115 C4
Skirsa Ct G23 ....97 A4
Skirsa PI G23 ....96 C4
Skirsa Sq G23 ....97 A4
Skirsa St G23 ....96 C4
Skirving St G41 ....136 C4
Skovlunde Way G75e ...180 C3
Skye G74 ....160 A4
Skye Ave PA4 ....94 B1
Skye Cres Gourock PA19 .44 B3
Old Kilpatrick G60 ....73 B3
Paisley PA2 ....133 B4
Skye Ct Cumbernauld G67 .82 B4
Irvine KA11 ....225 A4
Skye Dr Cumbernauld G67 .82 B4
Old Kilpatrick G60 ....73 B3
Skye Gdns Bearsden G61 .75 A3
Kilmarnock KA3 ....223 A3
Skye PI Cumbernauld G67 .82 B4
Stevenston KA20 ....206 C1
Skye Quadrant ML2 ....165 C3
Skye Rd Cumbernauld G67 .82 B4
Port Glasgow PA14 ....69 A3
Prestwick KA9 ....233 C2
Rutherglen G73 ....138 B2
Skye St PA16 ....45 B2
Skye Wynd ML3 ....161 C1
Skythorn Way FK1 ....41 C1
Slaemuir Ave PA14 ....68 C3
Slaemuir Gdns PA14 ....68 C3
Slaemuir Prim Sch PA14 .69 A3
Slakiewood Ave G69 ...100 C4
Slamannan Prim Sch
FK1 ....86 A4
Slamannan Rd
Avonbridge FK1 ....87 C3
Falkirk FK1 ....42 A1
Slamannan FK1 ....86 B4
Slatefield G66 ....57 B4
Slatefield Ct G11 ....118 A3
Slatefield St G31 ....118 A3
Sleaford Ave ML1 ....163 B2
Slenavon Ave G73 ....138 B2
Slessor Dr G75 ....180 C4
Slioch Sq ML1 ....143 B2
Sloan Ave KA12 ....219 B1
Sloan PI KA8 ....236 B1
Sloan St KA8 ....236 B1
Sloy St Glasgow G22 .....97 B2
Wishaw ML2 ....165 A1
Small Cres G72 ....161 B4
Smeaton Ave G64 ....78 A4
Smeaton Dr G64 ....78 A2
Smeaton St G20 ....96 C3
Smiddy Ct
Kilwinning KA13 ....207 C2
Lanark ML11 ....215 C2
Smiddy Wynd FK12 ....5 A3
Smillie PI KA1 ....227 B3
Smillie St PA15 ....46 C1
Smith Art Gallery & Mus*
FK8 ....7 A4
Smith Ave
Glengarnock KA14 ....170 B3
Irvine KA12 ....219 B2
Wishaw ML2 ....186 A4
Smith Cres Balloch G83 ..27 C4
Clydebank G81 ....74 A3
Kilwinning KA13 ....207 C1
Smith Dr KA21 ....217 A4
Smith PI FK6 ....21 B1
Smith Quadrant ML5 ...122 B4
Smith St Ayr KA7 ....239 A4
Dalry KA24 ....191 B4
Falkirk FK2 ....42 A4
Glasgow G14 ....95 C1
Greenock PA15 ....45 C3
Prestwick KA9 ....236 B4
Smith Terr G73 ....118 A1
Smith's La PA3 ....113 C3
Smithfield Loan FK10 ....9 C3
Smithhills St PA1 ....113 C3
Smithston Cres G65 .....60 C3
Smithstone Ct KA11 ....219 C3
Smithstone Terr KA11 .207 A4
Smithstone Way KA11 .219 C3

Smithview ML2 186 B4
Smithy Brae PA13 89 B4
Smithy Ct G82 48 A4
Smithy Rd G82 48 A4
Smithycroft ML3 163 A1
Smithycroft Rd G33 98 C1
Smithycroft Sec Sch G33 98 C1
Smithyends G67 62 A3
Smollett Rd G82 50 A2
Smollett St G83 27 B3
Smuggler's Way G84 15 B3
Smugglers Brig Rd ML8 201 A1
Smyllum Pk ML11 215 B2
Smyllum Rd ML11 215 B2
Snaefell Ave G73 138 B2
Snaefell Cres G73 138 B3
Snead View ML1 143 C1
Sneddon Ave ML2 165 B1
Sneddon St ML3 161 C3
Sneddon Terr ML3 161 C3
Snowden Sch Ltd FK8 7 A4
Snowdon Pl
14 Glasgow G5 117 B2
Stirling FK8 7 A3
Snowdon Place La FK7 7 A3
Snowdon St 15 G5 117 B2
Snowdon Terr KA23 190 A3
Snowdrop Sq KA7 239 A2
Snuff Mill Rd G44 137 A3
Society St G31 118 A3
Solar Ct ML9 199 A4
Sollas Pl G13 94 C4
Solvents Rd KA20 218 A3
Solway Ct ML3 183 A4
Solway Dr FK6 39 B4
Solway Pl Chryston G69 80 B1
Kilmarnock KA1 228 A2
Troon KA10 229 D3
Solway Rd G64 78 B1
Solway St G40 117 C1
Somerford Rd G61 75 C1
Somerled Ave PA3 94 A1
Somerset Ave ML3 162 A2
Somerset Pl G3 240 A4
Somerset Place Mews
G3 240 A4
Somerset Rd KA8 236 A1
Somervell St G72 138 C3
Somerville Ct KA15 150 A1
Somerville Dr
East Kilbride G75 180 C4
Glasgow G42 137 A4
Somerville La 14 G75 180 C4
Somerville Pk KA11 220 A4
Somerville Pl G84 25 A4
Somerville Terr 15 G75 180 C4
Somerville Way KA11 220 A4
Sommerville Dr KA20 217 C3
Sophia Cres KA12 219 A3
Sorbie Dr ML9 198 C1
Sorbie Rd
Ardrossan KA21,KA22 205 C2
Ardrossan, South Beach
KA22 205 B1
Sorby St G31 118 B3
Sorley St G11 95 C1
Sorn St G40 118 A2
Sorrel Dr KA7 239 B2
Souillac Dr FK6 21 B1
Soulis St KA3 223 A1
Sourlie Rdbt KA11 220 A4
Sourlie Terr KA11 219 C3
Souter Dr KA3 228 B4
Souter Pl KA7 239 A3
Souter Way FK5 23 B2
Souterhouse Path ML5 121 C3
Souterhouse Rd ML5 121 C3
South Annandale St
G42 117 A1
South Approach Rd FK2 24 C4
South Ave Carluke ML8 187 C1
Clydebank G81 74 A1
Hamilton G72 161 C3
Paisley PA2 133 C4
Renfrew PA4 94 B2
South Bank St G81 94 B4
South Bantaskine Dr FK1 42 A2
South Bantaskine Rd
FK1 42 A2
South Barrwood Rd G65 60 C4
South Beach KA10 229 C1
South Beach Espl KA10 229 C1
South Beach La KA10 229 C1
South Beach Rd
Ardrossan KA22 205 B1
Ayr KA7 235 C1
South Biggar Rd ML6 123 A4
South Brae G66 57 B4
South Bridge St ML6 123 A4
South Broomage Ave
FK5 23 B1
South Burn Rd ML6 122 B4
South Caldeen Rd ML5 122 A3
South Calder ML1 163 C4
South Campbell St PA2 113 C2
South Carbrain Rd G67 62 A1
South Chester St G32 119 A3
South Church Pl G83 27 C2
South Circular Rd ML5 122 A3
South Claremont La G62 55 A1
South Commonhead Ave
ML6 103 A1
South Crescent Rd
KA22 205 B1
South Crosshill Rd G64 78 A1
South Dean Park Ave
G71 141 A1
South Dean Rd KA3 223 A1
South Douglas St G81 94 B4
South Dr Kilbirnie KA25 170 A4
Linwood PA3 112 A3
Troon KA10 229 D2
South Dumbreck Rd G65 60 A4
South Elgin Pl G81 94 B4
South Elgin St G81 94 B4
South Erskine Pk G61 75 B3
South Exchange Ct G1 241 A2
South Frederick St G1 241 A2
South Gargieston Dr
KA1 227 B3
South Glassford St G62 55 A1
South Green Dr FK2 14 C2
South Hamilton Ct 1
KA1 227 C4
South Hamilton Pl KA1 227 C4
South Hamilton St KA1 227 C4
South Harbour St KA7 235 C1
South Hirst Rd ML7 126 B2
South Isle Rd KA22 205 B3
South King St G84 25 A4
South lanarkshire Coll
(Cambuslang Campus)
G72 139 A3
South Loan G69 100 B4
South Lodge Ct KA7 238 C3
South Mains Cotts PA6 91 C1
South Mains Rd G62 54 C1
South Medrox St ML5 101 B4
South Melville La FK1 42 A3
South Moraine La G15 75 B1
South Mound PA6 91 A1
South Muirhead Ct G67 62 A1
South Muirhead Rd G67 62 A1
South Neuk KA25 170 A4
South Newmoor Ave
KA11 219 C1
South Newmoor Ind Est
KA11 219 C1
South Nimmo St 8
ML6 123 A4
South Park Ave G78 134 B2
South Park Dr PA2 113 C1
South Park Gr ML3 162 B2
South Park Prim Sch
G75 180 B3
South Park Rd ML3 162 B1
South Park Sch KA7 239 A3
South Pl ML4 141 C2
South Pleasance Ave
FK1 42 A2
South Portland St 5
G5 117 A3
South Prim Sch PA2 113 C1
South Rd Clarkston G76 158 A3
Port Glasgow PA14 68 C4
West Kilbride KA23 190 B2
South Ring Rd KA20 218 A3
South Robertson Pl
ML6 122 C4
South Scott St G69 120 A2
South St Cambus FK10 9 A4
Glasgow G14 95 B2
Greenock PA16 45 B3
Houston PA6 91 A1
Inchinnan PA4 93 A2
Stirling FK9 2 B1
South Vennel
Irvine KA11 220 A2
Lanark ML11 215 A2
South Vesalius St G32 119 A3
South View Bellshill ML4 141 C2
Blantyre G72 140 B1
Clydebank G81 73 C2
Stenhousemuir FK5 23 B1
South William St PA5 111 C1
South Woodside Rd G4,
G20 96 C1
Southampton Dr G12 96 A3
Southampton La G12 96 A3
Southbank Bsns Pk G66 79 B4
Southbank Dr G66 79 B4
Southbank Rd G66 79 B4
Southbank St G31 118 B3
Southbar Ave G13 95 A4
Southbar Rd PA4,PA8 93 A4
Southbrae Ave PA11 110 A4
Southbrae Dr G13 95 B2
Southbrae La 9 G13 95 C3
Southburn Rd G63 31 B2
Southcraig Dr KA3 223 A3
Southcroft FK12 4 C3
Southcroft Rd G73 117 C1
Southcroft St G51 116 A4
Southdeen Ave G15 75 A2
Southdeen Rd G15 75 A2
Southend Pl ML4 141 C2
Southend Rd G81 74 A3
Southern Ave G73 138 A3
Southern General Hospl
G51 115 B4
Southerness Dr G68 62 A3
Southesk Ave G64 77 C1
Southesk Gdns G64 77 C2
Southfield Ave
Paisley PA2 133 C4
Port Glasgow PA14 68 C4
Shotts ML7 147 A2
Southfield Cres
Coatbridge ML5 122 B3
Glasgow G53 135 B4
Shotts ML7 147 A2
Stirling FK8 7 A3
Southfield Dr FK1 86 A3
Southfield Pk KA7 239 A3
Southfield Rd
Cumbernauld G68 61 B1
Southfield Rd *continued*
Shotts ML7 147 A2
Southgate
13 East Kilbride G74 159 C1
Milngavie G62 55 A1
Southgate Mall 2 G74 180 C4
Southhill Ave G73 138 B3
Southhook Rd
Kilmarnock KA1 222 B1
Knockentiber KA2 221 C2
Southinch Ave G14 94 C3
Southinch La G14 94 C3
Southlea Ave G46 136 A2
Southloch Gdns 12 G21 97 C2
Southloch St G21 97 C2
Southmuir Pl G20 96 B3
Southook Row KA11 220 A3
Southpark Ave
Glasgow G12 96 C1
Prestwick KA9 236 A4
Southpark La 1 G12 96 C1
Southpark Rd KA7 238 C3
Southpark Terr G12 96 C1
Southside Cres 2 G5 117 B2
Southview G61 75 B3
Southview Ave G76 157 C3
Southview Cres PA11 90 B1
Southview Ct 12 G64 97 C4
Southview Dr G63 31 A2
Southview Pl G69 100 C3
Southview Rd G63 31 B2
Southview Terr G64 97 C4
Southward Way KA10 229 D4
Southwold Rd PA1 114 C3
Southwood Dr G44 137 B3
Southwood Rd KA9 233 A3
Soutra Pl G33 119 A4
Spairdrum Rd Airdrie ML6 83 A2
Cumbernauld G67,ML6 82 C2
Spalehall Dr ML1 143 C2
Spallander Rd KA10 229 D3
Sparrow Gdns KA1 228 B4
Spateston Rd PA5 131 B4
Spean Ave G74 160 A1
Spean St G44 137 A3
Speedwell Sq KA7 239 A2
Speirs Pl PA3 112 B4
Speirs Rd G61 76 A2
Speirsfield Gdns PA2 113 C2
Speirshall Cl G14 94 C3
Speirshall Terr G14 94 C3
Spence St
Bonnybridge FK4 40 A3
Glasgow G20 96 B4
Spencer Dr PA2 132 C4
Spencer St Clydebank G81 74 A2
Glasgow G13 95 C4
Spencerfield Gdns ML3 162 C2
Spey Ave Kilmarnock KA1 228 A3
Paisley PA2 112 C1
Spey Ct Airdrie ML6 123 B3
Stirling FK7 7 B3
22 Wishaw ML2 165 C3
Spey Dr Coatbridge ML5 121 C2
Renfrew PA4 94 C1
Spey Gdns ML3 183 A4
Spey Gr G75 179 C4
Spey Pl PA5 131 B4
Spey Rd Bearsden G61 75 B1
Troon KA10 229 D2
Spey St G33 118 C4
Spey Terr G75 179 C4
Spey Wlk ML1 143 A3
Spey Wynd ML9 199 A4
Speyburn Pl KA11 219 C3
Spiers Ave KA15 171 A4
Spiers Gr G46 135 C2
Spiers Rd Houston PA6 91 A1
Johnstone PA5 112 A2
Lochwinnoch PA12 129 A2
Spiers Wharf G4 97 A1
Spiersbridge Ave G46 135 C2
Spiersbridge La G46 135 C2
Spiersbridge Rd G46 135 C2
Spiersbridge Terr G46 135 C2
Spiersland Way KA15 171 B4
Spindlehowe Rd
Uddingston G71 140 C3
Uddingston, Tannochside
G71 141 A4
Spindleside Rd ML1 144 B1
Spinkhill FK2 42 C1
Spinners Gdns PA2 113 A2
Spinners La G81 74 A4
Spinningdale ML9 198 B1
Spital Rd ML9 198 C1
Spittal Hill FK9 2 B2
Spittal Prim Sch G73 137 C3
Spittal Rd G73 137 C3
Spittal St FK8 7 A4
Spoolers Rd PA1 113 B2
Spoutmouth G1 241 B1
Sprig Way ML7 127 C3
Spring La ML6 104 C2
Springbank Gdns
Falkirk FK2 42 B3
Irvine KA11 220 A4
Springbank Ind Est
KA12 224 C4
Springbank Rd Ayr KA8 236 A2
Paisley PA3 113 B4
Shotts ML7 146 B3
Stirling FK7 7 B3
Springbank St G20 97 A2
Springbank Terr
Paisley PA3 113 B4
Plains ML6 103 C2
Springbank View ML6 103 C2
Springboig Ave G32 119 B3
Springboig Rd G32 119 B3
Springboig St John's Sch
G33 119 B4
Springburn Mus* G21 97 C2
Springburn Pl G74 159 A2
Springburn Rd G21 97 C2
Springburn Sta G21 97 C2
Springburn Way 4 G21 97 C2
Springcroft Ave G69 120 A3
Springcroft Cres G69 120 A3
Springcroft Dr G69 120 A3
Springcroft Gdns G69 120 B3
Springcroft Gr G69 120 A3
Springcroft Rd G69 120 B3
Springcroft Wynd G69 120 A3
Springfield Ave
Bishopbriggs G64 98 A4
Paisley PA1 114 A2
Prestwick KA9 236 B4
Uddingston G71 140 C3
Springfield Cres
Bishopbriggs G64 98 A4
Blantyre G72 161 B4
Carluke ML8 201 C4
Uddingston G71 140 C3
Springfield Ct G1 241 A2
Springfield Dr
Barrhead G78 134 C1
Falkirk FK1 41 C3
Springfield Gdns
Irvine KA11 220 A4
Lanark ML11 214 C3
Springfield Gr G78 155 B4
Springfield Park Rd
G73 138 B3
Springfield Pk PA5 112 A1
Springfield Prim Sch
Glasgow G40 118 A1
Gourock PA16 44 B2
Springfield Quay G5 240 A1
Springfield Rd
Airdrie ML6 123 C4
Alloa FK10 10 B4
Barrhead G78 155 B4
Bishopbriggs G64 78 A1
Crosshouse KA2 221 C1
Cumbernauld G67 62 A2
Denny FK6 21 C1
Glasgow G40 118 A2
Salsburgh ML7 125 A1
Stirling FK7 7 B3
Springfield Sq G64 98 A4
Springfield Woods PA5 112 A1
Springhead Rd ML7 167 A4
Springhill & Leadloch Rd
ML7,EH47 147 C1
Springhill Ave
Airdrie ML6 123 A4
Coatbridge ML5 121 B2
Crosshouse KA2 226 C4
Springhill Farm Gr 3
G69 120 A3
Springhill Farm Pl 1
G69 120 A3
Springhill Farm Rd G69 120 A3
Springhill Farm Way 2
G69 120 A3
Springhill Gdns
Glasgow G41 116 C1
Kilmarnock KA1 227 C4
Springhill Pl
Coatbridge ML5 121 B2
Kilmarnock KA1 227 C4
Springhill Prim Sch
G78 134 A1
Springhill Rd
Barrhead G78 155 A3
Clarkston G76 157 C4
Glasgow G69 120 A3
Port Glasgow PA14 47 B1
Shotts ML7 147 A2
Springhill Terr KA11 220 C1
Springhill View ML7 147 A2
Springholm Dr ML6 102 C1
Springkell Ave G41 116 B1
Springkell Dr G41 116 A1
Springkell Gate G41 116 B1
Springkell Gdns G41 116 B1
Springkell St PA15 46 A2
Springkerse Ind Est FK7 7 B3
Springkerse Rd FK7 7 B3
Springkerse Rdbt FK7 7 C4
Springside KA23 190 C4
Springside Gdns G15 75 A3
Springside Pl G15 75 A2
Springside Prim Sch
KA11 220 C1
Springside Terr KA11 220 C1
Springvale Ct KA21 216 C4
Springvale Dr PA2 112 C1
Springvale Pk KA7 238 C3
Springvale Pl KA21 216 C4
Springvale Rd KA7 238 C3
Springvale St KA21 216 C4
Springvale Terr 9 G21 97 C2
Springwell Cres G72 161 C4
Springwell Pl KA3 195 C1
Springwells Ave ML6 123 B4
Springwells Cres ML6 123 B4
Springwood FK7 6 C3
Springwood Ave FK8 6 C3
Springwood Dr PA13 69 B1
Sprotwell Terr FK10 5 B1
Spruce Ave Blantyre G72 161 B4
Hamilton ML3 162 C1
Johnstone PA5 112 A1
Spruce Ct
Coatbridge ML5 121 C2
Hamilton ML3 162 C1
Spruce Dr
Cambuslang G72 139 C2
Kirkintilloch G66 79 A3
Spruce Ho KA9 236 A3
Spruce Pk KA7 239 B3
Spruce Rd
Cumbernauld G67 62 B2
Uddingston G71 121 B1
Spruce St G22 97 B3
Spruce Way
Cambuslang G72 139 C2
Motherwell ML1 143 A2
Sprucebank Ave PA14 70 B4
Spur Rd KA8 235 C1
Spy's La G84 15 C2
Spynie Pl G64 78 B1
Spynie Way 1 ML2 165 C3
Square The FK7 8 B2
Squire St G14 95 C1
Sraehouse Wynd ML8 188 A1
Stable Gr PA1 113 A2
Stable Pl G62 54 C2
Stable Rd Milngavie G62 54 C2
Shotts ML7 147 A3
Stable Wynd KA10 230 A2
Stables The
Glasgow G52 115 A2
Mugdock G62 55 A3
Paisley PA1 113 A2
Staffa G74 181 B4
Staffa Ave
Port Glasgow PA14 69 A4
Renfrew PA4 94 B1
Staffa Ct KA11 225 A4
Staffa Dr Airdrie ML6 123 C4
Kirkintilloch G66 80 A4
Paisley PA2 133 C4
Staffa Pl FK1 42 A1
Staffa Rd G72 138 C2
Staffa St Glasgow G31 118 A4
Gourock PA19 44 C3
Staffin Dr G23 76 B1
Staffin Rd KA10 229 D3
Staffin St G23 76 C1
Stafflar Dr KA1 227 C2
Stafford Cres PA16 44 C2
Stafford Rd PA16 44 C2
Stafford St Bellshill ML4 141 C2
Glasgow G4 241 B4
Helensburgh G84 16 B1
Kilmarnock KA3 222 C1
Stafford St W G84 16 B2
Staffordway S PA16 44 C2
Stag Ct G71 141 B3
Stag St G51 116 A4
Staig Wynd ML1 164 A2
Staikhill ML11 214 C3
Staineybraes Pl ML6 102 C1
Stairlie Cres KA23 190 B3
Stalker St ML2 164 B2
Stamford St G31 118 A3
Stamperland Ave G76 157 C4
Stamperland Cres G76 157 C4
Stamperland Dr G76 157 C4
Stamperland Gdns G76 157 C4
Stamperland Hill G76 157 C4
Stanalane St G46 135 C2
Standalane Kilmaurs KA3 222 B4
Stewarton KA3 211 B4
Standburn Rd G33 98 B3
Stane Prim Sch ML7 147 A2
Stane Rd
Port Glasgow PA14 68 C4
Shotts ML7 147 A1
Staneacre Pk ML3 162 C2
Stanecastle Dr KA11 219 C3
Stanecastle Gate KA11 219 C3
Stanecastle Intc KA12 219 C2
Stanecastle Rd KA11 219 C2
Stanecastle Sch KA11 220 A3
Stanecraigs Pl 20 ML2 165 C3
Stanefield Dr ML1 143 C2
Stanely Cres PA2 133 A4
Stanely Dr PA2 113 B1
Stanely Gr PA2 133 A4
Stanely Rd PA2 113 B1
Stanford St G81 74 B1
Stanhope Dr G73 138 B3
Stanhope Pl ML2 186 A4
Stanistone Rd ML8 188 A1
Stanley Ave
Ardrossan KA22 205 B2
Paisley PA2 113 A1
Stanley Bvd ML3 161 B2
Stanley Dr
Ardrossan KA22 205 B2
Bellshill ML4 142 A3
Bishopbriggs G64 78 A1
Bridge of A FK9 2 A4
Brookfield PA5 111 B3
Stanley La PA5 111 B3
Stanley Pk ML6 123 A4
Stanley Pl Blantyre G72 140 B1
Saltcoats KA21 205 C1
Stanley Prim Sch KA22 205 B2
Stanley Rd
Ardrossan KA22 205 B2
Saltcoats KA21 216 C4
Stanley St Glasgow G41 116 C3
Hamilton ML3 161 C2
Stanley Street La G41 116 C3
Stanmore Ave ML11 215 A3

Stanmore Cres ML11 ....215 B3
Stanmore Gdns ML11 ...215 B3
Stanmore House Sch
  ML11 ....215 B3
Stanmore Rd
  Glasgow G42 ....137 A4
  Lanark ML11 ....215 B3
Stanners La PA15 ....46 A2
Stanrigg St ML6 ....104 A1
Stanton Ave FK10 ....9 C3
Stark Ave Clydebank G81 ..73 C3
  Falkirk FK1 ....41 B3
Starling Way ML4 ....141 C4
Starryshaw Rd ML7 ....146 C3
Startpoint St G33 ....119 A4
Station Ave
  Greenock PA15 ....46 A2
  Howwood PA9 ....130 C3
Station Brae Irvine KA11 ..220 B1
  Neilston G78 ....154 B4
Station Bridge KA7 ....239 A4
Station Cres PA4 ....94 C2
Station Ct
  Glengarnock KA14 ....170 B3
  Netherburn ML9 ....200 B2
Station Dr Hurlford KA1 ..228 B3
  Prestwick KA9 ....233 B1
  Springside KA11 ....221 A2
Station La KA3 ....211 B4
Station Pl ML8 ....187 A3
Station Rd Airdrie ML6 ..123 C4
  Ayr KA7,KA8 ....239 A4
  Bannockburn FK7 ....7 C1
  Bardowie G62 ....77 A4
  Bearsden G61 ....75 B2
  Bishopton PA7 ....72 A1
  Blackridge EH48 ....107 B1
  Blantyre G72 ....140 C1
  Bothwell G71 ....141 A1
  Bridge of A FK9 ....1 C4
  Caldercruix ML6 ....104 C2
  Cambus FK10 ....4 A1
  Cardross G82 ....48 A4
  Carluke ML8 ....187 C1
  Clarkston G76 ....158 A3
  Cleland ML1 ....144 A1
  Cowie FK7 ....12 B3
  Dumbarton G82 ....49 C2
  Dunlop KA3 ....195 A4
  Glasgow G69 ....120 B2
  Glasgow, Giffnock G46 ....136 B2
  Glasgow, Maryhill G20 ....96 B4
  Gourock PA19 ....44 C4
  Hamilton ML3 ....162 C2
  Helensburgh G84 ....25 A4
  Howwood PA9 ....130 C3
  Kilbarchan PA10 ....111 A1
  Kilsyth G65 ....36 B1
  Langbank PA14 ....70 B3
  Larkhall ML9 ....185 A2
  Law ML8 ....187 A3
  Lennoxtown G66 ....57 B4
  Longcroft FK4 ....39 A2
  Millerston G33 ....99 A3
  Milngavie G62 ....55 A1
  Motherwell ML1 ....143 A2
  Muirhead G69 ....100 B4
  Neilston G78 ....154 B4
  Netherburn ML9 ....200 B2
  Old Kilpatrick G60 ....73 A3
  Paisley PA1 ....113 A2
  Plains ML6 ....104 A1
  Port Glasgow PA14 ....47 B1
  Prestwick KA9 ....233 B1
  Prestwick, Monkton KA9 ..233 B2
  Renfrew PA4 ....94 C2
  Rhu G84 ....15 C3
  Shotts ML7 ....146 C2
  Slamannan FK1 ....86 A3
  Springside KA11 ....220 C1
  Stevenston KA20 ....217 B4
  Stirling FK8 ....7 A4
  Strathblane G63 ....31 A2
  Uddingston G71 ....140 C3
  Wishaw ML2 ....165 A1
Station Rise ML2 ....99 B3
Station Row Irvine KA11 ..225 C3
  Law ML8 ....187 A3
  Slamannan FK1 ....86 A3
Station St G82 ....27 B1
Station Way G71 ....140 C3
Station Wynd PA10 ....111 A1
Staybrae Dr G53 ....114 C1
Staybrae Gr G53 ....114 C1
Steading The ML2 ......165 A3
Steadings Dr G83 ....28 A3
Steadman Pl KA11 ....225 A4
Steel St Glasgow G1 ......241 B1
  Gourock PA19 ....44 C4
  Wishaw ML2 ....165 A1
Steele Cres G83 ....28 A4
Steele Wlk G83 ....28 A4
Steeple Sq PA10 ....111 A2
Steeple St PA10 ....111 A2
Steeples View KA10 ......229 D4
Stein Sq FK7 ....7 A2
Stemac La ML4 ....104 A1
Stenhouse Ave G69 ....100 B4
Stenhouse Rd FK5 ....23 C1
Stenhousemuir Prim Sch
  FK5 ....23 B2
Stenton Cres ML2 ....164 B1
Stenton Pl ML2 ....164 B1
Stenton St G32 ....118 C4

Stepends Rd Airdrie ML6 .124 B4
  Plains ML6 ....104 B1
Stepford Pl G33 ....119 C4
Stepford Rd G33 ....120 A4
Stephen Cres G69 ....119 C3
Stephen Pl 17 G75 ....180 B4
Stephenson Sq 16 G75 ...180 B4
Stephenson St G52 ....114 C4
Stephenson Terr G75 ...180 B4
Stepps Prim Sch G33 ....99 C3
Stepps Rd Glasgow G33 ..119 B4
  Kirkintilloch G66 ....79 C1
Stepps Sta G33 ....99 C3
Steps Rd KA12 ....219 B3
Steps St FK5 ....23 C2
Sterling (annexe) YH*
  FK8 ....2 A1
Steuart Rd FK9 ....1 C4
Steven St G83 ....27 C3
Stevens La ML1 ....143 A2
Stevens Pl PA19 ....44 C3
Stevenson Ct FK9 ....2 A3
Stevenson Pl ML4 ....142 A4
Stevenson St
  Carluke ML8 ....187 C1
  Clydebank G81 ....73 C2
  Glasgow G40 ....241 C1
  Kilmarnock KA1 ....222 B1
  Paisley PA2 ....113 C2
  Glasgow G40 ....117 C3
Stevenson Ct ML1 ....143 A2
Stevenson Ind Est
  KA20 ....217 C4
Stevenson St ML1 ....143 A2
Stevenson Sta KA20 .....217 B4
Stewart Ave
  Blantyre G72 ....161 B4
  Falkirk FK2 ....24 A1
  Hamilton ML3 ....183 A4
  Newton Mearns G77 ......156 C3
  Renfrew PA4 ....94 A1
Stewart Cres
  Barrhead G78 ....134 B2
  Wishaw ML2 ....166 A3
Stewart Ct Barrhead G78 .134 B2
  Coatbridge ML5 ....122 B2
  Rutherglen G73 ....138 B4
Stewart Ctr PA15 ....45 C3
Stewart Dr
  Bargeddie G69 ....121 A3
  Clarkston G76 ....157 C4
  Clydebank G81 ....74 A3
  Irvine KA12 ....219 B2
Stewart Gr ML7 ....127 C3
Stewart Pl G78 ....134 B2
Stewart Quadrant ML1 ...143 A3
Stewart Rd Ayr KA8 .....236 B2
  Falkirk FK2 ....42 B3
  Paisley PA2 ....133 C4
Stewart Sq FK8 ....2 A1
Stewart St Barrhead G78 .134 B2
  Bellshill ML4 ....142 B3
  Bonnybridge FK4 ....39 C3
  Cambusbarron FK7 ....6 B3
  Carluke ML8 ....187 C1
  Coatbridge ML5 ....122 A4
  Glasgow G4 ....240 C4
  Hamilton ML3 ....162 A3
  Milngavie G62 ....55 A1
Stewartfield Cres G74 ...159 B2
Stewartfield Dr G74 ......159 B2
Stewartfield Rd G74 .....159 B2
Stewartfield Way G74 ....159 B2
Stewartgill Pl ML9 ....185 C1
Stewarton Acad KA3 ....195 C1
Stewarton Cres KA3 ......223 A3
Stewarton Dr G72 ....138 C3
Stewarton Rd
  Dunlop KA3 ....195 A4
  Fenwick KA3 ....213 A2
  Glasgow G46 ....135 C1
  Newton Mearns G77 ......156 B4
Stewarton St ML2 ....165 B1
Stewarton Sta KA3 ....195 B1
Stewarton Terr ML2 ......165 B1
Stewarts La ML1 ....165 B2
Stewartville St G11 ......96 A1
Stirling Ave Bearsden G61 .75 C1
  Kilmarnock KA1 ....222 B1
Stirling Bsns Ctr FK8 .....7 A3
Stirling Castle* FK8 ......1 C1
Stirling Cres KA1 ....222 B1
Stirling Dr Bearsden G61 ..75 B3
  Bishopbriggs G64 ....77 C2
  East Kilbride G74 ....160 A2
  Gourock PA19 ....43 C3
  Hamilton ML3 ....161 C2
  Johnstone PA5 ....111 B1
  Linwood PA3 ....112 A3
  Rutherglen G73 ....138 A3
Stirling Ent Pk FK7 ....7 B4
Stirling F Ed Ctr FK7 .....7 B3
Stirling Gdns G64 ....77 C2
Stirling High Sch FK8 ....7 A3
Stirling Pl
  Lennoxtown G66 ....57 C4
  Plean FK7 ....12 B2
Stirling Rd Airdrie ML6 ..103 A3
  Alexandria G83 ....27 C1
  Alloa FK10 ....9 C4
  Alva FK12 ....4 C4
  Balloch G83 ....20 A1
  Carluke ML8 ....187 C2
  Chapelhall ML6 ....123 B2
  Cumbernauld G67 ....83 A3

Stirling Rd continued
  Dumbarton G82 ....50 B2
  Falkirk FK1,FK5 ....41 B4
  Fallin FK7 ....8 B2
  Glasgow G4 ....241 B3
  Kilsyth G65 ....36 C1
  Rogend ML6 ....83 A2
  Torwood FK5 ....22 C3
  Tullibody FK10 ....4 A2
Stirling Royal Infmy FK8 ..7 A3
Stirling St Airdrie ML6 ...123 A4
  Alva FK12 ....5 A2
  Coatbridge ML5 ....121 B2
  Cumbernauld G67 ....62 A2
  Denny FK6 ....21 B2
  Motherwell ML1 ....164 A2
  Renton G82 ....27 B1
Stirling Sta FK8 ....7 A4
Stirling Way
  Bishopbriggs G69 ....120 A2
  8 Renfrew PA4 ....94 B1
Stirlingfauld Pl 7 G5 ...117 A3
Stirrat St Glasgow G20 ..96 B3
  Paisley PA3 ....113 B4
Stobbs Cres KA13 ....207 C1
Stobbs Terr KA13 ....207 C1
Stobcross Bsns Pk 6
  G3 ....116 C4
Stobcross Rd G3 ....116 B4
Stobcross St
  Coatbridge ML5 ....122 A3
  Glasgow G3 ....240 A2
Stobcross Wynd G3 ......116 B4
Stobhill Cotts G21 ....98 A4
Stobhill Cres KA7 ....239 B3
Stobhill Hospl G21 ....98 A3
Stobhill Rd G21 ....97 C4
Stobo G74 ....160 B2
Stobo Ct G74 ....160 B2
Stobo St ML2 ....165 B3
Stobs Dr G78 ....134 A2
Stobs Pl G34 ....100 B1
Stock Ave PA2 ....113 C1
Stock St PA2 ....113 C1
Stockbridge Cres KA25 ..149 A2
Stockholm Cres PA2 .....113 C2
Stockiemuir Ave G61 ....75 C4
Stockiemuir Rd
  Bearsden G61 ....75 B4
  Milngavie G61,G62 ....54 B1
Stocks Rd ML1 ....144 C1
Stockwell Pl G1 ....241 A1
Stockwell St G1 ....241 A1
Stoddard Sq PA5 ....112 B2
Stonebank Gr G45 ....137 B2
Stonebyres Ct ML3 ......162 A2
Stonecraig Rd ML2 ....165 B1
Stonecrop Pl KA7 ....239 B2
Stonedyke Cres ML8 .....188 A2
Stonedyke Gr G15 ....75 A1
Stonedyke Prim Sch G15 ..75 A1
Stonedyke Rd ML8 ....188 A2
Stonefield Ave
  Glasgow G12 ....96 B3
  Paisley PA2 ....113 C1
Stonefield Cres
  Blantyre G72 ....161 B3
  Paisley PA2 ....113 C1
  Paisley PA2 ....113 C1
Stonefield Dr PA2 ....113 C1
Stonefield Gdns
  Carluke ML8 ....187 C2
  Paisley PA2 ....113 C1
Stonefield Gn PA2 ....113 C1
Stonefield Park Gdns
  G72 ....161 C4
Stonefield Pk Ayr KA7 ...238 B1
  Paisley PA2 ....113 C4
Stonefield Pl G72 ....161 B3
Stonefield Rd G72 ....161 B4
Stonefield St ML6 ....103 A1
Stonehall Ave ML3 ......162 A1
Stonehaven Cres ML6 ...122 C3
Stonehaven Rd PA16 ....44 C2
Stonehouse Hospl ML9 ..198 B1
Stonehouse Prim Sch
  ML9 ....198 C1
Stonelaw Dr G73 ....138 A3
Stonelaw High Sch
  G73 ....138 A4
Stonelaw High Sch Annexe
  G73 ....138 A4
Stonelaw Rd G73 ....138 A4
Stonelaw Twrs G73 ......138 B3
Stoneleigh Pl PA16 .....45 B4
Stoneleigh Rd PA16 .....45 B4
Stoneside Dr G43 ....136 A3
Stoneside Sq G43 ....136 A3
Stoney Brae Paisley PA2 .113 C4
  2 Paisley, Laigh Pk PA3 ..113 C3
Stonepetts Rd G69 ......80 C1
Stoneyholm Rd KA25 ....149 A1
Stoneymeadow Rd G72 ..139 C1
Stoneymollan Rd G82 ...26 A3
Stoneyetts Rd ML6 ......21 A1
Stonyflatt Ave G82 ......50 A3
Stonyflatt Rd G82 ....50 A3
Stonyhill Ave KA1 ....227 C3
Stonyhurst St
  Glasgow G22 ....97 B2
  Glasgow, Firhill G22 .....97 A2
Stonylee Rd G67 ....62 A1
Stoopshill Cres KA24 ....191 C4
Storie St PA1 ....113 C2
Stormyland Way G78 ....134 B1
Stornaway Dr KA3 ....223 A3

Stornoway Cres ML2 .....165 C3
Stornoway St G22 ....97 B4
Stow Brae PA1 ....113 C2
Stow Coll G3 ....97 A1
Stow Coll (West Campus)
  G20 ....96 C2
Stow Coll of Engineering
  G3 ....240 B4
Strachan St Bellshill ML4 .142 A2
Strachur St Glasgow G22 ..97 A4
  Falkirk FK1 ....41 C2
Strachur St G22 ....97 A4
Strain Cres ML6 ....123 A3
Straiton Dr ML3 ....161 B1
Straiton Pl G72 ....161 B4
Straiton St G32 ....118 C4
Strand KA15 ....171 A4
Strand St KA1 ....222 C1
Strandhead KA3 ....211 B4
Strang Pl KA9 ....236 B3
Strang's Pl FK1 ....66 C3
Stranka Ave PA2 ....113 B2
Stranraer Dr G15 ....75 B1
Stratford G74 ....160 B3
Stratford St G20 ....96 C3
Strath Carron ML8 ......187 A3
Strath Dearn ML8 ....187 A3
Strath Elgin ML8 ....187 A3
Strath Halladale ML8 ....187 A3
Strath Nairn ML8 ....187 A3
Strath Naver ML8 ....187 A3
Strath Peffer ML8 ....186 C3
Strathallan Ct ML3 ......161 C1
Strathallan Gdns 5 G66 .79 A4
Strathallan Rd FK9 ......2 A3
Strathallon Pl G73 ....138 B2
Strathaven Rd
  Eaglesham G76 ....178 C2
  East Kilbride G74,G75 ....181 A4
  Hamilton ML3 ....183 B3
  Stonehouse ML9 ....198 B1
Strathavon Cres ML6 ....103 A1
Strathaye Pl ML8 ....187 A3
Strathblane Cres ML6 ...103 A2
Strathblane Dr G75 ......179 C4
Strathblane Gdns G13 ...95 C4
Strathblane Prim Sch
  G63 ....31 B2
Strathblane Rd
  Clachan of C G66 ....32 C2
  Milngavie G62 ....55 B2
Strathboil Cres ML6 ......103 A2
Strathbran St G31 ....118 B2
Strathcarron Cres PA2 ...134 A3
Strathcarron Dr PA2 .....114 A1
Strathcarron Pl
  18 Glasgow G22 ....96 B3
Strathcarron Rd PA2 ....114 A1
Strathcarron Way PA2 ..114 A1
Strathclyde Arts Ctr G3 ..240 B2
Strathclyde Bsns Ctr
  Cambuslang G72 ....139 C2
  Greenock PA15 ....46 C2
  Motherwell ML1 ....142 C2
Strathclyde Bsns Pk
  ML4 ....141 C4
Strathclyde Ct G84 ......16 A2
Strathclyde Ctry Pk*
  ML1 ....141 C1
Strathclyde Hospl ML1 ...163 B3
Strathclyde Pl G84 ......16 A1
Strathclyde Rd
  Dumbarton G82 ....50 A3
  Motherwell ML1 ....163 A3
Strathclyde St G40 ......137 C1
Strathclyde View G71 ...141 A1
Strathclyde Way ML4 ....141 C4
Strathcona Dr G13 ......96 A4
Strathcona Gdns G13 ...96 A4
Strathcona La 8 G75 ....180 C4
Strathcona Pl
  East Kilbride G75 ....180 C4
  Rutherglen G73 ....138 B2
Strathcona St G13 ....95 C3
Strathclyde Dr G73 ......138 A3
Strathdearn Gr G75 .....179 C4
Strathdee Ave G75 ......74 A3
Strathdee Rd G44 ....136 C1
Strathdon Ave
  Glasgow G44 ....136 C1
  Paisley PA2 ....113 B1
Strathdon Dr G44 ....136 C1
Strathdon Pl KA7 ....238 B1
Strathdoon Pl KA7 ......238 B1
Strathearn Gr G66 ....59 A1
Strathearn Rd G76 ......157 C2
Strathendrick Dr G44 ...136 C2
Strathfillan Rd G74 ......159 B1
Strathgryffe Cres PA11 ..90 B1
Strathhalladale Ct G75 ..179 C4
Strathlachan Ave ML8 ..188 A1
Strathleven Dr G83 ......27 C1
Strathleven Pl G82 ......49 C2
Strathmiglo Ct G75 .....179 C4
Strathmiglo Pl FK5 ......23 C2

Strathmore Ave
  Blantyre G72 ....140 B1
  Paisley PA1 ....114 B2
Strathmore Cres
  Airdrie ML6 ....103 A3
  Stirling FK9 ....2 A2
Strathmore Dr FK9 ......2 A2
Strathmore Gdns G73 ...138 B2
Strathmore Gr G75 ......179 C4
Strathmore Pk KA11 ....220 A3
Strathmore Pl ML5 ....122 B3
Strathmore Rd
  Glasgow G22 ....97 A4
  Hamilton ML3 ....162 C2
Strathmore Wlk ML5 ....122 B3
Strathmungo Cres ML6 ..102 C1
Strathnairn Ave G75 ....179 C4
Strathnairn Ct G75 ......179 C4
Strathnairn Dr G75 ......179 C4
Strathnairn Way G75 ...179 C4
Strathnaver Cres ML6 ...103 A2
Strathnaver Gdns G75 ...179 C4
Strathord Pl G69 ....81 A2
Strathord St G32 ....119 A2
Strathpeffer Cres ML6 ..103 A1
Strathpeffer Dr G75 .....179 C4
Strathspey Ave G75 .....179 C4
Strathspey Cres ML6 ....103 A2
Strathtay Ave
  East Kilbride G75 ....179 C4
  Glasgow G44 ....136 C1
Strathtummel Cres ML6 ..103 A2
Strathview Gr G44 ....136 C1
Strathview Pk G44 ......136 C1
Strathview Rd ML4 ......141 C2
Strathvithie Gr G75 .....179 C4
Strathy Pl 13 Glasgow G20 .96 B3
  Kilmarnock KA1 ....228 A3
Strathyre Gdns
  Bearsden G61 ....76 A3
  East Kilbride G75 ....179 C4
  Glenmavis ML6 ....102 C3
  Moodiesburn G69 ....83 A2
Strathyre Rd G72 ....161 C3
Strathyre St G41 ....136 C4
Stratton Dr G46 ....136 A1
Strauss Ave G81 ....74 C1
Stravaig Path PA2 ....133 A4
Stravaig Wlk PA2 ....133 A4
Stravanan Terr G45 .....137 B1
Stravanan Ct G45 ....137 C1
Stravanan Gdns G45 ....137 B1
Stravanan Rd G45 ......137 B1
Stravanan St G45 ....137 B1
Stravenhouse Rd ML8 ..188 A3
Strawberry Field Rd PA6 .91 A1
Strawberrybank Rd
  KA3 ....223 A1
Strawhill Cr G76 ....157 C4
Strawhill Rd G76 ....157 C4
Streamfield Gate G33 ...98 B4
Streamfield Gdns G33 ...98 C4
Streamfield Lea G33 .....98 C4
Streamfield Pl G33 ......98 B4
Strenaby Ave G73 ....138 B2
Stripehead 8 FK10 .....10 A3
Striven Cres ML2 ....165 A1
Striven Ct ML5 ....122 A2
Striven Dr FK2 ....24 A2
Striven Gdns G20 ....96 C2
Striven Terr ML3 ....162 A1
Stroma Ave PA14 ....69 A4
Stroma Ct KA11 ....225 B4
Stroma St G21 ....98 A1
Stromness St G15 ....117 A2
Strone Cres PA15 ....46 A2
Strone Gdns G65 ....60 A4
Strone Path ML5 ....101 B3
Strone Pl ML6 ....123 B3
Strone Rd Alexandria G83 .27 C3
  Glasgow G33 ....119 A4
Stronend St G22 ....97 A3
Stronsay Ct KA11 ....220 A1
Stronsay Pl
  Bishopbriggs G64 ....78 B1
  Kilmarnock KA3 ....223 A3
Stronsay St G21 ....98 A1
Stronsay Way KA11 .....220 A1
Stronvar Dr G14 ....95 A2
Stroud Rd G75 ....180 B3
Strowan Cres G32 ......119 A2
Strowan St G32 ....119 B2
Strowan's Well Rd G82 ..50 B2
Struan Ave G46 ....136 B2
Struan Gdns G44 ....137 A3
Struan Rd G44 ....137 A3
Strude Howe FK12 ......5 A4
Strude Mill FK12 ....5 A4
Strude St FK12 ....5 A4
Strule St G34 ....120 A4
Struma Dr G76 ....157 B4
Struther & Swinhill Rd
  ML9 ....199 B3
Struther St ML9 ....199 A4
Struthers Ave G74,ML1 ..199 B4
Struthers Ave KA1 ......228 B4
Struthers Cres G74 .....160 A2
Struthers Pl KA10 ......229 D4
Struthers Prim Sch
  KA10 ....229 D3
Stuart Ave
  Old Kilpatrick G60 ....73 A3
  Rutherglen G73 ....138 A3
Stuart Dr Bishopbriggs G64 .97 C4
  Lanark ML11 ....215 A3
  Larkhall ML9 ....185 B1
Stuart Pl KA2 ....225 C1

Stuart Quadrant ML2 . . . 164 C1
Stuart Rd Bishopton PA7 . . 72 A2
Carmunnock G76 . . . . 158 B4
Dumbarton G82 . . . . 50 B2
Stuart St
East Kilbride G74 . . . . . . 159 C1
Old Kilpatrick G60 . . . . 73 A3
Stuarton Pk G74 . . . . 159 C1
Stuckleckie Rd G84 . . . . . . 17 A1
Sturrock St KA1 . . . . 227 C4
Styles Pl FK1 . . . . 41 C1
Succoth St G13 . . . . 95 C4
Sudbury Cres 10 G75 . . 159 A1
Suffolk Rd PA16 . . . . 44 C2
Suffolk St Glasgow G40 . 241 B1
Helensburgh G84 . . . . 16 B1
Sugworth Ave G69 . . . . . 120 A3
Suisnish PA4 . . . . 93 B4
Summerburgh St G33 . . . 119 A4
Summer St G40 . . . . 117 C3
Summerfield Cotts G14 . . 95 C1
Summerfield Rd G67 . . . . 82 A3
Summerfield St G40 . . . . 118 A2
Summerford FK1 . . . . 41 B2
Summerford Gdns FK1 . . . 41 B2
Summerford Rd FK1 . . . . . 41 B2
Summerhill & Garngibbock
Rd G67 . . . . 82 B2
Summerhill Ave ML9 . . . 185 A1
Summerhill Dr G15 . . . . . . 75 A2
Summerhill Gdns G15 . . . 75 A2
Summerhill Pl
Glasgow G15 . . . . 75 A2
Shotts ML7 . . . . 166 C4
Summerhill Prim Sch
G15 . . . . 75 A2
Summerhill Rd
Clarkston G76 . . . . 157 C4
Glasgow G15 . . . . 75 A2
Summerhill Way ML4 . . . 141 C2
Summerlea Rd
Glasgow G46 . . . . 135 C2
Seamill KA23 . . . . 190 A2
Summerlee Cotts ML5 . . 121 C4
Summerlee Mus* ML5 . . 121 C4
Summerlee Rd
Larkhall ML9 . . . . 184 C3
Wishaw ML2 . . . . 164 B2
Summerlee St
Coatbridge ML5 . . . . 121 C4
Glasgow G33 . . . . 119 B4
Summerston Sta G20 . . . . 96 B4
Summertown Rd G51 . . . 116 A4
Suna Path ML7 . . . . 147 A2
Sunart Ave PA4 . . . . 94 A2
Sunart Ct ML3 . . . . 162 A1
Sunart Gdns G64 . . . . 78 B1
Sunart Rd
Bishopbriggs G64 . . . . . . 78 B1
Glasgow G52 . . . . 115 C3
Sunart St ML2 . . . . 165 A1
Sunbury Ave G76 . . . . . . 157 B4
Sundale Ave G76 . . . . . . 157 B3
Sunderland Ave G82 . . . . 49 A2
Sunderland Ct KA25 . . . . 170 A4
Sundrum Pl KA13 . . . . . . 207 B1
Sunflower Gdns ML1 . . . 163 C4
Sunningdale Ave
Ayr KA7 . . . . 239 A2
Newton Mearns G77 . . . 156 C3
Sunningdale Dr PA11 . . . 110 B3
Sunningdale Rd G23 . . . . . 96 C4
Sunningdale Wynd G71 . 140 C2
Sunnybank Ave G72 . . . . 146 C3
Sunnybank Dr G76 . . . . . 157 B4
Sunnybank Gr G76 . . . . . 157 B3
Sunnybank Rd FK7 . . . . 2 A3
Sunnybank St G40 . . . . . 118 A2
Sunnylaw Dr EH48 . . . . . 107 C2
Sunnylaw Rd EH48 . . . . . 107 C2
Sunnyhill G65 . . . . 59 C2
Sunnylaw Dr PA2 . . . . . . 113 A1
Sunnylaw Pl FK1 . . . . 41 C2
Sunnylaw St G22 . . . . 97 A2
Sunnyside Kilmaurs KA3 . 222 A4
Stirling FK7 . . . . 2 C2
Sunnyside Ave
Motherwell ML1 . . . . 143 A3
Port Glasgow PA14 . . . . . 69 A4
Uddingston G71 . . . . 140 C3
Sunnyside Cres ML1 . . . . 143 A3
Sunnyside Ct FK10 . . . . . . 10 A4
Sunnyside Dr
Bargeddie G69 . . . . 121 A3
Clarkston G76 . . . . 158 C2
Glasgow G15 . . . . 75 A1
Sunnyside Oval PA2 . . . . 113 C1
Sunnyside Pl
Barrhead G78 . . . . 134 A1
Glasgow G15 . . . . 75 A1
Motherwell ML1 . . . . 143 A3
Sunnyside Prim Sch
Alloa FK10 . . . . 10 A4
Glasgow G33 . . . . 99 B2
Sunnyside Rd Alloa FK10 . 10 A4
Cleland ML1 . . . . 165 A4
Coatbridge ML5 . . . . 122 A4
Falkirk FK1 . . . . 41 C3
Kilmarnock KA1 . . . . 227 C1
Kirkfieldbank ML11 . . . . 214 B3
Larkhall ML3,ML9 . . . . . 184 B2
Paisley PA2 . . . . 113 C1
Sunnyside Sq KA1 . . . . . 227 C1
Sunnyside Sq W KA1 . . . 227 C1
Sunnyside St Falkirk FK1 . 41 C3
Larkhall ML9 . . . . 184 C2

Sunnyside Sta ML5 . . . . . 122 A4
Sunnyside Terr ML1 . . . . 143 A3
Surcoat Loan FK7 . . . . 7 C2
Surrey La 5 G5 . . . . 117 A2
Surrey St 3 G5 . . . . 117 A2
Susannah St G83 . . . . 27 C3
Sussex St G41 . . . . 116 C3
Sutcliffe Ct G13 . . . . 95 C4
Sutcliffe Rd G13 . . . . 95 C4
Sutherland Ave
Alloa FK10 . . . . 10 B4
Bearsden G61 . . . . 75 C4
Glasgow G41 . . . . 116 C1
Stirling FK8 . . . . 2 B1
Sutherland Cres ML3 . . . 162 A2
Sutherland Dr
Airdrie ML6 . . . . 122 C3
Denny FK6 . . . . 39 B4
Dumbarton G82 . . . . 50 B2
Kilmarnock KA3 . . . . 223 B1
Sutherland La G12 . . . . . . 96 B1
Sutherland Pl ML4 . . . . . 141 C1
Sutherland Rd
Clydebank G81 . . . . 74 A1
Greenock PA16 . . . . 45 A2
Sutherland St
Blantyre G72 . . . . 161 B3
Helensburgh G84 . . . . . . 16 A1
Paisley PA1 . . . . 113 B3
Sutherland Way G60 . . . 160 B2
Sutherness Dr G33 . . . . . 119 A4
Suttie Way FK9 . . . . 1 C4
Sutton Ct KA13 . . . . 207 A2
Sutton Pk Cres FK5 . . . . . 23 C2
Sutton Pl FK2 . . . . 42 B3
Swaledale G74 . . . . 159 B2
Swallow Gdns G13 . . . . . . 94 C4
Swallow Pl KA3 . . . . 223 B4
Swallow Rd Clydebank G81 74 B4
Wishaw ML2 . . . . 165 A2
Swan Pl PA5 . . . . 131 B4
Swan St Clydebank G81 . . 73 C2
Glasgow G4 . . . . 241 A4
Swanson Rd G83 . . . . 27 B4
Swanston St G40 . . . . . . 118 A1
Sween Ave G44 . . . . 137 A2
Sween Dr ML3 . . . . 162 A1
Sween Path ML4 . . . . 142 B2
Sweethill Terr ML5 . . . . . 122 B3
Sweethill Wlk ML4 . . . . . 142 B4
Sweethope Gdns G71 . . . 141 A1
Sweethope Pl G71 . . . . . . 141 A2
Swift Bank ML3 . . . . 161 C1
Swift Cl ML2 . . . . 165 A2
Swift Cres G13 . . . . 94 C4
Swift Pl East Kilbride G75 . 179 C3
Johnstone PA5 . . . . 131 B4
Swinburne Ave G72 . . . . 161 B4
Swinburne Dr FK10 . . . . . . 5 A1
Swindon St G81 . . . . 73 C2
Swinhill Rd ML9 . . . . 199 B3
Swinstie Rd ML1 . . . . 165 B4
Swinstie View ML1 . . . . . 144 B1
Swinton Ave G69 . . . . . . 120 B3
Swinton Cres
Coatbridge ML5 . . . . 121 A2
Glasgow G69 . . . . 120 B3
Swinton Dr G52 . . . . 115 A3
Swinton Gdns G69 . . . . . 120 B3
Swinton Path G69 . . . . . . 120 B3
Swinton Pl Glasgow G52 . 115 A3
Irvine KA11 . . . . 220 A4
Swinton Prim Sch G69 . . 120 B3
Swinton Rd G69 . . . . 120 B3
Swinton View G69 . . . . . 120 B3
Swisscot Ave ML3 . . . . . 183 A4
Swisscot Wlk ML3 . . . . . 183 A4
Switchback Rd G61 . . . . . 75 C1
Sword St Airdrie ML6 . . . 122 C4
Glasgow G31 . . . . 117 C3
Sword's Way FK2 . . . . 24 C3
Swordale Pl G34 . . . . 120 A4
Sycamore Ave
Beith KA15 . . . . 150 A1
Johnstone PA5 . . . . 112 A1
Kirkintilloch G66 . . . . 79 B3
Uddingston G71 . . . . 141 B4
Sycamore Cres
Airdrie ML6 . . . . 123 B3
Ayr KA7 . . . . 239 B3
East Kilbride G75 . . . . . 180 B3
Sycamore Ct Beith KA15 . 150 A1
Coatbridge ML5 . . . . 121 C2
East Kilbride G75 . . . . . 180 B3
Sycamore Dr Airdrie ML6 123 B3
Clydebank G81 . . . . 74 A2
Hamilton ML3 . . . . 162 C1
Sycamore Gr G72 . . . . . . 161 B4
Sycamore Pl
East Kilbride G75 . . . . . 180 B3
Gourock PA19 . . . . 44 A3
Motherwell ML1 . . . . 143 B2
Stirling FK8 . . . . 6 C3
Sycamore Way
Cambuslang G72 . . . . . . 139 C2
Carmunnock G76 . . . . . 158 B4
Milton of C G66 . . . . 58 B3
Sycamores The FK10 . . . . . 4 A1
Sydenham La G12 . . . . . . 96 B2
Sydenham Rd G12 . . . . . . 96 B2
Sydes Brae G72 . . . . 161 A2
Sydney Pl G75 . . . . 180 B4
Sydney Pl 8 G75 . . . . . . 180 B4
Sydney St Clydebank G81 . 73 B2
Glasgow G31 . . . . 241 C1
Sykehead Ave ML4 . . . . . 142 A3
Sykes Terr G78 . . . . 154 C4

Sykeside Rd ML6 . . . . 122 C2
Sylvania Way 5 . . . . 74 A1
Sylvania Way S G81 . . . . . 74 A1
Symington Dr G81 . . . . . . 74 A1
Symington Pl Falkirk FK2 . 24 A2
Irvine KA11 . . . . 224 D4
Symington Prim Sch
Symington KA1 . . . . 231 B2
Symington Rd N KA1 . . . 231 B2
Symington Rd S KA1 . . . 231 B2
Symington Sq 11 G75 . . 180 C4
Syms La KA8 . . . . 236 A1
Syriam Pl 10 G21 . . . . 97 C2
Syriam St G21 . . . . 97 C3

T

Tabard Pl G13 . . . . 95 B4
Tabard Rd G13 . . . . 95 B4
Tabernacle La G72 . . . . . 139 A3
Tabernacle St G72 . . . . . 139 A3
Taggart Rd G65 . . . . 60 C2
Taig Rd G66 . . . . 80 A4
Tait Ave G78 . . . . 134 B2
Tait Dr FK5 . . . . 41 B4
Tait Wlk ML8 . . . . 201 A1
Takmadoon Rd G65 . . . . . 36 C2
Talbot G74 . . . . 160 B2
Talbot Ct G13 . . . . 95 A3
Talbot Dr G13 . . . . 95 A3
Talbot Pl G13 . . . . 95 A3
Talbot Rd G83 . . . . 28 A4
Talbot Terr Glasgow G13 . 95 A3
Uddingston G71 . . . . 140 C4
Talisker G74 . . . . 160 B1
Talisman Ave 2 G82 . . . . . 49 B2
Talisman Cres
Helensburgh G84 . . . . . . 25 A4
Motherwell ML1 . . . . 142 B3
Talisman Rd Glasgow G13 . 95 B3
Paisley PA2 . . . . 132 C4
Talisman Wlk KA21 . . . . 206 A1
Talla Rd G52 . . . . 115 A3
Tallant Rd G15 . . . . 75 B2
Tallant Terr G15 . . . . 75 B2
Tam O' Shanter
Experience* KA7 . . . . . . 238 C1
Tam O'Shanter Dr FK7 . . 12 B4
Tam's Brig KA8 . . . . 236 A2
Tamar Dr G75 . . . . 179 C3
Tamarack Cres G71 . . . . 141 B4
Tambowie Ave G62 . . . . . 54 C1
Tambowie Cres G62 . . . . 54 C1
Tambowie St G13 . . . . 95 C4
Tamfourhill Ave FK1 . . . . 41 B2
Tamfourhill Ind Est FK1 . 41 B2
Tamfourhill Rd FK1 . . . . . 41 B2
Tammy Dale's Rd KA13 . 207 C2
Tamshill St G20 . . . . 96 C3
Tanar Ave PA4 . . . . 94 C1
Tanar Way PA4 . . . . 94 C1
Tandlehill Rd PA10 . . . . . 111 A1
Tanera Ave G44 . . . . 137 B2
Tanera Ct KA1 . . . . 42 A1
Tanfield Pl G32 . . . . 119 B4
Tanfield St G32 . . . . 119 B4
Tankerland Rd G44 . . . . . 137 A3
Tanna Dr G52 . . . . 115 B2
Tannadice Ave G52 . . . . . 115 B2
Tannadice Cres PA5 . . . . 111 A1
Tannahill Dr G74 . . . . . . 160 B2
Tannahill Rd
Glasgow G43 . . . . 136 C3
Paisley PA3 . . . . 113 A3
Tannahill Terr PA3 . . . . . 113 A3
Tanners Rd FK1 . . . . 42 A1
Tannery La FK8 . . . . 2 A1
Tannoch Dr
Cumbernauld G67 . . . . . . 82 C4
Milngavie G62 . . . . 54 C2
Tannoch Pl G67 . . . . 82 C4
Tannoch Rd G78 . . . . 153 A2
Tannochside Bsns Pk
G71 . . . . 121 A1
Tannochside Dr G71 . . . . 121 A1
Tannochside Prim Sch
G71 . . . . 141 A4
Tannock St Glasgow G22 . 97 A2
Tantallon Ave PA19 . . . . . 43 C3
Tantallon Ct ML8 . . . . . . 187 C2
Tantallon Dr
Coatbridge ML5 . . . . 101 B1
Paisley PA2 . . . . 113 A1
Tantallon Pk G74 . . . . . . 159 B1
Tantallon Rd
9 Bothwell G71 . . . . . . 141 A2
Glasgow G69 . . . . 120 A2
Glasgow, Langside G41 . 136 C4
Tanzieknowe Ave G72 . . 139 A2
Tanzieknowe Dr G72 . . . 139 A2
Tanzieknowe Pl G72 . . . . 139 A2
Tanzieknowe Rd G72 . . . 139 A2
Tappoch Pl FK5 . . . . 23 A2
Taransay St G51 . . . . 116 A4
Tarbert Ave Blantyre G72 . 140 B3
West Kilbride KA23 . . . . 190 C3
Wishaw ML2 . . . . 165 B2
Tarbert Ct ML3 . . . . 162 A1
Tarbert Way G72 . . . . 121 C2
Tarbet Pl ML8 . . . . 188 A1
Tarbet St PA19 . . . . 44 C4
Tarbolton G74 . . . . 160 B2
Tarbolton Cres ML6 . . . . 123 B1
Tarbolton Dr G81 . . . . 74 B2

Tarbolton Path ML9 . . . . 184 C2
Tarbolton Rd KA3 . . . . . . 223 B3
Tarbolton Rd
Cumbernauld G67 . . . . . . 62 A1
Dundonald KA2 . . . . 225 C1
Glasgow G43 . . . . 136 B3
Monkton KA9 . . . . 233 C2
Prestwick KA9 . . . . 231 C3
Tarbolton Sq G81 . . . . 74 B2
Tarbrax Path ML7 . . . . . . 147 A2
Tarbrax Way ML3 . . . . . . 162 A2
Tarduff Pl FK6 . . . . 21 A1
Tarff Ave G76 . . . . 178 C3
Tarfside Ave G52 . . . . . . 115 B2
Tarfside Gdns G52 . . . . . 115 B2
Tarfside Oval G52 . . . . . . 115 B2
Targe Wynd FK7 . . . . 7 C2
Target Rd ML6 . . . . 123 A3
Tarland St G51 . . . . 115 C3
Tarn Gr G33 . . . . 98 C4
Tarquin Pl ML1 . . . . 163 B4
Tarras Dr PA4 . . . . 94 C1
Tarras Pl G72 . . . . 139 B3
Tarryholme Dr KA11 . . . 219 B1
Tarsan Dr ML1 . . . . 23 C1
Tasker St PA15 . . . . 45 B3
Tasman Dr G75 . . . . 180 A4
Tasmania Quadrant
ML2 . . . . 165 C2
Tassie Pl G74 . . . . 160 A1
Tassie St G41 . . . . 136 B4
Tattershall Rd G33 . . . . . . 99 B1
Tavistock Dr G43 . . . . . . 136 B3
Tay Ave PA4 . . . . 94 C2
Tay Cres Bishopbriggs G64 . 78 A1
Glasgow G33 . . . . 98 C1
Tay Ct Alloa FK10 . . . . 10 B3
East Kilbride G75 . . . . . 179 C4
Tay Gdns ML3 . . . . 183 A4
Tay Gr G75 . . . . 179 C4
Tay La ML2 . . . . 166 A3
Tay Loan ML1 . . . . 143 A3
Tay Pl Dumbarton G82 . . . 50 A4
East Kilbride G75 . . . . . 179 C4
Johnstone PA5 . . . . 131 B4
Kilmarnock KA1 . . . . 228 A3
Larkhall ML9 . . . . 199 A4
Shotts ML7 . . . . 146 C3
Tay Rd Bearsden G61 . . . . 75 B1
Bishopbriggs G64 . . . . . . 78 A1
Troon KA10 . . . . 229 D2
Tay St Coatbridge ML5 . . 101 B1
Falkirk FK2 . . . . 24 B1
Greenock PA15 . . . . 45 A3
Tay Terr G75 . . . . 179 C4
Taybank Dr KA7 . . . . 239 A2
Tayinloan Dr ML8 . . . . . . 202 A4
Taylor Ave
Kilbarchan PA10 . . . . . . 110 C2
Motherwell ML1 . . . . 143 B4
Taylor Brown Cl KA3 . . . 211 C4
Taylor Ct 4 KA3 . . . . 223 C1
Taylor Cl 11 KA3 . . . . . . 235 C1
Taylor High Sch ML1 . . . 143 A2
Taylor Pl G4 . . . . 241 B3
Taylor St Alexandria G83 . 27 B2
Ayr KA8 . . . . 235 C1
Clydebank G81 . . . . 94 B4
Glasgow G4 . . . . 241 B3
Taylor's Rd FK5 . . . . 23 B1
Taymouth Dr PA19 . . . . . 43 C3
Taymouth St G32 . . . . . . 119 A2
Taynish Dr G44 . . . . 137 A3
Tayside ML6 . . . . 102 C1
Teak Pl G71 . . . . 121 B1
Teal Cres G75 . . . . 179 C3
Teal Ct ML4 . . . . 141 C4
Teal Dr G13 . . . . 95 A4
Tealing Ave G52 . . . . 115 B2
Tealing Cres G52 . . . . . . 115 B2
Teasel Ave G53 . . . . 135 A2
Teawell Rd G77 . . . . 156 B3
Technology Ave G72 . . . 161 B3
Teesdale G74 . . . . 159 B2
Teign Gr G75 . . . . 179 C3
Teith Ave PA4 . . . . 94 C1
Teith Dr G61 . . . . 75 B2
Teith Pl Cambuslang G72 . 139 B3
Kilmarnock KA1 . . . . 228 A3
Teith St G33 . . . . 98 C1
Telegraph Rd ML6 . . . . . 105 A4
Telephone La G12 . . . . 96 B1
Telford Ave ML9 . . . . 199 B4
Telford Ct Bannockburn FK7 . 7 B1
Clydebank G81 . . . . 74 A1
Telford Pl
Cumbernauld G67 . . . . . . 83 A4
Irvine KA11 . . . . 219 C1
Telford Rd
Cumbernauld G67 . . . . . . 83 A4
East Kilbride G75 . . . . . 180 C4
Telford Sq FK1 . . . . 41 C3
Telford Sq W KA3 . . . . . . 14 A3
Telford Terr 6 G75 . . . . . 180 C4
Teme Pl G75 . . . . 179 C3
Templand Cres KA24 . . . 191 B4
Templand Rd KA24 . . . . . 191 B4
Templar Ave G13 . . . . 75 B1
Temple Denny Rd FK6 . . . 21 B1
Temple Gdns G13 . . . . 95 C4
Temple Locks Ct 1 G13 . 95 C4
Temple Locks Pl G13 . . . . 95 C4
Temple Prim Sch G13 . . . 95 C4
Temple Rd G13 . . . . 96 A4
Templehill KA10 . . . . 229 B2
Templeland Rd G53 . . . . 115 B1
Templerigg Ct KA9 . . . . . 233 B1
Templerigg St KA9 . . . . . 233 B1

Templeton Bsns Ctr
G40 . . . . 117 C3
Templeton Cres KA9 . . . 236 B4
Templeton Gdns KA9 . . . 236 B4
Templeton St G40 . . . . . 117 C3
Ten Acres FK10 . . . . 5 A1
Tennant Ave G74 . . . . . . 159 A1
Tennant Complex The
G74 . . . . 159 A1
Tennant St PA4 . . . . 94 B2
Tennent St ML5 . . . . 122 A3
Tennyson Dr G31 . . . . . . 118 C2
Tenters Way PA2 . . . . . . 113 A2
Tern Pl PA5 . . . . 131 B4
Terrace Rd PA15 . . . . 46 A2
Terregles Ave G41 . . . . . 116 B1
Terregles Cres G41 . . . . 116 B1
Terregles Dr G41 . . . . . . 116 B1
Teviot Ave
Bishopbriggs G64 . . . . . . 78 A2
Paisley PA2 . . . . 132 C4
Teviot Cres G61 . . . . 75 B1
Teviot Dr PA7 . . . . 72 B1
Teviot Pl
Cambuslang G72 . . . . . . 139 C3
Troon KA10 . . . . 229 D2
Teviot Rd PA14 . . . . 68 C3
Teviot Sq G67 . . . . 61 C1
Teviot St Ayr KA8 . . . . . . 236 A2
Coatbridge ML5 . . . . 101 B1
Falkirk FK1 . . . . 41 C2
Glasgow G3 . . . . 116 B4
Teviot Terr PA5 . . . . 131 B4
Teviot Way G72 . . . . 161 B4
Teviotdale G77 . . . . 157 A3
Tewkesbury Rd G74 . . . . 160 B2
Thane Rd G13 . . . . 95 B3
Thanes Gate G71 . . . . . . 140 C3
Thankerton Ave ML1 . . . 142 C3
Thankerton Rd ML9 . . . . 185 A1
Tharsis St G21 . . . . 97 C1
Thimble St G82 . . . . 27 C1
Third Ave Alexandria G83 . 27 C3
Dumbarton G82 . . . . 50 B1
Glasgow G44 . . . . 137 A4
Irvine KA12 . . . . 224 B4
Kirkintilloch G66 . . . . 79 B1
Millerston G33 . . . . 99 B3
Renfrew PA4 . . . . 94 B1
Third Ave La G44 . . . . . . 137 A4
Third Gdns G41 . . . . 116 A2
Third Rd G72 . . . . 161 C2
Third St G71 . . . . 140 C4
Thirdpart Cres G13 . . . . . 94 C3
Thirdpart Pl KA1 . . . . 227 B4
Thirlmere G75 . . . . 179 C3
Thistle Ave FK6 . . . . 21 B1
Thistle Bank G66 . . . . 79 B2
Thistle Cres ML9 . . . . . . 185 A1
Thistle Gdns ML1 . . . . . . 143 A3
Thistle Ind Est FK7 . . . . . . 7 B3
Thistle Pl
East Kilbride G74 . . . . . 159 B2
Stirling FK8 . . . . 2 B1
Thistle Quadrant ML6 . . 103 A1
Thistle Rd ML1 . . . . 143 A2
Thistle St Airdrie ML6 . . 103 A1
Glasgow G5 . . . . 10 B3
Cleland ML1 . . . . 144 B1
Falkirk FK2 . . . . 42 B3
Glasgow G5 . . . . 117 B3
Kirkintilloch G66 . . . . 79 B4
Paisley PA1 . . . . 113 B3
Thistle Terr Glasgow G5 . 117 B2
Stevenston KA20 . . . . . . 206 C1
Thistle Wlk KA7 . . . . 239 B2
Thistlebank PA11 . . . . 90 B1
Thistlebank Gdns ML5 . . 121 C2
Thistledown Gr ML5 . . . 122 B3
Thistleneuk G60 . . . . 73 A4
Thom St PA16 . . . . 45 B2
Thomas Baird Gdns
KA3 . . . . 223 A2
Thomas Campbell St
KA21 . . . . 217 A4
Thomas Muir Ave G64 . . . 97 C4
Thomas Muir High Sch
G64 . . . . 78 B1
Thomas Muir La PA15 . . . 46 C1
Thomas Muir St PA15 . . . 46 C1
Thomas St Alexandria G83 . 27 C2
Paisley PA1 . . . . 113 A2
Thompson Ave G66 . . . . . 79 C4
Thompson Pl
Clydebank G81 . . . . 74 B3
Slamannan FK1 . . . . 86 A2
Thompson St
Glasgow G31 . . . . 118 A3
Renfrew PA4 . . . . 94 B1
Thompson's Cl ML11 . . . 215 A2
Thomson Ave
Johnstone PA5 . . . . 111 C2
Wishaw ML2 . . . . 164 B1
Thomson Cres ML5 . . . . 121 B1
Thomson Ct W G71 . . . . 198 C2
Thomson Dr Airdrie ML6 . 123 B1
Bearsden G61 . . . . 75 C3
Bellshill ML4 . . . . 141 B3
Motherwell ML1 . . . . 163 B3
Thomson Gr G72 . . . . . . 139 A4
Thomson Pl FK7 . . . . 6 A3
Thomson St Ayr KA8 . . . 236 B1
Carluke ML8 . . . . 187 C1
Johnstone PA5 . . . . 111 C1
Kilmarnock KA3 . . . . 222 C1

Thomson Terr
Shotts ML7 .....146 B3
Stewarton KA3 .....211 B4
Thorn Ave G74 .....158 B2
Thorn Brae PA5 .....112 A2
Thorn Ct PA5 .....112 A1
Thorn Dr Bearsden G61 ...75 B3
Rutherglen G73 .....138 B2
Thorn Prim Sch PA5 ...112 A1
Thorn Rd Bearsden G61 ...75 B3
Bellshill ML4 .....142 A3
Thorn Terr KA3 .....112 A1
Thornbank St G3 .....116 B4
Thornbridge
1 Glasgow G12 .....96 B3
2 Glasgow, Garrowhill
G69 .....120 A3
Thornbridge Gdns
Falkirk FK2 .....42 C2
14 Glasgow G69 .....120 A3
Thornbridge Rd
Falkirk FK2 .....42 C2
Glasgow G69 .....120 A3
Thornbridge Sq FK2 ...42 C3
Thorncliffe Gdns G41 ...116 C1
Thorncroft Dr G44 ...137 B2
Thorndale Gdns H44 ...39 A1
Thorndean Ave ML4 ...142 A3
Thorndean Cres ML4 ...142 A2
Thornden La G14 .....95 A2
Thornden PA5 .....112 A2
Thorndene Ave ML1 ...143 B1
Thorndene Ct FK1 .....41 C1
Thorndene Terr FK1 ...86 A4
Thorndyke G74 .....160 B3
Thorne Rd FK10 .....4 C1
Thorneyflat Cres KA8 ...236 C1
Thorneyflat Pl KA8 ...236 C1
Thornhill PA5 .....112 A1
Thornhill Ave
Blantyre G72 .....161 B4
Elderslie PA5 .....112 A1
Thornhill Ct KA13 ...207 A2
Thornhill Dr PA5 .....112 A1
Thornhill Gdns G77 ...156 B1
Thornhill La 11 G71 ...141 A2
Thornhill Path G31 ...118 B3
Thornhill Pl KA1 .....227 C2
Thornhill Rd Falkirk FK2 ...42 B3
Hamilton ML3 .....161 C2
Thornhill Way ML5 ...122 B2
Thornhouse Ave KA12 ...219 B1
Thorniecroft Dr G67 ...82 B3
Thorniecroft Pl G67 ...82 B3
Thornielee G74 .....160 A1
Thorniewood Gdns G71 ...141 A4
Thorniewood Rd G71 ...140 C4
Thornkip Pl ML5 .....122 B3
Thornlea Dr G46 .....136 A3
Thornlea Pl ML11 ...215 C4
Thornlea St ML8 .....202 A4
Thornley Ave G13 .....95 A3
Thornlie Gill ML2 .....165 A1
Thornlie Prim Sch ML2 ...165 A1
Thornliebank Ind Est
G46 .....135 C2
Thornliebank Prim Sch
G46 .....136 A2
Thornliebank Rd G43 ...136 A3
Thornliebank Sta G46 ...136 A3
Thornly Park Ave PA2 ...133 C4
Thornly Park Dr PA2 ...133 C4
Thornly Park Gdns PA2 ...113 C1
Thornly Park Rd PA2 ...133 C4
Thornside Rd PA5 .....112 A2
Thornton Ave
Bonnybridge FK4 .....40 A3
Crosshouse KA2 .....221 C1
Thornton La G20 .....96 C4
Thornton Pl ML3 .....183 B3
Thornton Rd G74 .....158 B1
Thornton St
Coatbridge ML5 .....101 B1
Glasgow G20 .....96 C4
Thorntonhall Sta G74 ...158 A2
Thorntree Ave
Beith KA15 .....150 B1
Hamilton ML3 .....161 C3
Thorntree Prim Sch
G32 .....119 A3
Thorntree Way G71 ...141 A2
Thornwood Ave Ayr KA8 ...236 C1
Glasgow G11 .....96 A1
Kirkintilloch G66 .....79 A3
Thornwood Cres G11 ...95 C2
Thornwood Dr
Bridge of W PA11 .....110 A3
Glasgow G11 .....95 C1
Irvine KA12 .....219 B1
Paisley PA2 .....113 A1
Thornwood Gdns G11 ...96 A1
Thornwood Pl G11 ...96 A2
Thornwood Prim Sch
G11 .....95 C1
Thornwood Quadrant
G11 .....95 C2
Thornwood Rd G11 ...95 C1
Thornwood Terr G11 ...95 C1
Thornyburn Dr G69 ...120 B2
Thornyburn Pl G69 ...120 B2
Thornyflat Dr KA8 .....236 C1
Thornyflat Rd KA8 .....236 C1
Thornyflat St KA8 .....236 C1
Thrashbush Ave ML2 ...165 B2
Thrashbush Cres ML2 ...165 B2

Thrashbush Rd ML2 ...165 B2
Threave Ct ML8 .....187 C2
Threave Pl G77 .....156 A3
Three Rivers Wlk G75 ...180 A4
Three Sisters Ct KA21 ...205 C1
Three Stanes Rdbt
KA11 .....224 C3
Threepwood Rd KA15 ...150 C1
Threestonehill Ave G32 ...119 B3
Threshold G74 .....160 A1
Threshold Pk G74 .....160 A1
Thriplee Rd PA11 .....110 B4
Thrums G74 .....160 B3
Thrums Ave G64 .....78 B1
Thrums Gdns G64 .....78 B1
Thrush Pl PA5 .....131 B4
Thrushbush La ML6 ...103 A1
Thrushbush Quadrant
ML6 .....103 A1
Thrushbush Rd ML6 ...103 A1
Thrushcraig Cres PA2 ...113 C1
Thurso St G11 .....96 B1
Thurston Rd G52 .....115 A3
Thyme Sq ML1 .....163 C4
Tianavaig PA4 .....93 B4
Tibbermore Rd 15 G11 ...96 A2
Tibbies Loan FK7 .....12 B4
Tiber Ave ML1 .....142 B1
Tig Rd KA8 .....236 A2
Tighnasheen Way G72 ...140 B1
Til St ML2 .....165 A3
Tillanburn Rd ML1 ...143 C2
Tillet Oval PA3 .....113 B4
Tillie St G20 .....115 C4
Tillycairn Ave G33 ...99 B1
Tillycairn Dr G33 .....99 B1
Tillycairn Pl G33 .....99 C1
Tillycairn Rd G33 .....99 C1
Tillycairn St G33 .....99 C1
Tilt Rd ML2 .....165 C3
Tilt St G33 .....98 C1
Time Capsule* ML5 ...121 C3
Timmons Gr ML4 .....142 B3
Timmons Pl FK6 .....21 B1
Timmons Terr ML6 .....123 B1
Tinker's La ML1 .....163 B3
Tintagel Gdns G69 .....80 C2
Tinto Ave G74 .....228 A2
Tinto Cres ML2 .....165 B1
Tinto Ct ML5 .....122 B2
Tinto Dr Barrhead G78 ...134 B1
Cumbernauld G68 .....61 B1
Tinto Rd Airdrie ML6 ...123 A3
Bargeddie G69 .....121 A3
Bearsden G61 .....75 B3
Bishopbriggs G64 .....78 B1
Glasgow G43 .....136 B3
Tinto St ML2 .....165 B1
Tinto View ML3 .....183 C4
Tinto View Rd ML9 ...199 B4
Tintock Dr G66 .....58 C1
Tintock Pl G68 .....61 A3
Tinto St G66 .....59 A1
Tinwald Path G52 .....115 A3
Tipperary Pl FK5 .....23 C1
Tiree G74 .....181 B4
Tiree Ave Paisley PA2 ...133 B4
Port Glasgow PA14 .....69 A4
Renfrew PA4 .....94 B1
Tiree Cres ML2 .....165 C3
Tiree Ct Cumbernauld G67 ...82 B4
Irvine KA11 .....225 A4
Tiree Dr G67 .....82 B4
Tiree Gdns Bearsden G61 ...75 A3
Glenmavis ML6 .....102 C3
Old Kilpatrick G60 .....73 B3
Tiree Grange ML3 .....161 C1
Tiree Pl Coatbridge ML5 ...121 B2
Falkirk FK1 .....42 A3
Newton Mearns G77 ...156 A3
Old Kilpatrick G60 .....73 B3
Stevenston KA20 .....206 C1
Tiree Rd G67 .....82 B4
Tiree Sq G21 .....98 B1
Tirry Ave PA4 .....94 C1
Tirry Way PA4 .....94 C1
Titania G40 .....117 C4
Titchfield Rd KA10 ...229 B1
Titchfield St KA1 .....227 C4
Titchfield Way KA11 ...225 A4
Titwood Dr KA3 .....222 C2
Titwood Rd Glasgow G41 ...116 B1
Newton Mearns G77 ...156 C1
Tiverton Ave G32 .....119 B2
Tivoli Ct G75 .....180 C3
Tobago Pl
East Kilbride G75 .....159 A1
Glasgow G40 .....117 C3
Tobago St Glasgow G40 ...117 C3
Greenock PA15 .....45 C3
Tobermory Rd G73 ...138 B2
Todburn Dr PA2 .....133 C4
Todburn Pl ML2 .....165 A1
Toddhill Ave KA3 .....222 C2
Todhills N G75 .....180 C4
Todhills S G75 .....180 C4
Todholm Cres PA2 ...114 A1
Todholm Prim Sch PA2 ...114 A1
Todholm Rd PA2 .....114 A1
Todholm Terr PA2 .....114 A1
Todrig Dr KA1 .....227 C2
Toft St G31 .....118 B4
Toftcombs Ave KA3 ...222 C2
Tofthill Ave G64 .....77 C1
Tofthill Gdns G64 .....77 C1
Tofts KA24 .....191 B4

Tofts Cres KA24 .....191 B4
Togo Pl PA15 .....45 C2
Tolbooth St 3 FK1 ...42 A2
Toll La G51 .....116 C3
Toll St ML1 .....163 C3
Toll Wynd ML3 .....183 B4
Tollbrae Ave ML6 .....123 A4
Tollbrae Prim Sch ML6 ...123 A4
Tollcross Children's Mus*
G32 .....118 C2
Tollcross Park Gr G32 ...118 C2
Tollcross Park View
G32 .....118 C2
Tollcross Rd G31, G32 ...118 C2
Tollerton Dr KA12 ...219 B2
Tollhouse Gdns ML4 ...142 B2
Tollhouse Way KA11 ...218 C3
Tollpark Cres ML2 ...166 A3
Tollpark Pl G68 .....62 C4
Tollpark Rd G68 .....62 C4
Tolsta St 2 G23 .....76 C1
Tom-A-Mhoid G84 ...15 A2
Tomtain Brae G68 .....81 C4
Tomtain Ct G68 .....81 C4
Toner Gdns ML2 .....186 A4
Tontine Cres G82 .....49 B4
Tontine La G1 .....241 B1
Tontine Pk G82 .....49 B4
Tontine Pl G73 .....138 C2
Tontine Rd 7 Ayr KA8 ...142 A2
Tophill Entry FK1 .....41 C3
Toponthank La KA3 ...223 A3
Toppersfield PA10 ...111 B1
Topshill Gdns G75 .....180 A2
Torbeg Ho KA9 .....236 A3
Torbothie Rd ML7 ...147 A2
Torbrackan Park PA9 ...131 A3
Torbreck St G52 .....115 C3
Torbrex Farm Rd FK7 ...7 A2
Torbrex Rd FK7 .....7 A2
Torbrex Rd
Cumbernauld G67 .....62 A1
Stirling FK7,FK8 .....7 A2
Torburn Ave
Glasgow G46 .....136 A2
Plean FK7 .....12 B2
Tordene Path G68 .....61 B2
Torgyle St G23 .....76 B1
Torlea Pl FK5 .....23 A2
Tormeadow Rd G77 ...156 B3
Tormore St G51 .....115 B3
Tormusk Dr G45 .....138 A2
Tormusk Gdns G45 ...138 A2
Tormusk Gr G45 .....138 A2
Tormusk Prim Sch G45 ...138 A2
Tormusk Rd G45 .....138 A2
Torness St G11 .....96 B1
Torogay Pl G22 .....97 C4
Torogay St G22 .....97 B4
Torogay Terr G22 .....97 C4
Toronto Wlk G32 ...139 B4
Torphin Cres G32 .....119 A4
Torr Ave PA11 .....89 C1
Torr Cres G84 .....15 C3
Torr La PA11 .....89 C1
Torr Rd Bishopbriggs G64 ...78 B1
Bridge of W PA11 .....110 B4
Torr St G22 .....97 B2
Torran Rd G33 .....119 C4
Torrance Ave ML6 ...123 B4
Torrance Prim Sch G64 ...57 A1
Torrance Rd
East Kilbride G74 ...159 C1
Greenock PA15 .....46 A1
Torrance G64 .....78 B4
Torrance Rdbt G75 ...181 A3
Torrance St G21 .....97 C2
Torranyard Cvn Pk
KA11, KA13 .....209 B2
Torrin Rd G23 .....76 B1
Torrington Ave G46 ...157 A4
Torrington Cres G32 ...119 B2
Torrisdale Pl ML5 .....121 C4
Torrisdale St
Coatbridge ML5 .....121 C4
1 Glasgow G42 .....117 A1
Torry Dr FK12 .....4 C4
Torryburn Rd G21 .....98 B2
Torwood Ave FK5 .....23 A1
Torwood Brae ML3 ...160 C1
Torwood La G69 .....81 A1
Torwood Sch FK5 .....22 C3
Torwoodhill Pl G84 ...15 C2
Torwoodhill Rd G84 ...15 C2
Toryglen Prim Sch G42 ...137 C4
Toryglen Rd G73 .....137 C4
Toryglen St G5 .....117 C2
Touch Rd FK7,FK8 .....6 A3
Touchhill Cres FK7 ...12 B2
Tourhill Rd KA3 .....222 C2
Tourmaline Terr ML4 ...142 A2
Tournai Path G72 .....161 B4
Towans Ct KA9 .....233 B1
Toward Ct G72 .....161 C4

Toward Rd G33 .....119 B4
Tower Ave G74 .....134 B2
Tower Cres PA4 .....94 A1
Tower Dr Gourock PA19 ...44 B3
Renfrew PA4 .....94 A1
Tower Pl
Clackmannan FK10 ...10 C3
Helensburgh G84 .....16 B1
Johnstone PA5 .....112 A1
Kilmarnock KA1 .....227 B2
Milngavie G62 .....55 A1
Tower Rd Airdrie G67 ...83 A3
Fluchter G64 .....56 C2
Johnstone PA5 .....111 C1
Tower Sq FK10 .....10 A4
Tower St Alloa FK10 ...10 A4
Glasgow G41 .....116 C3
Tower Terr PA1 .....113 B2
Tower View FK10 .....10 A4
Towerhill Ave KA3 ...222 B3
Towerhill Rd G13 .....75 B1
Towerlands Farm Rd
KA11 .....220 B1
Towerlands Gate KA11 ...220 A1
Towerlands Intc KA11 ...219 C2
Towerlands Prim Sch
KA11 .....220 B1
Towerlands Rd KA11 ...220 B1
Towers Ct 7 FK2 .....42 A3
Towers Pl 9 Airdrie ML6 ...123 C4
Stirling FK9 .....2 B2
Towie Pl 10 Glasgow G20 ...96 B3
Uddingston G71 .....140 C3
Town Burn FK7 .....6 C2
Town House St FK6 ...21 C1
Townend La KA24 ...191 B4
Townend s KA24 .....191 B4
Townend Rd
Dumbarton G82 .....50 A3
Kilmarnock KA1 .....227 C2
Townend St KA24 ...191 B4
Townfoot KA11 .....220 B1
Townhead Irvine KA12 ...219 B1
Kilbirnie KA25 .....149 A1
Kilmaurs KA3 .....222 B4
Kirkintilloch KA13 ...207 B2
Kirkintilloch G66 .....79 B4
Townhead Ave ML1 ...142 C4
Townhead Dr ML1 ...143 C2
Townhead Pl G71 ...141 A4
Townhead Prim Sch
ML5 .....101 B1
Townhead Rd
Coatbridge ML5 .....101 B1
Helensburgh G84 .....17 A1
Newton Mearns G77 ...156 B2
Saltcoats KA21 .....217 A4
Townhead St Beith KA15 ...171 A4
Hamilton ML3 .....162 C2
Kilsyth G65 .....60 B4
Stevenston KA20 .....206 B1
Townhill Prim Sch ML3 ...161 C1
Townhill Rd ML3 ...161 C2
Townhill Terr ML3 ...161 C2
Townholm KA3 .....223 A1
Townmill Rd G31 ...118 A4
Townsend St G4 .....97 B1
Tradeston Ind Est G5 ...117 B2
Tradeston St G5 ...240 B1
Trafalgar Ct G68 ...61 A3
Trafalgar St
Clydebank G81 .....73 C1
Glasgow G40 .....117 C2
Greenock PA15 .....45 C2
Trainard Ave G32 ...118 C2
Tramore Cres KA9 ...236 B4
Tranent Pl Cleland ML1 ...144 B1
Glasgow G33 .....118 C4
Traquair Ave
Paisley PA2 .....132 C4
Wishaw ML2 .....165 B3
Traquair Dr G52 .....115 A3
Traquair Wynd G72 ...161 B4
Treebank Cres KA7 ...239 B3
Treebank Gr G46 ...136 A2
Treebank Rd G46 ...157 A4
Trees Park Ave G78 ...134 A2
Treesbank KA13 .....207 B1
Treesbank Rd KA1 ...227 C2
Treeswoodhead Rd
KA1 .....228 A1
Trefoil Ave G41 ...136 B4
Trefoil Pl KA7 .....239 B3
Trelawney Terr KA20 ...217 C3
Trent Pl G75 .....179 C3
Trent Rd G75 .....179 C3
Tresta Rd G23 .....96 C4
Triangle Sh Ctr The G64 ...78 A1
Tribboch St ML9 ...184 C2
Trident Way PA4 .....94 A1
Trinidad Gn 3 G75 ...159 A1
Trinidad Way G75 ...159 A1
Trinity Ave G52 ...115 B3
Trinity Cres KA15 ...150 B1
Trinity Dr
Cambuslang G72 ...139 A2
Dalry KA24 .....191 A3
Trinity High Sch
Renfrew PA4 .....94 B2
Rutherglen G73 .....138 B4
Trinity Way 22 ML9 ...185 B1
Trinley Rd G13 .....75 B1

Triton Pl ML4 .....142 C3
Tron Ct FK10 .....4 A1
Trondra Gdns KA3 ...223 A3
Trondra Path G34 ...119 C4
Trondra Pl G34 .....119 C4
Trongate Glasgow G1 ...241 A1
Stonehouse ML9 .....198 C1
Troon Ave G75 .....180 A3
Troon Ct G75 .....180 A3
Troon Dr PA11 .....110 B4
Troon Gdns G68 .....61 C3
Troon Pl G77 .....157 A2
Troon Prim Sch KA10 ...229 C2
Troon Rd KA10 .....230 A2
Troon St G40 .....118 A2
Troon Sta KA10 .....229 C1
Trossachs Ave ML1 ...143 A3
Trossachs Ct G20 .....97 A2
Trossachs Rd G73 ...138 B1
Trossachs St G20 ...97 A2
Troubridge Ave PA10 ...111 A1
Troubridge Cres PA10 ...111 A1
Trows Rd ML2 .....186 A3
Truce Rd G13 .....95 A4
Truro Ave G69 .....80 C2
Tryfield Pl KA8 .....236 A1
Tryst Pk FK5 .....23 B3
Tryst Rd Cumbernauld G67 ...61 C1
Cumbernauld, Carbrain G67 ...62 A1
Cumbernauld FK5 .....23 B2
Tudhope Cres G83 ...27 B4
Tudor La S G14 .....95 C2
Tudor Rd G14 .....95 C2
Tudor St G69 .....119 C2
Tullallan Pl
East Kilbride G74 ...181 A4
Stenhousemuir FK5 ...24 A2
Tullibody Rd FK10 .....4 C1
Tullichewan Cres G83 ...27 B4
Tullichewan Dr G83 ...27 B4
Tulligarth Pk FK10 ...10 A4
Tullis St G40 .....117 C2
Tulloch Gdns ML1 ...164 A2
Tulloch Rd ML7 .....147 A2
Tulloch-Ard Pl G73 ...138 B2
Tully Wynd ML1 .....142 B1
Tullymet Rd ML3 .....183 B4
Tummel Dr ML6 .....102 C1
Tummel Gn G74 .....159 C2
Tummel Pl FK5 .....23 C3
Tummel St G33 .....98 C1
Tummell Way PA2 ...112 C1
Tunnel St G3 .....116 C4
Tuphall Rd ML3 .....162 B1
Turnberry Ave
5 Glasgow G11 .....96 A2
Gourock PA19 .....44 A3
Turnberry Cres
Chapelhall ML6 .....123 C1
Coatbridge ML5 .....121 C2
Turnberry Ct KA13 ...207 A2
Turnberry Dr
Bridge of W PA11 .....110 B3
Hamilton ML3 .....161 B1
Kilmarnock KA1 .....227 C2
Newton Mearns G77 ...157 A3
Rutherglen G73 .....137 C3
Turnberry Gdns G68 ...61 C3
Turnberry Pl
Dumbarton G82 .....49 B3
East Kilbride G75 ...180 A3
Rutherglen G73 .....137 C2
Turnberry Rd G11 ...96 A2
Turnberry Wynd
Bothwell G71 .....140 C1
Irvine KA11 .....224 C4
Turnbull Ave G65 .....27 B2
Turnbull Cres G83 ...27 B2
Turnbull High Sch G64 ...77 C1
Turnbull St G1 .....241 B1
Turner Pl KA1 .....223 A2
Turner Rd Glasgow G21 ...97 C1
Paisley PA3 .....113 C4
Turner St ML1 .....121 C3
Turners Ave PA1 .....113 A2
Turnhill Ave PA8 .....93 A4
Turnhill Cres PA8 ...93 A4
Turnhill Dr PA8 .....93 A4
Turnhill Gdns PA8 ...93 A4
Turninghaw Rd PA6 ...91 C3
Turnlaw G75 .....180 B3
Turnlaw Rd G72 .....139 A1
Turnlaw St G5 .....117 B2
Turnyland Mdws PA8 ...93 A4
Turnyland Way PA8 ...93 A4
Turquoise Terr ML4 ...142 A2
Turret Cres G13 .....95 B4
Turret Ct G13 .....95 B4
Turret Rd G13 .....95 B4
Turriff St G5 .....117 A2
Twain Ave FK5 .....24 A2
Twechar Prim Sch G65 ...60 A2
Tweed Ave PA2 .....112 C1
Tweed Cres Glasgow G33 ...98 C1
Kilmarnock KA1 .....228 A3
Renfrew PA4 .....94 C1
Wishaw ML2 .....165 C3
Tweed Dr G61 .....75 B2
Tweed La ML1 .....143 A3
Tweed Pl PA5 .....131 B4
Tweed St East Kilbride G75 ...179 C4
Coatbridge ML5 .....122 A2
East Kilbride G75 .....179 C4
Greenock PA16 .....45 A3
Larkhall ML9 .....185 A1

Tweedmuir Pl ML5 .... 122 B2
Tweedsmuir G64 .... 78 B1
Tweedsmuir Cres G61 ...... 75 C4
Tweedsmuir Rd ML3 ...... 183 B4
Tweedsmuir Rd G52 ...... 115 A3
Tweedvale Ave G14 .... 94 C3
Tweedvale Pl G14 .... 94 C3
Twinlaw St G34 .... 100 B1
Tygetshaugh Ct FK6 .... 21 B2
Tylney Rd ML1 .... 114 B3
Tyndrum Rd G64 .... 76 A3
Tyndrum St G4 .... 241 A4
Tyne Pl G5 .... 179 C3
Tynecastle Cres G32 ...... 119 A4
Tynecastle Path G32 ...... 119 A4
Tynecastle Pl G32 .... 119 A4
Tynecastle St G32 .... 119 A4
Tynron Ct ML3 .... 161 C1
Tynwald Ave G73 .... 138 B2

U

Uddingston Gram Sch
G71 .... 140 C3
Uddingston Rd G71 .... 141 A2
Uddingston Sta G71 ...... 140 C3
Udston Hospl ML3 .... 161 C2
Udston Prim Sch ML3 .... 161 C2
Udston Rd ML3 .... 161 C3
Udston Terr ML3 .... 161 C3
Uig Pl G33 .... 119 C3
Uist Ave PA14 .... 69 A4
Uist Cres G33 .... 99 C2
Uist Dr G66 .... 80 A4
Uist Pl ML6 .... 123 B3
Uist St G51 .... 115 C4
Uist Way ML2 .... 165 C3
Ulg Way ML7 .... 147 A2
Ullswater G75 .... 179 C3
Ulundi Rd PA5 .... 111 C1
Ulva St G52 .... 115 B3
Ulverston Terr ML3 .... 183 B3
Umachan PA4 .... 93 B4
Umberly Rd KA1 .... 227 C2
Underwood KA13 .... 207 B3
Underwood Cotts FK7 ...... 6 B3
Underwood Dr ML2 .... 166 A4
Underwood La PA1 .... 113 B3
Underwood Pl KA1 .... 227 C2
Underwood Rd
Cambusbarron FK7 .... 6 B3
Paisley PA3 .... 113 B3
Prestwick KA9 .... 236 B4
Rutherglen G73 .... 138 B3
Underwood St G41 .... 136 C4
Union Arc KA7 .... 236 A2
Union Gdns FK1 .... 41 B3
Union Pl Glasgow G1 .... 240 C2
Larbert FK5 .... 23 A1
Union Rd FK1 .... 41 B3
Union St Alexandria G83 .. 27 C2
    Alloa FK10 .... 10 A3
Bridge of A FK9 .... 2 A4
Carluke ML8 .... 187 C1
Falkirk FK2 .... 42 A4
Glasgow G1 .... 240 C2
Greenock PA16 .... 45 C3
Hamilton ML3 .... 162 B2
Hurlford KA1 .... 228 C3
Kilmarnock KA3 .... 222 C1
Kirkintilloch G66 .... 79 B4
Larkhall ML9 .... 185 A2
Motherwell ML1 .... 143 A2
Paisley PA2 .... 113 C1
Saltcoats KA21 .... 216 C4
Shotts ML7 .... 146 B3
Stenhousemuir FK5 ...... 23 C2
Stirling FK8 .... 2 A1
Stonehouse ML9 .... 198 C1
Troon KA10 .... 229 B2
Union Street La G83 ...... 27 C2
Unitas Cres ML8 .... 187 C1
Unitas Rd ML4 .... 142 B3
Unity Pk ML7 .... 146 B2
Unity Pl G4 .... 97 A1
Univ of Glasgow (Kelvin
Campus) G20 .... 96 A1
Univ of Glasgow (St Andrew's
Campus) G11 .... 75 B4
Univ of Glasgow (Veterinary
Medicine) G61 .... 96 A4
Univ of Paisley Ayr KA8 .. 239 B4
Paisley PA1 .... 113 C2
Univ of Paisley (Thornly Park
Campus) PA2 .... 133 C4
Univ of Strathclyde G1
G4 .... 241 B3
Universal Rd FK2 .... 42 C4
University Ave G12 .... 96 B1
University Gdns G12 .... 96 B1
University Pl G12 .... 96 B1
University Rd W FK9 .... 2 B3
Unsted Pl PA1 .... 114 A3
Unthank Rd ML1 .... 142 B3
Up La G65 .... 60 B4
UP Rd G65 .... 60 B4
Uphall Pl G33 .... 118 C3
Upland La G73 .... 95 B2
Upland Rd G14 .... 95 B2
Uplawmoor Prim Sch
G78 .... 153 C2
Uplawmoor Rd G78 ...... 153 C2
Upper Adelaide St G84 .. 16 C1
Upper Arthur St G83 ..... 27 B2
Upper Bourtree Ct G73 .. 138 B2

Upper Bourtree Dr G73 .. 138 B2
Upper Bridge St
Alexandria G83 .... 27 B2
Stirling FK8 .... 2 A1
Upper Cartsburn St PA15 . 46 A2
Upper Castlehill FK8 .... 7 A4
Upper Colquhoun St G84 . 16 B2
Upper Craigs FK8 .... 7 A4
Upper Crofts KA3 .... 238 C1
Upper Glenburn Rd G61 ... 75 B3
Upper Glenfinlas St G84 .. 16 C1
Upper Hall Rd G84 .... 15 B3
Upper Loaning KA7 .... 238 C1
Upper Mill St ML6 .... 123 A4
Upper Mill St Ind Est
ML6 .... 123 A4
Upper Newmarket St
FK1 .... 42 A3
Upper Smollett St G83 ... 27 B2
Upper Stoneymollan Rd
G83 .... 27 A4
Upper Sutherland Cres
G84 .... 16 A2
Upper Sutherland St G84 . 16 A2
Upper Torwoodhill Rd
G84 .... 15 C2
Ure Cres FK4 .... 40 A3
Urquhart Cres PA4 .... 94 B1
Urquhart Dr
East Kilbride G74 .... 160 A2
Gourock PA19 .... 43 C3
Urquhart Pl G84 .... 16 B2
Urrdale Rd G41 .... 116 A3
Usmore Pl G33 .... 119 C3

V

Vaila Pl G23 .... 97 A4
Vaila St G23 .... 96 C4
Vale Gr FK9 .... 1 C3
Vale of Leven Acad G83 .. 27 B2
Vale of Leven Hospl
(General) G83 .... 27 B3
Vale of Leven Ind Est
Renton G82 .... 27 C1
Renton G82 .... 49 C4
Vale Pl FK6 .... 21 C2
Valentine Cres G71 .... 141 A4
Valerio Ct G72 .... 161 B4
Valetta Pl G81 .... 73 B2
Valeview FK5 .... 23 B1
Valeview Terr
Dumbarton G82 .... 50 A3
Glasgow G42 .... 137 A4
Vallantine Cres G71 ...... 141 A4
Vallay St G22 .... 97 B4
Valley Ct ML3 .... 162 B1
Valley View
Cambuslang G72 .... 139 B3
Motherwell ML1 .... 164 A2
Valleybank G65 .... 37 B2
Valleyfield
East Kilbride G75 .... 159 B1
Milton of C G66 .... 58 A3
Valleyfield Dr G68 .... 60 C1
Valleyfield Pl FK7 .... 7 B3
Valleyfield St ☑ G21 ...... 97 C2
Valleyview Dr FK2 .... 42 A4
Valleyview Pl FK2 .... 42 A4
Vancouver Ct ☑ G75 ... 159 A1
Vancouver Dr G75 .... 159 A1
Vancouver La
☑ Glasgow G14 .... 95 B3
☑ Glasgow G14 .... 95 B3
Vancouver Rd G14 .... 95 B2
Vanguard St G81 .... 74 B1
Vanguard Way PA4 .... 94 B1
Vardar Ave G76 .... 157 B4
Vardon Lea ML1 .... 143 C1
Varna La G14 .... 95 C2
Varna Rd G14 .... 95 C2
Varnsdorf Way ML6 ...... 123 C3
Vaults La KA13 .... 207 C2
Veir Terr G81 .... 74 A3
Veitch Pl G66 .... 57 B4
Veitches Ct G81 .... 74 A3
Vennachar St ML7 .... 146 C3
Vennacher Rd PA4 .... 94 A2
Vennal St KA24 .... 191 A4
Vennel Gdns G41 .... 116 C1
Vennel La KA11 .... 211 C4
Vennel St KA11 .... 211 C4
Vennel The FK6 .... 21 C1
Vermont Ave G73 .... 138 A4
Vermont St G41 .... 116 C3
Vernon Bank G74 .... 159 C2
Vernon Dr PA3 .... 112 A3
Vernon Pl KA2 .... 225 C1
Vernon St KA1 .... 216 C4
Verona Ave G14 .... 95 B3
Verona Gdns ☑ G14 ..... 95 B3
Verona La G14 .... 95 B2
Verona Pl KA22 .... 205 B1
Vesalius St G32 .... 119 A3
Viaduct Circ KA13 .... 207 C3
Viaduct Rd G76 .... 157 C4
Vicar St FK1 .... 42 A3
Vicarfield St G51 .... 116 A4
Vicarland Pl G72 .... 139 A2
Vicarland Rd G72 .... 139 A3
Vicars Rd ML9 .... 199 B1
Vicars Wlk G72 .... 139 A3
Vickers St ML1 .... 163 A4

Victor St ML6 .... 104 A1
Victoria Ave
Barrhead G78 .... 134 A2
Carluke ML8 .... 187 C1
Victoria Cir G12 .... 96 B2
Victoria Cres
Airdrie ML6 .... 122 C3
Barrhead G78 .... 134 A2
Clarkston G76 .... 157 C4
Kilmacolm PA13 .... 111 A4
Kilsyth G65 .... 60 A4
Wishaw ML2 .... 166 A4
Victoria Crescent La G12 . 96 B2
Victoria Crescent Rd ☑
G12 .... 96 B2
Victoria Crescent Rd
G12 .... 96 B2
Victoria Cross G42 .... 117 A1
Victoria Ct Larkhall ML9 . 185 A2
Newton Mearns G77 .... 156 B1
Victoria Dr Barrhead G78 . 134 A2
Troon KA10 .... 229 C1
Victoria Dr E PA4 .... 94 B1
Victoria Dr W PA4 .... 94 A2
Victoria East Rd KA1 .... 228 A4
Victoria Gdns
Airdrie ML6 .... 122 C4
Barrhead G78 .... 134 A2
Victoria Glade G68 .... 61 B3
Victoria Gr G78 .... 134 A2
Victoria Infmy
Glasgow G42 .... 137 A4
Helensburgh G84 .... 16 C1
Victoria La G77 .... 156 B1
Victoria Meml Cottage Hospl
G65 .... 60 A4
Victoria Park Cnr G14 .... 95 B2
Victoria Park Dr N G14 .. 95 C2
Victoria Park Dr S G14 .. 95 C2
Victoria Park Gdns N
G11 .... 95 C2
Victoria Park Gdns S
G11 .... 95 C2
Victoria Park La N G14 .. 95 C2
Victoria Park La S G14 .. 95 C2
Victoria Park Sta ☑ G14 . 95 B2
Victoria Pk ☑ Ayr KA7 .. 238 C3
☑ Glasgow G14 .... 95 C2
Kilsyth G65 .... 60 A4
Victoria Pl Airdrie ML6 .. 122 C3
Barrhead G78 .... 134 B2
Bellshill ML4 .... 142 A3
Kilsyth G65 .... 60 B4
Milngavie G62 .... 55 A1
☑ Rutherglen G73 ...... 138 A4
Stirling FK8 .... 7 A3
Victoria Prim Sch
Airdrie ML6 .... 122 C4
Falkirk FK2 .... 42 B3
Glasgow G42 .... 117 A1
Victoria Quadrant ML1 .. 142 C3
Victoria Rd
Barrhead G78 .... 134 A2
Brookfield PA5 .... 111 B3
Dullatur G68 .... 61 B3
Falkirk FK2 .... 42 B3
Glasgow G42 .... 117 A2
Gourock PA19 .... 44 B4
Harthill ML7 .... 127 C3
Helensburgh G84 .... 16 C1
Kirkintilloch G66 .... 79 B2
Lennoxtown G66 .... 57 B4
Paisley PA2 .... 113 B1
Rutherglen G73 .... 138 A3
Saltcoats KA21 .... 217 A4
Stepps G33 .... 99 B3
Stirling FK8 .... 7 A3
Victoria Rdbt KA12 ...... 219 A1
Victoria Sq
Newton Mearns G77 .... 156 B1
☑ Troon KA10 .... 229 C3
Victoria St
Alexandria G83 .... 27 C2
Alloa FK10 .... 10 A4
Ayr KA8 .... 236 A1
Blantyre G72 .... 161 B4
Dumbarton G82 .... 50 A2
Hamilton ML3 .... 162 A3
Harthill ML7 .... 127 C3
Kirkintilloch G66 .... 79 B4
Larkhall ML9 .... 185 A2
Rutherglen G73 .... 138 A4
Wishaw ML2 .... 166 A2
Victoria Terr Dullatur G68 . 61 B3
Menstrie FK11 .... 4 A4
Victoria Way G72 .... 139 A2
Victory Dr PA10 .... 111 A2
Victory Way G72 .... 120 A2
Viewbank G46 .... 136 A2
Viewbank Ave ML6 ...... 123 A1
Viewbank St ML5 .... 101 C3
Viewfield Airdrie ML6 ... 122 C4
Moodiesburn G69 .... 80 C2
Viewfield Ave
Bishopbriggs G64 .... 97 C4
Blantyre G72 .... 140 C1
Kirkintilloch G66 .... 59 A3
Lochwinnoch PA12 ...... 129 A1
Milton of C G66 .... 58 A3
Viewfield Bsns Ctr KA8 . 236 A1
Viewfield Dr Airdrie ML6 . 122 C4
☑ Bishopbriggs G64 ..... 97 C4
Glasgow G69 .... 100 A3
Viewfield La G12 .... 96 C1
Viewfield Rd Ayr KA8 .... 236 A1

Viewfield Rd continued
Banknock FK4 .... 38 B2
Bellshill ML4 .... 141 C2
Bishopbriggs G64 .... 97 C4
Coatbridge ML5 .... 121 B2
Viewfield St Harthill ML7 . 127 C3
Stirling FK8 .... 7 A4
Viewforth FK8 .... 7 A3
Viewglen Ct G45 .... 137 B1
Viewmount Dr G20 .... 96 B4
Viewpark Beith KA15 .... 150 A1
Viewpark Rd ML1 .... 163 A2
Viewpark Ave G31 .... 118 A4
Viewpark Cir G73 .... 138 B3
Viewpark Dr G73 .... 138 A3
Viewpark Gdns PA4 ...... 94 A1
Viewpark Pl ML1 .... 163 B3
Viewpark Rd ML1 .... 163 B3
Viewpark Sch Ctr G71 .. 141 B3
Viewpoint Pl G21 .... 97 C3
Viewpoint Rd G21 .... 97 C3
Viking Cres PA6 .... 111 B4
Viking Rd ML6 .... 123 A3
Viking Terr G75 .... 180 C3
Viking Way Glasgow G46 . 135 C3
Renfrew PA4 .... 94 B1
Villa Bank FK6 .... 21 C1
Villafield Ave G64 .... 78 A2
Villafield Dr G64 .... 78 A2
Villafield Loan G64 .... 78 A2
Victoria Glade G68 ...... 140 C1
Village Gdns G72 .... 140 C1
Village Rd G72 .... 139 C2
Vincent St ML4 .... 142 A2
Vine Park Ave KA12 ..... 222 A4
Vine Park Dr KA12 ...... 222 A4
Vine St G11 .... 96 A1
Vinebugh Ave KA12 ..... 219 A2
Vinebugh Ct KA12 .... 219 A2
Vinicombe La ☑ G12 .... 96 B2
Vinicombe St G12 .... 96 B2
Vintner St G4 .... 97 B1
Viola Pl G64 .... 78 B4
Violet Gdns ML8 .... 201 C4
Violet Pl ML1 .... 143 A3
Virginia Ct G1 .... 241 A2
Virginia Gdns Ayr KA8 .. 236 A1
Milngavie G62 .... 76 B4
Virginia Pl G1 .... 241 A2
Virginia St Glasgow G1 .. 241 A2
Viscount Ave PA4 .... 94 A1
Viscount Gate G71 ...... 140 C3
Vivian Ave G62 .... 54 C1
Voil Dr G44 .... 137 A2
Voil Rd FK9 .... 2 A3
Vorlich Ct G78 .... 134 B1
Vorlich Dr FK1 .... 66 C4
Vorlich Gdns G61 .... 75 B4
Vorlich Pl
Kilmarnock KA1 .... 228 A2
Stirling FK9 .... 2 A2
Vorlich Wynd ML1 .... 143 B2
Vrackie Pl KA1 .... 228 A2
Vryburg Cres G75 .... 180 A2
Vulcan St ☑ Glasgow G21 . 97 C2
Motherwell ML1 .... 163 C4

W

Waddell Ave ML6 .... 102 B2
Waddell Ct Glasgow G5 . 117 B3
Kilmarnock KA3 .... 222 C2
Waddell St Airdrie ML6 .. 103 A1
Glasgow G5 .... 117 B2
Waggon Rd Ayr KA8 ..... 235 C1
Falkirk FK2 .... 42 A4
Waid Ave G77 .... 156 B3
Waldemar Rd G13 .... 95 B4
Walden Rd KA1 .... 228 C3
Waldo St ☑ G13 .... 95 C4
Walk The FK10 .... 10 A4
Walker Ave
Kilmarnock KA1 .... 228 A4
Troon KA10 .... 229 C3
Walker Ct Glasgow G11 .. 96 A1
Hurlford KA1 .... 228 A3
Walker Dr
Bonnybridge FK4 .... 39 B3
Elderslie PA5 .... 112 B1
Walker Path ☑ G71 ..... 141 A4
Walker Rd KA1 .... 228 A4
Walker St Glasgow G11 .. 96 A1
Greenock PA16 .... 45 B3
☑ Kilbirnie KA25 .... 149 A1
Paisley PA1 .... 113 B2
Walkerburn Dr ML2 ...... 165 B3
Walkerburn Rd G52 ...... 115 A2
Walkinshaw Pl ML1 ...... 143 A2
Walkinshaw St
Glasgow G40 .... 118 A2
Johnstone PA5 .... 112 A2
Walkinshaw Way PA3 ... 113 C4
Walkmill La G81 .... 74 A3
Wall Gdns FK1 .... 41 B3
Wall St FK1 .... 41 C3
Wallace Ave
Bishopton PA7 .... 72 A2
Dundonald KA2 .... 225 C1
Elderslie PA5 .... 112 B1
Troon KA10 .... 229 C3
Wallace Cres Denny FK6 . 21 C1
Plean FK7 .... 12 B2
Wallace Ct
Kilmarnock KA1 .... 228 C3

Wallace Ct continued
Prestwick KA9 .... 236 B4
Stirling FK9 .... 2 A1
Wallace Dr Wynd ML9 .. 185 B1
Wallace Gate FK8 .... 7 A4
Wallace Gdns Stirling FK9 . 2 B2
Torrance G64 .... 57 A1
Wallace High Sch FK9 ..... 2 A2
Wallace Ho G67 .... 61 C1
Wallace Monument* FK9 . 2 C2
Wallace Pl Blantyre G72 . 140 C1
Cambusbarron FK7 .... 6 B3
Falkirk FK2 .... 42 B3
Fallin FK7 .... 8 B2
Greenock PA15 .... 45 C3
Hamilton ML3 .... 162 B1
Wallace Rd Irvine KA12 . 219 B2
Motherwell ML1 .... 143 A1
Renfrew PA4 .... 94 A1
Wallace St Alloa FK10 ... 10 B4
Bannockburn FK7 .... 7 C1
Clydebank G81 .... 74 A1
Coatbridge ML5 .... 122 A3
Dumbarton G82 .... 50 A2
Falkirk FK2 .... 42 A3
Glasgow G5 .... 117 A3
Kilmarnock KA1 .... 227 C4
Greenock PA16 .... 45 B2
Plains ML6 .... 104 A1
Port Glasgow PA14 .... 47 C1
Rutherglen G73 .... 138 A4
Stirling FK8 .... 2 A1
Wallace View
Kilmarnock KA1 .... 227 C3
Shieldhill FK1 .... 66 B4
Tullibody ML10 .... 4 B2
Wallace Way ML11 ...... 215 B2
Wallace Wynd ML8 ...... 187 A3
Wallacefield Rd KA10 ... 229 C2
Wallacehill Rd KA1 ...... 227 C4
Wallacewell Cres G21 .. 98 A3
Wallacewell Pl G21 ..... 98 B3
Wallacewell Quadrant
G21 .... 98 B3
Wallacewell Rd G21 ..... 98 B3
Wallbrae Rd G67 .... 83 A4
Wallneuk ☑ PA1 .... 113 C3
Wallneuk Rd PA3 .... 113 C3
Walls St G1 .... 241 B2
Wallstale Rd FK7 .... 7 A2
Walmer Cres G51 .... 116 B3
Walnut Cres Glasgow G22 . 97 B3
Johnstone PA5 .... 112 A1
Walnut Ct G66 .... 58 A3
Walnut Dr G66 .... 79 A3
Walnut Gate G72 .... 139 C2
Walnut Pl Glasgow G22 . 97 B3
Uddingston G71 .... 121 B1
Walnut Rd Glasgow G22 . 97 B3
Kilmarnock KA1 .... 222 B2
Walpole Pl PA5 .... 131 B4
Walter St Glasgow G31 . 118 B4
Wishaw ML2 .... 165 B2
Walton Ave G77 .... 156 B3
Walton St Barrhead G78 . 134 B2
Glasgow G41 .... 136 C4
Wamba Ave G13 .... 95 C4
Wamphray Pl G75 .... 179 B4
Wandilla Ave G81 .... 74 B1
Wanlock St G51 .... 116 A4
Ward Ct KA8 .... 236 A2
Ward Rd KA8 .... 236 A2
Ward St FK10 .... 10 A3
Wardend Rd G64 .... 95 B4
Wardend Rd G64 .... 57 A1
Wardhill Rd G21 .... 98 A3
Wardhouse Rd PA2 ..... 133 B4
Wardie Pl G33 .... 119 C3
Wardie Rd G34 .... 120 A4
Wardlaw Ave G73 .... 138 A4
Wardlaw Cres
East Kilbride G75 .... 181 A4
Troon KA10 .... 230 B2
Wardlaw Dr ☑ G73 ...... 138 A4
Wardlaw Gdns KA11 .... 220 A4
Wardlaw Pl ML7 .... 24 B1
Wardlaw Rd
Bearsden G61 .... 75 C1
Kilmarnock KA3 .... 223 C3
Wardneuk Ave G14 .... 95 A3
Wardneuk Ct KA11 ...... 220 A3
Wardneuk Dr KA3 .... 223 A2
Wardpark Ct G67 .... 62 B3
Wardpark East Ind Est
G68 .... 62 C4
Wardpark North Ind Est
G68 .... 62 B4
Wardpark Rd G67 .... 62 B4
Wardpark Rdbt G68 ...... 62 B4
Wardpark South Ind Est
G67 .... 62 C4
Wardrop Pl G74 .... 159 C2
Wardrop St ☑ Beith KA15 . 171 A4
☑ Glasgow G51 .... 116 A4
Paisley PA1 .... 113 C2
Wardrop Terr KA15 ...... 171 B4
Wards Cres ML5 .... 121 C3
Wards Pl KA1 .... 227 C4
Ware Rd G34 .... 120 A4
Warilda Ave G81 .... 74 B1

Warlock Dr PA11 . . . . .90 B1
Warlock Rd PA11 . . . . .90 B2
Warly Dr KA2 . . . . .225 C1
Warly Pl KA2 . . . . .225 C1
Warner St KA20 . . . . .217 B4
Warnock Cres ML4 . . . . .142 A2
Warnock Rd G77 . . . . .156 B4
Warnock St G31 . . . . .241 C3
Warren Rd ML3 . . . . .183 B4
Warren St G42 . . . . .117 A1
Warren Wlk G66 . . . . .57 C4
Warriston Cres G33 . . . . . . .118 C4
Warriston Ct G33 . . . . .118 C4
Warriston Pl G32 . . . . .119 A4
Warriston St G33 . . . . .118 C4
Warriston Way G73 . . . . .138 B2
Warrix Ave KA12 . . . . .219 B1
Warrix Gdns KA10 . . . . .232 C4
Warrix Intc KA12 . . . . .219 C1
Warroch St G3 . . . . .240 A2
Warwick G74 . . . . .160 B2
Warwick Gr ML3 . . . . .161 C3
Warwick Hill KA11 . . . . .220 A3
Warwick Rd PA16 . . . . .44 C2
Warwickhill Pl KA11 . . . . . . .222 C1
Warwickhill Rd KA1 . . . . . . .222 B1
Washington Rd
 Kirkintilloch G66 . . . . .79 A4
 Paisley PA3 . . . . .113 C4
Washington St G3 . . . . .240 B2
Watchmeal Cres G81 . . . . . . .74 B4
Water La [8] KA1 . . . . .227 C4
Water Rd G78 . . . . .134 B2
Water Row G51 . . . . .116 A4
Water St PA14 . . . . .47 B1
Waterbank Rd G76 . . . . .158 B3
Watercut Rd KA13 . . . . .219 A4
Waterfoot Ave G53 . . . . .135 B4
Waterfoot Rd G76, G77 . . . . .157 A2
Waterfoot Row G76 . . . . .157 B2
Waterfoot Terr G53 . . . . .135 B4
Waterford Ct G46 . . . . .136 A2
Waterford Rd G46 . . . . .136 A2
Waterhaughs Gdns G33 . . . . . .98 B4
Waterhaughs Gr G33 . . . . .98 B4
Waterlands Gdns ML8 . . . . . .188 A2
Waterlands Pl ML8 . . . . .187 A2
Waterlands Rd ML8 . . . . .187 A3
Waterloo Cl G66 . . . . .58 B1
Waterloo Dr ML11 . . . . .215 A3
Waterloo Gdns [6] G66 . . . . . .58 B1
Waterloo La G2 . . . . .240 C2
Waterloo Rd
 Lanark ML11 . . . . .215 A3
 Prestwick KA9 . . . . .236 A3
Waterloo St G2 . . . . .240 C2
Watermill Gr PA2 . . . . .112 C1
Waters End PA2 . . . . .112 A4
Watersaugh Dr ML1 . . . . . . .144 A1
Watersedge Ct G84 . . . . .15 B2
Waterside Ave KA12 . . . . . . .219 A2
Waterside Ave G77 . . . . .156 B2
Waterside Ct
 Carmunnock G76 . . . . .158 B4
 Kilmarnock KA1 . . . . .227 C4
Waterside Dr G77 . . . . .156 B2
Waterside Gdns
 Cambuslang G72 . . . . .139 C2
 Carmunnock G76 . . . . .158 B4
 Hamilton ML3 . . . . .162 C1
Waterside La PA5 . . . . .111 B1
Waterside Pl G5 . . . . .117 B2
Waterside Rd
 Carmunnock G76 . . . . .158 B3
 Kilwinning KA13 . . . . .207 C2
 Kirkintilloch G66 . . . . .79 C4
Waterside St
 Glasgow G5 . . . . .117 B2
 Kilmarnock KA1 . . . . .227 C4
Waterside Terr PA5 . . . . .111 B1
Waterside Way PA5 . . . . .111 B1
Waterslap KA3 . . . . .213 A1
Waterston Way PA12 . . . . . . .129 B2
Waterworks Cotts G77 . . . . . .177 A2
Wateryetts Dr PA13 . . . . .69 B1
Watling Ave FK1 . . . . .41 B3
Watling Dr FK1 . . . . .41 B3
Watling Gdns FK1 . . . . .41 A3
Watling Pl [7] G75 . . . . .159 A1
Watling St Falkirk FK1 . . . . . . .41 B3
 Motherwell ML1 . . . . .142 B1
 Uddingston G71 . . . . .140 C4
Watson Ave Linwood PA3 . .112 A3
 Rutherglen G73 . . . . .138 A4
 Stonehouse ML9 . . . . .199 A2
Watson Cres G65 . . . . .60 C4
Watson Pl Blantyre G72 . . . .161 A4
 Bonnybridge FK4 . . . . .39 B2
Watson St Blantyre G72 . . . .161 B4
 Falkirk FK2 . . . . .42 A3
 Glasgow G1 . . . . .241 B1
 Kilmarnock KA3 . . . . .228 A4
 Larkhall ML9 . . . . .184 C2
 Motherwell ML1 . . . . .163 C3
 Uddingston G71 . . . . .140 C3
Watson Terr KA12 . . . . .219 B1
Watsonville Pk [3] ML1 . . . .163 C3
Watstone Rd ML9 . . . . .199 A3
Watt Ave G33 . . . . .99 C3
Watt Cres ML4 . . . . .142 A4
Watt St Dalry KA24 . . . . .191 B4
 Stonehouse ML9 . . . . .198 C1
Watt Gdns FK1 . . . . .41 C3
Watt La PA11 . . . . .110 C4

Watt Low Ave G73 . . . . .137 C3
Watt Pl Greenock PA15 . . . . . .46 A3
 Milngavie G62 . . . . .54 C2
Watt Rd Bridge of W PA11 . .110 B4
 Glasgow G52 . . . . .115 A4
Watt St Airdrie ML6 . . . . .103 B1
 Glasgow G5 . . . . .116 C3
 Greenock PA16 . . . . .45 C3
Wattfield Rd KA7 . . . . .238 C3
Waukglen Ave G53 . . . . .135 A1
Waukglen Cres G53 . . . . . . .135 B1
Waukglen Dr G53 . . . . .135 A2
Waukglen Gdns G53 . . . . . . .135 A1
Waukglen Path G53 . . . . .135 A2
Waukglen Pl G53 . . . . .135 A2
Waukglen Rd G53 . . . . .135 A2
Waulking Mill Rd G81 . . . . . . .74 B4
Waulkmill Ave G78 . . . . .134 B2
Waulkmill Pl KA1 . . . . .228 A4
Waulkmill St G46 . . . . .135 C2
Waulkmill Way G78 . . . . .134 B2
Waverley G74 . . . . .160 B2
Waverley Ave
 Helensburgh G84 . . . . .25 B4
 Kilmarnock KA1 . . . . .222 B1
Waverley Cres
 Cumbernauld G67 . . . . .82 B4
 Hamilton ML3 . . . . .161 C2
 High Bonnybridge FK4 . . . . . . .40 A2
 Kirkintilloch G66 . . . . .79 B4
 Lanark ML11 . . . . .215 B2
 Stirling FK8 . . . . .7 B3
Waverley Ct
 Bothwell G71 . . . . .141 A1
 Helensburgh G84 . . . . .25 B4
Waverley Dr Airdrie ML6 . . .103 A1
 Rutherglen G73 . . . . .138 B4
 Wishaw ML2 . . . . .165 A2
Waverley Gdns
 Elderslie PA5 . . . . .112 B1
 Glasgow G41 . . . . .116 C1
 Glasgow G66 . . . . .79 B4
Waverley Pk KA21 . . . . .205 C1
Waverley Rd Paisley PA2 . . .132 C4
 Stenhousemuir FK5 . . . . .23 B1
Waverley St
 Coatbridge ML5 . . . . .102 A1
 Falkirk FK2 . . . . .42 A4
 Glasgow G41 . . . . .116 C1
 Greenock PA16 . . . . .45 B2
 Hamilton ML3 . . . . .161 C2
 Larkhall ML9 . . . . .199 A4
Waverley Terr
 Blantyre G72 . . . . .161 B3
 Dumbarton G82 . . . . .49 A2
 Stenhousemuir FK5 . . . . .23 B1
Waverley Way PA2 . . . . .132 C4
Weardale La G33 . . . . .119 B4
Weardale St G33 . . . . .119 B4
Weaver Ave G77 . . . . .156 B4
Weaver Cres ML6 . . . . .123 A3
Weaver La PA10 . . . . .111 A2
Weaver Pl G75 . . . . .179 C4
Weaver Row FK7 . . . . .8 C2
Weaver St Ayr KA8 . . . . .235 C1
 Glasgow G4 . . . . .241 B2
Weaver Terr PA2 . . . . .114 A2
Weaver's Ct PA10 . . . . .111 A2
Weavers Ave PA2 . . . . .113 C1
Weavers Cott [4] PA10 . . . . .111 A2
Weavers Ct
 [2] East Kilbride G74 . . . . . .159 C1
 [3] Hamilton ML3 . . . . .162 C1
Weavers Gate PA1 . . . . .113 A2
Weavers Rd PA2 . . . . .113 A2
Weavers Way ML9 . . . . .198 C1
Weavers Wlk ML11 . . . . .215 A2
Webster Ave FK2 . . . . .24 A2
Webster Groves ML2 . . . . . .165 B2
Webster St Clydebank G81 . . .94 C4
 Glasgow G40 . . . . .118 A2
Wedderlea Dr G52 . . . . .115 A3
Wee Cl KA15 . . . . .171 A4
Wee Row FK2 . . . . .42 A3
Wee Sunnyside Rd ML3 . .184 A1
Weensmoor Rd G53 . . . . . . .134 C2
Weeple Dr PA3 . . . . .112 A3
Weighhouse Cl PA1 . . . . . . .113 C2
Weighhouse Rd ML8 . . . . . . .187 C2
Weir Ave Barrhead G78 . . . .134 B1
 Prestwick KA9 . . . . .213 B1
Weir Dr FK7 . . . . .8 B2
Weir Pl Greenock PA15 . . . . . .46 B2
 Kilbirnie KA25 . . . . .149 A1
 Law ML8 . . . . .186 C2
Weir Rd Ardrossan KA22 . . . .205 B2
 Ayr KA8 . . . . .235 C2
Weir St Coatbridge ML5 . . . .122 A4
 Falkirk FK1 . . . . .42 B3
 Greenock PA15 . . . . .46 B1
 Paisley PA3 . . . . .113 C3
 Stirling FK8 . . . . .7 B3
Weirston Rd KA13 . . . . .208 A2
Weirwood Ave G69 . . . . .120 A3
Weirwood Gdns G69 . . . . . . .119 C2
Welbeck Cres KA10 . . . . .229 B1
Welbeck Dr KA10 . . . . .229 B1
Welbeck Ho G74 . . . . .159 C1
Welbeck Mews KA10 . . . . . . .229 B1
Welbeck Rd G53 . . . . .135 A2
Welbeck St
 Greenock PA16 . . . . .45 C3
 Kilmarnock KA1 . . . . .228 A4
Weldon Pl G65 . . . . .36 A1
Welfare Ave G72 . . . . .139 B2
Well Gn G43 . . . . .136 B4
Well Gn Ct G43 . . . . .136 B4
Well La G66 . . . . .57 B4

Well Rd Bridge of A FK9 . . . . . .2 A4
 Kilbarchan PA10 . . . . .111 A2
 Lanark ML11 . . . . .215 A2
Well St Paisley PA1 . . . . .113 B3
 West Kilbride KA23 . . . . .190 B3
Welland Pl G75 . . . . .179 C4
Wellbank Gdns KA23 . . . . . .190 B3
Wellbank Pl G71 . . . . .140 C3
Wellbrae Larkhall ML9 . . . . .185 A1
 Stonehouse ML9 . . . . .198 C1
Wellbrae Rd ML3 . . . . .162 A1
Wellbrae Terr G69 . . . . .80 C1
Wellbuttslea Dr ML11 . . . . . .214 C2
Wellcroft Pl G5 . . . . .117 A2
Wellcroft Rd ML1 . . . . .161 C2
Wellcroft Terr ML3 . . . . .161 C2
Wellesley Cres
 Cumbernauld G68 . . . . .60 C1
 East Kilbride G75 . . . . .179 C4
Wellesley Dr
 Cumbernauld G68 . . . . .60 B1
 East Kilbride G75 . . . . .179 C4
Wellesley Pl G68 . . . . .60 B1
Wellfield Ave G46 . . . . .136 A2
Wellfield St G21 . . . . .97 C2
Wellgate ML1 . . . . .215 A2
Wellgate Ct ML9 . . . . .185 A2
Wellgate Dr FK9 . . . . .2 B4
Wellgate St ML9 . . . . .185 A2
Wellgatehead ML11 . . . . .215 A2
Wellgreen Pl FK8 . . . . .7 A3
Wellhall Ct ML3 . . . . .162 A2
Wellhall Rd ML11 . . . . .162 A2
Wellhead Ct ML11 . . . . .215 A2
Wellhouse Cres G33 . . . . . . .119 C4
Wellhouse Gdns G33 . . . . . . .119 C4
Wellhouse Prim Sch
 G33 . . . . .119 C4
Wellhouse Rd G33 . . . . .119 C4
Wellington G75 . . . . .180 A4
Wellington Acad PA15 . . . . . .45 C2
Wellington Ave KA3 . . . . . . .222 B1
Wellington La Ayr KA7 . . . . .238 C4
Wellington Pl
 Clydebank G81 . . . . .73 B2
 Coatbridge ML5 . . . . .121 B3
 Kilmarnock KA3 . . . . .222 C1
 Paisley PA3 . . . . .113 B3
 Prestwick KA9 . . . . .236 A3
 Wishaw ML2 . . . . .164 B3
Wellington Terr ML1 . . . . . . .214 C3
Wellington Way
 Greenock PA15 . . . . .45 C2
 [5] Renfrew PA4 . . . . .94 B1
Wellknowe Ave G74 . . . . . . .158 B1
Wellknowe Pl G74 . . . . .158 B1
Wellknowe Rd G74 . . . . .158 B1
Wellmeadow Annexe (Univ of
 Paisley) PA1 . . . . .113 B2
Wellmeadow Cl G77 . . . . . . .156 B3
Wellmeadow Gn G77 . . . . . .156 B3
Wellmeadow St PA1 . . . . . . .113 B2
Wellmeadow Way G77 . . . . .156 B3
Wellpark Ave G77 . . . . .238 C1
Wellpark Bldgs PA15 . . . . . . .46 A2
Wellpark Cres FK7 . . . . .6 C2
Wellpark Ct
 Greenock PA15 . . . . .45 C2
 Kilmarnock KA3 . . . . .228 B4
Wellpark Gr KA10 . . . . .229 B1
Wellpark La KA21 . . . . .216 C4
Wellpark Rd Banknock FK4 . .38 B1
 Motherwell ML1 . . . . .163 B3
 Saltcoats KA21 . . . . .216 C4
Wellpark St G31 . . . . .241 C2
Wellpark Terr
 Bonnybridge FK4 . . . . .40 A3
 Neilston G78 . . . . .154 B3
Wellpark Gr KA3 . . . . .228 B4
Wells St G81 . . . . .73 C2
Wellshot Dr G72 . . . . .138 C3
Wellshot Rd G32 . . . . .118 C2
Wellside Ave ML6 . . . . .103 A1
Wellside Ct FK1 . . . . .42 A3
Wellside Dr G72 . . . . .139 B2
Wellside La ML6 . . . . .103 A1
Wellside Pl FK1 . . . . .42 A3
Wellside Quadrant ML6 . . . .103 A1
Wellsquarry Rd C74,C76 . . . .159 B3
Wellview Dr ML1 . . . . .163 B3
Wellwood Ave KA13 . . . . . . .207 B1
Wellwood Ave ML11 . . . . . . .215 A3
Wellwynd ML6 . . . . .122 C4
Wellyard La PA16 . . . . .44 B1
Wellyard Way PA16 . . . . .44 B1
Welsh Dr Blantyre G72 . . . . .161 B3
 Hamilton ML3 . . . . .183 B4
Welsh Gdns FK9 . . . . .2 A4
Welsh Pl KA21 . . . . .205 C1
Welsh Rd KA9 . . . . .236 C4
Welsh Row ML6 . . . . .123 B2
Wemyss Ave G77 . . . . .156 B4
Wemyss Bay St PA15 . . . . . . .45 C2
Wemyss Dr G68 . . . . .60 C1

Wendur Way [6] PA3 . . . . . .113 B4
Wenlock Rd PA2 . . . . .113 C1
Wensleydale G74 . . . . .159 B2
Wentworth Dr [8] G23 . . . . . .76 C1
Wentworth Sq KA12 . . . . . . .207 B2
Wesley St Ayr KA8 . . . . .16 B2
West Abercromby St G84 . .16 B2
West Ave Carluke ML8 . . . . .187 C1
 Hamilton G72 . . . . .161 C3
 Motherwell ML1 . . . . .143 A1
 Paisley PA1 . . . . .112 B2
 Plains ML6 . . . . .104 A2
 Renfrew PA4 . . . . .94 B2
 Stepps G33 . . . . .99 B3
 Uddingston G71 . . . . .141 B2
West Balgrochan Rd G64 . . .57 A1
West Barmoss Ave PA14 . . . .68 C4
West Benhar Rd ML7 . . . . . .127 A2
West Blackhall St PA15 . . . . .45 C3
West Boreland Rd FK6 . . . . . .21 B1
West Bowhouse Gdns
 KA11 . . . . .220 A3
West Bowhouse Head
 KA11 . . . . .220 A3
West Bowhouse Way
 KA11 . . . . .220 A3
West Bowhouse Workshops
 KA11 . . . . .220 A3
West Brae PA1 . . . . .113 B2
West Bridge St FK1 . . . . .42 A3
West Bridgend G82 . . . . .49 C2
West Buchanan Pl PA1 . . . .113 B2
West Burn St PA15 . . . . .45 C3
West Burnside St G65 . . . . . .60 B4
West Byrehill Ind Est
 KA13 . . . . .207 A1
West Campbell St
 Glasgow G2 . . . . .240 C3
 Paisley PA1 . . . . .113 A2
West Canal St ML5 . . . . .121 C4
West Carmuirs Loan FK5 . . .40 C3
West Chapelton Ave G61 . . . .75 C2
West Chapelton Cres
 G61 .75 C2
West Chapelton Dr G61 . . . . .75 C2
West Chapelton La G61 . . . . .75 C2
West Clyde St
 Helensburgh G84 . . . . .16 B1
 Larkhall ML9 . . . . .185 A2
West Coats Prim Sch
 G72 . . . . .138 C3
West Coats Rd G72 . . . . .138 C3
West Cres KA10 . . . . .229 D2
West Cross ML2 . . . . .165 A2
West St Clydebank G81 . . . . . .73 C2
 Irvine KA12 . . . . .219 A1
West Dhuhill Dr G84 . . . . . . .16 A1
West Doura Ave KA21 . . . . . .205 C1
West Doura Way KA13 . . . . .207 B2
West Dr Airdrie ML6 . . . . . . .123 C3
 Stenhousemuir FK5 . . . . .23 B1
West End Dr ML4 . . . . .141 C2
West End Gdns FK10 . . . . . . .10 A3
West End Pl ML4 . . . . .141 C2
West Fairholm St ML9 . . . . .184 C3
West Faulds Rd ML11 . . . . . .215 C3
West Fullarton St KA1 . . . . .222 C1
West Gate ML2 . . . . .165 B2
West George La G2 . . . . .240 C3
West George St
 Coatbridge ML5 . . . . .122 A4
 Glasgow G2 . . . . .240 C3
 Kilmarnock KA1 . . . . .222 C1
West Glebe G76 . . . . .178 C3
West Glebe Terr ML3 . . . . . .162 B1
West Glen Gdns PA13 . . . . . . .69 B1
West Glen Rd
 Kilmacolm PA13 . . . . .69 C1
 Kilmacolm PA13 . . . . .70 A1
West Graham St G4 . . . . . . .240 C4
West Greenhill Pl G3 . . . . . .116 C4
West Hamilton St ML1 . . . . .163 C3
West High St G66 . . . . .58 B1
West James St FK12 . . . . .5 A3
West Johnstone St FK12 . . . .5 A3
West Kilbride Mus *
 KA23 . . . . .190 B3
West Kilbride Prim Sch
 KA23 . . . . .190 B3
West Kilbride Rd KA24 . . . . .191 A4
West Kilbride Sta KA23 . . . .190 B3
West King St G84 . . . . .16 A1
West Kirk St ML6 . . . . .122 C4
West Kirklands Pl KA24 . . . .191 A4
West La PA1 . . . . .113 A2
West Langlands St KA1 . . . .222 C1
West Lennox Dr G84 . . . . . . .16 B2
West Link Rd FK9 . . . . .2 A3
West Lodge Gdns FK10 . . . . .9 C4
West Lodge Rd PA4 . . . . .94 A2
West Main St ML7 . . . . .127 C3
West Mains Ind Est FK3 . . . . .42 C4
West Mains Rd
 East Kilbride G74 . . . . .159 B1
 Falkirk FK3 . . . . .22 C3
West Montrose St G84 . . . . . .16 B1
West Murrayfield FK7 . . . . .7 B1
West Nemphlar Rd
 ML11 . . . . .214 B3
West Netherton St KA1 . . . .227 C4
West Nile St G1 . . . . .241 A3
West Park Ave G53 . . . . .135 C1
West Park Cres KA3 . . . . . . .222 A4
West Park Dr KA3 . . . . .222 A4
West Park Sch KA2 . . . . .221 C1
West Pl ML2 . . . . .166 A3
West Portland St KA10 . . . . .229 B1

West Porton Pl PA7 . . . . .71 C2
West Prince's St G4 . . . . .96 C1
West Princes St G4 . . . . .16 B1
West Quay PA14 . . . . .47 B1
West Rd Irvine KA12 . . . . . . .219 A2
 Irvine KA12 . . . . .219 A4
 Kilbarchan PA10 . . . . .111 A2
 Port Glasgow PA14 . . . . .68 C4
 Stevenston KA20 . . . . .218 A3
 Torrance G64 . . . . .57 A1
West Regent La G2 . . . . .240 C3
West Regent St G2 . . . . .240 C3
West Rossdhu Dr G84 . . . . . .16 B2
West Row G63 . . . . .31 A2
West Sanquhar Ave
 KA8 .236 A1
West Sanquhar Rd KA8 . . . .236 A1
West Sanquhar Sch KA8 . . .236 A2
West Scott Terr ML3 . . . . . . .162 B1
West Shaw St
 Greenock PA15 . . . . .45 C3
 Kilmarnock KA1 . . . . .227 C3
West St Clydebank G81 . . . . . .94 A4
 Glasgow G5 . . . . .117 A3
 Paisley PA1 . . . . .113 B2
 West Sta ML3 . . . . .162 B2
West Stewart St
 Greenock PA15 . . . . .45 C3
 Hamilton ML3 . . . . .162 B2
West Stirling St FK12 . . . . .4 C4
West Street Underground Sta
 G5 . . . . .117 A3
West Thomson St G81 . . . . . .74 A2
West Thornlie St ML2 . . . . . .165 A1
West Vennel [7] FK10 . . . . . . .10 A3
West View Dunlop KA3 . . . . .195 A4
 Waterside KA3 . . . . .213 C2
West Wellbrae Cres
 ML3 .183 A4
West Whitby St G31 . . . . . . .118 B2
West Woodside Ave
 PA14 . . . . .68 C3
West Woodstock St
 KA1 .227 C4
Westacres Rd G77 . . . . .156 A2
Westbank Ct [7] G12 . . . . . . .96 C1
Westbank La G12 . . . . .96 C1
Westbank Quadrant G12 . . . .96 C1
Westbourne Ave G64 . . . . . . .16 B1
Westbourne Ave KA9 . . . . . .236 B4
Westbourne Cres G61 . . . . . .75 B3
Westbourne Dr G61 . . . . .75 B3
Westbourne Gardens La [26]
 G12 .96 B2
Westbourne Gdns KA9 . . . . .236 B4
Westbourne Gdns N [27]
 G12 .96 B2
Westbourne Gdns S [28]
 G12 .96 B2
Westbourne Gdns W [28]
 G12 .96 B2
Westbourne Rd G12 . . . . .96 B2
Westbourne Terrace La N [29]
 G12 .96 B2
Westbourne Terrace La S [3]
 G12 .96 B2
Westbrae Dr G14,G13 . . . . . . .95 C2
Westbrae Rd G77 . . . . .156 C3
Westburn Ave
 Cambuslang G72 . . . . .139 B3
 Falkirk FK1 . . . . .41 C2
 Paisley PA3 . . . . .113 A3
Westburn Cres
 Clydebank G81 . . . . .74 A4
 Rutherglen G73 . . . . .137 C4
Westburn Farm Rd G72 . . . .139 C4
Westburn Rd
 Cambuslang G72 . . . . .140 A3
 Cambuslang, Westburn
 G72 . . . . .139 B3
 Stewarton KA3 . . . . .195 C1
Westcastle Cres G45 . . . . . .137 B2
Westcastle Ct G45 . . . . .137 B2
Westcastle Gdns G45 . . . . . .137 B2
Westcastle Gr G45 . . . . .137 B2
Westcliff G82 . . . . .49 A3
Westclyffe St [3] G41 . . . . . .116 C1
Westcott Pl ML11 . . . . .215 B3
Westcraigs Pk EH48 . . . . . . .107 B2
Westcraigs Rd
 Blackridge EH48 . . . . .107 B2
 Harthill ML7 . . . . .127 C3
Westend G61 . . . . .76 A1
Westend Ct ML8 . . . . .186 C2
Westend Park St G3 . . . . . . .240 A4
Westend Pk St G3 . . . . .96 A1
Wester Carriagehill
 PA2 .113 C1
Wester Cleddens Prim Sch
 G64 .78 B1
Wester Cleddens Rd G64 . . .78 B1
Wester Common Dr G22 . . . .97 A2
Wester Common Prim Sch
 G22 .97 A2
Wester Common Rd G22 . . .97 A2
Wester Mavisbank Ave
 ML6 . . . . .122 C4
Wester Moffat Ave ML6 . . . .123 C4
Wester Moffat Cres [7]
 ML6 . . . . .123 C4
Wester Moffat Hospl
 ML6 . . . . .123 C4
Wester Myvot Rd G67 . . . . . . .82 A2
Wester Rd G32 . . . . .119 B2
Westerburn St G32 . . . . .118 C3
Westercraigs G31 . . . . .117 C4
Westerdale G74 . . . . .159 B2

Westerfield Rd G76 .....158 B2
Westergate Sh Ctr G2 ...240 C2
Westergill Ave ML6 .....123 C3
Westerglen Rd FK1 ....42 A1
Westergreens Ave G66 ...79 B3
Westerhill Rd G64 ....78 B2
Westerhouse Ct ML8 ....187 B1
Westerhouse Rd G34 ...120 A4
Westerkirk Dr G23 ....76 C1
Westerlands G12 ....96 A3
Westerlands Dr
Newton Mearns G77 ......156 A2
Stirling FK8 ....7 A3
Westerlands Gdns G77 ..156 A2
Westerlands Gr G77 ....156 A2
Westerlands Pl G77 ....156 A3
Westerlea Ct FK9 ....2 A3
Westerlea Dr FK9 ....2 A3
Westermains Ave G66 ....79 A4
Western Ave Falkirk FK2 ..42 A3
Rutherglen G73 ....137 C4
Western Cres KA25 .....170 A4
Western Infmy G11 ....96 B1
Western Isles Rd G60 ....73 B3
Western Rd
Cambuslang G72 ....138 C2
Kilmarnock KA3 ....223 A2
Westerpark Ave G72,
ML3 ....161 B2
Westerton Cowie FK7 .....12 B4
Lennoxtown G66 ....57 C4
Westerton Ave
Clarkston G76 ....158 A3
Glasgow G61 ....95 C4
Larkhall ML9 ....185 A1
Westerton Ct G76 ....158 A3
Westerton Dr FK9 ....2 A4
Westerton La G76 ....158 A3
Westerton Prim Sch G61 .75 C2
Westerton Rd G68 ....61 B3
Westerton Sta G61 ....75 C1
Westerton Terr FK2 ....24 B2
Westfield Dumbarton G82 ..49 B2
Kilbirnie KA25 ....170 A4
Westfield Ave G73 ......137 C4
Westfield Cres G61 ......75 C1
Westfield Dr
Bearsden G61 ....75 C1
Cumbernauld G68 ....81 C4
Glasgow G52 ....115 A3
Greenock PA16 ....45 B4
Kilmacolm PA13 ....89 A4
Westfield Ind Area G68 ...81 B3
Westfield Pl
Cumbernauld G68 ....81 B3
Denny FK6 ....21 C1
Westfield Prim Sch G68 ..81 C4
Westfield Rd Ayr KA7 ...238 C3
Cumbernauld G68 ....81 C4
Glasgow G46 ....136 A2
Kilmarnock KA3 ....223 B3
Kilsyth G65 ....36 A1
Motherwell ML1 ....143 B4
Port Glasgow PA14 ....68 C4
Westfield Rdbt FK2 ......42 C3
Westfield St FK2 ....42 C3
Westfield Trad Est FK6 ...21 C1
Westfields G64 ....77 C2
Westgarth Pl G74 ....159 A2
Westgate Way ML4 ......141 C2
Westhaugh Rd FK9 ....2 A2
Westhorn Dr G32 ....119 A1
Westhouse Ave G73 .....137 C4
Westhouse Gdns G73 ...137 C4
Westknowe Gdns G73 ...138 A3
Westland Dr G14 ....95 B2
Westland Drive La 28
G14 ....95 B2
Westlands Gdns PA2 ....113 B1
Westlea Pl ML6 ....123 A3
Westminster Pl FK5 ......23 C2
Westminster Terr 3
G3 ....116 C4
Westmoor Cres KA1 .....227 B4
Westmoreland St G42 ...117 A1
Westmorland Rd PA16 ....44 C2
Westmuir Pl G73 ....137 C4
Westmuir St G31 ....118 B3
Weston Pl KA9 ....236 B3
Weston Terr KA23 ....190 B3
Westpark Ct KA20 ....217 B4
Westpark Dr PA3 ....113 A3
Westpark Wynd KA24 ...191 A4
Westport
East Kilbride G75 ....159 A1
Lanark ML11 ....214 C2
Westport St 10 G65 ....60 B4
Westray Ave
Newton Mearns G77 .....156 B4
Port Glasgow PA14 ....69 A3
Westray Cir G22 ....97 B3
Westray Ct G67 ....82 C4
Westray Dr KA3 ....223 A3
Westray Pl
Bishopbriggs G64 ....78 B1
Glasgow G22 ....97 B4
Westray Rd G67 ....82 C4
Westray Sq G22 ....97 B4
Westray St G22 ....97 B4
Westray Terr FK1 ....42 B1
Westray Wynd 2 ML2 ...165 C3
Westside Gdns G11 ......96 B1
Westview Cres FK10 ....4 B1
Westward Way KA10 ....229 D4
Westwood Ave Ayr KA8 ..236 C1
Glasgow G46 ....136 A2
Westwood Cres Ayr KA8 .236 C1
Hamilton ML3 ....162 B1
Westwood Dr ML1 ......144 C1
Westwood Gdns PA3 ....113 A3
Westwood Hill G75 .....180 A4
Westwood Quadrant G81 .74 B1
Westwood Rd
East Kilbride G75 ....180 A4
Glasgow G43 ....136 A3
Wishaw ML2 ....166 A3
Westwood Sq G75 ......180 A4
Weymouth Cres PA19 .....44 C3
Weymouth Dr G12 ....96 A3
Whamflet Ave G34 ......120 B4
Whangie The* G63 ....29 A3
Wharf Rd KA12 ....218 B2
Wharry Rd FK12 ....4 C4
Whatriggs Rd KA1 ......228 A2
Wheatfield Rd Ayr KA7 ..238 C4
Bearsden G61 ....75 B1
Wheatholm Cres ML6 ....103 A1
Wheatholm St ML6 .....103 A1
Wheatland Ave G72 .....161 B4
Wheatland Dr ML11 .....214 C3
Wheatlandhead Ct G72 .161 B4
Wheatlands Ave FK4 .....40 A3
Wheatlands Dr PA10 ....111 A2
Wheatlands Farm Rd
PA10 ....111 A2
Wheatlandside ML11 ....214 C3
Wheatley Cres G65 ......60 B4
Wheatley Ct G32 ....119 A3
Wheatley Dr G32 ....119 A3
Wheatley Loan G64 ......98 B4
Wheatley Pl G32 ....119 A3
Wheatley Rd
Saltcoats KA21 ....206 A1
Stevenston KA20 ....206 C1
Wheatpark Pl KA8 ......236 C2
Wheatpark Rd Ayr KA8 ..236 C2
Lanark ML11 ....214 C2
Wheatsheaf Pend 8
G74 ....159 C1
Whifflet Ct ML5 ....122 A3
Whifflet St ML5 ....122 A2
Whifflet Sta ML5 ....122 A3
Whin Ave G78 ....134 A2
Whin Hill G74 ....160 A2
Whin Hill Rd KA7 ....239 A1
Whin Loan G65,G66 ......59 B4
Whin Pl G74 ....160 A3
Whin St G81 ....74 A2
Whinfell Dr G75 ....180 A3
Whinfell Gdns G75 .....180 A3
Whinfield Ave KA9 .....236 B3
Whinfield Gdns KA9 ....236 A3
Whinfield Rd
Glasgow G53 ....135 A2
Prestwick KA9 ....236 A3
Whinhall Ave ML6 ......102 C1
Whinhall Rd ML6 ....102 C1
Whinhill Cres PA15 ......46 A1
Whinhill Gdns G53 .....115 A2
Whinhill Pl G53 ....115 A2
Whinhill Rd
Glasgow G53 ....115 A2
Greenock PA15 ....46 A2
Paisley PA2 ....114 A1
Whinhill Sta PA15 ....46 A2
Whinknowe ML9 ....199 C4
Whinney Gr ML2 ....165 C2
Whinnie Knowe ML9 ....184 C1
Whinpark Ave ML4 .....141 C2
Whinriggs ML9 ....198 B1
Whins of Milton Sch FK7 ..7 A1
Whins Rd Alloa FK10 .....10 B4
Glasgow G41 ....116 B1
Stirling FK7 ....7 A1
Troon KA10 ....229 D4
Whinwell Rd FK8 ....2 A1
Whirlie Dr PA6 ....111 A4
Whirlie Rd PA6 ....91 A1
Whirlies Rdbt The G74 ..160 A2
Whirlow Gdns G69 ......120 A3
Whirlow Rd G69 ....120 A3
Whistleberry Cres ML3 ..162 A4
Whistleberry Dr ML3 ....162 A4
Whistleberry Ind Est
ML3 ....162 A4
Whistleberry Pk ML3 ....162 A4
Whistleberry Rd ML3 ...162 A4
Whistleberry Ret Pk
G72 ....161 C4
Whistlefield Ct G61 ......75 C2
Whitacres Path G53 ....135 A2
Whitacres Rd G53 ......135 A2
Whitburn St G32 ....118 C4
White Ave G82 ....50 A2
White Cart Rd PA3 ......113 C4
White Craig Rd KA22 ...205 B2
White St Ayr KA8 ....236 A2
Clydebank G81 ....94 B4
Glasgow G11 ....96 B1
White's Neuk ML11 .....215 B3
White-cart Twr G74 .....181 A4
Whiteadder Pl G75 ......179 B4
Whitecraigs Pl G23 ......96 C4
Whitecraigs Sta G46 ....157 A4
Whitecrook Prim Sch
G81 ....74 B1
Whitecrook St G81 ....74 B1
Whitefield Ave G72 .....139 A2
Whitefield Rd G51 ......116 B3
Whitefield Terr G66 ......33 B1
Whiteford Ave G82 ....50 B3
Whiteford Cres G82 ......50 B3
Whiteford Ct ML3 ....183 B3
Whiteford Pl G82 ....50 B3
Whiteford Rd
Paisley PA2 ....114 A1
Whiteford Rd *continued*
Stepps G33 ....100 A3
Whiteford View KA7 ....239 B4
Whitegates Pl FK1 ....41 B2
Whitehall Ave KA9 ......236 B4
Whitehall St G3 ....240 A2
Whitehaugh Ave PA1 ....114 A3
Whitehaugh Cres G53 ...135 A2
Whitehaugh Dr PA1 .....114 A3
Whitehaugh Rd G53 .....135 A2
Whitehill Ave
Airdrie ML6 ....103 A1
Cumbernauld G68 ....61 B1
Kirkintilloch G66 ....58 C1
Stepps G33 ....99 B3
Whitehill Cres
Carluke ML8 ....187 C2
Clydebank G81 ....74 C4
Kirkintilloch G66 ....58 C1
Lanark ML11 ....214 C2
Whitehill Farm Rd G33 ...99 B3
Whitehill Gdns G31 ....118 A4
Whitehill Gr G77 ....156 C1
Whitehill Pl FK8 ....7 A3
Whitehill Rd
Bearsden G61 ....75 B2
Hamilton ML3 ....162 A3
Whitehill Sec Sch G31 ..118 A4
Whitehill St G31 ....118 A4
Whitehill Street La G31 .118 A4
Whitehill Terr ML11 ....214 C2
Whitehills PA8 ....73 A1
Whitehills Dr G75 ......180 C4
Whitehills Pl G75 ......180 C4
Whitehills Terr G75 ....180 C4
Whitehirst Park Rd
KA13 ....207 A2
Whitehope Gn KA11 ....220 A2
Whitehorse Wlk G75 ....180 A4
Whitehouse Rd FK7 ....7 B4
Whitehurst G61 ....75 B3
Whitehurst Park Prim Sch
KA13 ....207 B2
Whitehurst Pk G61 ....75 B3
Whiteinch Prim Sch G14 .95 C1
Whitekirk Pl G15 ....75 A1
Whitelaw Ave ML5 ......101 C3
Whitelaw Cres ML4 .....142 B2
Whitelaw St
Blackridge EH48 ....107 B1
Glasgow G20 ....96 B4
Whitelaw Terr G65 ....59 C2
Whitelea Ave PA13 ....89 B4
Whitelea Cres PA13 ......89 B4
Whitelea Rd PA13 ....89 B4
Whitelee G75 ....180 B3
Whitelee Cres G77 .....156 A3
Whitelee Gate G77 .....156 A3
Whitelees Prim Sch G67 .62 C3
Whitelees Rd
Cumbernauld G67 ....62 C3
Greenock PA15 ....46 C1
Lanark ML11 ....215 B2
Lanark, Carstairs ML11 ..203 C1
Whitelees Rdbt G67 ......62 C3
Whiteloans G71 ....141 A2
Whitemoss Ave
East Kilbride G74 ....159 C1
Glasgow G44 ....136 C2
Whitemoss Gr G74 ......160 A1
Whitemoss Rdbt G74 ...160 A1
Whitepond Ave ML4 ....141 C2
Whites Bridge Ave PA3 .112 C2
Whites Bridge Cl PA3 ...113 A3
Whiteshaw Ave ML8 ....187 B1
Whiteshaw Dr ML8 .....187 B1
Whiteshaw Rd ML8 .....187 A2
Whiteside Rd KA9 ....236 B4
Whiteside Terr KA9 ....236 B4
Whitestone Ave G68 ......61 A1
Whitevale St G31 ....118 A3
Whitewisp Ct KA11 .....220 A2
Whitfield Dr KA8 ....236 B2
Whithope Rd G53 ....134 C2
Whithope Terr G53 .....134 C2
Whithorn Cres G69 ....80 C2
Whitlawburn Ave G72 ...138 C2
Whitlawburn Rd G72 ....138 C2
Whitlawburn Terr G72 ..138 C2
Whitlees Cres KA22 .....205 B2
Whitlees Ct KA22 ....205 C2
Whitletts Ct KA8 ....236 C1
Whitletts Prim Sch KA8 .236 C2
Whitletts Rd KA8 ....236 B1
Whitletts Rdbt KA6 .....236 C2
Whitriggs Rd G53 ......134 C2
Whitslade Pl G34 ....99 C1
Whitslade St G34 ....100 A1
Whitsun Dale G74 ......159 B2
Whittagreen Ave ML1 ...143 B2
Whittagreen Cres ML1 ..143 B1
Whittagreen Ct ML1 ....143 B2
Whittingehame Dr G12 ...96 A3
Whittingehame La G12 ...95 C3
Whittingehame Pk G12 ..95 C3
Whittington St ML5 .....122 A3
Whittle Pl KA11 ....219 C1
Whittle Rd KA8 ....236 B2
Whittlemuir Ave G44 ....136 C2
Whitton Dr G46 ....136 C2
Whitton St G20 ....96 B4
Whitworth Dr
Clydebank G81 ....74 A1
Glasgow G20 ....97 A3
Whitworth Gate G20 .....97 A3
Whyte Ave
Cambuslang G72 ....138 C3
Irvine KA12 ....219 B1
Whyte Cnr G82 ....50 C1
Whyte St ML7 ....127 C3
Whyteyetts FK10 ....5 B1
Wick Ave ML6 ....122 C2
Wickets The PA1 ....114 A2
Wickham Ave G77 ......156 B3
Wide Cl ML11 ....215 A2
Wigton Ave G77 ....156 B4
Wigtoun Pl G67 ....62 A2
Wildcat Rd KA23 ....190 A2
Wilderness The FK2 ......14 B2
Wildman Rd ML8 ....187 A4
Wilfred Ave G13 ....95 B4
Wilkie Cres ML9 ....185 A1
Wilkie Loan ML4 ....142 A4
Wilkie Rd G71 ....141 A3
William Booth Pl FK7 ......7 A2
William Burns Pl KA11 ..220 B1
William Dr ML3 ....183 B4
William Mann Dr G77 ...156 B2
William Spiers Pl ML9 ..185 A1
William St Clydebank G81 ..74 A3
Coatbridge ML5 ....122 A3
Glasgow G3 ....240 A3
Greenock PA15 ....46 A3
Hamilton ML3 ....162 A3
Helensburgh G84 ....16 B1
Johnstone PA5 ....111 C2
Kilmarnock KA3 ....222 C1
11 Kilsyth G65 ....60 B4
Paisley PA1 ....113 B2
Port Glasgow PA14 ....47 A1
William Tricker Cres
KA15 ....171 B4
William Ure Pl G64 ......78 A3
Williamfield Ave FK7 ......7 A2
Williamfield Gr KA12 ....219 A2
Williamfield Pk KA12 ...219 A2
Williamsburgh Prim Sch
PA1 ....114 A3
Williamsburgh Terr
PA1 ....114 A3
Williamson Ave
Dumbarton G82 ....50 A2
Falkirk FK2 ....24 A1
Williamson Dr G84 ....16 C1
Williamson Pl Falkirk FK2 .42 B4
Johnstone PA5 ....112 A1
Williamson St
Clydebank G81 ....74 A2
Falkirk FK1 ....42 A2
Glasgow G31 ....118 B2
Williamwood Dr G44 ....136 C1
Williamwood High Sch
G76 ....157 B4
Williamwood Pk G44 ....136 C1
Williamwood Pk W G44 .136 C1
Williamwood Sta G46 ...136 B1
Willie Mair's Brae KA3 ..223 A1
Willie Ross Pl KA3 ......223 B2
Willison's La PA14 ....47 B1
Willock Pl G20 ....96 C4
Willock St KA1 ....227 C3
Willockston Rd KA10 ....229 D1
Willoughby Dr G13 ....95 C3
Willoughby La G13 ....95 C3
Willow Ave
Bishopbriggs G64 ....98 A4
Elderslie PA5 ....112 B1
Kirkintilloch G66 ....79 B3
Motherwell ML1 ....143 A1
Willow Cres ML5 ....122 A2
Willow Ct G75 ....180 A3
Willow Dr Airdrie ML6 ...123 B4
Banknock FK4 ....38 C1
Blantyre G72 ....161 B4
Johnstone PA5 ....112 A1
Kilmacolm PA13 ....89 B4
Milton of C G66 ....58 B3
Willow Gdns KA11 ......219 C3
Willow Gr ML1 ....143 A3
Willow La Glasgow G32 ..119 A1
Troon KA10 ....229 C2
Willow Pk KA7 ....239 B2
Willow Pl Johnstone PA5 .112 A1
Uddingston G71 ....141 B4
Willow Rd KA1 ....227 B4
Willow St G13 ....95 C4
Willow Way ML3 ....162 C1
Willowbank ML9 ....185 A3
Willowbank Cres 8 G3 ...96 C1
Willowbank Gdns G66 ....79 B4
Willowbank Prim Sch
G3 ....96 C1
Willowbank Sch ML5 ....121 C3
Willowbank St G3 ......240 A4
Willowburn Rd KA15 ....170 C4
Willowdale Cres G69 ....120 A2
Willowdale Gdns G69 ...120 A2
Willowford Rd G53 .....135 A2
Willows The
Carmunnock G76 ....158 C4
Tullibody FK10 ....4 A1
Willowyard Ind Est
KA15 ....170 C4
Willowyard Rd KA15 ....170 C4
Wills Rd KA8 ....236 B1
Willwood Rd ML2 ....165 B4
Wilmot Rd G13 ....95 B3
Wilsgait St ML1 ....144 B1
Wilson Ave Denny FK6 .....21 B1
Falkirk FK1 ....41 B3
Irvine KA12 ....219 B2
Kilmarnock KA3 ....228 A4
Linwood PA3 ....112 A3
Troon KA10 ....230 A1
Wilson Ct Beith KA15 ...150 A1
Bellshill ML4 ....141 C3
Wilson Dr Bannockburn FK7 ..7 B1
Falkirk FK1 ....41 B3
Wilson Gdns FK1 ....41 B3
Wilson Pl Dundonald KA2 .225 C1
East Kilbride G74 ....160 A2
High Bonnybridge FK4 .....40 A2
Newton Mearns G77 .....156 B2
Wilson Rd Falkirk FK1 .....41 B3
Shotts ML7 ....167 A4
Wilson St Airdrie ML6 ...122 C4
Alexandria G83 ....27 C3
Ayr KA8 ....236 A1
Beith KA15 ....150 B1
Coatbridge ML5 ....122 B4
Glasgow G1 ....241 A2
Hamilton ML3 ....162 A3
Larkhall ML9 ....185 A1
Motherwell ML1 ....163 C4
Paisley PA1 ....113 B2
Port Glasgow PA14 ....47 B1
Renfrew PA4 ....94 B2
Wilson's Rd ML1 ....144 C4
Wilton Crescent La G20 ..96 C2
Wilton Ct 7 ML3 ....162 C1
Wilton Dr G20 ....96 C2
Wilton Rd ML8 ....202 A4
Wilton St Coatbridge ML5 .101 B1
Glasgow G20 ....96 C2
Wiltonburn Path G53 ...135 A2
Wiltonburn Rd G53 .....135 A2
Wilverton Rd G13 ....95 C4
Winburne Cres ML3 .....162 A2
Winchester Ave FK6 ......21 C2
Winchester Avenue Ind Est
FK6 ....21 C2
Winchester Ct FK6 ....21 C2
Winchester Dr G12 ....96 A3
Windelstraw Ct KA11 ...220 A2
Windemere Gdns ML3 ...183 B3
Winderemere St ML4 ....141 C2
Windermere G75 ....179 C3
Windhill Cres G43 ......136 A3
Windhill Pl G43 ....136 B3
Windhill Rd G43 ....136 B3
Windlaw Ct G45 ....137 B1
Windlaw Gdns G44 .....136 C2
Windlaw Park Gdns
G44 ....136 C2
Windlaw Prim Sch G45 .137 C1
Windlaw Rd
Carmunnock G76 ....158 B4
Glasgow G45 ....137 B1
Windmill Ct 4 ML1 .....163 C3
Windmill Gdns ML8 ....187 C1
Windmill Rd ML3 ....162 B2
Windmill St KA21 ....216 C4
Windmillhill St ML1 ....163 C3
Windrow Terr ML2 ......165 B4
Windsor Ave Falkirk FK1 ..41 C2
Newton Mearns G77 .....156 C3
Windsor Cres
Clydebank G81 ....74 A2
Elderslie PA5 ....112 A1
Falkirk FK1 ....41 C2
Paisley PA1 ....114 A3
Windsor Ct ML8 ....187 C1
Windsor Dr Denny FK6 ....21 B2
Falkirk FK1 ....41 C2
Glenmavis ML6 ....102 C2
Windsor Gdns Alloa FK10 ..9 C4
Falkirk FK1 ....41 C2
Hamilton ML3 ....162 A3
Windsor Path 8 ML9 ...185 B1
Windsor Pl Shotts ML7 ..146 C3
Stirling FK8 ....7 A4
Windsor Quadrant ML8 .187 C1
Windsor Rd Falkirk FK1 ...41 C2
Motherwell ML1 ....143 A3
Renfrew PA4 ....94 B1
Windsor St
Coatbridge ML5 ....121 C2
Glasgow G32 ....119 B3
4 Glasgow, Woodside G20 .97 A1
Menstrie FK11 ....3 C3
Shotts ML7 ....146 C3
Windsor Terr G20 ....97 A1
Windsor Wlk G71 ....141 A4
Windward Pk KA7 ......239 A1
Windward Rd G75 ......159 A1
Windy Yetts G65 ....59 C2
Windyedge Cres G13 .....95 B3
Windyedge Pl G13 ....95 B3
Windyedge Rd ML1 .....144 B2
Windyhill Pk G76 ....157 C1
Windyridge ML3 ....162 C1
Windyridge Pl G72 .....161 B4
Winehouse Yett KA2 ....225 C1
Winfield Ave G72 ....138 C4
Wingate Ave KA24 ......191 A4
Wingate Cres G74 ......160 B2
Wingate Dr G74 ....160 B2
Wingate Pk G74 ....160 B2
Wingate St ML2 ....164 C2
Wingfaulds Ave KA24 ...191 A4
Wingfield Gdns G71 ....141 A1
Winifred St G33 ....98 B2
Winning Ct G72 ....140 C1
Winning Quadrant ML2 .164 B2
Winning Row G31 ....118 B3
Winnipeg Dr G75 ....180 A4
Winstanley Wynd KA13 ..207 B3
Winston Ave KA9 ....236 B4
Winston Cres G66 ....57 B4
Winston Rd G84 ....17 A1
Wintergreen Ct G74 ....159 B2

Wintergreen Dr G74 ....159 B2
Winton Ave
Eaglesham G76 ....178 C2
Glasgow G46 ....136 B1
Kilwinning KA13 ......207 B2
Saltcoats KA21 ....216 C4
Winton Cres G72 ......161 B4
Winton Ct KA22 ....205 B1
Winton Dr G12 ....96 B3
Winton Gdns G71 ......140 C4
Winton La
Ardrossan KA22 ....205 B1
Glasgow G12 ....96 B3
Winton Pk G75 ....159 A1
Winton Pl
Ardrossan KA22 ....205 B1
Irvine KA12 ....219 B2
Winton Prim Sch KA22 .205 B1
Winton St
Ardrossan KA22 ....205 B1
Glasgow G46 ....216 C4
Wiran Pl G13 ....94 C4
Wishart Ave G81 ....74 B4
Wishart Dr FK7 ....7 B2
Wishart St G4, G31 ....241 C3
Wishaw Acad (Prim Sch)
ML2 ....165 A1
Wishaw General Hospl
ML2 ....164 C2
Wishaw High Rd ML1 ..165 B4
Wishaw Low Rd ML1,
ML2 ....165 A4
Wishaw Rd ML2 ....186 C4
Wishaw Sta ML2 ....165 A1
Wishawhill St ML2 .....164 C2
Wisner Ct G46 ....135 A3
Wisteria La ML8 ....201 C4
Wiston St G72 ....139 C3
Witch Rd KA3 ....222 C1
Witches Linn KA22 ....205 A2
Witchill Pl KA3 ....222 C1
Witchill Sch KA3 ......222 C1
Witchknowe Ave KA1 ..227 C3
Witchknowe Ct KA1 ...227 C2
Witchknowe Rd KA1 ...227 C2
Witchwood Ct ML5 ....101 B1
Witcutt Way ML2 ......164 C1
Wodrow St G40 ....118 A1
Wolcott Dr G72 ....161 B4
Wolfe Ave G77 ....156 B4
Wolfe Rd KA1 ....42 B2
Wolseley St G5 ....117 B2
Wood Aven Dr G74 ....159 B2
Wood Avens FK10 ....4 B1
Wood Cres
Kilwinning KA13 ......207 C2
Motherwell ML1 ......142 C1
Wood Ct KA10 ....229 B1
Wood Farm Rd G46 ...136 A1
Wood La KA1 ....220 B1
Wood La G64 ....98 B4
Wood Pk KA7 ....239 A2
Wood Pl G63 ....133 B4
Wood Quadrant G81 ...94 C4
Wood Rd KA10 ....229 B1
Wood St Airdrie ML6 ..103 B1
Coatbridge ML5 ....121 C4
Glasgow G31 ....118 A4
Greenock PA16 ....45 B4
Kilwinning KA13 ......207 C2
Motherwell ML1 ......163 C4
Paisley PA2 ....114 A2
Wood View
Motherwell ML1 ......143 A3
Shotts ML7 ....166 C4
Woodbank Cres
Clarkston G76 ....157 C3
Johnstone PA5 ....111 C1
Woodbank Ct G83 .....27 B4
Woodbank Gdns G83 ...27 B4
Woodbank Rd KA2 ....221 C1
Woodburn Ave
Airdrie ML6 ....122 C3
Balloch G83 ....28 A4
Blantyre G72 ....161 C4
Clarkston G76 ....157 C3
Kilwinning KA13 ......207 C2
Woodburn Cres FK4 ...39 C2
Woodburn Ct G73 .....138 A4
Woodburn Dr FK10 .....4 C1
Woodburn Gdns FK2 ..42 C3
Woodburn Gr ML3 ....162 C2
Woodburn Pl PA6 .....111 C4
Woodburn Rd
Beith KA15 ....171 B4
Falkirk FK2 ....42 B3
Glasgow G43 ....136 B3
Motherwell ML1 ......143 B4
Woodburn St
Falkirk FK2 ....42 C3
Motherwell ML1 ......163 C4
Woodburn Terr [9] ML9 .185 B1

Woodburn Way Alva FK12 ..5 A3
Cumbernauld G68 ......61 B1
Milngavie G62 ....55 A1
Woodcroft Ave G11 ....95 C2
Woodcroft Ave ML1 ...163 B2
Woodend Ct G32 .....119 C1
Woodend Dr
Airdrie ML6 ....103 B1
Glasgow G13 ....95 C3
Paisley PA1 ....114 B2
Woodend Gdns G32 ..119 B1
Woodend La [8] G13 ...95 C3
Woodend Oval KA6 ...239 C1
Woodend Pl PA5 ......112 A1
Woodend Rd Ayr KA7 .239 A1
Carluke ML8 ....188 A1
Glasgow G32 ....119 C1
Rutherglen G73 ......138 A2
Woodend St G84 ......16 A1
Woodfarm High Sch
G46 ....136 A2
Woodfield G11 ....141 B3
Woodfield Ave Ayr KA8 .236 A3
Bishopbriggs G64 .....98 A4
Woodfield Cres KA8 ..236 A2
Woodfield Rd KA8 ....236 A2
Woodfoot Path G53 ...135 A2
Woodfoot Quadrant
G53 ....135 A2
Woodfoot Rd
Glasgow G53 ....135 A2
Hamilton ML3 ....162 A1
Woodford Pl PA3 .....112 A3
Woodford St G41 .....136 C4
Woodgreen Ave G44 ..137 B3
Woodgreen Ct ML2 ...186 A4
Woodgreen Wynd KA13 .207 B3
Woodhall ML1 ....143 A4
Woodhall Ave
Calderbank ML6 ......123 A1
Coatbridge ML5 ......121 C2
Hamilton ML3 ....162 A2
Motherwell ML1 ......142 C3
Woodhall Cottage Rd
ML6 ....123 B1
Woodhall Mill Rd ML6 .123 A1
Woodhall Pl ML5 .....121 C2
Woodhall Rd
Braidwood ML8 ......201 B1
Calderbank ML6 ......123 A1
Glasgow G53 ....135 A2
Woodhall St
Chapelhall ML6 ......123 B1
Glasgow G40 ....118 A1
Woodhall Sta PA14 ....48 A1
Woodhall Terr PA14 ...69 A4
Woodhead Ave
Bothwell G71 ....141 A1
Cumbernauld G68 .....81 C4
Kirkintilloch G66 ......79 B4
Woodhead Cres
Hamilton ML3 ....183 A4
Uddingston G71 ......140 C4
Woodhead Ct G68 .....81 C4
Woodhead Gdns G71 ..162 A4
Woodhead Gr G68 .....81 C4
Woodhead Pl G68 .....81 C4
Woodhead Prim Sch
ML3 ....183 A4
Woodhead Rd
Cumbernauld G68 .....81 C1
Glasgow G53 ....135 A3
Stepps G69 ....100 A3
Woodhead Terr G69 ..100 A4
Woodhead View G68 ..81 C4
Woodhill Cres KA11 ..220 A3
Woodhill Pl KA3 ......222 A3
Woodhill Prim Sch G64 .78 B1
Woodhill Rd
Blackridge EH48 ......107 A2
Glasgow G21 ....98 A3
Kilmarnock KA3 ......222 C2
Hamilton Ave G44 ...137 B3
Woodhouse Ct G76 ..158 A3
Woodhouse St G13 ....95 C4
Woodilee Cotts G66 ...79 C3
Woodilee Ind Est G66 .79 C3
Woodilee Rd
Kirkintilloch G66 ......79 C3
Motherwell ML1 ......143 C2
Woodland Ave
Airdrie ML6 ....123 B2
Kirkintilloch G66 ......79 A4
Paisley PA2 ....133 C4
Woodland Cres
Cambuslang G72 .....139 B2
Eaglesham G76 ....178 B3
Woodland Gdns
Carmunnock G76 ....158 B4
Hamilton ML3 ....162 C1
Woodland Park Nature
Reserve* FK12 ....5 B4
Woodland Pk* FK12 ...5 B4
Woodland Pl KA22 ...205 B2
Woodland Terr ML9 ..185 B1

Woodland Way
Cumbernauld G67 .....62 A2
Denny FK6 ....39 B4
Woodlands Alloa FK10 ..3 C1
Glasgow G46 ....135 C2
Woodlands Ave
Bothwell G71 ....141 A2
Gartcosh G69 ....100 C3
Irvine KA12 ....219 B2
Law ML8 ....187 A3
Woodlands Cres Ayr KA2 .239 A2
Bothwell G71 ....141 A2
Falkirk FK1 ....42 A2
Glasgow G46 ....135 C2
Johnstone PA5 ....131 C4
Woodlands Ct
Alexandria G83 ....27 B4
Glasgow G46 ....135 C1
Woodlands Dr
Bothwell G71 ....121 B4
Glasgow G4 ....96 C1
Motherwell ML1 ......142 C3
Woodlands Gate
Glasgow G3 ....240 A4
Glasgow, Thornliebank
G46 ....135 C2
Woodlands Gdns G71 ..141 A2
Woodlands Gr
Kilmarnock KA3 ......223 A2
Milngavie G62 ....55 A1
Woodlands Pk G46 ...135 C2
Woodlands Pl
Coatbridge ML5 ......121 B4
Kilmarnock KA3 ......223 A2
Woodlands Prim Sch
Irvine KA12 ....219 B2
Linwood PA3 ....112 A3
Woodlands Rd
Glasgow G3 ....240 A4
Glasgow, Thornliebank
G46 ....135 C1
Motherwell ML1 ......163 C2
Woodlands St
Milngavie G62 ....55 A1
Motherwell ML1 ......163 C2
Prestwick KA9 ....236 A4
Woodlands Terr
Bothwell G71 ....141 A2
Glasgow G3 ....240 A4
Glasgow The ML4 ....142 B2
Woodlea Ave ML6 ....123 B2
Woodlea Cres KA2 ...221 C1
Woodlea Ct KA21 ....205 C1
Woodlea Dr
Glasgow G46 ....136 B2
Hamilton ML3 ....183 B4
Woodlea Gdns Alloa FK10 .5 A1
Bonnybridge FK4 ......39 C3
Woodlea La PA19 ......45 A4
Woodlinn Ave G44 ...137 A3
Woodmill KA13 ....207 C1
Woodmill Gdns G67 ..57 B1
Woodmill Gdns G67 ..81 C3
Woodneuk La G69 ...100 C3
Woodneuk Rd
Gartcosh G69 ....100 C3
Cumbernauld G68 .....81 C4
Glasgow G53 ....135 A3
Woodneuk St ML6 ...123 B1
Woodneuk Terr G69 ..100 C3
Woodrow ML1 ....143 A4
Woodrow Ave
Kilmalcolm PA13 ......69 B1
Motherwell ML1 ......143 A1
Woodrow Cir G41 ....116 B2
Woodrow Pl G41 .....116 B2
Woodrow Rd G41 ....116 B2
Woodside Houston PA6 ..91 B1
West Kilbride KA23 ..190 B2
Woodside Ave
Bridge of W PA11 .....90 B1
Glasgow G46 ....136 A2
Hamilton ML3 ....162 C1
Kilmarnock KA1 ......227 B3
Kilsyth G65 ....60 C4
Kirkintilloch G66 ......79 B3
Rutherglen G73 ......138 B4
Woodside Cres
Alexandria G83 ....27 C3
Barrhead G78 ....134 B1
Glasgow G3 ....240 A4
Paisley PA1 ....113 B2
Wishaw ML2 ....166 A3
Woodside Ct
Coatbridge ML5 ......121 B3
Falkirk FK1 ....42 A2
[4] Hamilton ML3 .....162 C1
Woodside Dr
Calderbank ML6 ......123 A1
Eaglesham G76 ....157 B1

Woodside Gdns
Carmunnock G76 ....158 B4
Clarkston G76 ....157 B4
Coatbridge ML5 ......121 B2
Woodside Gr
Glasgow G73 ....138 B4
Larbert FK5 ....41 B4
Woodside La PA5 .....111 B3
Woodside Pl Dunlop KA3 .195 B4
Fallin FK7 ....8 B2
Glasgow G3 ....240 A4
Uddingston G71 ......141 A2
Woodside Place La G3 .240 A4
Woodside Prim Sch
ML3 ....162 B1
Woodside Rd Alloa FK10 ..4 C1
Beith KA15 ....150 A1
Brookfield PA5 ....111 B3
Carmunnock G76 ....158 B4
Forrestfield ML6 .....106 A2
Kilwinning KA13 ......207 B2
Stirling FK8 ....2 A1
Tullibody FK10 ....4 A1
Woodside St
Chapelhall ML6 ......123 B1
Coatbridge ML5 ......121 B2
Motherwell ML1 ......164 A2
Motherwell, New Stevenston
ML1 ....143 A2
Woodside Terr
Clackmannan FK10 ...10 C2
Falkirk FK1 ....42 A2
Glasgow G3 ....240 A4
Woodside Terrace La
G3 ....240 A4
Woodside Way ML1 ...164 A2
Woodside Wlk ML3 ..162 C1
Woodstock Ave
Glasgow G41 ....116 B1
Kirkintilloch G66 ......79 C4
Lanark ML11 ....215 B2
Paisley PA2 ....132 C4
Woodstock Dr
Lanark ML11 ....215 A2
Wishaw ML2 ....165 B2
Woodstock Pl KA1 ...222 C1
Woodstock Rd
Greenock PA16 ....45 B2
Lanark ML11 ....215 A2
Woodstock Sch KA1 ..227 C4
Woodstock Way PA2 .132 C4
Woodstone Ct G84 ...15 C2
Woodvale Ave
Airdrie ML6 ....123 B2
Bearsden G61 ....96 C4
Rutherglen G46 .....157 A4
Woodvale Dr PA3 ....113 A3
Woodview G71 ....141 B4
Woodview Dr
Airdrie ML6 ....123 A3
Bellshill ML4 ....142 B4
Woodview La ML6 ...123 A3
Woodview Rd ML9 ...199 A4
Woodview Terr ML3 ..162 A2
Woodville Pk G51 ...116 A3
Woodville St G51 ....116 A3
Woodwynd KA13 .....207 C2
Woodyard Rd G82 ...49 C2
Woodyett Pk G76 ...157 C3
Woodyett Rd G76 ...157 C3
Wooer St [4] FK1 .....42 A2
Wordie Rd FK7 ....6 C2
Wordsworth Way G71 ..141 A2
Works Ave G72 ....139 C3
Workington Rd KA20 .218 A3
Workshops ML5 ......122 A3
Worsley Cres G77 ....156 B4
Wotherspoon Dr KA15 .150 A1
Wraes Ave G78 ....134 B2
Wraes View G78 .....153 C1
Wrangholm Cres PA7 .71 C2
Wrangholm Cres ML1 .143 A2
Wrangholm Dr ML1 ...143 A2
Wren Ct ML4 ....141 C4
Wren Pl Johnstone PA5 .131 B4
Wishaw ML2 ....165 A2
Wren Rd PA16 ....45 A2
Wright Ave G78 .....134 A1
Wright St Falkirk FK2 .42 A3
Renfrew PA4 ....94 A1
Wright Way ML1 .....143 A2
Wrightfield Pl KA7 ...238 C1
Wrightlands Cres PA8 .93 C4
Wyburn Pl KA8 ......236 A2
Wye Cres ML5 ....101 B1
Wykeham Pl G13 .....95 B3
Wykeham Rd G13 ....95 B3
Wylie G74 ....160 B3
Wylie Ave Alexandria G83 .27 B2
Newton Mearns G77 ..156 B4
Wylie Pl G82 ....27 C2
Wylie St G31 ....162 B1
Wylie Rd KA21 ......217 A4
Wynd The FK12 ....5 A4

Cumbernauld G67 .....62 A3
Wyndford Dr G20 .....96 B3
Wyndford Pl [5] G20 ..96 B3
Wyndford Prim Sch G20 .96 B3
Wyndford Rd
Cumbernauld G68 .....62 B4
Glasgow G20 ....96 B3
Wyndford Terr G71 ...141 A4
Wyndham Ct G12 ....96 B2
Wyndham St G12 ....96 B2
Wynyard Gn G75 ....180 A4
Wyper Pl G31 ....118 A3
Wyvil Ave G13 ....75 C4
Wyvis Ave Bearsden G61 .75 B4
Glasgow G13 ....94 C4
Wyvis Ct G77 ....156 B1
Wyvis Gdns KA1 .....228 A2
Wyvis Pl Glasgow G13 .94 C4
Irvine KA11 ....228 A2
Newton Mearns G77 ..156 B1
Shotts ML7 ....147 A2
Wyvis Quadrant G13 ..94 C4
Wyvis Rd KA1 ....228 A2

Y

Yair Dr G52 ....115 A3
Yardley Pl FK2 ....24 A1
Yardside Rd KA3 .....222 A4
Yarrow Cres
Bishopton PA7 ....72 B1
Wishaw ML2 ....165 A2
Yarrow Ct G72 ....139 C3
Yarrow Gardens La [1]
G20 ....96 C2
Yarrow Gdns G20 .....96 C2
Yarrow Pk G74 ....160 A1
Yarrow Rd G64 ....78 A2
Yate St G31 ....118 A3
Yerton Brae KA23 ...190 B2
Yetholm Gdns G74 ..159 C2
Yetholm St G14 ....94 C3
Yetholm Terr ML3 ...161 C2
Yett Rd ML1 ....143 B2
Yetts Ave PA13 ....69 B1
Yetts Cres G66 ....79 C4
Yetts Hole Rd ML6 ..102 A3
Yetts The FK7 ....6 B3
Yew Dr G21 ....98 A2
Yew Pl PA5 ....111 C1
Yews Cres ML3 ......162 A3
Yieldshields Rd ML8 ..189 B2
Yoker Ferry Rd G14 ..94 C3
Yoker Mill Gdns G13 ..94 C4
Yoker Mill Rd G13 ....94 C4
Yoker Prim Sch G14 ..94 C4
Yoker Sta G81 ....94 C4
Yokerburn Terr G81 ..94 C4
Yonderton Pl KA23 ..190 B2
York Dr Falkirk FK2 ...42 A3
Rutherglen G73 ......138 B3
York Pl KA8 ....235 C1
Motherwell ML6 .....143 B4
York St Ayr KA8 .....235 C1
Clydebank G81 ....74 B1
Falkirk FK2 ....42 A3
Glasgow G2 ....240 B2
Wishaw ML2 ....165 A1
York Street La KA8 ..235 C1
York Way PA4 ....94 B1
Yorke Pl KA1 ....222 B1
Yorke Rd KA10 ......229 C1
Yorkhill Pde G3 .....116 B4
Yorkhill St G3 ....116 B4
Young Ave KA10 ....229 C3
Young Pl
East Kilbride G75 ....181 A3
[1] Uddingston G71 ...141 A4
Wishaw ML2 ....166 A3
Young Rd ML11 .....215 C3
Young St Ardrossan KA22 .205 B1
Ayr KA8 ....236 A3
Clydebank G81 ....74 A2
Wishaw ML2 ....165 A2
Young Terr G21 ....98 A2
Young Wynd ML4 ...142 A4
Younger Dr KA9 .....233 B2
Younger Quadrant
G64 ....78 A1
Yukon Terr G75 ......180 A4
Yvetot Ave ML11 ....215 A2
Yvetot Ct ML8 ....187 C2

Z

Zambesi Dr G72 .....140 B1
Zena Cres G33 ....98 B2
Zena Pl G33 ....98 B2
Zena St G33 ....98 B2
Zetland Pl FK2 ....24 C2
Zetland Rd G52 .....114 C4

Any feature in this atlas can be given a unique reference to help you find the same feature on other Ordnance Survey maps of the area, or to help someone else locate you if they do not have a Street Atlas.

The grid squares in this atlas match the Ordnance Survey National Grid and are at 1 kilometre intervals. The small figures at the bottom and sides of every other grid line are the National Grid kilometre values (**00** to **99** km) and are repeated across the country every 100 km (see left).

To give a unique National Grid reference you need to locate where in the country you are. The country is divided into 100 km squares with each square given a unique two-letter reference. Use the administrative map to determine in which 100 km square a particular page of this atlas falls.

The bold letters and numbers between each grid line (**A** to **C**, **1** to **4**) are for use within a specific Street Atlas only, and when used with the page number, are a convenient way of referencing these grid squares.

Step 1: Identify the two-letter reference, in this example the page is in **SP**

Step 2: Identify the 1 km square in which the railway bridge falls. Use the figures in the southwest corner of this square: Eastings **17**, Northings **74**. This gives a unique reference: **SP 17 74**, accurate to 1 km.

Step 3: To give a more precise reference accurate to 100 m you need to estimate how many tenths along and how many tenths up this 1 km square the feature is. This makes the bridge about **8** tenths along and about **1** tenth up from the southwest corner.

This gives a unique reference: **SP 178 741**, accurate to 100 m.

Eastings (read from left to right along the bottom) come before Northings (read from bottom to top). If you have trouble remembering say to yourself "Along the hall, THEN up the stairs"!

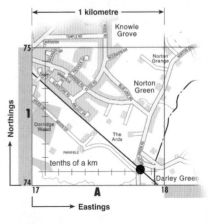